# The biological bases of behaviour

D1341105

# The biological bases of behaviour

*Edited by*

**Neil Chalmers**
**Roberta Crawley**
**Steven P R Rose**
assisted by Judy Hicklin

*at the Open University*

*Published for*
The Open University Press
by Harper & Row, Publishers
London New York Evanston San Francisco

This selection copyright © 1971 by The Open University
Introduction and Notes copyright © 1971 by The Open University
All rights reserved
First published 1971
Reprinted 1972
No part of this book may be used or reproduced in any manner
whatsoever without written permission except in the case of brief
quotations embodied in critical articles and reviews

Published by Harper & Row Ltd
28 Tavistock Street, London WC2E 7PN


Standard Book Number 06-318006-5 (cloth)
Standard Book Number 06-318007-3 (paper)


Designed and produced by Pica Editorial Ltd


Filmset in Photon Times 10 on 12 pt by
Richard Clay (The Chaucer Press) Ltd, Bungay, Suffolk
and printed in Great Britain by
Fletcher & Son Ltd, Norwich

# Preface

This book sprang from the Open University second level course on the biological bases of behaviour. The course itself is an attempt to blend the disciplines of biochemistry, physiology, developmental biology, ethology and experimental psychology into something approaching that new discipline of neurobiology whose growth is charted in the Introduction. The attempt – at least at the undergraduate level – is, so far as we know, unique in Britain, though there is an increasing demand for such courses at postgraduate level, for most of the new generation of researchers come into neurobiology from a single-disciplinary background and are expected to pick up the rest by a sort of osmosis.

Needless to say, when we came to look for books which we could recommend to our students, we ran into difficulties. There were many specialist works, of course, some quite excellent, but oriented towards the medical student, or the psychologist, for instance, and lacking the breadth of our course. There are also a number of collections of specialist papers in particular areas of brain research and psychology, edited often by distinguished researchers. But once again they did not really do the job we wanted. We therefore decided to make our own reader. Having done so, it seemed equally sensible to make it available, as cheaply as possible, to an audience beyond just the students of the Open University, for we believe that access to this material, collected into one volume, will be of value to many students, researchers and those only peripherally interested alike.

The plan of the book is as follows. It is divided into six sections. The first deals with the hardware and mechanics of the brain signalling and processing system and its evolution. It corresponds approximately to Units 1–4 of the OU course. The second is concerned with the biology of the special senses and psychological aspects of attention and perception, corresponding to OU units 5–7. Some of the articles in these two sections, notably those by Alfred S. Romer and E. J. W. Barrington, use a large number of zoological terms which might not be familiar to the reader. We have included a glossary of these terms at the end of the book. The third section deals primarily with the bio-chemistry, physiology, anatomy and psychology of emotion and motivation, and it corresponds to OU units 8–10. The "higher" cerebral functions, crucial to man as *Homo sapiens*: learning, remembering and forgetting, are handled in section four (OU units 11–13). At this point it becomes proper to turn from an examination of the brain and the behaviour of the individual organism to consider the relationships between brains – that is of organisms interacting in a natural environment. This, the province of ethology, is represented by five chapters, forming section five (OU units 14 and 15). Having come so far along the road provided by the experimental sciences, in the final section we can explore at last what the whole enterprise of the brain is about – the suggestive, confused and uncertain relationships of brains with models, machines and minds (OU units 16 and 17).

It should be emphasized, however, that throughout the reader, we have sought also to choose articles that illumine the relationship between the work of the neurobiologist and its social implications. Hence we include in their appropriate place critical discussions of the nature and significance of psychoactive agents, of the ethologizing tendencies of some recent attempts to "explain" man and the vexed nature–nurture conflict, transmuted as it is in its present version, to the topic of "race, intelligence and IQ".

The book has been produced at great speed to meet the deadlines which the Open University habitually sets its academics, administrators and students. As it is a compilation of original articles, we have retained where necessary the original style, spelling and figures, thus keeping alterations to the minimum, even at the risk of a certain inconsistency of style. The achievement of getting it out on time owes much to the tenacious editorial assistance of Judy Hicklin, and the co-operation of the publishers and their designers.

**N Chalmers**
**R Crawley**
**S P R Rose**

September 1971

# Contents

# Introduction
# The biological bases
# of behaviour
*Steven P R Rose and*
*Neil Chalmers*

If the reader has skimmed through the pages of this book, he might have been surprised to find within it articles by authors with interests as diverse as neuroanatomy, experimental psychology, philosophy, ethology, biochemistry and neurophysiology, to say nothing of areas less easily classifiable. The fact that all these people can have something important and different to say about the problems of nervous systems and behaviour is remarkable, and is one which raises mixed emotions in those currently engaged in behavioural and neurological research. That the problems of behaviour are being attacked by so many different people from so many different angles is heartening, and is a convincing sign that the nervous control of behaviour is nowadays coming to be regarded as one of the central problems of biology. With new and powerful experimental techniques as diverse as the ultracentrifuge, the electron microscope and the on-line computer, and with more sophisticated techniques of analysing behaviour, the whole field is wide open for exploration. There is, of course, another side to the coin. With a subject as complex as this, how can one ever hope to master all its aspects? How can a neurochemist talk meaningfully to a psychologist, or an information technologist to an ethologist? This difficulty has become particularly apparent over recent years, and in an attempt to overcome it there have been an increasingly large number of conferences and publications with an interdisciplinary approach. What has come out of these cooperative ventures is virtually a new science, one which as yet does not even have a satisfactory name. Its area is that of neurobiology and behaviour, and it is upon this area that the articles in this book concentrate.

It is a wide area, and it is useful to survey it now very briefly to see in which parts our knowledge is already substantial, which parts are at present being actively investigated and providing results, and which parts remain at present unapproachable.

The nervous system did not escape the nineteenth century biologist's passion for meticulous description, and so it is that our knowledge of the gross anatomy of nervous systems and sense organs of a wide variety of animals is both comprehensive and has a historical depth that is unusual in the neurobehavioural sciences. At a finer level, however, the situation is more fluid. We know that nervous systems contain varying numbers of nerve cells, from just a few hundred in some invertebrates to the $10^{10}$ nerve cells in the human cortex. Once one of these nerve cells fires, we can explain fairly well in physiological terms how the impulse travels down the nerve. (See "How cells communicate" by Bernhard Katz, chapter 2). A more complicated problem concerns what happens at the junctions between the nerve cells, at the synapses. Some idea of the complexity of the situation appears when it is realized that each nerve cell in the human cortex may make up to 10 000 connexions with its neighbours by way of synapses. It is at the synapse that the electrical transmission down the nerve is replaced by chemical transmission, and, because a synapse is the only place where one nerve cell interacts with another, it is the most likely site of any coding or information-transducing properties of the entire brain system. The synapse has been likened to the "and/or" gate of a computer. The release of a transmitter from the presynaptic cell can either trigger or inhibit the firing of the postsynaptic cell. (See "The synapse", by John Eccles, chapter 1).

Remarkable advances in the understanding of synaptic mechanisms have been made possible by two technological developments: the ultracentrifuge, which can separate purified preparation of synapses from the rest of the brain tissue; and multi-barrelled injection and recording electrodes, which, placed adjacent to individual nerve cells or inserted intracellularly, have been used both to examine the electrical responses of the cell membrane to impulses arriving upon it, and the effect of microapplication of putative transmitter substances. In parallel with these developments, techniques for studying single nerve cells and isolating them in bulk from brain tissue have begun to build up a model of the biochemical properties of the functioning cell and its reaction to changes in its environment.

At a more complex level than the study of single cells and their interactions with their immediate neighbours, we are concerned with the integration of functionally specialized nerve cells into blocks with particular roles, and input and output properties. Working on the assumption that such integration must result in recognizable behaviour patterns, earlier research attacked the problem in two ways. Careful observations of the behaviour of animals provided in many cases indicators of what sorts of nervous control must underlie the behaviour. Parallel to this, but at a more experimental level, were developed techniques involving anatomical assault on the brain — extirpation of specific areas and examination of the subsequent behaviour of the organism. (See, for example, chapter 16 by James Olds.)

To these have been added more sophisticated experimental techniques. These include the mapping of connexions of individual cells with each other, and the intracellular recording of the electrical events within a given cell consequent upon changes in the input message — either by artificial stimulation of the cells or brain regions known to be connected to the cell under study, or by behavioural changes in the animal's environment.

These various techniques have led to a much greater understanding of the nervous control of behaviour. The work of Pantin and, more recently, of several other people on coelenterates provides a clear example of the nervous control of movement in animals with simple nervous systems. In the fifties, E. S. Hodgson showed how the feeding response of blowflies fitted in with the neurophysiological properties of neurons situated in hairs on the flies' mouthparts. Another example comes from the work of Kenneth Roeder and his colleagues on the escape responses which certain moths make to the calls of bats which are hunting them. Roeder showed that various properties of the nerves connected with the moth's auditory system correlated well with the behaviour the moth showed when stimulated by sound. In vertebrates, too, there are encouraging results. The area of the brain whose function and anatomy has most satisfactorily been resolved by such techniques is undoubtedly the cerebellum, a large mass of highly convoluted tissue at the rear of the brain whose major function is the control of fine movement A combination of anatomical mapping, physiological recording techniques and mathematical analysis, mainly by Eccles and his collaborators, has produced a convincing solution to some of the questions relating to the internal and external interactions of this particular brain region. (See "How the cerebellum may be used" by Stephen Blomfield and David Marr, chapter 3.)

Far less tractable, because of its complexity, has proved the cerebral cortex, the thin sheet of "grey matter" which skims the top surface of the brain and is responsible for most of its higher nervous function. There are many different types of nerve cells in the cortex — different in shape,

connectivity and perhaps function — and their relations are unclear. A step towards understanding their operation, however, has been made by the detailed studies of David Hubel and Torsten Wiesel at Harvard University. (See "The visual cortex of the brain" by David Hubel, chapter 10.) They have been able to show, within that portion of the visual cortex which integrates visual input, that it is organized into "columns" of cells. These relate to different parts of the visual field, and contain cells which fire in response to inputs of differing types — such as, for instance, light followed by dark, or dark followed by light, or movement to the right or left. The existence of cells, or groups of cells, which can thus classify and analyse information arriving from the sense receptors, seems a major clue to our understanding of the integrative function of the brain. Just as in animals with less complex nervous systems the relationships between behavioural and neurophysiological data are becoming clearer, so here we can be hopeful that this neurophysiological information will eventually join up with the work of psychologists who are studying sensory processes and perception from the behavioural end.

At the highest level of complexity — the integration of total brain function — the last decade has seen the identification of several groups of cells connected to one another but scattered through the brain (for instance, the so-called reticular formation which is described by J. D. French, chapter 18). The past ten years have also seen the identification of particular brain regions (such as the hypothalamus), which have been shown by techniques of ablation, and of chemical or electrical stimulation, to control whole patterns of behaviour. These range from eliciting specific responses such as anger, fear, hunger or pleasure, to such less well defined brain "states" as arousal, attention or sleep. Several hormones, drugs and other psychoactive agents clearly affect the functioning of these groups of cells. Many of these topics are reviewed in section III of this volume.

Sophisticated and diverse these studies may be, but they do not cover all the problems in the field of neurobiology and behaviour. Another major area concerns the way the nervous system changes in an animal with time. On the broadest temporal canvas we may ask how nervous systems have evolved. At what evolutionary stage did nerves first appear? At what stage did they first collect together into ganglia, so forming the rudiments of a central nervous system which controlled behaviour? By what evolutionary stages were these ganglia elaborated to give the complex brains of, say, the octopus, or of vertebrates, including man himself? At what stage did consciousness arise? The earliest forbears of such characteristics are being pushed steadily back; papers have appeared claiming that even unicellular organisms, like Paramoecium, with no nervous system at all, can show simple behavioural repertoires. Meanwhile, allegations that flatworms – the simplest animals to show anything approximately equivalent to a central nervous system – can learn, have been made frequently and have been the subject of a number of rather sensational experiments.

Next in order as a temporal question comes that of identifying the pattern of development of the individual brain. Particular nerve cells during development and growth of the brain show a remarkable combination of specificity and plasticity. Specificity lies within the "wiring diagram" of many parts of the brain which is laid down with astonishing precision. A notable example is the visual pathway, where each retinal cell seems in some way to know with which cells on each of the various staging posts to the cerebral cortex it should make contact – and can find them again to develop connexions against severe experimental obstacles. Such specificity is one of the most intriguing of neurobiological problems (and ranks equally as a problem in developmental biology as a whole). Current theories often invoke "gradients" of chemical concentration which specify the pathways individual cells must take, and some chemical coding must clearly be involved. But theory has for long lagged behind the spectacular experimental results obtained in this area.

The specificity of the wiring diagram ensures, for instance, that the eye can communicate meaningfully with the brain. There remains the plasticity which has to ensure that this communication can be interpreted appropriately depending upon past experience and information – in other words, the capacity of the brain system to show memory and learning. Here indeed experiment and theory have been prolific. For many years now psychologists have been investigating learning and memory from a behavioural point of view, and more recently biochemists and neurophysiologists have attacked the same problem, trying to find tangible, physical changes which accompany learning. In such investigations it is usually assumed that the physical changes in the brain during the laying down of a memory trace result from the activity of modifiable synapses so as to provide a new pattern of connectivity between the cells, each "pattern" of connected cells representing a unique memory trace. Other theories, popular among mathematicians, substitute a "field" for a "point" theory of memory; arguing by analogy with the hologram, they see memory as a function of the total "state" of the brain at any given time. The differences between these models are not as yet resolved at the experimental level. (See section IV.)

There are still more complex problems in the field of behaviour: problems very much in the psychologists' and the philosophers' domain, such as cognition, thinking and consciousness (as section VI will show). Are our experimental techniques capable of approaching these problems too? This remains an unanswered question. Certainly the brain sciences of the sixties and early seventies, while producing fresh insights into what mechanisms might conceivably have been involved in these processes, have yet to provide us with either a technique or an experiment which can supplement the theoretical models which have been suggested.

Finally, there is one other major area in the field of neurobiology and behaviour. Given that an animal has a set of behavioural abilities, one has to ask how these abilities adapt the animal to the life it leads: how they help it in finding food and in escaping from predators, for example, and how animals of the same species interact with one another. In short, these are questions of the function, adaptiveness and evolution of behaviour. The work of Konrad Lorenz, Niko Tinbergen, and in more recent years, of many other ethologists, has been devoted to answering such questions – but in answering them, has raised questions concerning the validity of extrapolation of this work to man. (See section V.)

The last decade has thus pulled together a number of threads in the fabric of explanation of nervous system function and behaviour. As progress is made towards a fuller understanding of these problems, there remain those who argue that an explanation of behaviour in terms of mechanisms of brain function (reductionism) is impossible, that there is more to behaviour than this. There are others who feel that application of analytical techniques to the human brain is somehow degrading man and reducing him to a mere machine. The case against reductionism is made eloquently by Donald MacKay in "The bankruptcy of determinism" (chapter 33).

There are certainly some levels of description of brain function – one's feelings in the act of love, or of creative thought, for instance – which are best and most economically described using a language system which refers to the whole organism and not its molecular or cellular parts. It is not that it is impossible to use the molecular or submolecular language system, at least theoretically, albeit that it is beyond our range at present; it is simply that it is an inappropriate language to deal conveniently with these phenomena. Understanding the human brain is a way of recognizing and contributing to its uniqueness; it does not diminish it any more than understanding the mechanisms of genetics diminishes the act of love. Nor need we accept that it is theoretically impossible for one to "know oneself", to provide a satisfactory general description of brain function in molecular or cellular terms, although it will take a good deal longer to do that than the next decade or so. We are the beginning, not the end, of this particular road of research.

Which brings us to our final question: do we want to travel this road, to understand the brain? So far it has not been the case that advances in biological research have led to a conspicuous diminution in the quality of human life; rather the reverse. For other sciences, especially physics, such a diminution is today at least an arguable proposition. Can we be sure that a greater understanding of brain function would be applied to the benefit of mankind?

The air is dark with gloomy warnings of prospects of biological abuses, ranging from ecological death, test tube babies and genetic engineering, to mind and thought control. It is not easy to see how research into memory mechanisms, for instance, can readily lead to a greater abuse of individual humans by powerful manipulators – not on grounds of a belief in basic human virtue, but on the purely technical consideration that at this stage in our understanding of these mechanisms it is hard to see how they can be abused in a way subtle enough to achieve what the mind-bender may want. Experience of the relatively unpredictable effects of psychoactive agents on a population basis would seem to us to be a sufficient warning against too ready a belief that such a hazard is really imminent.

Such sanguinity may seem cold comfort to the doom watchers. It may appear as a sort of special pleading for the immunity of the neurobiologist's domain. At present, it appears that good can come out of understanding brain mechanisms – intellectual good, as a contribution towards the proper task of science, helping us to know ourselves; and material good in terms of the development of techniques for aiding the mentally ill or handicapped, and possibly also of techniques for helping us to improve or enrich the development of our children. Like all such scientific predictions in our uncertain world, this one can be only conditionally valid. A proportion of brain research, for example, is sponsored by organizations not noted for their benevolence, the US Department of Defence, NATO and the Ministry of Defence (Porton Down) among others. Those of us who, as neurobiologists, feel that we know the limits of our science better than these organizations must therefore remain vigilant.

# Section I
# Structure, function and development of the nervous system

In this section, we consider the hardware of the brain and its basic operating mechanisms both in the highly developed form of the adult mammal and in its evolutionary history. The majority of articles in the section are chosen to illustrate two main themes: those of *specificity*, the way the nervous system is rigidly structured in order to conduct certain operations with a degree of invariance, and *plasticity*, the way the system is capable of modifying its responses to changing circumstances – the key to the learning capacity of the brain, as we shall see in a later section.

The units of which the brain's hardware is composed are its nerve cells, the neurons, of which there have been estimated to be some $10^{10}$ in the cortex of the human brain, each making $10^3 - 10^4$ connexions with its neighbours. These synapses are the switches of the nervous system, which ensure one-way signal conduction and, because of their capacity to be turned on and off, provide a coding potential to the system.

Their analysis has been contributed to by biochemists, pharmacologists and physiologists. It is one of the latter, John Eccles, whose work has been responsible for many of our present views on the workings of the synapse, who contributes the first chapter of this reader.

There are four major components to the nervous system at the level of its individual units: the nerve cell itself, its dendrites, on which other cells synapse, its own synapses, and, connecting cell body to synapses, the nerve fibre or axon. Unlike the synapse, axonal conduction is invariant; it functions like a telephone wire. Much of the biochemistry, physiology and some of the biophysics, of its functioning have been resolved in the last two decades, and the author of chapter 2, Bernhard Katz, has been at the forefront of this field.

To relate the properties of individual cells and their connexions to those of the system as a whole, one needs to analyse the interactions of groups of cells and the various possible modes of their communication. This has presented a more formidable task, and the methodology to achieve it is only slowly being worked out. It demands a macrophysiological rather than a microphysiological approach, some of the techniques of classical anatomy, and often, the help of computer simulation and some of the mathematic armoury of the newly developing field of theoretical biology. There are no hard and fast answers here, but one of the younger researchers who has produced a series of papers which have caused considerable ripples is David Marr; his theories of cerebellar and cerebral working have attracted wide attention, and are represented here by a short paper with Stephen Blomfield on a possible mechanism for cerebellar function. A similar type of analysis, but more closely linked with neurophysiological data, is provided by David Hubel for the visual cortex and is included in section II.

The specificity and precision of the nervous system raise in acute form the question of its evolutionary origin: did it arise from a random collection of interacting cells, achieving greater precision of connectivity as evolution proceeded, or as an entire system gradually evolving the units required for efficient function? The extract from Alfred Romer's book throws some light on this question.

Finally, no account of the nervous system can omit a discussion either of the sense organs providing the information which the system processes, and the effectors which carry out the results of this processing. The sense organs warrant a full section to themselves (section II), but we feel it proper to conclude this section with an account of the working of the use of the major effector organs, the striated (voluntary) muscle, provided by one of the leading exponents of the "sliding filaments" model of muscle action, Hugh Huxley.

# 1 The synapse
## by *Sir John Eccles*

The human brain is the most highly organized form of matter known, and in complexity the brains of the other higher animals are not greatly inferior. For certain purposes it is expedient to regard the brain as being analogous to a machine. Even if it is so regarded, however, it is a machine of a totally different kind from those made by man. In trying to understand the workings of his own brain man meets his highest challenge. Nothing is given; there are no operating diagrams, no maker's instructions.

The first step in trying to understand the brain is to examine its structure in order to discover the components from which it is built and how they are related to one another. After that one can attempt to understand the mode of operation of the simplest components. These two modes of investigation – the morphological and the physiological – have now become complementary. In studying the nervous system with today's sensitive electrical devices, however, it

*first published in* Scientific American, *January 1965.*

*Reprinted with permission. Copyright © 1965 by Scientific American, Inc. All rights reserved.*

is all too easy to find physiological events that cannot be correlated with any known anatomical structure. Conversely, the electron microscope reveals many structural details whose physiological significance is obscure or unknown.

At the close of the past century the Spanish anatomist Santiago Ramón y Cajal showed how all parts of the nervous system are built up of individual nerve cells of many different shapes and sizes. Like other cells, each nerve cell has a nucleus and a surrounding cytoplasm. Its outer surface consists of numerous fine branches – the dendrites – that receive nerve impulses from other nerve cells, and one relatively long branch – the axon – that transmits nerve impulses. Near its end the axon divides into branches that terminate at the dendrites or bodies of other nerve cells. The axon can be as short as a fraction of a millimeter or as long as a meter, depending on its place and function. It has many of the properties of an electric cable and is uniquely specialized to conduct the brief electrical waves called nerve impulses. In very thin axons these impulses travel at less than one meter per second; in others, for example in the

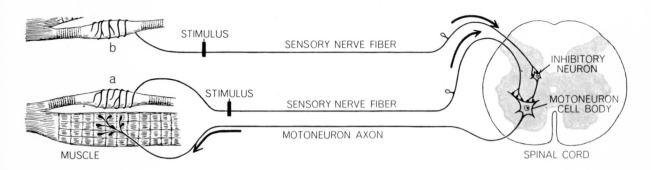

**Figure 1.1 Reflex arcs** provide simple pathways for studying the transmission of nerve impulses from one nerve cell to another. This transmission is effectuated at the junction points called synapses. In the illustration the sensory fiber from one muscle stretch receptor (*a*) makes direct synaptic contact with a motoneuron in the spinal cord. Nerve impulses generated by the motoneuron activate the muscle to which the stretch receptor is attached. Stretch receptor *b* responds to the tension in a neighboring antagonistic muscle and sends impulses to a nerve cell that can inhibit the firing of the motoneuron. By electrically stimulating the appropriate stretch-receptor fibers one can study the effect of excitatory and inhibitory impulses on motoneurons.

large axons of the nerve cells that activate muscles, they travel as fast as 100 meters per second.

The electrical impulse that travels along the axon ceases abruptly when it comes to the point where the axon's terminal fibers make contact with another nerve cell. These junction points were given the name "synapses" by Sir Charles Sherrington, who laid the foundations of what is sometimes called synaptology. If the nerve impulse is to continue beyond the synapse, it must be regenerated afresh on the other side. As recently as 1950 some physiologists held that transmission at the synapse was predominantly, if not exclusively, an electrical phenomenon. Now, however, there is abundant evidence that transmission is effectuated by the release of specific chemical substances that trigger a regeneration of the impulse. In fact, the first strong evidence showing that a transmitter substance acts across the synapse was provided in the early 1920s by Sir Henry Dale and Otto Loewi.

It has been estimated that the human central nervous system, which of course includes the spinal cord as well as the brain itself, consists of about 10 billion ($10^{10}$) nerve cells. With rare exceptions each nerve cell receives information directly in the form of impulses from many other nerve cells – often hundreds – and transmits information to a like number. Depending on its threshold of response, a given nerve cell may fire an impulse when stimulated by only a few incoming fibers or it may not fire until stimulated by many incoming fibers. It has long been known that this threshold can be raised or lowered by various factors. Moreover, it was conjectured some 65 years ago that some of the incoming fibers must inhibit the firing of the receiving cell rather than excite it (figure 1.2). The conjecture was subsequently confirmed, and the mechanism of the inhibitory effect has now been clarified. This mechanism and its equally fundamental counterpart – nerve-cell excitation – are the subject of this article.

## Probing the nerve cell

At the level of anatomy there are some clues to indicate how the fine axon terminals impinging on a nerve cell can make the cell regenerate a nerve impulse of its own. Figure 1.3 shows how a nerve cell and its dendrites are covered by fine branches of nerve fibers that terminate in knoblike structures. These structures are the synapses.

The electron microscope has revealed structural details of synapses that fit in nicely with the view that a chemical transmitter is involved in nerve transmission (figures 1.4 and 1.5). Enclosed in the synaptic knob are many vesicles, or tiny sacs, which appear to contain the transmitter substances that induce synaptic transmission. Between the

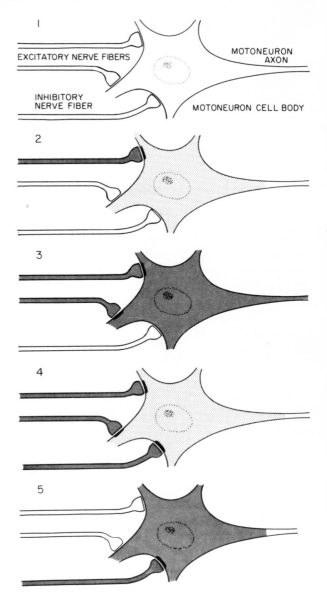

**Figure 1.2 Excitation and inhibition** of a nerve cell are accomplished by the nerve fibers that form synapses on its surface. *1* shows a motoneuron in the resting state. In *2* impulses received from one excitatory fiber are inadequate to cause the motoneuron to fire. In *3* impulses from a second excitatory fiber raise the motoneuron to firing threshold. In *4* impulses carried by an inhibitory fiber restore the subthreshold condition. In *5* the inhibitory fiber alone is carrying impulses. There is no difference in the electrical impulses carried by excitatory and inhibitory nerve fibers. They achieve opposite effects because they release different chemical transmitter substances at their synaptic endings.

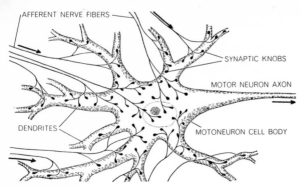

**Figure 1.3 Motoneuron cell body** and branches called dendrites are covered with synaptic knobs, which represent the terminals of axons, or impulse-carrying fibers, from other nerve cells. The axon of each motoneuron, in turn, terminates at a muscle fiber.

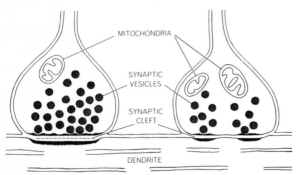

**Figure 1.4 Synaptic knobs** are designed to deliver short bursts of a chemical transmitter substance into the synaptic cleft, where it can act on the surface of the nerve-cell membrane below. Before release, molecules of the chemical transmitter are stored in numerous vesicles, or sacs. Mitochondria are specialized structures that help to supply the cell with energy.

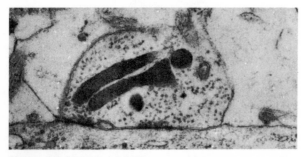

**Figure 1.5 Assumed inhibitory synapse** on a nerve cell is magnified 28 000 diameters in this electron micrograph by the late L. H. Hamlyn of University College, London. Synaptic vesicles, believed to contain the transmitter substance, are bunched in two regions along the synaptic cleft. The darkening of the cleft in these regions is so far unexplained.

synaptic knob and the synaptic membrane of the adjoining nerve cell is a remarkably uniform space of about 20 millimicrons that is termed the synaptic cleft. Many of the synaptic vesicles are concentrated adjacent to this cleft; it seems plausible that the transmitter substance is discharged from the nearest vesicles into the cleft, where it can act on the adjacent cell membrane. This hypothesis is supported by the discovery that the transmitter is released in packets of a few thousand molecules.

The study of synaptic transmission was revolutionized in 1951 by the introduction of delicate techniques for recording electrically from the interior of single nerve cells. This is done by inserting into the nerve cell an extremely fine glass pipette with a diameter of 0.5 micron – about a fifty-thousandth of an inch. The pipette is filled with an electrically conducting salt solution such as concentrated potassium chloride. If the pipette is carefully inserted and held rigidly in place, the cell membrane appears to seal quickly around the glass, thus preventing the flow of a short-circuiting current through the puncture in the cell membrane. Impaled in this fashion, nerve cells can function normally for hours. Although there is no way of observing the cells during the insertion of the pipette, the insertion can be guided by using as clues the electric signals that the pipette picks up when close to active nerve cells.

When my colleagues and I in New Zealand and later at the John Curtin School of Medical Research in Canberra first employed this technique, we chose to study the large nerve cells called motoneurons, which lie in the spinal cord and whose function is to activate muscles. This was a fortunate choice: intracellular investigations with motoneurons have proved to be easier and more rewarding than those with any other kind of mammalian nerve cell.

We soon found that when the nerve cell responds to the chemical synaptic transmitter, the response depends in part on characteristic features of ionic composition that are also concerned with the transmission of impulses in the cell and along its axon. When the nerve cell is at rest, its physiological makeup resembles that of most other cells in that the water solution inside the cell is quite different in composition from the solution in which the cell is bathed. The nerve cell is able to exploit this difference between external and internal composition and use it in quite different ways for generating an electrical impulse and for synaptic transmission.

The composition of the external solution is well established because the solution is essentially the same as blood from which cells and proteins have been removed. The composition of the internal solution is known only approximately. Indirect evidence indicates that the concentrations of sodium and chloride ions outside the cell are respectively

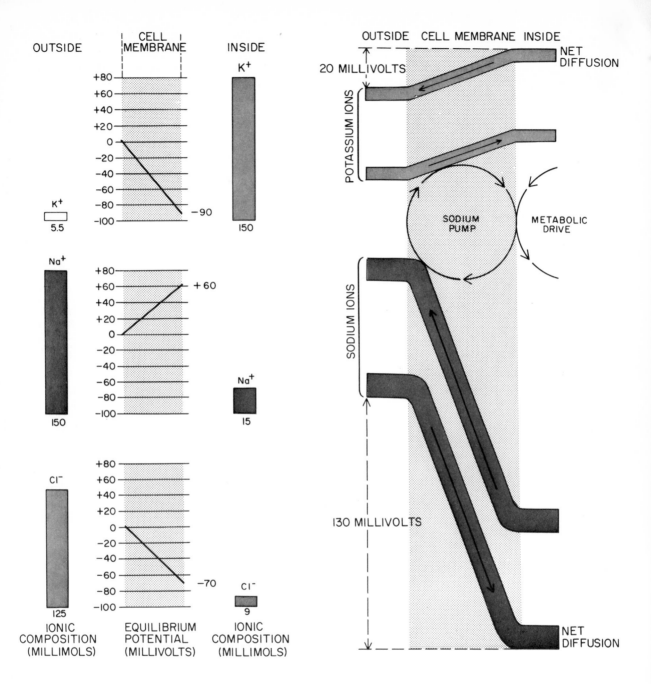

**Figure 1.6 Ionic composition** outside and inside the nerve cell is markedly different. The "equilibrium potential" is the voltage drop that would have to exist across the membrane of the nerve cell to produce the observed difference in concentration for each type of ion. The actual voltage drop is about 70 millivolts, with the inside being negative. Given this drop, chloride ions diffuse inward and outward at equal rates, but the concentration of sodium and potassium must be maintained by some auxiliary mechanism (figure 1.7).

**Figure 1.7 Metabolic pump** must be postulated to account for the observed concentrations of potassium and sodium ions on opposite sides of the nerve-cell membrane. The negative potential inside is 20 millivolts short of the equilibrium potential for potassium ions. Thus there is a net outward diffusion of potassium ions that must be balanced by the pump. For sodium ions the potential across the membrane is 130 millivolts in the wrong direction, so very energetic pumping is needed. Chloride ions are in equilibrium.

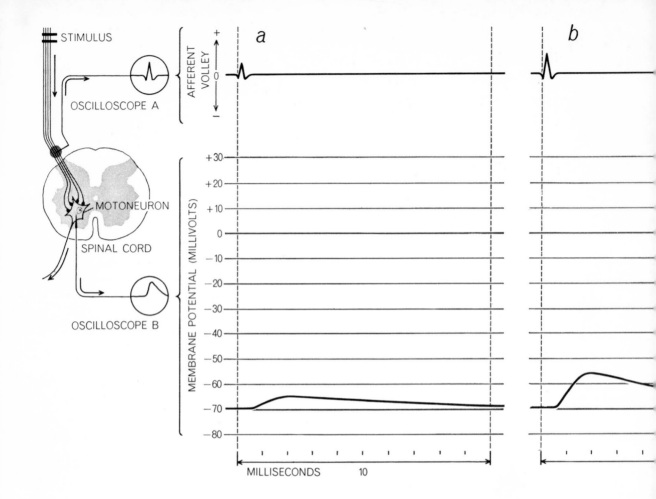

**Figure 1.8 Excitation of a motoneuron** is studied by stimulating the sensory fibers that send impulses to it. The size of the "afferent volleys" reaching the motoneuron is displayed on oscilloscope *A*. A microelectrode implanted in the motoneuron measures the changes in the cell's internal electric potential. These changes, called excitatory postsynaptic potentials (EPSPs), appear on oscilloscope *B*. The size of the afferent volley is proportional to the number of fibers stimulated to fire. It is assumed here that one to four fibers can be activated. When only one fiber is activated (*a*), the potential inside the motoneuron shifts only slightly. When two fibers are activated (*b*), the shift is somewhat greater. When three fibers are

some 10 and 14 times higher than the concentrations inside the cell. In contrast, the concentration of potassium ions inside the cell is about 30 times higher than the concentration outside.

How can one account for this remarkable state of affairs? Part of the explanation is that the inside of the cell is negatively charged with respect to the outside of the cell by about 70 millivolts. Since like charges repel each other, this internal negative charge tends to drive chloride ions (Cl⁻) outward through the cell membrane and, at the same time, to impede their inward movement. In fact, a potential difference of 70 millivolts is just sufficient to maintain the

observed disparity in the concentration of chloride ions inside the cell and outside it; chloride ions diffuse inward and outward at equal rates. A drop of 70 millivolts across the membrane therefore defines the "equilibrium potential" for chloride ions.

To obtain a concentration of potassium ions ($K^+$) that is 30 times higher inside the cell than outside would require that the interior of the cell membrane be about 90 millivolts negative with respect to the exterior. Since the actual interior is only 70 millivolts negative, it falls short of the equilibrium potential for potassium ions by 20 millivolts. Evidently the thirtyfold concentration can be achieved

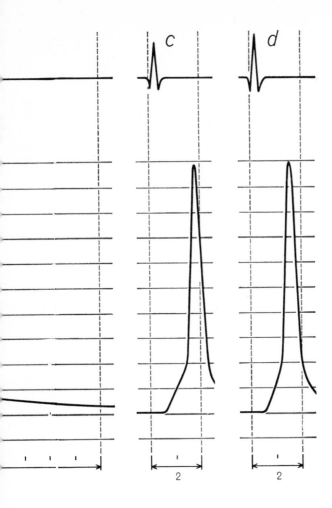

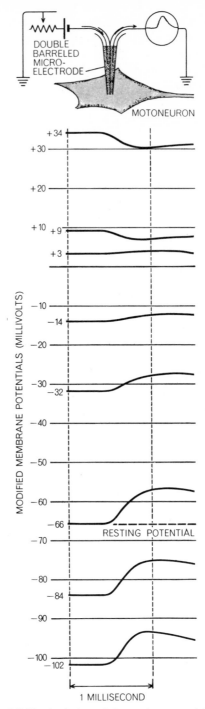

activated (c), the potential reaches the threshold at which depolarization proceeds swiftly and a spike appears on oscilloscope B. The spike signifies that the motoneuron has generated a nerve impulse of its own. When four or more fibers are activated (d), the motoneuron reaches the threshold more quickly.

and maintained only if there is some auxiliary mechanism for "pumping" potassium ions into the cell at a rate equal to their spontaneous net outward diffusion.

The pumping mechanism has the still more difficult task of pumping sodium ions ($Na^+$) out of the cell against a potential gradient of 130 millivolts. This figure is obtained by adding the 70 millivolts of internal negative charge to the equilibrium potential for sodium ions, which is 60 millivolts of internal *positive* charge (figures 1.6 and 1.7). If it were not for this postulated pump, the concentration of sodium ions inside and outside the cell would be almost the reverse of what is observed.

**Figure 1.9 Manipulation** of the resting potential of a motoneuron clarifies the nature of the EPSP. A steady background current applied through the left barrel of a microelectrode (*top*) shifts the membrane potential away from its normal resting level (minus 66 millivolts in this particular cell). The other barrel records the EPSP. The equilibrium potential, the potential at which the EPSP reverses direction, is about zero millivolts.

In their classic studies of nerve-impulse transmission in the giant axon of the squid, A. L. Hodgkin, A. F. Huxley and Bernhard Katz of Britain demonstrated that the propagation of the impulse coincides with abrupt changes in the permeability of the axon membrane. When a nerve impulse has been triggered in some way, what can be described as a gate opens and lets sodium ions pour into the axon during the advance of the impulse, making the interior of the axon locally positive. The process is self-reinforcing in that the flow of some sodium ions through the membrane opens the gate further and makes it easier for others to follow. The sharp reversal of the internal polarity of the membrane constitutes the nerve impulse, which moves like a wave until it has traveled the length of the axon. In the wake of the impulse the sodium gate closes and a potassium gate opens, thereby restoring the normal polarity of the membrane within a millisecond or less.

With this understanding of the nerve impulse in hand, one is ready to follow the electrical events at the excitatory synapse. One might guess that if the nerve impulse results from an abrupt inflow of sodium ions and a rapid change in the electrical polarity of the axon's interior, something similar must happen at the body and dendrites of the nerve cell in order to generate the impulse in the first place. Indeed, the function of the excitatory synaptic terminals on the cell body and its dendrites is to depolarize the interior of the cell membrane essentially by permitting an inflow of sodium ions. When the depolarization reaches a threshold value, a nerve impulse is triggered.

As a simple instance of this phenomenon we have recorded the depolarization that occurs in a single motoneuron activated directly by the large nerve fibers that enter the spinal cord from special stretch-receptors known as annulospiral endings. These receptors in turn are located in the same muscle that is activated by the motoneuron under study. Thus the whole system forms a typical reflex arc, such as the arc responsible for the patellar reflex, or "knee jerk" (figure 1.1).

To conduct the experiment we anesthetize an animal (most often a cat) and free by dissection a muscle nerve that contains these large nerve fibers. By applying a mild electric shock to the exposed nerve one can produce a single impulse in each of the fibers; since the impulses travel to the spinal cord almost synchronously they are referred to collectively as a volley. The number of impulses contained in the volley can be reduced by reducing the stimulation applied to the nerve. The volley strength is measured at a point just outside the spinal cord and is displayed on an oscilloscope. About half a millisecond after detection of a volley there is a wavelike change in the voltage inside the motoneuron that

has received the volley. The change is detected by a microelectrode inserted in the motoneuron and is displayed on another oscilloscope.

What we find is that the negative voltage inside the cell becomes progressively less negative as more of the fibers impinging on the cell are stimulated to fire. This observed depolarization is in fact a simple summation of the depolarizations produced by each individual synapse. When the depolarization of the interior of the motoneuron reaches a critical point, a "spike" suddenly appears on the second oscilloscope, showing that a nerve impulse has been generated. During the spike the voltage inside the cell changes from about 70 millivolts negative to as much as 30 millivolts positive. The spike regularly appears when the depolarization, or reduction of membrane potential, reaches a critical level, which is usually between 10 and 18 millivolts. The only effect of a further strengthening of the synaptic stimulus is to shorten the time needed for the motoneuron to reach the firing threshold (figure 1.8). The depolarizing potentials produced in the cell membrane by excitatory synapses are called excitatory postsynaptic potentials, or EPSPs.

Through one barrel of a double-barreled microelectrode one can apply a background current to change the resting potential of the interior of the cell membrane, either increasing it or decreasing it. When the potential is made more negative, the EPSP rises more steeply to an earlier peak. When the potential is made less negative, the EPSP rises more slowly to a lower peak. Finally, when the charge inside the cell is reversed so as to be positive with respect to the exterior, the excitatory synapses give rise to an EPSP that is actually the reverse of the normal one (figure 1.9).

These observations support the hypothesis that excitatory synapses produce what amounts virtually to a short circuit in the synaptic membrane potential. When this occurs, the membrane no longer acts as a barrier to the passage of ions but lets them flow through in response to the differing electric potential on the two sides of the membrane (figure 1.10a). In other words, the ions are momentarily allowed to travel freely down their electrochemical gradients, which means that sodium ions flow into the cell and, to a lesser degree, potassium ions flow out. It is this net flow of positive ions that creates the excitatory postsynaptic potential. The flow of negative ions, such as the chloride ion, is apparently not involved. By artificially altering the potential inside the cell one can establish that there is no flow of ions, and therefore no EPSP, when the voltage drop across the membrane is zero.

How is the synaptic membrane converted from a strong ionic barrier into an ion-permeable state? It is currently

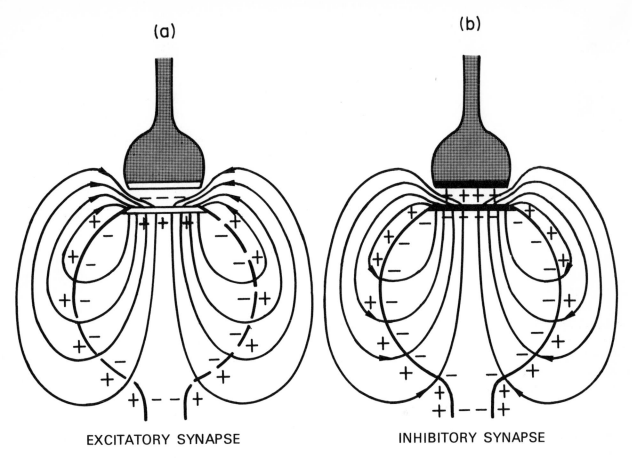

|  |  |
|---|---|
| **(a)** | **(b)** |
| EXCITATORY SYNAPSE | INHIBITORY SYNAPSE |

**Figure 1.10 Current flows** induced by excitatory and inhibitory synapses are shown at *a* and *b*. When the nerve cell is at rest, the interior of the cell membrane is uniformly negative with respect to the exterior. The excitatory synapse releases a chemical substance that depolarizes the cell membrane below the synaptic cleft, thus letting current flow into the cell at that point. At an inhibitory synapse the current flow is reversed.

accepted that the agency of conversion is the chemical transmitter substance contained in the vesicles inside the synaptic knob. When a nerve impulse reaches the synaptic knob, some of the vesicles are caused to eject the transmitter substance into the synaptic cleft (figure 1.11). The molecules of the substance would take only a few microseconds to diffuse across the cleft and become attached to specific receptor sites on the surface membrane of the adjacent nerve cell.

Presumably the receptor sites are associated with fine channels in the membrane that are opened in some way by the attachment of the transmitter-substance molecules to the receptor sites. With the channels thus opened, sodium and potassium ions flow through the membrane thousands of

times more readily than they normally do, thereby producing the intense ionic flux that depolarizes the cell membrane and produces the EPSP. In many synapses the current flows strongly for only about a millisecond before the transmitter substance is eliminated from the synaptic cleft, either by diffusion into the surrounding regions or as a result of being destroyed by enzymes. The latter process is known to occur when the transmitter substance is acetylcholine, which is destroyed by the enzyme acetylcholinesterase.

The substantiation of this general picture of synaptic transmission requires the solution of many fundamental problems. Since we do not know the specific transmitter substance for the vast majority of synapses in the nervous system we do not know if there are many different substances or only a few. The only one identified with reasonable certainty in the mammalian central nervous system is acetylcholine. We know practically nothing about the mechanism by which a presynaptic nerve impulse causes the transmitter substance to be injected into the synaptic cleft. Nor do we know how the synaptic vesicles not immediately adjacent to the synaptic cleft are moved up to the firing line to replace the emptied vesicles. It is conjectured that the vesicles contain the enzyme systems needed to recharge

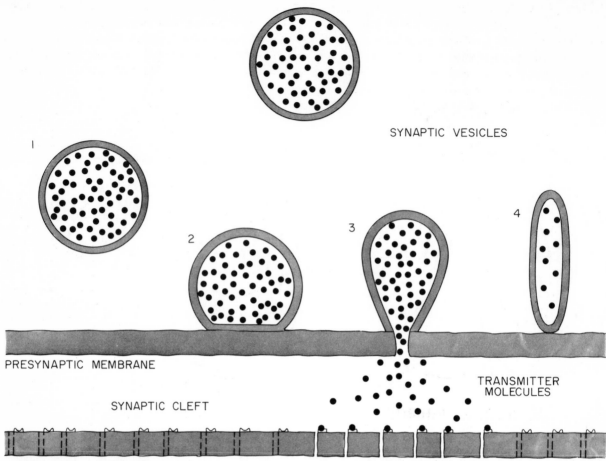

SYNAPTIC VESICLES

PRESYNAPTIC MEMBRANE

SYNAPTIC CLEFT

TRANSMITTER MOLECULES

SUBSYNAPTIC MEMBRANE

**Figure 1.11 Synaptic vesicles** containing a chemical transmitter are distributed throughout the synaptic knob. They are arranged here in a probable sequence, showing how they move up to the synaptic cleft, discharge their contents and return to the interior for recharging.

themselves. The entire process must be swift and efficient: the total amount of transmitter substance in synaptic terminals is enough for only a few minutes of synaptic activity at normal operating rates. There are also knotty problems to be solved on the other side of the synaptic cleft. What, for example, is the nature of the receptor sites? How are the ionic channels in the membrane opened up?

## The inhibitory synapse

Let us turn now to the second type of synapse that has been identified in the nervous system. These are the synapses that can inhibit the firing of a nerve cell even though it may be receiving a volley of excitatory impulses. When inhibitory synapses are examined in the electron microscope, they look

very much like excitatory synapses. (There are probably some subtle differences, but they need not concern us here.) Microelectrode recordings of the activity of single motoneurons and other nerve cells have now shown that the inhibitory postsynaptic potential (IPSP) is virtually a mirror image of the EPSP (figure 1.12). Moreover, individual inhibitory synapses, like excitatory synapses, have a cumulative effect. The chief difference is simply that the IPSP makes the cell's internal voltage more negative than it is normally, which is in a direction opposite to that needed for generating a spike discharge.

By driving the internal voltage of a nerve cell in the negative direction inhibitory synapses oppose the action of excitatory synapses (figure 1.10b), which of course drive it in the positive direction. Hence if the potential inside a resting cell is 70 millivolts negative, a strong volley of inhibitory impulses can drive the potential to 75 or 80 millivolts negative. One can easily see that if the potential is made more negative in this way the excitatory synapses find it more difficult to raise the internal voltage to the threshold

**Figure 1.12 Inhibition of a motoneuron** is investigated by methods like those used for studying the EPSP. The inhibitory counterpart of the EPSP is the IPSP: the inhibitory postsynaptic potential. Oscilloscope *A* records an afferent volley that travels to a number of inhibitory nerve cells whose axons form synapses on a nearby motoneuron (see figure 1.2). A microelectrode in the motoneuron is connected to oscilloscope *B*. The sequence *a*, *b* and *c* shows how successively larger afferent volleys produce successively deeper IPSPs. Curves at right show how the IPSP is modified when a background current is used to change the motoneuron's resting potential. The equilibrium potential where the IPSP reverses direction is about minus 80 millivolts.

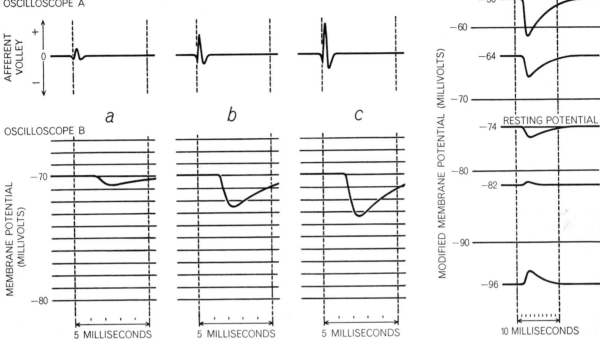

point for the generation of a spike. Thus the nerve cell responds to the algebraic sum of the internal voltage changes produced by excitatory and inhibitory synapses (figure 1.13).

If, as in the experiment described earlier, the internal membrane potential is altered by the flow of an electric current through one barrel of a double-barreled microelectrode, one can observe the effect of such changes on the inhibitory postsynaptic potential. When the internal potential is made less negative, the inhibitory postsynaptic potential is deepened. Conversely, when the potential is made more negative, the IPSP diminishes; it finally reverses when the internal potential is driven below minus 80 millivolts.

One can therefore conclude that inhibitory synapses share with excitatory synapses the ability to change the ionic permeability of the synaptic membrane. The difference is that inhibitory synapses enable ions to flow freely down an electrochemical gradient that has an equilibrium point at minus 80 millivolts rather than at zero, as is the case for excitatory synapses. This effect could be achieved by the outward flow of positively charged ions such as potassium or the inward flow of negatively charged ions such as chloride, or by a combination of negative and positive ionic flows such that the interior reaches equilibrium at minus 80 millivolts.

In an effort to discover the permeability changes associated with the inhibitory potential my colleagues and I have altered the concentration of ions normally found in motoneurons and have introduced a variety of other ions that are not normally present. This can be done by impaling nerve cells with micropipettes that are filled with a salt solution containing the ion to be injected. The actual injection is achieved by passing a brief current through the micropipette.

If the concentration of chloride ions within the cell is in this way increased as much as three times, the inhibitory postsynaptic potential reverses and acts as a depolarizing current; that is, it resembles an excitatory potential. On the other hand, if the cell is heavily injected with sulfate ions, which are also negatively charged, there is no such reversal

23

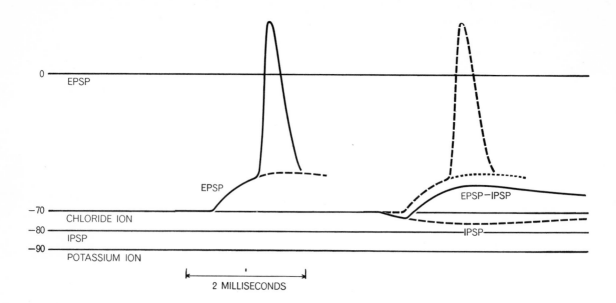

+60 ────── 
SODIUM ION

0 ────── 
EPSP

EPSP

EPSP−IPSP

−70 ────── 
CHLORIDE ION
−80 ────── 
IPSP
−90 ────── 
POTASSIUM ION

IPSP

|← 2 MILLISECONDS →|

**Figure 1.13 Inhibition of a spike discharge** is an electrical subtraction process. When a normal EPSP reaches a threshold (*left*), it will ordinarily produce a spike. An IPSP widens the gap between the cell's internal potential and the firing threshold. Thus if a cell is simultaneously subjected to both excitatory and inhibitory stimulation, the IPSP is subtracted from the EPSP (*right*) and no spike occurs. The five horizontal lines show equilibrium potentials for the three principal ions as well as for the EPSP and IPSP.

(figure 1.14). This simple test shows that under the influence of the inhibitory transmitter substance, which is still unidentified, the subsynaptic membrane becomes permeable momentarily to chloride ions but not to sulfate ions. During the generation of the IPSP the outflow of chloride ions is so rapid that it more than outweighs the flow of other ions that generate the normal inhibitory potential.

My colleagues have now tested the effect of injecting motoneurons with more than 30 kinds of negatively charged ion. With one exception the hydrated ions (ions bound to water) to which the cell membrane is permeable under the influence of the inhibitory transmitter substance are smaller than the hydrated ions to which the membrane is impermeable. The exception is the formate ion ($HCO_2^-$), which may have an ellipsoidal shape and so be able to pass through membrane pores that block smaller spherical ions.

Apart from the formate ion all the ions to which the membrane is permeable have a diameter not greater than 1.14 times the diameter of the potassium ion; that is, they are less than 2.9 angstrom units in diameter. Comparable investigations in other laboratories have found the same permeability effects, including the exceptional behavior of the formate ion, in fishes, toads and snails. It may well be that the ionic mechanism responsible for synaptic inhibition is the same throughout the animal kingdom.

The significance of these and other studies is that they strongly indicate that the inhibitory transmitter substance opens the membrane to the flow of potassium ions but not to sodium ions. It is known that the sodium ion is somewhat larger than any of the negatively charged ions, including the formate ion, that are able to pass through the membrane during synaptic inhibition. It is not possible, however, to test the effectiveness of potassium ions by injecting excess amounts into the cell because the excess is immediately diluted by an osmotic flow of water into the cell.

As I have indicated, the concentration of potassium ions inside the nerve cell is about 30 times greater than the concentration outside, and to maintain this large difference in concentration without the help of a metabolic pump the inside of the membrane would have to be charged 90 millivolts negative with respect to the exterior. This implies that if the membrane were suddenly made porous to potassium ions, the resulting outflow of ions would make the inside

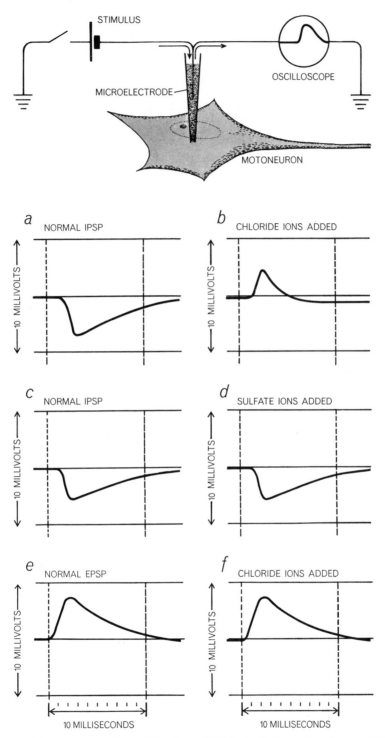

**Figure 1.14 Modification of ion concentration** within the nerve cell gives information about the permeability of the cell membrane. The internal ionic composition is altered by injecting selected ions through a microelectrode a minute or so before applying an afferent volley and recording the EPSP or IPSP. In the first experiment a normal IPSP (a) is changed to a pseudo EPSP (b) by an injection of chloride ions. When sulfate ions are similarly injected, the IPSP is practically unchanged (b, c). The third experiment shows that an injection of chloride ions has no significant effect on the EPSP (e, f).

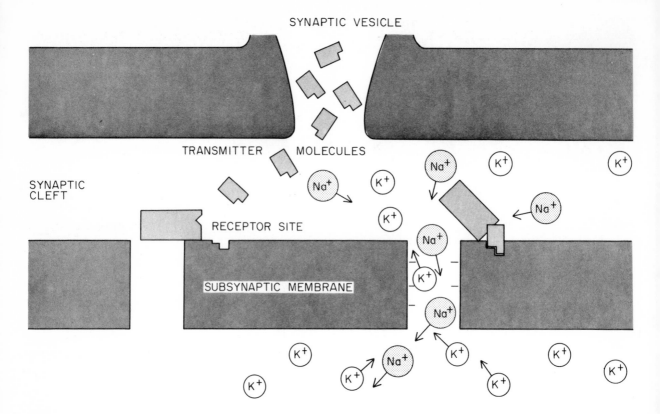

SYNAPTIC VESICLE

TRANSMITTER MOLECULES

SYNAPTIC CLEFT

RECEPTOR SITE

SUBSYNAPTIC MEMBRANE

**Figure 1.15 Excitatory synapse** may employ transmitter molecules that open large channels in the nerve-cell membrane. This would permit sodium ions, which are plentiful outside the cell, to pour through the membrane freely. The outward flow of potassium ions, driven by a smaller potential gradient, would be at a much slower rate. Chloride ions (*not shown*) may be prevented from flowing by negative charges on the channel walls.

potential of the membrane even more negative than it is in the resting state, and that is just what happens during synaptic inhibition. The membrane must not simultaneously become porous to sodium ions, because they exist in much higher concentration outside the cell than inside and their rapid inflow would more than compensate for the potassium outflow. In fact, the fundamental difference between synaptic excitation and synaptic inhibition is that the membrane freely passes sodium ions in response to the former and largely excludes the passage of sodium ions in response to the latter.

## Channels in the membrane

This fine discrimination between ions that are not very different in size must be explained by any hypothesis of synaptic action. It is most unlikely that the channels through the membrane are created afresh and accurately maintained for a thousandth of a second every time a burst of transmitter substance is released into the synaptic cleft. It is more likely that channels of at least two different sizes are built directly into the membrane structure. In some way the excitatory transmitter substance would selectively unplug the larger channels and permit the free inflow of sodium ions. Potassium ions would simultaneously flow out and thus would tend to counteract the large potential change that would be produced by the massive sodium inflow. The inhibitory transmitter substance would selectively unplug the smaller channels that are large enough to pass potassium and chloride ions but not sodium ions (figures 1.15 and 1.16).

To explain certain types of inhibition other features must be added to this hypothesis of synaptic transmission. In the simple hypothesis chloride and potassium ions can flow freely through pores of all inhibitory synapses. It has been shown, however, that the inhibition of the contraction of heart muscle by the vagus nerve is due almost exclusively to potassium-ion flow. On the other hand, in the muscles of

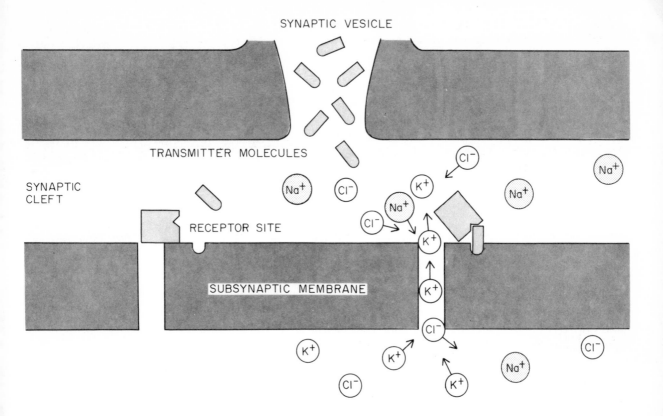

**Figure 1.16 Inhibitory synapse** may employ another type of transmitter molecule that opens channels too small to pass sodium ions. The net outflow of potassium ions and inflow of chloride ions would account for the hyperpolarization that is observed as an IPSP.

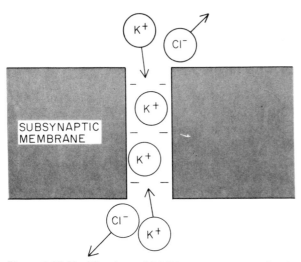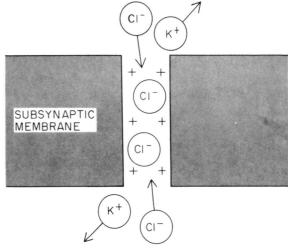

**Figure 1.17 Modifications of inhibitory synapse** may involve channels that carry either negative or positive charges on their walls. Negative charges (*left*) would permit only potassium ions to pass. Positive charges (*right*) would permit only chloride ions to pass.

crustaceans and in nerve cells in the snail's brain synaptic inhibition is due largely to the flow of chloride ions. This selective permeability could be explained if there were fixed charges along the walls of the channels. If such charges were negative, they would repel negatively charged ions and prevent their passage; if they were positive, they would similarly prevent the passage of positively charged ions. One can now suggest that the channels opened by the excitatory transmitter are negatively charged and so do not permit the passage of the negatively charged chloride ion, even though it is small enough to move through the channel freely (figure 1.17).

One might wonder if a given nerve cell can have excitatory synaptic action at some of its axon terminals and inhibitory action at others. The answer is no. Two different kinds of nerve cell are needed, one for each type of transmission and synaptic transmitter substance. This can readily be demonstrated by the effect of strychnine and tetanus toxin in the spinal cord; they specifically prevent inhibitory synaptic action and leave excitatory action unaltered. As a result the synaptic excitation of nerve cells is uncontrolled and convulsions result. The special types of cell responsible for inhibitory synaptic action are now being recognized in many parts of the central nervous system.

This account of communication between nerve cells is necessarily oversimplified, yet it shows that some significant advances are being made at the level of individual components of the nervous system. By selecting the most favorable situations we have been able to throw light on some details of nerve-cell behavior. We can be encouraged by these limited successes. But the task of understanding in a comprehensive way how the human brain operates staggers its own imagination.

## Bibliography

Excitation and Inhibition in Single Nerve Cells, Stephen W. Kuffler in *The Harvey Lectures, Series 54*, Academic Press, 1960

Physiology of Nerve Cells, John C. Eccles, Johns Hopkins Press, 1957

The Physiology of Synapses, John C. Eccles, Academic Press, 1964

The Transmission of Impulses from Nerve to Muscle, and the Subcellular Unit of Synaptic Action, B. Katz in *Proceedings of the Royal Society*, Vol. 155, No. 961, Series B, pages 455–77; April 1962

# 2 How cells communicate
## by Bernhard Katz

In the animal kingdom, the "higher" the organism, the more important becomes the system of cells set aside for coordinating its activities. Nature has developed two distinct coordinating mechanisms. One depends on the release and circulation of "chemical messengers", the hormones that are manufactured by certain specialized cells and that are capable of regulating the activity of cells in other parts of the body. The second mechanism, which is in general far superior in speed and selectivity, depends on a specialized system of nerve cells, or neurons, whose function is to receive and to give instructions by means of electrical impulses directed over specific pathways. Both coordinating mechanisms are ancient from the viewpoint of evolution, but it is the second – the nervous system – that has lent itself to the greater evolutionary development, culminating in that wonderful and mysterious structure, the human brain.

Man's understanding of the working of his millions of brain cells is still at a primitive stage. But our knowledge is reasonably adequate to a more restricted task, which is to describe and partially explain how individual cells – the neurons – generate and transmit the electrical impulses that form the basic code element of our internal communication system.

A large fraction of the neuronal cell population can be divided into two classes: sensory and motor. The sensory neurons collect and relay to higher centers in the nervous system the impulses that arise at special receptor sites, whose function is to monitor the organism's external and internal environments. The motor neurons carry impulses from the higher centers to the "working" cells, usually muscle cells, which provide the organism's response to changes in the two environments. In simple reflex reactions the transfer of signals from sensory to motor neurons is automatic and involves relatively simple synaptic mechanisms, which are fairly well understood.

first published in Scientific American, *September 1961*.
*Reprinted with permission. Copyright © 1961 by Scientific American, Inc. All rights reserved.*

When a nerve cell, either motor (figure 2.2) or sensory, begins to differentiate in the embryo, the cell body sends out a long fiber – the axon – which in some unknown way grows toward its proper peripheral station to make contact with muscle or skin. In man the adult axon may be several feet long, although it is less than 0.001 inch thick. It forms a kind of miniature cable for conducting messages between the periphery and the central terminus, which lies protected together with the nerve-cell body inside the spinal canal or the skull. Isolated peripheral nerve fibers probably have been subjected to more intense experimental study than any other tissue, in spite of the fact that they are only fragments of cells severed from their central nuclei as well as their terminal connections. Even so, isolated axons are capable of conducting tens of thousands of impulses before they fail to work. This fact and other observations make it clear that the nucleated body of the nerve cell is concerned with long-term maintenance of the nerve fibers – with growth and repair rather than with the immediate signaling mechanism.

For years there was controversy as to whether or not our fundamental concept of the existence of individual cell units could be applied at all to the nervous system and to its functional connections. Some investigators believed that the developing nerve cell literally grows into the cytoplasm of all cells with which it establishes a functional relationship. The matter could not be settled convincingly until the advent of high-resolution electron microscopy. It turns out that most of the surface of a nerve cell, including all its extensions, is indeed closely invested and enveloped with other cells, but that the cytoplasm of adjacent cells remains separated by distinct membranes. Moreover, there is a small extracellular gap, usually of 100 to 200 angstrom units, between adjoining cell membranes.

A fraction of these cell contacts are functional synapses: the points at which signals are transferred from one cell to the next link in the chain (figure 2.3). But synapses are found only at and near the cell body of the neuron or at the terminals of the axon. Most of the investing cells, particularly those clinging to the axon, are not nerve cells at all. Their function is still a puzzle. Some of these satellite cells

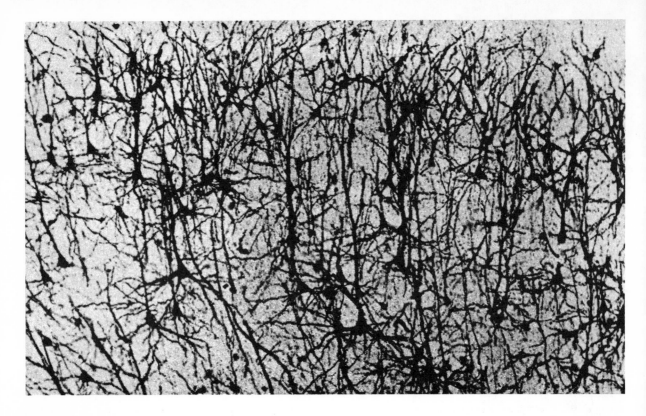

**Figure 2.1 Cerebral cortex** is densely packed with the bodies of nerve cells and the fibers called dendrites that branch from the cell body. This section through the sensory-motor cortex of a cat is enlarged some 150 diameters. Only about 1.5 per cent of the cells and dendrites actually present are stained and show here. The nerve axons, the fibers that carry impulses away from the cell body, are not usually shown at all by this staining method. The photomicrograph was made by the late D. A. Scholl of University College, London.

are called Schwann cells, others glia cells; they do not appear to take any part in the immediate process of impulse transmission except perhaps indirectly to modify the pathway of electric current flow around the axon. It is significant, for example, that very few scattered satellites are to be found on the exposed cell surfaces of muscle fibers, which closely resemble nerve fibers in their ability to conduct electrical impulses from one end to the other.

One of the known functions of the axon satellites is the formation of the so-called myelin sheath, a segmented insulating jacket that improves the signaling efficiency of peripheral nerve fibers in vertebrate animals. Thanks to the electron microscope studies of Betty Ben Geren-Uzman and Francis O. Schmitt of the Massachusetts Institute of Technology, we now know that each myelin segment is produced by a nucleated Schwann cell that winds its cytoplasm tightly around the surface of the axon, forming a spiral envelope of many turns (figure 2.4). The segments are separated by gaps – the nodes of Ranvier – which mark the points along the axon where the electrical signal is regenerated.

There are other types of nerve fiber that do not have a myelin sheath, but even these are covered by simple layers of Schwann cells. Perhaps because the axon extends so far from the nucleus of the nerve cell it requires close association with nucleated satellite cells all along its length. Muscle fibers, unlike the isolated axons, are self-contained cells with nuclei distributed along their cytoplasm, which may explain why these fibers can manage to exist without an investing layer of satellite cells. Whatever the function of the satellites, they cannot maintain the life of an axon for long once it has been severed from the main cell body; after a number of days the peripheral segment of the nerve cell disintegrates. How the nerve cell nucleus acts as a lifelong center of repair and brings its influence to bear on the distant parts of the axon – which in terms of ordinary diffusion would be years away – remains a mystery.

The experimental methods of physiology have been much more successful in dealing with the immediate processes of

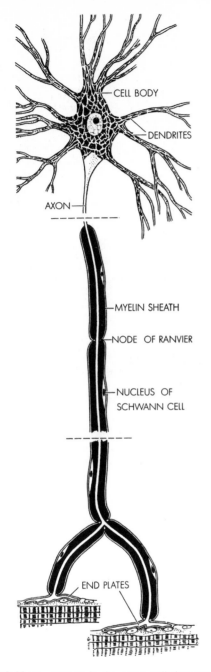

**Figure 2.2 Motor neuron** is the nerve cell that carries electrical impulses to activate muscle fibers. The cell body (*top*) fans out into a number of twigs, the dendrites, which make synaptic contact with other nerve fibers (figure 2.3). Nerve impulses arising at the cell body travel through the axon to the motor-plate endings, which are embedded in muscle fibers. Myelin sheath is formed by Schwann cells as shown in figure 2.4. By insulating the axon the myelin wrapping increases the speed of signal transmission.

Labels in figure: CELL BODY, DENDRITES, AXON, MYELIN SHEATH, NODE OF RANVIER, NUCLEUS OF SCHWANN CELL, END PLATES

nerve communication than with the equally important but much more intractable long-term events. We know very little about the chemical interactions between nerve and satellite, or about the forces that guide and attract growing nerves along specific pathways and that induce the formation of synaptic contacts with other cells. Nor do we know how cells store information and provide us with memory. The rest of this article will therefore be concerned almost solely with nerve signals and the method by which they pass across the narrow synaptic gaps separating one nerve cell from another.

Much of our knowledge of the nerve cell has been obtained from the giant axon of the squid, which is nearly a millimeter in diameter. It is fairly easy to probe this useful fiber with microelectrodes and to follow the movement of radioactively labeled substances into it and out of it. The axon membrane separates two aqueous solutions that are almost equally electroconductive and that contain approximately the same number of electrically charged particles, or ions. But the chemical composition of the two solutions is quite different. In the external solution more than 90 per cent of the charged particles are sodium ions (positively charged) and chloride ions (negatively charged). Inside the cell these ions together account for less than 10 per cent of the solutes; there the principal positive ion is potassium and the negative ions are a variety of organic particles (doubtless synthesized within the cell itself) that are too large to diffuse easily through the axon membrane. Therefore the concentration of sodium is about 10 times higher *outside* the axon, and the concentration of potassium is about 30 times higher *inside* the axon. Although the permeability of the membrane to ions is low, it is not indiscriminate; potassium and chloride ions can move through the membrane much more easily than sodium and the large organic ions can. This gives rise to a voltage drop of some 60 to 90 millivolts across the membrane, with the inside of the cell being negative with respect to the outside.

To maintain these differences in ion concentration the nerve cell contains a kind of pump that forces sodium ions "uphill" and outward through the cell membrane as fast as they leak into the cell in the direction of the electrochemical gradient (figure 2.11). The permeability of the resting cell surface to sodium is normally so low that the rate of leakage remains very small, and the work required of the pumping process amounts to only a fraction of the energy that is continuously being made available by the metabolism of the cell. We do not know in detail how this pump works, but it appears to trade sodium and potassium ions; that is, for each sodium ion ejected through the membrane it accepts

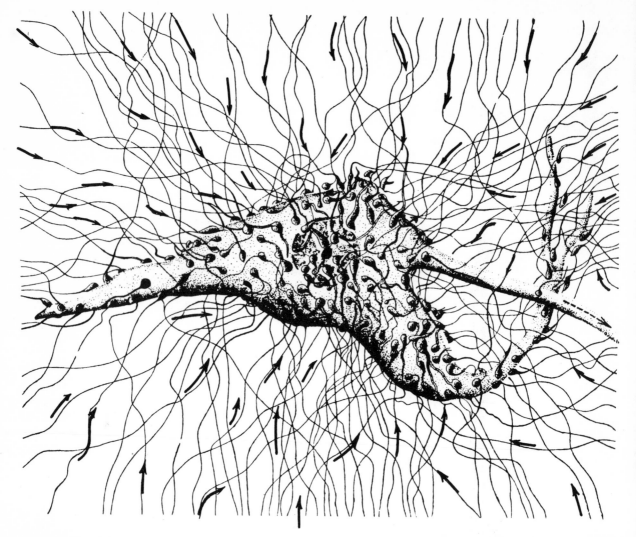

**Figure 2.3 Synaptic knobs**. The terminals of axons from other nerve cells cover the surface of a motoneuron cell body and its processes except for the axon.

one potassium ion. Once transported inside the axon the potassium ions move about as freely as the ions in any simple salt solution. When the cell is resting, they tend to leak "downhill" and outward through the membrane, but at a slow rate.

The axon membrane resembles the membrane of other cells. It is about 50 to 100 angstroms thick and incorporates a thin layer of fatty insulating material. Its specific resistance to the passage of an electric current is at least 10 million times greater than that of the salt solutions bathing it on each side. On the other hand, the axon would be quite worthless if it were employed simply as the equivalent of an electric cable. The electrical resistance of the axon's fluid core is about 100 million times greater than that of copper wire, and the axon membrane is about a million times leakier to electric current than the sheath of a good cable. If an electric pulse too weak to trigger a nerve impulse is fed into an axon, the pulse fades out and becomes badly blunted after traveling only a few millimeters.

How, then, can the axon transmit a nerve impulse for several feet without decrement and without distortion?

As one steps up the intensity of a voltage signal impressed on the membrane of a nerve cell a point is reached where the signal no longer fades and dies. Instead (if the voltage is of the right sign), a threshold is crossed and the cell becomes "excited" (figures 2.8 and 2.9). The axon of the cell no longer behaves like a passive cable but produces an extra current pulse of its own that amplifies the original

32

**Figure 2.4 Myelin sheath** is created when a Schwann cell wraps itself around the nerve axon (1–3). After the enfolding is complete (4), the cytoplasm of the Schwann cell is expelled and the cell's folded membranes fuse into a tough, compact wrapping. Diagrams are based on studies of chick-embryo neurons by Betty Ben Geren-Uzman of Children's Medical Center in Boston.

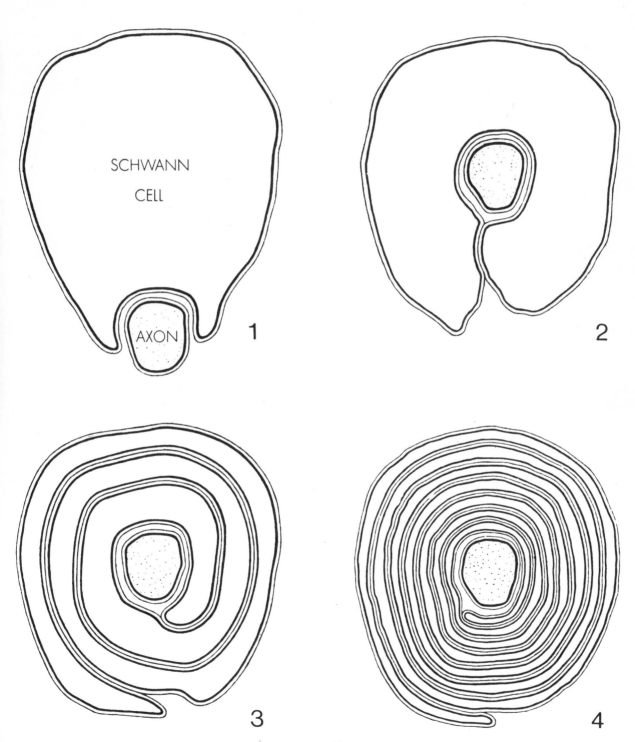

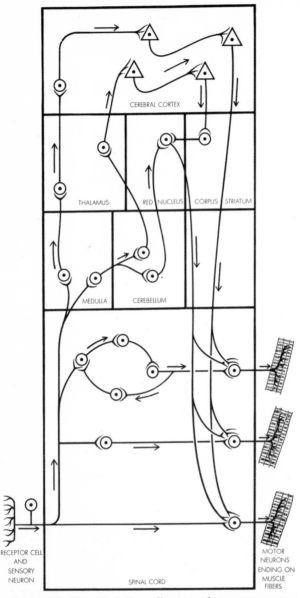

CEREBRAL CORTEX

THALAMUS

RED NUCLEUS CORPUS STRIATUM

MEDULLA CEREBELLUM

RECEPTOR CELL
AND
SENSORY
NEURON

MOTOR
NEURONS
ENDING ON
MUSCLE
FIBERS

SPINAL CORD

**Figure 2.5 Simplified flow diagram of nervous system** barely hints at the many possible pathways open to an impulse entering the spinal cord from a receptor cell and its sensory fiber. Rarely does the incoming signal directly activate a motor neuron leading to a muscle fiber. Typically it travels upward through the spinal cord and through several relay centers before arriving at the cerebral cortex. There (if not elsewhere) a "command" may be given (or withheld) that sends nerve impulses back down the spinal cord to fire a motor neuron.

input pulse. The amplified pulse, or "spike", regenerates itself from point to point without loss of amplitude and travels at constant speed down the whole length of the axon. The speed of transmission in vertebrate nerve fibers ranges from a few meters per second, for thin nonmyelinated fibers, to about 100 meters per second in the thickest myelinated fibers. The highest speeds, equivalent to some 200 miles per hour, are found in the sensory and motor fibers concerned with body balance and fast reflex movements. After transmitting an impulse the nerve is left briefly in a refractory, or inexcitable, state, but within one or two milliseconds it is ready to fire again.

The electrochemical events that underlie the nerve impulse – or action potential, as it is called – have been greatly clarified since the mid 1940s. As we have seen, the voltage difference across the membrane is determined largely by the membrane's differential permeability to sodium and potassium ions. Many kinds of selective membrane, natural and artificial, show such differences. What makes the nerve membrane distinctive is that its permeability is in turn regulated by the voltage difference across the membrane, and this peculiar mutual influence is in fact the basis of the signaling process.

It was shown by A. L. Hodgkin and A. F. Huxley of the University of Cambridge that when the voltage difference across the membrane is artificially lowered, the immediate effect is to increase its sodium permeability. We do not know why the ionic insulation of the membrane is altered in this specific way, but the consequences are far-reaching. As sodium ions, with their positive charges, leak through the membrane they cancel out locally a portion of the excess negative charge inside the axon, thereby further reducing the voltage drop across the membrane. This is a regenerative process that leads to automatic self-reinforcement; the flow of some sodium ions through the membrane makes it easier for others to follow. When the voltage drop across the membrane has been reduced to the threshold level, sodium ions enter in such numbers that they change the internal potential of the membrane from negative to positive; the process "ignites" and flares up to create the nerve impulse, or action potential. The impulse, which shows up as a spike on the oscilloscope, changes the permeability of the axon membrane immediately ahead of it and sets up the conditions for sodium to flow into the axon, repeating the whole regenerative process in a progressive wave until the spike has traveled the length of the axon (figure 2.10).

Immediately after the peak of the wave other events are taking place. The "sodium gates", which had opened during the rise of the spike, are closed again, and the "potassium gates" are opened briefly. This causes a rapid outflow of the

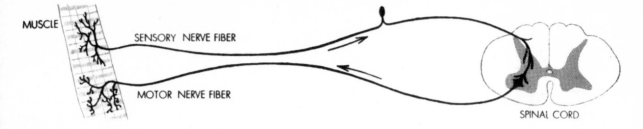

MUSCLE

SENSORY NERVE FIBER

MOTOR NERVE FIBER

SPINAL CORD

**Figure 2.6 Reflex arc** illustrates the minimum nerve circuit between stimulus and response. A sensory fiber arising in a muscle spindle enters the spinal cord, where it makes synaptic contact with a motor neuron whose axon returns to the muscle containing the spindle.

positive potassium ions, which restores the original negative charge of the interior of the axon. For a few milliseconds after the membrane voltage has been driven toward its initial level it is difficult to displace the voltage and set up another impulse. But the ionic permeabilities quickly return to their initial condition and the cell is ready to fire another impulse.

The inflow of sodium ions and subsequent outflow of potassium ions is so brief and involves so few particles that the over-all internal composition of the axon is scarcely affected. Even without replenishment the store of potassium ions inside the axon is sufficient to provide tens of thousands of impulses. In the living organism the cellular enzyme system that runs the sodium pump has no difficulty keeping nerves in continuous firing condition.

This intricate process – signal conduction through a leaky cable coupled with repeated automatic boosting along the transmission path – provides the long-distance communication needs of our nervous system. It imposes a certain stereotyped form of "coding" on our signaling channels: brief pulses of almost constant amplitude following each other at variable intervals, limited only by the refractory period of the nerve cell. To make up for the limitations of this simple coding system, large numbers of axon channels, each a separate nerve cell, are provided and arranged in parallel. For example, in the optic nerve trunk emerging from the eye there are more than a million channels running close together, all capable of transmitting separate signals to the higher centers of the brain.

Let us now turn to the question of what happens at a synapse, the point at which the impulse reaches the end of one cell and encounters another nerve cell. The self-amplifying cable process that serves within the borders of any one cell is not designed to jump automatically across

the border to adjacent cells. Indeed, if there were such "cross talk" between adjacent channels, for instance among the fibers closely packed together in our nerve bundles, the system would become quite useless. It is true that at functional synaptic contacts the separation between the cell membranes is only 100 to a few hundred angstroms. But from what we know of the dimensions of the contact area, and of the insulating properties of cell membranes, it is unlikely that an effective cable connection could exist between the terminal of one nerve cell and the interior of its neighbor. This can easily be demonstrated by trying to pass a subthreshold pulse – that is, one that does not trigger a spike – across the synapse that separates a motor nerve from a muscle fiber. A recording probe located just inside the muscle detects no signal when a weak pulse is applied to the motor nerve close to the synapse. Clearly the cable linkage is broken at the synapse and some other process must take its place.

The nature of this process was discovered some 35 years ago by Sir Henry Dale and his collaborators at the National Institute for Medical Research in London. In some ways it resembles the hormonal mechanism mentioned at the beginning of this article. The motor nerve terminals act rather like glands secreting a chemical messenger. Upon arrival of an impulse, the terminals release a special substance, acetylcholine, that quickly and efficiently diffuses across the short synaptic gap. Acetylcholine molecules combine with receptor molecules in the contact area of the muscle fiber and somehow open its ionic gates, allowing sodium to flow in and trigger an impulse. The same result can be obtained by artificially applying acetylcholine to the contact region of the muscle fiber. It is probable that similar processes of chemical mediation take place at the majority of cell contacts in our central nervous system. But it is most unlikely that acetylcholine is the universal mediator at all these points, and an intensive search is being made by many workers for other naturally occurring transmitter substances.

Synaptic transmission presents two quite distinct sets of problems. First, exactly how does a nerve impulse manage to cause the secretion of the chemical mediator? Second,

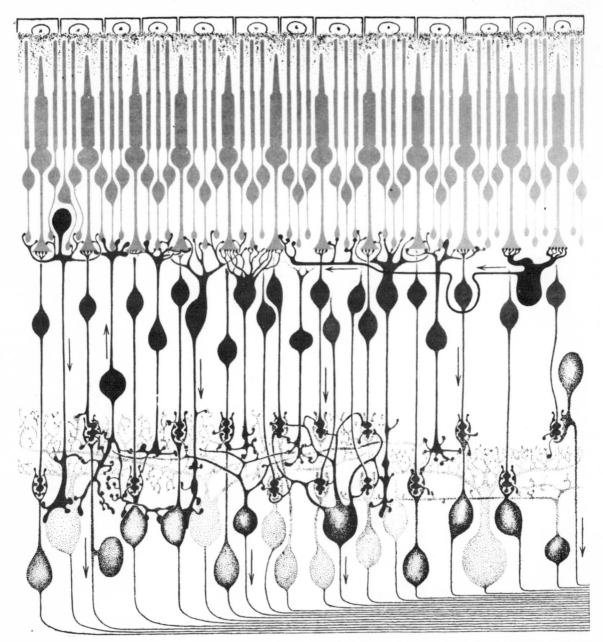

**Figure 2.7 Nerve-cell network in the retina,** here magnified about 600 diameters, exemplifies the retinal complexity in man and apes. The photoreceptors are the densely packed cells near the top; the thinner ones are rods, the thicker ones cones. To reach them the incoming light must traverse a dense but transparent layer of neurons (*dark shapes*) that have rich interconnections with the photoreceptors and with each other. The output of these neurons finally feeds into the optic nerve shown at the bottom of the diagram.

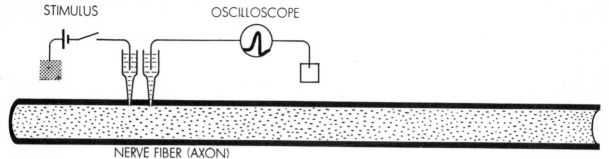

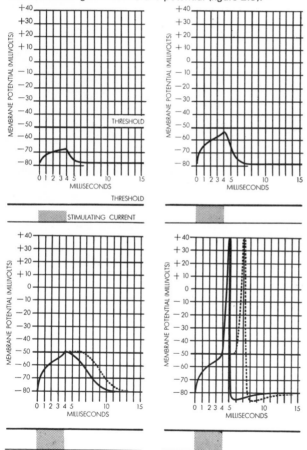

**Figure 2.8 Investigation of nerve fiber** is carried out with two microelectrodes. One provides a stimulating pulse, the other measures changes in membrane potential (figure 2.9).

**Figure 2.9 Electrical properties of nerve fiber** are elucidated by measuring voltage changes across the axon membrane when stimulating pulses of varying size are applied. In the resting state the interior of the axon is about 80 millivolts negative. Subthreshold stimulating pulses (*top left and top right*) shift the potential upward momentarily. Larger pulses push the potential to its threshold, where it becomes unstable, either subsiding (*bottom left*) or flaring up into an "action potential" (*bottom right*) with a variable delay (*broken curve*).

what are the physicochemical factors that decide whether a mediator will stimulate the next cell to fire in some cases or inhibit it from firing in others? So far we have said nothing about inhibition, even though it occurs throughout the nervous system and is one of the most curious modes of nervous activity. Inhibition takes place when a nerve impulse acts as a brake on the next cell, preventing it from becoming activated by excitatory messages that may be arriving along other channels at the same time. The impulse that travels along an inhibitory axon cannot be distinguished electrically from an impulse traveling in an excitatory axon. But the physiochemical effect that it induces at a synapse must be different in kind. Presumably inhibition results from a process that in some way stabilizes the membrane potential (degree of electrification) of the receiving cell and prevents it from being driven to its unstable threshold, or "ignition" point.

There are several processes by which such a stabilization could be achieved. One of them has already been mentioned; it occurs in the refractory period immediately after a spike has been generated. In this period the membrane potential is driven to a high stable level (some 80 to 90 millivolts negative inside the membrane) because, to put it somewhat crudely, the potassium gates are wide open and the sodium gates are firmly shut. If the transmitter substance can produce one or both of these states of ionic permeability, it will undoubtedly act as an inhibitor. There are good reasons for believing that this is the way impulses from the vagus nerve slow down and inhibit the heartbeat; incidentally, the transmitter substance released from the vagus nerve is again acetylcholine, as was discovered by Otto Loewi round about 1920. Similar effects occur at various inhibitory synapses in the spinal cord, but there the chemical nature of the transmitter has so far eluded identification.

Inhibition would also result if two "antagonistic" axons converged on the same spot of a third nerve cell and released chemically competing molecules. Although a natural example of this kind has not yet been demonstrated, the chemical and pharmacological use of competitive

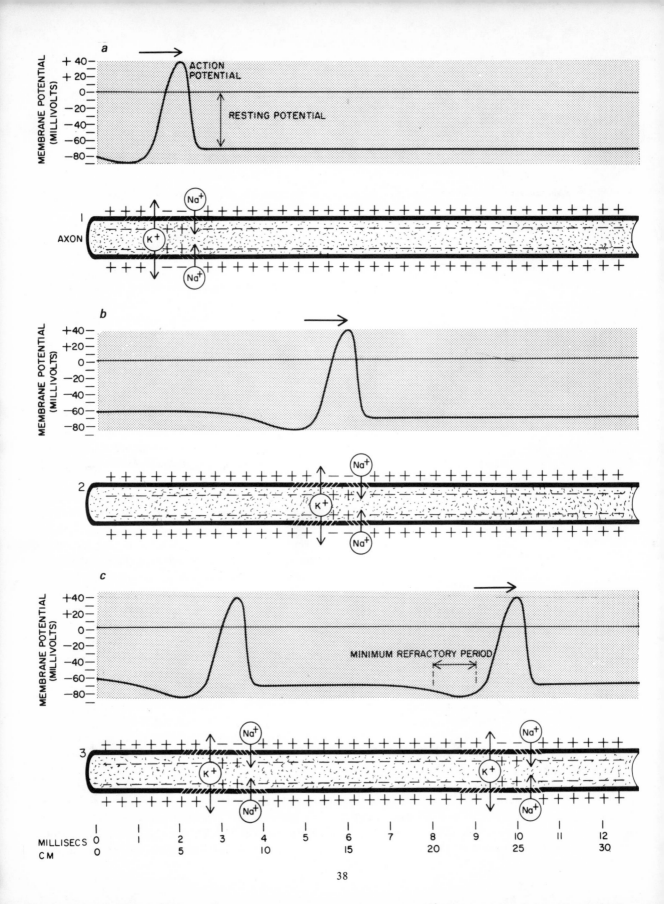

**Figure 2.10 Propagation of nerve impulse** coincides with changes in the permeability of the axon membrane. Normally the axon interior is rich in potassium ions and poor in sodium ions; the fluid outside has a reverse composition. When a nerve impulse arises, having been triggered in some fashion, a "gate" opens and lets sodium ions pour into the axon in advance of the impulse, making the axon interior locally positive. In the wake of the impulse the sodium gate closes and a potassium gate opens, allowing potassium ions to flow out, restoring the normal negative potential. As the nerve impulse moves along the axon (*a* and *b*) it leaves the axon in a refractory state briefly, after which a second impulse can follow (*c*). The impulse propagation speed is that of a squid axon.

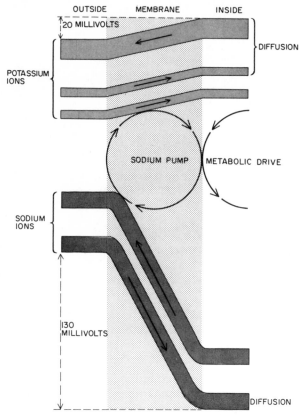

**Figure 2.11 "Sodium pump"**, details unknown, is required to expel sodium ions from the interior of the nerve axon so that the interior sodium-ion concentration is held to about 10 per cent that of the exterior fluid. At the same time the pump drives potassium ions "uphill" from a low external concentration to a 30-times-higher internal concentration. The pumping rate must keep up with the "downhill" leakage of the two kinds of ion. Since both are positively charged, sodium ions have the higher leakage rate (expressed in terms of millivolts of driving force) because they are attracted to the negatively charged interior of the axon, whereas potassium ions tend to be retained. But there is still a net outward leakage of potassium.

inhibitors is well established. (For example, the paralyzing effect of the drug curare arises from its competitive attachment to the region of the muscle fiber that is normally free to react with acetylcholine.) Alternatively, a substance released by an inhibitory nerve ending could act on the excitatory nerve terminal in such a way as to reduce its secretory power, thereby causing less of the excitatory transmitter substance to be released.

This brings us back to the question: How does a nerve impulse lead to the secretion of transmitter substances? Recent experiments on the nerve-muscle junction have shown that the effect of the nerve impulse is not to initiate a process of secretion but rather, by altering the membrane potential, to change the rate of a secretory process that goes on all the time. Even in the absence of any form of stimulation, packets of acetylcholine are released from discrete spots of the nerve terminals at random intervals, each packet containing a large number – probably thousands – of molecules.

Each time one of these quanta of transmitter molecules is liberated spontaneously, it is possible to detect a sudden minute local response in the muscle fiber on the other side of the synapse. Within a millisecond there is a drop of 0.5 millivolt in the potential of the muscle membrane, which takes about 20 milliseconds to recover. By systematically altering the potential of the membrane of the nerve ending it has been possible to work out the characteristic relation between the membrane potential of the axon terminal and the rate of secretion of transmitter packets. It appears that the rate of release increases by a factor of about 100 times for each 30-millivolt lowering of membrane potential. In the resting condition there is a random discharge of about one packet per second at each nerve-muscle junction. But during the brief 120-millivolt change associated with the nerve impulse the frequency rises momentarily by a factor of nearly a million, providing a synchronous release of a few hundred packets within a fraction of a millisecond.

It is significant that the transmitter is released not in independent molecular doses but always in multimolecular parcels of standard size. The explanation of this feature is probably to be found in the microstructural make-up of the nerve terminals. They contain a characteristic accumulation of so-called vesicles, each about 500 angstroms in diameter, which may contain the transmitter substance parceled and ready for release (figure 2.12). Conceivably when the vesicles collide with the axon membrane, as they often must, the collision may sometimes cause the vesicular content to spill into the synaptic cleft. Such ideas have yet to be proved by direct evidence, but they provide a reasonable explanation of all that is known about the quantal spontaneous

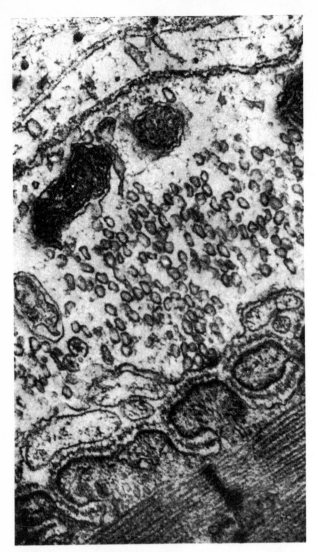

Because of the sparseness of existing knowledge, we have left out of this discussion many fascinating problems of the long-term interactions and adaptive modifications that must certainly take place in nerve pathways. For handling such problems investigators will probably have to develop very different methods from those followed in the past. It may be that our preoccupation with the techniques that have been so successful in illuminating the brief reactions of excitable cells has prevented us from making inroads on the problems of learning, of memory, of conditioning and of the structural and operating relations between nerve cells and their neighbors.

## Bibliography

Biophysical aspects of neuro-muscular transmission, J. del Castillo and B. Katz in *Progress in Biophysics and Biophysical Chemistry*, Vol. 6, pages 121–70; 1956

Ionic movement and electrical activity in giant nerve fibres, A. L. Hodgkin in *Proceedings of the Royal Society*, Series B, Vol. 148, No. 930, pages 1–37; 1 January 1958

Microphysiology of the neuro-muscular junction, a physiological "quantum of action" at the myoneural junction, Bernhard Katz in *Bulletin of the Johns Hopkins Hospital*, Vol. 102, No. 6, pages 275–312; June 1958

The physiology of nerve cells, John Carew Eccles, The Johns Hopkins Press, 1957

**Figure 2.12 Nerve muscle synapse** is the site at which a nerve impulse activates the contraction of a muscle fiber. In this electron micrograph (made by R. Birks, H. E. Huxley and the author) the region of the synapse is enlarged 53 000 diameters. Motor nerve terminal runs diagonally from lower left to upper right, being bounded at upper left by a Schwann cell. Muscle fiber is the dark striated area at lower right, with a folded membrane. Nerve terminal is populated with "synaptic vesicles" that may contain acetylcholine, which is released into the synaptic cleft by a nerve impulse and evokes electrical activity in the muscle.

release of acetylcholine and its accelerated release under various natural and experimental conditions. At any rate, the ideas provide an interesting meeting point between the functional and structural approaches to a common problem.

# 3 How the cerebellum may be used

## by Stephen Blomfield and David Marr

The vertebrate cerebellar cortex has a very uniform structure, and may, for the purpose of this article, be regarded as being composed of many units like that appearing in figure 3.1. Its only output is the projection of large inhibitory cells, the Purkinje cells (*Pu*), to the intracerebellar nuclei, and to some of the vestibular nuclei.[1,2] In man, a major projection from the intracerebellar nuclei is to the ventro-lateral nucleus of the thalamus (*VL*).[1,2] *VL* cells project to the motor cortex.

There are two kinds of input to the cerebellar cortex: the mossy fibres, which synapse with the numerous granule cells; and the climbing fibres, which project directly to the Purkinje cells and wrap themselves around their dendrites. Each Purkinje cell receives one climbing fibre,[1] and can be powerfully excited by it. The climbing fibres arise from a group of cells in the contralateral brain stem;[1] the curious shape of this group has led to its being named the olive. The inferior olive (*IO*) receives connexions from a wide variety of sources, in particular from the cerebral cortex.[2] The mossy fibres have several different sites of origin;[2] particularly important are the pontine nuclei (*PN*) of the brain stem. The cerebellar granule cells, with which the mossy fibres synapse, send axons (the parallel fibres) to the Purkinje cells, and to the inhibitory interneurones of the cortex.

In a recent article,[3] it was shown that the known anatomy and physiology of the cerebellar cortex are consistent with its interpretation as a simple memorizing device. It was predicted that the synapses between parallel fibres and Purkinje cells are modifiable, being facilitated by the conjunction of pre-synaptic and climbing fibre activity. It was shown how this would allow any single Purkinje cell to learn to recognize, without appreciable confusion, more than 200 different mossy fibre input patterns. Two methods were outlined by which such a memorizing device might learn to perform motor actions and maintain voluntary postures initially organized elsewhere. Since then, three relevant facts have come to our attention: (i), anatomical

information concerning the origin of the cortico-olivary and cortico-pontine projections:[4] (ii), the discovery that the olivo-cerebellar (that is, climbing) fibres branch;[5,6] and (iii), the prediction that climbing fibres can organize more than simple memorizing phenomena.[7] These facts have implications about the way the cerebellum may be used by the rest of the nervous system that will be of interest to experimenters, and we therefore give here an outline of their principal consequences.

(i) The origin of the descending projection to the olive has long been known to include cortical cells, of which the majority lie in the motor and pre-motor areas. But it has recently been shown that these fibres arise almost entirely from small pyramidal cells.[4] In contrast, the pontine nuclei receive collaterals from both large and small pyramidal cells.[4] The distinction may be that superficial pyramidal cells project to the inferior olive, while deep pyramidal cells give off collaterals to the pontine nuclei on their way to the spinal cord.[4,8] Further, the projection from the ventro-lateral thalamic nucleus to the motor cortex is direct to the deep pyramidal cells, and perhaps by way of an excitatory interneurone to both the superficial and the deep pyramidals (figure 3.1 [2,8,9]).

(ii) The inferior olive contains fewer cells than there are cerebellar Purkinje cells.[10] This means that either there are other sources of climbing fibres or the olivo-cere-bellar fibres branch. It seems that the latter explanation is correct.[5,6] The distribution of the branches of one climbing fibre also seems to be restricted to a parasagittal plane.[6]

(iii) The hypothesis[3] that the parallel fibre–Purkinje cell synapses are facilitated by simultaneous pre-synaptic and climbing fibre activity has implications deeper than merely allowing each Purkinje cell to memorize 200 or so different mossy fibre inputs. If a number of similar mossy fibre inputs have been learned and later an unlearned input is presented which is near enough to those which have been learned, then the Purkinje cell may treat the new input as if it had been learned. This is probably not the

*first published in* Nature, *London, 1970, Vol. 227, pages 1224–1228.*

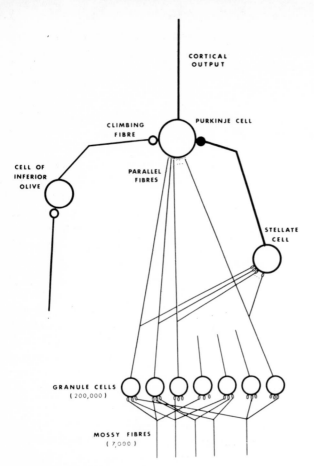

CORTICAL OUTPUT

PURKINJE CELL

CLIMBING FIBRE

CELL OF INFERIOR OLIVE

PARALLEL FIBRES

STELLATE CELL

GRANULE CELLS (200,000)

MOSSY FIBRES (7,000)

**Figure 3.1 The diagram** selects the principal elements of the cerebellar cortex. There is one output system, the Purkinje cell axons, and two input systems, the climbing and the mossy fibres. The climbing fibres originate in the inferior olivary nucleus, and each Purkinje cell usually receives exactly one. The mossy fibres, which come from many parts of the body and brain, are imagined to convey information about the state of the animal – information referred to as the "context" at that time. The mossy fibre input is translated by the granule cells into a language of subsets, and the granule cell axons become the parallel fibres. It is predicted that the parallel fibre synapses with a Purkinje cell that are coactive with its climbing fibre are facilitated. The inhibitory cell prevents the Purkinje cell from firing unless almost all its active afferent synapses have been facilitated. The numbers of the various kinds of fibre projecting to one Purkinje cell in cat are as shown: this enables a single cell to learn at least 200 different mossy fibre inputs, without confusion between learned and unlearned events.

disadvantage it was once thought.[3] It means that a Purkinje cell will generalize its response to all events in those regions where learned events are sufficiently clustered together. The implications of this generalization are set out elsewhere.[7]

*Input–output relations*

In figure 3.2, the new information (i) is combined with the previous knowledge of cerebellar anatomy. All the synapses in the diagram are excitatory, except those from the Purkinje cells to the cells of the cerebellar nuclei. One very striking feature of this circuit diagram is the loop formed from the deep pyramidals through the pontine nuclei, cerebellar nuclei and *VL* nucleus of thalamus back to the deep (and also superficial) pyramidals. This arrangement has been commented on before.[1,11] A necessary assumption of the present theory is that this loop, which will provide a positive feedback from the deep pyramidals to themselves, is so arranged as to give rise to temporally extended pyramidal cell outputs. One possibility would be that the feedback is chiefly to the original area, so that a movement – once initiated – will tend to continue indefinitely (at least well beyond the normal firing period of pyramidal cells in response to an excitatory input): and this will only be terminated either by applying direct inhibition to the deep pyramidal cells or by breaking the feedback loop. In the original cerebellar theory,[3] two possible forms of input–output relation were described, both of which required that each individual Purkinje cell could initiate one of the elemental movements into which it was postulated all actions were broken down. For executing actions it was thought necessary only to copy the correct pattern of elemental movements. It was shown how the cerebellar cortex could arrange this by having every elemental movement driven by the context in which it is required.

The anatomy of figure 3.2 is not wholly compatible with this simple programme for copying patterned sequences of elemental movements. In general, if a machine has to execute a sequence of movements, it can operate either by turning on the correct elemental movements at any instant, or by turning off all the incorrect ones. We believe that the design of the cerebellum suggests that the second scheme, the converse of the original input–output relations, is in fact used for learning motor actions. The second scheme is at first sight absurd, because the number of elemental movements required at any instant is far smaller than the number of possible elemental movements. It only becomes more economical than the first scheme if the number required exceeds the number which need to be turned off. In practice, this means that some agency must, at any instant, select from the vocabulary of elemental movements a particular set of "possibles", which includes all those actually required. If this can be done so that the number of "actuals" is greater than the number of "possibles" minus "actuals", it becomes cheaper to operate by deleting unwanted elemental movements from the set of "possibles".

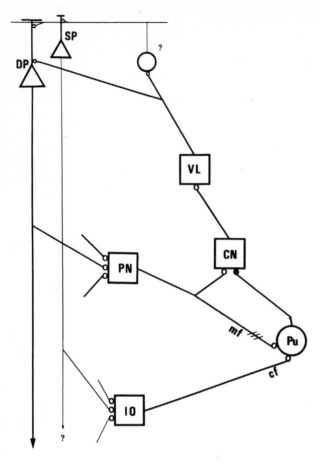

Such an agency would have to satisfy the following properties: (*a*), it must consist of cells capable of driving elemental movements; (*b*), these cells must be capable of

**Figure 3.2 There are two** relevant kinds of cell in the motor cortex: small, superficial pyramids (*SP*) and large, deep pyramids (*DP*). The *DP* cells send collaterals to the pontine nuclei (*PN*), and the *SP* cells to the inferior olive (*IO*). The axons from the inferior olive terminate as climbing fibres (*cf*) on the Purkinje cells (*Pu*) in the cerebellar cortex; those from the pontine nuclei become mossy fibres (*mf*). Purkinje cells are inhibitory, and send synapses to the various cerebellar nuclei (*CN*): these nuclei also receive excitatory synapses from mossy fibre and climbing fibre collaterals. The cerebellar nuclei send excitatory synapses to the ventro-lateral nucleus of the thalamus (*VL*). VL projects back to the motor cortex by way of a fast and a slow path: the fast path goes only to the large, deep pyramids; the slow path goes to both deep and superficial pyramidal cells, perhaps by way of an interneurone.

being context-driven; (*c*), the set of situations to which each cell responds must include those in which it is needed; and (*d*), cerebellar action upon it must be such that Purkinje cell activity turns off instructions for one (or more) elemental movements. We propose that the set of deep pyramidal cells in the motor cortex is such an agency, and that the conditions (*a*) to (*d*) are satisfied by them.

One can now assign a definite role to the small superficial[8] pyramidal cells which project to the inferior olive. These, we assume, project to regions of the inferior olive which drive climbing fibres in the same general region of the cerebellum as that which projects back to the deep pyramidal cell beneath them. If the ideas described earlier are correct, these cells must fire when the large pyramidal cells related to them are firing but should not. That is, the small superficial pyramidal cells should detect the need to correct the current motor activity by deleting the messages from their corresponding deep pyramidal cells. In this respect it is of interest that the *VL* nucleus of the thalamus sends excitatory connexions to both deep and superficial pyramidals; this will inform the superficial pyramidals of the feedback excitatory input to the deep pyramidals; clearly there is no point in the superficial pyramidals making deletions when the deep pyramidals are, in fact, not going to be fired. Learning may be necessary for organizing the details of the projection from the *VL* nucleus to the cortex.

Superficial pyramidal cells therefore recognize the classes of events which are incompatible with the current firing of the corresponding deep pyramidals. The analysis behind the recognition of the need for such corrections may be complicated, because it involves ideas about what the animal is trying to do. Its results can, however, be tied to specific contexts, using the kind of learning of which the cerebellar cortex may be capable.[3] There is thus a clear advantage to be gained by storing the corrections in the cerebellum.

It may fairly be objected that nothing has been said about the way in which the small pyramidal cells detect the need for the corrections which they can implement. This problem is in principle no greater, however, than the analogous assumption concerning the deep pyramidal cells: how do they recognize the need for their elemental movements? On a superficial level it is clear that all pyramidal cells could be capable of learning contexts[7] using the same mechanisms that have been described for the cerebellar Purkinje cells.[3] The deeper aspects of these problems have also begun to yield,[7] and a full account of them will appear elsewhere.

The following summary states the conditions under

which the inverted input–output relations could work, and hence the experimental findings needed to prove or disprove the hypothesis:

A  Elemental movements are coded by deep pyramidal cells in the motor cortex.

B  The set of situations to which such cells respond includes those in which they are needed.

C  Their axon collaterals to the pontine nuclei provide a positive feedback loop (via the cerebellar nuclei) which is necessary, during normal operation of the system, for the proper initiation and continuation of their elemental movements.

D  Small, superficial pyramidal cells recognize the need for correction of current motor cortex output. These corrections involve the prevention of firing of certain deep pyramidal cells.

E  These corrections, whose initial computation is not necessarily easy, can eventually be run by the cerebellar Purkinje cells – in the same way as Purkinje cells were originally thought to drive the elemental movements themselves.[3]

### Branching climbing fibres

Purkinje cells in different regions of the cerebellar cortex are exposed to information, through the mossy fibres, that originates in different parts of the body and brain. A full description of the state of the body and brain as transmitted through mossy fibres will be called a full context, and a similar description of part of the body or brain a partial context. Then each Purkinje cell has access to a partial context; and the kind of contextual information which may reach each cell is probably fixed.

Each Purkinje cell usually receives exactly one climbing fibre. Hence if the axon from a single olivary cell gives rise to ten climbing fibres, the firing of that olivary cell effectively signals modification conditions to ten, presumably different, partial contexts. During the rehearsal necessary for the cerebellum to learn a given action, some of these partial contexts will recur and some, because they carry information which is essentially irrelevant, will not. Those Purkinje cells, the firing of whose climbing fibres is associated with a relatively unchanging partial context will learn that context – and this will be useful. Those which receive a different partial context each time will not learn (provided synaptic modification does not work first time); nor would it be of any use if they did. Indeed, it would be a disadvantage on two grounds. First, it would reduce the effective capacity of the Purkinje cell to learn useful contexts; second, it might cause incorrect deletions during an action in which an irrelevant partial context arises and the elemental movement is required.

There are many related questions concerning the number of corrections a Purkinje cell discharge can implement, the kind of convergence there is in the cerebellar nuclei, and so on, which cannot be properly studied until more information becomes available. The parasagittal distribution [6,12] of the climbing fibres may, however, shed some light on these problems. It is known that the cerebellar cortex tends to be organized into longitudinal strips, whose Purkinje cells project to restricted regions in the intracerebellar nuclei; [2,12] so the climbing fibres from a single olivary cell will tend to cause modification of Purkinje cells whose influences converge on a restricted zone of the cerebellar nuclei. One can even devise a plausible embryological model which ensures that the Purkinje cells related to one olivary cell all converge on a single cerebellar nuclear cell – so that there is a one to one correspondence between olivary cells and cerebellar nuclear cells. But such a restriction is by no means necessary for the theory.

### Detection of clusters by Purkinje cells and climbing fibres

It seems likely that two parts of the theory developed by one of us [7] for the cerebral pyramidal cells also apply to the cerebellar Purkinje cells. The first concerns the nature of the signals which the Purkinje cells actually transmit. It is possible that these cells do give a response which is strictly all-or-none, depending on whether the current input has been learned. We feel, however, that it is more likely that they signal a measure of how similar their current output is to the structure of the events that they have learned. It seems that the most suitable measure of this similarity is the fraction of the currently active afferent synapses to a cell which have been modified,[7] provided that fraction is greater than some fixed lower bound p (say). A model has been proposed by which this quantity could be measured by a single cell,[7] and we feel that this is likely to be more suitable for the theory of Purkinje cell dendrites than the simple one developed earlier.[3]

This raises important questions concerning the need for convergence of Purkinje cell discharge on to cerebellar nuclear cells. Is it possible for a single maximally firing Purkinje cell to turn off a cerebellar nuclear cell completely, or does it need convergence from several Purkinje cells? And if several converging Purkinje cells are firing submaximally – in response to inputs rather dissimilar to their learned partial contexts – then is their summed effect sufficient to turn off the cerebellar nuclear cell?

The second application of the cerebral theory to the cerebellum concerns the discovery that a climbing fibre can organize a kind of cluster analysis.[7] Provided the information arriving at Purkinje cells is clustered and that the climbing fibre is coactive with enough events in a cluster, then the cell will respond to many more events, whether or not they have ever been associated with the climbing fibre activity. We think that this effect, certainly vital in the cerebral cortex,[7] is probably important in the cerebellum also. It is a mechanism which can provide a kind of generalization to events which should "obviously" initiate the same responses as their neighbours without the necessity for a specific new learning trial.

The next topic we wish to raise concerns the Purkinje axon collaterals.[1] It has been pointed out[3] that the effect produced by them through their connexions with basket and stellate cells is simple, whereas their effect through the Golgi cells is not. One possible explanation of their existence is that, when active in the region of a particular Purkinje cell $P$, they cause $P$ to relax the scale on which it measures the similarity of the current input to the events it has learned. This is suggested by two facts: first, the inhibition reaching $P$ will be decreased by collateral stimulation; and second, the Purkinje axon collateral inhibition of the Golgi cells will cause a slight decrease in the local granule cell threshold. This is the correct step for interpreting the current mossy fibre input within the structure formed by the other mossy fibre inputs which it has learned (by the interpretation theorem[7]).

It is therefore possible not only that direct generalization, of the sort described above, can occur in the cerebellar cortex, but also that the extent to which this generalization is permitted (that is, lowering the value of p) can be varied by Purkinje axon collateral activity. If this is so, it has implications about the distribution of these collaterals that one would expect to find: because the cues to lower p for a particular cell $P$ must arise from information suggesting that it would be appropriate to do so. This means that the Purkinje axon collaterals ending in one region of cortex should fire only when it is likely that the corrections controlled from these are wanted; and in general, the more likely they are to be wanted, the greater will be the permissible degree of generalization there (that is, the lower p can be), and so the more activity there should be in the Purkinje axon collaterals terminating there. This implies that the collaterals from each Purkinje cell $P_1$ tend to be distributed to regions of cortex containing Purkinje cells which are needed after or at the same time as $P_1$. The most obvious of such regions would be those containing the Purkinje cells which are fired by the other branches of the olivo-cerebellar axon which sends a branch to $P_1$. (It is interesting to note that Purkinje axon collaterals are often closely related to climbing fibres.) Those regions of cortex receiving collaterals from many currently active Purkinje cells would then be more likely to be needed next than those regions receiving from only a few. The known distribution of Purkinje axon collaterals tends to support this notion. The Purkinje axons first contribute collaterals to the transversely running infraganglionic plexus, whose fibres often bridge across several folia; branches are given off from this plexus to the longitudinally running supraganglionic plexus, whose distribution is much more limited. Hence Purkinje axon collateral effects will tend to be restricted to the parasagittal plane. We have already shown that there is reason to suppose that the Purkinje cells have closer relations to other Purkinje cells within such a plane than without.

There is one other piece of evidence in favour of this rather complex view of the Purkinje axon collaterals. It is that it also accounts for the climbing fibre collateral effects.[1,3] For, during learning, any instruction to generalize must be annulled, in order that a true record of the mossy fibre input may be stored. According to the theory,[3] learning occurs at $P$ when the relevant climbing fibre is also active; and when it is, the effect of its collaterals could roughly balance the effect of the Purkinje axon collateral near $P$. According to the available evidence,[1] both types of collateral are weak and their effects are opposite.

## Timing relationships

We have argued that the small, superficial pyramidal cells of the cerebral cortex detect incompatibilities in the current deep pyramidal cell activity, and that they modify the behaviour of the cerebro–cerebellar–cerebral loop to cope with this. We now consider the timing relationships involved.

The speed of the main "feedback" loop is astounding. It incorporates some of the fastest pathways in the nervous system, and its major links all include monosynaptic connexions.[1,11] In the cat, discharges in the pontine nuclei follow stimulation of the cerebral white matter by as little as 2 ms.[4] The corresponding times for the other stages are: pontine nuclei to cerebellar nuclei, 1 ms;[11] cerebellar nuclei to *VL* nucleus of thalamus, 2 ms;[1] *VL* nucleus of thalamus to cerebral pyramidal cells, an estimated 1 ms. The whole loop may therefore be traversed in as little as 6 ms, and certainly within 10 ms. Such a fast mechanism is clearly required in voluntary movements, especially those of a more complex kind when muscular groups have to be set into action in rapid sequence and at closely defined times.

Contextual information reaching the cerebellar cortex through the mossy fibres is also rapidly transmitted; indeed, it involves almost the same pathways. The time taken for stimulation of the subcortical white matter to evoke a mossy fibre response is 2.7 ms.[4] Mossy fibre responses to stimulation of forelimb and hindlimb peripheral nerves have delays as short as 5 ms and 7 ms respectively.[4]

On the other hand, the cortico–olivary–climbing fibre pathway is quite slow. The climbing fibre discharge evoked by stimulation of the cerebral subcortical white matter has a delay of 15 ms.[4] At first sight, it would therefore seem impossible that the superficial pyramidals could signal that the currently active deep pyramidals should be deleted: their commands would arrive too late to be effective.

It is, however, necessary to consider the time scale of the context in which these instructions are being made. The overall context of the movement changes much more slowly than the individual components of that movement. That a given group of deep pyramidal cells should not fire is not merely a decision whose effects last for a few milliseconds: the group will be required to be off for an extended period of time. The decision may have to be made and implemented quickly, but it will remain in force for much longer. This means that the modification conditions refer to extended contexts, of perhaps as long as 100 ms, rather than to instantaneous contexts.

It is therefore proposed that the inferior olive cells should fire in prolonged bursts, of up to 100 ms. During this time, the currently active synapses to the related Purkinje cells should be strengthened in proportion to their degree of activity. This allows the Golgi cell threshold system to be reset by the climbing fibre collaterals, so as to give the "correct" parallel fibre pattern during modification. More important, this ensures that the Purkinje cells can respond in good time to inhibit the cerebellar nuclei cells – because the mossy fibre context just before the climbing fibre activity (that is, when the input reaches the pontine nuclei) will differ only slightly from that during it. The ability of Purkinje cells to generalize will also help in this effect.

It may be found that the small, superficial pyramidal cells anticipate the large, deep pyramidal cells, and signal in advance that certain cerebellar nuclei cells must be inhibited within the context of the present developing movement.

## Cerebellar disorders

The present theory can provide a tentative explanation for many of the disorders arising from damage to the cerebellum. One of the most striking effects of acute cerebellar lesions is the delay in the initiation and termination of movements.[13] The delay in initiation is probably caused by malfunction of the cerebellar nuclei. In the acute stage of such lesions, there is considerable oedema and consequently raised pressure in the cerebellum; this could account for such malfunction. The result is that, when the cerebral cortex tries to initiate the movement, there is little or no excitatory feedback to the motor cortex. The movement can only be got going by a considerably greater voluntary effort, and this involves both delay and slow pick-up. With recovery of functioning of the cerebellar nuclei (that is, in those lesions which are more superficial), such delays will tend to disappear.[13]

Delay in termination[13] probably results from a combination of two factors. First, there is an inability to initiate the muscular contractions which are required to stop the movement: this again involves the cerebellar nuclei. Second, there is delay in switching off the current movement: this results from the malfunction of the cerebellar cortex. This latter effect should become more apparent as recovery proceeds, for the cerebellar nuclei will be functioning normally while the damage to the cerebellar cortex persists. In other words, the context which signifies that the movement should stop is no longer able to implement this operation, because the relevant Purkinje cells are lacking. This argument receives support from the observations of Gordon Holmes[13] that the start of relaxation in a movement is usually more markedly affected than the start of contraction.

The inability of patients with unilateral cerebellar lesions to maintain voluntary postures on the affected side, and the greater sense of effort involved in making any voluntary movements, are both common features in the early acute stages. Both are consequences of inadequate excitatory feedback from the cerebellar nuclei.

The phenomena of dysmetria,[13] in cases of acute cerebellar lesions, and of hypermetria, which occurs in more persistent cases, are probably related to these disorders. Dysmetria will result from the malfunctioning of both cerebellar nuclei and cerebellar cortex. Movements, once initiated, are ill-gauged and tend to undershoot or overshoot the mark. Undershoot will be caused by an inability to maintain a voluntary movement (a symptom of cerebellar nuclei malfunction); overshoot will be caused by inability to stop voluntary movements (already considered). It is particularly interesting that hypermetria should ensue – this is exactly what the theory would predict. It results from the lack of inhibitory control from the cerebellar cortex; as a result the movements consistently overshoot and are excessively forceful.

The decomposition of complex movements[13] is a natural consequence of any cerebellar malfunction. The errors arising in the initiation, continuation and termination of successive and concurrently running elemental movements should lead to hopeless confusion. The only hope for success would be to deal with one elemental movement at a time, so that errors may be consciously and deliberately dealt with as they arise.

An interesting disability which arises in cerebellar patients is that on trying to flex just one finger (in order to bring it into apposition with the thumb), they frequently flex all four fingers at the same time.[13] In this case, it may be that normally the cerebral command is to flex all four fingers but suppress flexion on the unwanted three. Certainly in early hand movements, flexion of all four fingers appears before flexion of individual fingers – though there is a cortical representation for each individual finger flexion. The suppression of the unwanted flexions is learned by the cerebellum during the early development of the child. Damage to the cerebellar cortex will interfere with the suppression, and a command to move one finger will initiate movement in all four.

We shall make just one reference to observations made on animals with lesions placed in the cerebellum. This concerns the effects of such lesions on the placing reaction.[14] Lesions which involve the dentate nucleus are found to abolish the placing reaction. In contrast, lesions confined to the cerebellar cortex may actually enhance it. Ablation of parts of the cerebral cortex which include the motor area is known to abolish the placing reaction. This is compatible with a learned reflex which passes through the cerebral motor cortex and whose output depends on positive feedback through the cerebro–cerebellar–cerebral loop. Clearly such a reflex is of use to the animal in standing and walking. Inhibitory control of this reflex is then exerted by the cerebellar cortex.

# References

1 Eccles, J. D., Ito, M., and Szentagothai, J., *The Cerebellum as a Neuronal Machine* (Springer-Verlag, Berlin, 1967)

2 Jansen, J., and Brodal, A., *Aspects of Cerebellar Anatomy* (Johan Grundt Tanum Forlag, Oslo, 1954)

3 Marr, David, *J. Physiol.*, Vol. 202, page 437 (1969)

4 Kitai, S. T. Oshima, T., Provini, L., and Tsukahara, N., *Brain Res.*, Vol. 15, page 267 (1969)

5 Armstrong, D. M., Harvey, R. J., and Schild, R. F., *J. Physiol.*, Vol. 202, page 106P (1969)

6 Faber, D. S., and Murphy, J. T., *Brain Res.*, Vol. 15, page 267 (1969)

7 Marr, David, A Theory for Cerebral Neocortex, *Proc. Roy. Soc.*, B, Vol. 176, pages 161–234, 1970

8 Towe, A. L., Patton, H. D., and Kennedy, T. T., *Exp. Neurol.*, Vol. 8, page 220 (1963)

9 Branch, C. L., and Martin, A. R., *J. Neurophysiol.*, Vol. 21, page 380 (1958)

10 Escobar, A., Sampedro, E. D., and Dow, R. S., *J. Comp. Neurol.*, Vol. 132, page 397 (1968)

11 Tsukahara, N., Korn, H., and Stone, J., *Brain Res.*, Vol. 10, page 448

12 Voogd, J., *Prog. Brain Res.*, Vol. 25, page 94 (1967)

13 Holmes, Gordon, *Brain*, Vol. 40, page 461 (1917)

14 Dow, R. S., and Moruzzi, G., *The Physiology and Pathology of the Cerebellum* (University of Minnesota Press, Minneapolis, 1958)

# 4 The evolution of the central nervous system
## by Alfred Sherwood Romer

The spinal cord (figure 4.1*A*), extending most of the length of the body, is a little-modified adult representative of the nerve tube formed in the early embryo. It still contains, as did that of the embryo, a centrally situated, fluid-filled canal; this, however, has become relatively tiny in diameter, owing to the great growth of the nervous tissues surrounding it.

The spinal cord is subcircular or oval in section in lower vertebrates, but in higher groups it tends to expand in bilateral fashion, and pronounced grooves may be present in the midline dorsally and ventrally. The cord tends to taper distally; in many forms (notably in mammals) it may be shorter than the vertebral column, and in the distal part of the vertebral canal there may be merely a series of nerves running back from the cord termination to serve the most posterior tail segments. Two layers of material can be readily distinguished in the cord, a central area of *gray matter* surrounding the canal of the cord, and a peripheral region of *white matter*. The former consists mainly of cell bodies, the latter of countless myelinated fibers coursing up and down the cord.

Primitively, the gray substance was, it seems, arranged in a fairly even fashion about the central cavity; in most vertebrates, however, there is a bilaterally symmetric arrangement, as seen in section, into an H-shape, or that of a butterfly's wings. Such a pattern gives the appearance of a pair of "horns" on either side, dorsally and ventrally. Actually, of course, each "horn" is merely a section of a longitudinal structure, and we should speak rather of a dorsal column and a ventral column.

The *ventral column* is the seat of the cell bodies of the efferent or motor neurons of the spinal nerves, their axons typically passing out through successive ventral nerve roots. The number of neurons in any given part of the cord will, naturally, vary with the volume of musculature at that level of the body, and in land vertebrates the ventral column

(indeed, the entire cord) may be much expanded in the regions supplying the limbs. Most of the motor supply is to somatic muscles; but visceral efferents may be present over much of the length of the trunk. The cell bodies of these latter neurons are situated above and lateral to those of the somatic motor type, and sometimes are distinguishable as a *ventrolateral column.*

The *dorsal column* of the gray matter is associated with the dorsal, sensory roots of the spinal nerves; it is the seat of the cell bodies of association neurons through which impulses brought in from sense organs may be relayed and distributed. These neurons have processes which may ascend and descend the cord to connect with motor neurons of the same side, may cross to connect with motor neurons of the opposite side of the cord, or, still further, may ascend the cord to the brain. The arrangement of various clusters of these sensory association cells in the dorsal column is complex and variable, but in some cases (particularly in certain embryos) it appears that we can distinguish a larger series associated with somatic sensory reception, situated dorsally and medially, and a smaller, visceral sensory group situated more ventrally and laterally. There thus appear to be in the gray matter four areas on either side related to the four

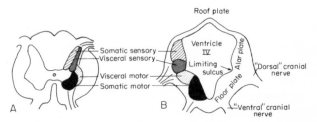

**Figure 4.1 Diagrams showing the distribution of sensory and motor columns.** *A*, The spinal cord of the adult of certain lower vertebrates. *B*, The embryonic medulla oblongata; the embryonic spinal cord shows a similar arrangement of the columns. The plate of tissue lying below the limiting sulcus is termed the floor plate; from this, motor centers arise. The sensory region above is the "wing" or alar plate. (Partly after Herrick.)

*first published in* The Vertebrate Body, *4th edition, 1970, pages 501–28 (W. B. Saunders Co., Philadelphia and London).*

nerve components, the four being in sequence, from dorsal to ventral: somatic sensory, visceral sensory, visceral motor and somatic motor. It is of interest that the same arrangement is found in the gray matter of the brain stem (figure 4.1B).

The *white matter* is composed, as has been said, of innumerable myelinated fibers. These include ascending and descending fibers of sensory nerve cells which enter the cord through the dorsal nerve roots, and of similar fibers taking origin from association cells. Present as well are fibers which carry sensory stimuli forward to the brain, and fibers returning from brain centers to act (usually via association neurons) on motor neurons. Fibers of these latter categories are especially abundant in higher vertebrate groups, in which the trunk loses the semi-autonomous nature which it has in fishes and comes more directly under the influence of the brain. Topographically, the white matter is more or less subdivided by the dorsal and ventral "horns" into major areas: dorsal, lateral and ventral *funiculi*. Anatomic and physiologic investigation enables one to distinguish in these areas *fiber tracts* with the varied types of connections noted above. These tracts, however, vary too greatly in nature and position from group to group to be described here in detail, although in general the dorsal funiculi mainly carry ascending, sensory fibers, the ventral ones descending fibers to motor neurons.

In all vertebrates, as well as in the more highly organized invertebrates, we find a concentration of nervous tissues at the anterior end of the body in the form of a brain or brainlike structure of some sort. Such a concentration is to be expected. In an actively moving, bilaterally symmetric animal this region is that which first makes contact with environmental situations to which response must be made. It is, in consequence, the region in which the major sensory structures come to be situated, and in which, hence, it is most advantageous to locate correlation and integration of sensory impulses.

Primitively, we may believe, the vertebrate brain was merely a modestly developed anterior region of the neural tube in which, in addition to facilities for local reflexes to the head and throat region, special sensory stimuli were assembled and "referred for action" to the semi-autonomous body region via the spinal cord. Within the vertebrates, however, there has occurred a strong trend for the concentration in the brain of command over bodily functions (except for the simplest reflexes), with the development of a series of complex, intercommunicating brain centers. We have noted, in discussing the elementary composition of the nervous system, the way in which the intercalation of an association neuron into the simple reflex arc greatly broadens the field of possible responses to a sensory stimulus and, conversely, greatly increases the variety of stimuli which may excite a specific motor response. The brain pattern is essentially an elaboration of this principle – the interposition of further series of neurons between primary areas of sensory reception and final motor paths. These intermediate neuron groups are clustered in functional centers. In such centers afferent impulses may be correlated and integrated for appropriate responses, or motor mechanisms coordinated; on still higher levels there may develop association centers of whose activity memory, learning and consciousness may be the products.

# Brain development

The general topography of the brain and its parts is best understood through a consideration of its development (figure 4.2). The brain develops rapidly in the embryo – much more rapidly than almost any other organ – and there is early established a generalized structural pattern upon which the numerous variations seen in the adult brains of different groups are superposed. In early stages the future brain is merely an expanded area of the neural tube. With continued increase in size, its anterior end tends to fold downward, forming a *cephalic flexure*. This distinguishes a median, terminal saclike structure, the primitive forebrain or *prosencephalon*, from the remainder of the tube. Somewhat later a second flexure, in a reverse direction, is found more posteriorly at the *isthmus*. This separates the midbrain, or *mesencephalon*, from the primitive hindbrain, the *rhombencephalon*, in which develops the *medulla oblongata* of the adult. Posteriorly, the rhombencephalon tapers gradually, without any abrupt change, into the spinal cord.

Prosencephalon, mesencephalon, and rhombencephalon are the three primary subdivisions of the brain. The three successive "segments" of the brain tube which constitute them in early stages are still recognizable in the adult, where they are termed collectively the *brain stem* – that part of the brain which is presumably phylogenetically the oldest and in which are persistently located centers for many simple but basically important reactions within the nervous system.* Subdivision of the brain stem into three parts

---

* The cerebellum and the cerebral hemispheres are "new additions" not developed at this stage and not included in the brain stem. Also excluded by neurologists in defining the brain stem are certain structures (such as the pons), lodged in the brain stem, but intimately connected with the functioning of cerebellum or hemispheres.

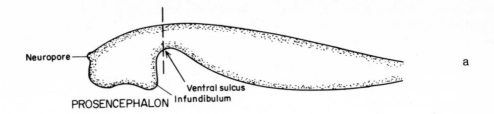

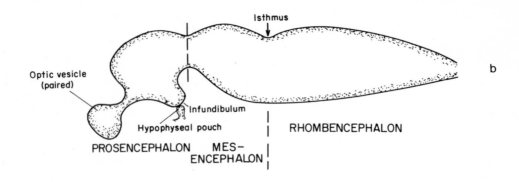

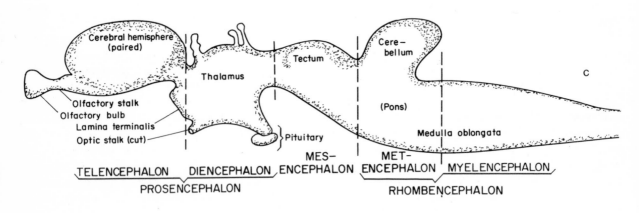

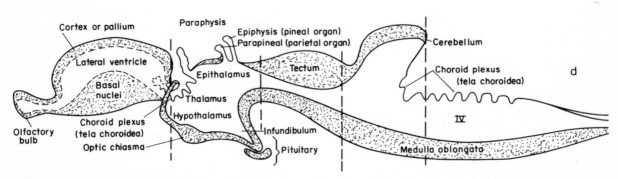

**Figure 4.2 Diagrams to show the development of the principal brain divisions and structures.** *a*, Only prosencephalon (primitive forebrain) distinct from remainder of neural tube. *b*, Three main divisions established. *c*, More mature stage in lateral view. *d*, The same in median section. (Partly after Bütschli.)

would have been pointless, one may believe, were it not that there presumably appeared at an early stage in phylogeny three major sense organs: nose, eye and ear + lateral line. In primitive vertebrates each of the three becomes associated with one of the three brain subdivisions, and for each of the three there tends to develop a dorsal outgrowth of laminated "gray matter" from its proper section of the stem (figure 4.3). These three outgrowths are respectively cerebrum, midbrain roof (tectum), and cerebellum.*

At the three-vesicle stage midbrain and hindbrain regions are simple in construction, but in the primitive forebrain region special structures appear early. Most notably, the optic vesicles push out at either side; the optic stalks, in which the optic nerves later develop, remain attached anteriorly to the base of the primitive forebrain at the optic chiasma. More posteriorly, there is a down-growing median projection from the diencephalon, the *infundibulum*. Concomitantly a pocket of epithelium, the *hypophyseal pouch* (Rathke's pouch) grows upward from the roof of the embryonic mouth. In later stages modified infundibular tissues and those derived from the pouch combine to form the pituitary gland. Dorsally there grows presently from the roof of the primitive forebrain a series of median processes, the paraphysis and a median "eye stalk" (sometimes two) which are described elsewhere.

Further developments occur to transform the tripartite brain stem into a brain of five regions. The midbrain shows little important change except for paired dorsal swellings which form the *tectum* (prominent in lower vertebrates), but both hindbrain and forebrain regions become subdivided. In the hindbrain a dorsal outgrowth from the roof of the front of the rhombencephalon becomes the *cerebellum*. The region of the medulla oblongata beneath the cerebellum is little changed in most vertebrates, but in mammals is expanded into the structure termed the *pons*. Pons and overlying cerebellum are distinguished as the *metencephalon* from the more posterior part of the oblongata, the *myelencephalon*.

Still more striking is the development anteriorly of paired outgrowths from the primitive forebrain. These are hollow pockets of brain tissue (at first somewhat analogous to the optic cups) which grow forward toward the basal region; from them develop the *cerebral hemispheres* and, still farther anteriorly, the *olfactory bulbs*. These structures constitute the *telencephalon*, the anterior terminal segment of the brain; the unpaired part of the forebrain is the *diencephalon*.

* In mammals the eye, as we shall see, has "deserted" the midbrain in favor of the hemispheres as a major brain connection.

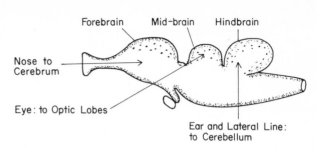

**Figure 4.3 Diagram** to show the relation in lower vertebrates of the three major sense organs to the three dorsal areas of gray matter in the three major subdivisions of the brain. (In mammals the midbrain tectum is reduced and optic sensations are relayed to the cerebrum instead.)

(It must be noted, however, that, by definition, the most anterior tip of the median forebrain pocket, between the foramina leading to the paired vesicles of the hemispheres, is reckoned as part of the telencephalon.)

The principal brain structures of the adult may be tabulated according to the divisions established in the embryo as shown below.

## Ventricles

The original cavity of the embryonic neural tube persists in the adult brain in the form of a series of cavities and passages filled with cerebrospinal fluid (figures 4.4, 4.8, 4.21). A cavity, or *lateral ventricle*, is present in each of the cerebral hemispheres. These cavities connect posteriorly through an *interventricular foramen* (foramen of Monro) with a median *third ventricle*, situated in the diencephalon. Within the midbrain there is in lower vertebrates a well

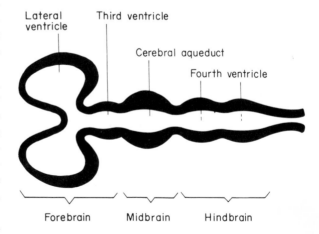

**Figure 4.4 Diagram** showing position of brain ventricles. (From Gardner.)

| **Prosencephalon** | Telencephalon | Cerebral hemispheres, including olfactory lobes, basal nuclei (corpus striatum) and cerebral cortex (pallium); olfactory bulbs |
| | Diencephalon | Epithalamus; thalamus; hypothalamus; and appendages |
| **Mesencephalon** | | Tectum, including optic lobes (corpora quadrigemina in mammals); tegmentum; crura cerebri (cerebral peduncles) in mammals |
| **Rhombencephalon** | Metencephalon | Part of medulla oblongata; cerebellum; pons of mammals |
| | Myelencephalon | Part of medulla oblongata |

developed ventricle, but in amniotes this becomes a narrow channel termed the *cerebral aqueduct* (aqueduct of Sylvius). Within the medulla oblongata is a *fourth ventricle*; this tapers posteriorly into the canal of the spinal cord. Over most of the extent of the brain the ventricles are surrounded by thick walls of nervous tissue. The walls are commonly thin, however, in two roof regions, one at the junction of the hemispheres with the diencephalon, the other forming the roof of the fourth ventricle. In each of these areas there develops a *choroid plexus* (or tela choroidea) – a highly folded area of richly vascular tissue. Through these plexuses exchange of materials takes place between the blood and cerebrospinal fluid.

## Brain architecture

In the present elementary account of the vertebrate brain our attention will be mainly centered on external features and gross structures (figures 4.5–4.13). But while such superficial aspects of brain anatomy are significant, an adequate understanding of the working of the brain can no more be gained from them than a knowledge of the working of a telephone system can be had from an acquaintance with the external appearance and room plan of the telephone exchange. What is of importance in a telephone system is the arrangement of switchboards and wiring; in a brain it is the centers which act as switchboards, in a sense, and the tracts of fibers, which form the wiring between them.

It may well be that the brain "wiring" was primitively much like that of the spinal cord – a general crisscross of fibers interconnecting all areas. Generally, however, there is a strong tendency for the clustering together of nerve cells of specific functions in centers, and the assembling of fibers with like connections into definite bundles.

Although certain special centers have special names, most are termed *ganglia* or *nuclei* (making an unfortunate, duplicate, biologic use of this latter word). Nuclei, or centers, in a broad sense, range in size from tiny clusters of

cells embedded in the gray matter of the brain stem and discernible only on microscopic study, to such massive structures as the cerebellum or cerebral cortex. Fiber bundles connecting nuclei with one another are in general termed *tracts*; the fibers constituting such a tract are, of course, axons of neurons whose cell bodies lie in the nucleus of origin. A tract is generally given a compound name, the two parts of which designate its origin and termination; thus the corticospinal tract carries impulses from the cortex of

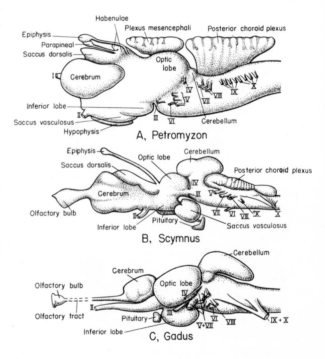

**Figure 4.5 Lateral views of brain** of *A*, a lamprey; *B*, a shark; *C*, a codfish. In the lamprey an exceptional condition is the development of a vascular choroid area, the plexus mesencephali, on the roof of the midbrain. (After Bütschli, Ahlborn.)

52

the cerebral hemispheres to or toward the motor cells of the spinal cord.

Despite the general tendency of brain cells and fibers to organize into clean-cut centers and tracts, a primitive condition persists in the *reticular system*. This is a band of interlacing cells and fibers associated with the motor columns in the brain stem and anterior part of the spinal cord, and particularly well developed in the anterior part of the brain stem. This system is important in motor coordination. Still further, the reticular network appears to function in carrying stimuli downward from the anterior brain regions to the motor centers of the oblongata and cord. This function is an essential one in lower vertebrates, in which motor tracts giving the brain control over trunk activities are poorly developed (*cf.* figures 4.23, 4.24); the reticular system is still important in mammals, not only as a persistent "low level" path to motor centers, but also (working in the opposite direction) as an agent which tends to promote activation of the higher centers of the cerebral cortex.

The brain is constructed on a bilaterally symmetric pattern; in consequence, cross connections must be established in order that an animal may not have a literally dual personality. We have noted that even in the spinal cord there are numbers of association neurons whose fibers cross to the opposite side, and in the brain such connections are numerous. There are a number of *commissures*, fiber tracts which connect corresponding regions of the two sides. In addition, there are cases where tracts in their course along the brain cross over from one side to the other (i.e. decussate), sometimes without apparent reason. We have described such a decussation in the case of the optic nerves (which are really brain tracts). Another example is recalled by the well-known fact that movements of one side of the body are controlled by the gray matter of the brain hemisphere of the opposite side – a situation caused by a decussation of the corticospinal tracts of the two sides as they pass backward along the brain stem.

The discussion above of the "wiring" of the brain was stated in terms comparable to those of a telephone system, a pattern of end-to-end connections of series of neurons straight through the system from receptor to effector. But actually, as has been increasingly realized in recent years, the general patterns of brain activity are far more intricate in nature, and include "feedbacks", resonating systems

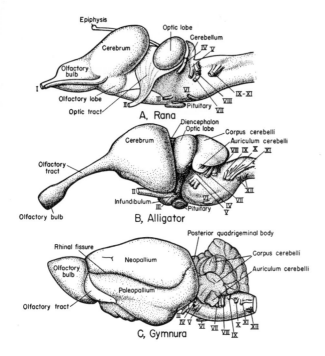

**Figure 4.6 Lateral views of brain** of *A*, a frog; *B*, an alligator; *C*, an insectivore representing a primitive mammalian type. (In normal head posture the front end of the alligator brain is tilted upward.) (After Bütschli, Clark, Crosby, Gaupp, Wettstein.)

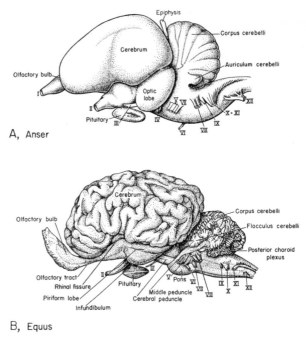

**Figure 4.7 Lateral views of brain** of *A*, a goose; *B*, a horse. (The goose brain, like that of the alligator, is tilted upward anteriorly in life.) (After Bütschli, Kuenzi, Sisson.)

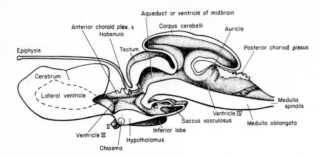

**Figure 4.8 Right half of the brain of a shark** (Scyllium) in median aspect. Unshaded areas are those sectioned. (After Haller, Bruckhardt.)

associated with memory and learning, and other complexities – into which we shall not attempt to enter here – which are being increasingly approached in the development of computing machines.

## Medulla oblongata

Approach to the study of brain architecture is best made by first considering those brain parts which are simplest in construction and most closely resemble the spinal cord. The brain stem, including the three primary vesicles of the embryo, is simpler than its specialized outgrowths, the cerebral hemispheres and cerebellum. Even in the stem, however, the anterior part appears to have been the seat of complex nervous centers from the beginning of vertebrate history. It is in the hindbrain region, the medulla oblongata, that we find the closest structural approach to the cord. Further, with the oblongata and the adjacent parts of the midbrain are connected all the cranial nerves except the atypical ones from nose and eye.

The medulla oblongata is, particularly in lower vertebrates, closely comparable to an anterior section of the spinal cord – enlarged, however, through the expansion of the central canal to form the fourth ventricle, and with the columns of gray matter of either side widely separated dorsally as a consequence. For most of its length the roof of the oblongata is thin, membranous, and infolded to form the *posterior choroid plexus*; anteriorly, the oblongata is covered by the cerebellum.

In the gray matter of the oblongata and the posterior part of the midbrain, there is found a series of columns or nuclei of gray matter basically similar to those present in the cord (figures 4.1*B*, 4.16). In that region we have noted the presence of a dorsal column, containing association centers for the reception and distribution of sensory impulses, and a ventral column containing motor neurons; we have further noted evidence that both columns may be subdivided into

somatic and visceral components. A similar situation is found in the oblongata and the posterior part of the midbrain, although the widely expanded ventricle makes for a somewhat different appearance. A horizontal groove, running along the inner surface of the brain stem on either side, separates a dorsal sensory region from a ventral motor region. Further, here, as in the cord, each of these two can be subdivided into somatic and visceral components.

In the embryo each subdivision appears to be formed as an essentially continuous fore and aft column. Most ventrally is a somatic motor column. Dorsal to this, but still below the limiting sulcus, are visceral motor columns for both branchial muscle and autonomic efferents. Above the sulcus are, in order, visceral sensory and somatic sensory columns, the primary areas of reception for sensations from gut and skin, respectively. The ventralmost column is that from which the ventral cranial nerves – III, IV, VI, XII – arise; the others are the areas of central connection of the dorsal root or branchial nerves – including V, VII, IX, X.

In the adults of lower vertebrate groups much of the embryonic longitudinal continuity of the column is preserved; in higher types, however, there is a strong trend for

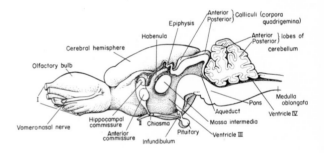

A, Didelphys

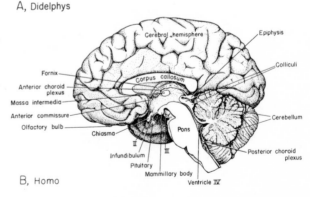

B, Homo

**Figure 4.9. Right half of the brain,** in median aspect, of *A*, an opossum; *B*, man. Unshaded areas are those sectioned. The internally bulging side walls of the diencephalon may meet and fuse in the midline, forming a "massa intermedia", which, however, has no functional importance. (*A* after Loo.)

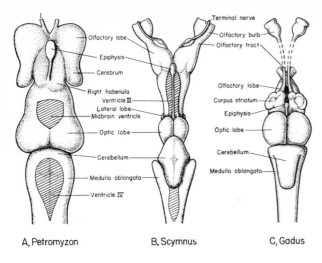

A, Petromyzon          B, Scymnus          C, Gadus

**Figure 4.10 Dorsal views of the brain** of *A*, a lamprey; *B*, a shark; *C*, a teleost (codfish). Hatched areas are those in which a choroid plexus has been removed, exposing the underlying ventricle. (After Bütschli, Ahlborn.)

a breaking down of the columns into discrete nuclei for the cranial nerves concerned and as centers for various body activities which are controlled or influenced by the brain stem. Thus in mammals the somatic motor column is fragmented into (1) several small anterior nuclei in the midbrain and in the anterior end of the oblongata for the eye muscle nerves, and (2) a more posterior nucleus for the hypoglossal. The special visceral motor column for branchial musculature is broken up into separate special visceral motor nuclei for nerves V, VII, and IX and X (*nucleus ambiguus*), and in this column there develops a center concerned with respiratory rhythm. Small autonomic nuclei are present in the midbrain for eye reflexes, farther back in the oblongata for salivary glands, and still farther back for the autonomic component of the vagus. In vertebrates generally the nuclei associated with the normal visceral sensory fibers remain concentrated in a *nucleus solitarius* of the oblongata, but a parallel *gustatory nucleus* is present for the special visceral sense of taste. The somatic sensory column remains as a single elongate nucleus which, primarily associated with the trigeminal nerve, extends much of the length of the brain stem and even back into the cord.

In mammals a great mass of fibers connecting with the cerebellum bridge over the base of the oblongata anteriorly, causing so prominent a swelling that this region is termed the *pons*. Even apart from this, the gray matter of the oblongata is thickly sheathed, in amniotes, with white tracts of fibers passing between body and more anterior brain centers. In lower classes the sheathing is relatively thin, for trunk and tail are semi-autonomous and perform most movements reflexly, without referring them to the brain. In fishes generally a limited number only of sensory fibers from the body reach the brain stem, cerebellum and midbrain; in amniotes such fibers reach forebrain centers. Conversely, there is little positive control by the higher brain centers over body movement below the stage of birds and mammals except through the rather indirect means of the reticular system mentioned above. A striking exception is the presence in fishes and tailed amphibians of a pair of spectacular *giant cells* (*cells of Mauthner*) in the medulla. Their cell bodies, closely associated with the acoustico-lateralis centers, lie in the floor of the medulla; their large axons extend the entire length of the cord. Locomotion in fishes and primitive tetrapods is mainly accomplished by rhythmic undulations of the body. To some extent this could be (and presumably is) regulated by local cord reflexes. This pair of cells, however, appears to exercise general control over these movements. In adult frogs, typical reptiles, and higher forms this type of locomotion disappears and these giant cells disappear likewise.

The series of motor and sensory columns or nuclei of the medulla give us all the elements required for reflex circuits in the brain between sensory reception and the responding effector organs of the head and gill region. But brain mechanisms are not built solely on such a simple plan. In addition to ordinary sensory receptors in the skin, muscles and gut tube, such as are found throughout the body, we

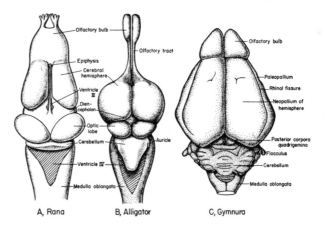

A, Rana          B, Alligator          C, Gymnura

**Figure 4.11 Dorsal views of the brain** of *A*, a frog; *B*, an alligator; *C*, a tree shrew. Hatched areas are those in which a choroid plexus has been removed, exposing the underlying ventricle. (After Gaupp, Crosby, Wettstein, Clark.)

have in the head region special sensory organs. Centers must be present for the primary reception of sensations from these organs; and higher centers must be built up for the association and correlation of these sensations before final "directions" can be issued to the motor columns of brain stem and cord. Much of this apparatus is situated elsewhere in the brain. But even in the relatively simple brain stem region here considered we find the primary area of reception of one of the main sensory systems – the acoustico-lateralis system.

The lateral line organs and the ear, a special development from them, are somatic sensory structures; as such, sensations from them were primitively received, we may reason-

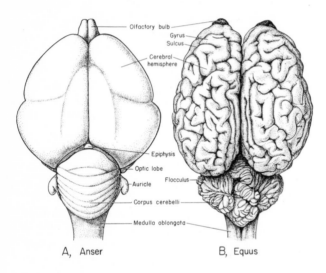

**Figure 4.12 Dorsal views of the brain** of *A*. a goose; *B*, a horse. (After Bütschli, Kuenzi, Sisson.)

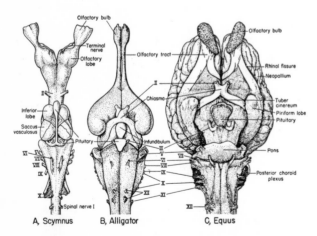

**Figure 4.13 Ventral views of the brain** of *A*, a shark; *B*, an alligator; *C*, a horse. (After Bütschli, Wettstein, Sisson.)

ably assume, in the somatic sensory column of the oblongata. So special are they, however, that in fishes a specific *acoustico-lateralis area*, often of considerable size, develops above the normal somatic sensory column in the anterior part of the oblongata. In land vertebrates the lateralis system disappears, but acoustic nuclei persist; in mammals there are distinct centers for the vestibular and cochlear parts of the ear.

## Cerebellum

Rising above the brain stem at the anterior end of the medulla oblongata is the cerebellum (figures 4.14, 4.15), a brain center, often of large size, which is of extreme importance in the coordination and regulation of motor activities and the maintenance of posture. The cerebellum acts in a passive, essentially reflex fashion in the maintenance of equilibrium and body orientation. In addition it plays a major positive role – particularly in mammals – in locomotion. Its function in regulating muscular activity may be compared to that of "staff work" in the movement of an army. To carry out the general orders of an army commander it is necessary that there be in hand information as to the position, current movements, condition and equipment of the bodies of troops concerned. A "directive" from the higher brain centers (hemispheres or tectum) for a muscular action – say, the movement of a limb – cannot be carried out efficiently unless there are available data as to the current position and movement of the limb, the state of relaxation or contraction of the muscles involved, the general position of the body, and its relation to the outside world. Such data are assembled in the cerebellum and synthesized there, and resulting "orders" issued by efferent pathways render the movement effective.

The data upon which the cerebellum acts are derived from two main sources. One is the acoustic area of the medulla – acoustico-lateralis area of lower vertebrates – in which are registered equilibrium sensations from the ear and lateral line sensations. The base of the cerebellum lies immediately above this area, and the cerebellum obviously originated as a specialized part of this sensory center. The second main source of cerebellar data is the system of muscle and tendon spindles. Into the cerebellum are directed fibers of this proprioceptive system carrying data regarding the position of the body parts and the state of muscle tension.

In addition to these two primary sources, the sensory picture assembled in the cerebellum is rounded out by additional fiber relays from skin sensory areas, from the optic centers, and, in lower vertebrates, even from the nose. Information, further, is supplied regarding muscular move-

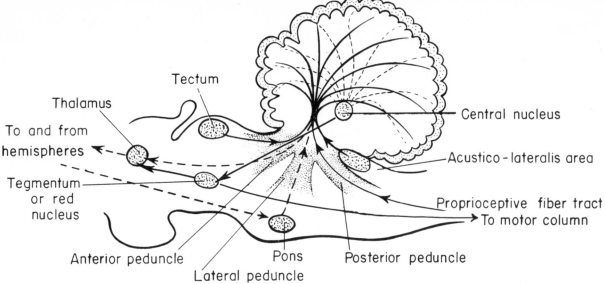

Thalamus

Tectum

Central nucleus

To and from hemispheres

Acustico-lateralis area

Tegmentum or red nucleus

Proprioceptive fiber tract
To motor column

Anterior peduncle

Pons

Posterior peduncle

Lateral peduncle

**Figure 4.14 Diagram to show the main connections of the cerebellum.** The connections with the cerebral cortex, peculiar to mammals, are shown in broken line.

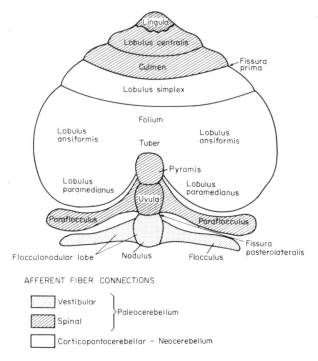

Lingula

Lobulus centralis

Culmen

Fissura prima

Lobulus simplex

Folium

Lobulus ansiformis

Lobulus ansiformis

Tuber

Pyramis

Lobulus paramedianus

Lobulus paramedianus

Uvula

Paraflocculus

Paraflocculus

Fissura posterolateralis

Flocculonodular lobe

Nodulus

Flocculus

AFFERENT FIBER CONNECTIONS

| | | |
|---|---|---|
| ☐ Vestibular | ⎫ | |
| ▨ Spinal | ⎬ Paleocerebellum | |
| ☐ Corticopontocerebellar – Neocerebellum | | |

**Figure 4.15 Diagram of a surface view of a mammalian cerebellum** (showing details not discussed in the text). The stippled and hatched portions, associated with equilibrium (vestibular) and with muscle sensations (spinal), are the phylogenetically oldest parts of the cerebellum; the white area is a mammalian addition associated with the cortex of the cerebral hemispheres. (From Fulton, after Larsell.)

ments which are directed by higher brain centers, but upon which the cerebellum has influence. In lower vertebrates these data are furnished by fibers from the midbrain, where such impulses in great measure originate; in mammals, where the cerebral cortex dominates motor functions, strong fiber tracts connect cortex with cerebellum via the pons.

After integration of data by the cerebellum, outgoing fiber tracts carry impulses forward and downward on either side of the brain stem to the side walls of the midbrain (the tegmental region), whence they continue (in part after a relay there) to the appropriate motor nuclei of head or body or, in mammals, to the thalamus and thence to the cerebral cortex also.

In forms in which the cerebellum is well developed the fiber tracts leading to and from it are prominent features in the architecture of the brain stem. In mammals, for example, these fibers form three pairs of pillar-like structures, the *cerebellar peduncles* (or *brachia*, figure 4.14). Anterior peduncles, mainly composed of efferent fiber tracts, connect cerebellum and midbrain. A middle, or lateral, pair of peduncles rise straight upward along the sides of the metencephalon from the pons; these carry fibers running from cerebral cortex to cerebellum, which cross and are relayed ventrally in the pons. Posterior peduncles rise up through the oblongata and carry proprioceptive fiber bundles from the cord.

The cerebellum varies greatly in size and shape from group to group. Its degree of development is correlated with the intricacy of bodily movements; it is large and elaborately constructed in many fishes and in birds and mammals, small in reptiles, little developed in cyclostomes and amphibians, where it is little more than a pair of small centers lying just above the acoustico-lateralis nuclei and hardly distinct from them. This most ancient part of the cerebellum persists in all groups as the *auricles* (or flocculi), especially concerned with equilibrium and closely connected with the inner ear.

Even in lampreys and amphibians, however, there is some development of a median cerebellar region between the two auricles above the front end of the fourth ventricle. To this come fibers from the organs of muscle sense and from sensory centers in the brain for integration and correlation with stimuli from the organs of equilibrium in the ear. This primary structure, the *corpus cerebelli*, constitutes the main mass of the cerebellum in typical fishes, reptiles and birds. In mammals the rise of the cerebral cortex to command of motor functions, and the development of powerful tracts from motor cortex to cerebellum and return, is correlated with the appearance of large paired and convoluted structures – "cerebellar hemispheres" – which make up much of the bulk of the mammalian organ.

In contrast to every other area of the central nervous system except the cerebral hemispheres and midbrain roof, the cerebellum is a region in which the gray cellular material is superficially placed as a laminated cortex, the white matter internal. In a well developed cerebellum the gray matter is spread out as a surface sheet which is often highly convoluted and thus gains greater area. Beneath this is the white matter, principally a fan-shaped radiation of incoming fibers spreading out in all directions to the surface, and of fibers returning from the gray matter. The cerebellar cortex contains cells of several quite distinctive types, arranged in layers, between which sensory data are interchanged by a complex fiber network. Most remarkable of cellular elements are the *Purkinje cells*, whose dendrites form highly branched "trees", collecting data from a large area of the cortex and sending the outgoing impulses via their axons to a relay in a *central nucleus*. There is evidence of some degree of localization of function in the cerebellum but, especially in mammals, in many respects the corpus cerebelli appears to act as an integrated unit.

## Midbrain and diencephalon

In contrast with the posterior part of the brain stem, the mesencephalon and diencephalon show specialized functional features in vertebrates of all classes. Sensory and motor nuclei connected with cranial nerves extend some distance into the midbrain from the oblongata. Farther forward, however, such structures are absent. The anterior brain stem centers have in general no direct connection with afferent or efferent impulses apart from those of the optic nerve. This region serves two main functions. In higher

vertebrates, more particularly, it is a principal way station between "lower" brain areas and the cerebral hemispheres. In all groups it is important to at least some degree as a locus of centers of nervous correlation and coordination. In mammals the latter functions are overshadowed by those of the cerebral cortex, but in many lower groups the most

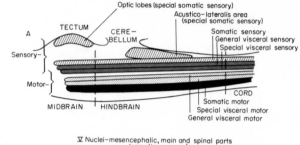

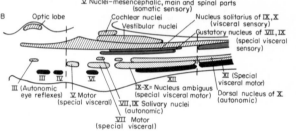

**Figure 4.16 Diagrams of midbrain and hindbrain regions** in lateral view to show the arrangement of sensory and motor nuclei. Somatic sensory and special somatic sensory, hatched; visceral sensory and special visceral sensory, light gray; visceral motor and special visceral motor, stippled; somatic motor, black. *A*, Hypothetic primitive stage, in which brain stem centers were continuous with one another and with the columns of the cord. Even at such a stage, however, it would be assumed that special somatic centers would have developed for eye and ear. The brain region includes a special visceral motor column for the branchial muscles. *B*, Comparable diagram of the mammalian situation. The somatic sensory column is still essentially continuous (almost entirely associated with nerve *V*), but the other columns are broken into discrete nuclei. The visceral sensory column includes both a general visceral nucleus (mainly for afferent fibers from the viscera via the vagus) and a special nucleus for the important sense of taste. Of efferent visceral nuclei, there are small anterior ones for autonomic eye reflexes and the salivary glands, and a large nucleus for parasympathetic fibers to the viscera via the vagus. There are important branchial motor nuclei for *V*, *VI*, and *IX*, *X* (ambiguus). The somatic motor column includes small nuclei for eye muscles anteriorly and a hypoglossal nucleus posteriorly.

highly developed association mechanisms lie in the midbrain and thalamus. In a mammal, destruction of the hemispheres results in functional disability; a frog, on the other hand, can go about its business in nearly normal fashion without cerebral hemispheres as long as the brain stem and the structures surmounting it are intact.

The topography of the midbrain and diencephalon and their annexes may be described before dealing with the functions and connections of the various nuclei of their gray matter (figure 4.17).

The midbrain is that part of the brain tube traversed by the cerebral aqueduct; the diencephalon is a region lying about the third ventricle. Diencephalon and midbrain lie on the lines of communication between anterior and posterior brain areas. In mammals the diencephalon is buried below and between the expanded hemispheres, and fiber tracts of white matter form the greater part of the midbrain walls and floor, these including great motor fiber bundles (the pyramidal tracts descending from the hemispheres) which form the *cerebral peduncles* (crura cerebri).

In the midbrain the gray matter above the aqueduct is greatly thickened to form the mesencephalic *tectum*; thinner areas of gray matter in the side walls are termed the *tegmentum*.

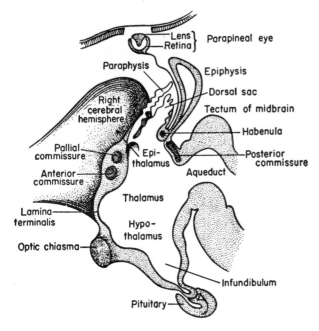

**Figure 4.17 Right half of the diencephalon,** midbrain and neighboring structures of a lizard to show, particularly, the various outgrowths. The arrow indicates the position of the interventricular foramen leading from ventricle III into the right lateral ventricle. (After von Kupfer, Nowikoff.)

Of the areas bounding the third ventricle, the anterior wall, the *lamina terminalis* in which the brain stem ends, is technically considered to form part of the telencephalon; the remainder forms the diencephalon. Accessory structures, described below, are present in the roof and floor of the diencephalon; the main substance of this brain subdivision consists of the lateral walls of the ventricle, which contain in their gray matter a host of nuclei. These wall areas are termed collectively the *thalamus*, because of the fancy that the diencephalon forms a "couch" upon which rest in higher vertebrates the great cerebral hemispheres. Dorsal and ventral parts — roof and floor — of the diencephalon are called the *epithalamus* and *hypothalamus*. Thickened parts of the hypothalamus may cause swellings of the brain surface as *inferior lobes* in fishes (figure 4.5) or *lateral lobes* in amphibians and reptiles. The thalamus proper is further divided, on the basis of the centers contained within it, into a *dorsal thalamus* and a *ventral thalamus*.

The roof of the third ventricle is for the most part a thin, non-nervous structure. In it develop a varied series of outgrowths. Most anteriorly, in that part of the roof which pertains to the telencephalic region, there grows upward in embryos of most groups a thin-walled sac, the *paraphysis*; this structure disappears in the adult in most cases. Almost nothing is known of its function, except that it may produce glycogen to be passed into the cerebrospinal fluid. Adjacent to it, in the anterior part of the diencephalic roof, is the region of the *anterior choroid plexus*. In higher vertebrate classes this is typically invaginated into the cavity of the ventricles; in lower groups, however, it is more generally an extroverted dorsal sac. Still more posteriorly in the diencephalic roof there may develop one or both of a pair of median, stalked eyelike structures, the parietal and pineal organs.

In the floor of the diencephalon the *optic chiasma* is a prominent feature anteriorly. Posteriorly, we find in most fishes the *saccus vasculosus*, a thin vesicle which may reach considerable size. Its function is unknown. Possibly it may register fluid pressure, internal and external; the sac is generally best developed, it may be noted, in deep sea fishes (figure 4.5). Below the diencephalon lies the *pituitary gland* or *hypophysis cerebri*, most important of all the endocrine structures of the body.

The eyes appear to have been responsible in great measure for the development, in lower vertebrates, of important association centers in the anterior region of the brain stem (just as the acoustico-lateralis system is related to cerebellar development in the hindbrain and the olfactory sense to cerebral development). The optic nerves enter ventroanteriorly at the chiasma. In all vertebrates except mammals, however, most of their fibers do not tarry in the diencephalon, but proceed, almost without exception, upward and backward to the roof of the midbrain, where the primary visual center is located. The midbrain roof, the tectum, became, early in vertebrate history, the seat of an important association center; it is the dominant brain region, it would appear, in fishes and amphibians, but became of lessened importance in amniotes with increased development of the cerebral hemispheres (cf. figures 4.23–4.25).

This center developed in connection with visual reception. A greater part of it develops as a pair of optic lobes, varying in size with the importance of the eyes, and becoming particularly large in birds and many teleosts. The histologic pattern of the optic lobes of nonmammalian vertebrates is complex, with successive layers of cell and fiber areas, giving them a structure broadly comparable to the laminated gray matter of the cerebellar or cerebral cortex. It appears probable that a visual pattern is here laid out in a fashion similar to that developed in our own case in the cerebral gray matter.

The presence of this visual center in lower vertebrates was, it would seem, responsible for the attraction to the tectal region of stimuli from other sensory areas. Fiber paths lead hither from the acoustico-lateralis area, from the somatic sensory column, and from the olfactory region via the diencephalon, and connections with the cerebellum are developed. Sensory stimuli from all somatic sources are here associated and synthesized, and motor responses originated. Primitively, these motor stimuli were relayed, it would seem, by way of the reticular formation lying more ventrally in the tegmental region of the midbrain. In amphibians and reptiles, however, direct motor paths are developed, with the formation of a definite tract from the tectum to the motor columns of the brain stem and cord.

In fishes and amphibians the tectum appears to be the true "heart" of the nervous system – the center which wields the greatest influence on body activity. In reptiles and birds the tectum is still an area of great importance, but is rivaled, particularly in birds, by the development of higher centers in the hemispheres.

In mammals the midbrain has undergone a great reduction in relative importance; most of its functions have been transferred to the gray matter of the cerebral hemispheres, and most of the sensory stimuli which are integrated in the midbrain in lower vertebrates are, instead, projected to the hemispheres in mammals. Most auditory and other somatic sensations which reach the midbrain are, in mammals, relayed onward by way of the thalamus to the hemispheres. It is especially notable that few of the optic fibers in mammals follow the original course to the midbrain; most are interrupted in the thalamus, and visual stimuli are shunted forward to the hemispheres. The tectum retains little function except that of serving in a limited way as a center for visual and auditory reflexes. In mammals it takes the form of four small swellings of the midbrain roof, the corpora quadrigemina. Of these the anterior pair deal with visual reflexes and represent the optic lobes of lower vertebrates. In amphibians, with the development of hearing functions in the ear, secondary auditory centers develop on either side of the midbrain adjacent to the optic tectum. These develop into the posterior pair of elements of the corpora quadrigemina, which attain considerable size in some groups of mammals; they function as a relay station for auditory stimuli on their way to the thalamus and thence to the cerebral hemispheres.

The region on either wall of the midbrain termed the tegmentum is essentially a forward continuation of the motor areas of the oblongata. As such it functions as a region in which varied stimuli from diencephalon, tectum, and cerebellum are coordinated and transmitted downward to the motor nuclei of the brain stem and spinal cord. In lower vertebrate groups it consists in general of the rather diffuse series of nerve cells and fibers of the reticular system. In some instances, however, well defined nuclei may be formed; we may note, for example, the presence in this region in mammals of the red nucleus through which are relayed efferent impulses from the cerebellum.

Of diencephalic regions, the epithalamus is of little importance as a brain center. We may note the constant presence here in all vertebrates of the habenular body, a group of small nuclei through which olfactory stimuli pass on their way back from hemispheres to brain stem. We have mentioned elsewhere that it is from this area there extend upward the paraphysis, the anterior choroid plexus, and the pineal and parietal (parapineal) bodies.

The hypothalamus contains olfactory centers, notably the tuber cinereum and, in mammals, the mamillary bodies adjacent to the pituitary region. Its main importance, however, is that of a visceral brain center; other major centers are almost exclusively somatic in their activities. Many of the visceral nervous functions are carried out by reflexes in the cord or medulla, but the hypothalamus is in all vertebrate classes a region which serves as a major integrative center for the body's visceral activities, and there are fiber connections with the autonomic centers of the brain stem and cord. A number of nuclei are present in this region. To them pass stimuli from olfactory and taste organs as well as sensations from various visceral structures of the body. Particularly important are connections with the more strictly olfactory areas of the cerebral hemispheres; the sense of smell plays a large role in visceral nervous activities. These nuclei have efferent connections, posteriorly, with autonomic centers. The hypothalamus controls to a considerable degree the activity of the pituitary; as noted elsewhere, some hypothalamic nuclei actually secrete hormones which pass to the neurohypophysis. The range of hypothalamic regulatory functions is incompletely known. It is, however, of interest that (for example) temperature regulation in reptiles, birds and mammals is accomplished by a sensory "thermostat" in the hypothalamus, and that in mammals heart beat, respiration rate, blood pressure, sleep and gut activities are controlled or influenced by the hypothalamus.

The thalamus proper is in lower vertebrate classes an area of modest importance. Its ventral, motor part may be considered an anterior outpost of the motor column of the brain stem; it is in every class a motor coordinating center, and is further a relay center on the motor path from the basal nuclei of the hemispheres back to the brain stem.

In lower vertebrates the dorsal, sensory region of the thalamus appears to be merely an anterior extension of the sensory correlation areas connected with the tectal region of the midbrain. Its importance increases proportionately with the increased development of association centers in the cerebral hemispheres. Even in vertebrates with a lowly brain organization, a certain amount of sensory data may be passed forward from the brain stem, particularly the reticular system, by relay in the thalamus to the cerebral hemispheres for synthesis there with olfactory stimuli. With a high degree of development of association centers in the hemispheres of amniotes, there is a great development of nuclei in the dorsal thalamus for relay purposes. In the mammalian stage (with the practical abandonment of the tectal association center) the thalamus reaches the height of its development. In mammals all somatic sensations are assembled in the gray matter of the cerebral cortex; and all this sensory material (excepting, of course, olfaction) is relayed to it via the dorsal thalamus. Conspicuous elements in its structure are the *lateral geniculate body*, whence optic stimuli are projected upward to the hemispheres, the *medial geniculate body*, which relays auditory stimuli, and the *ventral nucleus*, which transmits somatic sensory stimuli.

## Cerebral hemispheres

The evolution of the cerebral hemispheres is the most spectacular story in comparative anatomy. These paired outgrowths of the forebrain began their history, it would seem, simply as loci of olfactory reception. Early in tetrapod history they became large and important centers of sensory

correlation; by the time the mammalian stage is reached, the greatly expanded surfaces of the hemispheres have become the dominant association center, seat of the highest mental faculties. The development of centers of such importance in this anterior, originally olfactory, segment of the brain emphasizes the importance of the sense of smell in vertebrates generally. The acoustico-lateralis system and vision, are, as we have seen, senses upon which important correlation mechanisms were erected early in vertebrate history, but in the long run smell has proved dominant. Smell is of little account in higher primates, such as ourselves. But in

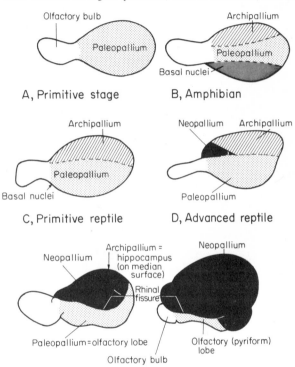

Figure 4.18 **Diagrams to show progressive differentiation of the cerebral hemisphere** (*cf.* figure 4.19). Lateral views of left hemisphere and olfactory bulb. In *A* the hemisphere is merely an olfactory lobe. *B*, Dorsal and ventral areas, archipallium (=hippocampus) and basal nuclei (corpus striatum) are differentiated. *C*, The basal nuclei have moved to the inner part of the hemisphere. *D*, The neopallium appears as a small area (in many reptiles). *E*, The archipallium is forced to the median surface, but the neopallium is still of modest dimensions, and the olfactory areas are still prominent below the rhinal fissure (as in primitive mammals). *F*, The primitive olfactory area is restricted to the ventral aspect, and the neopallial areas are greatly enlarged (as in advanced mammals). The various cellular components of the hemispheres are distinguished by shading.

following down the ancestral line to early mammals and on down to their early vertebrate ancestors, it appears that this sense has been throughout a main channel through which information concerning the outside world has been received. It is thus but natural that its brain centers should form a base upon which higher correlative and associative mechanisms have been built.

Presumably the brain tube of the earliest vertebrates was, like that of Amphioxus, a single, unpaired structure all the way forward to its anterior end; the cavity of the telencephalon was a median, unpaired terminal ventricle, as it is today in the early embryo of every type. In all vertebrates the most anterior part of the wall of the third ventricle is considered as belonging to the telencephalon, but in land vertebrates most of that brain segment consists of distinct paired structures, the *lateral ventricles* and the tissues surrounding them. Most fishes – cyclostomes, Chondrichthyes, actinopterygians – show a transitional condition, for there is, for much of the length of the end brain, a single ventrilar cavity which bifurcates only distally.

In even the lowest of living vertebrates, the cyclostomes, each half of the end brain is subdivided into two parts, the *olfactory bulb* and the *cerebral hemisphere*. The bulb is a terminal swelling in which the fibers of the olfactory nerve end; its size varies with the acuteness of the sense of smell; it is, for example, small to minute in birds. Here is located the primary olfactory nucleus. From its cells, fibers pass back (sometimes with a relay en route) to be distributed to the various regions of the hemisphere. Depending on the configuration of the head and braincase, bulb and hemisphere may be in close contact or may be well separated, with a distinct *olfactory tract* between them.

Primitively, as seen in cyclostomes, the hemisphere is merely an *olfactory lobe* – an area in which olfactory sensations are assembled and learned olfactory reactions relayed to more posterior centers for correlation with other sensory impulses (figures 4.18A, 4.19A). At this level of development few if any fibers ascend from the stem to the hemispheres for correlation there. In general, fiber paths from olfactory areas follow two routes: ventrally to end in visceral centers in the hypothalamus, or dorsally to the habenulae in the epithalamus and thence to the tectum or motor areas of the brain stem.

A higher stage, although still primitive, is that seen in the amphibians (figures 4.18B, 4.19B); sharks are at approximately the same stage of cerebral development. Here most of the tissues of the hemispheres can be divided regionally into three areas, of interest because of their history in more progressive types. All three areas receive olfactory stimuli and exchange fibers with one another; all three discharge to the brain stem. Ventrally lies the region of the *basal nuclei*, essentially equivalent to the corpus striatum of mammals, and destined in higher stages to move into the central parts of the hemisphere. The basal nuclei form a correlation center at an early evolutionary stage and become increasingly more important in this regard in more advanced groups.

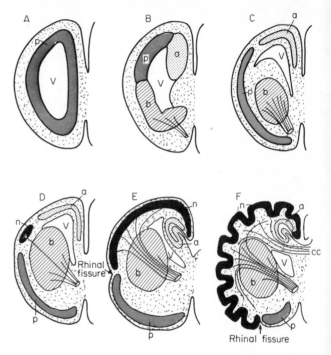

**Figure 4.19 Diagrammatic cross sections of left cerebral hemisphere** to show stages in the evolution of the corpus striatum and cerebral cortex. A, Primitive stage, essentially an olfactory lobe; gray matter internal and little differentiated. B, Stage seen in modern amphibians. Gray matter still deep to surface, but differentiated into paleopallium (=olfactory lobe), archipallium (=hippocampus), and basal nuclei (=corpus striatum), the last becoming an association center, with connections from and to the thalamus (indicated by lines representing cut fiber bundles). C, More progressive stage, in which basal nuclei have moved to interior, and pallial areas are moving toward surface. D, Advanced reptilian stage; beginnings of neopallium. E, Primitive mammalian stage; neopallium expanded, with strong connections with brain stem; archipallium rolled medially as hippocampus; paleopallial area still prominent. F, Progressive mammal; neopallium greatly expanded and convoluted; paleopallium confined to restricted ventral area as pyriform lobe. The corpus callosum developed as a great commissure connecting the two neopallial areas. *a*, Archipallium; *b*, basal nuclei; *cc*, corpus callosum; *n*, neopallium; *p*, paleopallium; *V*, ventricle. The different types of "gray matter" shaded as in figure 4.18.

Sensory impulses are "projected" upward into the basal nuclei from the thalamus for correlation with olfactory sensations; descending fibers carry impulses from the basal nuclei to centers in the thalamus and midbrain tegmental region.

The gray matter of all parts of the hemisphere except the basal nuclei tends progressively to move outward toward the surface, and thus becomes the *cerebral cortex*, or *pallium* ("cloak"). In the amphibian stage the gray matter is still largely internal, but these terms may nevertheless be used in the light of later history. A band of tissue along the lateral surface of the hemisphere is termed the *paleopallium*. This area remains largely olfactory in character, and the paleopallial region is that of the olfactory lobes in higher stages. Dorsally and medially lies the *archipallium*, which is antecedent to the hippocampus of mammals. This area is to a minor extent a correlation center in all land vertebrates, with ascending fibers from the diencephalon as well as fibers from olfactory bulb and lobe, and appears to be related to "emotional" behavior. The tract from this region to the hypothalamus is the main component of the fiber bundle termed the *fornix* in mammals.

An aberrant, "everted" type of forebrain is seen in the dominant fishes of today, the teleosts and their lower ray-finned relatives (figure 4.20A). Here the gray matter of the hemispheres has been crowded downward and inward to form massive structures bulging up into the ventricles from below. These masses include both the basal nuclei or striatum and tissues above it representing the pallial areas,

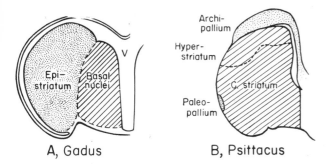

A, Gadus  B, Psittacus

**Figure 4.20 Aberrant types of forebrains.** Section of left hemispheres of *A*, a teleost (codfish); *B*, a bird (parrot). In teleosts the roof of the ventricles is only a membrane; the gray matter has been pushed downward and inward to join the basal nuclei (or striatum) as an epistriatum. In birds the cortex is little developed but there is (analogous to the teleosts) a great development of the basal nuclei (or corpus striatum); a dorsal region termed the hyperstriatum is believed to be a correlation center of high order. *v*, Ventricle. Basal nuclei hatched.

which in some teleosts includes a cortex of complex structure. The roof of the hemispheres is but a thin, non-nervous membrane. This peculiar development is probably to be correlated with the fact that olfaction is relatively unimportant in teleosts.

The reptile hemispheres are advanced over the amphibian type in both complexity of organization and relative size compared with other brain parts. Roof and side walls of the hemispheres show in the main an essentially primitive arrangement of the pallial areas, but some of the gray matter has spread outward toward the surface. The basal nuclei are large and have moved inward to occupy a considerable area in the floor. Strong projection fiber bundles run to the basal nuclei from the thalamus and back from them to the brain stem; the basal nuclei are obviously correlation centers of importance.

In birds (figure 4.20B) the hemispheres are further enlarged. Their evolutionary development, however, has taken place in a fashion radically different from that seen in mammals. Presumably correlated, as in teleosts, with the great reduction of the sense of smell in birds generally, there is very little development of the cerebral cortex; there is a very small area of paleopallium, and a modest development, at the medial posterior areas of the hemispheres, of a cortical area of archipallial nature; despite some current uncertainty there appears to be nothing in the bird brain to correspond to the neopallium, described below, which is the seat of the highest brain activities of a mammal. Instead, there is an enormous expansion of the basal ganglia, or *corpus striatum*. Even leaving out of the picture the hyperstriatum, mentioned subsequently, the corpus striatum proper is a large solid and complex mass of cells and fibers occupying much of the inside of the hemispheres. Birds are notable as having born in them a complex series of stereotyped action patterns which may be called forth to meet a great variety of situations. Presumably these are lodged in the highly developed corpus striatum. However, many birds, notably the crows and ravens, have been shown to possess, in addition to these innate patterns, a considerable ability to learn by experience. In mammals, memory and learning are associated with the cerebral cortex, little developed in birds. Instead (as proved experimentally), these powers reside in the *hyperstriatum*, an internal development of the hemispheres situated above the striatum proper. Extirpation of this region (particularly its uppermost part) destroys the bird's memory and learning ability, while leaving its normal reflex activities undisturbed.

The first faint traces of mammalian cortical development are to be seen in certain reptiles (figures 4.18D, 4.19D). In the hemispheres of these forms we find, between paleopallium and archipallium, a small area of superficial gray matter of a new type, that of the *neopallium*. Even at its inception it is an association center, receiving, like the basal nuclei, fibers which relay to it sensory stimuli from the brain stem and, in turn, sending "commands" directly to the motor columns.

The evolutionary history of the mammal brain is essentially a story of neopallial expansion and elaboration. The cerebral hemispheres have attained a bulk exceeding that of all other parts of the brain, particularly through the growth of the neopallium, and dominate functionally as well. This dominance is apparent in mammals of all types, but is particularly marked in a variety of progressive forms, most especially in man. In even the more primitive mammals (figures 4.18E, 4.19E) the neopallium has expanded over the roof and side walls of the hemispheres. It has crowded the archipallium on to the median surface above; the paleopallium is restricted to the ventrolateral part of the hemispheres, below the *rhinal fissure* – a furrow which marks the boundary between olfactory and nonolfactory areas of the cortex. With still further neopallial growth (figures 4.18F, 4.19F) the archipallium is folded into a restricted area on the median part of the hemispheres, where it remains as the *hippocampus*,* and the olfactory lobes, which include the paleopallium, come to constitute but a small ventral hemisphere region – the *pyriform lobe*. The corpus striatum persists as a relay center for the more automatic reactions.

As it develops in mammalian evolution, the neopallium assumes newer and higher types of neural activity in correlation and association and also takes over many of the functions previously exercised by brain stem centers and many of those of the basal nuclei. The midbrain tectum loses its former importance and is reduced to a reflex and relay center. Auditory and other somatic sensations are relayed on forward to the thalamus, most of the optic fibers are intercepted there, and all are projected from thalamus to hemispheres by great fiber tracts. We have seen thalamic connections of this sort for the basal nuclei had evolved in lower vertebrate groups, and in birds powerful projection tracts evolved in connection with that dominant brain region. In mammals, however, the greater part of these fibers plunge on through the basal nuclei – here termed the *corpus striatum*† – to radiate out to the neopallial surface. With all the sensory data thus made available, the appro-

priate motor "decision" is made by the cortex. As mentioned earlier, one set of stimuli is sent from cortex to cerebellum by way of the pons for appropriate regulatory effects; there are cortical connections to the corpus striatum and even some discharge to the hypothalamus and thence to the autonomic system. The main motor discharge, however, is by way of the *pyramidal tract*, a fiber bundle which extends directly, without intervening relay, from the neopallial cortex to "voluntary" motor regions of brain stem and cord – a feature emphasizing the dominating position of the cerebral cortex in mammals.

With expansion, the cerebral hemispheres tend to cover and envelop the other brain structures. In a primitive mammalian brain (figure 4.9A) the cerebrum leaves much of the midbrain exposed; but in a majority of living mammals (as in figure 4.7B) the midbrain and part of the cerebellum are overlapped. The paired ventricles and the "old-fashioned" areas associated more purely with olfaction – olfactory bulb, pyriform lobe, hippocampus and related tracts and nuclei – have been shifted and distorted, with the growth of the mammalian hemispheres, into patterns which are difficult to compare with those of lower and more simply built brains (figure 4.21).

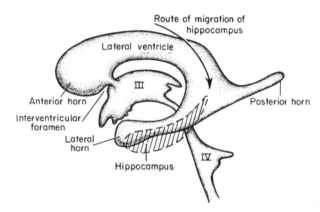

**Figure 4.21 The brain ventricles of an advanced mammalian type** (Homo) in lateral view from the left. The ventricles are represented as solid objects, the brain tissue being removed. With expansion of the cerebral hemisphere, the lateral ventricle has expanded backward to a posterior horn in the occipital lobe, and downward and forward laterally to a lateral horn in the temporal lobe. With this backward and downward expansion, various shifts in position of brain parts occurred. The hippocampus, which developed dorsally on the median surface of the hemisphere (*cf.* figure 4.19F) has been rotated in advanced mammals, backward and downward into a ventral position near the midline.

---

* So called because of its fancied resemblance (in section) to a sea horse, with its coiled tail.

† The name is due to the striated appearance caused by the passage of the fiber bundles through the gray matter of the basal nuclei.

Since the neopallium is essentially a thin sheet of laminated cellular material, underlain by the white fibrous mass of the cerebrum, simple increase in hemisphere bulk fails to keep cortical expansion in step with increase in fiber volume; surface folding is necessary. In small or primitive mammals the neopallial surface is often smooth; in large or more progressive types the surface is generally highly convoluted – thrown into folds which greatly increase the surface area. The folds are termed *gyri*, the furrows between, *sulci*. These are prominent landmarks on the brain surface, and it was once believed that in some cases they are structural boundary markers for specific cortical areas. Further study, however, shows that (apart from the rhinal fissure and, to some degree, a central sulcus in primates) there is no fixed relationship between the convolution pattern and the structural subdivisions of the cortex.

In man, most particularly, the hemisphere is often described as composed of a series of lobes – a *frontal lobe* anteriorly, a *parietal lobe* at the summit, an *occipital lobe* at the posterior end, and a lateral *temporal lobe*. These terms are, however, purely topographic, and have no precise meaning as regards the architecture or functioning of cortical areas.

The gray matter of the neopallium has a complex histologic structure with, in placentals, as many as six superposed cellular layers and masses of intervening fibrils – this in contrast to paleopallial and archipallial regions, in which but two to four cell layers are present. It is estimated that in some of the larger mammalian brains the number of neopallial cells may run into the billions. The white matter internal to the gray includes, besides a fan of cortical connections to and from lower brain regions, a great interweaving meshwork of fibers which connect every part of the cortex with every other. An *anterior commissure* (figure 4.17), connecting olfactory portions of the two hemispheres, is present in all vertebrates, and other commissural fibers are present in the fornix; to connect the neopallial structures, a massive new commissure, the *corpus callosum* figure 4.9*b*), develops in placental mammals, functioning to allow both hemispheres to share memory and learning.

The complex "wiring" system connecting all parts of the cortex with one another would suggest that the gray matter is essentially a unit, equipotent in all its parts for any cerebral activity. This is to some extent true; experiments show that in laboratory animals a good part of the neopallium may be destroyed without permanently interfering with normal activity, and the results of injury and disease conditions show that the same holds for certain areas of the human brain. On the other hand, it is clear that certain cortical areas are normally associated with specific functions (figure 4.22). We have previously discussed the "old-fashioned" cortical regions devoted mainly to olfactory sensations – the paleopallium and archipallium, represented in mammals in the pyriform lobe and hippocampus, respectively. Regional differentiation is present in the neopallium as well. The front part of the hemispheres includes a motor area. The posterior part is associated with sensory perception. Special regions are associated with eye and ear, in occipital and temporal lobes, while the areas for sensations received from the skin and proprioceptive organs are situated farther forward, close to the motor area. In primates a *central sulcus* which crosses the top of the hemisphere from medial to lateral surfaces divides (although not exactly) motor and sensory areas. Along its front margin are specific motor areas for each subdivision of the body and limbs, arranged in linear order; along the back margin is an exactly parallel arrangement of loci for sensory reception from the various members. In many mammals nearly the entire surface of the neopallium is occupied by areas associated more or less closely with specific sensory or motor functions. Although

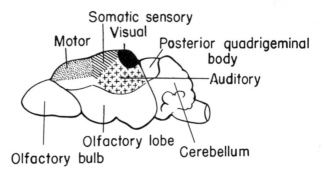

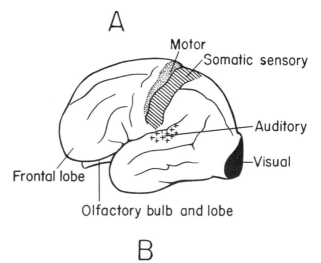

Figure 4.22 Lateral view of A, **the brain of a shrew;** B the cerebrum of man; to show cortical areas.

65

the central sulcus may not be present, placental mammals generally have a similar linear arrangement of sensory and motor areas opposite one another. Marsupials have a similar "layout" of body regions, but sensory and motor areas are combined rather than separate. In man, particularly, however, we find that these specific functional areas occupy only a relatively small part of the neopallium. Between them have developed large areas of gray matter, most conspicuously one occupying much of the frontal lobe, which are not associated with specific sensory or motor functions. They are, in consequence, sometimes termed "blank areas". This is the reverse of the case; as shown by injury to these areas, they are the seat of our highest mental properties, including learning ability, initiative, foresight and judgment.

Size of cerebral hemispheres might be thought of as giving a clue to the mental abilities of a mammal. This is true in a sense, but subject to strong qualification. If the amount of cortical surface present is related in any way to intelligence, it is obvious that of two brains of the same size, one with convoluted hemispheres is better than one with a smooth surface. The bulk of the animal concerned affects brain size, presumably because of the need of greater terminal areas for the increased sensory and motor connections, but the increase in brain size as a whole is not absolutely proportionate to body bulk, and large animals tend to have relatively small brains without, it seems, any loss of mental powers. That absolute brain size is not a criterion of intellect is indicated by the fact that the brain of a whale may have five times the volume of that of a man. Nor is the proportion of brain size to body size a perfect criterion, for small South American monkeys may have a brain one fifteenth or one twentieth of body weight, while the brain weight of an average man is but one fortieth that of the body. A final and most important factor that must be taken into account is the relative complexity of the cortical sheet.

## Brain patterns: summary

In earlier sections of this chapter we described the principal structural and functional elements of the brain and certain of their interconnections. The more important features may be summarized here.

In the posterior part of the brain stem — the medulla oblongata — there is present a series of sensory and motor columns closely comparable to those of the spinal cord and connected with them by the reticular system. As in the cord, direct reflexes may take place between sensory and motor columns. The history of brain evolution, however, has been mainly one of the development, above and in front of the medulla, of higher centers of coordination and association,

interposed between sensory and motor areas. In such centers sensory data are assembled and synthesized and resultant motor stimuli sent out to the motor columns of brain stem and cord. These centers have been in the main built up, as dorsal outgrowths of laminated gray matter, about areas primarily concerned with the special senses of the head region — acoustico-lateralis, visual and olfactory.

1. The primary area of reception for equilibrium and lateral line stimuli lies in the sensory columns of the medulla oblongata; above this developed the cerebellum, important in all vertebrates. This organ initiates no bodily movement, apart from adjustments in posture, but insures that motor directives initiated in other centers be carried out in proper fashion. It may receive fibers from all the somatic senses, but is principally informed by the adjacent acoustico-lateralis centers and by fibers from the proprioceptive system of the muscles and tendons. Its outgoing, regulatory stimuli are for the most part sent to the midbrain and thence distributed to the motor areas. In mammals, where the cortex assumes direct control over most motor responses, powerful circuits are established connecting cerebellum and cortex in both directions (figure 4.14).

2. In lower vertebrates the main centers dominating nervous activity are situated in the anterior regions of the brain stem. (a) A great center of coordination in which motor activity is initiated is established in the tectum of the midbrain, in which the primary visual center is situated (figure 4.23). To this region are relayed also stimuli from the nose, ear, and other somatic senses; from it are sent out stimuli to the motor columns. As we ascend the vertebrate scale the tectal area becomes rivalled and then exceeded by the association centers of the cerebral hemispheres; in birds, despite the great development of the corpus striatum, the tectum is still prominent, but in mammals most of the sensory data formerly assembled in the tectum are, instead, relayed to the neopallium via the thalamus, and the tectum is reduced to a reflex center. (b) The tectal centers are somatic in nature; corresponding centers for visceral sensations and visceral motor responses were early established farther anteriorly and ventrally, in the hypothalamus. This situation remains little changed throughout the vertebrate series.

3. As the vertebrate scale is ascended, the cerebral hemispheres, originally only a center for olfactory sensation, have become more and more important as association centers. (a) First of cerebral areas to gain importance is that of the basal nuclei, the corpus striatum. Fiber tracts from the thalamus relay somatic sensations to this body, and return fibers carry motor stimuli back to the midbrain and thence to the motor columns. In reptiles the corpus striatum is a prominent structure which rivals the older tectal center in

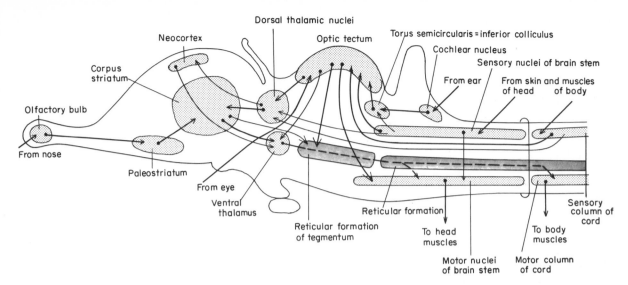

**Figure 4.23 Diagram of the main centers and "wiring" arrangement of a reptile,** in which the tectal region of the midbrain plays a dominant role; the corpus striatum (basal ganglia) is of some importance as a correlation center, but the neocortex (neopallium) is unimportant. The reticular formation of the brain stem (stippled) is important in carrying motor impulses to nuclei of the stem and cord. In this oversimplified diagram only a limited number of paths between somatic receptor and effectors are included; visceral centers and paths are omitted, as are cerebellar connections (shown in figure 4.14).

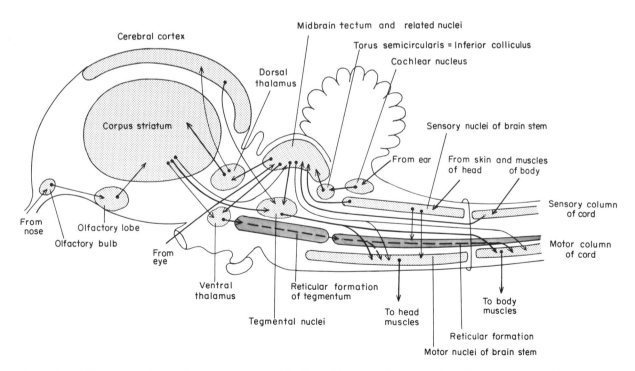

**Figure 4.24 Diagram of the main centers and "wiring" arrangement of a bird.** Here the corpus striatum plays a dominant role; the midbrain tectal centre is well-developed, with sensory tracts reaching it from ears, eyes and body, motor tracts to the body via the ventral thalamus. There is no direct connection between cerebellum and forebrain.

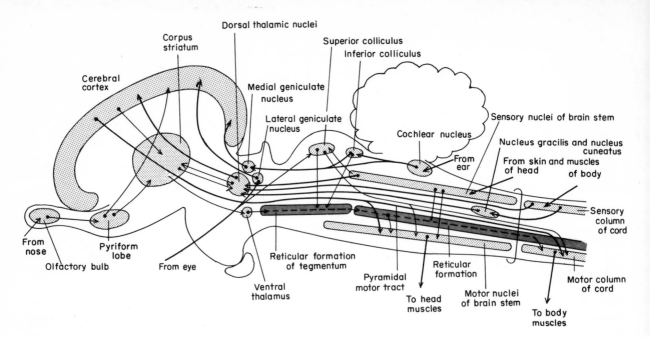

**Figure 4.25 A "wiring diagram" of a mammalian brain** comparable to figures 4.23 and 4.24. The midbrain tectum is reduced to a minor reflex center, and the corpus striatum is relatively unimportant; most sensory impulses are projected "upward" to the cerebral cortex, whence a direct motor path (pyramidal tract) extends to the motor centers of brain stem and cord.

importance, and in birds the corpus striatum, with the new addition of the hyperstriatum, becomes a large complex, and dominant center (figure 4.24). (*b*) In mammals, descended along a different evolutionary line from that leading to birds, a different development has occurred. The new master organ is the neopallium, a greatly expanded gray cortical area for correlation, association and learning. This assumes the greater part of the higher functions once concentrated in the tectum or corpus striatum, gains a complete array of somatic sensory data through projection fibers from the thalamus, and develops direct motor paths to the motor columns of the brain stem and spinal cord (figure 4.25).

# 5 The contraction of muscle
## by H E Huxley

A basic characteristic of all animals is their ability to move in a purposeful fashion. Animals move by contracting their muscles (or some primitive version of them), so muscle contraction is one of the key processes of animal life. Muscle contraction has been intensively studied by a host of investigators, and their labors have yielded much valuable information. We still, however, cannot answer the fundamental question: How does the molecular machinery of muscle convert the chemical energy stored by metabolism into mechanical work? Recent studies, notably those utilizing the great magnifications of the electron microscope, have nonetheless enabled us to begin to relate the behavior of muscle to events at the molecular level. At the very least we are now in a position to ask the right sort of question about the detailed molecular processes which remain unknown.

Muscles are usually classified as "striated" or "smooth," depending on how they look under the ordinary light microscope. The classification has a good deal of functional significance. The muscles which vertebrates such as mice or men use to move their bodies or limbs – muscles which act quickly and under voluntary control – are crossed by microscopic striations. The muscles of the gut or uterus or capillaries – muscles which act slowly and involuntarily – have no striations; they are "smooth." In this article I shall discuss only striated muscles, because our knowledge of them is in a much more advanced state. I shall be surprised, however, if nothing I say is relevant to smooth muscles.

Striated muscles are made up of muscle fibers, each of which has a diameter of between 10 and 100 microns (a micron is a thousandth of a millimeter). The fibers may run the whole length of the muscle and join with the tendons at its ends. About 20 per cent of the weight of a muscle fiber is represented by protein; the rest is water, plus a small amount of salts and of substances utilized in metabolism. Around each fiber is an electrically polarized membrane, the inside of which is about a 10th of a volt negative with respect to the outside.

first published in Scientific American, November 1958.
Reprinted with permission. Copyright © 1958 by Scientific American, Inc. All rights reserved.

If the membrane is temporarily depolarized, the muscle fiber contracts; it is by this means that the activity of muscles is controlled by the nervous system. An impulse traveling down a motor nerve is transmitted to the muscle membrane at the motor "end-plate"; then a wave of depolarization (the "action potential") sweeps down the muscle fiber and in some unknown way causes a single twitch. Even when a frog muscle is cooled to the freezing point of water, the depolarization of the muscle membrane throws the whole fiber into action within 40 thousandths of a second. When nerve impulses arrive on the motor nerve in rapid succession, the twitches run together and the muscle maintains its contraction as long as the stimulation continues (or the muscle becomes exhausted). When the nerve stimulation stops, the muscle automatically relaxes.

## The energy budget of muscle

Striated muscles can shorten at speeds up to 10 times their length in a second, though of course the amount of shortening is restricted by the way in which the animal is put together. Such muscles can exert a tension of about three kilograms for each square centimeter of their cross section – some 42 pounds per square inch. They exert maximum tension when held at constant length, so that the speed of shortening is zero. Even though a muscle in this state does no external work, it needs energy to maintain its contraction; and since the energy can do no work, it must be dissipated as heat. This so-called "maintenance heat" slightly warms the muscle.

When the muscle shortens, it exerts less tension; the tension decreases as the speed of shortening increases. One might suspect that the decrease of tension is due to the internal viscosity or friction in the muscle, but it is not. If it were, a muscle shortening rapidly would liberate more heat than one shortening slowly over the same distance, and this effect is not observed.

The energy budget of muscle has been investigated in great detail, particularly by A. V. Hill of England and his colleagues. Studies of this kind have shown that a shortening muscle does liberate extra heat, but in proportion to the

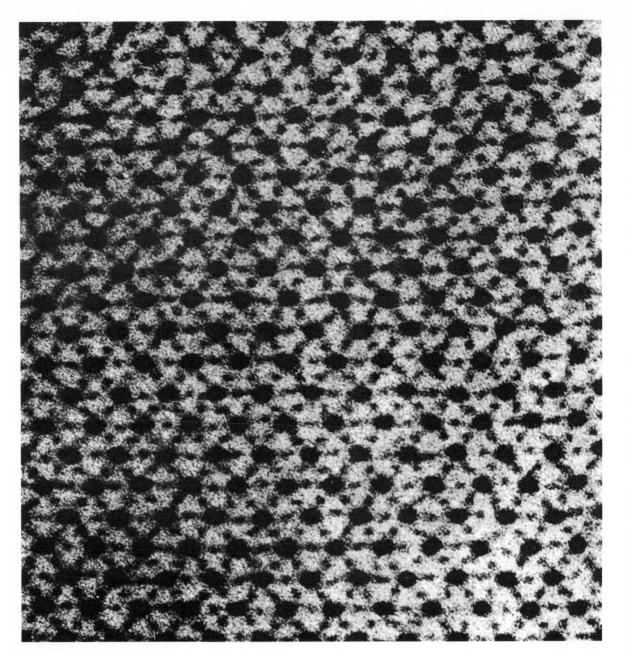

**Figure 5.1 Filaments** in an insect flight-muscle are seen from the end in the electron micrograph. Thick filaments (*larger spots*) and thin filaments (*smaller spots*) lie beside one another in a remarkably regular hexagonal array. Some of the thick filaments appear to be hollow. This electron micrograph, which enlarges the filaments some 400 000 diameters, was made by Jean Hanson of the Medical Research Council Unit at King's College and the author.

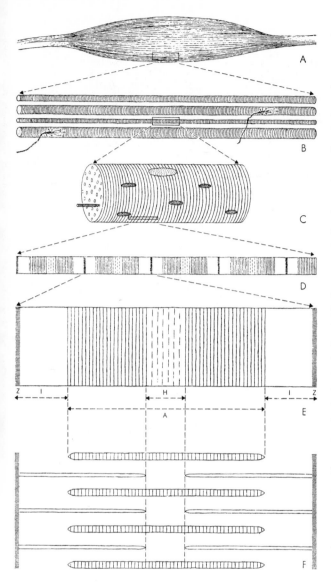

**Figure 5.2 Striated muscle is dissected** in these schematic drawings. A muscle (*A*) is made up of muscle fibers (*B*) which appear striated in the light microscope. The small branching structures at the surface of the fibers are the "end-plates" of motor nerves, which signal the fibers to contract. A single muscle fiber (*C*) is made up of myofibrils, beside which lie cell nuclei and mitochondria. In a single myofibril (*D*) the striations are resolved into a repeating pattern of light and dark bands. A single unit of this pattern (*E*) consists of a "Z-line", then an "I-band" then an "A-band" which is interrupted by an "H-zone", then the next I-band and finally the next Z-line. Electron micrographs (see figures 5.3, 5.4) have shown that the repeating band pattern is due to the overlapping of thick and thin filaments (*F*).

*distance* of shortening rather than to the speed. Curiously this "shortening heat" is independent of the load on the muscle: a muscle produces no more – and no less – shortening heat when it lifts a large load than when it lifts a small one through the same distance.

But a muscle lifting a large load obviously does more work than a muscle lifting a small load, so if the shortening heat remains constant, the total energy (heat plus work) expended by the contracting muscle must increase with the load. The chemical reactions which provide the energy for contraction must therefore be controlled not only by the change in the length of the muscle, but also by the tension placed on the muscle during the change. This is a remarkable property, of great importance to the efficiency of muscle, and new information about the structure of muscle has begun to explain it.

From the chemical point of view, the contractile structure of muscle consists almost entirely of protein. Perhaps 90 per cent of this substance is represented by the three proteins myosin, actin and tropomyosin. Myosin is especially abundant: about half the dry weight of the contractile part of the muscle consists of myosin. This is particularly significant because myosin is also the enzyme which can catalyze the removal of a phosphate group from adenosine triphosphate (ATP). And this energy-liberating reaction is known to be closely associated with the event of contraction, if not actually part of it.

Myosin and actin can be separately extracted from muscle and purified. When these proteins are in solution together, they combine to form a complex known as actomyosin. Some years ago Albert Szent-Györgyi, the noted Hungarian biochemist who now lives in the US, made the striking discovery that if actomyosin is precipitated and artificial fibers are prepared from it, the fibers will contract when they are immersed in a solution of ATP! It seems that in the interaction of myosin, actin and ATP we have all the essentials of a contractile system. This view is borne out by experiments on muscles which have been placed in a solution of 50 per cent glycerol and 50 per cent water, and soaked for a time in a deep-freeze. After this procedure, and some further washing, practically everything can be removed from the muscle except myosin, actin and tropomyosin; and this residual structure will still contract when it is supplied with ATP.

## The structure of the fiber

The most straightforward way to try to find out how the muscle machine works is to study its structure in as much detail as possible, using all the techniques now at our disposal. This has proved to be a fruitful approach, and I shall briefly

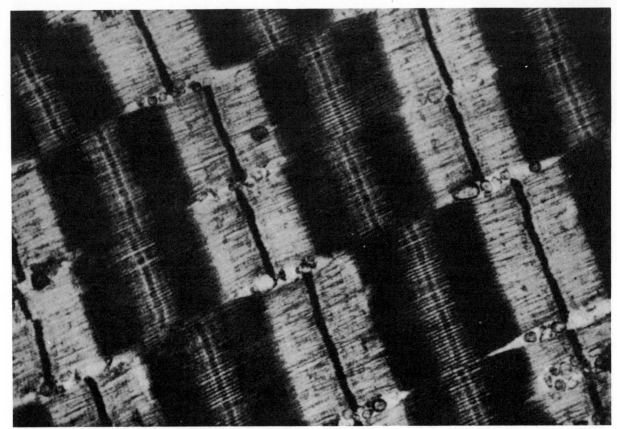

**Figure 5.3 Striated muscle** from a rabbit is enlarged 24 000 diameters in this electron micrograph. Each of the diagonal ribbons is a thin section of a muscle fibril. Clearly visible are the dense A-bands, bisected by H-zones; and the lighter I-bands, bisected by Z-lines.

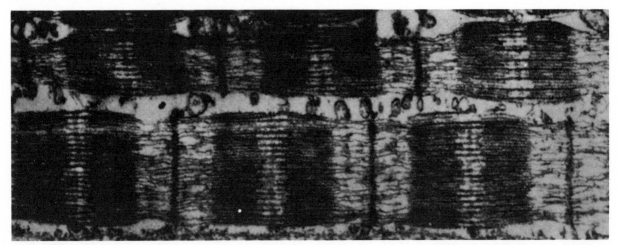

**Figure 5.4 Extremely thin section** of a striated muscle is shown at much greater magnification. The section is so thin that in some places it contains only one layer of filaments. The way in which overlapping thick and thin filaments give rise to the band pattern can be clearly seen. Although the magnification of this electron micrograph is much larger than that of the micrograph at top of page, distance between the narrow Z-lines is less. This is because the section was longitudinally compressed by the slicing process.

**Figure 5.5 Transverse sections** through a three-dimensional array of filaments in vertebrate striated muscle (**a**) show how the thick and thin filaments are arranged in a hexagonal pattern (**b**). At **c** are electron micrographs of the corresponding sections.

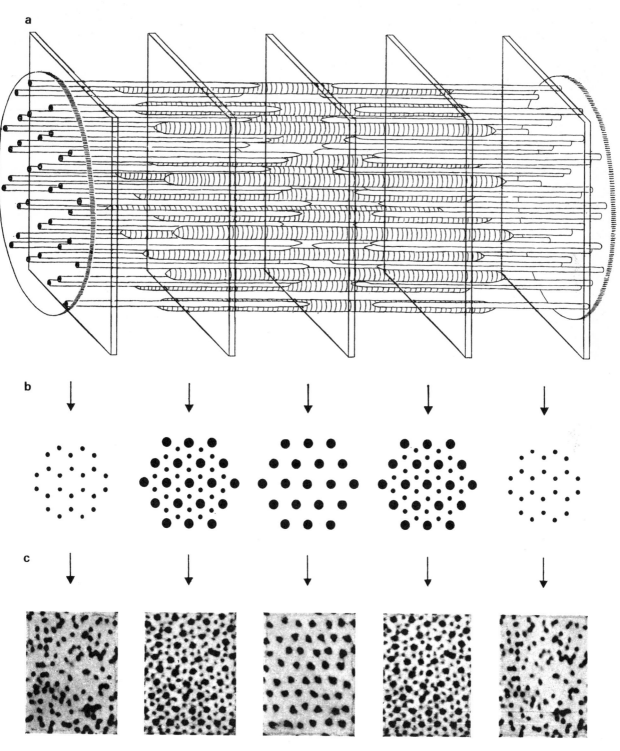

**Figure 5.6 Longitudinal section** (b) through the same array (a) shows how two thin filaments lie between two thick ones. This pattern is a consequence of the fact that one thin filament is centered among three thick ones. At (c) is a micrograph of the corresponding section.

a

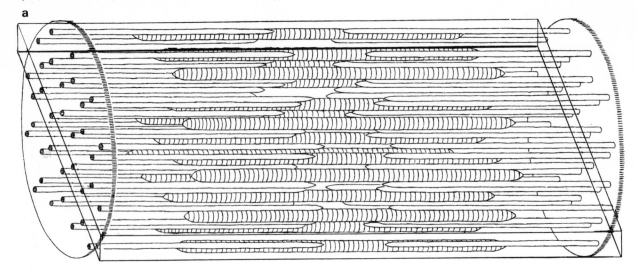

b

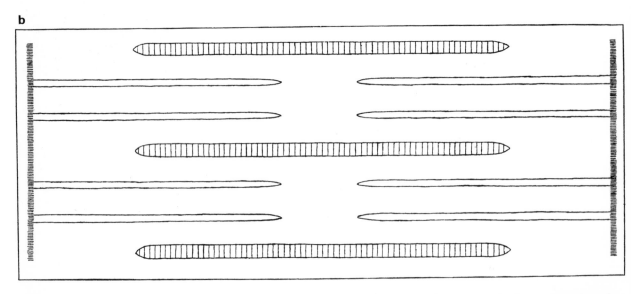

c

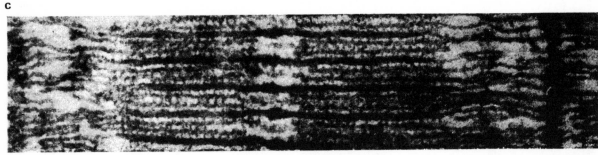

**Figure 5.7 Several fibrils** in a vertebrate striated muscle are seen from the end in an electron micrograph which enlarges them 90 000 diameters. Within each fibril is the hexagonal array of its filaments. This pattern, in which one thin filament lies symmetrically among three thick ones, differs from the pattern in the insect muscle figure 5.1, in which one thin filament lies between two thick ones.

describe its results. Much of the work I shall discuss I have done in collaboration with Jean Hanson of the Medical Research Council Unit at King's College in London.

The contractile structure of a muscle fiber is made up of long, thin elements which we call myofibrils. A myofibril is about a micron in diameter, and is cross-striated like the fiber of which it is a part. Indeed, the striations of the fiber are due to the striations of the myofibril, which are in register in adjacent myofibrils. The striations arise from a repeating variation in the density, *i.e.*, the concentration of protein along the myofibrils.

The pattern of the striations can be seen clearly in isolated myofibrils, which are obtained by whipping muscle in a Waring blendor. Under a powerful light microscope there is a regular alternation of dense bands (called A-bands) and lighter bands (called I-bands). The central region of the A-band is often less dense than the rest of the band, and is known as the H-zone (figure 5.2). When a striated muscle from a vertebrate is near its full relaxed length, the length of one of its A-bands is commonly about 1.5 microns, and the length of one of its I-bands about 0.8 micron. The I-band is bisected by a dense narrow line, the Z-membrane or Z-line. From one Z-line to the next the repeating unit of the myofibril structure is thus: Z-line, I-band, A-band (interrupted by the H-zone), I-band and Z-line.

When myofibrils are examined in the electron microscope, a whole new world of structure comes into view. It can be seen that the myofibril is made up of still smaller filaments, each of which is 50 or 100 angstrom units in diameter (an angstrom unit is a 10 000th of a micron). These filaments were observed in the earliest electron micrographs of muscle, made by Cecil E. Hall, Marie A. Jakus and Francis O. Schmitt of the Massachusetts Institute of Technology, and by M. F. Draper and Alan J. Hodge of Australia. And now thanks to recent advances in the technique of preparing specimens for the electron microscope, it is possible to examine the arrangement of the filaments in considerable detail (figure 5.7).

For this purpose a piece of muscle is first "fixed", that is, treated with a chemical which preserves its detailed structure during subsequent manipulations. Then the muscle is "stained" with a compound of a heavy metal, which increases its ability to deflect electrons and thus enhances its contrast in the electron microscope. Next it is placed in a solution of plastic which penetrates its entire structure. After the plastic is made to solidify, the block of embedded tissue can be sliced into sections 100 or 200 angstrom units thick by means of a microtome which employs a piece of broken glass as a knife. When we look at these very thin sections in the electron microscope, we can see immediately that muscle is constructed in an extraordinarily regular and specific manner.

A myofibril is made up of two kinds of filament, one of which is twice as thick as the other. In the psoas muscle from the back of a rabbit the thicker filaments are about 100 angstroms in diameter and 1.5 microns long; the thinner filaments are about 50 angstroms in diameter and two microns long. Each filament is arrayed in register with other filaments of the same kind, and the two arrays overlap for part of their length. It is this overlapping which gives rise to the cross-bands of the myofibril: the dense A-band consists of overlapping thick and thin filaments; the lighter I-band, of thin filaments alone; the H-zone, of thick filaments alone. Halfway along their length the thin filaments pass through a narrow zone of dense material; this comprises the Z-line. Where the two kinds of filament overlap, they lie together in a remarkably regular hexagonal array. In many vertebrate muscles the filaments are arranged so that each thin filament lies symmetrically among three thick ones; in some insect flight-muscles each thin filament lies midway between two thick ones (figures 5.1 and 5.7).

The two kinds of filament are linked together by an intricate system of crossbridges which, as we shall see, probably play an important role in muscle contraction (figure 5.11). The bridges seem to project outward from a thick filament at a fairly regular interval of 60 or 70 angstroms, and each bridge is 60 degrees around the axis of the filament with respect to the adjacent bridge. Thus the bridges form a

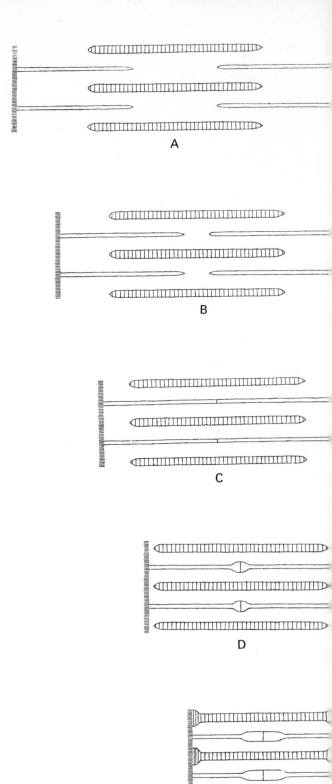

**Figure 5.8 Change in length** of the muscle changes the arrangement of the filaments. In A the muscle is stretched; in B it is at its resting length; in C, D and E it is contracted. In C the thin filaments meet; in D and E they crumple up. In E the thick filaments also meet adjacent thick filaments (*not shown*) and crumple. The crumpling gives rise to new band patterns.

76

helical pattern which repeats every six bridges, or about every 400 angstroms along the filament. This pattern joins the thick filament to each one of its six adjacent filaments once every 400 angstroms.

The arrangement of the filaments and their cross-bridges, as seen in the electron microscope, is so extraordinarily well ordered that one may wonder whether the fixing and staining procedures have somehow improved on nature. Fortunately this regularity is also apparent when we examine muscle by another method: X-ray diffraction. Muscle which has not been stained and fixed deflects X-rays in a regular pattern, indicating that the internal structure of muscle is

**Figure 5.9 Different chemical composition** of the thick and thin filaments is demonstrated. At **a** is a myofibril photographed in the phase-contrast light microscope. The wide dark regions are A-bands; between them are I-bands bisected by Z-lines. **b** is a simplified schematic drawing of how the thick and thin filaments give rise to this pattern. **c** is a photomicrograph of a myofibril from which the protein myosin has been chemically removed. The A-bands have disappeared, leaving only the I-bands and Z-lines. At **d** is a drawing which shows how this pattern is explained on the assumption that the thick filaments have been removed. Thus it appears that the thick filaments are composed of myosin, and the thin filaments of other material.

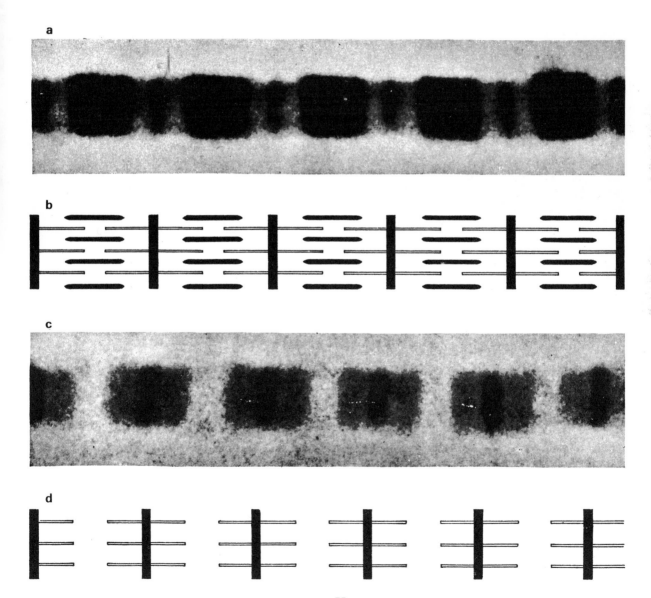

also regular. The details of the diffraction pattern are in accord with the structural features observed in the electron microscope. Indeed, many of these features were originally predicted on the basis of X-ray diffraction patterns alone.

## The sliding-filament model

As soon as the meaning of the band pattern of striated muscle became apparent, it was obvious that changes in the pattern during contraction should give us new insight into the molecular nature of the process. Such changes can be unambiguously observed in modern light microscopes, notably the phase-contrast microscope and the interference microscope. They can be studied in living muscle fibers (as they were by A. F. Huxley and R. Niedergerke at the University of Cambridge) or in isolated myofibrils contracting in a solution of ATP (as they were by Jean Hanson and myself at M.I.T.). We all came to the same conclusions.

It has been found that over a wide range of muscle lengths, during both contraction and stretching, the length of the A-bands remains constant. The length of the I-bands, on the other hand, changes in accord with the length of the muscle. Now the length of the A-band is equal to the length of the thick filaments, so we can assume that the length of these filaments is also constant. But the length of the H-zone – the lighter region in the middle of the A-band – increases and decreases with the length of the I-band, so that the distance from the end of one H-zone through the Z-line to the beginning of the next H-zone remains approximately the same. This distance is equal to the length of the thin filaments, so they too do not alter their length by any large amount.

The only conclusion one can draw from these observations is that, when the muscle changes length, the two sets of filaments slide past each other. Of course when the muscle shortens enough, the ends of filaments will meet; this happens first with the thin filaments, and then with the thick (see figure 5.8). Under such conditions, in fact, new bands are observed which suggest that the ends of the filaments crumple or overlap. But these effects seem to occur as a *result* of the shortening process, and not as causes of contraction.

It has often been suggested that the contraction of muscle results from the extensive folding or coiling of the filaments. The new observations compel us to discard this idea. Instead we are obliged to look for processes which could cause the filaments to slide past one another. Although this search is only beginning, it is already apparent that the sliding concept places us in a much more favorable position with respect to what we might call the intermediate levels of explanation: the description of the behavior of muscle in terms of molecular changes whose detailed nature we do not know, but whose consequences we can now compute.

There is more to be said about such matters, but first let us return to the chemical structure of muscle (figure 5.9). If a muscle is treated with an appropriate salt solution, and then examined under the light microscope, it is observed that the A-bands are no longer present. It is also known that such a salt solution will remove myosin from muscle. This demonstrates that the thick filaments of the A-band are composed of myosin, a conclusion which has been quantitatively confirmed by comparing measurements made by chemical methods with those made by the interference microscope. Moreover, when myofibrils which have been treated with salt solution are examined in the electron microscope, they lack the thick filaments. The "ghost" myofibril that remains consists of segments of material which correspond to the arrays of thin filaments in the I-

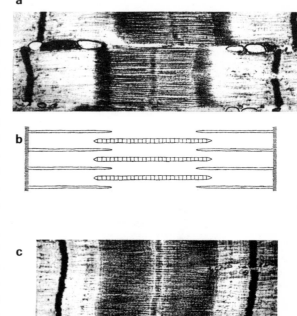

**Figure 5.10 Stretching** of muscle changes its band pattern. At **a** is an electron micrograph showing two myofibrils in a stretched muscle. **b** is a drawing of the position of their filaments. The thick and thin filaments overlap only at their ends. **c** is a micrograph of a myofibril at its resting length. At **d** is a drawing showing the position of the filaments.

bands. If the myofibril is treated so as to extract its actin, a large part of the material in these segments is removed. This indicates that the thin filaments of the I-band are composed of actin and (probably) tropomyosin.

Thus the two main structural proteins of muscle are separated in the two kinds of filaments. As noted earlier, actin and myosin can be made to contract in a solution of ATP, but only when they are combined. We therefore conclude that the physical expression of the combination of actin and myosin is to be found in the bridges between the two kinds of filaments. It should also be said that the thick and thin filaments are too far apart for any plausible "action at a distance", so it would seem likely that the sliding movement is mediated by the bridges (figure 5.11).

## The cross-bridges

The bridges seem to form a permanent part of the myosin filaments; presumably they are those parts of myosin molecules which are directly involved in the combination with actin. In fact, when we calculate the number of myosin molecules in a given volume of muscle, we find that it is surprisingly close to the number of bridges in the same volume. This suggests that each bridge is part of a single myosin molecule.

How could the bridges cause contraction? One can imagine that they are able to oscillate back and forth, and to hook up with specific sites on the actin filament. Then they could pull the filament a short distance (say 100 angstroms) and return to their original configuration, ready for another pull (figure 5.12). One would expect that each time a bridge went through such a cycle, a phosphate group would be split from a single molecule of ATP; this reaction would provide the energy for the cycle.

To account for the rate of shortening and of energy liberation in the psoas muscle of a rabbit, each bridge would have to go through 50 to 100 cycles of operation a second. This figure is compatible with the rate at which myosin catalyzes the removal of phosphate groups from ATP. When the muscle has relaxed, we suppose that the removal of phosphate groups from ATP has stopped, and that the myosin bridges can no longer combine with the actin filaments; the muscle can then return to its uncontracted length. Indeed, there is evidence from various experiments that ATP from which phosphate has *not* been split can break the combination of actin and myosin. The reverse effect – the formation of permanent links between the actin and myosin filaments in the total absence of ATP – would explain the rigidity of muscles in *rigor mortis*: when the muscles' supply of ATP has been used up, they "seize" like a piston which has been deprived of lubrication.

The system I have described is sharply distinguished from most other suggested muscle mechanisms by one

**Figure 5.11 Cross-bridges** between thick and thin filaments may be seen in this electron micrograph of the central region of an A-band. The micrograph enlarges the filaments 600 000 diameters. Three thick filaments are seen; between each pair are two thin filaments.

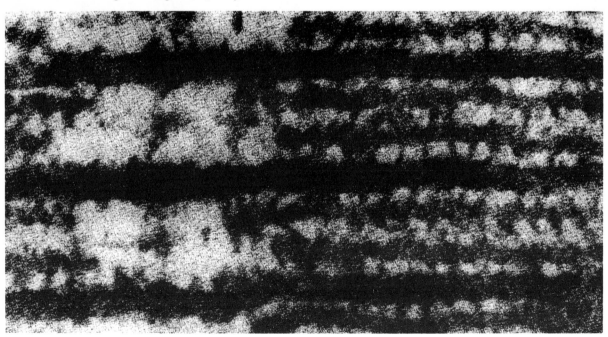

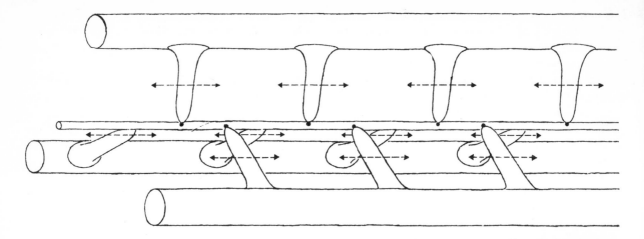

**Figure 5.12 Arrangement of cross-bridges** suggests that they enable the thick filaments to pull the thin filaments by a kind of ratchet action. In this schematic drawing one thin filament lies among three thick ones. Each bridge is a part of a thick filament, but it is able to hook onto a thin filament at an active site (*dot*). Presumably the bridges are able to bend back and forth (*arrows*). A single bridge might thus hook onto an active site, pull the thin filament a short distance, then release it and hook onto the next active site.

significant feature: a ratchet device in the linkage between the detailed molecular changes and the contraction of the muscle. This makes it possible for a movement at the molecular level to reverse direction without reversing the contraction. Thus during each contraction the molecular events responsible for the contraction can occur repeatedly at each active site in the muscle. As a result the muscle can do much more work during a single contraction than it could if only one event could occur at each active site.

Earlier in this article I mentioned that the tension exerted by a muscle falls off as its speed of shortening increases. This phenomenon can now be explained quite simply if we assume that the process by which a cross-bridge is attached to an active site on the actin filament occurs at a definite rate. There is only a certain period of time available for a bridge to become attached to an actin site moving past it, and the time decreases as the speed of shortening increases. Thus during shortening not all the bridges are attached at a given moment; the number of ineffective bridges increases with increasing speed of shortening, and the tension consequently decreases. A. F. Huxley has worked out a detailed scheme of this general nature, and has shown that it can account for many features of contraction.

It was also indicated earlier that the total energy (heat

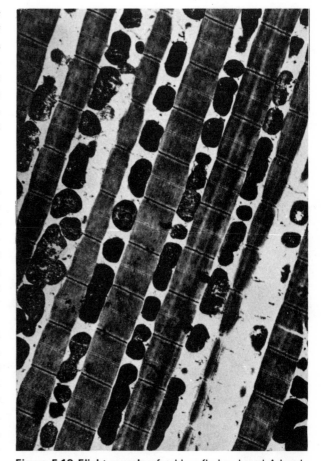

**Figure 5.13 Flight muscle** of a blow fly has broad A-bands and narrow I-bands. This is consistent with the sliding-filament hypothesis because the flight muscle of the blow fly contracts only a few per cent of its length (though it must do so several hundred times a second). The dense bodies between the myofibrils are mitochondria, particles in which foodstuff is oxidized to provide the energy for contraction.

plus work) developed by a muscle contracting over a given distance increases with the tension or load placed on the muscle. This can be explained by our mechanism if the chemical reaction which delivers the energy – say the removal of phosphate groups from ATP – proceeds slowly at bridges which are not attached to an actin filament, and rapidly at bridges which are attached. Since the number of bridges attached at any moment is determined by the load on the muscle, the amount of energy released in a given distance of shortening is automatically varied according to the amount of external work done. This assumption of a difference in the reaction rate at unattached bridges and at attached bridges is plausible: when myosin is placed in a solution approximating the environment of muscle, it splits ATP rather slowly; when the myosin is allowed to combine with actin, the splitting is greatly accelerated.

There are other reasons, with which I shall not burden the general reader, for believing that the sliding-filament model of muscle accords rather well with our chemical and physiological knowledge of striated muscle. The model provides a frame of reference in which we can relate to one another many different kinds of information: about muscle itself, about artificial contractile systems and about muscle proteins. The situation is promising and stimulating, and we seem to be on the right track, but we are still far from being able to describe the contraction of muscle in detailed molecular terms – perhaps farther than we think!

There remains the most fundamental question of all: Exactly how does a chemical reaction provide the motive force for the molecular movements of contraction? We have made little progress toward answering the question; indeed, the recent studies have made the problem more difficult by seeming to require that a movement of 100 angstroms in part of the muscle structure be the consequence of a single chemical event. But it may be that the sliding process is effected by a more subtle mechanism than the one described here, perhaps a caterpillar-like action, in which one kind of filament crawls past the other by small repetitive changes of length, will be closer to the truth.

Two things are certain. The problem of muscular contraction will not be solved independently of other modern biological problems those of the structure of proteins, of the action of enzymes, and of energy transfer in biological systems. And muscle itself provides as promising a system for attacking these problems as any we know.

## Bibliography

Chemistry of Muscular Contraction. 2nd edition, revised and enlarged, A. Szent-Györgyi, Academic Press, Inc., 1951

The Double Array of Filaments in Cross-striated Muscle, H. E. Huxley in *The Journal of Biophysical and Biochemical Cytology*, Vol. 3, No. 5, pages 631–46, 25 September 1957

Facts and Theories about Muscle, D. R. Wilkie in *Progress in Biophysics and Biophysical Chemistry*, Vol. 4, pages 288–322, 1954

Muscle Structure and Theories of Contraction, H. E. Huxley in *Progress in Biophysics and Biophysical Chemistry*, Vol. 7, pages 255–312, 1957

The Transference of the Muscle Energy in the Contraction Cycle, H. H. Weber and Hildegard Portzehl in *Progress in Biophysics and Biophysical Chemistry*, Vol. 4, pages 60–107, 1954

# Section II
# Sensory processes
# and perception

An animal is constantly being bombarded by stimuli from its environment. It is subjected to mechanical stimulation, to electromagnetic radiation, and comes into contact with a host of chemical substances in the surrounding medium. For all its complexity and sophistication, the animal's nervous system, when faced with such stimuli, can do virtually nothing. The reason is simple. The nervous system uses one type of language, the environment uses others. The language of the nervous system is one of electrochemical events, and so the nervous system cannot deal directly with electromagnetic radiation or the other forms of stimulation mentioned above. For each form of stimulation there is an intermediary which translates from the environmental language into that of the nervous system. These intermediaries are the sense organs.

Sense organs, however, are not merely passive translators and transmitters of information. They actively process the input from the environment, so that what the nervous system receives is a censored version of that input. Stimuli that are too weak, or outside certain limits of frequency, say, are not passed on; complex stimuli may be split down into simpler components. After leaving the sense organs, the nervous system itself then processes the input further, often in several stages, until the animal perceives the stimuli in their familiar form.

Any study of sensory processes and perception, then, must consider the way in which sense organs convert changes in the environment into nerve impulses with which the nervous system can deal, and the subsequent steps by which the information from the environment is processed. These two problems form the main theme of this section. Rather than surveying all of the senses, the articles chosen concentrate upon two: hearing and vision. Alfred Romer's article on the origin of the ear sets the scene by giving an anatomical account of these structures in a wide variety of vertebrates. The article describes the evolutionary changes which have occurred in the vertebrates, through ancestral amphibia, reptiles and mammal-like reptiles to give the more familiar mammalian condition. The next article, by Georg von Békésy, describes in detail the structure and function of the human ear.

Nearly all of the remaining articles deal with vision. E. J. W. Barrington and Alfred Romer describe the anatomy and, at a gross level, the function of light-sensitive organs in a wide variety of invertebrates and vertebrates. How the information which reaches the eye is processed on its way to and in the brain is described in subsequent articles. David Hubel discusses how cells of the visual cortex respond when objects of different shapes and orientation are presented to the eye, and the article by Edward MacNichol is concerned with the perception of colour.

# 6 The origin of the ear
## by Alfred Sherwood Romer

A highly developed sensory system of a type quite unknown in land vertebrates is that of the lateral line organs (figures 6.1–6.3) found in fishes and in aquatic and larval amphibians. The receptors are clusters of sensory cells termed neuromasts; these may be found distributed in isolated fashion in the skin, but are generally located along a series of canals or grooves on the head and body.

A main element of the system is the *lateral line* in the narrower sense of the term. In typical fishes this is a long canal running the length of either flank (parallel secondary lines sometimes develop). The canal continues forward onto the head, where similar canals form a complex pattern. Generally, a major canal runs forward over the temporal region, then curves downward and forward beneath the orbit to the snout as an infraorbital canal. A second cranial canal is supraorbital in position in its forward course. The canals of the two sides may have a transverse connection across the occiput; a canal generally crosses the cheek and then runs downward and forward along the lower jaw. Other accessory canals may be present on the head and gill region, and in some cases there are accessory body lines. Isolated neuromasts, *pit organs*, may also be found on the head, often in linear arrangements.

In most fishes the lateral line organs are contained in closed canals, opening at intervals to the surface. In many bony fishes this canal system may be sunk within the substance of the head plates and within or below the body scales; in cyclostomes the neuromasts, on the contrary, are in isolated pits, although the pits are arranged in roughly linear order. In a few cartilaginous and bony fishes open grooves take the place of canals, and the same appears to have been true among the ancient fossil amphibians. In modern amphibians the neuromasts lie in the skin in more or less isolated fashion, although preserving in part a linear arrangement.

*first published in* The Vertebrate Body, *4th edition, 1970, pages 461–475 (W. B. Saunders Co., Philadelphia and London).*

The sense organs of the lateral line system are the *neuromasts*, consisting of bundles of cells, often with much the appearance of taste buds. The neuromast cells are elongated, and each bears a projecting hairlike structure. Invariably there is present above the "hairs", and enclosing their tips, a mass of gelatinous material which may be termed a *cupula*, secreted by the neuromast cells, which waves freely in the surrounding water (figure 6.3). Lacking structures at all comparable ourselves (except, as we shall see, in the internal ear), the nature of the sensations registered has been difficult for us to determine. It appears that the neuromasts respond to waves or disturbances in the water through movement of the cupula and consequent bending of the hairlike processes and supplement vision by making the fish aware of nearby moving objects – prey, enemies – or of fixed "obstructions to navigation". A fish seldom has visible "landmarks" against which to measure its progress through the water; sensory structures of this sort will at least tell it of water movements and the pressure of currents against its body and thus be of great aid in locomotion.

The neuromasts and their nerve cells are derived embryologically (as are certain other nervous and sensory structures)

**Figure 6.1 Section through the skin of a teleost,** to show the lateral line canal, *lc*, piercing a series of scales, and opening at intervals to the surface. The canal is followed by the lateral line nerve, *ln*, which sends branches to the sensory organs, *so*; *ep*, epithelium. (After Goodrich.)

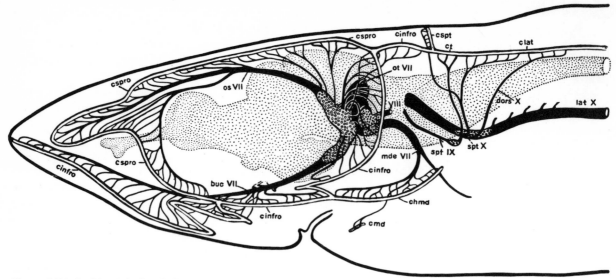

**Figure 6.2 Left side of the head of a shark** to show the lateral line canals (parallel lines) and the nerves (black) supplying them. Pit organs are not shown: *buc VII*, buccal ramus of nerve VII; *chmd*, hyomandibular canal; *cinfro*, infraorbital canal; *clat*, lateral line canal proper; *cmd*, mandibular canal, *cspro*, supra-orbital canal; *cspt*, supratemporal (or occipital) canals; *ct*, temporal canal; *dors X*, dorsal ramus of nerve X; *lat X*, lateral line ramus of nerve X; *mde VII*, external mandibular ramus of nerve VII; *os VII*, superficial ophthalmic ramus of nerve VII; *ot VII*, otic ramus of nerve VII; *spt IX*, supratemporal ramus of nerve IX; *spt* X, supratemporal ramus of nerve X. (From Norris and Hughes.)

from thickenings of the ectoderm on either side of the neural tissues of the head, termed *placodes*. The lateral line placodes become associated with three of the cranial nerves. Much of the system of head canals is formed from an anterior placode associated with cranial nerve VII. A short segment in the temporal region is formed from a small placode related to nerve IX. A posterior placode forms the posterior part of the head system and grows backward the length of the trunk; it is associated with cranial nerve X (the vagus), which sends a branch along the flank to accompany it.

Although the lateral line system is present in larval amphibians, it was lost, it seems, in the earliest reptiles. Many reptiles and mammals have returned to a water-dwelling life, but, useful as it would be to them, this sensory system, once lost, never reappears.

Related to the lateral line system in development and probably in phylogeny, although differing in structure and probable function, are the *Ampullae of Lorenzini*, clusters of jelly-filled little tubules scattered over the head region —

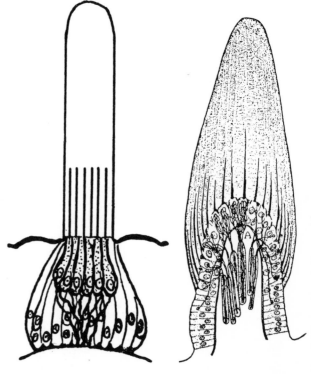

**Figure 6.3 Neuromast sensory organs.** *Left*, an organ from a lateral line canal; *right*, the crista from a semicircular canal. In both are seen supporting cells and sensory cells, the latter with hairlike processes extending into the flexible, gelatinous cupula. (Partly after Fulton.)

particularly the snout – of elasmobranchs and containing at their bases sensory cells. It is possible that, like the proper lateral line organs, they are sensitive to hydrostatic pressure; they appear, however, to be most especially highly sensitive receptors for temperature changes in the water and may be sensitive to electrical charges. Somewhat similar structures are present in certain primitive freshwater teleosts (notably the African mormyrids), where they act as "radar" receptors for electric impulses sent out by the fish.

First thoughts as to the primary anatomic or functional aspects of the vertebrate ear are liable to be misleading when based on familiar human features. One tends to think, when the word is mentioned, of the ornamental pinna of the mammalian external ear, or, perhaps, of the middle ear cavity behind the drum, with its contained ear ossicles. These items, however, are entirely lacking in fishes; the basic ear structures of all vertebrates are those of the internal ear, the sensory organs buried deep within the ear capsule. We naturally think of hearing as the proper ear function; but in the ancestral vertebrates audition was apparently unimportant and perhaps absent; equilibrium was the basic sensory attribute of the "auditory" organ.

## The ear as an organ of equilibrium

Before considering the hearing function, which becomes increasingly important as we ascend the scale of vertebrates, we may discuss the ear as an organ of equilibrium, a basic and relatively unchanged function from fish to man. Equilibrium is a type of sensation produced by the internal ear alone; all accessory ear structures are related to the hearing sense and need not concern us for the moment.

In a variety of fishes, amphibians and reptiles the paired internal ears are built upon a relatively uniform pattern in which most of the structures present are related to equilibration (figure 6.4, *A–D*). The *membranous labyrinth* consists of a series of sacs and canals contained within the otic region on either side of the braincase. These form a closed system of cavities, lined by an epithelium and containing a liquid, the *endolymph*, not dissimilar to that of the interstitial fluid.

Two distinct, major saclike structures are generally present in jawed vertebrates, the *utriculus* and the *sacculus*. A slender tube, the *endolymphatic duct*, usually extends upward and inward from them to terminate within the braincase in an *endolymphatic sac*. In general, the sacculus lies below the utriculus. In both there is found a large oval "spot" consisting of a sensory epithelium associated with branches of the auditory nerve; these areas are the *utricular macula* and *saccular macula*. The utricular macula lies on the floor of that sac, in a horizontal plane; the saccular element is typically in a vertical plane on the inner wall of the sacculus. A pocket-like depression is found in the floor of the sacculus near the posterior end; this is the *lagena*, which contains a smaller *lagenar macula*.

The sensory cells of these maculae (and, indeed, of the entire internal ear) are comparable to the neuromasts of the lateral line system. During development there forms over the combined tips of the sensory hairs of these cells a gelatinous membrane or cupula. In the utricular and saccular maculae, and often that of the lagena as well, this material becomes a thickened structure, weighed down by the deposition in it of a mass of crystals of calcium carbonate termed an *otolith*. The nature of this "ear stone" varies. It may remain a rather amorphous mass of crystals. In ray-finned fishes, however, the otoliths develop into compact structures. The saccular otolith is generally the best developed; in teleosts it is so large as practically to fill the sacculus and reflect in its outlines the shape of that cavity. This shape varies from genus to genus and from species to species; a single tiny otolith will often furnish positive identification of the fish which bore it.

The utricular macula and, to a much lesser degree, those of the sacculus and lagena, register by the tilt of the otolith and its enclosed sensory "hairs" the tilt of the head and linear acceleration; somewhat similar organs are found in a number of invertebrate types. They do not, however, furnish data as to turning movements. This is the function of another series of structures, the *semicircular canals*.

These tiny tubes are dorsal elements of the endolymphatic system, springing out from the utriculus and connected at either end with this sac. In every jawed vertebrate, without exception, three such canals are present; each of the three lies in a plane at right angles to the other two, so that one is present for each of the three planes of space. Two canals lie in vertical planes, an *anterior vertical* (or superior) *canal*, angled forward and outward from the upper surface of the utriculus, and a *posterior vertical canal*, running backward and outward; a *horizontal canal* extends laterally from that body. Often the two vertical canals arise at their proximal ends by a common stalk, a *crus commune*, from the upper surface of the utriculus. Each semicircular canal has at one end a spherical expansion, an *ampulla*. The vertical canals bear these ampullae at their distal ends, anteriorly and posteriorly; the horizontal canal (for no known reason in particular) has its ampulla anteriorly placed. Within each ampulla is a sensory area, usually elevated, termed a *crista* (figure 6.3). Here we find again the familiar hair cells, or neuromasts; their tips are embedded in a common membrane or mass of gelatinous substance, a tall

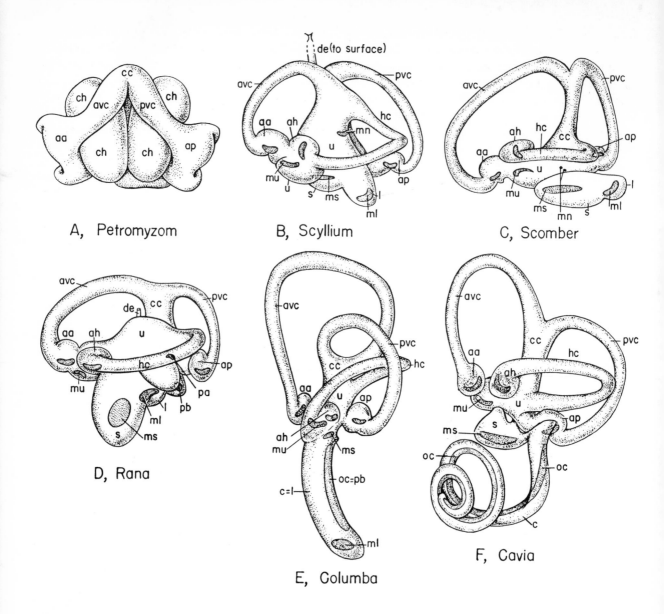

**Figure 6.4 Membranous labyrinth** of *A*, lamprey; *B*, shark; *C*, teleost; *D*, frog; *E*, bird; *F*, mammal; all external views of the left ear. Sensory areas are shown (except in *a*) as if the membrane were transparent. *aa*, Ampulla of anterior canal; *ah*, ampulla of horizontal canal; *ap*, ampulla of posterior canal; *avc*, anterior vertical canal; *c*, cochlear duct; *cc*, crus commune with which both vertical canals connect; *ch*, chambers in the lamprey ear lined with a ciliated epithelium; *de*, endolymphatic duct; *hc*, horizontal canal; *l*, lagena; *ml*, macula of lagena; *mn*, macula neglecta; *ms*, macula of sacculus; *mu*, macula of utriculus; *oc*, organ of Corti; *pa*, papilla amphibiorum; *pb*, papilla basilaris; *pvc*, posterior vertical canal; *s*, sacculus; *u*, utriculus. (After Retzius.)

cupula, which nearly blocks the ampulla and can move to and fro like a swing door.

The arrangement of the canals and their sensory structures makes it seem clear that their function is to register turning movements of the animal in the several planes of space. Displacement of liquid in one or more of the canals displaces the cupulae, and a consequent bending of their sensory hairs.

## Hearing in fishes

Whether or not fish hear is a topic that was long disputed. A considerable body of evidence, however, indicates that hearing is certainly present in many teleosts, but in elasmobranchs there is merely indication of response to very low vibrations. Localization of the sensory uptake of vibrations is difficult. In most cases the saccular macula appears to be the major receptor, but in some forms the utriculus is apparently concerned as well. A suspect is the *macula neglecta* (figure 6.4*A* and *C*), a small sensory spot found in the utriculus in a variety of fish and lower land vertebrates. The hearing organs of land vertebrates develop in connection with the lagenar pocket, but in fishes the macula of the lagena appears to be concerned only with gravity.

Fishes in general lack the various accessory devices by which in higher vertebrates sound waves reach the internal ear. But, as shown by studies on men with hearing deficiences, the conduction of vibrations through the head skeleton to the internal ear can produce some degree of hearing (and lateral line sensations are closely allied to hearing, of course). In most fishes water vibrations, to be heard, must set up head vibrations, and these in turn produce endolymphatic vibrations which can be picked up by the hair cells of the internal ear.

Some bony fishes, however, have accessory structures which parallel in a way the "hearing aids" found in land vertebrates, although evolved quite independently and along other lines. In these fishes, it appears, the swim bladder is utilized as a device for the reception of vibrations. In herring-like teleosts this air bladder sends forward a tubular extension which comes to lie alongside part of the membrane system of either ear and can thus induce vibrations in the endolymph. In a group of teleosts termed the Ostariophysi, which includes the catfishes, carp and relatives, in which hearing is unquestionably developed, another method is used. Processes of the most anterior vertebrae develop on either side as small detached bones termed the *weberian ossicles* (figure 6.5). These articulate in series to form a chain extending from the air bladder forward to the ear region. The ossicles operate somewhat in the fashion of the little ear bones of a mammal, transmitting air bladder vibrations to the liquids of the internal ear system.

## The internal ear in reptiles

In tetrapods, as already indicated, the parts of the internal ear devoted to equilibrium remain little changed from the fish condition. The auditory apparatus, however, gradually develops into structures which attain such size and importance that the older regions of the sacs and canals are often termed (rather slightingly) the *vestibule* of the internal ear.

It is the lagenar region in which this expansion takes place. The macula of the lagena, mentioned earlier as present in fishes, persists in all tetrapods, except mammals above the monotreme level, but never develops to any de-

gree; if it has an auditory function in land vertebrates, this function cannot be significant. The lagena itself, however, is important as a basal structure in the development of the cochlea.

The sensory area vital in the development of hearing in tetrapods is that termed the *basilar papilla* (figure 6.4). This area is unknown in fishes, but is characteristically developed in many amphibians and in typical reptiles. In these forms it is an area of hair cells, covered by a common gelatinous membrane, situated on the posterior wall of the sacculus at the base of the lagena. It is here that vibrations, brought in from without by the stapes, are received.

In general the sacs and canals of the inner ear are not adherent to the skeletal walls of the auditory capsule that surround them. They are separated from them by spaces filled with liquid and crossed by connective tissue strands. This liquid is the *perilymph* (figure 6.8). It surrounds the membranous labyrinth and thus is quite distinct from the endolymph within. From the perilymph, there develops in land vertebrates a conduction system which leads from the fenestra ovalis to the basilar papilla and forms the last link

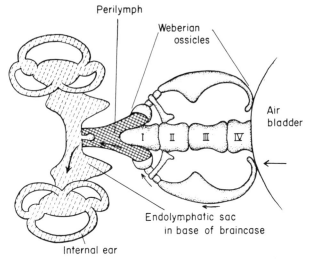

**Figure 6.5 Diagrammatic horizontal section** of the posterior part of the head and anterior part of the body of a teleost with weberian ossicles. Vibrations in an anterior subdivision of the air bladder set up corresponding vibrations in a series of small ossicles which in turn set up waves in a perilymphatic sac. This, again, sets up vibrations in an endolymphatic sac at the base of the braincase. Arrows show the course of transmission of the vibrations. Roman numerals indicate the vertebrae from which the weberian ossicles are derived. (After Chvanilov.)

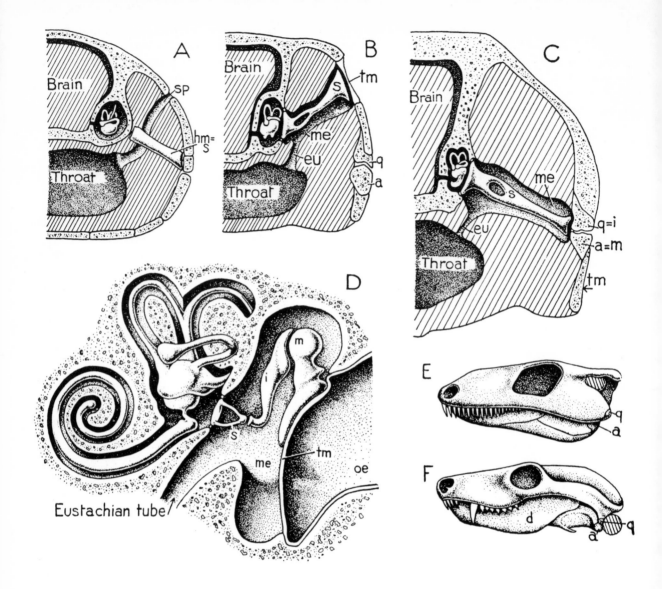

**Figure 6.6 Diagrams to show the evolution of the middle ear and auditory ossicles.** Diagrammatic sections through the otic region of the head of *A*, a fish; *B*, a primitive amphibian; *C*, a primitive reptile; *D*, a mammal (showing the ear region only); *E*, side view of the skull of a primitive land vertebrate; *F*, of a mammal-like reptile to show the shift of the eardrum from the otic notch of the skull to the region of the jaw articulation. *a*, Articular; *d*, dentary; *eu*, eustachian tube; *hm*, hyomandibular; *i*, incus; *m*, malleus; *me*, middle ear cavity; *oe*, outer ear cavity; *q*, quadrate; *s*, stapes; *sp*, spiracle; *tm*, timpanic membrane. (From Romer, *Man and the Vertebrates*, University of Chicago Press.)

in the chain of structures by which potentially audible vibrations reach the auditory sensory areas.

Internal to the oval window in lower tetrapods there develops a large *perilymphatic cistern*, against which the stapes plays (figures 6.7, 6.8, 6.9). Vibrations received here are, in typical reptiles, carried around the lagena to its posterior border in a perilymph-filled canal. This duct passes just outside the area of the basilar papilla, and is separated from the base of its sensory cells only by a thin *basilar membrane*. Vibrations in this membrane agitate the hair cells and at long last, in this roundabout fashion, the sensory organ is reached. This situation – an auditory sen-

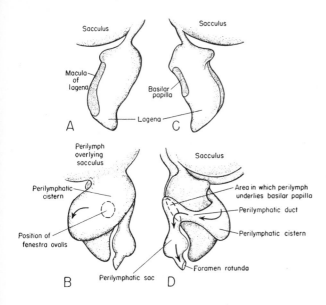

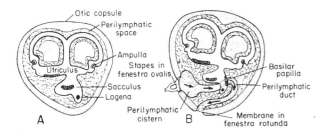

Figure 6.7 The ear of a late embryo of a lizard (Lacerta). *A*, Left ear, lateral view of the membranous labyrinth in the floor of the sacculus and the lagena. *B*, The same with the perilymphatic system shown in addition. *C, D*, Medial views comparable to *A* and *B*, respectively. Arrows indicate course of conduction of vibrations from stapes to basilar papilla and on to the "round window" at the distal end, beyond the perilymphatic duct.

Figure 6.8 *A*, Schematic section through the ear capsule of a fish, to show the perilymphatic space surrounding the membranous labyrinth containing endolymph. *B*, Similar scheme of a tetrapod; in which a part of the perilymph area (arrows) is specialized to conduct sound from the fenestra ovalis to and past the auditory sensory area. The maculae are darkly shaded. (After de Burlet.)

sory structure agitated by vibrations of the membrane at its base – is a fundamental feature in the construction of the hearing apparatus in all amniotes. We shall find it repeated, and capable of description in much the same words, in birds and mammals.

As a final point here, it must be noted that for vibrations set up by the stapes in the perilymph and carried along by the perilymphatic duct, some release mechanism, allowing a corresponding vibration, must be set up at the far end of the perilymph system. In many amphibians this consists of a *perilymphatic sac*, which projects from the auditory capsule into the braincase. In some amphibians and in reptiles (except the turtles) a further development takes place. There is a large, rather tubular foramen (primarily for the vagus nerve) in the braincase wall which runs out from a point near this sac. We find that the perilymphatic duct system may, instead of terminating in a sac, run outward through this foramen – or a separate one formed close by, the *fenestra rotunda* (figure 6.9) – and terminate in a membrane which vibrates in phase with the impulses received through the fenestra ovalis at the other end of the perilymph system. Primitively, this membrane is buried in the tissues at the margin of the skull; in more advanced forms this round window opens back into the middle ear chamber.

## Development of the cochlea

Both birds and mammals have greatly extended their hearing ability by the evolution of a *cochlea* – a highly developed structure for auditory reception. The crocodilians, related to the birds, demonstrate the manner in which the cochlea was developed. Three structural features are involved: the lagena, the perilymphatic duct, and the basilar papilla.

In the crocodiles and birds (figure 6.9*B*) the finger-like lagena has become expanded into a long but essentially straight tube, filled of course with endolymph; this is the *cochlear duct* or *scala media*. At the tip in these forms (and monotreme mammals) persists the original macula of the lagena, of doubtful function. The important sensory structure is the basilar papilla, which is here greatly expanded into an elongate area running the length of the cochlear duct, and generally termed the *organ of Corti*. It has a complicated series of sensory hair cells and supporting cells; over them folds a membranous flap, the *tectorial membrane*, corresponding to the cupula in other neuromast structures; beneath is an elongate fiber-supported and vibratile basilar membrane. With the lengthening of this sensory organ the perilymphatic duct, which remains closely applied to its base, expands in a double loop. The part of this tube leading inward from the oval window is termed the *scala*

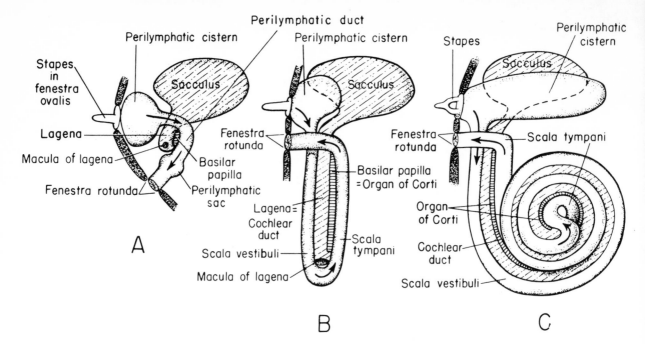

**Figure 6.9 Diagrammatic sections** through the saccular region to show the evolution of the cochlea. *A*, Primitive reptile with a small basilar papilla adjacent to the perilymphatic duct. *B*, The crocodile or bird type; the lagena has elongated to form a cochlear duct, the basilar sense organ with it, and a loop of the perilymphatic duct follows the cochlear duct in its elongation. *C*, The mammalian type; the cochlea is further elongated and coiled in a fashion economical of space.

*vestibuli* (so called because the fenestra ovalis is considered to lie in the vestibular part of the inner ear). The distal limb of the tube, leading to the round window with its membrane, or "tympanum", is the *scala tympani*. It is in this distal segment of the loop that the perilymphatic duct underlies the basilar membrane and the sensory organ.

These modifications of the primitive reptilian system result in the development, in birds and their crocodilian relatives, of a true, although simply constructed, cochlea. This consists of three associated tubular structures – one endolymphatic, and two filled with perilymph – and, in the central duct, the organ of Corti. This sensory organ is separated from the distal perilymphatic tube – the scala tympani – only by the basilar membrane and from the proximal perilymph duct – the scala vestibuli – by a still thinner membrane, lying across from it on the other side of the cochlear duct. Crudely one may visualize the formation of this type of cochlea by imagining that he has grasped the

region of the lagena and the perilymphatic duct crossing its base and pulled this area outward. This pull has stretched the lagena out into a long blind tube as the cochlear duct; the perilymphatic duct, attached at both ends, has pulled out as a double-looped structure, the two scalae.

The mammalian cochlea (figures 6.10, 6.11), we believe, has developed independently of that of birds, but in closely parallel fashion. In monotremes it is still a simple, uncoiled structure, readily comparable to that of birds. The typical mammalian cochlea is, however, much more elongated than that of birds or crocodiles. If it were to remain straight, it could not be comfortably accommodated within the ear capsule, and in relation to this we find that (as the name implies) the mammalian cochlea of three tubes has been coiled into a tidy spiral structure.

The mammalian organ of Corti is, like that of a bird, readily derivable, by elongation and increased complexity of structure, from the primitive basilar papilla. Beneath it, adjacent to the scala tympani, is the basilar membrane, crossed by numerous fibers. Above is, as in birds and crocodiles, a tectorial membrane in which, as always, the tip of the hair cells are engaged. Centrally there is a curious little triangular tunnel, braced by pillar cells on either side; on either side of this structure are rows of sensory hair cells, running the length of the cochlea – typically three or four rows toward the center of the cochlea, a single row externally. Rows of supporting cells are present farther toward either edge of the membrane. As in lower tetrapods, vibrations in the basilar membrane caused by waves in the perilymph system cause hearing sensations through displacement

**Figure 6.10 Diagrammatic section** through a mammalian cochlea. (After Finnerty and Cowdry.)

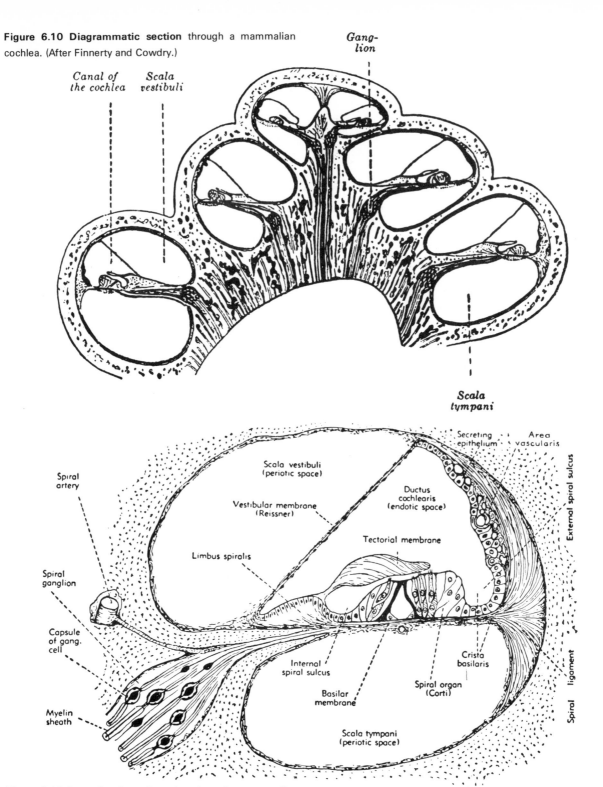

*Gang-lion*

*Canal of the cochlea*

*Scala vestibuli*

*Scala tympani*

Secreting epithelium · · Area vascularis

Scala vestibuli (periotic space)

Ductus cochlearis (endotic space)

Spiral artery

Vestibular membrane (Reissner)

Tectorial membrane

External spiral sulcus

Limbus spiralis

Spiral ganglion

Capsule of gang. cell

Internal spiral sulcus

Crista basilaris

Spiral organ (Corti)

Basilar membrane

Myelin sheath

Scala tympani (periotic space)

Spiral ligament

**Figure 6.11 A much enlarged section** through a mammalian cochlea to show details of the organ of Corti (*cf.* figure 6.10). (From Ruch and Fulton, *Medical Physiology and Biophysics*.)

of the hairs of the sensory cells above the membrane. Although in a primitive tetrapod hearing system the vibrations reach the basilar membrane and basilar papilla (organ of Corti) only from below (*cf.* figure 6.9*A*), here vibrations entering this triple system via the scala vestibuli can "short circuit" the double loop and send impulses through the vestibular membrane and down to the basilar structures through the liquid of the cochlear duct. The functional "reason" for elongation of the basilar papilla into the formed organ of Corti appears to be the discrimination of sounds of different pitch – *i.e.* of different wavelengths. Differences in the transverse span of the basilar membrane, which grades in width from one end of the cochlea to the other, appear to result in making the membrane sensitive to different wavelengths at different parts of its extent and thus render tone distinctions possible. The apex of the cochlea, where the basilar membrane is broadest, is most sensitive to the lowest tones, the narrow region of the membrane at the base of the cochlea to high notes. Even in the relatively short avian cochlea, there is excellent discrimination of tone, and in mammals the range of vibrations heard may be extremely wide. The human ear, for example, can respond to frequencies ranging from about 15 to 16 000 or so cycles per second; typical bats (Microchiroptera) can emit and receive sounds in pitch far above those audible to a human ear, and have evolved an "echolocation" system which aids them in flying in the dark and in capturing insect prey on the wing.

# 7 The ear

## by Georg von Békésy

Even in our era of technological wonders, the performances of our most amazing machines are still put in the shade by the sense organs of the human body. Consider the accomplishments of the ear. It is so sensitive that it can almost hear the random rain of air molecules bouncing against the eardrum. Yet in spite of its extraordinary sensitivity the ear can withstand the pounding of sound waves strong enough to set the body vibrating. The ear is equipped, moreover, with a truly impressive selectivity. In a room crowded with people talking, it can suppress most of the noise and concentrate on one speaker. From the blended sounds of a symphony orchestra the ear of the conductor can single out the one instrument that is not performing to his satisfaction.

In structure and in operation the ear is extraordinarily delicate. One measure of its fineness is the tiny vibrations to which it will respond. At some sound frequencies the vibrations of the eardrum are as small as one billionth of a centimeter – about one tenth the diameter of the hydrogen atom! And the vibrations of the very fine membrane in the inner ear which transmits this stimulation to the auditory nerve are nearly 100 times smaller in amplitude. This fact alone is enough to explain why hearing has so long been one of the mysteries of physiology. Even today we do not know how these minute vibrations stimulate the nerve endings. But thanks to refined electro-acoustical instruments we do know quite a bit now about how the ear functions.

What are the ear's abilities? We can get a quick picture of the working condition of an ear by taking an audiogram, which is a measure of the threshold of hearing at the various sound frequencies. The hearing is tested with pure tones at various frequencies, and the audiogram tells how much sound pressure on the eardrum (*i.e.* what intensity of sound) is necessary for the sound at each frequency to be just barely audible. Curiously, the audiogram curve often is very

*first published in* Scientific American, *August 1957.*

*Reprinted with permission. Copyright* © *1957 by Scientific American, Inc. All rights reserved.*

much the same for the various members of a family; possibly this is connected in some way with the similarity in the shape of the face.

The ear is least sensitive at the low frequencies (figure 7.7): for instance, its sensitivity for a tone of 100 cycles per second is 1 000 times lower than for one at 1 000 cycles per second. This comparative insensitivity to the slower vibrations is an obvious physical necessity, because otherwise we would hear all the vibrations of our own bodies. If you stick a finger in each ear, closing it to air-borne sounds, you hear a very low, irregular tone, produced by the contractions of the muscles of the arms and finger. It is interesting that the ear is just insensitive enough to low frequencies to avoid the disturbing effect of the noises produced by muscles, bodily movements, etc. If it were any more sensitive to these frequencies than it is, we would even hear the vibrations of the head that are produced by the shock of every step we take when walking.

On the high-frequency side the range that the ear covers is remarkable. In childhood some of us can hear well at frequencies as high as 40 000 cycles per second. But with age our acuteness of hearing in the high-frequency range steadily falls. Normally the drop is almost as regular as clockwork: testing several persons in their 40s with tones at a fixed level of intensity, we found that over a period of five years their upper limit dropped about 80 cycles per second every six months. (The experiment was quite depressing to most of the participants.) The aging of the ear is not difficult to understand if we assume that the elasticity of the tissues in the inner ear declines in the same way as that of the skin: it is well known that the skin becomes less resilient as we grow old – a phenomenon anyone can test by lifting the skin on the back of his hand and measuring the time it takes to fall back.

However, the loss of hearing sensitivity with age may also be due to nerve deterioration. Damage to the auditory nervous system by extremely loud noises, by drugs or by inflammation of the inner ear can impair hearing. Sometimes after such damage the hearing improves with time; sometimes (*e.g.* when the damaging agent is streptomycin) the loss is permanent. Unfortunately a physician cannot predict the prospects for recovery of hearing loss, because they vary from person to person.

Psychological factors seem to be involved. Occasionally, especially after an ear operation, a patient appears to improve in hearing only to relapse after a short time. Some reports have even suggested that operating on one ear has improved the unoperated ear as well. Since such an interaction between the two ears would be of considerable neurological interest, I have investigated the matter, but I have never found an improvement in the untreated ear that could be validated by an objective test.

## Structure of the ear

To understand how the ear achieves its sensitivity, we must take a look at the anatomy of the middle and the inner ear (figure 7.1). When sound waves start the eardrum (tympanic membrane) vibrating, the vibrations are trans-mitted via certain small bones (ossicles) to the fluid of the inner ear (figure 7.2). One of the ossicles, the tiny stirrup (weighing only about 1.2 milligrams), acts on the fluid like a piston, driving it back and forth in the rhythm of the sound pressure. These movements of the fluid force into vibration a thin membrane, called the basilar membrane. The latter in turn finally transmits the stimulus to the organ of Corti, a complex structure which contains the endings of the auditory nerves. The question immediately comes up: Why is this long and complicated chain of transmission necessary?

The reason is that we have a formidable mechanical problem if we are to extract the utmost energy from the sound waves striking the eardrum. Usually when a sound hits a solid surface, most of its energy is reflected away. The problem the ear has to solve is to absorb this energy. To do so it has to act as a kind of mechanical transformer, converting the large amplitude of the sound pressure waves in the air into more forceful vibrations of smaller amplitude. A

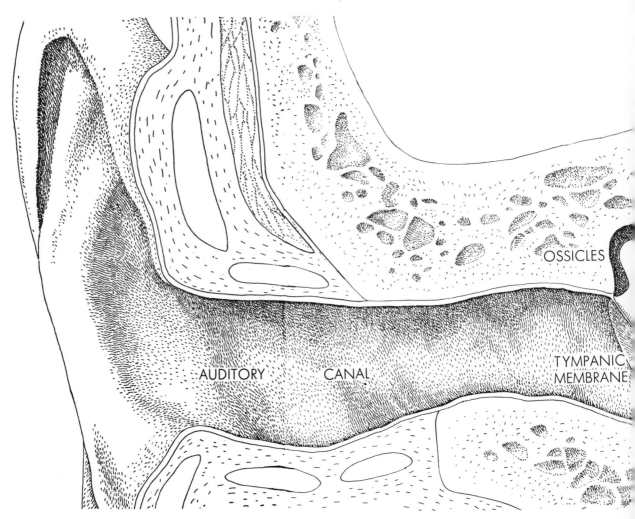

OSSICLES

AUDITORY CANAL

TYMPANIC MEMBRANE

hydraulic press is such a transformer: it multiplies the pressure acting on the surface of a piston by concentrating the force of the pressure upon a second piston of smaller area. The middle ear acts exactly like a hydraulic press: the tiny footplate of the stirrup transforms the small pressure on the surface of the eardrum into a 22-fold greater pressure on the fluid of the inner ear. In this way the ear absorbs the greater part of the sound energy and transmits it to the inner ear without much loss (figure 7.3).

But it needs another transformer to amplify the pressure of the fluid into a still larger force upon the tissues to which the nerves are attached. I think the ear's mechanism for this purpose is very ingenious indeed. It is based on the fact that a flat membrane, stretched to cover the opening of a tube, has a lateral tension along its surface. This tension can be increased tremendously if pressure is applied to one side of the membrane. And that is the function of the organ of Corti. It is constructed in such a way that pressure on the

basilar membrane is transformed into shearing forces many times larger on the other side of the organ (figures 7.4, 7.5 and 7.6). The enhanced shearing forces rub upon extremely sensitive cells attached to the nerve endings.

The eardrum is not by any means the only avenue through which we hear. We also hear through our skull, which is to say, by bone conduction. When we click our teeth or chew a cracker, the sounds come mainly by way of vibrations of the skull. Some of the vibrations are transmitted directly to the inner ear, by-passing the middle ear. This fact helps in the diagnosis of hearing difficulties. If a person can hear bone-conducted sounds but is comparatively deaf to air-borne sounds, we know that the trouble lies in the middle ear. But if he hears no sound by bone conduction, then his auditory nerves are gone, and there is no cure for his deafness. This is an old test, long used by deaf musicians. If a violin player cannot hear his violin even when he touches his teeth to the vibrating instrument, then he knows he suffers from nerve deafness, and there is no cure.

## Speaking and hearing

Hearing by bone conduction plays an important role in the process of speaking. The vibrations of our vocal cords not only produce sounds which go to our ears via the air but also cause the body to vibrate, and the vibration of the jawbone is transmitted to the ear canal. When you hum with closed lips, the sounds you hear are to a large degree heard by bone conduction. (If you stop your ears with your fingers, the hum sounds much louder.) During speaking and singing, therefore, you hear two different sounds – one by bone conduction and the other by air conduction. Of course another listener hears only the air-conducted sounds. In these sounds some of the low-frequency components of the vocal cords' vibrations are lost. This explains why one can hardly recognize his own voice when he listens to a recording of his speech. As we normally hear ourselves, the low-frequency vibrations of our vocal cords, conducted to our own ears by the bones, make our speech sound much more powerful and dynamic than the pure sound waves heard by a second person or through a recording system. Consequently the recording of our voice may strike us as very thin and disappointing. From this point of view we

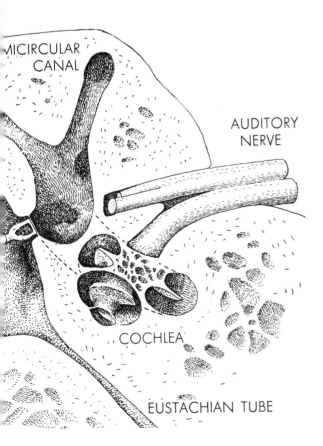

SEMICIRCULAR CANAL

AUDITORY NERVE

COCHLEA

EUSTACHIAN TUBE

**Figure 7.1 Parts of the ear** are illustrated in somewhat simplified cross section. Between the eardrum (tympanic membrane) and the fluid-filled inner ear are the three small bones (ossicles) of the middle ear. The auditory nerve endings are in an organ (*not shown*) between the plate of bone which spirals up the cochlea and the outer wall of the cochlea.

have to admire the astonishing performance of an opera singer. The singer and the audience hear rather different sounds, and it is a miracle to me that they understand each other so well. Perhaps young singers would progress faster if during their training they spent more time studying recordings of their voices.

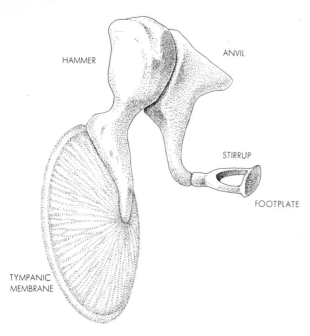

**Figure 7.2 Three ossicles** transmit the vibrations of the tympanic membrane to the inner ear. The footplate of stirrup, surrounded by a narrow membrane, presses against inner-ear fluid.

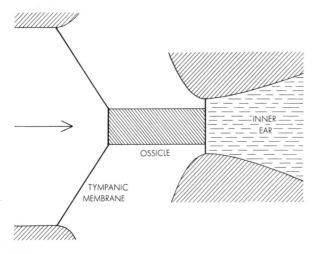

**Figure 7.3 How ossicles act** as a piston pressing against the fluid of the inner ear is indicated by this drawing. Pressure of the vibrations of tympanic membrane are amplified 22 times.

# Feedback to the voice

The control of speaking and singing involves a complicated feedback system. Just as feedback between the eyes and the muscles guides the hand when it moves to pick up an object, so feedback continually adjusts and corrects the voice as we speak or sing. When we start to sing, the beginning of the sound tells us the pitch, and we immediately adjust the tension of the vocal cords if the pitch is wrong. This feedback requires an exceedingly elaborate and rapid mechanism. How it works is not yet entirely understood. But it is small wonder that it takes a child years to learn to speak, or that it is almost impossible for an adult to learn to speak a foreign language with the native accents.

Any disturbance in the feedback immediately disturbs the speech. For instance, if, while a person is speaking, his speech is fed back to him with a time delay by means of a microphone and receivers at his ears, his pronunciation and accent will change, and if the delay interval is made long enough, he will find it impossible to speak at all. This phenomenon affords an easy test for exposing pretended deafness. If the subject can continue speaking normally in the face of a delayed feedback through the machine to his ears, we can be sure that he is really deaf.

The same technique can be used to assess the skill of a pianist. A piano player generally adjusts his touch to the acoustics of the room: if the room is very reverberant, so that the music sounds too loud, he uses a lighter touch; if the sound is damped by the walls, he strengthens his touch. We had a number of pianists play in a room where the damping could be varied, and recorded the amplitude of the vibrations of the piano's sounding board while the musicians played various pieces. When they played an easy piece, their adjustment to the acoustics was very clear: as the sound absorption of the room was increased, the pianist played more loudly, and when the damping on the walls was taken away, the pianist's touch became lighter. But when the piece was difficult, many of the pianists concentrated so hard on the problems of the music that they failed to adjust to the feedback of the room. A master musician, however, was not lost to the sound effects. Taking the technical difficulties of the music in stride, he was able to adjust the sound level to the damping of the room with the same accuracy as for an easy piece. Our rating of the pianists by this test closely matched their reputation among musical experts.

In connection with room acoustics, I should like to mention one of the ear's most amazing performances. How is it that we can locate a speaker, even without seeing him, in a bare-walled room where reflections of his voice come at us from every side? This is an almost unbelievable performance by the ear. It is as if, looking into a room completely

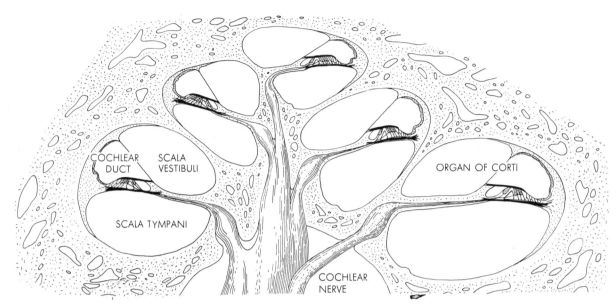

**Figure 7.4 Tube of the cochlea,** coiled like the shell of a snail, is depicted in cross section. The plate of bone which appears in the cross section in figure 7.1 juts from the inside of the tube. Between it and the outside of the tube is the sensitive organ of Corti.

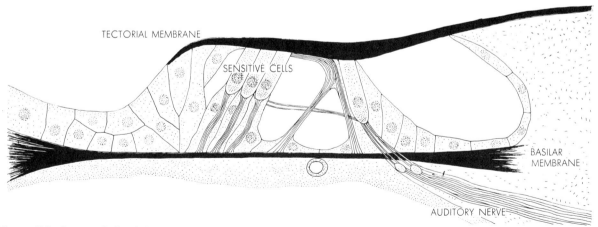

**Figure 7.5 Organ of Corti** lies between the basilar and tectorial membranes. Within it are sensitive cells which are attached to a branch of the auditory nerve (*lower right*). When fluid in scala tympani (*see figure 7.4*) vibrates, these cells are stimulated.

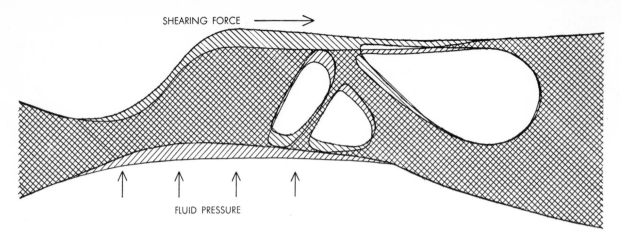

SHEARING FORCE →

FLUID PRESSURE

**Figure 7.6 How vibration forces are amplified** by the organ of Corti is indicated by this drawing. When the vibration of the fluid in the scala tympani exerts a force on the basilar membrane, a larger shearing force is brought to bear on tectorial membrane.

lined with mirrors, we saw only the real figure and none of the hundreds of reflected images. The eye cannot suppress the reflections, but the ear can. The ear is able to ignore all the sounds except the first that strikes it. It has a built-in inhibitory mechanism.

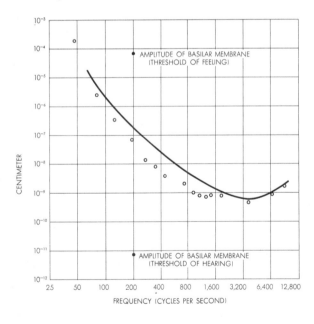

**Figure 7.7 Sensitivity of the ear** is indicated by this curve, in which the amplitude of the vibrations of the tympanic membrane in fractions of a centimeter is plotted against the frequency of sound impinging on the membrane. Diameter of hydrogen atom is $10^{-8}$ centimeter.

## Suppressed sounds

One of the most important factors that subordinate the reflected sounds is the delay in their arrival; necessarily they come to the ear only after the sound that has traveled directly from the speaker to the listener. The reflected sounds reinforce the loudness and tone volume of the direct sound, and perhaps even modify its localization, but by and large, they are not distinguishable from it. Only when the delay is appreciable does a reflected sound appear as a separate unit – an echo. Echoes often are heard in a large church, where reflections may lag more than half a second behind the direct sound. They are apt to be a problem in a concert hall. Dead walls are not desirable, because the music would sound weak. For every size of concert room there is an optimal compromise on wall reflectivity which will give amplification to the music but prevent disturbing echoes.

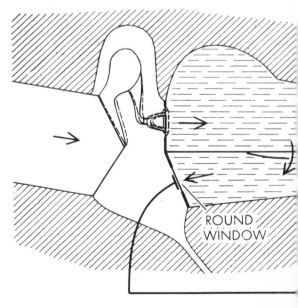

ROUND WINDOW

In addition to time delay, there are other factors that act to inhibit some sounds and favor others. Strong sounds generally suppress weaker ones. Sounds in which we are interested take precedence over those that concern us less, as I pointed out in the examples of the speaker in a noisy room and the orchestra conductor detecting an errant instrument. This brings us to the intimate collaboration between the ear and the nervous system.

Any stimulation of the ear (*e.g.* any change in pressure) is translated into electrical messages to the brain via the nerves. We can therefore draw information about the ear from an analysis of these electrical impulses, now made possible by electronic instruments. There are two principal types of electric potential that carry the messages. One is a continuous, wavelike potential which has been given the name microphonic. In experimental animals such as guinea pigs and cats the microphonics are large enough to be easily measured (they range up to about half a millivolt (figure 7.8)). It has turned out that the magnitude of the microphonics produced in the inner ear is directly proportional to the displacements of the stirrup footplate that set the fluid in the inner ear in motion. The microphonics therefore permit us to determine directly to what extent the sound pressure applied to the eardrum is transmitted to the inner ear, and they have become one of the most useful tools for exploring sound transmission in the middle ear. For instance, there used to be endless discussion of the simple question: Just how much does perforation of the eardrum affect hearing? The question has now been answered with mathematical precision by experiments on animals. A hole of precisely measured size is drilled in the eardrum, and the amount of hearing loss is determined by the change in the microphonics. This type of observation on cats has shown that a perforation about one millimeter in diameter destroys hearing at the frequencies below 100 cycles per second but causes almost no impairment of hearing in the range of frequencies above 1 000 cycles per second. From studies of the physical properties of the human ear we can judge that the findings on animals apply fairly closely to man also.

The second type of electric potential takes the form of sharp pulses, which appear as spikes in the recording instrument. The sound of a sharp click produces a series of brief spikes; a pure tone generates volleys of spikes, generally in the rhythm of the period of the tone. We can follow the spikes along the nerve pathways all the way from the inner ear up to the cortex of the brain. And when we do, we find that stimulation of specific spots on the membrane of the inner ear seems to be projected to corresponding spots in the auditory area of the cortex (figure 7.12). This is reminiscent of the projection of images on the retina of the eye to

**Figure 7.8 Electrical potentials** of the microphonic type generated by the inner ear of an experimental animal can be detected by this arrangement. At left is a highly schematic diagram of the ear, the cochlea is represented in cross section by the fluid-filled chamber and the organ of Corti by the horizontal line in this chamber. When the vibrations of the eardrum are transmitted to the organ of Corti, its microphonic potentials can be picked up at the round window of the cochlea and displayed on the face of an oscilloscope (*right*).

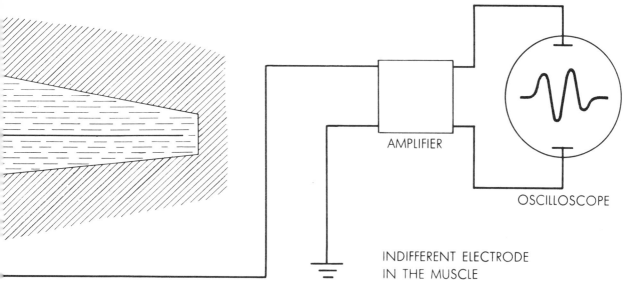

AMPLIFIER

OSCILLOSCOPE

INDIFFERENT ELECTRODE
IN THE MUSCLE

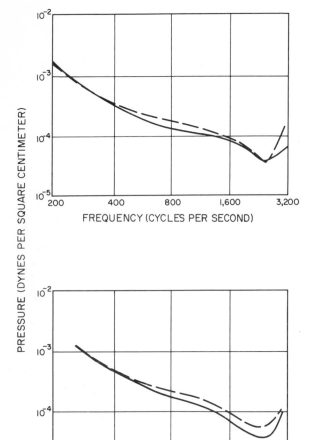

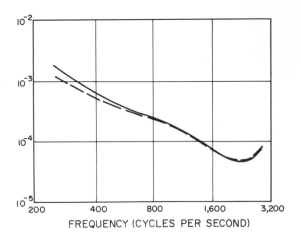

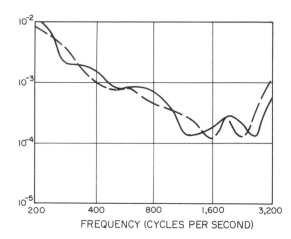

PRESSURE (DYNES PER SQUARE CENTIMETER)

FREQUENCY (CYCLES PER SECOND)

FREQUENCY (CYCLES PER SECOND)

FREQUENCY (CYCLES PER SECOND)

FREQUENCY (CYCLES PER SECOND)

**Figure 7.9 Audiograms** plot the threshold of hearing (in terms of pressure on the tympanic membrane) against the frequency of sound. The first three audiograms show the threshold for three members of the same family; the fourth, the threshold for an unrelated person. The continuous curves represent the threshold for one ear of the subject; the broken curves, for the other ear of the same subject. The audiogram curves indicate that in normal hearing the threshold in both ears, and the threshold in members of the same family, are remarkably similar.

**Figure 7.10 Stirrup** of the normal human ear is enlarged 19 ▶ times in the photograph at the top of the opposite page. The thin line at the top of the photograph is the tympanic membrane seen in cross section. The hammer and anvil do not appear. The narrow membrane around the footplate of the stirrup may be seen as a translucent area between the footplate and the surrounding bone. The photograph at the bottom shows the immobilized footplate of an otosclerotic ear. In this photograph only the left side of the stirrup appears; the footplate is the dark area at the bottom center. The membrane around the footplate has been converted into a rigid bony growth.

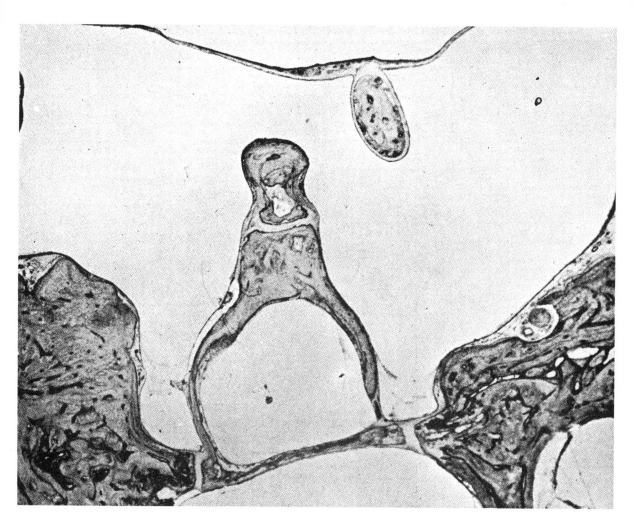

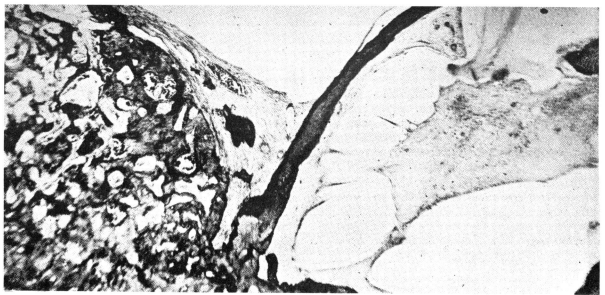

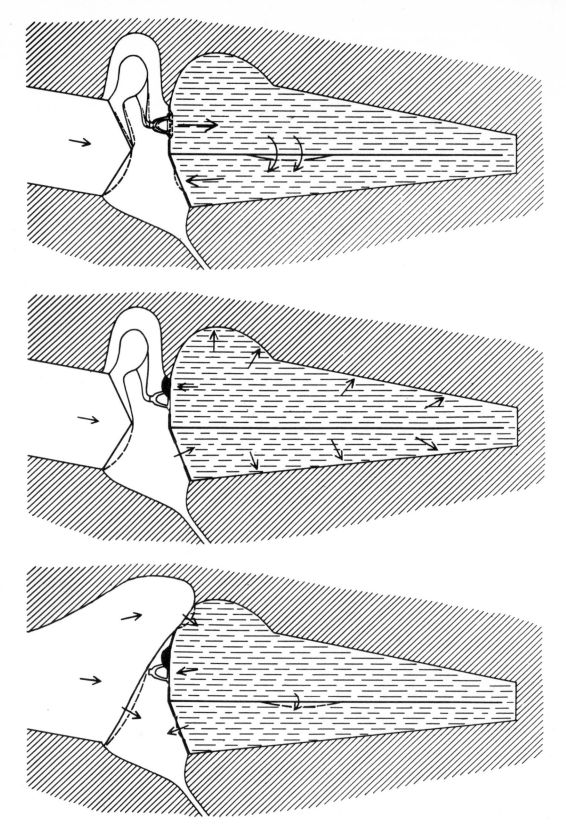

**Figure 7.11 Fenestration operation** can alleviate the effects of otosclerosis. The drawing at the top schematically depicts the normal human ear as described in the caption to figure 7.8. The pressure on the components of the ear is indicated by the arrows. The drawing in the middle shows an otosclerotic ear; the otosclerotic growth is represented as a black protuberance. Because the stirrup cannot move, the pressure on the tympanic membrane is transmitted to the organ of Corti only through the round window of the cochlea; and because the fluid in the cochlea is incompressible, the organ of Corti cannot vibrate. The drawing at the bottom shows how the fenestration operation makes a new window into the cochlea to permit the organ of Corti to vibrate freely.

the visual area of the brain. But in the case of the ear the situation must be more complex, because there are nerve branches leading to the opposite ear and there seem to be several auditory projection areas on the surface of the brain. At the moment research is going on to find out how the secondary areas function and what their purpose is.

## Detecting pitch

The orderly projection of the sensitive area of the inner ear onto the higher brain levels is probably connected with the resolution of pitch. The ear itself can analyze sounds and separate one tone from another. There are limits to this ability, but if the frequencies of the tones presented are not too close together, they are discriminated pretty well. Long ago this raised the question: How is the ear able to discriminate the pitch of a tone? Many theories have been argued, but only within the last decade has it been possible to plan pertinent experiments.

In the low-frequency range up to 60 cycles per second the vibration of the basilar membrane produces in the auditory nerve volleys of electric spikes synchronous with the rhythm of the sound. As the sound pressure increases, the number of spikes packed into each period increases. Thus two variables are transmitted to the cortex: (1) the number of spikes and (2) their rhythm. These two variables alone convey the loudness and the pitch of the sound.

Above 60 cycles per second a new phenomenon comes in. The basilar membrane now begins to vibrate unequally over its area: each tone produces a maximal vibration in a different area of the membrane. Gradually this selectivity takes over the determination of pitch, for the rhythm of the spikes, which indicates the pitch at low frequencies, becomes irregular at the higher ones. Above 4 000 cycles per second pitch is determined entirely by the location of the maximal vibration amplitude along the basilar mem-

brane. Apparently there is an inhibitory mechanism which suppresses the weaker stimuli and thus sharpens considerably the sensation around the maximum. This type of inhibition can also operate in sense organs such as the skin and the eye. In order to see sharply we need not only a sharp image of the object on the retina but also an inhibitory system to suppress stray light entering the eye. Otherwise

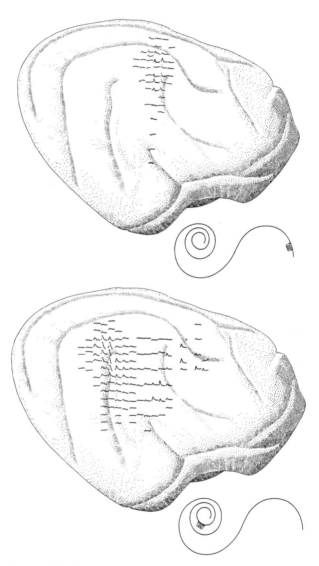

**Figure 7.12 Nerve impulses** due to the electrical stimulation of the organ of Corti were localized on the surface of the brain of a cat. The spirals below each of these drawings of a cat's brain represent the full length of the organ of Corti. The pairs of arrows on each spiral indicate the point at which the organ was stimulated. The peaks superimposed on the brains represent the electrical potentials detected by an electrode placed at that point.

we would see the object surrounded by a halo. The ear is much the same. Without inhibitory effects a tone would sound like a noise of a certain pitch but not like a pure tone.

We can sum up by saying that the basilar membrane makes a rough, mechanical frequency analysis, and the auditory nervous system sharpens the analysis in some manner not yet understood. It is a part of the general functioning of the higher nerve centers, and it will be understood only when we know more about the functioning of these centers. If the answer is found for the ear, it will probably apply to the other sense organs as well.

## Deafness

Now let us run briefly over some of the types of hearing disorders, which have become much more understandable as a result of recent experimental researches.

Infections of the ear used to be responsible for the overwhelming majority of the cases of deafness. Twenty years ago in a large city hospital there was a death almost every day from such infections. Thanks to antibiotics, they can now be arrested, and, if treated in time, an ear infection is seldom either fatal or destructive of hearing, though occasionally an operation is necessary to scoop out the diseased part of the mastoid bone.

The two other principal types of deafness are those caused by destruction of the auditory nerves and by otosclerosis (a tumorous bone growth). Nerve deafness cannot be cured: no drug or mechanical manipulation or operation can restore the victim's hearing. But the impairment of hearing caused by otosclerosis can usually be repaired, at least in part.

Otosclerosis is an abnormal but painless growth in a temporal bone (i.e. at the side of the skull, near the middle ear; figure 7.10). If it does not invade a part of the ear that participates in the transmission of sound, no harm is done to the hearing. But if the growth happens to involve the stirrup footplate, it will reduce or even completely freeze the footplate's ability to make its piston-like movements; the vibrations of the eardrum then can no longer be transmitted to the inner ear. An otosclerotic growth can occur at any age, may slow down for many years, and may suddenly start up again. It is found more often in women than in men and seems to be accelerated by pregnancy.

Immobilization of the stirrup blocks the hearing of air-borne sound but leaves hearing by bone conduction unimpaired. This fact is used for diagnosis. A patient who has lost part of his hearing ability because of otosclerosis does not find noise disturbing to his understanding of speech; in fact, noise may even improve his discrimination of speech. There is an old story about a somewhat deaf English earl (in France it is a count) who trained his servant to beat a drum whenever someone else spoke, so that he could understand the speaker better. The noise of the drum made the speaker raise his voice to the earl's hearing range. For the hard-of-hearing earl the noise of the drum was tolerable, but for other listeners it masked what the speaker was saying, so that the earl enjoyed exclusive rights to his conversation.

Difficulty in hearing air-borne sound can be corrected by a hearing aid. Theoretically it should be possible to compensate almost any amount of such hearing loss, because techniques for amplifying sound are highly developed, particularly now with the help of the transistor. But there is a physiological limit to the amount of pressure amplification that the ear will stand. Heightening of the pressure eventually produces an unpleasant tickling sensation through its effect on skin tissue in the middle ear. The sensation can be avoided by using a bone-conduction earphone, pressed firmly against the surface of the skull, but this constant pressure is unpleasant to many people.

## Operations

As is widely known, there are now operations (e.g. "fenestration") which can cure otosclerotic deafness (figure 7.11). In the 19th century physicians realized that if they could somehow dislodge or loosen the immobilized stirrup footplate, they might restore hearing. Experimenters in France found that they could sometimes free the footplate sufficiently merely by pressing a blunt needle against the right spot on the stirrup. Although it works only occasionally, the procedure seems so simple that it has recently had a revival of popularity in the US. If the maneuver is successful (and I am told that 30 per cent of these operations are) the hearing improves immediately. But unfortunately the surgeon cannot get a clear look at the scene of the operation and must apply the pushing force at random. This makes the operation something of a gamble, and the patient's hearing may not only fail to be improved but may even be reduced. Moreover, the operation is bound to be ineffectual when a large portion of the footplate is fixed. There are other important objections to the operation. After all, it involves the breaking of bone, to free the adhering part of the stirrup. I do not think that bone-breaking can be improved to a standard procedure. In any case, precision cutting seems to me always superior to breaking, in surgery as in mechanics. This brings us to the operation called fenestration.

For many decades it has been known that drilling a small opening, even the size of a pinhead, in the bony wall of the inner ear on the footplate side can produce a remarkable improvement in hearing. The reason, now well understood, is quite simple. If a hole is made in the bone and then covered again with a flexible membrane, movements of the fluid in, for instance, the lateral canal of the vestibular organ can be transmitted to the fluid of the inner ear, and so vibrations are once again communicable from the middle to the inner ear. In the typical present fenestration operation the surgeon bores a small hole in the canal wall with a dental drill and then covers the hole with a flap of skin. The operation today is a straightforward surgical procedure, and all its steps are under accurate control.

## Hazards to hearing

I want to conclude by mentioning the problem of nerve deafness. Many cases of nerve deafness are produced by intense noise, especially noise with high-frequency components. Since there is no cure, it behoves us to look out for such exposures. Nerve deafness creeps up on us slowly, and we are not as careful as we should be to avoid exposure to intense noise. We should also be more vigilant about other hazards capable of producing nerve deafness, notably certain drugs and certain diseases.

We could do much to ameliorate the tragedy of deafness if we changed some of our attitudes toward it. Blindness evokes our instant sympathy, and we go out of our way to help the blind person. But deafness often goes unrecognized. If a deaf person misunderstands what we say, we are apt to attribute it to lack of intelligence instead of to faulty hearing. Very few people have the patience to help the deafened. To a deaf man the outside world appears unfriendly. He tries to hide his deafness, and this only brings on more problems.

## Bibliography

The early history of hearing – observations and theories, Georg von Békésy and Walter A. Rosenblith in *The Journal of the Acoustical Society of America*, Vol. 20, No. 6, pages 727–48, November 1948

Hearing: its psychology and physiology, Stanley Smith Stevens and Hallowell Davis, John Wiley & Sons, Inc., 1938

Physiological acoustics, Ernest Glen Wever and Merle Lawrence, Princeton University Press, 1954

# 8 Photoreception

## by E J W Barrington

Two main types of highly differentiated photoreceptor system have appeared in the invertebrates: the compound eyes of arthropods and the camera-type eyes of cephalopods. Enough is known of the mode of functioning of these, and of their probable past history, to show that they represent the evolution, along two very different lines, of organs that have some striking points of similarity with the vertebrate eye, not only in their pigments but also in certain details of their structural organization. Indeed, this is an aspect of animal organization which is of considerable significance – a convergence resulting from the widespread distribution of a common biochemical ground plan. In this instance the common feature is, of course, the nature of the photosensitive pigments.

Simple types of eyes are seen in the free-living Platyhelminthes and in the Annelida, where they are often composed of sensory cells associated with screening pigment cells. In their simplest form they may be no more than pigment spots, forming part of the general epithelium, but more usually they sink inwards to form cups. In the Turbellaria the pigment cells are often arranged to form the wall of an open bowl, the bipolar receptor cells projecting into this through its aperture. In such an eye there can be no possibility of forming an image, for there is no refractive structure. These organs are doubtless restricted to the differentiation of light and darkness, and in this way they make it possible for the animal to orientate itself with respect both to the intensity and to the source of the illumination. The distal ends of the receptor cells are differentiated to form a rod border, in which longitudinal striations can be seen with the light microscope. The function of this border is unknown, but it may have something in common with the rod-like differentiations that are seen in the receptor cells of more complex eyes, and that are known, as we shall see below, to be an essential element of these photoreceptors.

Cup-like arrangements of pigment cells are common in the eyes of polychaetes, but a higher level of differentiation is reached in this group. Not only do the receptor cells themselves have a rod-like tip, but the epithelium of the cup may produce secretions that fuse to form one or more lenses. Moreover, groups of sensory cells may be closely collected together to form ommatidia, recalling the unit structures of the compound eye of arthropods. Indeed, in sabellids (*Branchiomma*, for example) the ommatidia themselves may be grouped together to form a rudimentary type of compound eye. No doubt a similar tendency played an

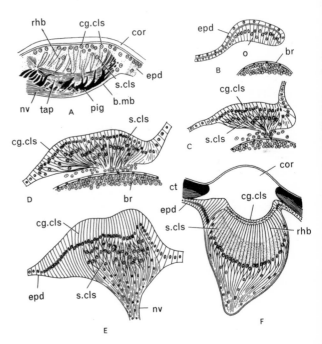

**Figure 8.1 Examples of the structure** and development of dorsal ocelli of insects. *A*, dorsal ocellus of *Machilis*. *B–F*, stages in the development of a dorsal ocellus of male of *Formica pratensis*, and mature median ocellus of same. *b.mb*, basement membrane; *br*, brain; *cg.cls*, corneagenous cells; *cor*, cornea; *ct*, cuticula; *epd*, epidermis; *nv*, nerve; *o*, ocellar rudiment in epidermis; *pig*, pigment; *rhb*, rhabdome; *s.cls*, sense cells; *tap*, tapetum. (Adapted from Snodgrass and used with permission.)

*first published in* Invertebrate Structure and Function, *1967, pages 282–90 (Nelson, London).*

important part in the ancestors of arthropods, contributing to the establishment of their characteristic compound eyes. Convergence was probably involved in the process of arthropodization, so much so that it is necessary to envisage the possibility of an independent evolution of compound eyes in more than one line. The situation in annelids goes some way to make the possibility of the independent evolution of compound eyes acceptable, although it does not reveal the actual ancestry of these organs.

Evidently the optic cup is the foundation upon which the varied types of arthropod eye have been formed. It is seen in the Onychophora, in which the eyes are a pair of closed vesicles into which a lens is secreted. It is seen also in the median eye of the nauplius larva, and in the dorsal ocelli of insects (figure 8.1). From a purely morphological point of view it is not difficult to visualize the evolution of such structures into the vertically elongated groups of cells that make up the ommatidia of the compound eye. This type of eye is seen at its simplest in the lateral eye of *Limulus*, which has provided material for experimental analysis of much elegance. It consists of about 1 000 ommatidia, each of which is formed of twelve retinula cells, together with an eccentrically placed nerve cell (figure 8.2). The retinula cells are arranged like the segments of an orange, packed radially around the dendrite of the nerve cell. Within the ommatidia is a photosensitive pigment based upon vitamin $A_1$ and retinene$_1$; these occur in the vertebrate eye, but the analogy with the latter is even closer than this.

Electron microscopy reveals that the rods and cones of the vertebrate retinula cells contain membranes arranged as closely packed discs. It is supposed that the visual pigments are arranged on or in these membranes, and that isomerization causes permeability changes, resulting in ionic movements and changes in membrane potential. Within the retinula cells of *Limulus* there are arrays of parallel tubules that suggest an obvious analogy with the ultrastructure of the vertebrate rods and cones. The similarity of the pigments makes it highly probable that the mechanisms of energy capture and transduction are fundamentally the same in the two groups. It is thus all the more significant that by using microelectrodes we can recognize generator potentials in the ommatidium of *Limulus*, and show that the eccentric nerve cell (the corresponding elements are, of course, arranged quite differently in the vertebrate retina) gives rise to the nerve impulses already mentioned.

Compound eyes of a more advanced type are found in crustaceans and insects; while varying greatly in detail, they are essentially of the plan in figure 8.3. Two refractive bodies are present: the lens, which is a biconvex thickening of the general cuticle, and the crystalline cone, secreted by a

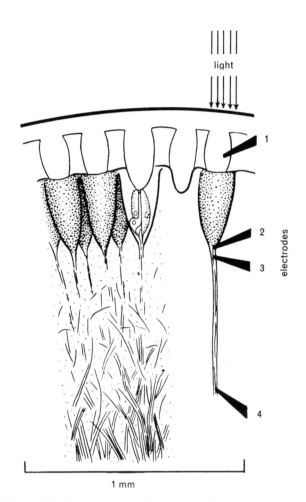

**Figure 8.2 Schematic drawing**, representing a section of lateral eye of *Limulus*, in a plane perpendicular to surface of cornea, as seen in fresh preparations. Transparent cornea at top, showing crystalline cones of the ommatidia; the heavily melanin-pigmented conical bodies of these form a layer on the inner surface of the cornea. On the left, a group of ommatidia is represented, with indications of bundles of nerve fibres traversing the plexus behind the ommatidia, collecting in larger bundles that become the optic nerve still farther back. One of these ommatidia has been represented as if the section had passed through it, revealing the sensory component, also as if sectioned. On the right an ommatidium with its nerve fibre bundle is represented as it appears after having been isolated by dissection and suspended, in air, on electrodes (moist cotton wicks, from chlorided silver tubes filled with sea water) represented by the solid black triangles. (From Hartline et al.)

107

group of vitrellar cells. Below these is a group of seven to eight receptor (retinula) cells, each of which forms a fibrillar rhabdomere along its length, the several rhabdomeres fusing to form the rhabdome. The visual pigment is probably located within the rhabdome, which may therefore be compared with the rods and cones of the vertebrate retina. Photostimulation is presumably initiated within the rhabdome, its result being the propagation of nerve impulses into the optic nerve along the nerve fibres that arise from the base of each retinula cell.

We can distinguish two main morphological types of compound eye, the apposition eye and the superposition eye (figures 8.4, 8.5). In both types the ommatidium is structurally a separate and self-contained unit, separated from its

**Figure 8.4 Diagram of an ommatidium** of an apposition eye. *c.l*, cornea lens; *c.c*, crystalline cone; *s.c*, sense cells. In the cross-section the individual rhabdomeres can be recognized in the rhabdome (*r.m*). (From Kuiper.)

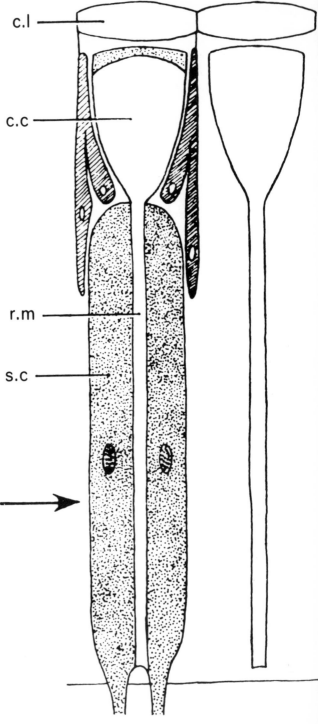

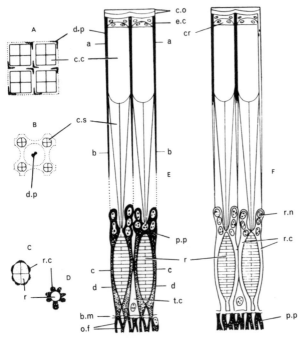

**Figure 8.3 Structure of the ommatidia** of *Astacus astacus* (redrawn from Bernhards). *A, B, C, D*, tangential cross sections of four (*A, B*) ommatidia or one (*C, D*) ommatidium at the levels indicated in *E* by *aa, bb, cc,* and *dd*, respectively. *E*, radial (axial) section of two ommatidia showing the pigment in the light-adapted condition providing maximum shielding of each single unit. *F*, similar view in the dark-adapted condition with a condition of minimum light shielding by pigment. The facet diameter of such an eye is about 60 $\mu$. *b.m*, basilar membrane; *c.c*, crystalline cone; *c.o*, cornea (lens); *c.s*, stalk of crystalline cone; *cr*, crystalline cone cells; *d.p*, distal pigment; *e.c*, corneagenous cells; *o.f*, optic nerve fibres of retinal cells; *p.p*, proximal pigment; *r*, rhabdome; *r.c*, retinular cells; *r.n*, retinular cell nucleus; *t.c*, tapetal cell. (From Waterman.)

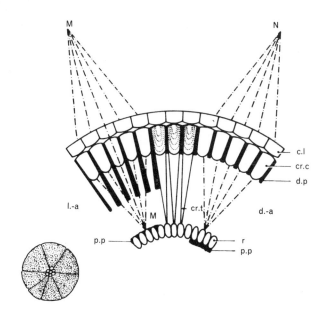

**Figure 8.5 Diagram of the light rays** in the superposition eye. The position of the distal pigment (*d.p*) and the proximal pigment (*p.p*) is shown in the light-adapted state (*l.-a*) and the dark-adapted state (*d.-a*). In the three central ommatidia the hypothetical laminated structure of the cones is indicated; here also the crystalline tracts (*cr.t*) are drawn. The corneal lenses (*c.l*) are usually not drawn in such diagrams though they often have a greater refractive power than the cones. *m* and *n* are two light sources and *r* is the retinula. (From Kuiper.)

neighbours by groups of distal and proximal pigment and reflecting cells. Where the types differ is in the degree of functional independence of the ommatidia, a factor that has an important influence on the mode of functioning of the eye.

The apposition type is particularly characteristic of terrestrial, littoral, and diurnal species, including the Hymenoptera and Diptera amongst the insects. Its receptor cells are greatly elongated, extending distally as far as the crystalline cone. According to the classical mosaic theory of vision, each ommatidium receives light from the very small area that corresponds to its geometrical projection. This means that the image formed by the eye as a whole must be a mosaic of areas corresponding in number to the ommatidia. In the superposition eye – found, for example, in lobsters, crabs, and nocturnal insects – the retinal cells are widely separated from the crystalline cone, and it is supposed that each receptor cell is stimulated by light that has entered through a number of ommatidial lenses. This type of

eye is suited for vision in dim light, which might not be an adequate stimulus if each receptor cell received only the rays that had entered through its own ommatidium. The resulting overlapping of images, however, will yield poor resolution, whereas much better resolution is to be expected from the isolated images formed by the apposition eye.

This interpretation would indicate that the pigment cells cooperate in visual function by modifying the degree of isolation of the ommatidia. Their behaviour varies greatly from species to species, but in general they seem to be of greater importance in the superposition eye. Here, in conditions of strong illumination, the pigment moves within the cells to screen the retinal cells, so that they can only be stimulated by light entering along the ommatidial axis. In this condition the eye is said to be light-adapted (figure 8.3). In dim light the pigment moves to expose the retinal cells, which can now be reached by light from a wider source, a condition in which the eye is said to be dark-adapted (figure 8.3).

Evidently, many arthropods are unable to secure precise discrimination of form in their visual field. Often they will only distinguish degrees of shade and illumination, but even so the compound structure of the eye probably aids detection of movement, because of the continuously changing pattern of ommatidial illumination. These matters are still very imperfectly understood, but new experimental approaches are leading to re-assessments of old problems. For example, it has been widely supposed that the apposition eye favours the discrimination of form through acuity of resolution. Recent electronic studies, however, have shown that the field of vision of a single ommatidium is much larger than was formerly believed. Thus a single ommatidium of the eye of *Locusta* receives light over an angle of 20°, which means that a single point source must stimulate many ommatidia. Yet this same eye can detect movement, and discriminate pattern, when the angle subtended by the movement or source is only of the order of 0.3°. The sensitivity of the compound eye in this instance is certainly much higher than might have been predicted – perhaps, according to a suggestion of Burtt and Catton, because additional images are formed deeper in the eye by groups of ommatidia. It is at least quite clear from behaviour studies, to which we shall be referring later, that some insects are well able to discriminate form and, by virtue of this capacity, to learn the landmarks in their neighbourhood.

It is equally clear that certain insects can discriminate colour, so that this capacity, too, must be latent in the structure of the compound eye. It has been supposed that the basis of colour vision in vertebrates is the presence of three pigments, differing from each other in their spectral sensitivity, and there are now some reasons for believing that a similar explanation may apply to the compound eye. This is a field of investigation only recently opened up with the aid of electronic techniques. Already, however, it has been possible to explore the responses of single retinal cells in the compound eyes of the blowfly, *Calliphora erythrocephala*, and to show that the degree of depolarization depends upon the wavelength of the light, as well as upon its intensity. This has led to the recognition of three types of receptor cell in this eye. All three show a peak response at a wavelength of about 350 mμ, in the ultraviolet range, but they differ from each other in respect of a second peak. In one of the types, the most abundant one, this peak lies at about 490 mμ (green-type receptor), while in the other two it lies respectively at below 470 mμ (blue-type receptor) and at above 520 mμ (yellow-green type). Obviously the differences between these several pigments are very small, and so the central nervous system must be highly specialized to differentiate between the varying patterns of excitation that are transmitted to it from the eyes. In this there is nothing either surprising or improbable. On the contrary, as Burkhardt points out in his discussion of these results, it is much easier to imagine the evolution of colour

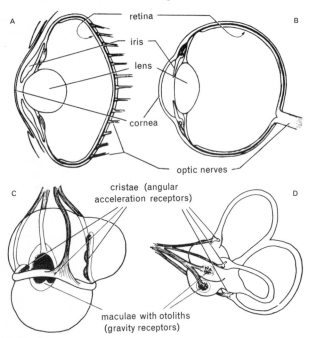

**Figure 8.6 Parallel development** of sensory receptors in man and the octopus. *A* and *B* are longitudinal vertical sections through the eyes of an octopus and of a man respectively. *C* and *D* show the statocysts of *Octopus* and the labyrinth of the inner ear of man. (After Young, and Wells.)

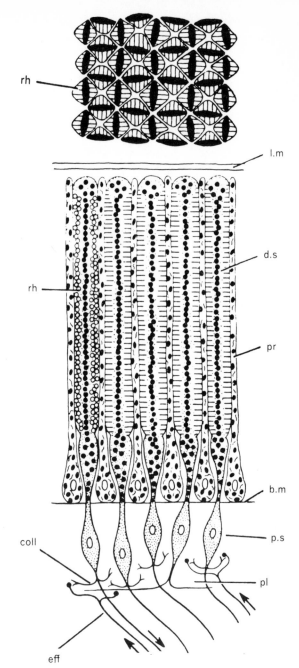

**Figure 8.7 Diagram of probable arrangement** of the elements of the retina of *Octopus*. *Above*, as seen in tangential section; *below*, in radial section. *b.m*, basal membrane; *coll*, collateral of retinal fibre; *eff*, efferent axon to the retina; *d.s*, distal segment of retinal cell; *l.m*, limiting membrane; *p.s*, proximal segment of retinal cell; *pl*, plexus beneath retina; *pr*, process of supporting cell (probably thinner); *rh*, rhabdomes. The second retinal cell from the right has been wrongly shown; it should carry a fibre to the optic nerve. (From Young.)

**Figure 8.8 Orientation of the eyes** before and after bilateral statocyst removal. In unoperated animals the slit-like pupil normally remains horizontal or very nearly so (*A–E*), whatever the position of the octopus. After removal of both statocysts this ceases to be true, and the orientation of the retina, as indicated by the position of the pupil, thereafter depends upon the position in which the animal is sitting (*F, G*). Pictures traced from projections of Kodachrome transparencies: *C, D,* and *E* are of comparatively large (500 g) octopuses, the rest of small (15–25 g) animals in an aquarium set up in front of a vertically striped background; in *B* and *F* the aquarium with the animals sitting on the bottom, has been tipped through 45°. (From Wells.)

vision by the accumulation of small changes in pigment properties rather than by the sudden emergence of entirely new types of photosensitive substance.

We have suggested that the history of the arthropod eye is to be traced through the increasing elaboration of the simple vesicular eyes found in lower invertebrates; this also seems to be the case in the molluscan eye. In the more primitive forms, as, for example, in *Patella*, the eyes are no more than open invaginations of the epidermis, lined with pigment and receptor cells, but with no lens. In more advanced forms the opening of the vesicle is narrowed and closed, the vesicle then containing either a fluid secretion or a lens. Such organs are presumably used for orientation,

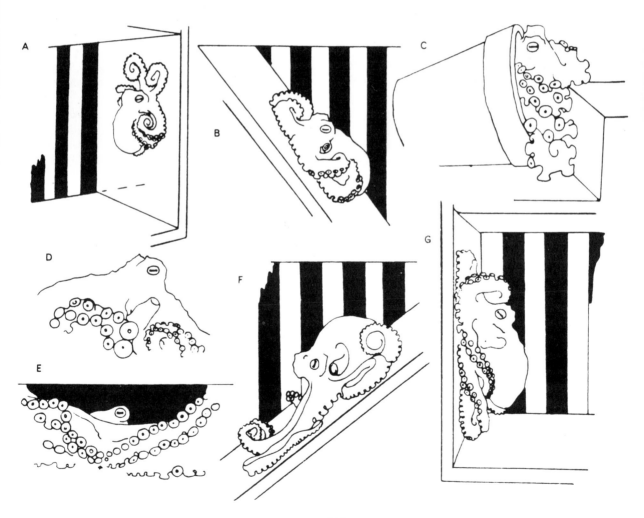

since they can have no capacity for form discrimination. More specialized arrangements are seen in the more active molluscs, such as *Pecten*, where the pallial tentacles bear highly differentiated eyes, each with a lens and an inverted retina. Even here, however, these organs can do no more than detect movements and shadows, capacities that are none the less of first importance in animals that are capable of such rapid swimming responses.

As might be expected, it is in the cephalopods, with their generally high level of activity and response, that the molluscan eye reaches its peak of differentiation. Superficially, the eye of dibranchiates such as *Octopus* greatly resembles that of vertebrates, and presents in this respect a classical example of convergence (figure 8.6). Yet its mode of development is different, while in some ways its retinal organization is more akin to that of the compound eye of arthropods. In *Nautilus* the eye is still simple, being a cup-shaped invagination with a small opening to the outside and lacking any lens. The dibranchiate eye still develops in this way, so that it is formed in its entirety direct from the epidermis; the vertebrate eye, by contrast, develops centrifugally as an outgrowth of the central nervous system. These differences in mode of development account for the cephalopod retina being the direct type, with the sensory ends of the receptor cells directed towards the source of light, whereas the retina of vertebrates is inverted, with the sensory ends turned away from the source of light. The eventual resemblances between the eyes, however, are all the more remarkable. In the cephalopod the invagination closes over, the lining forming the retina while a lens develops at the point of fusion. Later an iris is formed, so that a pupillary opening is delimited, and the whole becomes covered by a transparent cornea associated with eyelids. Focusing is effected through the ciliary muscle which contributes to the suspension of the lens, relaxation of the muscle leaving the lens in position for distant viewing.

The optic potentialities of this eye, by analogy with the vertebrate eye, would seem to be excellent, yet it is limited in its capacities by the organization of the retinal elements. These are arranged (figure 8.7) in groups that recall to some extent the ommatidia of the arthropod eye. The retinula cells, which are pigmented, are arranged in groups surrounding a rhabdome, which is composed of four rhabdomeres. Like the rods and cones of vertebrates, and the rhabdomes of arthropods, these rhabdomeres have a complex fine structure, each consisting of piles of tubules. The important feature of these piles, and one that probably has a fundamental effect upon the mode of behaviour of these animals, is that the piles are so arranged that two of them lie in the horizontal plane and two in the vertical plane. Each pair (vertical or horizontal, as the case may be) is related to a distinct nerve fibre.

Behaviour studies of the octopus show that this animal has marked powers of form discrimination, but that these depend largely upon the estimation and comparison of horizontal and vertical extents. Thus it can readily discriminate between horizontal and vertical rectangles but cannot discriminate between oblique ones. It has been suggested that this limitation is a consequence of the horizontal and vertical orientation within its receptor elements, an orientation that is also detectable in the dendrite fields of the optic lobes into which the impulses from the eyes are discharged. The importance of this orientation is further suggested by the octopus maintaining a constant orientation of its eyes, irrespective of the position in which the body may be held (figure 8.8). This orientation depends upon information received from the statocysts. If these organs are removed the orientation of the eyes is disturbed; for example, they may be held at an angle of 90° from their normal position, and in these circumstances the animal may interpret vertical rectangles as horizontal ones, and vice versa. Clearly the apparent convergence of the cephalopod and the vertebrate eye is superficial and deceptive, and is applicable only to the more general features of the structure of these organs. Closer analysis shows that the mode of functioning of the dibranchiate eye, and its relationships with the statocyst, attain a very high level of specialization in details that have no parallel in the vertebrates.

## Figure references

Snodgrass, R. E., *Principles of Insect Morphology* (McGraw-Hill, New York, 1935)

Hartline, H. K., Wagner, H. G. and MacNichol, E. F., Cold Spring Harb. Symp. quant, Biol., Vol. 17, pages 125–141 (1952)

Waterman, T. H., in *The Physiology of Crustacea*, Vol. 2, edit. T. H. Waterman, pages 1–64 (1961)

Kuiper, Symp. Soc. exp. Biol., Vol. 16, pages 58–71 (1961)

Wells, *Advmt Sci. Lond.*, Vol. 17, pages 461–471 (1961)

Young, J. Z., *Biol. Rev.*, Vol. 36, pages 32–96 (1961)

Wells, M., *J. exp. Biol.*, Vol. 37, pages 489–499 (1960)

# 9 The eye
## by Alfred Sherwood Romer

The vertebrate body is subjected constantly to radiations which may vary from the extremely short but rapid waves of cosmic rays and those from atomic disintegration to the long, slow undulations utilized for radio transmission; in figures, from waves with as high a frequency as some quintillion vibrations per second and a length of a fraction of a billionth of a centimeter, to others with only a few hundreds or thousands of oscillations per second and a theoretic wavelength measurable in miles. Many of these radiations affect protoplasm, but specific sensitivity to them appears to be limited to a narrow band part way between the two extremes; for knowledge of other wavelengths we must resort to mechanisms which transform their effects into terms receivable by our own limited senses. It is not unreasonable to find that the animal band of sensitivity corresponds in great measure to the range of radiations reaching the earth from the sun, since that body is the source of the vast bulk of the radiations that normally reach us. Of this band, slower waves are received as heat, faster, shorter waves perceived as light – the process of *photoreception*.

The general composition of the vertebrate eye (figures 9.1, 9.2) may first be noted before considerations of details. Leaving aside for the moment various accessories, we find that the essential structure is the roughly spherical *eyeball*, situated in a recess, the *orbit*, on either side of the braincase, and connected with the brain by an *optic nerve* contained in a stalk emerging from the internal surface. The eyeball has an essentially radial symmetry, with a main axis running from inner to outer aspects. Internally, there is a set of chambers filled with watery or gelatinous liquids. In the interior, well toward the front, lies a *lens*. The walls of the hollow sphere are formed basically of three layers, in order, from the outside inward, the *scleroid* and *choroid* coats, and the retina. The scleroid is a complete sphere, choroid and retinal coats are incomplete externally. The first two are of mesenchyme origin and are essentially supporting and nutri-

tive in function; the retina (actually a double layer) includes the sensory part of the eye system where visual stimuli are received and transferred to the brain via the optic nerve. At the outer end of the eyeball the scleroid coat is modified to form, with the overlying skin, the transparent *cornea*. Externally, choroid and retinal layers are fused and modified. Opposite the margins of the lens the conjoined layers usually expand to form a *ciliary body*, from which the lens may be suspended. Forward beyond this point the two fused layers curve inward parallel to the lens to form the *iris*, but leave a centrally situated opening, the *pupil*.

The general nature of the operation of the eye is commonly (and reasonably) compared to that of a simple box camera. The chamber of the eyeball corresponds to the dark interior of the camera box. In the eye the lens (and in land vertebrates the cornea as well) operates, like the camera lens, in focusing the light properly upon the sheet of sensitive materials in the back of the chamber; the retina functions in reception of the image as does the camera film. The iris of the eye is comparable to the similarly named diaphragm of the camera, regulating the size of the pupil.

## Sclera and cornea

The outermost eye sheath is that of the scleroid coat, or sclera, a stiff external structure which preserves the shape of the eye ball and resists pressure, internal or external, which might modify this shape. In cyclostomes and mammals, at the two extremes of the scale of living vertebrates, it consists entirely of dense connective tissue. In most groups, however, this is reinforced by the development of cartilage or bone. Often there is a cartilaginous cup enclosing much of the eyeball posteriorly; in birds this sometimes ossifies. Further protection against pressures is afforded by the frequent presence of a *scleral ring* (figure 9.3), a series of bony plates, fixed in position, lying in the sclera in front of the "equator". Fossil evidence shows that such a ring was present in ancestral vertebrates and continued onward along all the main lines of vertebrate evolution. It has, however, disappeared in many groups, and is found today only in actinopterygian fishes, numerous reptiles and birds.

*first published in* The Vertebrate Body, *4th edition, 1970, pages 447–60 (W. B. Saunders Co., Philadelphia and London).*

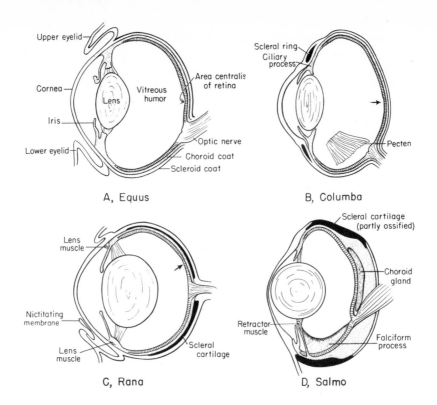

A, Equus

B, Columba

C, Rana

D, Salmo

**Figure 9.1 Diagrammatic vertical sections** through the eye of *A*, a horse; *B*, a dove; *C*, a common frog; *D*, a teleost (salmon). Connective tissue of sclera and cornea unshaded; scleral ring or cartilage black; choroid, ciliary body, and iris stippled; retina hatched. Arrows point to the fovea. In *B* is shown the pecten, lying to one side of the midline. In *D* the section is slightly to one side of the choroid fissure through which the falciform process enters the eyeball. (After Rochon-Duvigneaud, Walls.)

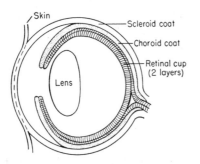

**Figure 9.2 Diagrammatic section** of an eye to show the arrangement of the successive embryonic layers.

Primitively, it appears, the ring consisted in fishes of four plates, but it is reduced in living ray-finned forms to two elements (or to one or none). In the crossopterygian ancestors of land vertebrates and the older fossil amphibians the number of plates was greatly increased, often to a score or more, and a high count is still present in reptiles and birds.

The superficial, external part of the sphere of sclerotic tissue is the translucent cornea, through which light enters the eyeball. Primitively, the cornea appears to have lain beneath the skin as a distinct structure, and this is still the case in lampreys. In all gnathostomes, however, the scleral coat and skin fuse inseparably in the adult; the skin component of the cornea and the sensitive skin area beneath the lid folds constitute the *conjunctiva*.

The refractive index of the cornea – its ability, that is, to deflect the course of light waves – is practically the same as that of water. Hence in primitive water-dwelling vertebrates the cornea has no power to act as a lens structure. In air, however, the curved cornea does much of the work of focusing and relieves the lens of much of this task. Its importance is shown by the fact that in ourselves many defects such as astigmatism calling for optical correction are due to departures of the cornea from its proper form as a segment of a sphere.

114

# Choroid

The inner of the two mesodermal layers of the eyeball is that of the choroid coat. This contrasts strongly with the sclera, for it is a soft material containing numerous blood vessels which are particularly important for the sustenance of the retina. The choroid is pigmented and absorbs most of the light reaching it after penetrating the retina. But in addition, the choroid of many vertebrates, from elasmobranchs to a variety of mammals, includes a light-reflecting device, most familiar to us as seen in the ghostly eyes of a night-prowling cat illuminated by automobile headlights. This phenomenon is due to the *tapetum lucidum*, generally developed in nocturnal terrestrial animals and in fishes which live deep in the water. With plenty of light coming to the eye, internal reflection is not needed and is in fact harmful, since it may confuse the details of the visual image. Where light is scarce, however, conservation of light rays, turned back to the retina by this mirror, more than makes up for the disadvantages.

Tapeta are variously constructed. In one type, common in hoofed mammals, the inner part of the choroid develops as a sheet of glistening connective tissue fibers which act as a mirror of sorts. In a second type, exemplified in carnivorous mammals, elasmobranchs and some marine teleosts, the cells of this part of the choroid form an epithelium filled with fiber-like crystals of guanine. Although the tapetum when present is normally formed in the choroid, some teleosts develop a guanine mirror in the pigment layer of the retina.

# Iris

This structure, universally present, is formed by a combination of modified segments of both choroid and retinal layers of the eyeball. Both layers have in this region lost their most characteristic functions – vascular supply and photorecep-

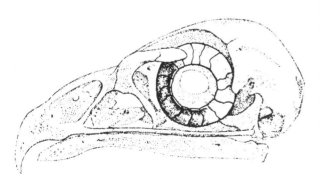

**Figure 9.3 A skull** of a bird (Aquila), showing the scleral ring in place. (From Edinger.)

tion, respectively. In attenuated form, they join to furnish an "external" covering for the lens and retinal cavity, and outline the pupil – the restricted opening through which light penetrates into the inner recesses of the eyeball. The iris is universally pigmented. Its inner (retinal) layer, for example, gives in man a blue effect, while brown pigments which may mask the blue are added by the outer (choroid) component. In a number of fish groups the iris is fixed in dimensions, except where forward or backward movement of the lens may affect its distension and the consequent size of the pupil. In sharks, however, some teleosts, and in tetrapods generally, muscle cells are present – striated fibers in most reptiles and birds, smooth in amphibians and mammals (mixed in crocodilians). Arranged in circular and radial patterns, as sphincters and dilators, these fibers may contract or expand the pupillary opening. This gives the iris the function of a camera diaphragm: the pupil may be expanded in dim light for maximum illumination, contracted in bright light for protection of the retina and for more precise definition. Nocturnal forms tend to have a slit-shaped pupil which closes more readily to exclude bright light.

# The lens and accommodation

In land vertebrates light rays are strongly refracted as they enter the cornea, which consequently does much of the work of focusing. In fishes this is not the case, and the entire task is thus performed by the lens itself. In consequence, we find that the fish lens has a spherical shape, which gives it the highest possible power, and is situated far outward in the eyeball to afford the maximum distance for the convergence of rays on to the retina. In land vertebrates, in which the cornea relieves it of its optical task except for "fine adjustment", the lens is less rounded (the primate lens is exceptionally flat) and is situated farther back in the eye cavity. The lens is formed of elongated collagen fibers, wound about in a complicated pattern of concentric layers; it nevertheless has excellent optical properties and is completely transparent. It is firm in shape and, in lower vertebrates, resistant to distortion.

In cyclostomes the lens is not attached to the walls of the eyeball; pressure from the "vitreous humor" behind it and the cornea in front fixes it in place. In all other groups, however, the lens is attached peripherally by a belt of tissues of some sort. This may be (as in elasmobranchs) a circular membrane or zonule, shaped like a plumber's washer; in most cases, however, the suspensory structure consists of a circular belt of zonule fibers. The area of attachment of these fibers is a ring-shaped region of conjoined choroid and retinal layers, the ciliary body, lying opposite the equator of the lens. The inner surface of this body is an epithelium formed by retinal tissue; its substance is derived from the choroid.

As every user of a camera is aware, it is impossible to obtain exact "definition" of objects at varied distances without adjustment of the lens focus. Such adjustment in the eye is termed *accommodation*. The eyes of most vertebrates are capable of accommodation; but, curiously, it is attained in a different fashion in almost every major group. The methods used may be broadly classified as follows:

A Lens moved to achieve accommodation:

   *1* Fixed position for near vision; moved backward to accommodate for distant objects (lampreys and teleosts)

   *2* Fixed position for far vision; moved forward to accommodate for near objects (elasmobranchs, amphibians)

B Shape of lens modified; fixed form for far vision, expanded shape for near objects (amniotes)

In lampreys and teleosts the lens is normally at its most "forward" position and is thus adjusted for nearby objects. For distant vision the lens is, in lampreys, pushed back by a flattening of the cornea, which it directly underlies (the flattening is accomplished by an external somatic muscle peculiar to these animals). In teleosts there is an unusual situation in that the embryonic choroid fissure in the floor of the eye remains open. Through it projects an elongated vascular structure, the *falciform process* (figure 9.1), serving a nutritive function for the interior of the eyeball. From the front edge of this process there generally takes origin a small *retractor lentis muscle* (of mesodermal origin) which attaches to the lower edge of the lens and pulls it backward.

In elasmobranchs the lens, most strongly suspended by a dorsal ligament, is fixed for distant vision; for close sight it is swung forward by the pull of a small protractor muscle attached to the ventral rim of the lens.

The amphibian lens movement is the same as that of sharks – a forward pull of the lens for close-up focus. All amphibians have a small ventral muscle which pulls forward on the lens, and in anurans there is a second, dorsal muscle as well.

In all amniotes the second principal mode of accommodation is present. The lens is somewhat flexible and capable of changing its shape from a flattened condition adjusted to far vision to more rounded contours for near sight. These changes in shape are accomplished by smooth muscles situated in the ciliary body. But despite this basic agreement among amniotes, we find that (perversely) reptiles and birds, on the one hand, and mammals on the other, do the trick in two different ways. In typical reptiles and in birds the greatly developed ciliary body has a ring of padlike processes which extend inward to gain a contact with the periphery of the lens. When circular muscle fibers of the ciliary body contract, these processes push in on the lens and force it to bulge into the more rounded shape suitable for near vision.

In reptiles and birds the zonule fibers are unimportant. In mammals, however, the ciliary body does not touch the lens; this is suspended by the fibers, which attach at the back edge of the ciliary region (figure 9.4). The pull of the fibers holds the lens, when the ciliary muscles are relaxed, in a flattened condition suitable for distant vision. Contraction of the ciliary muscles brings the region to which the fibers attach outward, closer to the lens; the fibers relax, and the elastic lens, released from tension, takes a more rounded shape. The amniote type of mechanism is efficient in many regards, but is effective only if the lens retains its elasticity. In man, as older readers know, it stiffens with age, accommodation diminishes, and without artificial aids a book can be read only at arm's length, if at all. Further, the ciliary musculature is poorly developed in many mammals, and a large variety of forms, ranging from rats to cows, lack powers of accommodation and are permanently far-sighted.

Why this great variety of methods to attain a single result? One may more than suspect that it is due to the absence of any device of this sort in the ancestral vertebrates (some fish still have none today). Over the long course of hundreds of millions of years various major vertebrate groups have all solved the problem of accommodation, but have solved it independently of one another, each in its own fashion.

## Cavities of the eyeball

Much of the eyeball is, as far as function goes, merely a blank space which need only be filled by some substance which will not block or distort light rays passing through. This filling is in the form of liquids, here known under the old-fashioned name of humors. The principal cavity of the eyeball, between lens and retina, is filled by the *vitreous humor*, a thick, jelly-like material. In front of the lens is the *aqueous humor*, a thinner watery liquid (as it needs particularly to be in lower vertebrates where the lens moves to and fro in this area). The cavity filled by aqueous humor between the cornea and iris is termed the *anterior chamber* of the eye, the *posterior chamber* is not, as one might think, that filled by the vitreous humor, but the area – never of any great dimensions – which the aqueous humor may occupy between iris and lens (figure 9.4).

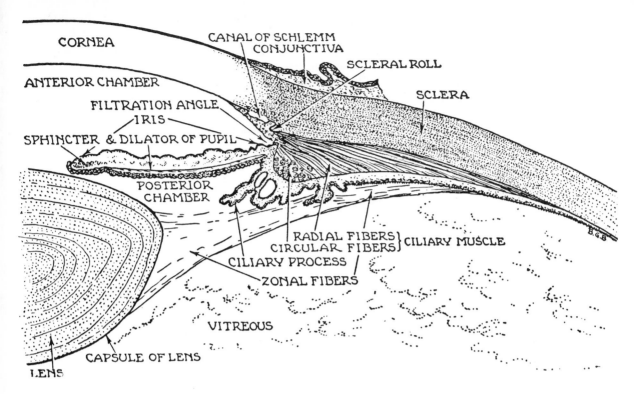

**Figure 9.4 Details of the outer segment** of the human eye. (From Fulton.)

Intrusive structures are sometimes found in the eye cavity occupied by the vitreous humor. We have already noted the intrusion of the falciform process of teleosts. In reptiles a *papillary cone* projects into this cavity from the region of attachment of the optic nerve. This is a highly vascular structure which presumably aids in the supply of nutritive substances to the retina by diffusion through the vitreous humor. In birds this projection has developed into the *pecten* (figure 9.1*B*), a characteristic structure of this class. The pecten is, like its reptilian homologue, a source of nutritive or oxygen supply, but its usual shape, with pronounced parallel ridges, leads to the belief that it is, in addition, a visual aid. It is suggested that the shadows of these ridges, falling on the retina, act as a grille ruling, and that small or distant moving objects are more readily discerned as their images pass from one component to another on this grille. The presence of a pecten may be responsible, in part at least, for the high visual powers attributed to many birds.

## Retina

All other parts of the eye are subordinate in importance to the retina; their duty is to see that the light rays are brought in proper arrangement and focus to this sensory structure for its stimulation and the transfer of these stimuli inward to the brain. Embryologically the retina is a double-layered structure; in the adult, however, the two layers are fused. The outer one is thin and unimportant; it contributes nothing but a set of pigment cells to reinforce the pigment present external to it in the choroid. The complex sensory and nervous mechanisms of the retina all develop from its inner layer.

The nature of the retina varies greatly from form to form and from one part to another of a single retina. Frequently, however, a sectioned retina has the general appearance seen at the left in figure 9.5. Externally, next to the choroid, there is the thin pigmented layer; just inside this, a zone showing perpendicular striations; inside this, again, three distinct zones containing circular objects recognizable as cell nuclei. Special methods of staining reveal the nature of this stratification. The striated zone contains the elongated tips of the light-receiving cells, the rods and cones; the outer nuclear zone contains the cell bodies and nuclei of these structures. The nuclear zone next in order is that of the bipolar cells, which transmit the impulses inward from the rods and cones, and of accessory types of retinal nerve cells. The innermost nuclei are those of ganglion cells which pick up the stimuli from the bipolar elements and send fibers along the optic nerve to the brain.

The *rods* and *cones* are the actual photoreceptors of the system. They receive their names from their usual shape in mammals. Each cell includes a sensory tip directed outward toward the choroid, a thickened section and (beneath a membrane lying at this level of the retina) a basal piece containing the nucleus. In most mammalian eyes the two types are readily distinguishable: the rod cell is slenderly built throughout; the cone cell has generally a short broad tip and broad "body". In other groups, however, rods and cones vary greatly in shape and are sometimes difficult to tell apart.

One is immediately impressed by the fact that rod and cone cells in the vertebrate retina are *pointing the wrong way!* In a "logically" constructed retina, the tips of the photoreceptors should point toward the light source, and the parts of the retina which carry the impulses inward toward the brain should be farther removed. Some invertebrate eyes are so built, but not those of vertebrates, in which the light has to plunge through the full depth of the retina before reaching the point of reception. Various theories have been made to account for this anomalous situation — theories based mainly on the fact that the retina is a brain outgrowth. A reasonable assumption is that visual cells first appeared in the floor (or side wall) of the brain cavity and were able to function with upwardly (and inwardly) pointing tips, owing to a translucent build of the head in ancestral chordates. (Such cells appear to be present in the Amphioxus spinal cord.) When such cell groups became outfolded optic vesicles, the retinal elements simply retained their original orientation.

Considerable data are currently at hand regarding the chemistry of photoreception. All sensitive retinal cells contain substances consisting of special retinal proteins plus some type of carotenoid pigment related to vitamin A. The tips of the rods in land-living vertebrates and most marine fishes contain a substance known as visual purple, chemically termed *rhodopsin*. Light reception causes a breaking down of the visual purple and nerve stimulation; in the dark rhodopsin is reconstituted. A more primitive vertebrate rod chemical, however, is a "visual red", *porphyropsin*, formed from a vitamin A of somewhat different composition than that of rhodopsin; this is present in lampreys, fresh water fishes and larval amphibians. The cones have visual pigments, *iodopsin* and *cyanopsin*, of violet and bluish tints, closely comparable to the two types in the rods.

Rods and cones differ markedly in their functions, as one can determine from his own eyes, where the cones are concentrated in the center of the field of vision, the rods situated, in the main, peripherally. (1) Good illumination is necessary before the cones come into play; rods are effective in faint light, and it is calculated that rod stimulation can be produced by a single quantum, the smallest theoretic unit of energy. At night one can often catch a glimpse of a faint star in the margin of the field of vision, but fail to see it if looking directly at it. (2) Cones as a group give good visual details; rods give a more blurred picture. For accurate detail we focus the cone-bearing center of the eye on the object; things seen peripherally with the rods are blurred and indistinct. (3) Cones give color vision; rods give black-and-white effects only. In one's visual field, peripheral objects are gray and colorless.

Color vision is widespread in vertebrates, but very far from universal. Obviously there is little if any color vision in forms in which cones are rare or absent. But it is none too certain that color vision is present, or if present is similar to our own, even where cones or cone-like structures are found in the retina. Observation and experiment on living animals are necessary to determine whether color sensitivity is present. Many teleosts have color vision, as do many reptiles and most birds, but there is no proof of color vision in elasmobranchs and amphibians. In mammals as a whole relatively few of those tested show much response to color; the ancestral mammals, it is believed, were mainly nocturnal forms, with rods predominating in the eyes. The high color sensitivity of higher primates, including man, is an exceptional situation in mammals; to a dog or cat the world is probably gray, or has at the most faint pastel tints.

The distribution of rods and cones in different animals and in different retinal regions is highly variable. As would be expected, rods dominate in nocturnal animals, or fishes dwelling in deeper waters; cones are more abundant in forms active by day. Since, however, members of a given order or class may differ widely in their habits, the distribution of rod and cone types of retinas does not sort out well taxonomically. In an "average" vertebrate probably not over 5 per cent or so of the total photoreceptive cells are cones. Retinas containing rods alone are found in many sharks and some deep sea teleosts, and a relatively few nocturnal forms in the amniote classes. Eyes which, on the other hand, have cones only are also known in a few amniotes of each class. A majority of reptiles and birds have eyes relatively rich in cones and hence mainly suited for daytime life. In teleosts there are to be found "twin" cones, with partially fused cell bodies.

Rods and cones may both be present in any retinal region. Often, however, in forms in which both types of cell are common, there develops a distribution such as that in our own eyes. In this pattern the cones are but sparingly present over most of the retinal area and concentrated, to the practical exclusion of rods, in a central region in which

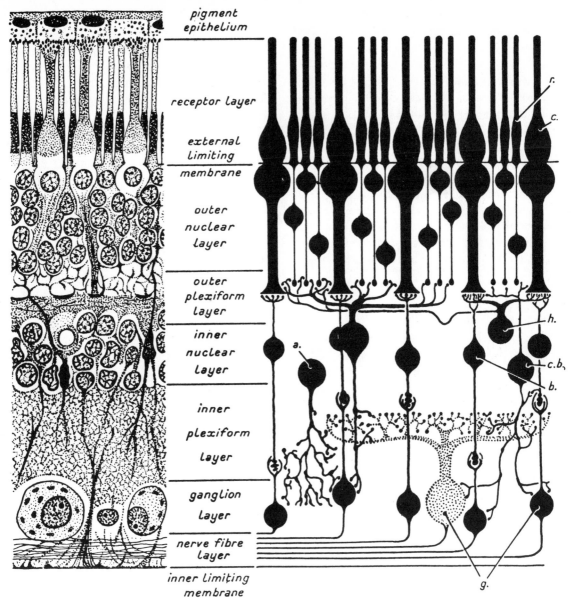

pigment
epithelium

receptor layer

external
limiting
membrane

outer
nuclear
layer

outer
plexiform
layer

inner
nuclear
layer

inner
plexiform
layer

ganglion
layer

nerve fibre
layer

inner limiting
membrane

**Figure 9.5** *Left*, Vertical section through the retina of a mammal; *Right*, retinal connections are revealed by silver impregnation. *a* and *h*, Nervous elements of more or less uncertain function. Other abbreviations: *b*, bipolar cells associated with single cones; *c*, cones; *cb*, bipolar cells, connecting with a series of rods; *g*, ganglion cells; *r*, rods. (From Walls, partly after Polyak.)

vision is most acute and perception of detail best developed. This is the *area centralis* (sometimes termed *macula lutea* because, exceptionally, the area has a yellow tinge in man). Frequently there is present here a *fovea* as well, a depression in the surface of the area centralis from which blood vessels and the inner layers of cells have been cleared away.

In many birds (and in some lizards as well) there is, curiously, a development of two central areas in each eye, one centrally situated, the other well toward the posterior or outer region. The bird's eye normally is pointed well to the side, and the primary central area is aimed at this lateral visual field. In bird flight, vision straight ahead is of great importance; the secondary center gives each eye a perception of detail in the anterior part of each visual field.

Inward from the rods and cones is a layer which consists for the most part of *bipolar cells*; and, well to the inner surface of the retina, a third cell layer is that of *ganglion cells.* The bipolar cells have short processes serving to connect with rods and cones on the one hand and with ganglion cells on the other; the latter cells are neurons from which long fibers relay on into the brain the impulses initiated by light reception. Both bipolar and ganglion layers include in addition peculiar types of cells which appear to make cross connections between the various direct pathways. It appears that often (although not always) one cone cell alone connects with a given bipolar cell, and only one such bipolar cell connects with an associated ganglion cell; thus each cone may have an individual pathway to optic nerve and brain. On the other hand, a considerable number of rods always converge into a single bipolar cell. In consequence, the brain obtains no information as to which of the group of rods has been stimulated, a condition which accounts for the lack of precision in rod vision as compared with that of cone areas.

## Optic nerve

The ganglion cells of the retina produce long nerve fibers which travel inwardly along the course of the original optic stalk to the forebrain region. The fibers originate on the inner surface of the retina, converge to a point opposite the attachment of the stalk and there plunge through the substance of the retina. At this point there can, of course, be no rods or cones, and there is, hence, a *blind spot* in the field of vision. In ourselves, at least, this blank area is "fudged" by the brain, which fills it in with the same materials seen in the surrounding region.

While the connection of retina with brain proper is customarily called a nerve, it differs from any normal nerve in two regards. Here, somewhat as in the olfactory nerve, we are dealing with fibers running inward toward the brain rather than outward from cells in or near that organ. Further, since the retina is, from an embryologic point of view, properly a part of the brain itself, the optic "nerve" is to be thought of not as a true external nerve, but rather as a fiber tract connecting two brain regions.

Reaching the floor of the forebrain, the optic nerve fibers enter via the X-shaped *optic chiasma* (figure 9.6). We find that frequently fiber bundles cross from one side to the other within the substance of the brain, without any immediately obvious reason, and this is the case also with the optic nerves. In the crossroads of the chiasma, in primitive vertebrates, nearly all the fibers of the right optic nerve cross to the left side of the brain, and vice versa; such a crossing of fibers is termed a *decussation.* The two sets of fibers in lower vertebrates run to the paired roof structures of the midbrain (tectum); in mammals most are relayed to special areas in the gray matter of the cerebral hemispheres. Details

are little known in lower vertebrates, but it appears that, as is known to be the case in mammals, the points in the brain receiving sensations from the different parts of the retina are arranged topographically in many if not all cases in such a fashion as to give a brain pattern – and a resulting mental "picture" – reproducing the arrangement of objects as "seen" by the retina.

In a majority of vertebrates the eyes are directed nearly straight laterally, and the two fields of vision are partially or totally different; the brain builds up two separate pictures of two quite separate views. In a number of higher types, however – such as birds of prey and many mammals – the eyes are turned forward, the two fields of vision overlap to a greater or lesser degree, and the two sets of impressions transmitted to the brain are more or less the same. Most notable is the case in primates, where, from Tarsius to man, the two fields of vision are practically identical.

In such cases the formation of two duplicate mental pictures seems an unnecessary procedure. Nevertheless, this is done, as far as can be discovered, in birds and other non-mammalian forms with overlapping visual fields. In mammals, however, we find a new development. *Stereoscopic vision* appears. The field of vision is unified: sensations from objects received in common by the two eyes are superposed. As a result such a form as man is aided, by the slight differences in point of view of the two eyes, in gaining effects of depth and three dimensional shape of objects – effects otherwise impossible of attainment.

An important anatomic phenomenon concerned with this development is *incomplete decussation* at the optic chiasma. In many mammals – and in mammals alone – we find that, for overlapping parts of the field of the two eyes, fibers from

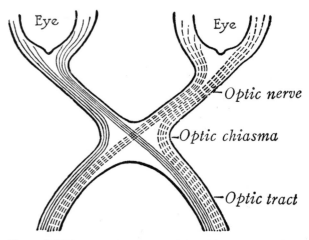

**Figure 9.6 Diagram of the optic chiasma** in a mammal with good stereoscopic vision. All fibers from the corresponding half of each eye pass to the same side of the brain. (From Arey.)

120

the areas which in both retinas view the same objects go to the same side of the brain. In consequence, certain groups of fibers do not cross (*i.e.*, decussate), but turn a right angle at the chiasma, to accompany their mates from the opposite eye. In man, for example, where the overlap of visual fields is nearly complete, practically all the fibers from the left halves of both retinas enter the left side of the brain, and all fibers from the right halves of the retinas enter the right side of the brain (figure 9.6). As a result, the visual area of each brain hemisphere builds up a half-picture of the total visual field as a "double exposure"; by further complicated interconnections between the hemispheres, the two halves of the picture are welded together to emerge into consciousness as a single stereoscopic view.

## Eye variations

Our previous comments on optic structures have given some faint idea of the great amount of adaptive variation seen in vertebrate eyes as a whole. Throughout the vertebrate series the basic eye pattern persists with remarkable consistency; nevertheless, entire volumes could be (and have been) devoted to an account of the wealth of changes rung on the basic eye structures in different groups. A few additional notes on variations may be given here.

Eyeballs are generally nearly spherical, but there are striking departures from this. "Tube eyes" – deep and narrow – are seen in deep-sea teleosts on the one hand, and in owls on the other. Both these forms operate in dim light; in this eye type all available illumination is concentrated on a narrow patch of sensory retina to bring the light intensity up to the minimum necessary for visibility. Typical day birds, in contrast with owls, have a broadly expanded retinal surface (as in figure 9.1*B*), making perception of small details possible. A curiosity is the little "four-eyed fish", Anableps of the American tropics, which has two separate corneas and retinal areas in each eye, so that, floating at the surface, it can simultaneously see both above and below water.

Eyes are relatively small in large animals, relatively large in little forms. This one might reasonably expect, for if an eye of a certain size furnishes satisfactory vision for a given animal, there is no selective advantage in a larger eye even if general body size has increased.

Eyes have degenerated and lost much of their structural niceties in a variety of forms from hagfishes to mammals. Such degeneration is, of course, usually correlated with a mode of life in which light is dim or absent. Among marine teleosts, those living at fairly considerable depths universally have large and specialized eyes which make the most of the faint illumination present; but in the great deeps some fishes have, so to speak, abandoned the struggle, and the eyes have degenerated. Cave life, too, has led to eye degeneration in various fishes and amphibians, some closely related to forms with normal eye structure. In land vertebrates burrowing forms usually exhibit a similar tendency. Snake eyes are in general well developed, but are peculiarly built and lack various structures, such as the scleral ring and certain of the usual eye muscles. It is suggested that the ancestral snakes were burrowers with reduced eyes, and that the typical ophidian eye of today has been secondarily built up from the remains of the degenerate ancestral organ.

# 10  The visual cortex of the brain
## by David H Hubel

An image of the outside world striking the retina of the eye activates a most intricate process that results in vision: the transformation of the retinal image into a perception. The transformation occurs partly in the retina but mostly in the brain, and it is, as one can recognize instantly by considering how modest in comparison is the achievement of a camera, a task of impressive magnitude.

The process begins with the responses of some 130 million light-sensitive receptor cells in each retina. From these cells messages are transmitted to other retinal cells and then sent on to the brain, where they must be analyzed and interpreted. To get an idea of the magnitude of the task, think what is involved in watching a moving animal, such as a horse. At a glance one takes in its size, form, color and rate of movement. From tiny differences in the two retinal images there results a three-dimensional picture. Somehow the brain manages to compare this picture with previous impressions; recognition occurs and then any appropriate action can be taken.

The organization of the visual system – a large, intricately connected population of nerve cells in the retina and brain – is still poorly understood. In recent years, however, various studies have begun to reveal something of the arrangement and function of these cells. In the early 1950s Stephen W. Kuffler, working with cats at the Johns Hopkins Hospital, discovered that some analysis of visual patterns takes place outside the brain, in the nerve cells of the retina. My colleague Torsten N. Wiesel and I at the Harvard Medical School, exploring the first stages of the processing that occurs in the brain of the cat, have mapped the visual pathway a little further: to what appears to be the sixth step from the retina to the cortex of the cerebrum. This kind of work falls far short of providing a full understanding of vision, but it does convey some idea of the mechanisms and circuitry of the visual system.

*first published in* Scientific American, *November 1963.*
*Reprinted with permission. Copyright © 1963 by Scientific American, Inc. All rights reserved.*

In broad outline the visual pathway is clearly defined (figure 10.2). From the retina of each eye visual messages travel along the optic nerve, which consists of about a million nerve fibers. At the junction known as the chiasm about half of the nerves cross over into opposite hemispheres of the brain, the other nerves remaining on the same side. The optic nerve fibers lead to the first way stations in the brain: a pair of cell clusters called the lateral geniculate bodies. From here new fibers course back through the brain to the visual area of the cerebral cortex (figure 10.1). It is convenient, although admittedly a gross oversimplification, to think of the pathway from retina to cortex as consisting of six types of nerve cells, of which three are in the retina, one is in the geniculate body and two are in the cortex.

Nerve cells, or neurons, transmit messages in the form of brief electrochemical impulses. These travel along the outer membrane of the cell, notably along the membrane of its long principal fiber, the axon. It is possible to obtain an electrical record of impulses of a single nerve cell by placing a fine electrode near the cell body or one of its fibers. Such measurements have shown that impulses travel along the nerves at velocities of between half a meter and 100 meters per second. The impulses in a given fiber all have about the same amplitude; the strength of the stimuli that give rise to them is reflected not in amplitude but in frequency.

At its terminus the fiber of a nerve cell makes contact with another nerve cell (or with a muscle cell or gland cell), forming the junction called the synapse. At most synapses an impulse on reaching the end of a fiber causes the release of a small amount of a specific substance, which diffuses outward to the membrane of the next cell. There the substance either excites the cell or inhibits it. In excitation the substance acts to bring the cell into a state in which it is more likely to "fire"; in inhibition the substance acts to prevent firing. For most synapses the substances that act as transmitters are unknown. Moreover, there is no sure way to determine from microscopic appearances alone whether a synapse is excitatory or inhibitory.

It is at the synapses that the modification and analysis of nerve messages take place. The kind of analysis depends

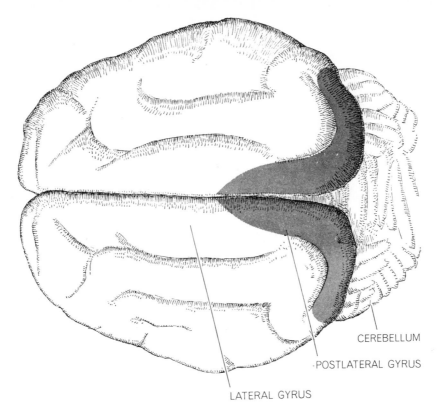

CEREBELLUM

POSTLATERAL GYRUS

LATERAL GYRUS

**Figure 10.2 Visual system** appears in this representation of the human brain as viewed from below. Visual pathway from retinas to cortex via the lateral geniculate body is shaded.

partly on the nature of the synapse: on how many nerve fibers converge on a single cell and on how the excitatory and inhibitory endings distribute themselves. In most parts of the nervous system the anatomy is too intricate to reveal much about function. One way to circumvent this difficulty is to record impulses with microelectrodes in anesthetized animals, first from the fibers coming into a structure of neurons and then from the neurons themselves, or from the fibers they send onward. Comparison of the behavior of incoming and outgoing fibers provides a basis for learning what the structure does. Through such exploration of the different parts of the brain concerned with vision one can hope to build up some idea of how the entire visual system works.

That is what Wiesel and I have undertaken, mainly through studies of the visual system of the cat. In our experiments the anesthetized animal faces a wide screen 1.5 meters away, and we shine various patterns of white light on the screen with a projector. Simultaneously we penetrate the visual portion of the cortex with microelectrodes. In that way we can record the responses of individual cells to the light patterns. Sometimes it takes many hours to find the region of the retina with which a particular visual cell is linked and to work out the optimum stimuli for that cell. The reader should bear in mind the relation between each visual cell — no matter how far along the visual pathway it may be — and the retina. It requires an image on the retina to evoke a meaningful response in any visual cell, however indirect and complex the linkage may be.

The retina is a complicated structure, in both its anatomy and its physiology, and the description I shall give is highly simplified. Light coming through the lens of the eye falls on the mosaic of receptor cells in the retina. The receptor cells do not send impulses directly through the optic nerve but instead connect with a set of retinal cells called bipolar cells. These in turn connect with retinal ganglion cells, and it is the latter set of cells, the third in the visual pathway, that sends its fibers — the optic nerve fibers — to the brain.

This series of cells and synapses is no simple bucket brigade for impulses: a receptor may send nerve endings to more than one bipolar cell, and several receptors may converge on one bipolar cell (figure 10.3). The same holds for the synapses between the bipolar cells and the retinal ganglion cells. Stimulating a single receptor by light might therefore be expected to have an influence on many

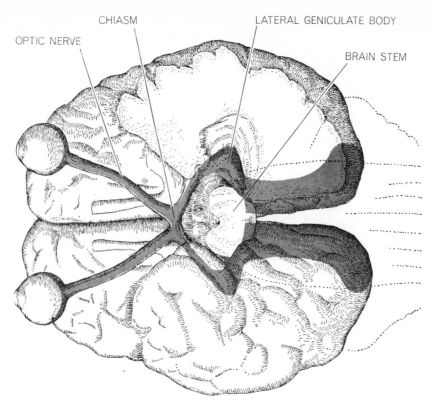

OPTIC NERVE CHIASM LATERAL GENICULATE BODY BRAIN STEM

**Figure 10.2 Visual system** appears in this representation of the human brain as viewed from below. Visual pathway from retinas to cortex via the lateral geniculate body is shaded.

bipolar or ganglion cells; conversely, it should be possible to influence one bipolar or retinal ganglion cell from a number of receptors and hence from a substantial area of the retina.

The area of receptor mosaic in the retina feeding into a single visual cell is called the receptive field of the cell. This term is applied to any cell in the visual system to refer to the area of retina with which the cell is connected – the retinal area that on stimulation produces a response from the cell.

Any of the synapses with a particular cell may be excitatory or inhibitory, so that stimulation of a particular point on the retina may either increase or decrease the cell's firing rate. Moreover, a single cell may receive several excitatory and inhibitory impulses at once, with the result that it will respond according to the net effect of these inputs. In considering the behavior of a single cell an observer should remember that it is just one of a huge population of cells: a stimulus that excites one cell will undoubtedly excite many others, meanwhile inhibiting yet another array of cells and leaving others entirely unaffected.

For many years it has been known that retinal ganglion cells fire at a fairly steady rate even in the absence of any stimulation. Kuffler was the first to observe how the retinal ganglion cells of mammals are influenced by small spots of light. He found that the resting discharges of a cell were intensified or diminished by light in a small and more or less circular region of the retina. That region was of course the cell's receptive field. Depending on where in the field a spot of light fell, either of two responses could be produced. One was an "on" response, in which the cell's firing rate increased under the stimulus of light. The other was an "off" response, in which the stimulus of light decreased the cell's firing rate. Moreover, turning the light off usually evoked a burst of impulses from the cell. Kuffler called the retinal regions from which these responses could be evoked "on" regions and "off" regions.

On mapping the receptive fields of a large number of retinal ganglion cells into "on" and "off" regions, Kuffler discovered that there were two distinct cell types. In one the receptive field consisted of a small circular "on" area and a surrounding zone that gave "off" responses. Kuffler termed this an "on"-center cell. The second type, which he called "off"-center, had just the reverse form of field – an "off" center and an "on" periphery (figure 10.5). For a given cell the effects of light varied markedly according to the place in which the light struck the receptive field. Two spots of light shone on separate parts of an "on" area produced a more vigorous "on" response than either spot alone, whereas if one spot was shone on an "on" area and the other on an "off" area, the two effects tended to neutralize each other, resulting in a very weak "on" or "off" response. In an "on"-center cell, illuminating the entire central "on" region evoked a maximum response; a smaller or larger spot of light was less effective.

Lighting up the whole retina diffusely, even though it may

Figure 10.3 Structure of retina is depicted schematically. Images fall on the receptor cells, of which there are about 130 million in each retina. Some analysis of an image occurs as the receptors transmit messages to the retinal ganglion cells via the bipolar cells. A group of receptors funnels into a particular ganglion cell, as indicated by the shading; that group forms the ganglion cell's receptive field. Inasmuch as the fields of several ganglion cells overlap, one receptor may send messages to several ganglion cells.

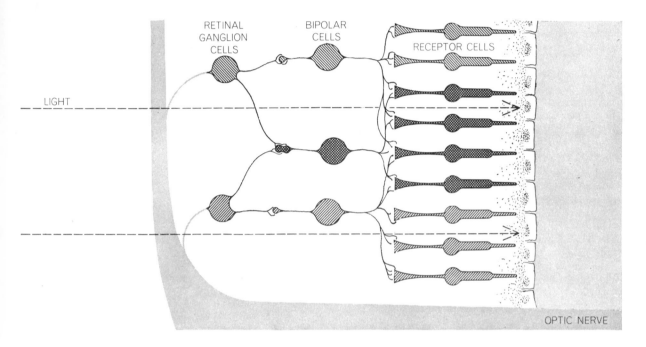

affect every receptor in the retina, does not affect a retinal ganglion cell nearly so strongly as a small circular spot of exactly the right size placed so as to cover precisely the receptive-field center. The main concern of these cells seems to be the contrast in illumination between one retinal region and surrounding regions.

Retinal ganglion cells differ greatly in the size of their receptive-field centers. Cells near the fovea (the part of the retina serving the center of gaze) are specialized for precise discrimination; in the monkey the field centers of these cells may be about the same size as a single cone — an area subtending a few minutes of arc at the cornea. On the other hand, some cells far out in the retinal periphery have field centers up to a millimeter or so in diameter. (In man one millimeter of retina corresponds to an arc of about three degrees in the 180-degree visual field.) Cells with such large receptive-field centers are probably specialized for work in very dim light, since they can sum up messages from a large number of receptors.

Given this knowledge of the kind of visual information brought to the brain by the optic nerve, our first problem was to learn how the messages were handled at the first central way station, the lateral geniculate body. Compared with the retina, the geniculate body is a relatively simple structure. In a sense there is only one synapse involved, since the incoming optic nerve fibers end in cells that send their fibers directly to the visual cortex. Yet in the cat many optic nerve fibers converge on each geniculate cell, and it is reasonable to expect some change in the visual messages from the optic nerve to the geniculate cells.

When we came to study the geniculate body, we found that the cells have many of the characteristics Kuffler described for retinal ganglion cells. Each geniculate cell is driven from a circumscribed retinal region (the receptive field) and has either an "on" center or an "off" center, with an opposing periphery. There are, however, differences between geniculate cells and retinal ganglion cells, the most important of which is the greatly enhanced capacity of the periphery of a

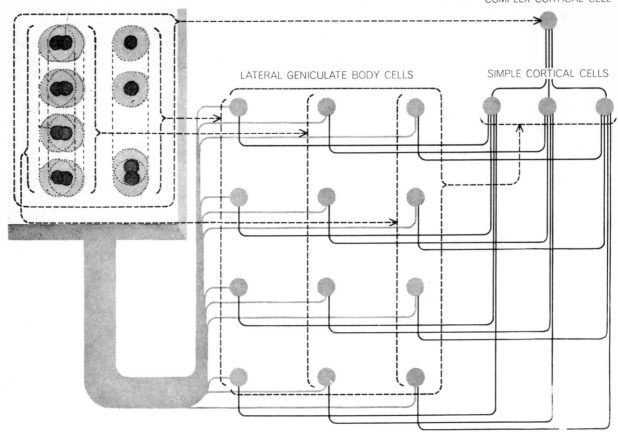

RETINA

LATERAL GENICULATE BODY CELLS

COMPLEX CORTICAL CELL

SIMPLE CORTICAL CELLS

**Figure 10.4 Visual processing by brain** begins in the lateral geniculate body, which continues the analysis made by retinal cells. In the cortex "simple" cells respond strongly to line stimuli, provided that the position and orientation of the line are suitable for a particular cell. "Complex" cells respond well to line stimuli, but the position of the line is not critical and the cell continues to respond even if a properly oriented stimulus is moved, as long as it remains in the cell's receptive field. Broken lines indicate how receptive fields of all these cells overlap on the retina; solid lines, how several cells at one stage affect a single cell at the next stage.

geniculate cell's receptive field to cancel the effects of the center. This means that the lateral geniculate cells must be even more specialized than retinal ganglion cells in responding to spatial differences in retinal illumination rather than to the illumination itself. The lateral geniculate body, in short, has the function of increasing the disparity – already present in retinal ganglion cells – between responses to a small, centered spot and to diffuse light.

In contrast to the comparatively simple lateral geniculate body, the cerebral cortex is a structure of stupendous complexity. The cells of this great plate of gray matter – a structure that would be about 20 square feet in area and a tenth of an inch thick if flattened out – are arranged in a number of more or less distinct layers. The millions of fibers that come in from the lateral geniculate body connect with cortical cells in the layer that is fourth from the top. From here the information is sooner or later disseminated to all layers of the cortex by rich interconnections between them. Many of the cells, particularly those of the third and fifth layers, send their fibers out of the cortex, projecting to centers deep in the brain or passing over to nearby cortical areas for further processing of the visual messages. Our problem was to learn how the information the visual cortex sends out differs from what it takes in.

Most connections between cortical cells are in a direction perpendicular to the surface; side-to-side connections are generally quite short. One might therefore predict that impulses arriving at a particular area of the cortex would

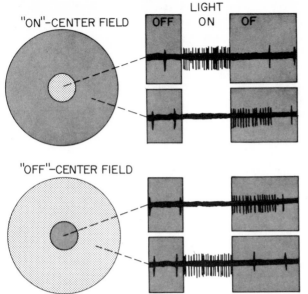

"ON"-CENTER FIELD

"OFF"-CENTER FIELD

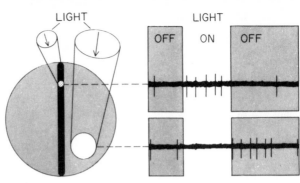

**Figure 10.5 Concentric fields** are characteristic of retinal ganglion cells and of geniculate cells. At top an oscilloscope recording shows strong firing by an "on"-center type of cell when a spot of light strikes the field center; if the spot hits an "off" area, the firing is suppressed until the light goes off. At bottom are responses of another cell of the "off"-center type.

**Figure 10.7 Response is weak** when a circular spot of light is shone on receptive field of a simple cortical cell. Such spots get a vigorous response from retinal and geniculate cells. This cell has a receptive field of type shown in Figure 10.6a.

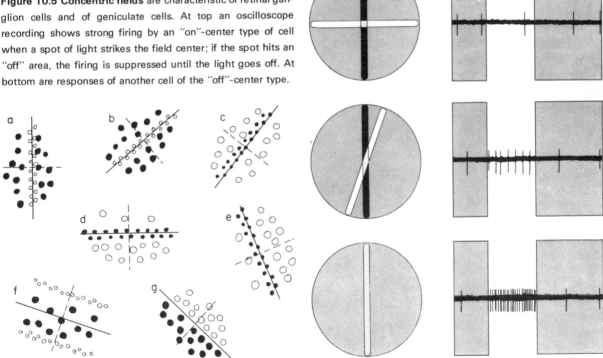

**Figure 10.6 Simple cortical cells** have receptive fields of various types. In all of them the "on" and "off" areas, represented by open and solid dots respectively, are separated by straight boundaries. Orientations of fields vary, as indicated particularly at a and b. In the cat's visual system such fields are generally one millimeter or less in diameter.

**Figure 10.8 Importance of orientation** to simple cortical cells is indicated by varying responses to a slit of light from a cell preferring a vertical orientation. Horizontal slit (*top*) produces no response, slight tilt a weak response, vertical slit a strong response.

exert their effects quite locally. Moreover, the retinas project to the visual cortex (via the lateral geniculate body) in a systematic topologic manner; that is, a given area of cortex gets its input ultimately from a circumscribed area of retina. These two observations suggest that a given cortical cell should have a small receptive field; it should be influenced from a circumscribed retinal region only, just as a geniculate or retinal ganglion cell is. Beyond this the anatomy provides no hint of what the cortex does with the information it receives about an image on the retina.

In the face of the anatomical complexity of the cortex, it would have been surprising if the cells had proved to have the concentric receptive fields characteristic of cells in the retina and the lateral geniculate body. Indeed, in the cat we have observed no cortical cells with concentric receptive fields; instead there are many different cell types, with fields markedly different from anything seen in the retinal and geniculate cells.

The many varieties of cortical cells may, however, be classified by function into two large groups. One we have called "simple"; the function of these cells is to respond to line stimuli − such shapes as slits, which we define as light lines on a dark background; dark bars (dark lines on a light background), and edges (straight-line boundaries between light and dark regions). Whether or not a given cell responds depends on the orientation of the shape and its position on the cell's receptive field. A bar shone vertically on the screen may activate a given cell, whereas the same cell will fail to respond (but others will respond) if the bar is displaced to one side or moved appreciably out of the vertical (figure 10.8). The second group of cortical cells we have called "complex"; they too respond best to bars, slits or edges, provided that, as with simple cells, the shape is suitably oriented for the particular cell under observation. Complex cells, however, are not so discriminating as to the exact position of the stimulus, provided that it is properly oriented. Moreover, unlike simple cells, they respond with sustained firing to moving lines (figure 10.9).

From the preference of simple and complex cells for specific orientation of light stimuli, it follows that there must be a multiplicity of cell types to handle the great number of possible positions and orientations. Wiesel and I have found a large variety of cortical cell responses, even though the

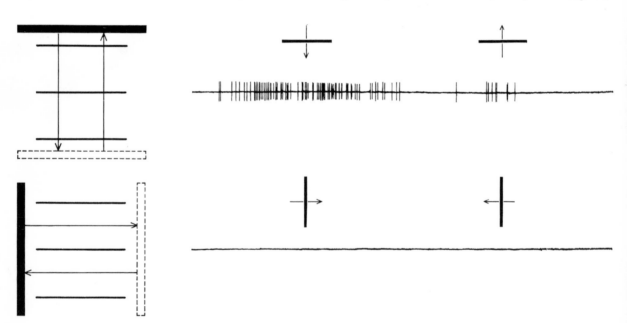

**Figure 10.9 Complex cortical cell** responded vigorously to slow downward movement of a dark, horizontal bar. Upward movement of bar produced a weak response and horizontal movement of a vertical bar produced no response. For other shapes, orientations and movements there are other complex cells showing maximum response. Such cells may figure in perception of form and movement.

number of individual cells we have studied runs only into the hundreds compared with the millions that exist. Among simple cells, the retinal region over which a cell can be influenced − the receptive field − is, like the fields of retinal and geniculate cells, divided into "on" and "off" areas. In simple cells, however, these areas are far from being circularly symmetrical. In a typical example the receptive field

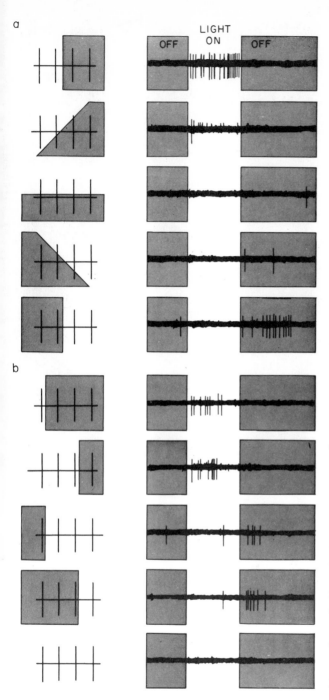

**Figure 10.10 Single complex cell** showed varying responses to an edge projected on the cell's receptive field in the retina. In group *a* the stimulus was presented in differing orientations. In group *b* all the edges were vertical and all but the last evoked responses regardless of where in the receptive field the light struck. When a large rectangle of light covered entire receptive field, however, as shown at bottom, cell failed to respond.

consists of a very long and narrow "on" area, which is adjoined on each side by larger "off" regions. The magnitude of an "on" response depends, as with retinal and geniculate cells, on how much either type of region is covered by the stimulating light. A long, narrow slit that just fills the elongated "on" region produces a powerful "on" response. Stimulation with the slit in a different orientation produces a much weaker effect, because the slit is now no longer illuminating all the "on" region but instead includes some of the antagonistic "off" region. A slit at right angles to the optimum orientation for a cell of this type is usually completely ineffective.

In the simple cortical cells the process of pitting these two antagonistic parts of a receptive field against each other is carried still further than it is in the lateral geniculate body. As a rule a large spot of light – or what amounts to the same thing, diffuse light covering the whole retina – evokes no response at all in simple cortical cells. Here the "on" and "off" effects apparently balance out with great precision.

Some other common types of simple receptive fields include an "on" center with a large "off" area to one side and a small one to the other; an "on" and an "off" area side by side; a narrow "off" center with "on" sides; a wide "on" center with narrow "off" sides. All these fields have in common that the border or borders separating "on" and "off" regions are straight and parallel rather than circular (figure 10.6). The most efficient stimuli – slits, edges or dark bars – all involve straight lines. Each cell responds best to a particular orientation of line; other orientations produce less vigorous responses, and usually the orientation perpendicular to the optimum evokes no response at all. A particular cell's optimum, which we term the receptive-field orientation, is thus a property built into the cell by its connections. In general the receptive-field orientation differs from one cell to the next, and it may be vertical, horizontal or oblique. We have no evidence that any one orientation, such as vertical or horizontal, is more common than any other.

How can one explain this specificity of simple cortical cells? We are inclined to think they receive their input directly from the incoming lateral geniculate fibers. We suppose a typical simple cell has for its input a large number of lateral geniculate cells whose "on" centers are arranged along a straight line; a spot of light shone anywhere along that line will activate some of the geniculate cells and lead to activation of the cortical cell (figure 10.7). A light shone over the entire area will activate all the geniculate cells and have a tremendous final impact on the cortical cell (figure 10.8).

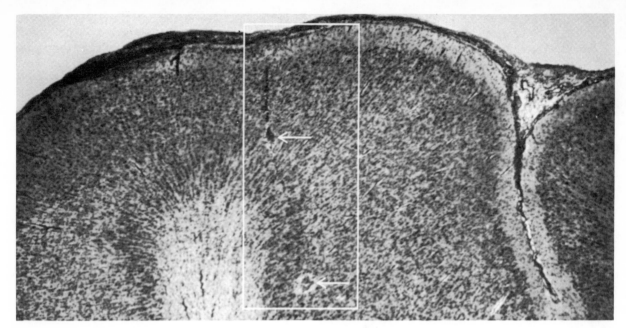

**Figure 10.11 Section of cat's visual cortex** shows track of microelectrode penetration and, at arrows, two points along the track where lesions were made so that it would be possible to ascertain later where the tip of the electrode was at certain times. This section of cortex is from a single gyrus, or fold of the brain; it was six millimeters wide and is shown here enlarged 30 diameters.

One can now begin to grasp the significance of the great number of cells in the visual cortex. Each cell seems to have its own specific duties; it takes care of one restricted part of the retina, responds best to one particular shape of stimulus and to one particular orientation. To look at the problem from the opposite direction, for each stimulus – each area of the retina stimulated, each type of line (edge, slit or bar) and each orientation of stimulus – there is a particular set of simple cortical cells that will respond; changing any of the stimulus arrangements will cause a whole new population of cells to respond. The number of populations responding successively as the eye watches a slowly rotating propeller is scarcely imaginable.

Such a profound rearrangement and analysis of the incoming messages might seem enough of a task for a single structure, but it turns out to be only part of what happens in the cortex. The next major transformation involves the cortical cells that occupy what is probably the sixth step in the visual pathway: the complex cells, which are also present in this cortical region and to some extent intermixed with the simple cells.

Complex cells are like simple ones in several ways. A cell responds to a stimulus only within a restricted region of retina: the receptive field. It responds best to the line stimuli (slits, edges or dark bars) and the stimulus must be oriented to suit the cell. But complex fields, unlike the simple ones, cannot be mapped into antagonistic "on" and "off" regions.

A typical complex cell we studied happened to fire to a vertical edge, and it gave "on" or "off" responses depending on whether light was to the left or to the right. Other orientations were almost completely without effect (figure 10.10). These responses are just what could be expected from a simple cell with a receptive field consisting of an excitatory area separated from an inhibitory one by a vertical boundary. In this case, however, the cell had an additional property that could not be explained by such an arrangement. A vertical edge evoked responses anywhere within the receptive field, "on" responses with light to the left, "off" responses with light to the right. Such behavior cannot be understood in terms of antagonistic "on" and "off" subdivisions of the receptive field, and when we explored the field with small spots we found no such regions. Instead the spot either produced responses at both "on" and "off" or evoked no responses at all.

Complex cells, then, respond like simple cells to one particular aspect of the stimulus, namely its orientation. But when the stimulus is moved, without changing the orientation, a complex cell differs from its simple counterpart chiefly in responding with sustained firing. The firing continues as the stimulus is moved over a substantial retinal area, usually the entire receptive field of the cell, whereas a simple cell will respond to movement only as the stimulus crosses a very narrow boundary separating "on" and "off" regions.

It is difficult to explain this behavior by any scheme in which geniculate cells project directly to complex cells. On the other hand, the findings can be explained fairly well by the supposition that a complex cell receives its input from a large number of simple cells. This supposition requires only that the simple cells have the same field orientation and be all of the same general type. A complex cell responding to vertical edges, for example, would thus receive fibers from simple cells that have vertically oriented receptive fields. All such a scheme needs to have added is the requirement that the retinal positions of these simple fields be arranged throughout the area occupied by the complex field.

The main difficulty with such a scheme is that it presupposes an enormous degree of cortical organization. What a vast network of connections must be needed if a single complex cell is to receive fibers from just the right simple cells, all with the appropriate field arrangements, tilts and positions! Yet there is unexpected and compelling evidence that such a system of connections exists. It comes from a study of what can be called the functional architecture of the cortex. By penetrating with a microelectrode through the cortex in many directions, perhaps many times in a single tiny region of the brain, we learned that the cells are arranged not in a haphazard manner but with a high degree of order. The physiological results show that functionally the cortex is subdivided like a beehive into tiny columns, or segments (figure 10.12), each of which extends from the surface to the

white matter lower in the brain. A column is defined not by any anatomically obvious wall – no columns are visible under the microscope – but by the fact that the thousands of cells it contains all have the same receptive-field orientation. The evidence for this is that in a typical microelectrode penetration through the cortex the cell – recorded in sequence as the electrode is pushed ahead – all have the same field orientation, provided that the penetration is made in a direction perpendicular to the surface of the cortical segment. If the penetration is oblique, as we pass from column to column we record several cells with one field orientation, then a new sequence of cells with a new orientation, and then still another.

The columns are irregular in cross-sectional shape, and on the average they are about half a millimeter across. In respects other than receptive-field orientation the cells in a particular column tend to differ; some are simple, others complex; some respond to slits, others prefer dark bars or edges.

Returning to the proposed scheme for explaining the properties of complex cells, one sees that gathered together in a single column are the very cells one should expect to be interconnected: cells whose fields have the same orientation and the same general retinal position, although not the same position. Furthermore, it is known from the anatomy that there are rich interconnections between neighboring cells, and the preponderance of these connections in a vertical direction fits well with the long, narrow, more or less cylindrical shape of the columns. This means that a column may be looked on as an independent functional unit of cortex, in which simple cells receive connections from lateral geniculate cells and send projections to complex cells.

It is possible to get an inkling of the part these different cell types play in vision by considering what must be happening in the brain when one looks at a form, such as, to take a relatively simple example, a black square on a white background. Suppose the eyes fix on some arbitrary point to the left of the square. On the reasonably safe assumption that the human visual cortex works something like the cat's and the monkey's, it can be predicted that the near edge of the square will activate a particular group of simple cells, namely cells that prefer edges with light to the left and dark to the right and whose fields are oriented vertically and are so placed on the retina that the boundary between "on" and "off" regions falls exactly along the image of the near edge of the square. Other populations of cells will obviously be called into action by the other three edges of the square. All the cell populations will change if the eye strays from the

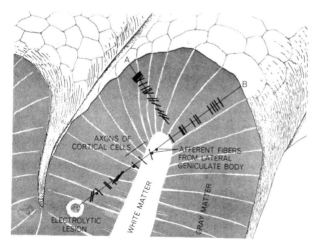

**Figure 10.12 Functional arrangement** of cells in visual cortex resembled columns, although columnar structure is not apparent under a microscope. Lines *A* and *B* show paths of two microelectrode penetrations; lines show receptive-field orientations encountered. Cells in a single column had same orientation; change of orientation showed new column.

point fixed on, or if the square is moved while the eye remains stationary, or if the square is rotated.

In the same way each edge will activate a population of complex cells, again cells that prefer edges in a specific orientation. But a given complex cell, unlike a simple cell, will continue to be activated when the eye moves or when the form moves, if the movement is not so large that the edge passes entirely outside the receptive field of the cell, and if there is no rotation. This means that the populations of complex cells affected by the whole square will be to some extent independent of the exact position of the image of the square on the retina.

Each of the cortical columns contains thousands of cells, some with simple fields and some with complex. Evidently the visual cortex analyzes an enormous amount of information, with each small region of visual field represented over and over again in column after column, first for one receptive-field orientation and then for another.

In sum, the visual cortex appears to have a rich assortment of functions. It rearranges the input from the lateral geniculate body in a way that makes lines and contours the most important stimuli. What appears to be a first step in perceptual generalization results from the response of cortical cells to the orientation of a stimulus, apart from its exact retinal position. Movement is also an important stimulus factor; its rate and direction must both be specified if a cell is to be effectively driven.

One cannot expect to "explain" vision, however, from a knowledge of the behavior of a single set of cells, geniculate or cortical, any more than one could understand a woodpulp mill from an examination of the machine that cuts the logs into chips. We are now studying how still "higher" structures build on the information they receive from these cortical cells, rearranging it to produce an even greater complexity of response.

In all of this work we have been particularly encouraged to find that the areas we study can be understood in terms of comparatively simple concepts such as the nerve impulse, convergence of many nerves on a single cell, excitation and inhibition. Moreover, if the connections suggested by these studies are remotely close to reality, one can conclude that at least some parts of the brain can be followed relatively easily, without necessarily requiring higher mathematics, computers or a knowledge of network theories.

## Bibliography

Discharge Patterns and Functional Organization of Mammalian Retina, Stephen W. Kuffler in *Journal of Neurophysiology*, Vol. 16, No. 1, pages 37–68, January 1953

Integrative Process in Central Visual Pathways of the Cat, David H. Hubel in *Journal of the Optical Society of America*, Vol. 53, No. 1, pages 58–66, January 1963

Receptive Fields, Binocular Interaction and Functional Architecture in the Cat's Visual Cortex, D. H. Hubel and T. N. Wiesel in *Journal of Physiology*, Vol. 160, No. 1, pages 196–254, January 1962

The Visual Pathway, Ragnar Granit in *The Eye, Volume II: The Visual Process*, edited by Hugh Davson, Academic Press, 1962

# 11 Three-pigment color vision
## by Edward F MacNichol Jr

Investigations have established that color vision in verte-brates is mediated by three light-sensitive pigments segregated in three different kinds of receptor cell in the retina, and that one of these pigments is primarily responsible for sensing blue light, one for sensing green and one for red. These findings solve one of the central problems of color vision: the nature of the primary receptors that discriminate light of various wavelengths. Large questions remain to be answered: How is the information from the receptors coded in the retina? How is it transmitted to the brain? How is it decoded there?

In 1802 the English physicist Thomas Young suggested that the retina probably contains three different kinds of light-sensitive substances, each maximally sensitive in a different region of the spectrum, and that the information from the excitation of each substance is separately transmitted to the brain and there combined to reproduce the colors of the outside world. Over the years investigators accumulated a great deal of information on the mechanisms of vision without being able to prove or disprove Young's simple postulates. They learned that rod-shaped and cone-shaped receptor cells in the retina contain pigments that are bleached by light, that the rods are responsible for vision in faint light and that the cones distinguish colors. Psychophysical experiments, in which a human subject is presented with visual stimuli and asked to tell what he sees, established that any color could be matched by a combination of three colors in different parts of the spectrum. This supported Young's trichromatic theory, but other psychophysical studies seemed to support different theories. The fact is that psychophysical investigation tells only what the visual system can do and not how it does it.

To learn what happens at various steps along the visual pathway one must measure directly the effect of light on the receptor cells and the generation of electrical impulses in the retinal nerve cells. Spectrophotometric measurements of individual cone cells in the retinas of the goldfish, the rhesus monkey and man, conducted in our laboratory at Johns Hopkins University and also at Harvard University and the University of Pennsylvania, have now confirmed Young's three-receptor hypothesis. Electrophysiological studies of nerve cells in the retina, on the other hand, suggest that Young was wrong about the transmission of color information to the brain along three discrete pathways.

A physiologist seeking to learn what message the eye sends the brain, and how, would like to start at the beginning – with the impact of light on a photoreceptor. Unfortunately the lack of suitable techniques ruled out this systematic approach: single-cell spectrophotometry has been possible only in very recent years. Electrophysiological methods, on the other hand, have been applicable since 1938, when H. K. Hartline, then at the University of Pennsylvania, isolated individual optic nerve fibers in the retina of the frog. Each such fiber originates in a single ganglion cell: a nerve cell that collects information from a large number of receptors. Hartline found that the ganglion cells responded to light by emitting showers of nerve impulses, and he classified the cells as "on", "off" or "on-off", depending on whether they responded to the onset or to the end of illumination or to both. In 1939 the Swedish physiologists Ragnar A. Granit and Gunnar Svaetichin and the Finnish physicist Alvar Wilska developed microelectrodes that could record directly from a cell, and since then microelectrode techniques have been used to trace nerve messages through many parts of the visual pathway as well as in other parts of the nervous system.

The ganglion cells are "third order" nerve cells, two steps behind the receptor cells along the visual pathway (although in front of them anatomically; the receptor cells are at the back of the translucent retina). With the development of micropipette electrodes after World War II it became possible to probe more precisely into individual cells, and in the 1950s Svaetichin recorded, in the retinas of certain fishes, the most peripheral localized sign of electrical activity

*first published in* Scientific American, *December 1964.*
*Reprinted with permission. Copyright © 1964 by Scientific American, Inc. All rights reserved.*

discovered up to that time: slow changes in potential in response to flashes of light. These S-potentials, as they came to be called, were of two types and were quite different from anything previously reported. One, which Svaetichin called the luminosity response, took the form of a sizable negative resting potential that increased in the presence of light; the wavelengths that are most effective in this regard are distributed in a broad peak across the center of the spectrum. The luminosity response has since been found in a large number of fishes and in the cat and the frog, and it probably occurs in all vertebrates. The other intraretinal response was similar in some respects: it was a steady negative resting potential that became more strongly negative when the stimulating light was at the short-wavelength, or blue, end of the spectrum. As progressively longer wavelengths were used for illumination, however, the responses diminished in

amplitude until a neutral point was reached at which there was no sustained change in potential; any increase in wavelength from that point on produced a positive potential! This unusual "chromatic" response suggested a possible mechanism of color vision. In 1957 I joined Svaetichin at the Venezuelan Institute for Scientific Research and we undertook a detailed study of both the nature and the exact source of the S-potentials.

We found the luminosity response in a number of different fishes but the chromatic response only in species that swim at levels to which a broad band of wavelengths, or colors, penetrates: no deeper than about 100 feet. The chromatic response of some fishes showed a negative peak in the green portion of the spectrum and a positive peak in the red; in other species the peaks were in the blue and yellow. Among the species we tested only the mullet (*Mugil*) had

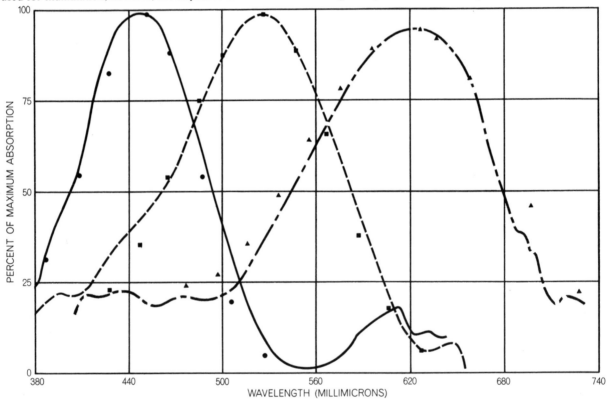

**Figure 11.1 Color vision** in primates is mediated by three cone pigments responsible for sensing light in the blue, green and red portions of the spectrum. Their spectral-sensitivity curves are shown here. For the three cone pigments the peak sensitivities are: 447 millimicrons (blue-violet), 540 (green) and 577 (yellow). Although the "red" receptor peaks in the yellow, it extends far enough into the red to sense red well. Symbols accompanying curves trace shapes of hypothetical pigments with peaks at each wavelength (*see text*).

both the "green-red" and the "blue-yellow" response. Further analysis of these chromatic responses showed that each was made up of two opposed processes — negative in the blue or green and positive in the yellow or red — combined algebraically. The independence of the two processes was demonstrated by adaptation experiments. Illumination of a retina with a steady blue light, for example, diminished the chromatic response in the short-wavelength region and increased it in the yellow or red. Similar experiments did not

134

change the shape of the luminosity response, only its amplitude. Clearly the chromatic response was made up of two distinct components, whereas the luminosity response was unitary.

To visualize the sites of origin we filled the micropipettes with dye that was forced out into the retinal tissue by electrophoresis after each recording. By sectioning and examining the specimens we could trace the luminosity response to the region just beyond the endings of the cone cells, where the fish retina has a layer of giant horizontal "glial" cells. The large size of the area in which the luminosity response arises, and the fact that it signals a change in brightness anywhere in an extensive area, seem to confirm its origin in these giant cells.

The chromatic response arises in the next layer of the retina. Genyo Mitarai of the University of Nagoya in Japan, working with Svaetichin, has secured evidence that they come from the so-called Müller fibers, which surround the "second order" nerve cells known as bipolar cells. The Müller fibers – like the giant horizontal cells – are glial elements: supporting or nutritive structures often seen in association with nerve cells. The S-potentials are quite different from the shower of short-lived "spike" impulses ordinarily emitted by nerve cells; Svaetichin has suggested that these slow changes in potential are signs of metabolic changes in the glial structures in which they originate, induced by the activity of adjacent nerve cells and able in turn to alter the nerve cells' activity. Glia have usually been assumed to play a passive role in the nervous system, but Holger Hydén of the University of Göteborg has shown that metabolic events in glial cells are correlated

Figure 11.2 Human receptor cells are seen end on in this photograph of a retinal specimen on the stage of the spectrophotometer that measures their light absorption. The well-defined small circles are the rod and cone outer segments, the parts of the receptors that contain the visual pigments. The rods are the more closely packed. The specimen is oriented so that the test beam of colored light comes through a cone outer segment (*black spot at middle left*) and the reference beam passes through an empty area (*right*).

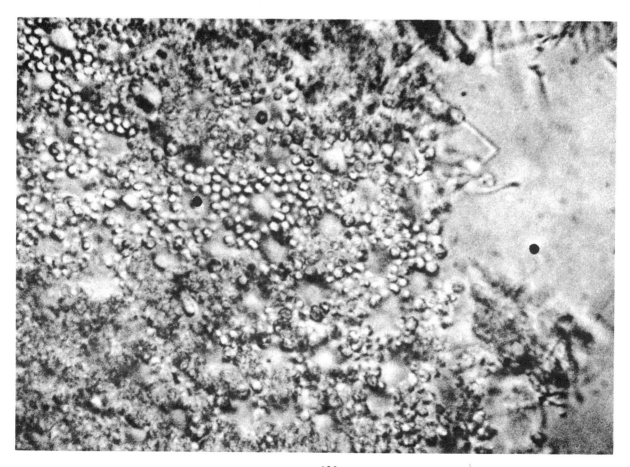

with certain forms of nervous activity and may even control them. This is a challenging area for further experimentation.

Whatever their exact explanation, if these intraretinal S-potentials did have something to do with color vision, we thought they should be correlated with the discharge patterns of the ganglion cells, which appear to be the only source of messages from the retina to the brain. Russel L. DeValois of Indiana University had found that spontaneously active nerve cells in a visual center of the monkey brain increase their rate of discharge when the eye is stimulated by light at one end of the spectrum and decrease it when the eye is stimulated by light at the other end. No one, however, had obtained chromatic responses from the monkey retina for comparison. Together with M. L. Wolbarsht and H. G. Wagner of the Naval Medical Research Institute I studied the effects of wavelength on the responses of retinal ganglion cells in the goldfish (*Carassius auratus*), which had been shown to have a well-developed color sense (figures 11.3 and 11.4).

First we established that the goldfish retina does produce both the luminosity and the chromatic S-potentials, both of them qualitatively the same as in the fishes we had studied previously. Then we went on to record with microelectrodes inserted into the ganglion cells. Most of these cells responded with a burst of impulses when a white light was turned on and another burst when the light was turned off. Colored light brought a response that in the manner of the chromatic response was peculiarly dependent on wavelength. At short wavelengths, where the chromatic response was large and negative, a typical ganglion cell produced vigorous "on" discharges; at intermediate wavelengths, where the chromatic potential went too zero, there was a transition from "on" to "off"; at long wavelengths, where the chromatic response was large and positive, the "off" responses reached a maximum and there was a suppression of activity during illumination (figure 11.5). The short wavelengths caused excitation; the long wavelengths had an inhibitory effect during illumination that was followed by an "off" discharge that seemed to be a "post-inhibitory rebound", a common phenomenon in nervous systems.

In addition to wavelength, the intensity of the stimulus

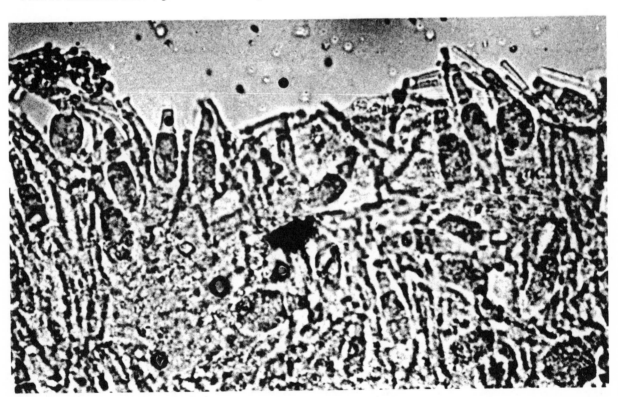

**Figure 11.3 Goldfish receptors** are seen from the side in a piece of retina squeezed between two cover slips and placed in the spectrophotometer. The three-micron test and reference beams (*black spots*) pass through a cone outer segment (*upper left*) and a clear area.

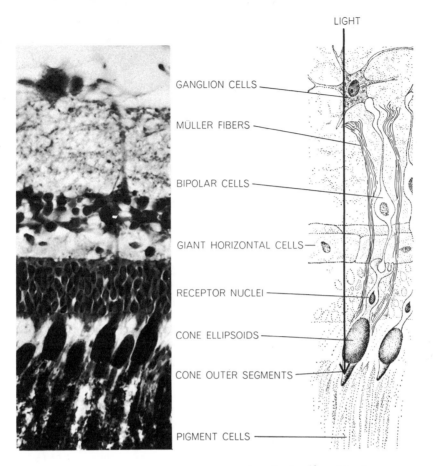

LIGHT

GANGLION CELLS

MÜLLER FIBERS

BIPOLAR CELLS

GIANT HORIZONTAL CELLS

RECEPTOR NUCLEI

CONE ELLIPSOIDS

CONE OUTER SEGMENTS

PIGMENT CELLS

**Figure 11.4 Goldfish retina,** magnified about 1 000 diameters, is seen in section in the photomicrograph (*left*). The various elements of the retina are identified in the drawing (*right*). They have been rendered schematically in an effort to suggest the connections between them on the basis of the information available from recent electron microscope studies.

also had an effect on the discharge. If we held the wavelength constant and increased the intensity of the illumination, the response pattern changed from excitation ("on") to both excitation and inhibition ("on-off") and eventually to inhibition alone ("off"). This held true only in a limited band of wavelengths.

The relation of these two factors – wavelength and intensity – became more evident when we ran a series of threshold experiments, adjusting the intensity of the stimulus to produce a constant response at various wavelengths; the intensity thus became a measure of the sensitivity of the process at a given wavelength. Measurements on a single ganglion cell usually defined two distinct luminosity functions of

wavelength: the intensities for a constant "on" and for a constant "off" response. In one of our early experiments (figure 11.6) the two curves overlapped from 530 to 610 millimicrons. It was in this region that a change in intensity was effective in converting "on" patterns to "off" patterns. The gray curve in the illustration traces the intensities that caused complete suppression of all activity during illumination; it is the "inhibition" curve. In the overlap region it illustrates the effect of increasing intensity mentioned above. Beyond that it coincides closely with the "off" response, again suggesting that the latter is a rebound phenomenon.

Experiments in which either the short-wavelength or the long-wavelength process was selectively light-adapted provided further evidence for the independence of the two processes and the idea that the "off" system is inhibitory in nature. Adaptation with red light, for example, depressed the "off" response and increased the sensitivity of the "on" process. The latter, moreover, could now be obtained throughout the spectrum: it had been released from inhibition.

The ganglion cells I have been discussing are "green-on, red-off" cells. We found others that gave an opposite

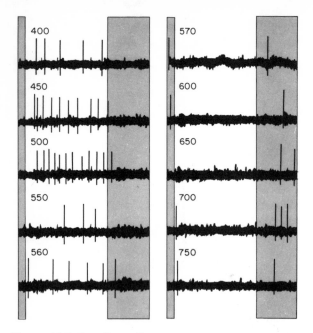

Figure 11.5 Ganglion-cell response varies with the wavelength of the stimulus, a half-second flash of light (*white area*). At short wavelengths (*left*) there is an "on" response, a burst of impulses during illumination. At long wavelengths (*right*) there is an "off" response instead. (Spikes at left side of some long-wavelength records are from preceding stimuli.)

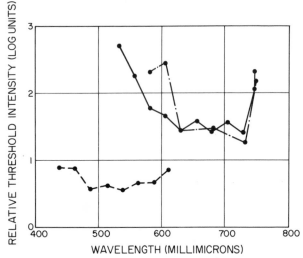

Figure 11.6 Threshold curves show the intensity necessary to elicit "on" and "off" responses from a ganglion cell at different wavelengths. The "on" response (*dashed*) was obtained at short wavelengths, the "off" (*continuous*) at long wavelengths. In the overlap region the "off" response required a higher-intensity stimulus. The dash and dot curve traces the inhibition threshold.

response ("green-off, red-on"), but in both cases the "off" response was associated with the inhibition of nerve-impulse activity during illumination, whether it was spontaneous activity, the result of background illumination or a carry-over of the "on" burst elicited by a previous stimulus.

Our results made it clear that in the goldfish information with regard to wavelength is carried up the optic nerve in the form of discharges from ganglion cells that are acted on by groups of receptors having sensitivities in different parts of the spectrum. These groups of receptors, presumably acting through the second-order bipolar cells, exert either excitatory or inhibitory effects on the ganglion cells. A given ganglion cell may, for example, be excited primarily by a group of red-sensitive receptors and inhibited mainly by a number of green-sensitive receptors. Other cells would be conversely affected. Some ganglion cells show no wavelength dependence but have about equal "on" and "off" thresholds throughout the spectrum; one would expect that they receive equal numbers of excitatory and inhibitory connections from each type of receptor. A few cells maintain a discharge throughout illumination; these presumably have only excitatory connections. Others discharge in the dark and are inhibited throughout prolonged illumination; they may only have inhibitory connections. David Hubel and Torsten Wiesel at the Harvard Medical School have found similar color-coded "on" and "off" responses in the optic nerve fibers of monkeys. The kind of coding we discovered in the retinal ganglion cells of fishes presumably holds true in man as well.

At this point in our investigation we had identified, at the level of the S-potentials and again at the level of the ganglion-cell discharge, elements of an "opponent color" coding system. The 19th-century German physiologist Ewald Hering had developed a color-vision theory based on such a process, perhaps involving a yellow-blue, a red-green and a black-white receptor. Hering's theory attempted to account for two-color phenomena — such as the fact that red and green (or blue and yellow) vary together in sensitivity and never appear subjectively mixed — that could not be easily

Figure 11.7 Microspectrophotometer measures the absorption of light by a single cone. Monochromatic light, held to a constant flux by a feedback loop, is formed into two beams. A rotating chopper disk allows the "test" (*A*) and the "reference" (*B*) beams alternately to pass through the specimen to the photomultiplier tube. Depending on which beam is passing through, photodiodes switch the photomultiplier output into a test or a reference channel. The transmissivity of the specimen, *A* over *B*, is recorded and punched on tape.

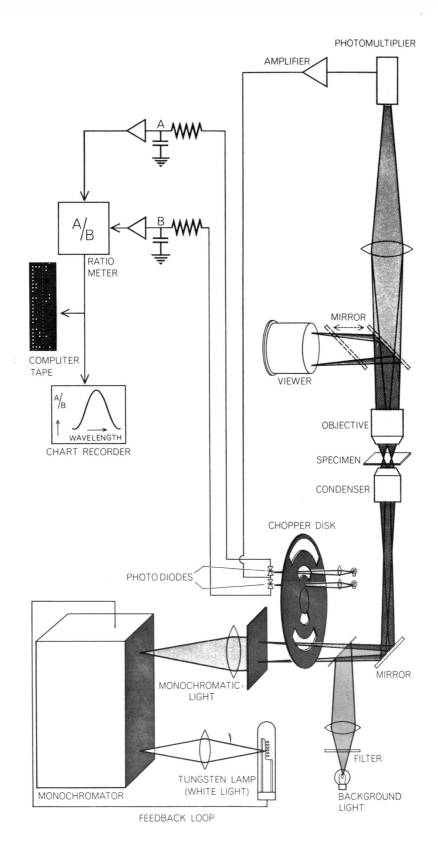

PHOTOMULTIPLIER

AMPLIFIER

A

A/B

RATIO
METER

B

COMPUTER
TAPE

A/B

WAVELENGTH

CHART RECORDER

MIRROR

VIEWER

OBJECTIVE

SPECIMEN

CONDENSER

CHOPPER DISK

PHOTO DIODES

MONOCHROMATIC
LIGHT

MIRROR

FILTER

TUNGSTEN LAMP
(WHITE LIGHT)

MONOCHROMATOR

BACKGROUND
LIGHT

FEEDBACK LOOP

explained by a trichromatic system of the sort suggested by Young and elaborated by Hering's contemporary Hermann von Helmholtz. There seemed to be no way to confirm or disprove either theory except by examining the sensitivity of the actual receptors at various wavelengths. This meant measuring the absorption characteristics of the pigments in the cones across the entire visible spectrum.

Cone pigments are difficult to extract and have yet to be separated from one another by standard biochemical methods. By analyzing a solution of chicken-retina pigments after partial bleaching, George Wald and his colleagues at Harvard University were able to distinguish a cone pigment, which they called iodopsin, from the known rod pigment rhodopsin, but this method has not been successful in mammals. The first successful method of distinguishing the various cone pigments *in situ* was devised by F. W. Campbell and W. A. H. Rushton at the University of Cambridge in 1955. They measured the intensity of light beamed into the human eye and reflected out again by the pigmented layer at the back of the retina. By selective bleaching and by comparing data from normal and color-blind people Rushton was able to identify two different pigments in the fovea, the central region of the retina where the cones are closely packed and there are no rods. One pigment, which he called chlorolabe, was most sensitive in the green part of the spectrum and another, erythrolabe, had its peak sensitivity in the yellow (see "Visual pigments in man", by W. A. H. Rushton, *Scientific American*, November 1962). At Harvard, Wald and Paul K. Brown were able to approach the problem even more directly, measuring with a spectrophotometer the absorption of light by dissected monkey and human foveas. They too were able to identify a green-sensitive and a red-sensitive pigment. Neither this method nor Rushton's, however, could specify whether the pigments were segregated in separate receptors or were mixed in a single receptor, nor could either method present clear evidence for any blue-sensitive pigment.

The best way to settle the question was somehow to measure with a spectrophotometer the absorption spectra of the pigments in individual cone cells. This is simple conceptually but quite difficult in practice. The outer segment of a cone cell, which contains the pigment, has a diameter ranging from perhaps five microns to less than two microns in various species: the small amount of pigment present in each cone requires that the beam of light passed through it be of low intensity, and the quantized nature of light then makes for "photon noise" in the record. Nevertheless, two Japanese investigators, T. Hanaoka and K. Fujimoto, did manage in 1957 to examine single cones in the retina of the

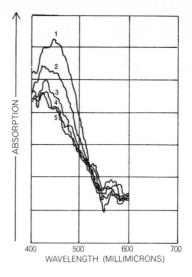

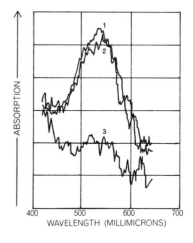

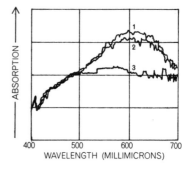

**Figure 11.8 Raw data** for blue (*top*), green (*middle*) and red (*bottom*) cones were recorded with varying gains and light intensities. The blue curves were done as described in the text and required correction for bleaching. Green and red curves 1 and 2, recorded at low intensities, bleached very little; after deliberate flash bleaching, the final curves (*3*) were recorded. Subtracting the last from the first curves yields difference spectra.

carp; they detected what appeared to be five or six different pigments, each in a different cone. For some reason they did not pursue this line of work. Brown at Harvard and Paul A. Liebman at the University of Pennsylvania made spectrophotometric measurements on the outer segment of frog rod cells, but their instruments were apparently not yet able to detect the pigments in the outer segment of cones, which are much smaller. William B. Marks and I set out to design an instrument sensitive enough to measure the absorption curves of goldfish cones.

Our microspectrophotometer directs two beams of colored light through a specimen of retinal tissue to a photomultiplier tube. The "test beam" passes through the outer segment of a cone; the "reference beam", through a clear area. The photomultiplier measures the amount of light transmitted by the cone pigment compared with the amount in the unobstructed reference beam (figure 11.7). Light generated in a monochromator passes through two small apertures in a piece of metal foil; the two resulting beams are focused on the specimen, a piece of goldfish retina squeezed flat between two glass cover slips. In order to keep the retina dark-adapted, or unbleached, we orient the

specimen under infrared background illumination, viewing it with an infrared image converter.

A mechanical "chopper" alternately selects the test and reference beams for passage through the specimen to the photomultiplier; photodiodes on the chopper alternately switch the corresponding signal from the photomultiplier into a chart recorder that takes the ratio of the two signals. This ratio, a measure of the relative absorption of the cone pigment across the visible spectrum, is simultaneously digitized and punched on tape to be analyzed and corrected by computer.

The simple absorption spectrum of a visual pigment is distorted by the presence of extraneous nonbleaching pigments, by the wavelength-dependent scattering caused by particulate matter and by diffraction and chromatic aberration in the optical system. The usual way of minimizing

**Figure 11.9 Goldfish cone pigment** spectral sensitivities are shown by these curves, the averages of eight difference spectra peaking in the blue, ten in the green and nine in the red. The small symbols outline the curves for hypothetical "Dartnall pigments" (*see text*).

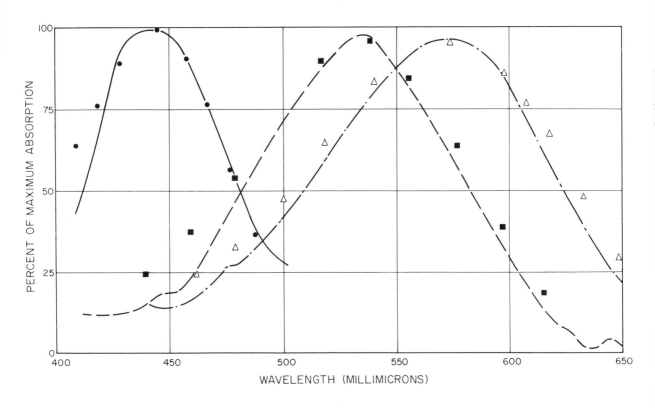

such effects is to record an absorption spectrum, bleach the specimen with white light, record another absorption spectrum and subtract it from the first. If colored products are not created in the process (often they are and must be corrected for), the resulting "difference spectrum" should provide the true spectral absorption curve of the bleachable pigment. This method requires that the intensity of the test beam be low in order not to bleach the pigment during a scan. In the early stages of his investigation Marks found that he had to step up the intensity of the beam in order to overcome photon noise; therefore he allowed the test beam to bleach the pigment, making several scans (figure 11.8) and subtracting the last from the first to get a difference spectrum. The peak of such a spectrum was displaced from the correct wavelength because there was progressively less pigment available at successive points in the scan. Marks worked out a correction procedure: he estimated the fraction of the original pigment remaining at each wavelength and divided the calculated difference at that point by the appropriate fraction. With W. E. Love, Marks wrote a computer program to perform the calculations, make the corrections and plot the corrected difference spectrum.

When a large number of difference spectra recorded in this way were printed together, it was evident that they fell into three groups with peaks in the blue, green and red. When he averaged the curves in each group, Marks came up with the three goldfish cone pigment spectra shown above, with peaks at wavelengths of about 455, 530 and 625 millimicrons (figure 11.9). For evidence whether or not these curves represent the spectral sensitivities of three cone pigments, Marks compared them with the curves for three hypothetical visual pigments with peaks at these wavelengths. These curves are based on a translation of the curve of rhodopsin to the specified wavelengths according to a graph devised in 1953 by H. J. A. Dartnall of the Institute of Ophthalmology in London. Iodopsin and other visual pigments discovered since then have conformed to such curves. Our goldfish curves conform rather well, although not perfectly.

The primary conclusion we could draw from the goldfish investigation was that it unequivocally verified Young's three-receptor prediction, at least in one species known to be capable of color vision. Liebman has since performed similar experiments, employing light intensities that do not cause appreciable bleaching. He has provided independent confirmation of the work by developing curves that are in generally good agreement with Marks's results. Marks was also able to determine the density of the pigment in the cones: it is about a million molecules per cubic micron, or nearly the same as in the density of the rhodopsin in the

rods. Since his measurements were made at right angles to the axis of the cones and could be repeated at several points in an outer segment with identical results, they showed further that the pigment is present throughout the outer segment (not concentrated in a minute granule, as Rushton had once suggested) and that such optical effects as filtering and focusing cannot play a significant role in color perception.

We were anxious to extend our investigation to individual human cone cells, not only because of the implicit interest of the human visual system but also because of the large amount of psychophysical data with which one can compare objective experimental results. William Dobelle, a graduate student, was able to obtain some human retinas through the cooperation of an eye bank, and along with them we used material from the rhesus monkeys *Macaca nemistrina* and *M. mulata*, obtained from the Naval Medical Research Institute. Monkey and human cones, like the cones of other primates, are much smaller than fish cones, measuring only about two microns in diameter at the base of the outer segment. If these cones were squeezed flat, as they were in the goldfish experiment, the light beam penetrated them from the side and not enough pigment molecules lay in its path to register a signal far enough above noise. Dobelle and Marks finally learned how to mount a piece of retina so that the cones are vertical and the beam of light traverses the main axis of the receptor, thus encountering more pigment molecules. They took specimens from the region of the retina just outside the fovea, where the cones are separated by closely packed rods, from which they can easily be discriminated, and proceeded to obtain difference spectra in the same way described earlier for goldfish cones (figure 11.2).

When the computer printed out the corrected spectra for 10 primate cones, the curves fell once again into three clearly defined groups (figure 11.10). Marks has since made some corrections in these original results; the best averages to date for the three receptors are shown in figure 11.1. The fact that in primates the "red" receptor's spectral curve peaks not in the red part of the spectrum but in the yellow seems remarkable but was not surprising. It has already been indicated by psychophysical results, notably those of W. S. Stiles of the National Physical Laboratory in England, who found a "red" maximum from 575 to 587 millimicrons. Although the curve peaks in the yellow, it extends far enough into the red to sense red light unambiguously. That is, these cones are at least substantially more sensitive to red than are the green receptors, and that is all that is necessary if red light is to stimulate the retina to send a message the brain can interpret as "red".

At about the same time as we were investigating primate

cones, Brown and Wald at Harvard modified the instrument with which they had examined frog rods and primate foveas so that it could record from individual cones. Their measurements of four cones in a single human retina also revealed three distinct absorption curves, although the peaks of the curves were somewhat different from ours: 450, 525 and 555 millimicrons. This could have been because there are in fact substantial differences among individual cones of the same type or because the methods by which Brown and Wald produced and corrected their spectra were different from ours. Liebman has also obtained data from individual human cones, but we have not yet been able to analyze his results. Many more measurements will have to be made before the exact spectral sensitivities of primate color-vision pigments are determined.

Single-cell microspectrophotometry develops the curve of whatever pigment material is in an individual cone, and not necessarily the curve of an individual pigment. Recently

Wald performed a series of psychophysical experiments to determine if the color sensitivity of the living human eye corresponds to the single-cone data. He measured threshold sensitivities after selective adaptation and derived three curves with peaks at 430, 540 and 575 millimicrons – in closer agreement with our spectrophotometric data than with his own. Since these pigment-specific curves obtained from the entire population of receptors agree so well with our cone-specific spectrophotometric data, it seems likely that there are indeed three types of cone, each of which contains principally one of three pigments.

**Figure 11.10 Primate cone** difference spectra are shown as plotted from spectrophotometer tapes by a digital computer. One blue and one green human cone and eight rhesus monkey cones are represented. These curves, after correction, are the basis of figure 11.1.

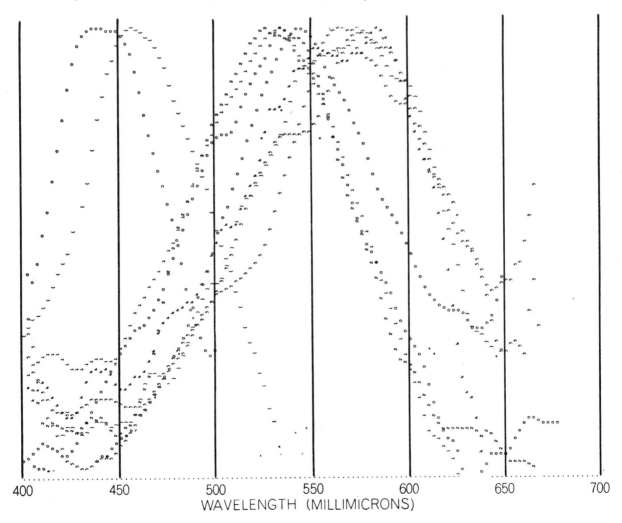

WAVELENGTH (MILLIMICRONS)

Electrophysiological evidence of what goes on in the vertebrate receptor cell has been difficult to obtain, but in 1963 Tsuneo Tomita of Keio University in Japan recorded slow potential changes that he is fairly sure originated in receptors in the retina of the carp, which is closely related to the goldfish. These signals vary in response to illumination by light of different wavelengths. They seem to reach a maximum amplitude at three points in the spectrum. And the three peaks correspond rather well with those Marks derived for the pigments of the goldfish cones.

All the evidence for a three-color, three-receptor cone system comes up against the earlier electrophysiological evidence for an opponent-color system farther along the visual pathway. Color vision is apparently at least a two-stage process, consistent with the Young–Helmholtz theory at the receptor level and with the Hering theory at the level of the optic nerve and beyond. Each receptor does not have its private route to the brain; three-color information is somehow processed in the retina and encoded into two-color on-off signals by each of the color-sensitive retinal ganglion cells for transmission to the higher visual centers.

## Bibliography

The Eye, edited by Hugh Davson, Academic Press, 1962

In Situ Microspectrophotometric Studies on the Pigments of Single Retinal Rods, Paul A. Liebman in *Biophysical Journal*, Vol. 2, No. 2, Part 1, pages 161–178, March 1962

Journal of the Optical Society of America, Vol. 53, No. 1, January 1963

Retinal Mechanisms of Color Vision, E. F. MacNichol Jr, in *Vision Research*, Vol. 4, Nos. 1/2, pages 119–133, June 1964

# Section III
# Emotion and motivation

This section is mainly concerned with the mechanisms underlying the genesis, persistence and character of behaviour which we call "motivated", "emotional", "goal-directed" and "purposeful". It seeks to explain the fact that animals are variable in their responsiveness to environmental stimulation even in situations where the environment itself remains unchanged.

Before certain physiological techniques were evolved, such as direct recording from and stimulation of the brain, psychologists suggested various hypothetical internal events and systems responsible for the fluctuation in responsiveness and the appearance of certain kinds of behaviour at certain times. Hypothetical internal states such as "drive", "arousal" and "motive" were suggested to account for the observed behaviour. More recently it has been possible to look inside the "black-box", as it were, and we are now closer to understanding the physiological bases of the fluctuations in behaviour such as eating, drinking, fear, anger, sexual behaviour and temperature control.

Analysis of the underlying mechanisms is one step towards the control of these behaviour patterns artificially, and, as such, is socially significant. There may be good arguments for controlling anger in a culture, but the morality of an external control of sleeping, fear and sex is debatable, to say the least.

The papers included in this section illustrate several quite different techniques in the study of behaviour. The article, "Ulcers in the executive monkey" by Joseph Brady, takes up the theme of the interdependence of "psyche" and "soma" and reports some interesting observations of the genesis of pychosomatic ulcers in monkeys experiencing environmental "stress" of specific periodicity.

"Attitude and pupil size" by Eckhard Hess looks at yet another response which is controlled by the autonomic nervous system, ANS; the pupillary light reflex and, using this as a gross indicator of ANS activity, he explores its relationship to the "emotive" and "motivating" aspects of environmental stimuli. The paper by S. P. Grossman, "Eating and drinking elicited by adrenergic and cholinergic stimulation of the hypothalamus", in marked contrast, describes a technique for exploring the hypothalamic systems subserving behaviour by direct stimulation with two common neurohumoural transmitters. In the following article Samuel Eiduson deals in greater detail with the biochemistry of neurohumoural transmitters in relation to psychoactive drugs and environmental factors.

"Emotional centres in the brain" by James Olds takes hedonism to the neuronal level and describes distinct reward and aversive systems in the brain. This is followed by an article by Ronald Melzack which discusses the problem of the perception of pain.

The last two articles in this section, "The reticular formation" by J. French and "The states of sleep" by Michel Jouvet, describe experiments using direct electrical stimulation and recording from the CNS which explore the systems underlying the arousal continuum. The former is included as it provides a readable introduction to the reticular formation (RF); it does, however, represent the classical view of this system as it was written at about the time when further research-findings modified this view. Briefly, the functions of the RF are approximately as stated by the classical theory, but the anatomy is quite different; it has been found that it is not a diffuse multisynaptic system and that not all major sensory pathways provide collateral input into the RF, as was earlier thought.

# 12 Ulcers in executive monkeys
## by Joseph V Brady

Physicians and laymen alike have long recognized that emotional stress can produce bodily disease. Psychic disturbances can induce certain skin and respiratory disorders, can set off attacks of allergic asthma and may even play a part in some forms of heart disease. Of all the body's systems, however, the gastrointestinal tract is perhaps the most vulnerable to emotional stress. The worries, fears, conflicts and anxieties of daily life can produce gastrointestinal disorders ranging from the "nervous stomach", which most of us know at first hand, to the painful and often disabling ulcers which are the traditional occupational disease of business executives.

Emotional stress appears to produce ulcers by increasing the flow of the stomach's acid juices. The connection between emotional disturbance, stomach secretion and ulcers is well documented. A recent study of 2 000 Army draftees, for example, found that those who showed emotional disturbance and excessive gastric secretion during their initial physical examination developed ulcers later on under the strains of military life.

But not every kind of emotional stress produces ulcers, and the same kind of stress will do so in one person and not in another. Experimental investigation of the problem is difficult. Animals obviously cannot provide wholly satisfactory experimental models of human mind-body interactions. They can, however, be studied under controlled conditions, and it is through animal experiments that we are finding leads to the cause of ulcers as well as to the effect of emotional stress on the organism in general.

Various investigators have succeeded in inducing ulcers in experimental animals by subjecting them to physical stress. But the role of the emotional processes in such experiments has been uncertain. Experiments on dogs by George F. Mahl of Yale University Medical School indicate that a "fear producing" situation lasting many hours increases the animals' gastric secretions, but these animals do not develop ulcers. William L. Sawrey and John D. Weisz of the University of Colorado produced ulcers in rats by subjecting them to a conflict situation: keeping them in a box where they could obtain food and water only by standing on a grid which gave them a mild electric shock. But this experiment, as Sawrey and Weisz themselves pointed out, did not prove conclusively that emotional stress was the crucial factor in producing the ulcers.

Our studies of ulcers in monkeys at the Walter Reed Army Institute of Research developed somewhat fortuitously. For several years we had been investigating the emotional behavior of these animals. In some of our experiments we had been keeping monkeys in "restraining chairs" (in which they could move their heads and limbs but not their bodies) while we conditioned them in various ways. Since these procedures seemed to impose considerable emotional stress on the animals, we decided that we ought to know something about their physiological reactions. Preliminary investigation showed that stress brought about dramatic alterations in the hormone content of the animals' blood, but a more extensive study of 19 monkeys was brought to a halt when many of them died.

At first we considered this merely a stroke of bad luck, but the post-mortem findings showed that more than bad luck was involved. Many of the dead monkeys had developed ulcers as well as other extensive gastrointestinal damage. Such pathological conditions are normally rare in laboratory animals, and previous experiments with monkeys kept in restraining chairs up to six months convinced us that restraint alone did not produce the ulcers. Evidently the conditioning procedures were to blame.

One of the procedures which showed a high correlation with ulcers involved training the monkey to avoid an electric shock by pressing a lever. The animal received a brief shock on the feet at regular intervals, say, every 20 seconds. It could avoid the shock if it learned to press the lever at least once in every 20-second interval. It does not take a monkey very long to master this problem; within a short

*first published in* Scientific American, *October 1958.*

*Reprinted with permission. Copyright © 1958 by Scientific American, Inc. All rights reserved.*

time it is pressing the lever far oftener than once in 20 seconds. Only occasionally does it slow down enough to receive a shock as a reminder.

One possibility, of course, was that the monkeys which had developed ulcers under this procedure had done so not because of the psychological stress involved but rather as a cumulative result of the shocks. To test this possibility we set up a controlled experiment, using two monkeys in "yoked chairs" in which both monkeys received shocks but only one monkey could prevent them. The experimental or "executive" monkey could prevent shocks to himself and his partner by pressing the lever; the control monkey's lever was a dummy. Thus both animals were subjected to the same physical stress (*i.e.*, both received the same number of shocks at the same time), but only the "executive" monkey was under the psychological stress of having to press the lever (figure 12.1).

We placed the monkeys on a continuous schedule of alternate periods of shock-avoidance and rest, arbitrarily choosing an interval of six hours for each period. As a cue

for the executive monkey we provided a red light which was turned on during the avoidance periods and turned off during the "off" hours. The animal soon learned to press its lever at a rate averaging between 15 and 20 times a minute during the avoidance periods, and to stop pressing the lever when the red light was turned off. These responses showed no change throughout the experiment. The control monkey at first pressed the lever sporadically during both the avoidance and rest sessions, but lost interest in the lever within a few days.

After 23 days of a continuous six-hours-on, six-hours-off

**Figure 12.1 Conditioning experiment** involves training monkeys in "restraining chairs". Both animals receive brief electric shocks at regular intervals. The "executive" monkey (*left*) has learned to press the lever in its left hand, which prevents shocks to both animals. The control monkey (*right*) has lost interest in its lever, which is a dummy. Only executive monkeys developed ulcers.

schedule the executive monkey died during one of the avoidance sessions. Our only advance warning had been the animal's failure to eat on the preceding day. It had lost no weight during the experiment, and it pressed the lever at an unflagging rate through the first two hours of its last avoidance session. Then it suddenly collapsed and had to be sacrificed. An autopsy revealed a large perforation in the wall of the duodenum – the upper part of the small intestine near its junction with the stomach, and a common site of ulcers in man. Microscopic analysis revealed both acute and chronic inflammation around this lesion. The control

**Figure 12.2 Responses of monkeys** were recorded automatically. Slope of the lines shows the rate of lever-pressing (*vertical lines indicate resetting of stylus*). Upper chart shows responses of an executive monkey during the last half of a six-hour avoidance session (*shaded area*) and the first half of a six-hour rest period; shocks were programmed every 20 seconds. Monkeys kept on this schedule developed ulcers. Lower chart shows responses during a 30-minutes-on, 30-minutes-off schedule with shocks programmed every two seconds. Monkeys on this schedule failed to develop ulcers, despite more intense activity and presumably greater psychic stress.

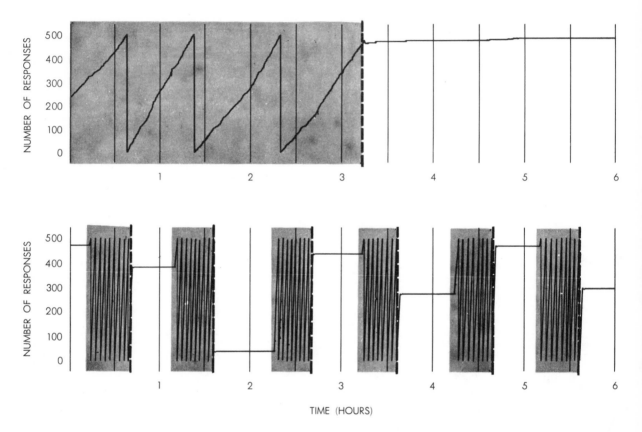

TIME (HOURS)

monkey, sacrificed in good health a few hours later, showed no gastrointestinal abnormalities. A second experiment using precisely the same procedure produced much the same results. This time the executive monkey developed ulcers in both the stomach and the duodenum; the control animal was again unaffected.

In a series of follow-up experiments which is still in progress we have tried to isolate the physiological and psychological factors which produce the "laboratory ulcers". For example, one of our groups suggested that the "social" interaction between the two monkeys might be important. Certainly the most casual observation showed that considerable "communication" was going on between the two animals, who were seated within easy chattering distance of each other. We therefore studied several pairs of animals isolated from each other in soundproof "telephone booths". Unfortunately isolation failed to protect the executive monkeys, for they continued to develop ulcers.

More recently, however, we have found a factor or group of factors which does seem to be critical in producing ulcers. What we have learned seems to pivot on our chance selection of six hours as the interval for shock-avoidance and for rest in the conditioning procedure. We made this discovery when we sought to improve on the results of our experiments. Though laboratory animals can rarely be made to develop ulcers, we had come upon a procedure that seemed to produce ulcers "to order". The only uncertainty was the length of exposure required. This varied greatly among individual monkeys; some came down with ulcers in 18 days, others took as long as six weeks. If we could develop a technique guaranteed to produce ulcers in, say, 10 days, we could stop the shock-avoidance sessions on the eighth or ninth day, apply various therapeutic measures and study the monkey's response to them.

It seemed reasonable to assume that we might induce ulcers more rapidly and dependably by simply increasing the stress on the animals. We therefore put several monkeys on an 18-hours-on, six-hours-off schedule. After a few weeks one of the animals died, but of tuberculosis, not ulcers. The rest continued to press their levers week after week with no apparent ill effects. Finally, when it began to seem as if we might have to wait for the animals to die of old age, we sacrificed them − and found no gastrointestinal abnormalities whatever!

We put another group on an even more strenuous schedule: 30 minutes on and 30 minutes off, with the shocks programmed for every two seconds rather than every 20. Again one of the animals died, this time of a generalized virus infection unrelated to ulcers. The others, after weeks of frantic lever pressing, showed no gastrointestinal changes (figure 12.2).

We had to conclude that the crucial factor was not the degree or even the frequency of stress but was to be sought in the relationship between the length of the stress period and that of the rest period. The six-hours-on, six-hours-off schedule had produced ulcers (and occasionally other somatic disorders) despite individual differences in monkeys, variations in diet and maintenance routines and gross alterations in preliminary physiological tests. No other schedule we had tried produced ulcers at all.

This unexpected finding suggested that we should investigate what was going on in the monkeys' stomachs during the conditioning procedure. A standard technique for investigating gastric processes in experimental animals makes use of an artificial opening, or fistula, in the animal's abdominal and stomach walls through which the contents of its stomach can be sampled. Such fistulas have played an important role in expanding our knowledge of the gastrointestinal system. In the early 19th century the famous US Army surgeon William Beaumont made the first systematic study of the digestive process with the cooperation of a young Canadian who had a fistula due to an imperfectly healed gunshot wound. More than a century later Stewart G. Wolf Jr, and Harold G. Wolff at the Cornell University Medical College, with the help of a man who had a similar injury, conducted a pioneer investigation of the relationship between emotional stress and ulcers. They found that situations

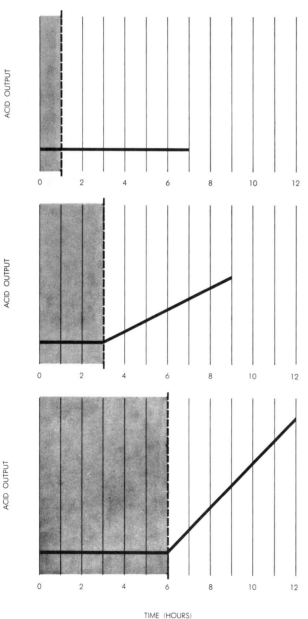

**Figure 12.3 Stomach acidity** of executive monkeys, as shown in these highly simplified charts, did not increase during avoidance sessions (*shaded*) but rather during the subsequent rest periods. The greatest increase followed a six-hour session; no rise followed a one-hour session.

which produced feelings of anxiety or aggression in their subject stepped up his gastric secretions and engorged his stomach wall with blood. Physiological changes of this sort, they believed, are the precursors of ulcers.

Edwin Polish of our department of neuroendocrinology has been studying the stomach acidity of some of our executive monkeys by means of artificial fistulas. His measurements, though far from complete, seem to provide one possible explanation of the results of our experiments.

The stomach secretions of the executive monkeys do indeed become considerably more acid, but not (as one might expect) during the avoidance periods. When the animals are actually pressing the levers the acidity of their stomachs rises little. The significant increase in acidity begins at the end of the avoidance session and reaches a peak several hours later, while the animal is presumably resting. This finding suggests a close relationship between the formation of ulcers and the cyclic character of the six-hours-on, six-hours-off procedure. Emotional stress, it appears, must be intermittent – turning the animal's system on and off, so to speak – if it is to cause ulcers. Continuous emotional stress seems to permit a stable adjustment (at least for a while) under which ulcers do not develop. It is tempting to consider the analogy of the vacuum tube or light bulb which seems to last much longer under conditions of continuous current than when it is subjected to frequent heating and cooling.

Like most analogies, this one limps badly and has its limitations. For example, our experiments show that periodic stress does not always bring on ulcers, and Polish's findings are consistent with this. His measurements indicate that the greatest increase in acidity occurs after a six-hour avoidance session. After a three-hour session acidity rises, but less sharply; after a one-hour session it does not rise at all (figure 12.3). Periodic emotional stress apparently causes ulcers only if its period coincides with that of some natural rhythm of the gastrointestinal system.

Obviously our knowledge of the physiological and psychological processes which produce ulcers is far from complete. Our understanding of even the relatively well-controlled experiments I have described is just beginning to progress beyond the primitive level. We have yet to discover why emotional stress steps up the stomach's acidity later rather than immediately. We are still looking for a method of producing ulcers at will, in days rather than weeks. Eventually we hope to learn to detect an incipient ulcer before the animal collapses, by examining the subject's blood, urine and other secretions, thus making post-mortem examinations unnecessary.

There are many other questions about the effects of emotional stress which we have not yet begun to investigate. Really thorough examination of the experimental animals might well show other types of damage of which we are at present unaware. The two monkeys which died of causes unrelated to ulcers, for example, may have succumbed because their resistance had been lowered in some way by psychological stress. It would be surprising to find physical processes wholly unimpaired in monkeys who have been on a 30-minutes-on, 30-minutes-off schedule for several weeks. The opportunity to bring psychosomatic relationships under experimental scrutiny in the laboratory seems to open broad horizons for research into the causes and alleviation of this poorly understood class of ills.

## Bibliography

Evidence on the Genesis of Peptic Ulcer in Man, Stewart Wolf and Harold Wolff in *The Journal of the American Medical Association*, Vol. 120, No. 9, pages 670–675, 31 October 1942

An Experimental Method of Producing Gastric Ulcers, William L. Sawrey and John D. Weisz in *Journal of Comparative and Physiological Psychology*, Vol. 49, No. 3, pages 269–270, June 1956

# 13 Attitude and pupil size
## by Richard H Hess

One night in 1960 I was lying in bed leafing through a book of strikingly beautiful animal photographs. My wife happened to glance over at me and remarked that the light must be bad – my pupils were unusually large. It seemed to me that there was plenty of light coming from the bedside lamp and I said so, but she insisted that my pupils were dilated. As a psychologist who is interested in visual perception, I was puzzled by this little episode. Later, as I was trying to go to sleep, I recalled that someone had once reported a correlation between a person's pupil size and his emotional response to certain aspects of his environment. In this case it was difficult to see an emotional component. It seemed more a matter of intellectual interest, and no increase in pupil size had been reported for that.

The next morning I went to my laboratory at the University of Chicago. As soon as I got there I collected a number of pictures – all landscapes except for one seminude "pinup". When my assistant, James M. Polt, came in, I made him the subject of a quick experiment. I shuffled the pictures and, holding them above my eyes where I could not see them, showed them to Polt one at a time and watched his eyes as he looked at them. When I displayed the seventh picture, I noted a distinct increase in the size of his pupils; I checked the picture, and of course it was the pinup he had been looking at. Polt and I then embarked on an investigation of the relation between pupil size and mental activity.

The idea that the eyes are clues to emotions – "windows of the soul", as the French poet Guillaume de Salluste wrote – is almost commonplace in literature and everyday language. We say "his eyes were like saucers" or "his eyes were pinpoints of hate"; we use such terms as "beady-eyed" or "bug-eyed" or "hard-eyed". In his *Expressions of Emotion in Man and Animals* Charles Darwin referred to the widening and narrowing of the eyes, accomplished by movements of the eyelids and eyebrows, as signs of human emotion; he apparently assumed that the pupil dilated and contracted only as a physiological mechanism responsive to changes in light intensity.

This light reflex is controlled by one of the two divisions of the autonomic nervous system: the parasympathetic system. Later investigators noted that pupil size is also governed by the other division of the autonomic system – the sympathetic system – in response to strong emotional states and that it can vary with the progress of mental activity. On a less sophisticated level some people to whom it is important to know what someone else is thinking appear to have been aware of the pupil-size phenomenon for a long time. It is said that magicians doing card tricks can identify the card a person is thinking about by watching his pupils enlarge when the card is turned up, and that Chinese jade dealers watch a buyer's pupils to know when he is impressed by a specimen and is likely to pay a high price. Polt and I have been able to study the pupil response in detail and to show what a remarkably sensitive indicator of certain mental activities it can be. We believe it can provide quantitative data on the effects of visual and other sensory stimulation, on cerebral processes and even on changes in fairly complex attitudes.

Most of our early experiments related pupil size to the interest value and "emotionality" of visual stimuli. Our techniques for these studies are quite simple. The subject peers into a box, looking at a screen on which we project the stimulus picture. A mirror reflects the image of his eye into a motion-picture camera (figure 13.2). First we show a control slide that is carefully matched in overall brightness to the stimulus slide that will follow it; this adapts the subject's eyes to the light intensity of the stimulus slide. At various points on the control slide are numbers that direct the subject's gaze to the center of the field. Meanwhile the camera, operating at the rate of two frames per second, records the size of his pupil. After 10 seconds the control slide is switched off and the stimulus slide is projected for 10 seconds (figure 13.3); as the subject looks at it the camera continues to make two pictures of his eye per second. The sequence of control and stimulus is repeated

*first published in* Scientific American, *April 1965.*
*Reprinted with permission. Copyright © 1965 by Scientific American, Inc. All rights reserved.*

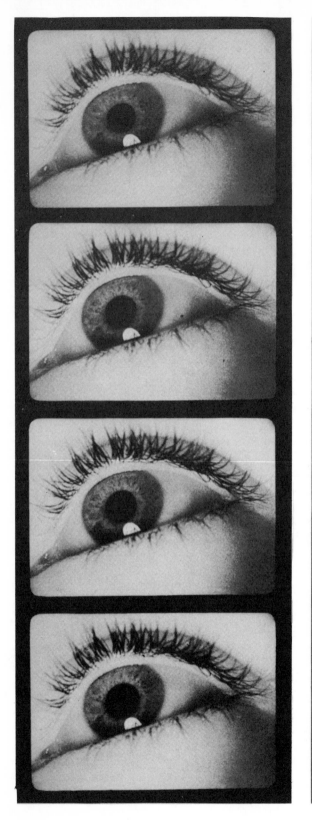
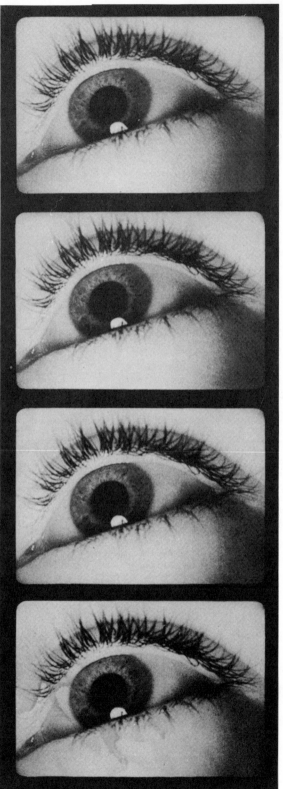

**Figure 13.1 Pupil size** varies with the interest value of a visual stimulus. In the author's laboratory a subject's eye is filmed as he looks at slides flashed on a screen. These consecutive frames (*top to bottom at left and top to bottom at right*) show the eye of a male subject during the first four seconds after a photograph of a woman's face appeared. His pupil increased in diameter 30 per cent.

**Figure 13.2 Subject** in pupil-response studies peers into a box, looking at a rear-projection screen on which slides are flashed from the projector at right. A motor-driven camera mounted on the box makes a continuous record of pupil size at the rate of two frames a second.

about 10 or 12 times a sitting. To score the response to a stimulus we compare the average size of the pupil as photographed during the showing of the control slide with its average size during the stimulus period. Usually we simply project the negative image of the pupil, a bright spot of light, on a screen and measure the diameter with a ruler; alternatively we record the changes in size electronically by measuring the area of the pupil spot with a photocell.

In our first experiment, before we were able to control accurately for brightness, we tested four men and two women, reasoning that a significant difference in the reactions of subjects of different sex to the same picture would

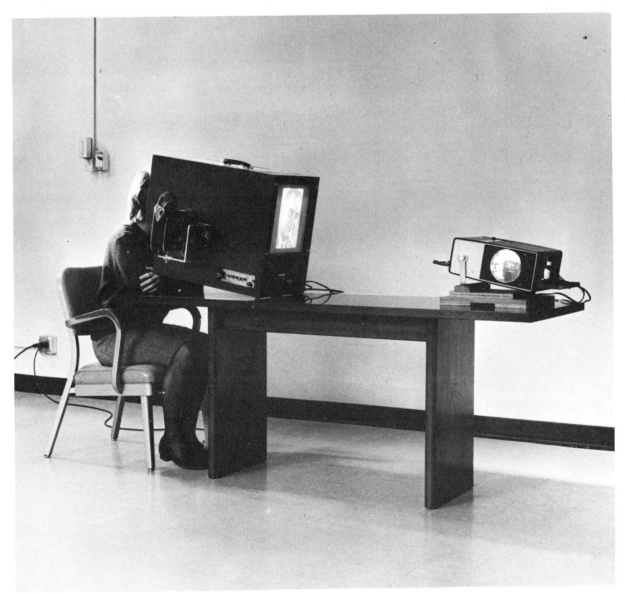

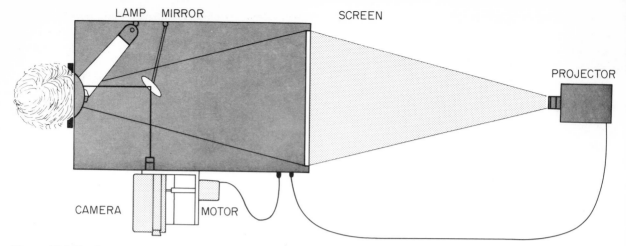

LAMP    MIRROR                    SCREEN

PROJECTOR

CAMERA          MOTOR

**Figure 13.3 Pupil-response apparatus** is simple. The lamp and the camera film work in the infrared. A timer advances the projector every 10 seconds, flashing a control slide and a stimulus slide alternately. The mirror is below eye level so that view of screen is clear.

be evidence of a pupil response to something other than light intensity. The results confirmed our expectations: the men's pupils dilated more at the sight of a female pinup (figure 13.1) than the women's did; the women showed a greater response than the men did to a picture of a baby or of a mother and baby and to a male pinup (figure 13.4). We interpreted dilation in these cases as an indication of interest.

We then undertook another demonstration designed to eliminate the role of brightness (figure 13.5). In this experiment we did not show a control slide; only the general room lighting illuminated the rear-projection screen of the apparatus during the control period. When the stimulus slide came on, every part of the screen was therefore at least somewhat brighter than it had been during the control period. If the eye responded only to changes in light intensity, then the response by all subjects to any stimulus ought to be negative; that is, the pupil should constrict slightly every time. This was not the case; we got positive responses in those subjects and for just those stimuli that would have been expected, on the basis of the results of the first study, to produce positive responses. We also got constriction, but only for stimuli that the person involved might be expected to find distasteful or unappealing.

These negative responses, exemplified by the reaction of most of our female subjects to pictures of sharks, were not isolated phenomena; constriction is as characteristic in the case of certain aversive stimuli as dilation is in the case of

interesting or pleasant pictures. We observed a strong negative response, for example, when subjects were shown a picture of a cross-eyed or crippled child; as those being tested said, they simply did not like to look at such pictures. One woman went so far as to close her eyes when one of the pictures was on the screen, giving what might be considered the ultimate in negative responses. The negative response also turned up in a number of subjects presented with examples of modern paintings, particularly abstract ones. (We were interested to note that some people who insisted that they liked modern art showed strong negative responses to almost all the modern paintings we showed them.) The results are consistent with a finding by the Soviet psychologist A. R. Shachnowich that a person's pupils may constrict when he looks at unfamiliar geometric patterns.

We have come on one special category of stimuli, examples of which are pictures of dead soldiers on a battlefield, piles of corpses in a concentration camp and the body of a murdered gangster. One might expect these to be "negative", and indeed they do produce extreme pupil constriction in some subjects, but they elicit a very different pattern of responses in others. On initial exposure the subject often responds with a large increase, rather than a decrease, in pupil size. Then, with repeated presentations, there is a shift to a negative response; the shift is usually accomplished after three to five exposures, and the time interval between those exposures seems to make little difference. Our impression was that these were negative stimuli with an additional "shock" content that prompted a strong emotional reaction. To check this hypothesis we attached electrodes to the hands of some of our volunteers and recorded their galvanic skin response, a measure of the electrical resistance of the skin that has been correlated with emotional level and is a component of most so-called lie-detector tests. As we had anticipated, stimuli we had classified as "shocking" got a

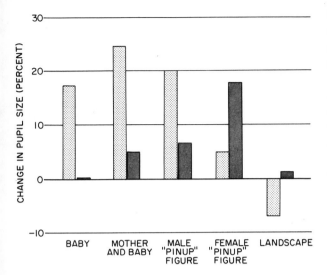

**Figure 13.4 Different responses** to the same picture by female subjects (*dotted bars*) and male (*gray bars*) established that the pupil response was independent of light intensity. The bars show changes in average area of pupils from the control period to the stimulus period.

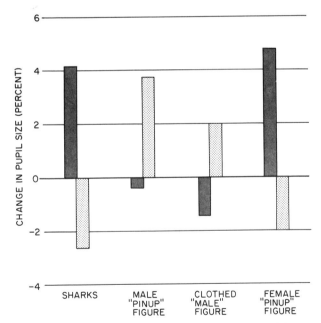

**Figure 13.5 Role of brightness** was also eliminated in an experiment in which the screen was unlighted before the stimulus appeared. Whereas responses to light alone would therefore have resulted in constriction, some pictures caused dilation in men (*gray·bars*) and women (*dotted*). In this experiment pupil diameter was tabulated rather than area.

high galvanic skin response along with the initial high pupil response in most subjects. After repeated presentations the skin response decreased rapidly as the pupil response shifted from dilation to constriction.

Although we have dealt primarily with positive stimuli, the evidence suggests that at least with respect to visual material there is a continuum of responses that ranges from extreme dilation for interesting or pleasing stimuli to extreme constriction for material that is unpleasant or distasteful to the viewer. In the presence of uninteresting or boring pictures we find only slight random variations in pupil size.

One of the most interesting things about the changes in pupil size is that they are extremely sensitive, sometimes revealing different responses to stimuli that at the verbal level seem to the person being tested quite similar. We once demonstrated this effect with a pair of stimulus photographs that in themselves provided an interesting illustration of the relation between pupil size and personality. In a series of pictures shown to a group of 20 men we included two photographs of an attractive young woman. These two slides were identical except for the fact that one had been retouched to make the woman's pupils extra large and the other to make them very small (figure 13.11). The average response to the picture with the large pupils was more than twice as strong as the response to the one with small pupils; nevertheless, when the men were questioned after the experimental session, most of them reported that the two pictures were identical. Some did say that one was "more feminine" or "prettier" or "softer". None noticed that one had larger pupils than the other. In fact, they had to be shown the difference. As long ago as the Middle Ages women dilated their pupils with the drug belladonna (which means "beautiful woman" in Italian). Clearly large pupils are attractive to men, but the response to them — at least in our subjects — is apparently at a nonverbal level. One might hazard a guess that what is appealing about large pupils in a woman is that they imply extraordinary interest in the man she is with!

Pupillary activity can serve as a measure of motivation. We have investigated the effect of hunger, which is a standard approach in psychological studies of motivation. It occurred to us that a person's physiological state might be a factor in the pupil response when we analyzed the results of a study in which several of the stimulus slides were pictures of food — rather attractive pictures to which we had expected the subjects to respond positively. The general response was positive, but about half of the people tested had much stronger responses than the others. After puzzling over this for a while we checked our logbook and found that about 90 per cent of the subjects who had evinced strong

155

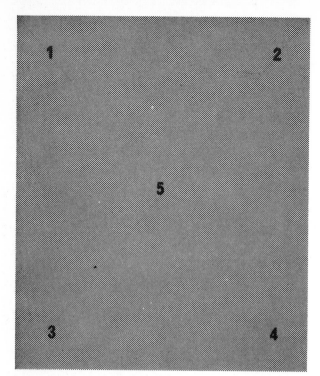

**Figure 13.6 Control slide** provides calibration for experiments involving direction of gaze (figure 13.7). The subject looks at the five numbers in sequence and the camera records the resulting movements of his pupil.

Our first study involved a variety of presumably pleasant-tasting liquids – carbonated drinks, chocolate drinks and milk – and some unpleasant-tasting ones, including concentrated lemon juice and a solution of quinine. We were surprised to find that both the pleasant and the unpleasant liquids brought an increase in pupil size compared with a "control" of water. Then we decided to test a series of similar liquids, all presumably on the positive side of the "pleasant–unpleasant" continuum, to see if, as in the case of visual material, some of the stimuli would elicit greater responses than others. We selected five "orange" beverages and had each subject alternate sips of water with sips of a beverage. One of the five orange beverages caused a significantly larger average increase in pupil size than the others did; the same drink also won on the basis of verbal preferences expressed by the subjects after they had been through the pupil-size test. Although we still have a good deal of work to do on taste, particularly with regard to the response to unpleasant stimuli, we are encouraged by the results so far. The essential sensitivity of the pupil response suggests that it can reveal preferences in some cases in which the actual taste differences are so slight that the subject cannot even articulate them – a possibility with interesting implications for market research.

We have also had our volunteers listen to taped excerpts of music while the camera monitors their pupil size. We find different responses to different compositions, apparently depending on individual preference. As in the case of the taste stimuli, however, the response to music seems always to be in a positive direction: the pupil becomes larger when music of any kind is being played. We have begun to test for the effect of taped verbal statements and individual words, which also seem to elicit different pupil responses. Research in these areas, together with some preliminary work concerning the sense of smell, supports the hypothesis that the pupil is closely associated not only with visual centers in the

responses had been tested in the late morning or late afternoon – when, it seemed obvious, they should have been hungrier than the people tested soon after breakfast or lunch.

To be sure, not everyone is equally hungry a given number of hours after eating, but when we tested two groups controlled for length of time without food, our results were unequivocal: the pupil responses of 10 subjects who were "deprived" for four or five hours were more than two and a half times larger than those of 10 subjects who had eaten a meal within an hour before being tested. The mean responses of the two groups were 11.3 per cent and 4.4 per cent respectively.

Interestingly enough the pupils respond not only to visual stimuli but also to stimuli affecting other senses. So far our most systematic research on non-visual stimuli has dealt with the sense of taste. The subject places his head in a modified apparatus that leaves his mouth free; he holds a flexible straw to which the experimenter can raise a cup of the liquid to be tasted. During the test the taster keeps his eyes on an *X* projected on the screen, and the camera records any changes in pupil size.

**Figure 13.7 Directional analysis** reveals where a subject was ▶ looking when each frame of film was made as well as how large his pupil was. Superposed on the upper reproduction of Leon Kroll's "Morning on the Cape" are symbols showing the sequence of fixations by a female subject looking at the painting; a man's responses are shown below. The stippled symbols indicate a pupil size about the same as during the preceding control period; open symbols denote smaller responses and black symbols larger responses. The experimenters determine the direction of gaze by shining light through the film negative; the beam that passes through the image of the pupil is projected on a photograph of the stimulus (in this case the painting) and its position is recorded.

brain but also with other brain centers. In general it strongly suggests that pupillary changes reflect ongoing activity in the brain.

It is not surprising that the response of the pupil should be intimately associated with mental activity. Embryologically and anatomically the eye is an extension of the brain; it is almost as though a portion of the brain were in plain sight for the psychologist to peer at. Once it is, so to speak, "calibrated" the pupil response should make it possible to observe ongoing mental behavior directly and without requiring the investigator to attach to his subject electrodes or other equipment that may affect the very behavior he seeks to observe.

At the beginning of the century German psychologists noted that mental activity (solving arithmetical problems, for example) caused a gross increase in pupil size. We decided this would be a good area for detailed study in an effort to see how precise and differentiated an indicator the response could be. We present mental-arithmetic problems

**Figure 13.8 Changes in pupil size** are traced in a subject doing the three mental-arithmetic problems shown at the top. Beginning when the problem is posed (*half black circle*), the pupil dilates until the answer is given (*solid black circles*). This subject appears to have reached a solution of the third problem (*open circle*) and then to have reconsidered, checking his answer before giving it.

of varying difficulty to volunteers and then obtain a continuous trace of their pupil response by measuring the filmed images of the pupil with a photocell (figure 13.8). As soon as the problem is presented the size of the pupil begins to increase. It reaches a maximum as the subject arrives at his solution and then immediately starts to decrease, returning to its base level as soon as the answer is verbalized. If the subject is told to solve the problem but not give the answer, there is some decrease at the instant of solution but the pupil remains abnormally large; then, when the experimenter asks for the solution, the pupil returns to its base level as the subject verbalizes the answer.

In one study we tested five people, two who seemed to be able to do mental arithmetic easily and three for whom even simple multiplication required a lot of effort. The pupil-response results reflect these individual differences (figure 13.9) and also show a fairly consistent increase in dilation as the problems increase in difficulty. Individual differences of another kind are revealed by the trace of a subject's pupil size. Most subjects do have a response that drops to normal as soon as they give the answer. In some people, however, the size of the pupil decreases momentarily after the answer is given and then goes up again, sometimes as high as the original peak, suggesting that the worried subject is working the problem over again to be sure he was correct. Other people, judging by the response record, tend to recheck their answers before announcing them.

We have found a similar response in spelling, with the

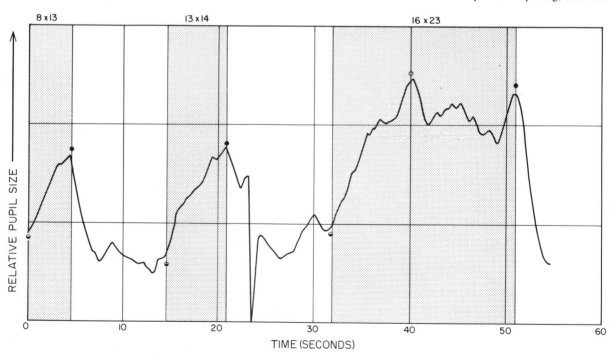

8 x 13     13 x 14     16 x 23

RELATIVE PUPIL SIZE

TIME (SECONDS)

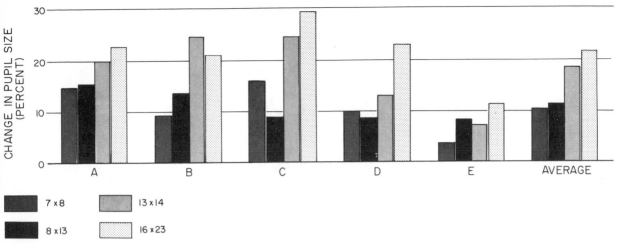

7 x 8    13 x 14

8 x 13    16 x 23

**Figure 13.9 Individual differences** in pupil response while solving multiplication problems reflect the fact that two of the five subjects, *D* and *E*, could do mental arithmetic with less effort than the others. The change in pupil size was computed by comparing the average size in the five frames before the problem was posed with the average in the five frames just before the answer was given.

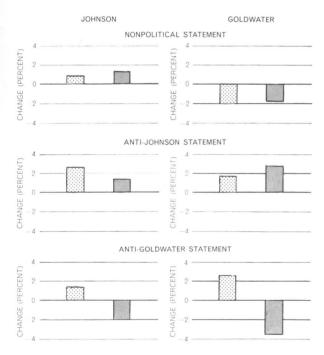

**Figure 13.10 Attitude changes** are revealed by responses to Johnson (*left*) and Goldwater (*right*) before (*light bars*) and after (*dark bars*) subjects read a statement supplied by the experimenter. Nonpolitical material had no appreciable effect. The anti-Johnson material had the expected effect. Bitter anti-Goldwater material made response to both candidates negative.

maximum pupil size correlated to the difficulty of the word. The response also appears when a subject is working an anagram, a situation that is not very different from the kind of mental activity associated with decision-making. We believe the pupil-response technique should be valuable for studying the course of decision-making and perhaps for assessing decision-making abilities in an individual.

It is always difficult to elicit from someone information that involves his private attitudes toward some person or concept or thing. The pupil-response technique can measure just such attitudes. We have established that the correlation between a person's expressed attitude and his "measured pupil" attitude can vary widely, depending on the topic. For example, we tested 64 people with five pictures of foods and also asked them to rank the foods from favorite to least preferred. When we matched each person's verbal report with his pupil response, we obtained 61 positive correlations – a result one could expect to get by chance only once in a million times.

The correlation is poor in an area that involves social values or pressures, however. For example, we do not get such good agreement between pupillary and verbal responses when we show women pictures of seminude men and women. Nor did we get good correlation when we did a political study in the fall of 1964. We showed photographs of President Johnson and Barry Goldwater to 34 University of Chicago students, faculty members and employees. Everyone professed to be in favor of Johnson and against Goldwater. The pupil-response test, however, had indicated that about a third of these people actually had a slightly more positive attitude toward Goldwater than toward Johnson.

To be sure, the pupil test may over-emphasize the effect of physical appearance; certainly our data do not prove that

**Figure 13.11 Two photographs,** almost identical, elicited very different responses from a group of male subjects. One in which a girl's eyes were retouched, as at left, to make the pupils large got a greater response than one in which the pupils were made small (*right*).

a third of the subjects went on to vote for Goldwater. But the results do raise the interesting possibility that at least some of them did, and that in the liberal atmosphere of the university these people found it difficult to utter any pro-Goldwater sentiment. The results suggest that our technique, by which we measure a response that is not under the control of the person being tested, may yield more accurate representations of an attitude than can be obtained with even a well-drawn questionnaire or with some devious "projective" technique in which a person's verbal or motor responses are recorded in an effort to uncover his real feelings.

For me the most interesting aspect of our work has been the measurement of changes in attitude. We begin by determining the pupil response of one of our volunteers to someone's picture. Then we have the subject read some kind of informative material, we retest for the response and compare the "before" and "after" scores. In one case the reading material consisted of a passage indicating that the man whose picture had been displayed was the former comman-

dant of the concentration camp at Auschwitz. When we then remeasured the subject's pupil response to the man in question, we found that a more negative attitude had clearly developed as a result of the intervening reading.

Take another and more hypothetical example: Suppose a patient seeking psychotherapy has a fear of people with beards. We ought to be able to get a pupillary measure of his attitude by showing him photographs of bearded men, among others, and then be able to check on the course of treatment by repeating the test later. Regardless of whether what intervenes is straightforward information, psychotherapy, political propaganda, advertising or any other material intended to change attitudes, it should be possible to monitor the effectiveness of that material by measuring changes in pupil size, and to do this with a number of people at any desired interval.

One recent study along these lines will illustrate the possibilities. We showed five different photographs of President Johnson and five of Goldwater, along with a single photograph of former presidents Kennedy and Eisenhower, to three groups of people. One group thereupon read anti-Johnson material, another read anti-Goldwater material and the third read some excerpts from a psychology journal that had no political content. Then each group was retested.

Now the people who had read the anti-Johnson material showed a slightly smaller response than before to Johnson and a slightly larger response than before to Goldwater.

160

Some extremely negative anti-Goldwater material, which one of my assistants apparently found very easy to write, had a different kind of effect. It did cause the expected decrease in the response to Goldwater, but it also caused a large drop in the response to Johnson (figure 13.10) and even to Eisenhower! The only person who was unaffected was Kennedy. This may indicate that bitter campaign propaganda can lower a person's attitude toward politicians in general, Kennedy alone being spared for obvious reasons.

The pupil response promises to be a new tool with which to probe the mind. We are applying it now in a variety of studies. One deals with the development in young people of sexual interest and of identification with parents from pre-school age to high school age. In an attempt to establish personality differences, we are tabulating the responses of a number of subjects to pictures of people under stress and pictures of the same people after they have been released from the stressful situation. Our other current study deals with volunteers who are experiencing changes in perception as the result of hypnotic suggestion. In the perception laboratory of Marplan, a communications-research organization that has supported much of our work, Paula Drillman is studying responses to packages, products and advertising on television and in other media. Several laboratories at Chicago and elsewhere are employing our techniques to study such diverse problems as the process of decision-making, the effect of certain kinds of experience on the attitudes of white people toward Negroes and the efficacy of different methods of problem-solving. Those of us engaged in this work have the feeling that we have only begun to understand and exploit the information implicit in the dilations and constrictions of the pupil.

## Bibliography

Pupil Size as Related to Interest Value of Visual Stimuli, Eckhard H. Hess and James M. Polt in *Science*, Vol. 132, No. 3423, pages 349–350, 5 August 1960

Pupil Size in Relation to Mental Activity during Simple Problem-solving, Eckhard H. Hess and James M. Polt in *Science*, Vol. 143, No. 3611, pages 1190–1192, 13 March 1964

# 14 Eating or drinking elicited by direct adrenergic or cholinergic stimulation of the hypothalamus

## by *S P Grossman*

The exploration of the central nervous system by means of electrical stimulation has provided a wealth of information of great interest to physiologists and psychologists alike. The usefulness of this technique is limited, however, because the effects of stimulation are not restricted to synaptic junctions but affect fibers of passage, causing conduction in both normal and antidromic directions.

It has long been recognized that chemical stimulation avoids these problems, but the technique has in the past been plagued by the problem of uncontrolled spread, which raises a serious objection to the injection of chemicals in solution. Attempts to control for this factor by minimizing the injected quantities have apparently not been completely successful in preventing the escape of the fluid along the shank of the needle, following the path of least resistance.

Depositing chemicals in solid form has been shown to reduce this problem greatly,[1] but this method has not allowed repeated stimulation of a selected locus. In the present study, a technique was developed which avoids this objection.

A double cannula system, consisting of two modified syringe needles, was permanently implanted unilaterally, by means of a stereotaxic instrument, into the lateral hypothalamus of each of 12 albino rats. Histological verification of the intended placements showed the tip of the cannula to be located in a circumscribed perifornical region at the same rostrocaudal coordinate as the ventromedial nucleus, an area corresponding to the ventral portion of Anand and Brobeck's "feeding area" of the lateral hypothalamus.[2]

After 5 days of postoperative recuperation, the inner cannula was removed and minute amounts (1 to 5 $\mu$g) of crystalline chemicals were tapped into its tip before it was returned to its usual position. Successive treatments were administered to all animals in a counterbalanced order, with a minimum of 3 days between injections. Both food and water were freely available throughout the experiment. The

*first published in* Science, *1960, Vol. 132, page 301. Copyright 1960 by the American Association for the Advancement of Science.*

food and water consumption of satiated rats was recorded for 1 hour immediately following stimulation and compared with the consumption in a comparable period immediately preceding the injection. Daily food and water consumption records were maintained.

None of the animals ever consumed food or water in measurable quantities during the prestimulation period. The injection of epinephrine or norepinephrine resulted in highly significant ($p < 0.01$) food consumption beginning 5–10 minutes after stimulation and persisting with variable intensity for 20–40 minutes. Food consumption averaged 3.0 gm under epinephrine and 4.3 gm under norepinephrine.

The injection of acetylcholine (capped by physostigmine) or carbachol into the identical loci in the same animals resulted in highly significant drinking ($p < 0.01$), the latency, duration and magnitude of the effect being comparable to those obtained for eating after the injection of adrenergic substances. Water consumption averaged 7.4 ml after the injection of acetylcholine and 12.8 ml after the injection of carbachol, this difference being highly significant ($p < 0.01$). There was no significant food consumption after cholinergic stimulation (figure 14.1).

The injection of adrenergic substances resulted in significantly less water intake than cholinergic stimulation ($p < 0.01$). Since in all but one animal the drinking occurred only after a considerable amount of dry food had been consumed, water consumption seemed to be secondary to the food intake rather than a direct consequence of stimulation. To establish further the specificity of the adrenergic effect, norepinephrine was deposited in the lateral hypothalamus of six food- and water-satiated animals, which were then placed in observation cages containing only water. For 30 minutes after the injection none of the animals consumed measurable quantities of water, though four of them repeatedly sampled the drinking tube very briefly. Food was then introduced, and all animals ate almost immediately, though total food consumption was lower than that normally observed, since the food was introduced only toward the end of the period previously established as the duration of the adrenergic effect.

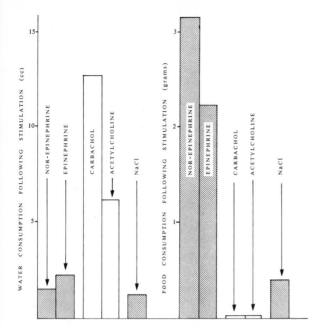

**Figure 14.1 Food and water intake** during 1 hour following stimulation. (The intake during a comparable period was zero in all cases and is not shown.)

In order to control for the effect of osmotic stimulation, comparable amounts of NaCl were deposited in all the animals. No significant food or water intake was observed. In order to control for general excitation effects, strychnine in comparable quantities was deposited in six animals which also showed the above-described effects of adrenergic and cholinergic stimulation. No consumatory behavior was observed following this stimulation.

The daily consumption records indicate that the amount of food or water consumed during the 1-hour period after stimulation, totaling as much as 40 per cent of the animal's normal daily intake, appeared to be consumed above and beyond the normal daily intake. Because of the variability of these records, no statistical evaluation of this effect can be presented, but the conclusion is supported, at least for eating, by the consistent weight gain observed on the day following adrenergic stimulation.

A control for the specificity of the localization of the observed effects was obtained in a preliminary study designed to yield optimal stereotaxic coordinates for the study reported here. It was found that very small deviations from the optimal position sufficed to eliminate the effects completely.

The results of this investigation indicate that (i) cell concentrations active in the regulation of both food and water intake are present in the lateral hypothalamus; (ii) cell con- centrations exerting this control appear to be highly localized but not clearly separate from each other, since stimulation of "identical" loci in the same animal can evoke both forms of behavior; and (iii) the feeding mechanism appears to be selectively activated by adrenergic stimulation, while the drinking mechanisms appear to respond selectively to cholinergic stimulation.

# References

1 MacLean, P. D., *A.M.A. Arch. Neurol. Psychiat.*, Vol. 78, page 113 (1957)
2 Anand, B. K. and Brobeck, J. R., *Proc. Soc. Exptl. Biol. Med.*, Vol. 77, page 323 (1951)

# 15  The biochemistry
# of behaviour
## by *Samuel Eiduson*

For centuries, man has used extracts obtained from various members of the plant kingdom (raw or fermented) to produce pleasurable inner feelings and perceptions which were alien to his everyday existence. The alcoholic brews of virtually all the agrarian cultures were used to alter perceived realities, and sacramental herbs were chewed to obtain a "religious experience". Scientific insight began to replace mystical insight when experiments began to show the possible relationships between the active ingredients of these extracts and the resultant behavioural phenomena on the one hand and, on the other, their effects on specific chemical substances in the body in general and the brain in particular.

The history of science tells us that at some point in time there usually occurs a confluence of seemingly disparate observations which leads to unifying notions in a particular scientific field. Thus, the knowledge that ingestion of minute amounts of an ergot derivative, lysergic acid diethylamide (LSD), resulted in marked changes in perception, emotion and thought, that the alkaloid, reserpine, resulted in sedation and that drugs such as chlorpromazine had the properties of "tranquillizers", excited the interests of students of biochemistry, pharmacology and behaviour. When the work of pioneering investigators such as J. H. Gaddum and M. Vogt in Scotland, D. W. Wooley in the United States, U. S. von Euler in Sweden and V. Erspamer in Italy suggested that these agents were also involved in the action of known biochemical substances in the brain, the biogenic amines, the interest for the biochemist heightened. Resulting experimental work clearly demonstrated a phenomenon frequently seen in the history of the biological sciences − namely, that when biochemistry serves in an interdisciplinary fashion, it has the unique function of being the "explanatory cement" tying up one field with another: in this case, psychology and pharmacology.

Concurrent with research into the biochemical action of the psychoactive drugs is the study of their impact on the individual and society as a whole. I will discuss these sociological effects in more detail later in the article but shall first describe briefly the biochemical action of the drugs and how they modify behaviour.

Two main research strategies have been employed during the past decade and a half to elucidate the relationship between the psychoactive agents, their biochemical mechanisms in the brain and their effects on behaviour. First, the drug is administered to an organism, changes in behaviour noted and the brain analysed for changes in levels of some chemical constituent or products of its metabolism. One of the difficulties which arises in such experiments is that one is never certain that the observed biochemical changes bear a relationship to the observed behaviour or even result directly from the action of the drug. Consequently, with the development of more sophisticated techniques, isolated biochemical systems have been directly investigated to ascertain the drug/system interaction. Conversely, the chemical constituent or its metabolites may be administered to ascertain whether changes in behaviour result and whether such changes are consistent with the observations using the drugs themselves.

The second research strategy is to modify the environmental situation to obtain a behavioural change and then to study concomitant changes in brain biochemistry. Mentally disturbed patients have been compared with non-disturbed ones and individuals subjected to various experimental behavioural problems. In both animals and humans, the effects of the drugs can then be observed upon environmentally induced behavioural changes and biochemical-behavioural hypotheses tested.

The behavioural effects of psychotomimetics such as LSD have been well chronicled. The marked changes that occur in perception, emotion and thought are now the commonplaces expected during the "trip", the LSD "experience". I shall not discuss these in detail but will refer to other, more subtle, aspects of this drug-induced behaviour which can lead to a greater understanding of the phenomena. The effect of the psychotomimetics is particu-

*first published in* Science Journal, *May 1967, page 113.*

larly influenced by such factors as the "setting" in which they are administered and the expectations of the drug taker. Many complications and adverse reactions – including chronic anxiety, depression and even acute paranoid behaviour – have been reported, particularly when the drug is used in an uncontrolled way without medical supervision. In addition, the "state" can re-occur spontaneously days to months after the drug has been taken.

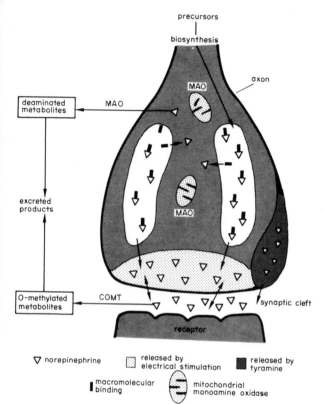

**Figure 15.1 Neurohumoral transmitter** storage and metabolism is shown schematically in the diagram above. Norepinephrine is located in two types of pool: in its unbound state it is found in labile pools (*stippled areas*) at nerve endings and can be readily released into the synaptic cleft by electrical stimulation; when bound to large molecules it is found in stable pools (*white areas*) and is not readily releasable by electrical stimulation. Mitochondrial monoamine oxidase catalyses the oxidation of any norepinephrine released from the stable pool which is then replenished primarily through biosynthesis of the amine from its precursor. Unbound norepinephrine released from the labile pool is converted to its methylated derivative by catechol-O-methyl transferase. The labile pool, which is in equilibrium with the stable pool, can receive amine from the latter but, more importantly, any amine released into the synaptic cleft can be transported back to the labile pool.

The action of these drugs appears to be linked to the biochemistry of the biogenic amines. Prior to Otto Loewi's classical experimental demonstration in 1921 of the concept of chemical transmission, it was thought that the transfer of electrical activity and information from one neuron to another across the synapse occurred by electrical rather than chemical means; as Sir Henry Dale pointed out, "transmission by chemical mediators was like a lady with whom the neurophysiologist was willing to live and to consort in private, but with whom he was reluctant to be seen in public". Now, however, it is generally accepted that electrical stimulation of a neuron and its axon causes release at the nerve ending of a chemical substance which diffuses across the synapse and, when in contact with the postsynaptic receptor site, results in excitation of the receptor. Compounds such as acetylcholine, norepinephrine, serotonin and dopamine are thought to be such chemical mediators or "neurohumoral transmitters".

In this article, I shall use norepinephrine as a "model" transmitter substance because its biosynthesis and metabolism have been well worked out. The amino acid tyrosine is first converted to dopamine. Dopamine in turn is converted to norepinephrine and, outside the central nervous system, norepinephrine is converted to epinephrine. In the brain, however, this final stage is thought not to take place to any appreciable extent. What does happen in the brain is that two important enzymes, catechol-O-methyl transferase (COMT) and monoamine oxidase (MAO), initiate the conversion of norepinephrine to its metabolites. Although the two major routes of metabolism of norepinephrine lead to the same end products, it is essential to know which of the enzymes, COMT or MAO, acts first on the amine before we can understand some of the observed drug effects; I shall explain this later in the article.

As with most small chemical substances in the brain, norepinephrine in its free state is found in "pools" rather than being randomly distributed. It is now believed that at least two such pools exist in which the amine is either bound to a large molecule or is unbound. Unbound norepinephrine, contained in vesicles at the nerve endings and thought to form a labile or unstable pool, is readily released into the synaptic cleft by electrical excitation of the neuron and its axon. The bound norepinephrine, on the other hand, exists in vesicles along the axon and is not readily releasable by electrical stimulation. Monoamine oxidase, which is contained in the mitochondria, catalyses the oxidation of any norepinephrine released in the neurons from the bound pool; these oxidation products are then transported to the periphery where they may be further metabolized. When any unbound norepinephrine is released by stimulation into the synapse it is acted upon first by COMT and is thus converted to its methylated derivative.

It is thought that the stable pool is replenished primarily through the biosynthesis of the amine from its precursor. On the other hand, the labile pool is replenished in at least two ways. It is in equilibrium with the stable pool and, therefore, when its supply of transmitter substance is depleted by stimulation it can receive the amine from the stable pool. Also, and perhaps more importantly, any norepinephrine released at the synapse may, in fact, be actively transported back into the vesicles of the labile pool (figure 15.1).

Assuming that the neurohumoral transmitters are stored in the way I have described, it is then possible to put forward a preliminary explanation of the way a number of the psychoactive drugs act and to examine where this action takes place. Drugs such as reserpine and tetrabenezine, which have a sedative or tranquillizing effect, are thought to release the neurohumoral transmitter from storage sites in the neurons. The amine is then oxidatively deaminated by MAO. In addition, these drugs may also prevent the reuptake by the intraneuronal storage granules of any available transmitter amine in the cytoplasm. As a result the brain stores become short of the amine. On the other hand, antidepressant drugs of the imipramine type act primarily on the membrane of the nerve endings by inhibiting the reuptake of transmitter amine from the synaptic cleft. This leads to a higher concentration of physiologically active transmitter substance at the receptor site. The labile stores of norepinephrine released by electrical stimulation are also released by drugs like amphetamine. In addition, amphetamine prevents the re-uptake of the norepinephrine into these same nerve ending storage vesicles; this again results in a greater concentration of physiologically active transmitter at the receptor site.

The MAO inhibitors can be interpreted as acting intraneuronally, inhibiting the mitochondrial MAO activity. Therefore, as norepinephrine is released from the intraneuronal storage sites, its oxidative deamination is prevented by the inhibitor and, as a result, the level of the amine rises intraneuronally as well as externally. Tranquillizers such as chlorpromazine also apparently enter this picture here in that they can occupy the same receptor site as the transmitter substance itself, and could thus prevent excitation of the receptor.

Although existing evidence supports this view of the metabolism of the neurohumoral transmitter norepinephrine, it is still too early to accept it categorically. For example, the magnitude of the drug dose plays an important

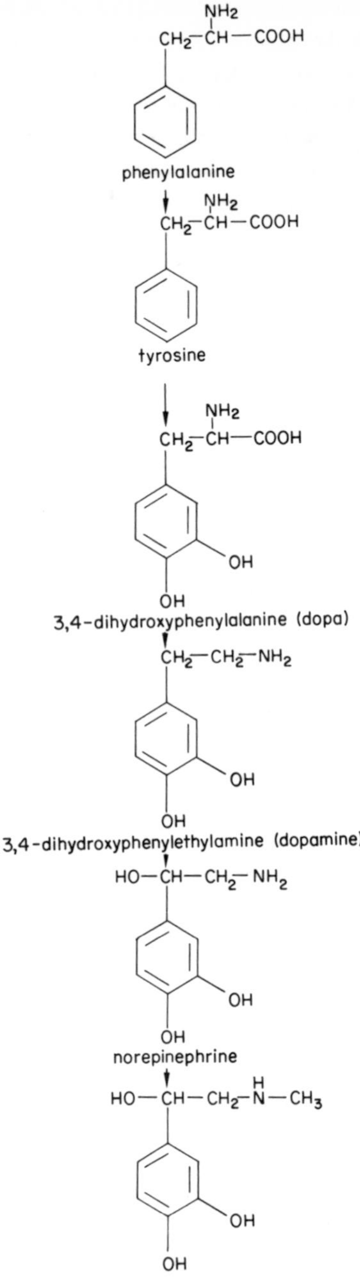

Figure 15.2 Biosynthesis of epinephrine and norepinephrine follows the route outlined above. Phenylalanine, an essential amino acid, is converted to tyrosine. Tyrosine is hydroxylated to give dopa which is, in turn, decarboxylated to dopamine – a compound with many of the physiological properties of norepinephrine to which it is converted by hydroxylation. Methylation of norepinephrine produces epinephrine. The enzymes responsible for the reactions are known and most have been found in the brain.

166

part in any observed behaviour; a low concentration of drug may affect the uptake of the amine into intraneuronal storage sites, while a higher dose will also affect the re-uptake mechanism at the membrane of the nerve terminals. Another complicating factor is that many drugs have a multiplicity of action, and one cannot always be certain that a particular result is due to only one particular action of a drug.

Complicating the picture still further is the problem of the state of the organism at the time of an experiment; during excitation and stress many other biochemical systems are mobilized which can affect a drug response. For example, endocrine activation as a consequence of stress may result in more or less of a particular enzyme being synthesized; this can affect the level of any of the amines and thus complicate the drug picture. Indeed, work in my laboratory at the Brain Research Institute has shown that brains of animals under certain stressful conditions take up less of an administered dose of drug than the brains of non-stressed animals.

One behavioural disturbance which appears to implicate the biogenic amine story is that known clinically as "depression" or the "affective disorders". According to J. J. Schild-kraut "the catecholamine hypothesis of affective disorders proposes that some, if not all, depressions are associated with an absolute or relative deficiency of catecholamine, particularly norepinephrine, at functionally important adrenergic receptor sites in the brain. Elation, conversely, may be associated with an excess of such amines." Irrespective of the ultimate truth or falsity of this particular hypothesis, it is clear that the knowledge of the metabolism, storage and function of the biogenic amines being uncovered almost daily offers hope that the molecular substrates of the affective disorders will become known. If true, then once again biochemistry will have served its historical role as an "explanatory cement", fusing in this instance physiology, pharmacology and psychiatry.

I mentioned earlier in the article that one of the approaches to the study of the relationship between biochemistry and behaviour was to alter or manipulate behaviour in some specific way and then to determine the effect of this manipulation upon some biochemical system or systems. A number of laboratories have made some headway with this approach although the meaning of their findings is not yet clear. D. Krech, M. R. Rosenzweig and E. L. Bennett have studied biochemical changes in the brain of rats placed in either a complex environmental setting or one in which the animals lived in isolation with little external stimulation. Under such conditions, it was found that the animals in the complex environment had significantly higher brain cortex weights than the isolated controls. In addition, these "environmental-rich" rats showed a different distribution and activity of brain acetylcholinesterase as compared to the isolated animals.

The observations have been extended more recently by E. Geller, A. Yuwiler and J. F. Zolman, who showed that the brains of rats from "enriched" environments contained less norepinephrine. Moreover, it appears that isolation was stressful to the animals because there was altered activity of some liver enzymes. Although these studies indicate an unmistakable correlation between the environmental-behavioural set of the animal and its chemistry, their meaning is still unclear.

A different behavioural pattern has been used by M. H. Aprison and co-workers to tease out some biochemical–behavioural correlates. They treated a subject by conditioning techniques involving approach-avoidance behaviour and observed that, following an intramuscular injection of 5-hydroxytryptophan, there was a disruption in the subject's behaviour which coincided with an increase of serotonin in certain parts of the brain. However, decreases in catechol-amine concentrations which did not appear to coincide with the behavioural changes were also noted.

These recent advances suggest that we are coming closer to knowing what are the specific biochemical substrates of specific forms of behaviour. Add to this the knowledge of the relationship of nucleic acid and protein synthesis to learning and memory, and what is already known about "inborn errors of metabolism" such as phenylketonuria, and it becomes apparent that the contagion of scientific excitement about the psychoactive drugs, neurohumoral transmitters and behaviour runs deep.

As more knowledge becomes available, the relationship of biochemistry to behaviour will become even clearer. In humans, the knowledge being adduced will undoubtedly stimulate further explorations into the wider implications of the drug–biochemistry–behaviour triad. Already, experimental results suggest that LSD, for example, may be useful in the treatment of the terminal cancer patient to give more prolonged and persistent relief from pain than the normally employed morphine-like drugs. In addition, there is speculation that LSD may be helpful to the chronic alcoholic, although the meagre data available at present are not yet convincing. The problem concerning the utilization of the drug in psychotherapy is also in the realm of speculation.

There are more general, and perhaps more important, social and cultural problems with which man is confronted as a consequence of the psychoactive agents in particular, and of the increase in biochemical and biological knowledge in general. It is not too presumptuous to assume that in the relatively near future we shall know quite precisely how the important neurohumoral substances work in the brain and even in which regional parts of the brain they operate, together with the kinds of behaviour which are influenced by them. Furthermore, our future knowledge of the mechanism of action of psychoactive agents may well permit us to manipulate biochemical–behavioural interactions in a variety of ways. What are the probable and possible consequences of this biological knowledge to the human condition?

Much has been said and written about the possible "mind-controlling" or "brain-washing" consequences of our increasing knowledge of biochemistry and behaviour. Throughout history, fear, isolation and extreme physical hardship have been used to coerce an individual into specific kinds of behaviour. Although at the present time there is no evidence that the psychoactive drugs – tranquillizers, energizers, psychotomimetics – have been used by one group of individuals for the precise purpose of imposing a set of attitudes or behaviour upon other individuals, it is not an inconceivable contingency. Brain washing or mind controlling correctly conjures up in the minds of many people a sordid picture of mindless and aimless men at the mercy of the brain washers. But "mind dulling" is also a possible consequence of our psychopharmacological knowledge. An equally appalling picture is that of a society (without coercion!) manipulating their central nervous systems *en masse* by the use of psychoactive agents. Different individuals, using different drugs to achieve different conditions of heightened sensory stimulation or tranquillization, may be unable or unmotivated to question existing social thought and standards of behaviour and thus become a conforming mass, sluggish to change in an ever-changing and complex environment.

We have learned from evolution that certain organisms, unable to adapt to a changing environment, have perished. Man has achieved his state of civilization perhaps mainly because his great diversity – genetic, anatomical and behavioural – has permitted an equally great diversity in response to an ever increasing environmental complexity. Because such frightening conditions as mind controlling or conforming may be possible, it is imperative that we recognize more clearly the extreme importance of maintaining this diversity of response to the demands of existence. The threat of our exploding knowledge in biochemistry and behaviour lies precisely in the abuse of this knowledge (to coerce, to control and to conform) to reduce the ways in

which man can act to achieve his needs in a complex world. Therefore, the recognition that drugs could be used to constrain our options in responding, and thus limit our freedom, makes it necessary to ask at every stage whether this or that drug related event will or will not diminish the number of possible choices we may make. Clearly, some diminution of alternative responses will occur as long as we are members of a society of other men. Indeed, some constraints, such as compulsory education, may be quite desirable and may even lead to greater potential for options of responding. But if we always consider the inevitable growth in our biological knowledge in terms of whether it maximizes or decreases our possible alternatives of response to the world, then the danger of mind control will be minimized.

Of equal importance is the effect of our exploding biochemical and biological knowledge in the area of memory and learning. Our concern here is what impact will the facilitation of memory and learning have on how we teach, when we teach and where we teach. Will schools and instruments of instruction have to undergo a revolution? At the very least, it seems to me, our quantitative kind of knowledge will have to be imparted at much earlier periods of life than is being done today. Thus, calculus and thermodynamics, computers and biostatistics will be occupying the fertile minds of the young. As we learn more about the biochemistry of the human nervous system, especially as it applies to the development of that system and of its "critical periods", our understanding of the mechanisms of learning may suggest that teaching is most effective at certain early stages of development. Certain kinds of human knowledge may be better understood and more easily stored at certain periods of development of the brain than at others. The work on imprinting, for example, indicates that the phenomenon, if it is to take place at all, must take place in the newborn chick's first hours or days of life. After this period passes, it is unlikely that the imprinting mechanism can be elicited.

We now know that much of the material substance and intricate chemistry of the brain is made during early development while that brain is functioning, while communication, integration and interpretation of internal and external events are in progress. Surely, all these sensory inputs, these internal and external influences, must have a modulating effect upon the maturation of the brain substance itself as well as on its biochemistry and its functioning? Our styles of thinking and perception may be laid down very early in life and, with the knowledge of developmental biochemistry and behaviour, such styles may indeed be altered, inhibited or facilitated.

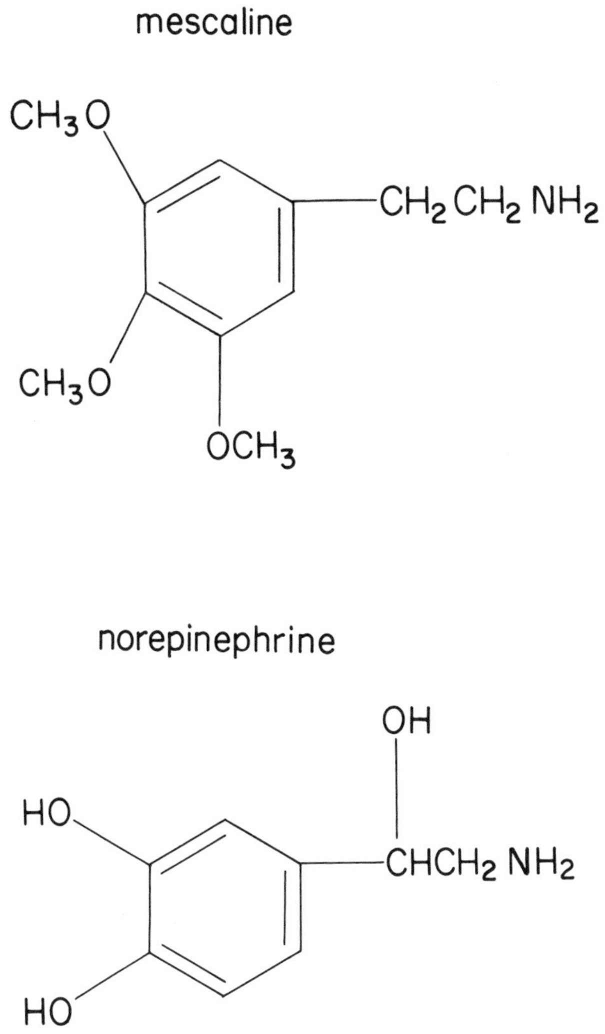

## mescaline

## norepinephrine

Figure 15.3 Mescaline is extracted from the cactus *Lophophora williamsi*. The psychoactive nature of mescaline was described at the turn of the century. It is now believed that the mescaline induced psychotic state results primarily from interference with norepinephrine to which it is closely related chemically.

If our increasing knowledge of the mechanism of memory and learning could have such widespread effects upon the young, it is certainly appropriate to ask what effect it would have upon the elderly. As length of life is extended, will we be able to facilitate memory and learning during this period? Although no evidence exists today that this can be done, experimental data suggest that it may be possible. What effect will this have upon the schooling of our population – new schools for older people? What effect will this have upon our working population and retirement? It appears probable that our concept of work and leisure may have to undergo drastic changes.

It seems plausible, too, to suppose that with a detailed knowledge of the mechanism of action of the neurohumoral substances, drugs and behaviour, certain areas of the brain can be stimulated and modulated such that growth and complexity of these areas can be fostered as never before. This could possibly mean that humans can be reared so that imagination and ambiguity are fostered and tolerated (creativity?), that heightened visual activity results (potential artist?) or that auditory sensitivity and discrimination are increased (potential musicians?). But with these potential gains in our advancing knowledge we may have to assess the price, the cost which may have to be borne. Our current biological knowledge tells us that a significant change in a particular biochemical system of the brain does not result in a solitary change but rather, due to the transactional character of the biological processes, to a complex of changes. This transactional process is so complex that it would be virtually impossible to affect one system without affecting another. Although in the future we may be able to manipulate and alter a part of the visual system of the organism, the same alteration could have a deleterious effect upon some other system such as the auditory sense, for example.

Here, then, we are confronted with the notions of "good" and "bad". These are value judgments, and science can offer no answer *per se* but only probabilities and statistics. As I have said, the diversity of man has permitted him to achieve his present stature in the animal kingdom. This diversity has permitted those adaptations required by a changing and complex environment, and it is clear that tampering with this individuality and uniqueness can have the effect of reducing the alternatives of response to future environments as yet not known or even imagined.

As Marsten Bates has pointed out, man has always been a medicine taker, a drug taker and, in all probability, will continue to be one. Therefore, this drug problem may always be with us. However, our increasing knowledge of the interaction of drugs, brain biochemistry and behaviour may permit man to alter his growth, his maturation and, therefore, the way he will perceive and react to the real world. Through all of this, the scientist will have continually to raise the question of what the social consequences will be and ask whether his alternatives of response are being seriously affected. In this way, the scientist, excited and exhilarated by experiments in his laboratory, can share with the social scientists and the humanists the responsibility for evaluating and utilizing his laboratory findings for the advancement of the human condition.

## Bibliography

Psychotomimetic Agents, Sidney Cohen in *Ann. Rev. of Pharmacol.* Vol. 7, 1967

*Neuropsychopharmacology*, edited by P. B. Bradley, F. Flugel and P. H. Hoch, Elsevier, New York, Vol. 3, 1964

*Antidepressant Drugs of Non-MAO Inhibitor Type*, edited by D. H. Efron and S. S. Kety, U.S. Dept. of Health, Education and Welfare, Washington D.C., 1966

*Biochemistry and Behavior*, by S. Eiduson, E. Geller, A. Yuwiler and B. Eiduson, Van Nostrand and Co., Philadelphia, 1964

The Social Responsibilities of the Behavioral Scientist in *Journal of Social Issues*, Vol. 21, April 1965

# 16 Emotional centres in the brain

## by James Olds

In 1939 H. Kleuver and P. C. Bucy at the University of Chicago damaged specific areas of the brains of monkeys and found that the animals subsequently behaved like emotional or motivational idiots: they ate nuts and bolts as happily as raisins and became confused as to when they should respond with appreciation and when with fear. Clearly, the part of the brain involved – the palaeocortex, a thin layer lying between the outer cortex and the centre of the brain – was in some way involved in emotional activity. Indeed, these experiments stemmed from the fact that rabies, which makes dogs "mad", also causes extensive damage of the palaeocortex.

Since the 1930s, interest in locating emotional centres in the brain has turned from the palaeocortex to a small part of the brain, the hypothalamus, situated deep inside the brain, which appears to provide the palaeocortex with information. Mapping of the hypothalamus is now well underway. Most interesting is the discovery of topographically separate regions with special relations to the basic "drives" of hunger, thirst and sex. A pair of larger topographic entities has also been discovered which includes these regions but extends beyond them. The pair has special relations to both the negative emotions which direct behaviour away from aversive objects, on the one hand, and to positive emotions which direct behaviour towards gratifying objects on the other.

The hypothalamus is best known for its relationship to feeding and drinking behaviour and, as a consequence, its role in the regulation of body weight. Lesions in this general region, it is known, cause obesity. When obesity is produced experimentally by electrical coagulation of small hypothalamic regions in rats, they gain weight not mainly because of a metabolic defect but rather because of overeating. They do not overeat indefinitely but only during a "dynamic" phase until they become excessively fat after which a "static" phase ensues and food intake levels off. And yet, as demonstrated by N. E. Miller, C. J. and J. A. F. Stevenson at Yale

*first published in* Science Journal, *May 1967.*

and by P. Teitelbaum, now at the University of Pennsylvania, the overeating is not accompanied by a corresponding increase in hunger drive; a relatively low drive state is indicated by the unwillingness of the animals to work for food as hard as other hungry rats, and their unwillingness to accept non-palatable food which is acceptable to starving rats.

Why did the rats in these experiments eat more even though they were not excessively hungry? It appeared that there was some failure of a satiety ("stop-eating") mechanism and also there was at times a state of craving or voracious appetite evidenced by their stuffing the mouth with food to the point of suffocation. How this voracious behaviour could have coexisted with a relatively low drive state has not yet been satisfactorily explained.

In the course of this series of studies, it was also found that the hypothalamus as a whole was divided into three parts so far as these lesion effects on food intake were concerned: there was a large area occupying more than half of the length and width of the hypothalamus within which small or large lesions caused obesity; there were far anterior and posterior regions where lesions were without clear effects on eating, and there was a very small "needle-in-the-haystack" region far out on each side where lesions caused another complex and partly opposite effect. It was opposite in the sense that the animals instead of overeating refused to eat and in fact died of starvation unless fed by stomach tube; but it was similar in that these animals showed little evidence of hunger drive and were exceptionally responsive to the palatability of the food that they were offered.

Since then Miller and J. M. R. Delgado at Yale, B. G. Hoebel and Teitelbaum at Pennsylvania, and members of my own laboratory, among others, have carried forward the study of motivational centres in the hypothalamus by creating excitatory pathological conditions. These studies were made mainly with a method developed by W. R. Hess of Zürich who discovered between 1924 and 1940 many of the phenomena which the rest of us have "discovered" during the past two decades. In his experiments fine wire needles insulated along their length but bared at the tip were inserted through small holes in the skull and advanced through the brain until the tip was in the target region. A connector or plug was arranged on the head so that after recovery from surgery an electrical cord could be plugged in to stimulate locally between any two of the implanted wires.

Hess found the hypothalamus to have two poles. In one region electric stimulation caused a group of involuntary responses of heart, respiratory apparatus and so forth, all of which could be considered as preparing the animal for violent action; most of the posterior parts of the hypothalamus together with adjacent tissues of the midbrain were included in this. In another region electric stimulation caused reactions associated with rest, recuperation and relaxation; much of the anterior part of the hypothalamus together with adjacent tissues in the direction of the olfactory cortex were included in this. Within the midbrain part of the posterior region, Hess found a subdivision where he could evoke a highly motivated behaviour which appeared to be characterized by a negative emotional state related to aggression or defence, or to both.

With probes in a region of the hypothalamus between the anterior and posterior region, M. Brugger working in Hess's laboratory in 1943 found that he could provoke "mouthing" and eating. The animal would lick or take into its mouth all objects with which it came in contact and if food was present it would eat voraciously during stimulation; immediately thereafter it would desist from this behaviour and resume whatever course of action had been underway before. In 1953 a somewhat similar observation was reported by Delgado and B. K. Anand. In this case, however, the excessive eating came several hours after the hypothalamic stimulation was completed and it was therefore unclear whether the result derived from temporary excitation or from some sort of temporary lesion.

Drinking behaviour was evoked in goats by B. Andersson of Uppsala in 1952 after application of sodium chloride to the hypothalamus. Later in 1955 Andersson and S. M. McCann produced the same effect by application of electrical stimuli. K. Akert, in his 1961 review of the work deriving from Hess's school, reports that when trains of pulses lasting 10 to 20 seconds were applied, "drinking occurred shortly after stimulation began and outlasted it for 2 to 3 seconds. The drinking was very forceful in character; even diluted urine was accepted. The hydration obtained by repeated periods of stimulation reached extreme values of up to 40 per cent of the pre-experimental body weight. In four hours and 40 minutes of intermittent stimulation, one goat drank 16 liters of water."

It remained to determine whether the eating and drinking responses resulted merely from the stimulation of motor centres – in which case the animals were only going through the motions and one might speak of sham hunger or thirst. Miller showed that stimulation in certain parts of the rat hypothalamus caused eating if food was presented. It caused instrumental responding in pursuit of food if food was absent and it caused a change of direction away from water and towards food in a thirsty and drinking animal. He was satisfied therefore that the electric stimulus in these cases had many of the behavioural consequences of ordinary hunger drive and he presumed, justifiably it seems, that the hypothalamus had some important role in coordinating this drive.

In 1953, in the laboratory of D. O. Hebb at McGill, I found that a rat stimulated in a region near the anterior hypothalamus behaved repeatedly as if it were "coming back for more". It came back to one particular corner of a large enclosure. Whenever it was in that corner, I would apply a brain stimulus and it seemed as if this stimulation supplied the purpose for the rat's return. Later the rat learned to run regularly, rapidly and without errors to the "correct" terminus of a "T"-shaped runway, the brain stimulus being the only reward.

P. M. Milner collaborated with me in a study exploiting this finding. We planted probe pairs in a number of rats and at a number of different brain points. To evaluate the effects we placed the animal in a small box with a large lever or pedal at one end. When the animal pressed the lever, the brain stimulus was applied automatically. If the animal under these conditions stimulated its brain at a high rate this created an impression that the stimulus was rewarding: it looked as if the rat worked because it wanted the brain shock. In these boxes, the random pedal rate – that with no brain shock or any other reward – rarely went above 50 responses in the first hour and far fewer thereafter. When each lever response initiated a brain stimulus in the appropriate anatomical region, rates of 5 000 responses an hour were often observed. As this amounted to more than one response a second, the pedal response often came to predominate in the animals' behaviour repertory and occurred in some cases at a maximum possible rate (figure 16.2).

We stimulated many different brain areas but found that the hypothalamus itself, particularly a large and diffuse pathway in its lateral part, formed the focus of the effect. This pathway is called the medial forebrain bundle; it leads back and forth from the hypothalamus to the nearby olfactory cortical systems; it or its terminals must certainly play a critical role in this phenomenon of producing gratification by electric stimulation of the brain.

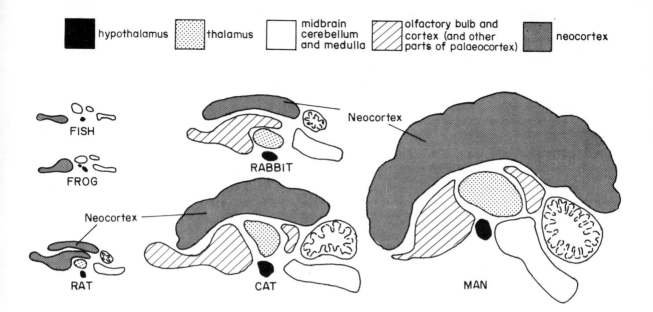

hypothalamus ▦ thalamus □ midbrain cerebellum and medulla ▨ olfactory bulb and cortex (and other parts of palaeocortex) ▨ neocortex

FISH

FROG

RABBIT

Neocortex

Neocortex

RAT

CAT

MAN

**Figure 16.1 Forebrain** has evolved from the simple olfactory bulb and hypothalamus in the fish to the large and complex structure in man. In the frog the thalamus appears and the olfactory bulb has a bulge, the olfactory cortex. In mammals the olfactory cortex is enlarged and gives rise to other parts of the palaeocortex and to the neocortex. Midbrain, medulla and cerebellum with its folds are shown white.

Later experiments made with a closed alley maze and with stimulation applied in regions near the medial forebrain bundle seemed to confirm this. Animals learned to run rapidly to the goal box and to eliminate errors along the way, with the brain shock as the only reward. Not only that but, when animals were brought back 24 hours after previous tests, they ran rapidly and with few errors to the goal box where stimulation was applied. Apparently, no simple response compulsion was involved nor was there only a momentary directed state produced as the immediate after-effect of the previous brain stimulation.

However, in other experiments "brain reward" behaviour has been found to be less persistent than food rewarded behaviour. And there is some evidence that several brain shocks are needed to produce the same reinforcement of behaviour as is obtained by one food pellet with a hungry rat. In fact, brain shock rewards may have more in common with sweets than with food because sweets are rewarding even to a food satiated rat. There is no steadily mounting drive state like hunger to motivate the striving for a brain

reward. As with a reward of sweets, the "temptation" of brain rewards probably declines with time after the last gratification but can still be aroused by the stimuli which cause anticipation of the reward. J. A. Deutsch has suggested that the rewarding brain stimulus supplies its own drive, which would account for the rapid drop in performance once stimulation ceased, but it would not account for the energetic striving which often occurs at the beginning of a day's test before any pre-stimulation.

Although brain reward behaviour sometimes does not persist for long after the shocks are cut off, while the reward is available the behaviour it motivates is intense. When attempts were made to satiate rats' appetite for brain rewards the animals worked steadily for periods of 4, 6, 8 or even 24 hours and returned for more after resting. To get these brain rewards they even crossed electrified grids which stopped rats starved for 24 hours from running for food. Even more remarkable is the fact that starving rats, forced to choose between food enough to keep them alive and brain rewards, chose the brain rewards.

Once it had been established that there was positive motivation here which had some psychological validity and that there was a hypothalamic focus, the question arose as to how this motivation would be related anatomically and functionally to the other functions already known to have some relation to the hypothalamus, particularly the defensive and aggressive reactions.

Dr Marianne E. Olds and I made a map of the hypothalamus and adjacent regions in rats, testing each

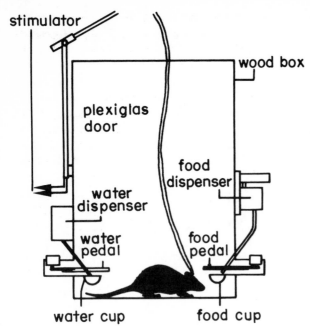

stimulator

wood box

plexiglas door

food dispenser

water dispenser

water pedal

food pedal

water cup

food cup

**Figure 16.2 Self stimulation** experiments were used to demonstrate and map the rewarding effects of electric stimulation in the brain. Each pedal response produced a quarter second train of electric impulses, after which the current was shut off automatically and the animal had to release the pedal and press again to get more. Stimulated drive effects in rats were demonstrated in several laboratories using boxes like the one illustrated. When the brain probe was appropriately placed, stimulation caused the satiated animal to work for food and to eat; when probe was differently placed, stimulation caused animal to work for water and to drink. In other cases, same stimulation caused both eating and drinking.

point first for production of rewarding effects and later for the production of aversive effects. We found that there was a lateral hypothalamic region where positive effects were induced without any clear negative side effects, and there were regions bordering the thalamus and midbrain where negative effects were produced without any signs of reward at all; but there was a large region, including many of the nuclear masses in the mid-hypothalamus, where electric stimulation caused mixed positive and negative effects. With probes in these places, animals in a lever box would learn to stimulate their brains and would respond often but sporadically to accomplish this. But they also performed well in tests in which they were trained to escape from the same stimulation.

One possible explanation was that in some of the midline hypothalamic regions there must be junctions, or synapses, between two opposing sets of nerve fibres. One

set entered from the lateral hypothalamic region where stimulation had pure positive effects. The other set entered from the thalamus and midbrain region where stimulation had pure negative effects. Stimulation of either set alone gave pure positive or negative effects; stimulation of the junction caused mixed effects, perhaps by simultaneously activating the two groups. Because of the opposite effects of stimulating the two fibre groups separately, it seemed appealing to suppose that they came together in the hypothalamus in order for one group to inhibit the other, or possibly for both groups to inhibit one another.

Tests with stimulation simultaneously applied in the "positive" and "negative" regions were made in order to find out whether any inhibitory relations might be detected. In the first series of these tests the animals responded in a lever box, thereby stimulating themselves via hypothalamic electrodes; while this self-stimulation behaviour was underway, the experimenter turned on a continuous stimulus in aversive regions of the midbrain. In many cases this caused a cessation of the positive behaviour – the lever pressing. Thus there was possibly some inhibition caused by the aversive stimulation acting upon the region where stimulation had rewarding effects; equally likely, however, was a more diffuse interaction, such that the aversive stimulus caused too much pain for enjoyment.

In a second series of tests the animals responded in a lever box with the opposite aim, namely to turn off the stimulus which was being repeatedly applied in aversive regions of the midbrain. The experimenter then turned on a stimulus in the positive regions of the hypothalamus. In many cases, this caused the unexpected effect of increasing the animal's escape behaviour. It was unclear why a background of rewarding stimulation should do this. The most appealing explanation to us was the possibility that the stimulus facilitated all ongoing behaviour, even that motivated by negative stimulation. Data such as these made us wonder whether part of the hypothalamic region supposedly involved in positive behaviour might not be a control region involved in the direction of both positively and negatively motivated voluntary behaviour.

The regions involved in the basic drives of hunger and thirst also appear to be related to those which produced positive and negative behaviour. It was found by E. E. Coons and Miller, by Hoebel and Teitelbaum and by D. L. Margules in our own laboratory that the lateral region where electric stimulation caused eating responses was to a large degree overlapped by lateral areas where electric stimulation caused positive reinforcement of behaviour. G. J. Mogensen has recently demonstrated that a nearby but perhaps slightly more anterior region exists where electric stimulation caused drinking behaviour in rats; this "drinking" region was also to a large extent included within the number of regions where electric stimulation caused positive reinforcement of behaviour. Similarly, for reproductive behaviour, L. J. Herberg, and A. R. Caggiula and Hoebel, showed that in a somewhat more posterior part of the mid-lateral hypothalamus, stimulation caused copulation and ejaculation; not surprisingly, this stimulation was also rewarding (figure 16.3).

Almost undoubtedly, further refinement of technique will allow a separation of the "drive" and "reward" effects, at least for feeding, as it is inconceivable that these two poles of the feeding cycle, namely the uphill behaviour towards food and the downhill consummatory process after food is reached, would be sustained by neural activity of one and the same set of neurons.

In earlier studies on the relations between these two aspects of motivation, the drives were manipulated to study their effects on behaviour rewarded with brain stimulation. The aim of these studies was partly to find out whether an appropriate drive could be found for each brain reward region. If an appropriate drive could be found, this might provide some clue to the meaning of the stimulus to the animal, some hint as to whether the animals were responding to this stimulus as though it were a food object, for example, in which case appetite might be expected to be augmented by hunger. These studies were also partly to test the degree to which this kind of behaviour needed a drive to maintain it and, on the other hand, the degree to which the brain stimulus might supply its own drive, as Deutsch later suggested it might do.

Hunger drive was manipulated by depriving the animals of food; sex drive was manipulated by castrating the animals or by administering hormones. The outcomes at first seemed to make good sense. In some cases, the self stimulation rates were augmented by hunger and depleted by satiety. In other cases, rates were depleted by castration and restored later by administration of sex hormones. There were also reversed cases for each drive where the high drive seemed to counteract the behaviour. Moreover, looking at all the cases, there was an inverse relation between the two drives. When the self stimulation rate was greatly augmented by hunger, it was apt to be depleted by a high level of sex hormones and vice versa. This suggested that the two drives are located in separate regions and that the behaviours related to sex and to hunger are mutually interfering. The main difficulty was that further efforts to specify these two regions anatomically failed.

In an attempt to sort out some of the supposedly interconnected effects several investigators have applied chemical stimuli. Would the different drive and reward systems be sensitive to different chemical stimuli so that these systems could be stimulated separately by local applications of chemicals, even though they were so close together that electrical stimuli always activated them together? A. E. Fisher of the University of Pittsburgh applied sodium testosterone sulphate, which is a water soluble form of the male sex hormone, to the hypothalamus. Nesting behaviour, infant retrieval and sexual behaviour were activated by these stimuli. R. G. Grossman, who was Miller's student at the time, applied the two best known "neurotransmitters" or chemical messengers: acetylcholine and epinephrine. When acetylcholine and carbamylcholine, a related compound, were applied in the hypothalamus they caused non-thirsty rats to drink; when compounds of the epinephrine or norepinephrine group were applied at the same sites, they caused satiated animals to eat. The experiments in which drinking was caused by acetylcholine or its relative have been repeated in several laboratories; Fisher showed that these compounds caused drinking when applied almost anywhere in the hypothalamus or palaeocortex or in some places outside this part of the brain. The experiments in which epinephrine or its relatives caused eating were also repeated in Fisher's laboratory. To me it appears that the eating might be due to an inhibitory effect of these epinephrine-like compounds in regions where lesions produce overeating.

In studies in our laboratory, animals were prepared with probes for the local application of chemicals in the lateral hypothalamus, where electric stimulation had caused positive effects, and in the midbrain regions where electric stimulation had caused negative effects. The animals with probes in the hypothalamus were tested in a cage where each lever response caused application of $3 \times 10^{-6}$ ml of fluid. Application of carbamylcholine caused excited behaviour and, therefore, much pedal pressing. A similar but more intense effect was caused by application of substances which caused depletion of calcium ions in the brain fluids; this was because calcium ions act as a damper on spontaneous neuronal activity. The excitatory effects of acetylcholine relatives and of calcium ion depletion were counteracted if norepinephrine or epinephrine was mixed into the applied solutions.

When the probes were in the midbrain "aversive" regions carbamylcholine and calcium ion depletors again proved to be excitatory and norepinephrine had counter-effects. There was a difference here, however: carbamylcholine caused the greater effect in midbrain aversive regions, calcium depletors in hypothalamic regions. This suggests that some special effect in the hypothalamus was produced by depletion of calcium ions but not by stimulation of acetylcholine receptors. The smaller number of pedal responses caused by application of carbamylcholine was perhaps evidence of mere activation rather than of rewarding effects; and the added influence of the calcium depletors might have derived from their evoking both the activation and the lateral hypothalamic rewarding effects.

This would be particularly interesting if true because there was one distant relative of the epinephrine group which counteracted only this added effect; it was effective against calcium depletors when these were applied in the hypothalamus but it failed to act against carbamylcholine and it had no effect against the responses evoked by chemical stimulation of the midbrain. This was serotonin. It was originally discovered as a factor in blood which caused vasoconstriction, thereby helping to stop the bleeding of a wound. This compound was later shown to have special relations to the hypothalamus and midbrain by Martha Vogt of Edinburgh and A. Heller, J. A. Harvey and R. Y. Moore of the University of Chicago. It has recently been suggested as a factor playing a major role in emotional disorders by D. W. Wooley and his co-workers at the Rockefeller University in New York. These workers now believe that disorders in the biochemistry of serotonin may lie at the root of some of the major mental illnesses.

One might assume from these chemical stimulation studies that it is possible to produce similar effects by administering drugs to the brain via the blood stream to augment the amount of acetylcholine-like compounds or epinephrine-like compounds in the central nervous system. However, drugs administered in this way have the opposite effects to those expected. For example, P. Stark and E. S. Boyd at Rochester showed that application of physostigmine via the blood stream, which augmented active acetylcholine in both central and peripheral nervous systems, inhibited hypothalamic self stimulation in dogs instead of promoting it. Similarly, L. Stein showed that administration of amphetamine via the blood stream, which augmented the amounts of epinephrine compounds in the central nervous system, caused an increase in hypothalamically rewarded behaviour.

Why there should be these striking differences between the effects of compounds administered via the blood stream and the effects of these same compounds administered direct to the brain is still a mystery. In the drug studies the change in concentration of the active chemicals occurred both in the blood stream and in brain tissue, whereas in the chemical stimulation studies it occurred in brain tissue alone. It would be appealing to suppose that the brain responded more to blood/brain differences in chemical levels than to chemical levels in the brain itself.

The pharmacological study of the hypothalamic rewarding effect also showed it to be surprisingly resistant to such drugs as alcohol, the sleeping pill pentobarbital and the popular tranquillizer called meprobamate or "Miltown". Alcohol effects were studied by J. St Laurent in our laboratory; it was interesting that an animal so drugged by alcohol that it could not stand would quickly be roused and brought into a state of good motor control by a few brain rewards after which it would self stimulate. It would relapse to the drugged condition if the brain shocks became no longer available. Pentobarbital and meprobamate also failed to counter self stimulation.

Speculation that the positive response to electrical stimulation of the hypothalamus might be peculiar to the rat was countered by the demonstration of the same behaviour in fish, birds, cats, dogs, monkeys and porpoises. Similar responses from human beings with brain probes implanted for therapeutic purposes were also observed by C. Sem Jacobsen of Norway, R. Heath of Tulane, Delgado of Yale and others.

The implantation of brain probes in human beings was undertaken in accordance with standard procedures for diagnosis or cure of major psychoses, epilepsies, Parkinson's tremors, protracted episodes of intolerable pain or for other similar reasons. The reports of conscious human beings who were stimulated in olfactory cortical areas or in the region of the hypothalamus have not been as illuminating as might have been hoped. The patients of Sem Jacobsen often showed appearances of positive emotion during the stimulation but their later reports as to why they "liked" it were often confused. The data of Heath and of Delgado indicated that stimulation of olfactory regions in or near the cortex often caused reduction of anxiety or pain or actual positive feelings sometimes related to sex. But the effects of stimulation in the hypothalamus were correlated with confusing behaviour and confusing reports.

In some experiments the patient would self stimulate by manipulating a switch which caused stimulation via hypothalamic probes. With certain probe placements this behaviour was very intense, appearing not unlike what would be expected on the basis of the animal experiments. However, there was a characteristic of the human behaviour which paralleled that of the monkey but differed from that of the rat, namely that the responding did not cease when the current was no longer available. In fact the behaviour would go on and on in repetitive fashion as if it were going on for ever. Observing the behaviour, one would not know that the current was turned off; and therefore one might guess that the patient did not know either. Furthering the view that the patient did not know what was going on was the fact that his report of his reasons for the self stimulation behaviour seemed at first glance to represent confabulations. One patient, for example, said he did it because the doctor wanted him to, or to earn favours from the hospital staff. This did not seem to make sense because he had started responding regularly only after the experimenter, unbeknown to him, turned on the hypothalamic stimulation.

The paradoxical behaviour was not incompatible with the possibility that hypothalamic stimulation had a general influence causing facilitation or repetition of ongoing behaviour without too much regard for its rational justification in terms of positive or negative motivational goals. The behaviour so determined might then have been justified in

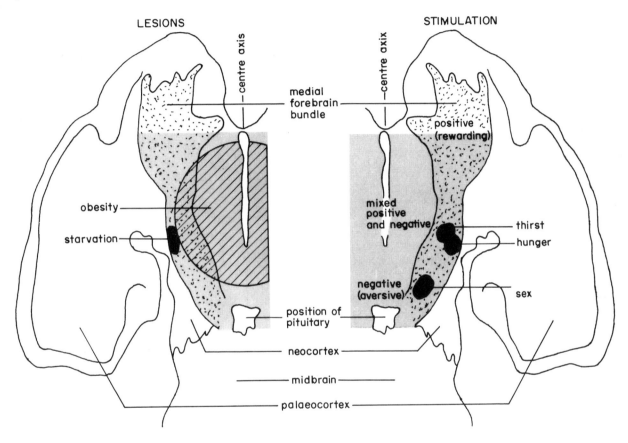

**Figure 16.3 Lesions** (*left*) produced by electrical coagulation in the hypothalamus (*grey*) leads to obesity when made in the large central region and to starvation when made in the small lateral regions. This obesity appears to result from overeating caused by failure of a satiety mechanism. Rat brain is shown in horizontal section through the hypothalamus. Electrical stimulation experiments (*right*) in different parts of the hypothalamus show "islands" of drive — hunger, thirst and sex — in a "river" of reward, the medial forebrain bundle. The most intense reward effects were obtained by stimulation in the most posterior parts of this "river". Other experiments reveal an aversive region in the posterior central hypothalamus and a region of mixed positive and negative responses in front of this.

the patient's mind by whatever explanation seemed to him to be the most plausible.

What kind of consequences can we expect from these findings? Eventually, neuron activity at sites in the olfactory forebrain may be manipulated by pharmacological means in the treatment of pathological conditions. It is not completely out of the question that devices might be surgically placed, above the roof of the nose for example, which would provide electrical stimulation as a therapy both less extreme and more effective than electroconvulsive shock in dangerous cases of severe psychotic depression. Research on these brain topics in laboratory animals will guide the way for pharmacological and surgical approaches if and when they are used.

But such consequences will be only "spin-off"; the main goal is to understand how the brain operates, by artificially stimulating regions which are clearly responsible for important aspects of behaviour. To clarify the meaning of the findings I have described in this article, we need to study in detail the inputs and outputs of the hypothalamic area.

To summarize these findings in terms of an organized psychological theory would be, I believe, to take unfair advantage of an interesting set of findings, treating them as if they suggested a relatively unique interpretation or as if they bore their meaning clearly on their face. Our knowledge of brain behaviour relations is primitive; we await a transition from the relatively descriptive level to the relatively organized. No one in our field has yet suggested to his colleagues a view of brain function of any complexity that was readily received. Simple and complex ideas come and go but they are highly personal; each of us strives for an idea which will take root; and one day, hopefully soon, we shall succeed.

## Bibliography

Appetitite, P. Teitelbaum in *Proceedings of the American Philosophical Society*, Vol. 108, pages 464–472, 1964

Hypothalamic Substrates of Reward, J. Olds in *Physiological Review*, Vol. 42, pages 554–604

Experiments on Motivation, N. E. Mille in *Science*, Vol. 126, pages 1271–1278

Self Stimulation of the Brain, J. Olds in *Science*, Vol. 127, pages 315–323

Diencephalon, K. Akert. Chapter 20 in *Electrical Stimulations of the Brain*, edited by D. E. Sheer (University of Texas Press, Austin, Texas), 1961

# 17  The perception of pain
## by Ronald Melzack

Even though pain is a private and personal experience, we rarely pause to define it in ordinary conversation. Indeed, no one who has worked on the problem of pain has ever been able to define pain to the satisfaction of all his colleagues. When compared with vision or hearing, for example, the perception of pain seems simple, urgent and primitive. We expect the nerve signals evoked by injury to "get through", unless we are unconscious or anesthetized. But experiments show that pain is not always perceived after injury even when we are fully conscious and alert. Thus a knowledge of pain perception goes beyond the problem of pain itself: it helps us to understand the enormous plasticity of the nervous system and how each of us responds to the world in a unique fashion.

A vast amount of study has been devoted to the perception of pain, especially in the last decade, and from it is emerging a concept of pain quite different from the classical view. Research shows that pain is much more variable and modifiable than many people have believed in the past. Moreover, direct recordings of nerve signals are helping us to see, in physiological detail, why pain is such a complex experience.

Anyone who has suffered prolonged, severe pain comes to regard it as an evil, punishing affliction that is harmful in its own right. Yet everyone recognizes the positive aspect of pain. It warns us that something biologically harmful is happening. The occasional reports of people who are born without the ability to feel pain provide convincing testimony on the value of pain. Such a person sustains extensive burns and bruises during childhood, frequently bites deep into his tongue while chewing food and learns only with difficulty to avoid inflicting severe wounds on himself.

It is the obvious biological significance of pain that leads most of us to expect that it must always occur after injury and that the intensity of pain we feel is proportional to the amount and extent of the damage. Actually, in higher species at least, there is much evidence that pain is not simply a function of the amount of bodily damage alone. Rather, the amount and quality of pain we feel are also determined by our previous experiences and how well we remember them, by our ability to understand the cause of the pain and to grasp its consequences. Even the significance pain has in the culture in which we have been brought up plays an essential role in how we feel and respond to it.

In our culture, for example, childbirth is widely regarded as a painful experience. Yet anthropologists have observed cultures in which the women show virtually no distress during childbirth. In some of these cultures a woman who is going to have a baby continues to work in the fields until the child is about to be born. Her husband then gets into bed and groans as though he were in great pain while she bears the child. The husband stays in bed with the baby to recover from the terrible ordeal he has just gone through, and the mother almost immediately returns to attend the crops.

Can this mean that all women in our culture are making up their pain? Not at all. It happens to be part of our culture to recognize childbirth as possibly endangering the life of the mother, and young girls learn to fear it in the course of growing up. Books on "natural childbirth" ("childbirth without fear") stress the extent to which fear increases the amount of pain felt during labor and birth and point out how difficult it is to dispel it.

The influence of early experience on the perception of pain was demonstrated a few years ago in experiments my colleagues and I conducted at McGill University. We raised Scottish terriers in isolation from infancy to maturity so that they were deprived of normal environmental stimuli, including the bodily knocks and scrapes that young animals get in the course of growing up. We were surprised to find that when these dogs grew up they failed to respond normally to a flaming match. Some of them repeatedly poked their noses into the flame and sniffed at it as long as it was present. If they snuffed it out, they reacted similarly to a second flaming match and even to a third. Others did not

*first published in* Scientific American, *February 1961.*

*Reprinted with permission. Copyright* © *1961 by Scientific American, Inc. All rights reserved.*

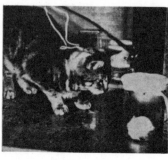

**Figure 17.1. Attentive cat** (*middle*) watching mouse in a jar presumably does not hear a click as loudly as when it is in repose (*top and bottom*). Assumption is based on shape of nerve-signal recordings picked up by electrode implanted in auditory pathway. Clicks were sounded at the dots. This experiment was performed at the School of Medicine of the University of California at Los Angeles by Raúl Hernández-Peon and his associates.

sniff at the match but made no effort to get away when we touched their noses with the flame repeatedly. These dogs also endured pinpricks with little or no evidence of pain. In contrast, littermates that had been reared in a normal environment recognized potential harm so quickly that we were usually unable to touch them with the flame or pin more than once.

This astonishing behaviour of dogs reared in isolation cannot be attributed to a general failure of the sensory conducting systems. Intense electric shock elicited violent excitement. Moreover, reflex movements made by the dogs during contact with fire and pinprick indicate that they may have felt something during stimulation; but the lack of any observable emotional disturbance, apart from reflex movements, suggests that their perception of actual damage to the skin was highly abnormal.

We have considerable evidence to show that people too attach variable meanings to pain-producing situations and that these meanings greatly influence the degree and quality of pain they feel. During World War II Henry K. Beecher of the Harvard Medical School observed the behavior of soldiers severely wounded in battle. He was astonished to find

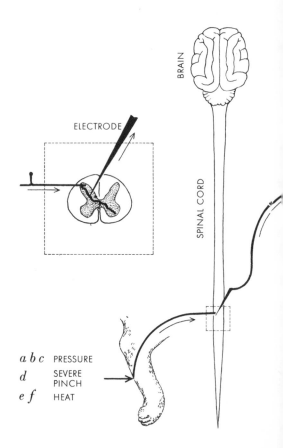

180

that when the wounded were carried into combat hospitals, only one out of three complained of enough pain to require morphine. Most of the soldiers either denied having pain from their extensive wounds or had so little that they did not want any medication to relieve it. These men, Beecher points out, were not in a state of shock, nor were they totally unable to feel pain, for they complained as vigorously as normal men at an inept vein puncture. When Beecher returned to clinical practice as an anesthesiologist, he asked a group of civilians who had just undergone major surgery and who had incisions similar to the wounds received by the soldiers whether they wanted morphine to alleviate their pain. In contrast with the wounded soldiers, four out of five claimed they were in severe pain and pleaded for a morphine injection.

Beecher concluded from his study that "the common belief that wounds are inevitably associated with pain, that the more extensive the wound the worse the pain, was not supported by observations made as carefully as possible in the combat zone". He goes on to say: "The data state in numerical terms what is known to all thoughtful clinical observers: There is no simple direct relationship between the wound *per se* and the pain experienced. The pain is in

very large part determined by other factors, and of great importance here is the significance of the wound. . . . In the wounded soldier [the response to injury] was relief, thankfulness at his escape alive from the battlefield, even euphoria; to the civilian, his major surgery was a depressing, calamitous event."

The importance of the meaning associated with a pain-

**Figure 17.2 Neuron-firing patterns,** recorded from single cells in the spinal cord of a cat, show the initial response in the central nervous system to various stimuli applied to the cat's leg. Pattern *a* was caused by hanging a two-gram weight on a single hair; *b* shows effect of a 20-gram weight; *c* is effect of a mild pinch. All three stimuli start at arrows and continue for duration of the recording. In *d* the skin was severely pinched for one minute. In *e* and *f* a heat lamp was directed at the skin for 15 seconds after the arrows, raising the skin temperature four and 12 degrees centigrade respectively. Each dot in the recordings represents a single nerve impulse; height above base line represents time interval between recorded impulse and preceding one. These experiments were performed by Patrick D. Wall at Massachusetts Institute of Technology.

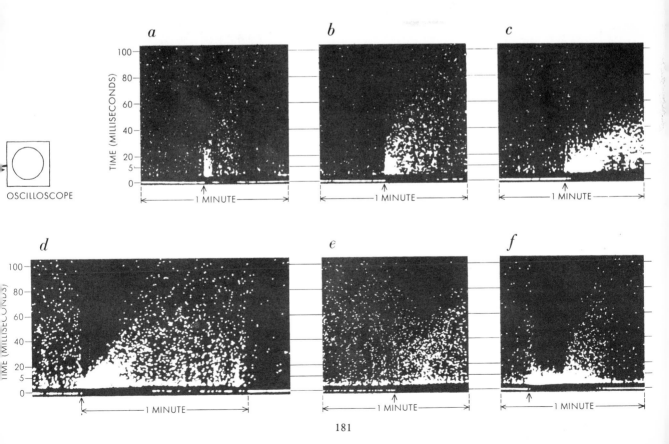

producing situation is made particularly clear in conditioning experiments carried out by the Russian physiologist Ivan Pavlov. Dogs normally react violently when they are given strong electric shocks to a paw. Pavlov found, however, that if he consistently presented food to a dog after each shock, the dog developed an entirely new response. Immediately after a shock the dog would salivate, wag its tail and turn eagerly toward the food dish. The electric shock now failed to evoke any responses indicative of pain and became instead a signal meaning that food was on the way. The dog's conditioned behavior persisted when Pavlov increased the intensity of the electric shocks and even when he supplemented them by burning and wounding the dog's skin. Jules H. Masserman of Northwestern University carried the experiment still further. After cats had been taught to respond to electric shock as a signal for feeding, they were trained to administer the shock themselves by walking up to a switch and closing it.

It is well known that prize fighters, football players and other athletes can sustain severe injuries without being aware that they have been hurt. In fact, almost any situation that attracts intense, prolonged attention may diminish or abo-

lish pain perception. Formal recognition of this fact has led to increasing medical interest in hypnosis. Like pain itself, the hypnotic state eludes precise definition. But, loosely speaking, hypnosis is a trance state in which the subject's attention is focused intensely on the hypnotist while attention to other stimuli is markedly diminished. Evidently a small percentage of people can be hypnotized deeply enough to undergo surgery entirely without anesthesia. For a larger number of people hypnosis reduces the amount of pain-killing drug required to produce successful analgesia.

If, however, the subject's attention is focused on a potentially painful experience, he will tend to perceive pain more intensely than he would normally. K. R. L. Hall and E. Stride in England found that the simple appearance of the word "pain" in a set of instructions made anxious subjects report as painful a level of electric shock they did not regard as painful when the word was absent from the instructions. Thus the mere anticipation of pain is sufficient to raise the level of anxiety and thereby the intensity of perceived pain. Similarly, experiments carried out by Harris E. Hill and his colleagues at the US Public Health Service Hospital in Lexington, Ky, have shown that if anxiety is dispelled (by reassuring a subject that he has control over the pain-

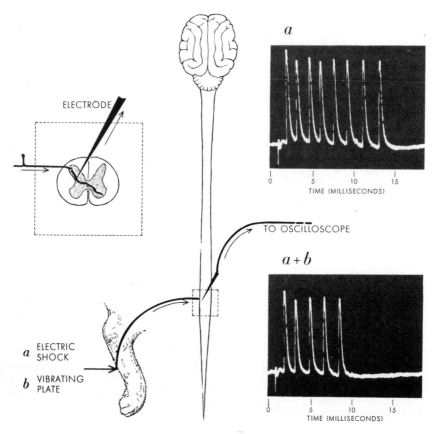

ELECTRODE

*a* ELECTRIC SHOCK

*b* VIBRATING PLATE

TO OSCILLOSCOPE

*a*

TIME (MILLISECONDS)

*a + b*

TIME (MILLISECONDS)

producing stimulus), a given level of electric shock or burning heat is perceived as significantly less painful than the same stimulus under conditions of high anxiety. Hill was also able to show that morphine diminishes pain if the anxiety level is high but has no demonstrable effect if the subject's anxiety has been dispelled.

The influence of psychological processes such as anxiety, attention and suggestion on the intensity of perceived pain is further demonstrated by studies of the effectiveness of placebos. Clinical investigators have found that severe pain (such as postsurgical pain) can be relieved in some patients by giving them a placebo, such as sugar solution or saline solution, in place of morphine or other analgesic drugs. About 35 per cent of the patients report marked relief from pain after being given a placebo. Since morphine, even in large doses, will relieve severe pain in only some 75 per cent of patients, one can conclude that nearly half of the drug's effectiveness is really a placebo effect. This is not to imply that people who are helped by a placebo do not have real pain; no one will deny the reality of postsurgical pain. Rather, it illustrates the powerful contribution of psychological processes to the perception of pain.

Taken together, the observations described so far indicate that the same injury can have different effects on different people or even on the same person at different times. A stimulus may be painful in one situation and not in another. How can we account for such variability in terms of what we know about the nervous system? First, we must recast the psychological facts into physiological terms. We must

**Figure 17.3 Modification of sensory messages** can take place within the spinal cord under certain conditions. In experiment at left, performed by Wall, the long train of nerve impulses following a single shock (a) is shortened when the skin around the shocked region is simultaneously vibrated by a metal plate (b). In experiment at right an afferent nerve fiber entering the spinal cord is electrically stimulated directly (a). The signal passes through a pool of neurons and is recorded on the other side of the cord (whence it ascends to the brain), producing tracing a. If the cerebellum (b) or cortex (c) is stimulated simultaneously, the afferent signal is almost completely suppressed, as shown in tracings a + b and a + c. These experiments were performed at the School of Medicine of the University of California at Los Angeles by K. E. Hagbarth and D. I. B. Kerr.

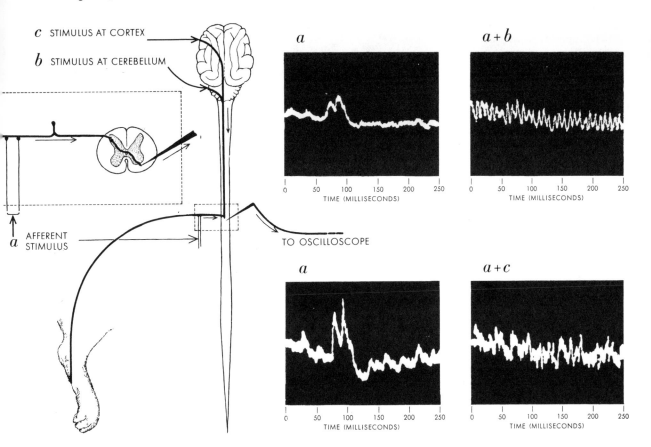

assume that psychological processes such as memories of previous experiences, thoughts, emotions and the focusing of attention are in some way functions of the higher areas of the brain – that they represent the actual activities of nerve impulses. What the psychological data suggest, then, is that these higher brain functions are able to modify the patterns of nerve impulses produced by an injury. Remarkable evidence for such complex neural interplay has recently been observed in physiological laboratories.

When energy from the environment stimulates the skin, a message is transmitted along nerve bundles to the spinal cord of the central nervous system. Until recently it was believed that the message, once fed in, was relayed without interference direct to a particular area of the brain cortex; the arrival of the message at this cortical area produced the sensation of pain, touch, warmth or cold, depending entirely on the physical characteristics of the initial stimulus. We now know that this is only a part of the picture. Investigators in a number of countries have recently demonstrated the presence of systems of nerve fibers that run from the higher areas of the brain downward to make connection with the message-carrying nerve pathways in the spinal cord. Electrical activity induced in these higher brain areas is capable of suppressing or modifying the message; it may never get beyond the lower levels of the central nervous system or an entirely different message may reach the brain (figure 17.3).

There is no longer any doubt that these message-modifying fibers exist; it has been found that electrical stimulation of widespread regions of the brain is able to modify the messages transmitted through every major sensory system. The origins and terminations of these message-controlling fibers have not yet been fully established. But even at this stage it is reasonable to speculate that the fibers provide the mechanism whereby higher brain activities such as memories, thoughts and emotions can modify the sensory messages after injury. We can assume, moreover, that this modification can occur throughout the entire axis of the central nervous system, at every junction at which nerve messages are relayed from one neuron to the next in the course of their ascent to the highest areas of the brain. If this view is right, we have a conceptual physiological model to account for the fact that psychological events play an essential role in determining the quality and intensity of the ultimate perceptual experience.

We may ask at this point: What is the nature of the sensory nerve signals or messages traveling to the brain after injury that permits them to be modified in the course of their transmission? Let us say we have burned a finger; what is the sequence of events that follows in the nervous system? To begin with, the intense heat energy is converted into a

code of electrical nerve impulses. These energy conversions occur in nerve endings in the skin called receptors, of which there are many different types. It was once popular to identify one of these types as the specific "pain receptor". We now believe that receptor mechanisms are more complicated. There is general agreement that the receptors that respond to noxious stimulation are widely branching, bushy networks of fibers that penetrate the layers of the skin in such a way their receptive fields heavily overlap with one another. Thus damage at any point on the skin will activate at least two or more of these networks and initiate the transmission of trains of nerve impulses along bundles of sensory nerve fibers that run from the finger into the spinal cord. What enters the spinal cord of the central nervous system is a coded pattern of nerve impulses, traveling along many fibers and moving at different speeds and with different frequencies (figure 17.2).

Before the nerve-impulse pattern can begin its ascent to the brain, a portion of it must first pass through a pool of short, densely packed nerve fibers that are diffusely interconnected. The fibers comprising these pools, found throughout the length of the spinal cord, are called internuncial neurons. It is in the course of transmission from the sensory fibers to the ascending spinal cord neurons that the pattern of signals may be modified. Patrick D. Wall of the Massachusetts Institute of Technology has been able to insert microelectrodes into single spinal cord neurons in cats and record the patterns of neural firing evoked when painful stimuli are applied to the skin. He has shown that these patterns of firing can be altered and limited in duration by subjecting the surrounding skin to a vibratory stimulus (figure 17.3). Wall has directly confirmed with human subjects that normally painful electric shocks and pinpricks are not perceived as painful when the surrounding skin is stimulated with a rapidly vibrating device.

Once the sensory patterns or signals have entered the spinal cord neurons they are transmitted to the brain along nerve bundles that occupy the anterolateral (front and side) portions of the spinal cord. Many fibers belonging to these bundles continue to the thalamus, forming the spinothalamic tract. The majority of the fibers, however, penetrate a tangled thicket of short, diffusely interconnected nerve fibers that form the central core of the lower part of the brain. Out of this formation of "reticulated" cells there emerges a series of pathways, so that the sensory patterns now stream along multiple routes to the higher regions of the brain.

When I was working with W. K. Livingston at the University of Oregon Medical School, our group found that electrical impulses evoked by painful stimuli are transmitted through the lower part of the brain along five distinct routes (figures 17.5, 17.6). Three of them — the spinothalamic tract, the central tegmental tract and the central gray pathway — appear to represent major conduction systems for sensory pain patterns since their electrical activity is significantly depressed by analgesic agents (such as nitrous oxide) that are capable of abolishing the awareness of pain in human patients without similarly affecting vision and hearing. Analgesic drugs also produce a striking reduction in the electrical activity in the fourth region, the central core of reticulated cells, which has been shown by other investigators to have the role of arousing the whole brain into alert activity. The final pathway, a major sensory system called the lemniscal tract, plays an undetermined role in the total pain process since its transmission capacity is unaffected by anesthetic or analgesic drugs.

In order to determine the role played by these various ascending pathways in the perception of pain, we studied the behavior of cats in which some of the pathways had been selectively destroyed (figure 17.7). We found that cats with lesions of the spinothalamic tract often failed to respond to normaly painful stimuli, confirming earlier evidence that had demonstrated the importance of this pathway in the sensory pain process. But we found that it is not the only pathway involved. Cats with lesions in the central gray pathway also failed to respond to the stimuli. In contrast, cats with the lemniscal tract made inactive responded immediately to the stimuli.

To our surprise, the picture turned out to be even more complex than this. Lesions of the central tegmental tract had the opposite effect of making the cats excessively responsive to some kinds of painful stimuli, and many of these cats showed behavior suggesting "spontaneous pain" in the absence of external stimulation.

A recent development in the surgical control of pain in human patients lends striking confirmation to the results obtained in the cat study. Frank R. Ervin and Vernon H. Mark of the departments of psychiatry and neurosurgery at the Massachusetts General Hospital have found that patients suffering unbearable pain from cancer and other pathological sources may obtain excellent relief from pain after a small surgical lesion is made in that part of the human thalamus which receives fibers from the spinothalamic tract as well as from the pathways that stem from the reticular formation. If, however, the lesion is made just a few millimeters in front of this area, destroying the thalamic fibers of the lemniscal pathway, the experience of pain remains unchanged. Direct observations such as these on the sensory mechanisms of the pain

**Figure 17.4 Stimulation of brain stem** impels a cat to rotate a paddle wheel that turns off the weak electric stimulus. The stimulus was turned on between top and middle photographs. The cat's quickly learned behavior has all the characteristics of pain avoidance. These are frames from a motion picture made by Neal E. Miller of Yale University.

185

process have provided us with valuable information on the nature of pain.

But we still cannot account for the complexity of many pain phenomena, especially bizarre pain syndromes sometimes encountered in hospital clinics. One in particular – phantom-limb pain – is both fascinating and terrible. In 1552 Ambroise Paré described it thus: "Verily it is a thing wondrous strange and prodigious, and which will scarce be credited, unless by such as have seen with their eyes, and heard with their ears, the patients who have many months after the cutting away of the leg, grievously complained that they yet felt exceeding great pain of that leg so cut off."

The majority of amputees report feeling a phantom limb soon after amputation and it may remain for years without bothering them. About 30 per cent, however, have the misfortune to develop pains in their phantom limbs, and in about 5 per cent the pain is severe. These pains may be occasional or continuous, but they are felt in definite parts of the phantom limb. W. K. Livingston reports the case of a young woman who described her phantom hand as being clenched, fingers bent over the thumb and digging into the palm of her hand, so that the whole hand became tired and painful. When she was able to open her phantom hand as a result of her physician's treatment, the pain vanished.

Phantom-limb pain tends to decrease and eventually disappear in most amputees. There are a few, however, for whom the pain increases in severity over the years. In addition, the disturbance spreads and other regions of the body may become so sensitized that merely touching them will evoke spasms of severe pain in the phantom limb. Even emotional upsets such as seeing a disturbing film may sharply increase the pain. Still worse, the conventional surgical procedures, such as cutting the spinothalamic tract, usually fail to bring permanent relief, so that these patients may undergo a series of such operations without any decrease in the severity of the pain. Phenomena such as these defy explanation in terms of our present physiological knowledge. A few psychiatrists have been tempted simply to label these amputees as neurotic, but the evidence argues against such an explanation for all cases.

So far we can only speculate on the nature of phantom-limb pain. We know that irritation of the nerves of the remaining part of the limb contributes to the pain process, since stimulation of these nerves can trigger severe pain. But the spread of the trigger sites and the frequent failure of conventional surgical procedures make it clear that this is not the whole story. All the evidence suggests that the primary focus of physiological disturbance lies in the central nervous system itself. Livingston believes that the initial damage to the limb, or perhaps the trauma associated with

its removal, disturbs the patterning of neural activity in the internuncial pools of the spinal cord, creating reverberating, abnormally patterned activity. Even minor irritations to the skin or nerves near the site of the operation can then feed into these active pools of neurons and keep them in an abnormal, disturbed state over periods of years. Impulse patterns that would normally be interpreted as touch may now trigger these neuron pools into greater activity, thereby sending volleys of abnormal patterns of impulses to the higher areas of the brain and bringing about the perception of pain. Although there is no direct evidence that the inter-

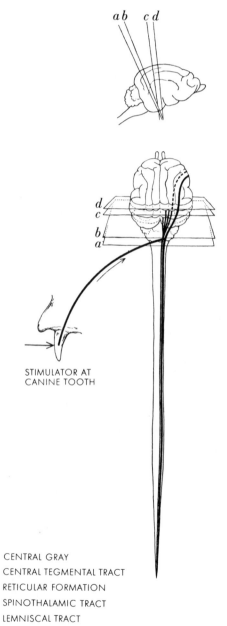

STIMULATOR AT
CANINE TOOTH

CENTRAL GRAY
CENTRAL TEGMENTAL TRACT
RETICULAR FORMATION
SPINOTHALAMIC TRACT
LEMNISCAL TRACT

nuncial pools play this role in phantom-limb pain, the concept helps us to understand facts that are otherwise difficult to explain.

So far we have been discussing pain primarily as a sensory experience somewhat similar to sight or hearing. But there is something missing. Pain has a unique, distinctly unpleasant quality that wells up in consciousness and obliterates anything we may have been thinking or doing at the time. It becomes overwhelming and demands immediate attention. Pain has a strong emotional quality that drives us

**Figure 17.5 Five pathways** in the brain stem transmit signals evoked by stimulating the nerve of a cat's tooth. The sections *a*, *b*, *c* and *d* show how the pathways progress through the midbrain and thalamus; two of the pathways, the spinothalamic and lemniscal, send projections to the cortex (*see also figure 17.6*). An analgesic mixture of nitrous oxide and oxygen largely blocks the signals in four (*2*) of the five pathways. The signal is not blocked, however, in the lemniscal pathway (*1*), which projects to the cortex. These experiments were performed by D. I. B. Kerr, Frederick P. Haugen and the author at the University of Oregon Medical School.

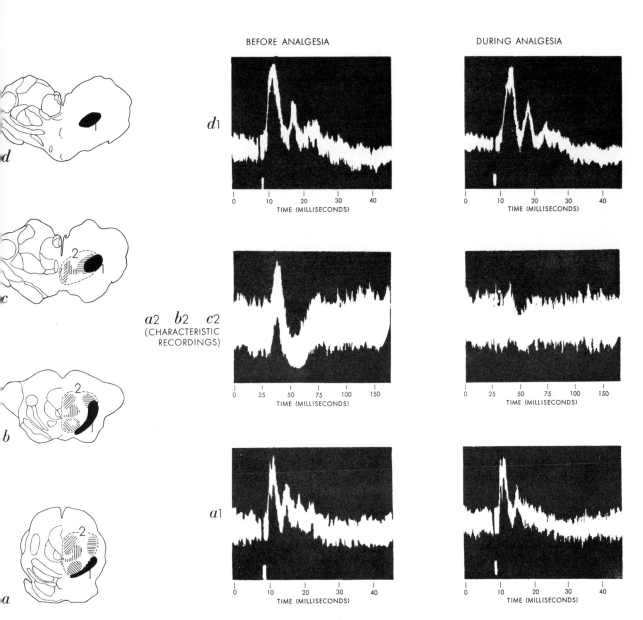

187

into doing something about it. We seek desperately to stop the pain as quickly as we can by whatever means we can.

Introspectionist psychologists at the turn of the century made a sharp distinction between the sensory and the emotional, or affective, dimensions of pain. The psychologist Edward B. Titchener was convinced that there is a continuum of *feeling* in conscious experience, distinctly different from sensation, that ranges through all the degrees of pleasantness and unpleasantness. "The pain of a toothache," Titchener wrote, "is localized at a particular place, 'in the tooth'; but the unpleasantness of it suffuses the whole of present experience, is as wide as consciousness. The word 'pain' . . . often means the whole toothache experience."

These two dimensions, the sensory and the affective, are brought clearly into focus by clinical studies on prefrontal

**Figure 17.6 Signals reach the cortex** via projections from at least two of the five pathways ascending through the brain stem: the spinothalamic and the dorsal column–medial lemniscal pathways. Fibers from the former also penetrate the brain stem reticular formation, which is capable of arousing the whole cortex into activity. Surgical experiments (*see figure 17.7*) and analgesia experiments, suggest that pain perception is associated least with signals reaching cortex from lemniscal pathway.

**Figure 17.7 Surgical inactivation of brain stem pathways** ▶ gives added evidence of complexity of pain perception. The surgery was performed on cats that had been trained to jump out of a box to avoid having their paws pricked or burned. Brain sections at left indicate the pathways inactivated in various animals. After surgery the animals were retested. The code number of each animal appears at the bottom of the bar graphs. Height of bar indicates percentage of avoidance responses when paws were pricked or heated. The marks + and ++ indicate, respectively, animals that became hyper-responsive to pain or that gave evidence of "spontaneous" pain. Inactivation of the spinothalamic and central gray pathways reduced the behavioral evidence of pain; inactivation of the lemniscal path had little or no effect. Inactivation of the central tegmental pathway seemed to heighten pain sensitivity.

lobotomy, a neurosurgical operation for intense pain in which the connections between the prefrontal lobes and the rest of the brain are severed. Typically, these patients report after the operation that they still have pain but it does not bother them; they simply no longer care about the pain and often forget it is there. When they are questioned more closely, they frequently say that they still have the "little" pain, but the "big" pain, the suffering, the anguish are gone. Yet they complain vociferously about pinprick and mild

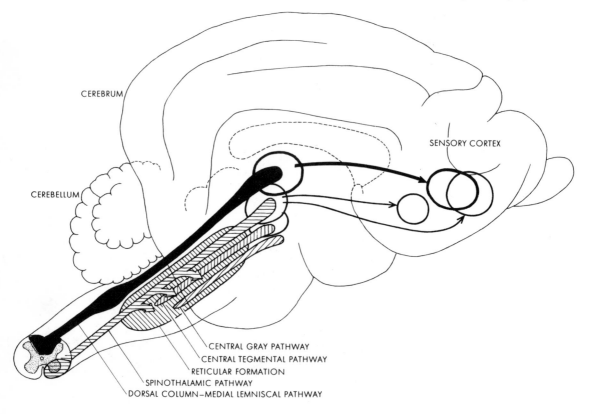

CEREBRUM

SENSORY CORTEX

CEREBELLUM

CENTRAL GRAY PATHWAY
CENTRAL TEGMENTAL PATHWAY
RETICULAR FORMATION
SPINOTHALAMIC PATHWAY
DORSAL COLUMN–MEDIAL LEMNISCAL PATHWAY

PATHWAY
INACTIVATED

HEAT                    PINPRICK

LEMNISCAL

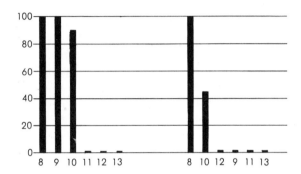

SPINOTHALAMIC

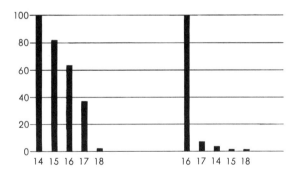

CENTRAL GRAY

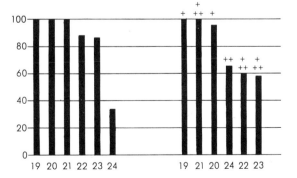

CENTRAL TEGMENTAL

189

burn. It is certain that the operation does not stop pain perception entirely, since the sensory component is still present. Its predominant effect appears to be on the emotional coloring of the total pain experience; the terribly unpleasant quality of the pain has been abolished.

How are we to account for these effects? It is known that prefrontal lobotomy lowers the anxiety associated with pain to a striking degree: the fear of death is greatly diminished as well as the patient's preoccupation with his painful disease. It is often suggested that the reduction of anxiety brings about a concomitant reduction of pain intensity; specifically that the brain's prefrontal lobes, which are presumably involved in higher psychological processes, fail to elaborate the sensory nerve patterns as they ascend from the source of the pain. Such an explanation is consistent with the perceptual approach to pain that we have been discussing.

But is it only this? The emotional quality of the pain experience and its remarkable capacity for acting as a drive are both so different from touch, warmth or cold that to explain its psychological and neural basis seems to require something more than different patterns of nerve impulses arriving at the higher sensory areas of the brain. We might infer that distinctly different parts of the brain are involved in addition to the sensory areas.

Where, then, do the streams of sensory nerve impulses go after they are transmitted through the lower portions of the brain? We know that the spinothalamic tract has a relay station in the thalamus and there is good evidence that at least a portion of its impulse patterns is transmitted upward to the sensory cortex. The central gray neurons and the central tegmental tract, however, make connection with other neural systems, so that impulse patterns produced by painful stimuli have access to large areas of the brain that lie beneath the cortex.

Various experiments suggest that some of these subcortical areas are particularly concerned with the "driving" or motivating aspects of behavior. Neal E. Miller and other investigators at Yale University have used implanted electrodes to make a systematic exploration of areas deep within the brains of cats and other animals. When certain areas are stimulated, the animals cry out and behave exactly as if they were in pain (figure 17.4). To call these areas "pain centers" would be misleading, since the evidence we have been discussing points to a complex interaction of sensory and cognitive processes involving other major portions of the brain. But there can be little doubt that these subcortical areas make a major contribution to the total pain process. Is it possible that the activities in these areas provide the neural substrate for the affective, "driving" component of pain perception? There is great temptation to speculate that they do – but in fact we do not know. All we can say for the present is that the ascending sensory patterns arouse activities in the brain that somehow subserve the broad category of perceptions we describe as "pain".

Some time ago W. K. Livingston attempted to answer the question "What is pain?" He argued against the classical conception that the intensity of pain sensation is always proportional to the stimulus. He proposed instead that pain, like all perceptions, is "subjective, individual and modified by degrees of attention, emotional states and the conditioning influence of past experience". Since that time we have moved still further away from the classical assumptions of specific "pain receptors", "pain pathways" and a "pain center" in the brain, all of which implied that stimulation of a "pain receptor" will invariably produce pain, that the pain will have only one specific quality and that it can vary only in intensity.

Pain, we now believe, refers to a category of complex experiences, not to a single sensation produced by a specific stimulus. In her essay "On being ill" Virginia Woolf touches on precisely this point. "English," she writes, "which can express the thoughts of Hamlet and the tragedy of Lear, has no words for the shiver and the headache. ... The merest schoolgirl, when she falls in love, has Shakespeare and Keats to speak for her, but let a sufferer try to describe a pain in his head to a doctor and language at once runs dry."

We are beginning to recognize the poverty of language for describing the many different qualities of sensory and affective experience that we simply categorize under the broad heading of "pain". We are more and more aware of the plasticity and modifiability of events occurring in the central nervous system. We are aware that in the lower part of the brain, at least, the patterns of impulses produced by painful stimuli travel over multiple pathways going to widespread regions of the brain and not along a single path going to a "pain center". The psychological evidence strongly supports the view of pain as a perceptual experience whose quality and intensity is influenced by the unique past history of the individual, by the meaning he gives to the pain-producing situation and by his "state of mind" at the moment. We believe that all these factors play a role in determining the actual patterns of nerve impulses ascending to the brain and traveling within the brain itself. In this way pain becomes a function of the whole individual, including his present thoughts and fears as well as his hopes for the future.

# 18 The reticular formation
## by J D French

The title "reticular formation" might suggest various things – a football line-up, a chess gambit, a geological structure or whatnot – but the phrase refers to a particular region of the brain, a once mysterious part which has recently come in for a great deal of attention from biologists. The reticular formation is a tiny nerve network in the central part of the brain stem (figures 18.1, 18.2). Investigators have discovered that this bit of nerve tissue, no bigger than your little finger, is a far more important structure than anyone had dreamed. It underlies our awareness of the world and our ability to think, to learn and to act. Without it, an individual is reduced to a helpless, senseless, paralyzed blob of protoplasm.

The actual seat of the power to think, to perceive, indeed to respond to a stimulus with anything more than a reflex reaction, lies in the cortex of the brain. But the cortex cannot perceive or think unless it is "awake". Consider the alarm ring that awakens you in the morning: several seconds pass before you recognize the disturbance and can respond to stop the painful jangle. A sensory signal arriving at the cortex while it is asleep goes unrecognized. Experiments on anesthetized individuals have shown further that stimulation of the cortex alone is not sufficient to awaken the brain. Something else must arouse the cortex; that something is the reticular formation.

It was not until the end of the 1940s that two eminent physiologists, H. W. Magoun of the US and Giuseppe Moruzzi of Italy, working together at Northwestern University, discovered this fact. They were exploring the mystery of the reticular formation's functions by means of an electrode planted in this area in the brain of a cat. They found that stimulation of the area with a small electric current would awaken a drowsing cat as peacefully as a scratch on the head. The animal's behavior, and recordings of changes in its brain waves with the electroencephalo-graph, showed all the signs of a normal arousal from sleep. Magoun and Moruzzi decided that the reticular formation acted as a kind of sentinel which aroused the cortex, and they named it the RAS (reticular activating system).

Now mysteries began to clear – not only with regard to the function of the reticular formation but also as to some previously puzzling features of the nervous system's anatomy. All the great sensory nerve trunks in the body have brush-like branches which stream into the reticular formation. Sensory signals from all parts of the body go to the cortex by direct pathways, but on the way through the brain stem they also feed into the reticular formation. Evidently the reticular formation, when so stimulated, sends arousing signals to the cortex. The awakened cortex can then interpret the sensory signals it is receiving directly (figures 18.2, 18.3).

The RAS is a kind of general alarm: that is to say, it responds in the same way to any sensory stimulus, whether from the organs of hearing, seeing, touch or whatever. Its response is simply to arouse the brain, not to relay any specific message. Its signals spray the entire cortex rather than any one center of sensation. A noise, a flash of light, a pinch on the hand, the smell of burning wood, a pain in the stomach – any of these excites the reticular formation to alert the cortex to a state of wakefulness, so that when the specific stimulus arrives at the appropriate center in the cortex, the brain can identify it.

Apparently the RAS learns to be selective in its sensitivity to particular stimuli. A mother may be instantly awakened by the faintest whimper of her baby. Father, on the other hand, may sleep through baby's fiercest bellowings but be aroused by a faint smell of smoke. A city dweller may sleep peacefully in the midst of the riotous din of traffic while his visitor from the country spends a sleepless night wishing he were elsewhere. It is as if the RAS becomes endowed by experience with the ability to discriminate among stimuli, disregarding those it has found unimportant and responding to those that are helpful. Happily so. Imagine how unbearable life would be if you could not

*first published in* Scientific American, *May 1957.*

*Reprinted with permission. Copyright © 1957 by Scientific American, Inc. All rights reserved.*

shut out most of the environment from consciousness and were at the mercy of the thousands of sights and sounds simultaneously clamoring for attention.

The RAS, like the starter in an automobile, starts the brain engine running, but this is by no means the end of its job. It goes on functioning to keep the individual in a conscious state. ("Consciousness" is a controversial word among psychologists, but for our purposes its meaning is clear enough.) If the RAS cannot function normally, consciousness is impossible. A person whose reticular formation has been permanently injured or destroyed falls into a

coma from which he can never recover. He may live on for a year or more, but he remains as helpless and shut off from communication as a vegetable.

If uninjured, the RAS can maintain a wakeful state (but not consciousness) even in the absence of the cortex. In a newborn baby the cortex has not yet begun to function, but the infant nevertheless has short periods of wakefulness throughout the day. The same is true of the tragic creatures born without any cortex at all (called anencephalic monsters). Such a child (sometimes kept alive for three or four years) never achieves any understanding or real contact with its surroundings, but it has periods of wakefulness during which it swallows and digests food, smiles and coos when fondled and cries when treated roughly. We must conclude, therefore, that wakefulness of a very crude sort is possible without the cortex, so long as the RAS can function.

For sustained wakefulness, however, the cortex certainly is essential. The alert state seems to depend upon an interplay between the cortex and the RAS. The reticular forma-

**Figure 18.1 The reticular formation** is the area stippled in this cross section of the brain. A sense organ (*lower right*) is connected to a sensory area in the brain (*upper left*) by a pathway extending up the spinal cord. This pathway branches into the reticular formation. When a stimulus travels along the pathway, the reticular formation may "awaken" the entire brain (*dashed black arrows*).

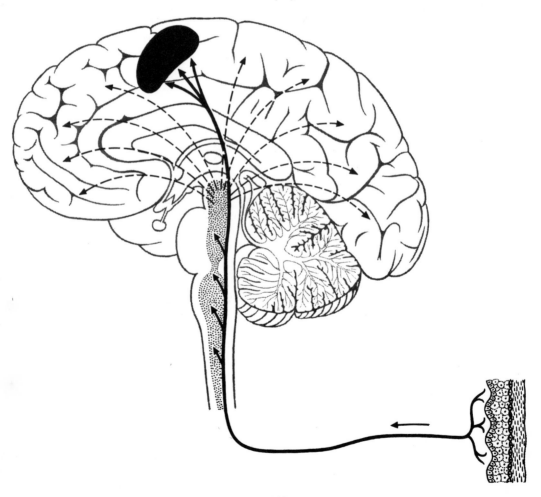

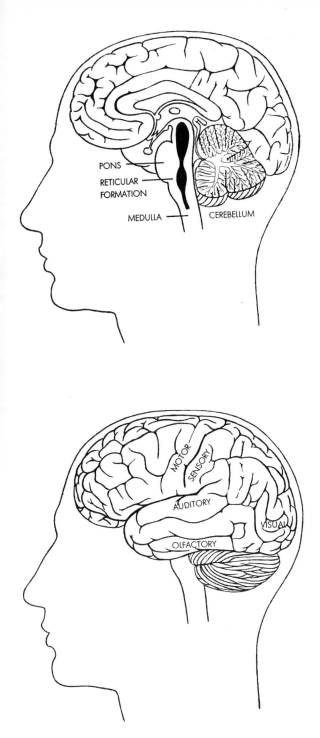

tion is stimulated not only by the sensory nerves but also by impulses from some parts of the cortex. This has been demonstrated by electrical stimulation of certain areas of the cortex in monkeys: such stimulation will awaken a sleeping monkey. When the experiment is tried on a monkey that is awake, it evokes a dramatic response. The monkey instantly stops whatever it is doing and looks about intently and slightly puzzled, as if to say: "What was that?" It does not seem distressed or agitated – only warily alert. So it would seem that in the waking state the RAS plays a part, in combination with the cortex, in focusing attention and probably in many other mental processes (figure 18.4).

All this raises the possibility that the RAS may be importantly involved in mental disorders. Investigations of this possibility have already begun by means of experiments with drugs. It is natural to start with anesthetic and sleep-inducing drugs, to see how they affect the RAS. The results of these experiments are illuminating but not surprising. They show that the drug blocks the flow of nerve impulses in the reticular formation but has little effect on the flow along the direct pathways from sense organs to the cortex. As the anesthesia wears off, the flow in the RAS returns to normal. A stimulating drug, on the other hand, has the opposite effect: it enhances the conduction of impulses in the RAS. It will be interesting to extend these experiments to the new tranquilizing drugs and the substances that produce experimental psychoses. Already there is evidence that these drugs do affect the functioning of the RAS.

Still another domain is under the control of this amazingly cogent bit of tissue in the brain. The RAS apparently has a hand in regulating all the motor activities of the body. It can modify muscle movements of both the voluntary type (controlled by the brain) and the reflex type (controlled in the spinal cord) (figure 18.5).

Just as the brain cortex has specific centers of sensation, it also has specific motor centers which generate muscle contractions. If one stimulates a motor center with an electric current, the appropriate muscles will respond but the resulting body movements are jerky and uncontrolled. These powerful movements are normally controlled and polished by other motor centers of the cortex, acting through the reticular formation. If the RAS is not stimulated or does not function properly, the movements will be jerky.

More surprising is the fact that the RAS can also act on the reflexes, centered in the spinal cord. The reflex apparatus has two functions. First, it generates automatic muscle movements. When signals from a sudden and alarming sensory stimulus (*e.g.* touching something hot) arrive at the

**Figure 18.2 Relationship of the reticular formation** (*black area*) to various parts of the brain is indicated at the top. The functional areas of the brain are outlined at bottom.

193

**Figure 18.3 Cat is awakened** by the sound of a bell. The sound stimuli reach the reticular activating system, or RAS, and the auditory area of the brain. The RAS acts to awaken the cortex so that it can "hear" signals arriving in the auditory area. The brain waves at the top change from a pattern of sleep to one of wakefulness. The RAS then integrates the brain's activity so that the brain can react as a whole. The cat finally responds with a motor impulse that is related by the RAS. The cat then jumps to its feet and runs away. The entire process takes place in a matter of a few seconds.

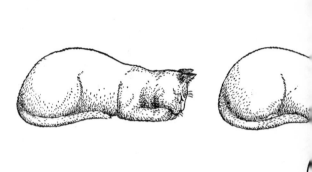

**Figure 18.4 Cortex is stimulated** by passing an electric current to the brain surface of a sleeping monkey. Six recording electrodes show the RAS has been activated to awaken the brain.

    **RAS is stimulated** by passing an electric current into the brain stem of a sleeping monkey. Recording electrodes show a more abrupt transition from sleep to wakefulness. The waves become sharp, short and more frequent. This is a typical waking pattern.

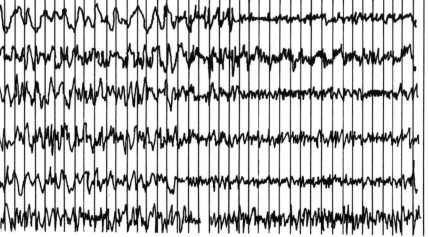

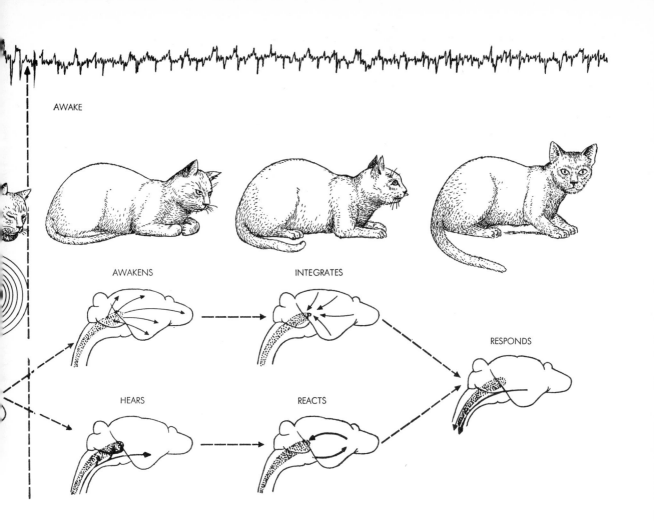

AWAKE

AWAKENS    INTEGRATES

RESPONDS

HEARS    REACTS

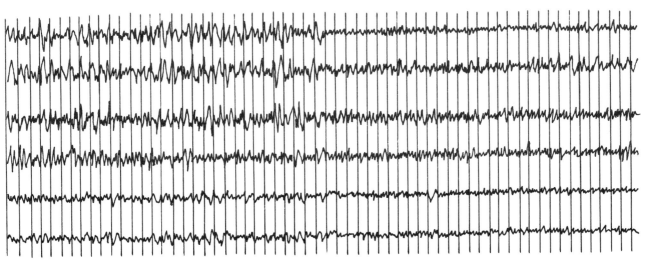

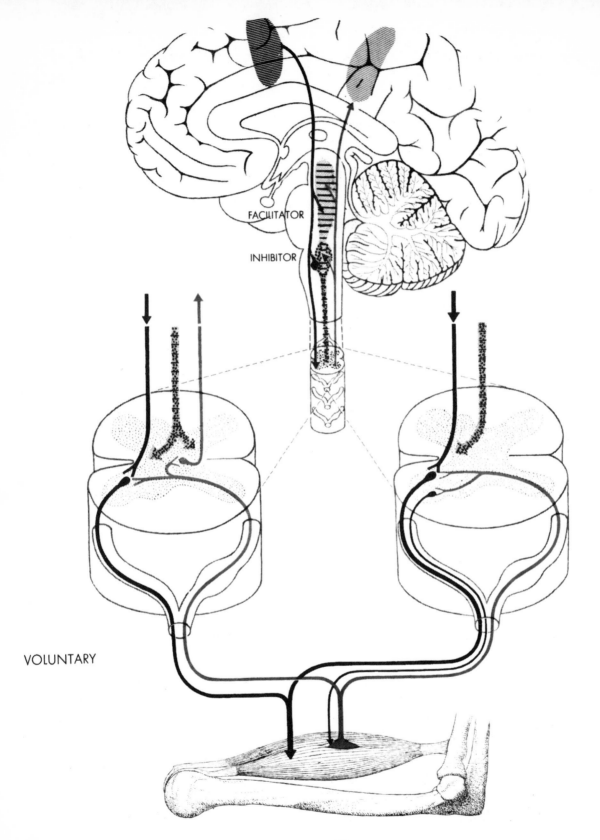

FACILITATOR

INHIBITOR

VOLUNTARY

REFLEX

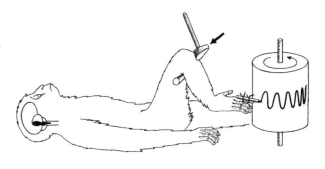

Figure 18.5 **Movements are modified** by the RAS. In voluntary movement sensory nerves (*gray*) conduct impulses from the muscle spindle (*bottom*) to a sensory area in the brain (*gray hatching*). Motor nerves (*black*) conduct impulses from the motor area (*black hatching*) to the muscle. Both nerve systems branch into the RAS (*horizontal stripes*). The RAS sends down impulses (*speckled arrows*) that facilitate or inhibit the response. In reflex movement sensory impulses are passed on immediately to motor nerves in the spinal cord. One nerve activates the muscle and maintains its "tone". The other (*thin black line*) sensitizes the spindle. The RAS controls both.

spinal cord, they are passed on immediately to an adjacent motor nerve and travel right back to the affected part of the body to jerk it away. In general, the automatic, reflex activities are protective – responses to danger or sudden challenges in the surroundings. But some of them can be tricked into action by suddenly stretching a muscle: for example, a tap on the knee elicits the well-known knee jerk.

The second function of the reflex system is to keep the muscles ready for action by maintaining "tone" – that is, a state of partial contraction. Just as a violin string must be stretched to a certain tension before it can emit music, so a muscle must be maintained at a certain tension to respond efficiently to a stimulus. The mechanism that regulates its resting tension, or "tone", is a small structure within the muscle called a "spindle". When a muscle contracts, it squeezes the spindle; when it relaxes, the pressure on the spindle loosens. Either departure from normal tone causes the spindle to send signals by way of a sensory nerve to the spinal cord; there they excite a motor nerve to correct the contraction or relaxation of the muscle. This feedback system automatically keeps each muscle at precisely the right tone. And the appropriate tone itself is adjusted to suit the needs of the moment by nerve impulses which regulate the sensitivity of the spindle.

Now experiments have clearly demonstrated that the RAS exerts some control over voluntary and reflex motor reactions. Let us take for illustration an experiment on the reflex knee jerk, which is easy and convenient to perform. A monkey is anesthetized and a pen is tied to its toe to record the size of its knee kicks on a rotating drum. We keep tapping its knee and we get a uniform response, recorded as a nice series of regular curves on the drum. Then we suddenly stimulate the reticular formation electrically. The knee jerks immediately become larger: the RAS has enhanced them. When we stop stimulating it, the kicks return to normal size. Now in the course of exploratory experiments along the reticular formation a new fact

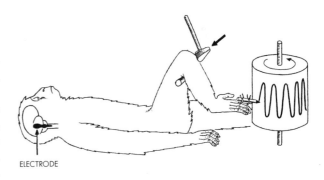

ELECTRODE

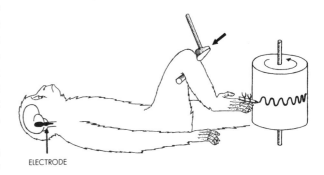

ELECTRODE

Figure 18.6 **Control of reflex motor reactions** by the reticular formation was demonstrated by this experiment on an anesthetized monkey. When the monkey's knee is tapped regularly, its knee jerks record a series of regular curves on a rotating drum (*top*). When the upper part of the monkey's reticular formation is stimulated, the jerks are larger (*middle*). When the lower part of the formation is stimulated, the jerks are smaller (*bottom*).

emerges. If we stimulate the formation at a point toward its lower end in the brain stem, the kicks are not enhanced but instead are inhibited! (figure 18.6).

Following up this finding, we discover that these centers can enhance or inhibit sensory as well as motor impulses. In short, the RAS acts as a kind of traffic control center, facilitating or inhibiting the flow of signals in the nervous system.

The astonishing generality of the RAS gives us a new outlook on the nervous system. Neurologists have tended to think of the nervous system as a collection of more or less separate circuits, each doing a particular job. It now appears that the system is much more closely integrated than had been thought. This should hardly surprise us. A simple organism such as the amoeba reacts with totality toward stimuli: the whole cell is occupied in the act of finding, engulfing and digesting food. Man, even with his 10 billion nerve cells, is not radically different. He must focus his sensory and motor systems on the problem in hand, and for this he obviously must be equipped with some integrating machine.

The RAS seems to be such a machine. It awakens the brain to consciousness and keeps it alert; it directs the traffic of messages in the nervous system; it monitors the myriads of stimuli that beat upon our senses, accepting what we need to perceive and rejecting what is irrelevant; it tempers and refines our muscular activity and bodily move-

ments. We can go even further and say that it contributes in an important way to the highest mental processes – the focusing of attention, introspection and doubtless all forms of reasoning.

## Bibliography

Brain Mechanisms and Consciousness, J. F. Delafresnaye, Blackwell Scientific Publications, 1954

Brain Stem Reticular Formation and Activation of the EEG, G. Moruzzi and H. W. Magoun in *Electroencephalography and Clinical Neurophysiology*, Vol. 1, No. 4, pages 455–473, November 1949

Patterns of Organization in the Central Nervous System, edited by Philip Bard, The Williams & Wilkins Company, 1952

Spasticity: the Stretch-Reflex and Extrapyramidal Systems, H. W. Magoun and Ruth Rhines, Charles C. Thomas, 1947

**Figure 18.7 Extensive branching of cells** in the reticular formation is depicted by this photomicrograph of a section of the reticular formation in the brain of a dog. The dark areas in the photomicrograph are cells of the formation which have been stained with silver. The section was lent by Drs. M. and A. Scheibel of the Medical School of the University of California at Los Angeles.

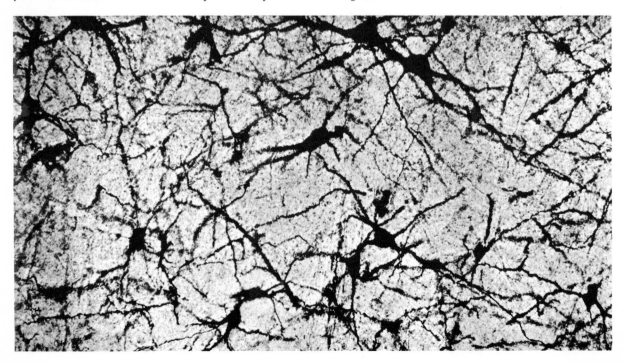

# 19  The states of sleep
## by Michel Jouvet

Early philosophers recognized that there are two distinctly different levels of sleep. An ancient Hindu tale described three states of mind in man: (1) wakefulness (*vaiswanara*), in which a person "is conscious only of external objects [and] is the enjoyer of the pleasures of sense"; (2) dreaming sleep (*taijasa*), in which one "is conscious only of his dreams [and] is the enjoyer of the subtle impressions in the mind of the deeds he has done in the past", and (3) dreamless sleep (*prajna*), a "blissful" state in which "the veil of unconsciousness envelops his thought and knowledge, and the subtle impressions of his mind apparently vanish".

States 2 and 3 obviously are rather difficult to investigate objectively, and until very recently the phases of sleep remained a subject of vague speculation. Within the past few years, however, studies with the aid of the electroencephalograph have begun to lift the veil. By recording brain waves, eye movements and other activities of the nervous system during the different sleep states neurophysiologists are beginning to identify the specific nervous-system structures involved, and we are now in a position to analyze some of the mechanisms responsible.

## Brain activities in sleep

Lucretius, that remarkably inquisitive and shrewd observer of nature, surmised that the fidgetings of animals during sleep were linked to dreaming. Some 30 years ago a German investigator, R. Klaue, made a significant discovery with the electroencephalograph. He found that sleep progressed in a characteristic sequence: a period of light sleep, during which the brain cortex produced slow brain waves, followed by a period of deep sleep, in which the cortical activity speeded up. Klaue's report was completely overlooked at the time. In the 1950s, however, Nathaniel Kleitman and his students at the University of Chicago took

*first published in* Scientific American, *February 1967.*

*Reprinted with permission. Copyright © 1967 by Scientific American, Inc. All rights reserved.*

up this line of investigation. Kleitman and Eugene Aserinsky found (in studies of infants) that periods of "active" sleep, alternating with quiescent periods, were marked by rapid eye movements under the closed lids. Later Kleitman and William C. Dement, in studies of adults, correlated the eye movements with certain brain-wave patterns and definitely linked these activities and patterns to periods of dreaming. In 1958 Dement showed that cats may have periods of sleep similarly marked by rapid eye movement and fast cortical activity. He called such periods "activated sleep".

Meanwhile at the University of Lyons, François Michel and I had been conducting a series of experiments with cats. In the cat, which spends about two-thirds of its time sleeping, the process of falling asleep follows a characteristic course, signaled by easily observable external signs. Typically the animal curls up in a ball with its neck bent. The flexing of the nape of its neck is a clear sign that the muscles there retain some tonus, that is, they are not completely relaxed. In this position the cat lapses into a light sleep from which it is easily awakened.

After about 10 to 20 minutes there comes a constellation of changes that mark passage over the brink into deep sleep. The cat's neck and back relax their curvature, showing that the muscles have completely lost tonus: they are now altogether slack. At the same time there are bursts of rapid eye movements (eight to 30 movements in each burst) in either the side-to-side or the up-and-down direction, like the movements in visual use of the eyes. Occasionally these eyeball movements behind the closed eyelids are accompanied by a sudden dilation of the pupils, which in the main are tightly constricted during sleep. Along with the eye movements go events involving many other parts of the body: small tremors of muscles at the ends of the extremities, causing rapid flexing of the digits and now and then small scratching motions; very rapid movements of the ears, the whiskers, the tail and the tongue, and an episode of fast and irregular breathing.

It is somewhat startling to realize that all this activity goes on during a period in which the animal's muscular system is totally atonic (lacking in tension). The activities are also the accompaniment of deep sleep, as is indicated by the fact that it takes an unusually high level of sound or electrical stimulation to arouse the cat during this phase. The state of deep sleep lasts about six or seven minutes and alternates with periods of lighter sleep that last for an average of about 25 minutes.

To obtain more objective and specific information about events in the brain during sleep we implanted electrodes in the muscles of the neck and in the midbrain of cats (figure 19.1). We used animals that were deprived of the brain cortex, since we wished to study the subcortical activities. In the course of extended recordings of the electrical events we were surprised to find that the electrical activity of the neck muscles disappeared completely for regular periods (six minutes long), and the condition persisted when sharp spikes of high voltage showed up now and then in the pontine reticular formation, situated just behind the "arousal center" of the midbrain. These electrical signs were correlated with eye movements of the sleeping animal. Further, we noted that in cats with intact brains both the abolition of muscle tonus and the sharp high-voltage spikes were strikingly correlated with the rapid eye movement and fast cortical activity Dement had described. These findings presented a paradox. It was surely strange to find fast cortical activity (generally a sign of wakefulness) coupled with complete muscular atony (invariably a sign of deep sleep)! (figure 19.2).

## The two sleep states

We named this strange state "paradoxical sleep". It is also called deep sleep, fast-wave sleep, rapid-eye-movement (REM) sleep and dreaming sleep, whereas the lighter sleep that precedes it is often called slow-wave sleep. We consider paradoxical sleep a qualitatively distinct state, not simply a deepened version of the first stage of sleep. Very schematically (for the cat) we can describe the three states – wakefulness, light sleep and paradoxical sleep – in the following physiological terms. Wakefulness is accompanied by fast, low-voltage electrical activity in the cortex and the subcortical structures of the brain and by a significant amount of tonus in the muscular system. The first stage of sleep, or light sleep, is characterized by a slackening of electrical activity in the cortex and subcortical structures, by the occurrence of "spindles", or groups of sharp jumps, in the brain waves and by retention of the muscular tension. Paradoxical sleep presents a more complex picture that we must consider in some detail.

We can classify the phenomena in paradoxical sleep under two heads: tonic (those having to do with continuous phenomena) and phasic (those of a periodic character). The principal tonic phenomena observed in the cat are fast electrical waves (almost like those of wakefulness) in the cortex and subcortical structures, very regular "theta" waves at the level of the hippocampus (a structure running from the front to the rear of the brain) and total disappearance of electrical activity in the muscles of the neck. The principal phasic phenomena are high-voltage spikes, isolated or grouped in volleys, that appear at the level of the pons and the rear part of the cortex (which is associated with the visual system). These spikes make their appearance about a minute before the tonic phenomena. Just as the latter show up, the peripheral phasic phenomena come into evidence: rapid eye movements, clawing movements of the paws and so on. The high-voltage spikes during paradoxical sleep in the cat come at a remarkably constant rate: about 60 to 70 per minute (figure 19.4).

Our continuous recordings around the clock in a sound-proofed cage have shown that cats spend about 35 per cent of the time (in the 24-hour day) in the state of wakefulness, 50 per cent in light sleep and 15 per cent in paradoxical sleep. In most cases the three states follow a regular cycle from wakefulness to light sleep to paradoxical sleep to wakefulness again. An adult cat never goes directly from wakefulness into paradoxical sleep. Thus we find that the two states of sleep have well-defined and clearly distinct electrical signatures. Equipped with this information, we are better prepared to search for the nervous structures and mechanisms that are responsible for sleep and dreaming.

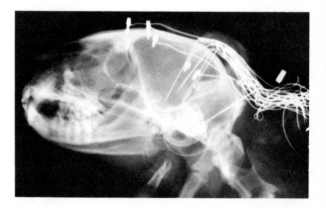

**Figure 19.1 X-ray of cat's head** shows a cluster of electrodes with which the author obtained a record of the electrical signals from various parts of the cat's brain. The cat's mouth is at the left; one electrode at far right measures the changes in the animal's neck-muscle tension.

**Figure 19.2 Characteristic rhythms** associated with deep sleep in a cat (*group of traces at right*) are so much like those of wakefulness (*left group*) and so different from those of light sleep (*middle group*) that the author has applied the term "paradoxical" to deep sleep. Normal cats spend about two-thirds of the time sleeping. They usually begin each sleep period with 25 minutes of light sleep, followed by six or seven minutes of paradoxical sleep. In the latter state they are hard to wake and their muscles are relaxed.

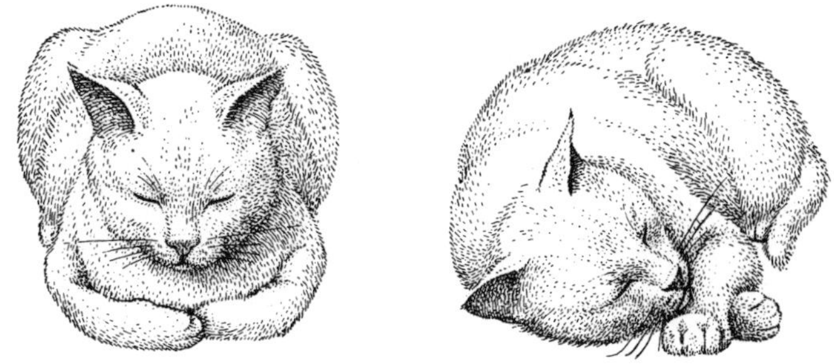

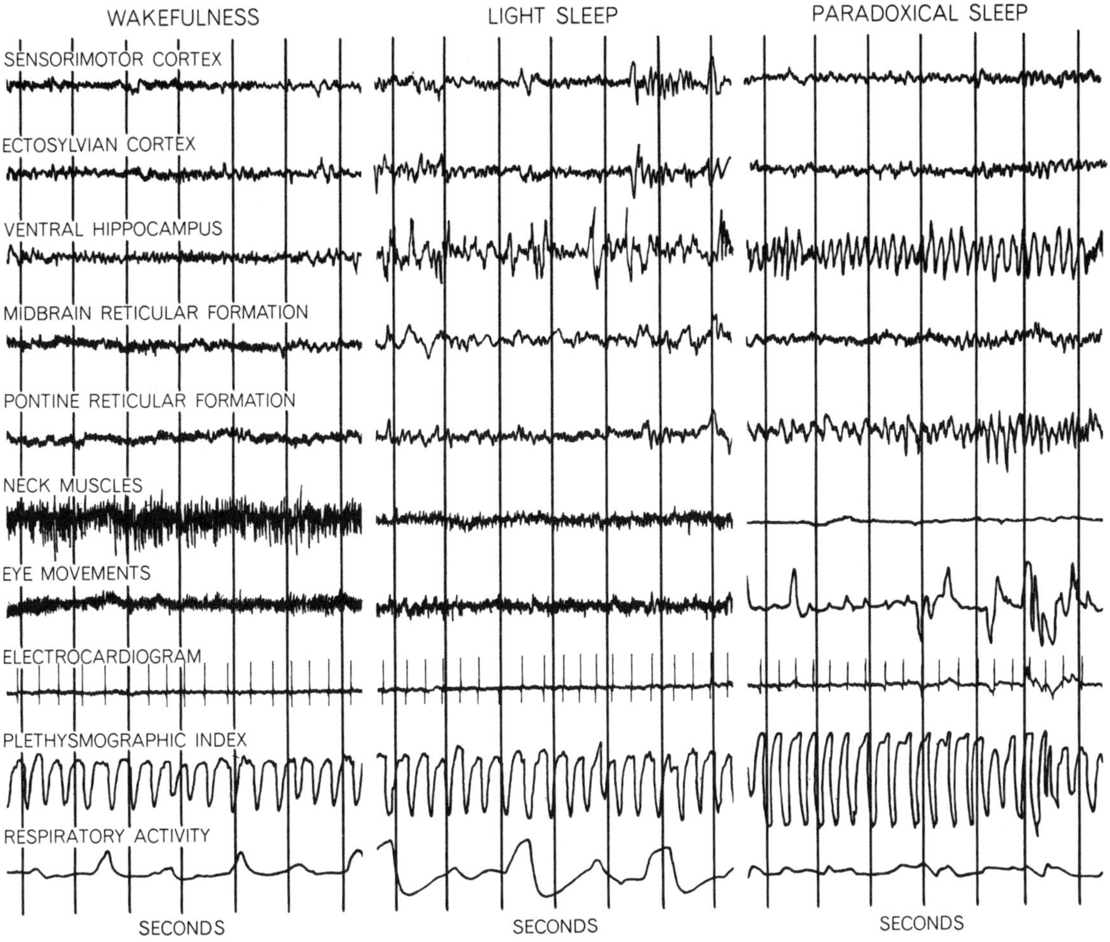

| WAKEFULNESS | LIGHT SLEEP | PARADOXICAL SLEEP |
|---|---|---|
| SENSORIMOTOR CORTEX | | |
| ECTOSYLVIAN CORTEX | | |
| VENTRAL HIPPOCAMPUS | | |
| MIDBRAIN RETICULAR FORMATION | | |
| PONTINE RETICULAR FORMATION | | |
| NECK MUSCLES | | |
| EYE MOVEMENTS | | |
| ELECTROCARDIOGRAM | | |
| PLETHYSMOGRAPHIC INDEX | | |
| RESPIRATORY ACTIVITY | | |
| SECONDS | SECONDS | SECONDS |

**Figure 19.3 Cat's brain,** seen in front-to-back section, has a number of segments. Some of the principal ones are identified in the illustration at the top of the opposite page. Many segments of the cat's brain, such as the cerebellum (*top right*), have no role to play in sleep.

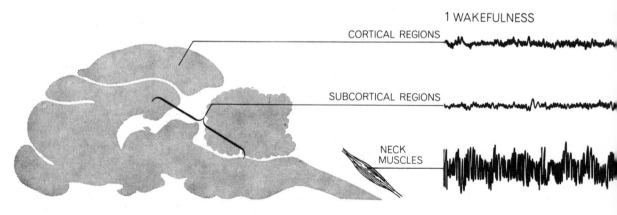

1 WAKEFULNESS

CORTICAL REGIONS

SUBCORTICAL REGIONS

NECK MUSCLES

**Figure 19.4 Varying rhythms** are identified with the various states of sleep. From left to right, a wakeful cat (*1*) shows high-speed alternations in electric potential in both cortical and subcortical regions of the brain, as well as neck-muscle tension. In light sleep (*2*) the cat shows a slower rhythm in the traces from the cortical and subcortical regions, but neck-muscle tension continues. The phasic, or periodic, aspects of paradoxical sleep (*3*) are marked by isolated spike discharges from the rear of the cortex and the pons, as well as by rapid eye movement and limb movements. Loss of neck-muscle tension is a tonic (*4*) rather than a phasic phenomenon. Other tonic, or continuous, aspects of paradoxical sleep are high-speed cortical rhythms and regular "theta" waves from hippocampus.

202

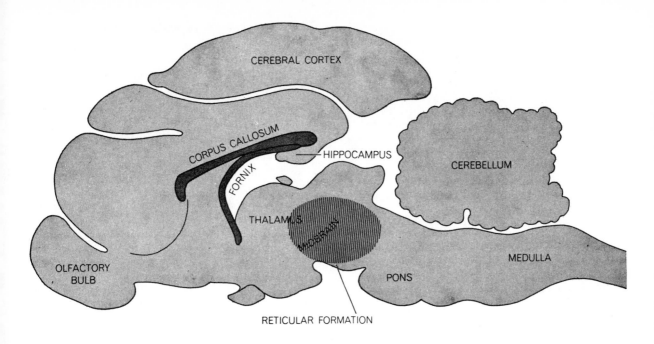

**Figure 19.5 Brain segments** associated with sleep include the reticular formation, which controls wakefulness. This region is under the control of an area in the lower brain. When the control is blocked by making a cut through the pons, a normal cat becomes insomniac.

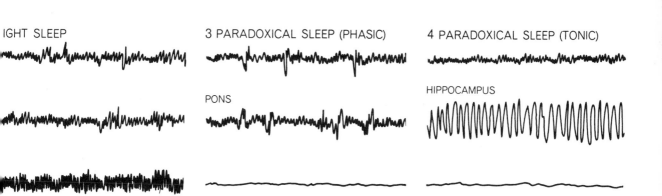

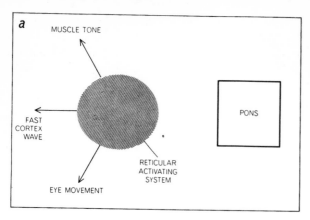

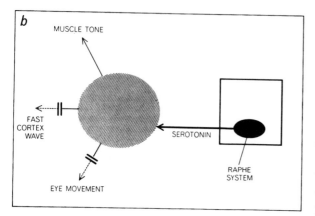

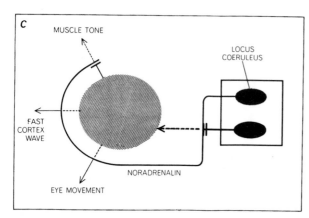

**Figure 19.6 Working hypothesis,** proposed by the author to provide a bridge between the neurophysiology and the biochemistry of sleep, suggests that the normal state of wakefulness (*a*) is transformed into light sleep (*b*) when a secretion produced by the nuclei of raphe modifies many effects of the reticular activating system. Paradoxical sleep follows (*c*) when a second secretion, produced by the locus coeruleus, supplants the raphe secretion and produces effects that resemble normal wakefulness except for the loss of muscle tension.

# The suppression of wakefulness

The first and most important question we must answer is this: does the nervous system possess a specific sleep-producing mechanism? In other words, should we not rather confine our research to the operations of the mechanism that keeps us awake? Kleitman has put the issue very clearly; he observes that to say one falls asleep or is put to sleep is not the same as saying one ceases to stay awake. The first statement implies that an active mechanism suppresses the state of wakefulness — a mechanism analogous to applying the brakes in an automobile. The second statement implies that the wakefulness-producing mechanism simply stops operating — a situation analogous to removing the foot from the accelerator. Thus the mechanism responsible for sleep would be negative or passive, not active.

Now, it has been known for nearly two decades that the brain contains a center specifically responsible for maintaining wakefulness. This was discovered by H. W. Magoun of the US and Giuseppe Moruzzi of Italy, working together at Northwestern University. They named this center, located in the midbrain, the reticular activating system (RAS) (figures 19.3 and 19.5). Stimulation of the RAS center in a slumbering animal arouses the animal; conversely, destruction of the center causes the animal to go into a permanent coma. To explain normal sleep, then, we must find out what process or mechanism brings about a deactivation of the RAS for the period of sleep.

On the basis of the known facts about the RAS there seemed at first no need to invoke the idea of a braking mechanism to account for deactivation of the system. The Belgian neurophysiologist Frédéric Bremer suggested that the RAS could simply lapse into quiescence as a result of a decline of stimuli (such as disturbing noise) from the surroundings.

Several years ago, however, explorations of the brain by the Swiss neurophysiologist W. R. Hess and others began to produce indications that the brain might contain centers that could suppress the activity of the RAS. In these experiments, conducted with cats, the cats fell asleep after electrical stimulation of various regions in the thalamus and elsewhere or after the injection of chemicals into the cerebrum. Interesting as these findings were, they were not very convincing on the question at issue. After all, since a cat normally sleeps about two-thirds of the time anyway, how could one be sure that the applied treatments acted through specific sleep-inducing centers? Moreover, the experiments seemed to implicate nearly all the nerve structures surrounding the RAS, from the cerebral cortex all the way down to the spinal cord, as being capable of inducing sleep.

**Figure 19.7 Brain structures** involved in light sleep include the raphe system, which, by producing the monoamine serotonin, serves to counteract the alerting effects of the brain's reticular formation (hatched). The author suggests that raphe system structures act to modulate the fast wave pattern of the alert cortex into the slower pattern typical of light sleep (*a*). Such slow activity, however, depends on higher as well as lower brain structures (*b*); when a cat is deprived of its cerebral cortex and thalamus, the brainstem wave pattern characteristic of light sleep disappears. The reason for this is not yet understood.

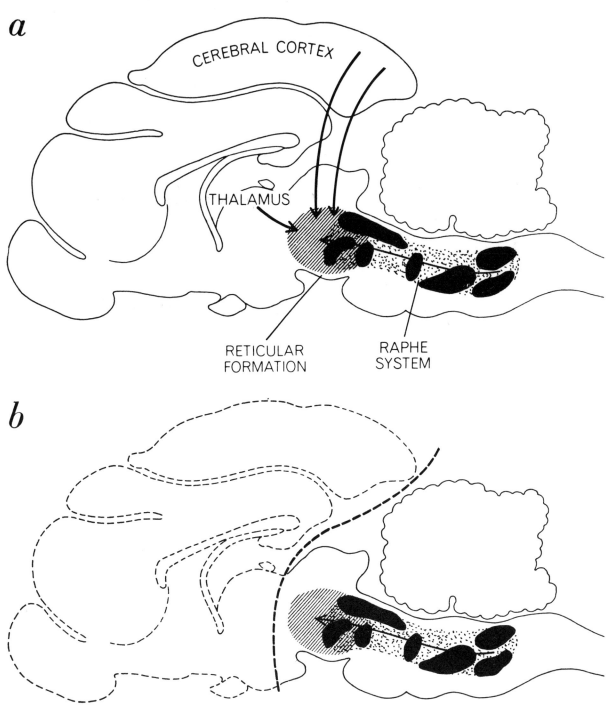

It was implausible that a sleep-inducing system could be so diffuse. Nevertheless, in spite of all these doubts, the experiments at least pointed to the possibility that the RAS might be influenced by other brain centers.

Moruzzi and his group in Italy proceeded to more definitive experiments. Seeking to pin down the location of a center capable of opposing the action of the RAS, they focused their search on the lower part of the brainstem. They chose a site at the middle of the pons in front of the trigeminal nerve, and with cats as subjects they cut completely through the brainstem at that point. The outcome of this operation was that the cats became insomniac: they slept only 20 per cent of the time instead of 65 per cent! The brain cortex showed the characteristic electrical activity of wakefulness (fast, low-voltage activity), and the eye movements also were those of a wakeful animal pursuing moving objects. The experiments left no doubt that the cut had disconnected the RAS from some structure in the lower part of the brainstem that normally exercised control over the waking center. It was as if a brake had been removed, so that the RAS was essentially unrestricted and kept the animal awake most of the time.

The new evidence leads, therefore, to the conclusion that sleeping is subject to both active and passive controls. The active type of control consists in the application of a brake on the RAS by some other brain structure or structures; the passive type corresponds to a letup on the accelerator in the RAS itself.

## Sleep centers

What, and where, are the sleep-inducing centers that act on the RAS? Our suspicions are now focused on a collection of nerve cells at the midline of the brainstem that are known as the "nuclei of raphe" (from a Greek work meaning "seam" and signifying the juncture of the two halves of the brain) (figures 19.7 and 19.9). In Sweden, Annica Dahlström and Kzell Fuxe have shown that under ultraviolet light these cells emit a yellow fluorescence that shows they are rich in the hormone-like substance serotonin, which is known to have a wide spectrum of powerful effects on the brain and other organs of the body. Suspecting from various preliminary pharmacological experiments that serotonin might play a role in sleep, we decided to test the effects of destroying the raphe cells, which are the principal source of the serotonin supply in the brain. We found that when we destroyed 80 per cent of these cells at the level of the medulla in cats (the animals could not have survived destruction of a larger percentage), the cats became even more sleepless than those on which Moruzzi had performed his operation. In more than 100 hours of continuous observation with electrical

recording instruments, our animals slept less than 10 per cent of the time. Our results were closely related to those of Moruzzi's. His operation dividing the brainstem cut through the raphe system. We found that when we destroyed only the raphe cells on one side or the other of the site of his cut, our animals were reduced to the same amount of sleep (20 per cent) as those on which he had performed his experiment. This gives us further reason to believe the raphe system may indeed be the main center responsible for bringing on sleep in cats.

These new developments bring serotonin into a prominent place in the research picture and offer an avenue for biochemical attack on the mysteries of sleep. The fact that the raphe cells are chiefly notable for their production of serotonin seems to nominate this substance for an important role in producing the onset of sleep. We have recently been able to demonstrate a significant correlation between the extent of the lesion of the raphe system, the decrease in sleep and the decrease in the amount of serotonin in the brain as measured by means of spectrofluorescent techniques.

*a*

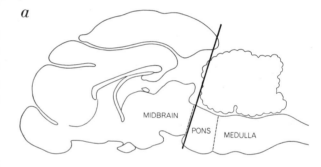

*b*

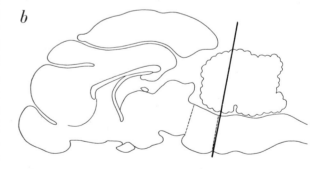

**Figure 19.8 Paradoxical sleep structures** evidently lie far back along the brainstem. A cat deprived of all its higher brain function by means of a cut through the pons (*a*) will live for months, alternately awake and in paradoxical sleep. If a cut is made lower (*b*) along the brainstem, however, the cat will no longer fall into paradoxical sleep, because the cut destroys some brain cells in that region, which produce another monoamine, noradrenalin.

In physiological terms we can begin to see the outlines of the system of brain structures involved in initiating the onset of sleep and maintaining the first stage of light slumber. At the level of the brainstem, probably within the raphe system, there are structures that apparently counteract the RAS and by their braking action cause the animal to fall asleep. Associated with these structures there presumably are nearby structures that account for the modulations of electrical activity (notably the slow brain waves) that have been observed to accompany light sleep. This slow activity seems to depend primarily, however, on the higher brain structures, particularly the cortex and the thalamus; in a decorticated animal the pattern characteristic of light sleep does not make its appearance. We must therefore conclude that the set of mechanisms brought into play during the process of falling asleep is a complicated one and that a number of steps in the process still remain to be discovered.

## Paradoxical sleep

In searching for the structures involved in paradoxical, or deep, sleep we are in a somewhat better position. When an animal is in that state, we have as clues to guide us not only the electrical activities in the brain but also conclusive and readily observable signs such as the disappearance of tonus in the muscles of the neck. This is the single most reliable mark of paradoxical sleep. Furthermore, it enables us to study animals that have been subjected to drastic operations we cannot use in the study of light sleep because they obliterate the electrical activities that identify the falling-asleep stage.

A cat whose brainstem has been cut through at the level of the pons, so that essentially all the upper part of the brain has been removed, still exhibits the cycle of waking and deep sleep. Such an animal can be kept alive for several months, and with the regularity of a biological clock it oscillates between wakefulness and the state of paradoxical sleep, in which it spends only about 10 per cent of the time. This state is signaled, as in normal animals, by the typical slackness of the neck muscles, by the electroencephalographic spikes denoting electrical activity in the pons structures and by lateral movements of the eyeballs.

When, however, we sever the brainstem at a lower level, in the lower part of the pons just ahead of the medulla, the animal no longer falls into paradoxical sleep (figure 19.8). The sign that marks this cyclical state — periodic loss of muscle tonus — disappears. It seems, therefore, that the onset of paradoxical sleep must be triggered by the action of structures somewhere in the middle portion of the pons. Further experiments have made it possible for us to locate these structures rather precisely. We have found that para-

doxical sleep can be abolished by destroying certain nerve cells in a dorsal area of the pons known as the locus coeruleus. Dahlström and Fuxe have shown that these cells have a green fluorescence under ultraviolet light and that they contain noradrenalin. Hence it seems that noradrenalin may play a role in producing paradoxical sleep similar to the one serotonin apparently plays in bringing about light sleep.

What mechanism is responsible for the elimination of muscular tonus that accompanies paradoxical sleep? It seems most likely that the source of this inhibition lies in the spinal cord, and Moruzzi and his colleague Ottavio Pompeiano are making a detailed investigation of this hypothesis.

The objective information about paradoxical sleep developed so far gives us some suggestions about the mechanisms involved in dreaming. The controlling structures apparently are located in the dorsal part of the pons. They give rise to spontaneous excitations that travel mainly to the brain's visual tracts, and it seems possible that this excitation is related to the formation of the images that one "sees" in dreams. Regardless of how strongly the brain is stimulated by these spontaneous impulses (as Edward V. Evarts of the National Institute of Mental Health and others have shown by means of microelectrode recordings of the visual system), during sleep the body's motor system remains inactive because a potent braking mechanism blocks electrical excitation of the motor nerves. This inhibitory mechanism seems to be controlled by the hormone-secreting nerves of the locus coeruleus structure (figure 19.9). If this structure is destroyed, the animal may periodically exhibit a spasm of active behavior, which looks very much as if it is generated by the hallucinations of a dream. In such episodes the cat, although it evinces the unmistakable signs of deep sleep and does not respond to external stimuli, will sometimes perform bodily movements of rage, fear or pursuit for a minute or two. The sleeping animal's behavior may even be so fierce as to make the experimenter recoil.

All in all the experimental evidence from mammals obliges us to conclude that sleep has a fundamental duality; deep sleep is distinctly different from light sleep, and the duality is founded on physiological mechanisms and probably on biochemical ones as well. Can we shed further light on the subject by examining animal evolution?

## The evolution of sleep

Looking into this question systematically in our laboratory, we failed to find any evidence of paradoxical sleep in the tortoise and concluded that probably reptiles in general were capable only of light sleep. Among birds, however, we

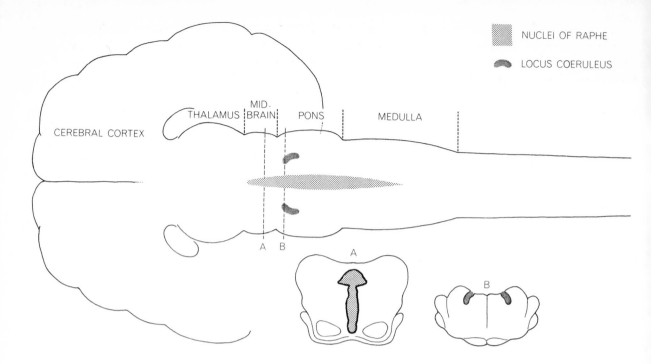

NUCLEI OF RAPHE

LOCUS COERULEUS

CEREBRAL CORTEX

THALAMUS | MID-BRAIN | PONS | MEDULLA

A B

A

B

**Figure 19.9 Cat's brainstem** is the site of the two groups of cells that produce the substances affecting light and paradoxical sleep. The nuclei of raphe (*stippled*) secrete serotonin; another cell group in the pons, known as the locus coeruleus (*gray*), secretes noradrenalin.

start to see a beginning of paradoxical sleep, albeit very brief. In our subjects – pigeons, chicks and other fowl – this state of sleep lasts no longer than 15 seconds at a time and makes up only 0.5 per cent of the total sleeping time, contrasted with the higher mammal's 20 to 30 per cent. In the mammalian order all the animals that have been studied, from the mouse to the chimpanzee, spend a substantial portion of their sleeping time in paradoxical sleep. We find a fairly strong indication that the hunting species (man, the cat, the dog) enjoy more deep sleep than the hunted (rabbits, ruminants). In our tests the former average 20 per cent of total sleep time in paradoxical sleep, whereas the latter average only 5 to 10 per cent (figure 19.10). Further studies are needed, however, to determine if what we found in our caged animals is also true of their sleep in their natural environments.

The evolutionary evidence shows, then, that the early vertebrates slept only lightly and deep sleep came as a rather late development in animal evolution. Curiously, however, it turns out that the opposite is true in the development of a young individual; in this case ontogeny does not follow

phylogeny. In the mammals (cat or man) light sleep does not occur until the nervous system has acquired a certain amount of maturity. A newborn kitten in its first days of life spends half of its time in the waking state and half in paradoxical sleep, going directly from one state into the other, whereas in the adult cat there is almost invariably a transitional period of light sleep. By the end of the first month the kitten's time is divided equally among wakefulness, light sleep and paradoxical sleep (that is, a third in each); thereafter both wakefulness and light sleep increase until adulthood stabilizes the proportions of the three states at 35, 50 and 15 per cent respectively.

Considering these facts of evolution and development, we are confronted with the question: what function does paradoxical sleep serve after all? Dement found that when he repeatedly interrupted people's dreams by waking them, this had the effect of making them dream more during their subsequent sleep periods. These results indicated that dreaming fulfills some genuine need. What that need may be remains a mystery. Dement's subjects showed no detectable disturbances of any importance – emotional or physiological – as a result of their deprivation of dreaming.

We have found much the same thing to be true of the deprivation of paradoxical sleep in cats. For such a test we place a cat on a small pedestal in a pool of water with the pedestal barely topping the water surface. Each time the cat drops off into paradoxical sleep the relaxation of its neck muscles causes its head to droop into the water and this wakes the animal up. Cats that have been deprived of paradoxical sleep in this way for several weeks show no profound disturbances, aside from a modest speeding up of the heart rate. They do, however, have a characteristic pattern of aftereffects with respect to paradoxical sleep. For several days following their removal from the pedestal they spend much more than the usual amount of time (up to 60 per cent) in paradoxical sleep, as if to catch up. After this rebound they gradually recover the normal rhythm (15 per cent in deep sleep), and only then does the heart slow to the normal rate. The recovery period depends on the length of the deprivation period: a cat that has gone without paradoxical sleep for 20 days takes about 10 days to return to normal.

## The chemistry of sleep

All of this suggests that some chemical process takes place during the recovery period. Let us suppose that the deprivation of paradoxical sleep causes a certain substance related to the nervous system to accumulate. The excess of paradoxical sleep during the recovery period will then be oc-

cupied with elimination of this "substance", presumably through the agency of "enzymatic" factors that act only during paradoxical sleep.

There is reason to believe that certain enzymes called monoamine oxidases, which oxidize substances having a single amine group, play a crucial role in bringing about the transition from light sleep to paradoxical sleep. We have found that drugs capable of inhibiting these enzymes can suppress paradoxical sleep in cats without affecting either light sleep or wakefulness. A single injection of the drug nialamide, for example, will eliminate paradoxical sleep from the cycle for a period of hundreds of hours. We have also found that this potent drug can suppress paradoxical sleep in cats that have first been deprived of such sleep for a long period in the pool experiment.

The findings concerning the probable importance of the monoamine oxidases in the sleep mechanism raise the hope that it may soon be possible to build a bridge between neurophysiology and biochemistry in the investigation of sleep. If it is indeed a fact that these enzymes play an important role in sleep, this tends to strengthen the hypothesis that serotonin and noradrenalin, which are monoamines, are involved in the two states of sleep – serotonin in light sleep and noradrenalin in paradoxical sleep. There are other bits of chemical evidence that support the same view. For example, the drug reserpine, which is known to prevent the accumulation of monoamines at places where these compounds are usually deposited, has been found to be capable of producing some specific electrical signs of paradoxical sleep in experimental animals. Further, the injection of certain precursors involved in the synthesis of serotonin in the brain can produce a state resembling light sleep, whereas drugs that selectively depress the serotonin level in the brain produce a state of permanent wakefulness.

We can put together a tentative working hypothesis about the brain mechanisms that control sleep. It seems that the raphe system is the seat responsible for the onset of light sleep, and that it operates through the secretion of serotonin. Similarly, the locus coeruleus harbors the system responsible for producing deep sleep, and this uses noradrenalin as its agent. In cyclic fashion these two systems apply brakes to the reticular activating system responsible for wakefulness and also influence all the other nerve systems in the brain, notably those involved in dreaming (figure 19.6).

Dreaming itself, particularly the question of its evolutionary origin and what function it serves, is still one of the great mysteries of biology. With the discovery of its objective accompaniments and the intriguing phenomenon of paradoxical sleep, however, it seems that we have set foot on a new continent that holds promise of exciting explorations.

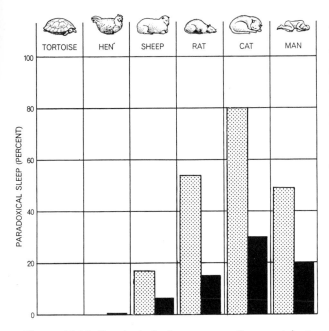

**Figure 19.10 Paradoxical sleep** among three vertebrate classes of increasing evolutionary complexity is shown as a percentage of each animal's time spent in light sleep. None is known in the case of the reptile, a tortoise; in the case of the hen it is only two-tenths of 1 per cent of the total. In the case of each of the four mammal species shown, the newborn spend at least twice as much time in paradoxical sleep (*stippled*) as do their adult counterparts (*black*).

# Bibliography

Aspects Anatomo-fonctionnels de la Physiologie du Sommeil, edited by M. Jouvet, Centre National de la Recherche Scientifique, 1965

An Essay on Dreams: the Role of Physiology in Understanding Their Nature, W. C. Dement in *New Directions in Psychology: Vol. II.*, Holt, Rinehart & Winston, Inc., 1965

Sleep and Wakefulness, Nathaniel Kleitman, The University of Chicago Press, 1963

Sleeping and Waking, Ian Oswald, American Elsevier Publishing Company, Inc., 1962

Sleep Mechanisms, edited by K. Akert, C. Bally and J. P. Schadé, American Elsevier Publishing Company, Inc., 1965

# Section IV
# Learning, memory and intelligence

This section is concerned with the closely related topics of memory and learning, both of which enable an organism to adapt to prevailing environmental circumstances, to retain this adaptive behaviour and to modify behaviour in the event of changes in the situation – mechanisms which are clearly essential to the survival of the animal. For learning to occur implies that there must be some form of storage of the information reaching the central nervous system via the sensory nerves; the actual form of the "memory mechanism" is still being investigated. Some animals learn faster than other members of their species and these differences in learning ability gave rise to the vexed question of intelligence and with it, the problem of whether intelligence is inherited or not. Such a question has obvious social implications, for whether it is believed that one can alter the level of learning ability of an animal by manipulation of the environment, or not, will affect the treatment of that individual. It is alarming to think that whole sections of the population may be neglected educationally while pseudo-scientific arguments are used to bolster political acts.

The articles included in this section cover a wide range of approaches to the subject from the philosophical to the biochemical. The first paper, "Information and memory" by George Miller, discusses some philosophical and early psychological studies of human memory span – the amount of information which can be retained at any one time. By contrast, an anatomical approach to the memory problem is provided by Roger Sperry's work on the question of transference of memory and skills between the two halves of the brain, and Steven Rose provides a biochemical viewpoint in the molecular approach to memory which discusses the possible mechanisms of memory at the cellular level and beyond. The selection from the *Bulletin of the Cambridge Society for Social Responsibility in Science* takes another look at the nature/nurture controversy centred around a recent provocative article published in the USA by Professor Arthur Jensen, which suggested that intelligence is largely inherited. Experimental investigations of human infants of the kind necessary to settle this issue are not possible for ethical reasons and are anyhow experimentally dubious, and so various investigators have attempted to answer the question by exploiting situations which occur naturally within the culture, for example the early separation of monozygotic twins. However, the statistical procedures employed and the so-called separation of environmental and inherited factors are frequently questionable and this selection of papers brings out some of the important points in this time-worn, but inflammatory debate.

The final paper by Harry Harlow and Margaret Kuenne Harlow, "Learning to think", suggests that problem-solving strategy can be greatly improved by repeated exposure to problem-solving situations, and that "insight" is not an automatic strategy present from birth but depends for its genesis upon earlier learning by trial and error. This takes us back to the nature/nurture question and suggests that environmental opportunities may be extremely important to the development of learning and ability to solve problems, contrary to Jensen's opinion.

# 20  Information and memory
## by George A Miller

Some things are easy to remember. A short poem is easier to memorize than a long one; an interesting story is better recalled than a dull one. But brevity and wit are not all that is involved. Equally important is the way things fit together. If a new task meshes well with what we have previously learned, our earlier learning can be transferred with profit to the novel situation. If not, the task is much harder to master.

Imagine that you are teaching geometry to children. You have covered the business of calculating the length of the hypotenuse of a right-angled triangle when the base and the altitude are given. Now you are about to take up the problem of finding the *area* of a right triangle when the base and the hypotenuse are given. Suppose you were given your choice of the following two methods of teaching the children to solve the problem. In method A you would help them to discover that the area of a right triangle is half that of a rectangle with the same base and altitude, that the unknown altitude of the triangle in this case can be calculated from the given base and hypotenuse by use of the Pythagorean theorem, and that the area of the triangle can therefore be found by deriving the altitude, computing the area of the rectangle and then taking half of that. In method B you would simply tell the class to memorize six steps: (1) add the length of the base to the length of the hypotenuse; (2) subtract the length of the base from the length of the hypotenuse; (3) multiply the first result by the second; (4) extract the square root of this product; (5) multiply the positive root by the length of the base; (6) divide this product by 2 (figure 20.1).

Which method of teaching would you choose? Probably no one but an experimental psychologist would ever consider method B. Method A is productive and insightful; method B is stupid and ugly. But just why do we find method B repulsive? What is repugnant about a procedure

that is logically impeccable and that leads always to the correct answer? This question is raised by the psychologist Max Wertheimer in his provocative little book, *Productive Thinking*. An obvious answer is that a child taught by method A will understand better what he is doing. But until we can say what it means to understand what one is doing, or what profit there is in such understanding, we have not really answered Wertheimer's question.

It is helpful to consider the interesting fact that method B is the procedure we would use to instruct a computing machine of the present-day type. The machine is able to perform arithmetical operations such as addition, subtraction, multiplication, division and the extraction of roots. Instruction for the machine consists in writing a "program" – like the series of steps used in method B except that the computer's program must be even more explicit and detailed, with even less hint of the basic strategy. Computing-machine engineers have their hearts set on some day designing machines which will construct programs for themselves: that is, given the strategy for handling a problem, the machine will understand the problem well enough to create all the appropriate operations or subroutines required to solve it. The desirability of such a development is obvious. In the first place, at present it takes many hours of drudgery to write the detailed instructions for all the steps a computer must take. Then, after the instructions have been written, they must be stored in the machine in some easily accessible form. In a large machine the number of subroutines may run into the thousands; it might actually be more economical to equip the machine with the ability to create them on demand rather than to build the necessary storage and access machinery. In other words, in a very elaborate computer it would be more efficient to store rules from which subroutines could be generated than to store the routines themselves.

It seems, therefore, that even the computing machine realizes that method B is ugly. Each subroutine is an isolated operation that must be stored in its proper place, and no attempt is made to tie these steps to other informa-

*first published in* Scientific American, *August 1956.*
*Reprinted with permission. Copyright © 1956 by Scientific American, Inc. All rights reserved.*

tion available to the machine. So we can see that one superiority of method A lies in the fact that it makes more efficient use of the capacity for storing information. In the teaching of geometry to a child, method A highlights the relations of the new problem to things that the child has already learned, and thus it provides the rules by which the child can write his own subroutines for computation. In essence the ugly method is less efficient because it requires the child to master more new information.

The intimate relation between memory and the ability to reason is demonstrated every time we fail to solve a problem because we fail to recall the necessary information. Since our capacity to remember limits our intelligence, we should try to organize material to make the most efficient use of the memory available to us. We cannot think simultaneously about everything we know. When we attempt to pursue a long argument, it is difficult to hold each step in mind as we proceed to the next, and we are apt to lose our way in the sheer mass of detail. Three hundred years ago René Descartes, in an unfinished treatise called *Rules for the Direction of the Mind*, wrote:

"If I have first found out by separate mental operations what the relation is between the magnitudes A and B, then that between B and C, between C and D, and finally between D and E, that does not entail my seeing what the relation is between A and E, nor can the truths previously learned give me a precise knowledge of it unless I recall them all. To remedy this I would run them over from time to time, keeping the imagination moving continuously in such a way that while it is intuitively perceiving each fact it simultaneously passes on to the next; and this I would do until I had learned to pass from the first to the last so quickly, that no stage in the process was left to the care of memory, but I seemed to have the whole in intuition before me at the same time. This method will relieve the memory, diminish the sluggishness of our thinking, and definitely enlarge our mental capacity."

Descartes's observation is familiar to anyone who has ever memorized a poem or a speech, or mastered a mathematical proof. Rehearsal or repetition has the very important effect of organizing many separate items into a single unit, thus reducing the load our memory must carry and leaving us free for further thinking. In terms of logic, the process is like the substitution of a single symbol for a longer expression which would be clumsy to write each time we wanted to use it.

The practical advantages of this unitizing process were vividly illustrated for me the first time I saw one of those digital computing machines that have small neon lights to show which relays are closed. There were 20 lights in a row, and I did not see how the men who ran the machine could grasp and remember a pattern involving so many elements. I quickly discovered that they did not try to deal with each light as an individual item of information. Instead, they translated the light pattern into a code. That is to say, they grouped the lights into successive triplets and gave each possible triplet pattern a number as its name, or symbol. The pattern all three lights off (000) was called 0; the pattern off-off-on (001) was called 1; off-on-off (010) was called 2, and so forth. Having memorized this simple translation, the engineers were able to look at a long string of lights such as 011000101001111 and break it down into triplets (011 000 101 001 111) which they immediately translated into 30517. It was much easier to remember these five digits than the string of 15 lit and unlit lights (figure 20.2).

Reorganization enabled the engineers to reduce the original complexity to something easily apprehended and remembered without changing or discarding any of the original data. There is an analogy between this simple trick and the process described by Descartes. Each step in a complex argument is like a single light in the binary sequence. Rehearsal organizes the steps into larger units similar to the engineers' triplets. Repeated rehearsal patterns the long argument into larger and larger units which are then replaced in thought by simpler symbols.

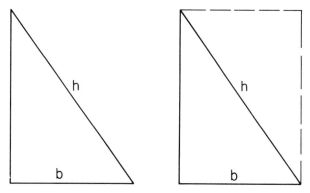

**Figure 20.1 Two methods** may be used to teach children how to find the area of a right-angled triangle. The method associated with the triangle at left has the following algebraic steps: (1) $h + b = v$, (2) $h - b = w$, (3) $v \times w = x$, (4) $\sqrt{x} = \pm y$, (5) $+ y \times b = z$, (6) $z/2 =$ area. The method associated with the triangle at right proceeds: (1) find altitude by the Pythagorean theorem, (2) find area of rectangle from base and altitude, (3) area of triangle is half the area of rectangle. The first method is considered ugly and the second efficient. Why?

| Binary lights | Octal code |
|:---:|:---:|
| 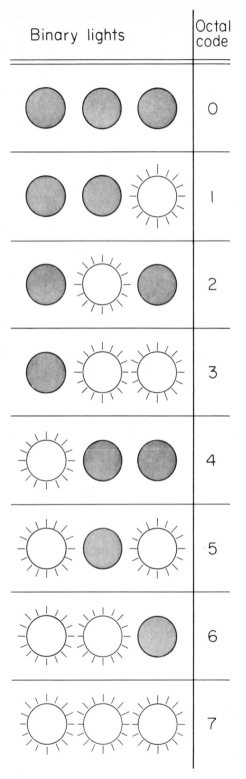 | 0 |
| | 1 |
| | 2 |
| | 3 |
| | 4 |
| | 5 |
| | 6 |
| | 7 |

**Figure 20.2 Computer lights** are quickly read by engineers using the code illustrated here.

The first person to propose an experimental test of the span of a man's instantaneous grasp seems to have been Sir William Hamilton, a 19th-century Scottish metaphysician. He wrote: "If you throw a handful of marbles on the floor, you will find it difficult to view at once more than six or seven at most, without confusion" (figure 20.3). It is not clear whether Hamilton himself actually threw marbles on the floor, for he remarked that the experiment could be performed also by an act of imagination, but at least one reader took him literally. In 1871 the English economist and logician William Stanley Jevons reported that when he threw beans into a box, he never made a mistake when there were three or four, was sometimes wrong if the number was five, was right about half the time if the beans numbered 10 and was usually wrong when the number reached 15. Hamilton's experiment has been repeated many times with better instrumentation and control, but refined techniques serve only to confirm his original intuition. We are able to perceive up to about six dots accurately without counting; beyond this errors become frequent.

But estimating the number of beans or dots is a perceptual task, not necessarily related to concepts or thinking. Each step in the development of an argument is a particular thing with its own structure, different from the other steps and quite different from one anonymous bean in Jevons's box. A better test of "apprehension" would be the ability to remember various symbols in a given sequence. Another Englishman, Joseph Jacobs, first performed this experiment with digits in 1887. He would read aloud a haphazard sequence of numbers and ask his listeners to write down the sequence from memory after he finished. The maximum number of digits a normal adult could repeat without error was about seven or eight.

From the first it was obvious that this span of immediate memory was intimately related to general intelligence. Jacobs reported that the span increased between the ages of 8 and 19, and his test was later incorporated by Alfred Binet, and is still used, in the Binet intelligence test. It is valuable principally because an unusually short span is a reliable indicator of mental deficiency; a long span does not necessarily mean high intelligence.

A person who can grasp eight decimal digits can usually manage about seven letters of the alphabet or six monosyllabic words (taken at random, of course). Now the interesting point about this is that six words contain much more information, as defined by information theory, than do seven letters or eight digits. We are therefore in a position analogous to carrying a purse which will hold no more than seven coins – whether pennies or dollars. Obviously we will carry more wealth if we fill the purse with silver dollars

rather than pennies. Similarly we can use our memory span most efficiently by stocking it with informationally rich symbols such as words, or perhaps images, rather than with poor coin such as digits.

The mathematical theory of communication developed by Norbert Wiener and Claude Shannon provides a precise measure of the amount of information carried. In the situation we are considering, the amount of information per item is simply the logarithm (to the base two) of the number of possible choices. Thus the information carried by a binary digit, where there are two alternatives, is $\log_2 2 = 1$ bit. In the case of decimal digits the amount of information per digit is $\log_2 10 = 3.32$ bits. Each letter of the alphabet carries $\log_2 26 = 4.70$ bits of information. When we come to make the calculation for words, we must take into account the size of the dictionary from which the words were drawn. There are perhaps 1 000 common monosyllables in English, so a rough estimate of the informational value of a monosyllabic word selected at random might be about 10 bits.

A person who can repeat nine binary digits can usually repeat five words. The informational value of the nine binary digits is nine bits; of the five words, about 50 bits. Thus the Wiener–Shannon measure gives us a quantitative indication of how much we can improve the efficiency of memory

**Figure 20.3 Sir William Hamilton**, a 19th-century Scottish philosopher (not to be confused with Sir William Rowan Hamilton, the mathematician), observed: "If you throw . . . marbles on the floor, you will find it difficult to view at once more than six . . . without confusion."

| Binary (1 bit) | Decimal (3.3 bits) | Alphabetic (4.7 bits) | Syllabic (10 bits) |
|---|---|---|---|
| 110100 | 4972 | XJR | for, line |
| 0100110 | 86515 | AYCZ | nice, it, act |
| 10010011 | 021942 | EDLYG | time, who, to, air |
| 101100010 | 3776380 | QJPEVJ | by, west, cent, or, law |
| 001010110 | 28201394 | DLXBAHC | boy, sea, ten, red, ask, mob |
| 1101000101 | 918374512 | HOKOMSFB | go, how, ice, save, hat, sue, way |
| 10100111010 | 1038204665 | FQGUJRZVM | odd, gas, call, at, ant, pay, get, was |
| 00010101110011 | 57048621937 | PNKSNWJUWT | by, game, log, free, so, you, car, big, why |

**Figure 20.4 Span of immediate memory** depends mainly on the number of items to be memorized and is relatively independent of the amount of information per item. In this table the amount of information is measured in "bits", or binary digits. A binary digit can be 1 or 0, and hence conveys a minimum amount of information. A person who can repeat nine binary digits can usually memorize seven decimal digits, six letters or five words (*row above broken line*). The other rows compare the span for other groups of items.

by using informationally rich units. The computer engineers who group the relay lights by threes and translate the triplets into a code can remember almost three times as much information as they would otherwise.

It is impressive to watch a trained person look at 40 consecutive binary digits, presented at the rate of one each second, and then immediately repeat the sequence without error. Such feats are called "mnemonic tricks" — a name that reveals the suspicious nature of psychologists. The idea that trickery is involved, that there is something bogus about it, has discouraged serious study of the psychological principles underlying such phenomena. Actually some of the best "memory crutches" we have are called laws of nature. As for the common criticism that artificial memory crutches are quickly forgotten, it seems to be largely a question of whether we have used a stupid crutch or a smart one.

When I was a boy I had a teacher who told us that memory crutches were only one grade better than cheating, and that we would never understand anything properly if we resorted to such underhanded tricks. She didn't stop us, of course, but she did make us conceal our method of learning. Our teacher, if her conscience had permitted it, no doubt could have shown us far more efficient systems than we were able to devise for ourselves. Another teacher who told me that the ordinate was vertical because my mouth went that way when I said it and that the abscissa was horizontal for the same reason saved me endless confusion, as did one who taught me to remember the number of days in each month by counting on my knuckles.

The course of our argument seems to lead to the conclusion that method A is superior to the ugly method B because it uses better mnemonic devices to represent exactly the same information. In method A the six apparently arbitrary steps of method B are organized around three aspects of the total problem so that each aspect can be represented by symbols which the student has already learned. The process is not essentially different from the engineers' method for recoding a sequence of binary lights.

It is conceivable that all complex, symbolic learning proceeds in this way. The material is first organized into parts which, once they cohere, can be replaced by other symbols – abbreviations, initial letters, schematic images, names or what have you – and eventually the whole scope of the argument is translated into a few symbols which can all be grasped at one time. In order to test this hypothesis we must look beyond experiments on the span of immediate memory.

Our question is: Does the amount of information per item (*i.e.*, the number of possible alternative choices per item) affect the number of items we can remember when there is a large amount of material to be mastered? For example, is it more difficult to memorize a random sequence of 100 monosyllabic words than 100 digits or 100 letters of the alphabet? The question is important because it has a bearing on how we can organize material most efficiently for learning.

In an exploratory study that S. L. Smith and I devised at the Harvard University Psychological Laboratories, the subjects were required to memorize three different kinds of lists of randomly chosen items. One list was constructed from a set of 32 alternatives (all the alphabet except Q plus the numerals 3, 4, 5, 6, 7, 8 and 9), another from a set of eight alternatives and the third from just two alternatives. The subject read a test list at the rate of one item every second and then had to write down as much of the list as he could remember in the correct order. The lists ran to 10, 20, 30 or 50 items. If the subject failed to reproduce the list exactly, it was presented again. The number of presentations required before the first perfect reproduction measured the difficulty of the task.

We were not greatly surprised to find that the subjects did somewhat better (*i.e.*, needed about 20 per cent fewer trials) on the binary-choice lists than on the other types (figure 20.4). After all, a run of, say, six zeros or six ones is easy to remember and therefore in effect shortens the list. But on the other two types of lists (eight alternatives and 32 alternatives) the subjects' performances were practically indistinguishable. In other words, it was just as easy to memorize a list containing a lot of information as one of the same length containing less information.

Very similar results have been obtained at the University of Wisconsin by W. J. Brogden and E. R. Schmidt, who did their experiments for other reasons and without knowledge of the hypothesis Smith and I were trying to test. They used verbal mazes with either 16 or 24 choice points and they varied the number of alternatives per choice point from two to 12. Here again the length of the list of points that had to be learned, and not the number of alternatives offered at each choice point, determined the difficulty of the test – with the same exception that we found, namely, that it was slightly easier to remember where only two choices were offered.

Tentatively, therefore, we are justified in assuming that our memories are limited by the number of units or symbols we must master, and not by the amount of information that these symbols represent. Thus it is helpful to organize material intelligently before we try to memorize it. The process of organization enables us to package the same total amount of information into far fewer symbols, and so eases the task of remembering (figure 20.4).

How much unitizing and symbolizing must we do, and how can we decide what the units are? The science of linguistics may come to our aid here. Language has a hierarchical structure of units – sounds, words, phrases, sentences, narratives – and it is there that one should seek evidence for a similar hierarchy of cognitive units.

It has been estimated that English sentences are about 75

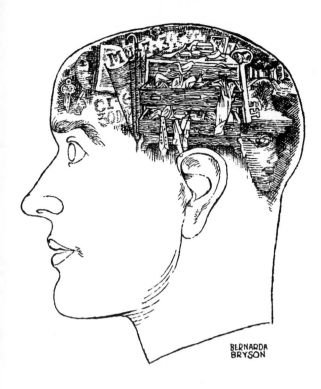 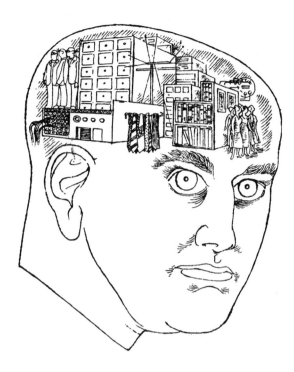

**Figure 20.5 Fanciful heads** were drawn by Bernarda Bryson to depict René Descartes's *Rules for the Direction of the Mind*, described in the text of the article. The individual at left has presumably not had the benefit of the rules, whereas the man at right has.

per cent redundant: that is, about four times as long as they would need to be if we used our alphabet with maximum efficiency. At first glance this fact seems paradoxical. If length is our major source of difficulty, why do we deliberately make our sentences longer than necessary? The paradox arises from a confusion about the definition of sentence length. Is a sentence 100 letters, or 25 words, or 6 phrases, or one proposition long? The fact that all our books contain 75 per cent more letters than necessary does not mean that 75 per cent of the ideas could be deleted. And it is those larger subjective units, loosely called ideas, that we must count to determine the psychological length of any text.

A sequence of 25 words in a sentence is easier to recall than a sequence of 25 words taken haphazardly from the dictionary. The sentence is easier because the words group themselves easily into familiar units. In terms of psychological units, a 25-word sentence is shorter than a sequence of 25 unrelated words. This means that the word is not the appropriate unit for measuring the psychological length of a sentence. Perhaps linguistic techniques for isolating larger units of verbal behaviour will provide an objective basis for settling the question.

When we memorize a sentence, all our previous familiarity with the lexicon and grammar of the language comes to our aid. It is one of the clearest possible examples of the transfer of previous learning to a new task. And the transfer is profitable because it serves to reduce the effective length of the material to be remembered. By learning the language, we have already acquired automatic habits for unitizing those sequences that obey the rules of the language.

There are three stages in the unitizing process. All three were described in the 17th century by John Locke in his famous *Essay Concerning Human Understanding*: "Wherein the mind does these three things: first, it chooses a certain number [of specific ideas]; secondly, it gives them connexion, and makes them into one idea; thirdly, it ties them together by a name." Men form such complex ideas, Locke said, "for the convenience of communication", but the combination of ideas sometimes leads to confusion because it is "the workmanship of the mind, and not referred to the real existence of things". The development in the 20th century of a mathematical theory of communication enables us to see more clearly how this process serves the convenience of communication and, coupled with the fact that it is the length, not the variety of the material that limits our memories, gives us an important insight into the economics of cognitive organization.

Organizing and symbolizing are pervasive human activities. If we can learn to perform them more efficiently, perhaps we shall indeed be able, as Descartes promised, to "relieve the memory, diminish the sluggishness of our thinking, and definitely enlarge our mental capacity".

## Bibliography

The Magical Number Seven, Plus-or-Minus Two: Some Limits on Our Capacity for Processing Information, George A. Miller in *Psychological Review*, Vol. 63, No. 2, pages 81–97, March 1956

# 21 The great cerebral commissure
## by R W Sperry

The body plan of a mammal provides for two lungs, two kidneys and paired organs such as eyes, ears and limbs. In a sense it also provides for a paired brain. In structural detail and functional capacity the two halves of the mammalian brain are mirror twins, each with a full set of centers for the sensory and motor activities of the body: vision, hearing, muscular movement and so on. Each hemisphere of the brain is mainly associated with one side of the body, the right brain presiding over the left side and the left brain over the right side. Each hemisphere's influence is not, however, always restricted in this way: when an area in one hemisphere is damaged, the corresponding area in the other often can take over its work and so control the functions involved for both sides of the body. In short, either half of the brain can to a large extent serve as a whole brain.

Anatomically, of course, the two halves of the brain are linked together and normally function as one organ. They are united not only by the common stem that descends from the brain into the spinal cord but also by a number of cross bridges between the hemispheres. Especially striking is the system of connections between the two halves of the cerebrum: the upper part of the brain. The cerebral hemispheres are linked by discrete bundles of nerve fibers, called commissures, that form reciprocal connections between parallel centers in the two hemispheres. By far the most prominent of these bridges is a broad cable known as the great cerebral commissure or, more technically, as the corpus callosum (figure 21.2). This massive structure, which is particularly large in primates and largest in man, contains most of the millions of nerve fibers that connect the two halves of the cerebral cortex, which is the highest integrating organ of the brain.

The size and obviously important position of the corpus callosum suggest that it must be crucial for the proper performance of the brain's functions. Many years ago,

however, brain surgeons discovered to their surprise that when the corpus callosum was cut into (as it sometimes had to be for medical reasons), this severing of fiber connections between the cerebral cortices produced little or no noticeable change in the patients' capacities. The same was true in the rare cases of individuals who lacked the corpus callosum because of a congenital failure in development. Experiments in severing the corpus callosum in monkeys tended to confirm the apparent harmlessness of the operation. Accordingly in the late 1930s surgeons tried cutting the entire corpus callosum in some cases of severe epilepsy as a measure to prevent the spread of epileptic seizures from one brain hemisphere to the other. Efforts to pinpoint losses of function in this series of cases were again unsuccessful.

Exactly what purpose the corpus callosum served became more and more a mystery. In 1940 the nerve physiologist Warren S. McCulloch, then working at the Yale University School of Medicine, summarized the situation with the remark that its only proved role seemed to be "to aid in the transmission of epileptic seizures from one to the other side of the body". As recently as 1951 the psychologist Karl S. Lashley, director of the Yerkes Laboratories of Primate Biology, was still offering his own jocular surmise that the corpus callosum's purpose "must be mainly mechanical . . . i.e., to keep the hemispheres from sagging". The curious capacity of the brain to carry on undisturbed after the destruction of what is by far its largest central fiber system came to be cited rather widely in support of some of the more mystical views in brain theory.

Intrigued by the problem of the great cerebral commissure and the theoretical implications of this problem, my colleagues and I began an intensive investigation of the matter, starting in the early 1950s at the University of Chicago and continuing after 1954 at the California Institute of Technology. This research, carried on by many workers at Cal Tech and elsewhere, has now largely resolved the mystery of the corpus callosum; today this bundle of fibers is probably the best understood of any of the large central

*first published in* Scientific American, *January 1964.*
*Reprinted with permission. Copyright © 1964 by Scientific American, Inc. All rights reserved.*

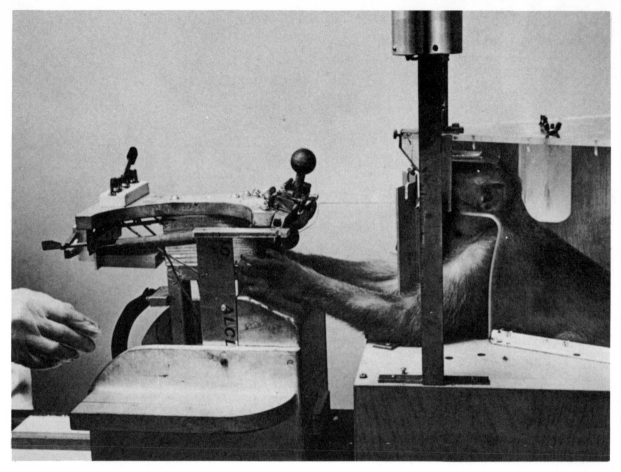

**Figure 21.1 Effect of brain division** is tested on animals trained to perform a variety of tasks in response to visual or tactile cues. In this test designed by the author the monkey must pull one or the other of two levers with differently shaped handles.

association systems of the brain. The investigation has gone considerably beyond the question of the corpus callosum's functions. From it has emerged a new technique for analyzing the organization and operation of the brain; this approach has already yielded much interesting information and promises to open up for detailed study many heretofore inaccessible features of brain activity.

The technique essentially consists in the study or application, in various ways, of the split brain: a brain divided surgically so that the performance of each half can be tested separately. It has entailed a series of experiments with animals, starting with cats and continuing with monkeys and chimpanzees. The findings are not confined to animals; there has also been opportunity to study human patients who had been operated on for severe epilepsy and emerged from the operation with a split brain but freed of convulsive attacks and still in possession of most of their faculties.

The split-brain studies have borne out the earlier observation that the cutting of the entire corpus callosum causes little disturbance of ordinary behavior. This is generally true even when the operation severs not only the corpus callosum but also all the other connections between the right and left sides of the brain down through the upper part of the brain stem. Cats and monkeys with split brains can hardly be distinguished from normal animals in most of their activities. They show no noticeable disturbance of co-ordination, maintain their internal functions, are alert and active, respond to situations in the usual manner and perform just about as well as normal animals in standard tests of learning ability. Their individual traits of personality and temperament remain the same.

It required specially designed tests to show that the split brain is not, after all, entirely normal in its function. The first convincing demonstration was provided by Ronald E. Myers, in his doctoral research started in 1951 in our laboratory at the University of Chicago and continued at Cal Tech. Testing the performance of the two brain halves separately, he found that when the corpus callosum was cut, what was learned by one side of the brain was not transferred to the other side. In fact, the two sides could learn diametrically opposed solutions to the same experimental problem, so that the animal's response in a given situation depended on which side of the brain was receiving the triggering stimulus. It was as though each hemisphere were a separate mental domain operating with complete disregard – indeed, with a complete lack of awareness – of what went on in the other. The split-brain animal behaved in the test situation as if it had two entirely separate brains.

The initial experiment involved segregating each eye with half of the brain as a separate system. This was accomplished by cutting both the corpus callosum and the structure called the optic chiasm, in which half the nerve fibers from each eye cross over to the brain hemisphere on the opposite side of the head (figure 21.3). The effect of this combined operation is to leave each eye feeding its messages solely to the hemisphere on the same side of the head.

The animal was then trained to solve a problem presented only to one eye, the other eye being covered with a patch. The problem might be, for example, to discriminate between a square and a circle; if the animal pushed a panel bearing the correct symbol, say the square, it got a reward of food. After it had learned to make the correct choice with one hemisphere, the problem was then presented to the other eye and hemisphere, the first eye now being blindfolded. When the subject used the second eye, it reacted as if it had never been faced with the problem before. The number of trials required to relearn the problem with the second eye showed that no benefit carried over from the earlier learning with the first eye. The transfer of learning and memory from one hemisphere to the other occurred readily in animals with the corpus callosum intact but failed completely in those with the corpus callosum cut. Each hemisphere, and its associated eye, was independent of the other.

This was again demonstrated when the two hemispheres were trained to make opposite choices. The animal was first trained to choose the square when the pair of symbols was seen through one eye. After learning was complete the eye patch was shifted and the animal was taught with the other eye to reject the square and pick the circle. This reversed training through the separate eyes gave rise to no sign of interference or conflict, as it does in an animal with an intact corpus callosum.

Subsequent studies, many dealing with forms of learning other than the visual – discrimination by touch, motor learning and so on – support the same conclusion. For example, in a special training box in which the animals could not see what their forepaws were doing, John S. Stamm and I trained cats to get food by using a paw to choose correctly between a hard pedal and a soft one, or a rough pedal and a smooth one, or two pedals of different shapes (figure 21.4). With the corpus callosum intact, an animal trained to use one paw is generally able to carry out the learned performance when it is made to use the untrained paw; normally the training transfers from one side to the other. But when the corpus callosum has been cut beforehand, the training of one paw does not help the other; on shifting from the first paw to the second the cat has to learn discrimination by touch all over again. The same applies to the learning of a motor task, such as the pattern of finger or paw movement necessary to push a lever or open the hasp and cover of a food well. What is learned with one hand or paw fails, as a rule, to carry over to the other when the corpus callosum has been severed, be it in a cat, a monkey, a chimpanzee or a man.

In short, it appears from the accumulated evidence that learning in one hemisphere is usually inaccessible to the other hemisphere if the commissures between the hemispheres are missing. This means that the corpus callosum has the important function of allowing the two hemispheres to share learning and memory. It can do this in either of two ways: by transmitting the information at the time the learning takes place, or by supplying it on demand later. In the first case the engrams, or memory traces, of what is learned are laid down both in the directly trained hemisphere and, by way of the corpus callosum, in the other hemisphere as well. In other words, intercommunication via the corpus callosum at the time of learning results in the formation of a double set of memory traces, one in each half of the brain. In the second case a set of engrams is established only in the directly trained half, but this information is available to the other hemisphere, when it is required, by way of the corpus callosum.

By cutting the corpus callosum after learning, and by other methods of investigation, it is possible to determine which of these two memory systems is used in different learning situations and in different species. It appears from present evidence that the cat tends to form engrams in both hemispheres when it is learning something. In man, where one hemisphere is nearly always dominant, the single-engram system tends to prevail, particularly in all memory relating to language. The monkey seems to fall somewhere in between. It sometimes uses the double-engram system, but under other conditions it may lay down engrams in only one of its hemispheres.

**Figure 21.2 Corpus callosum** and the other commissures connect the two halves of the mammalian brain. The drawings on these two pages show the brains of a cat (*left*), a monkey (*center*) and a human being (*right*). In each case the top drawing shows the top of the cerebral hemispheres, with the position of the corpus callosum indicated between the broken lines. The bottom drawings are sectional views of the right half of the brain as seen from the mid-line.

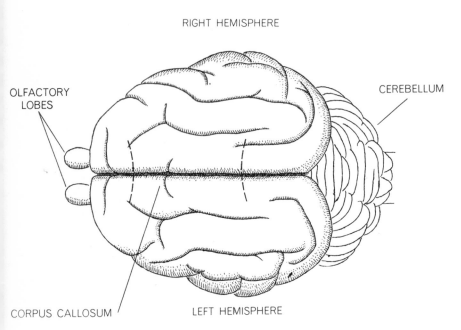

RIGHT HEMISPHERE

OLFACTORY LOBES

CEREBELLUM

CORPUS CALLOSUM

LEFT HEMISPHERE

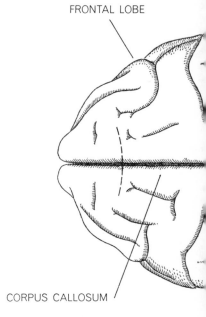

FRONTAL LOBE

CORPUS CALLOSUM

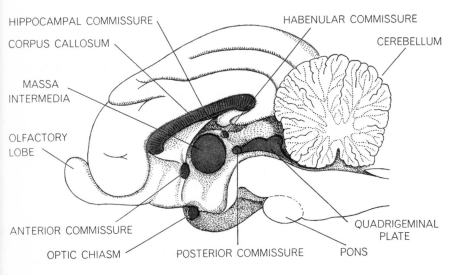

HIPPOCAMPAL COMMISSURE

CORPUS CALLOSUM

MASSA INTERMEDIA

OLFACTORY LOBE

HABENULAR COMMISSURE

CEREBELLUM

ANTERIOR COMMISSURE

OPTIC CHIASM

POSTERIOR COMMISSURE

PONS

QUADRIGEMINAL PLATE

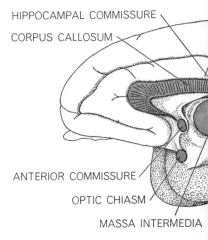

HIPPOCAMPAL COMMISSURE

CORPUS CALLOSUM

ANTERIOR COMMISSURE

OPTIC CHIASM

MASSA INTERMEDIA

ARIETAL LOBE

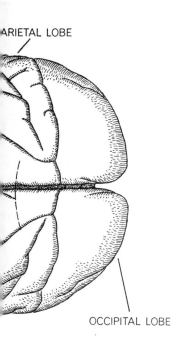

OCCIPITAL LOBE

FRONTAL LOBE

PARIETAL LOBE

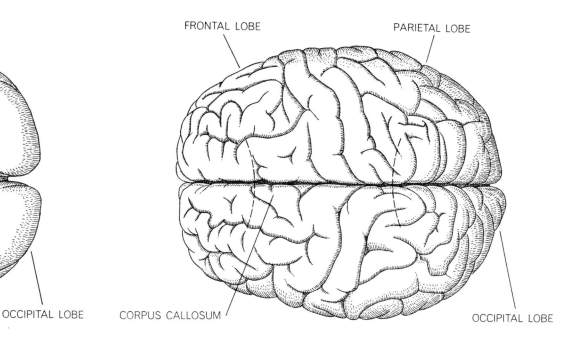

CORPUS CALLOSUM

OCCIPITAL LOBE

HABENULAR COMMISSURE

POSTERIOR COMMISSURE

QUADRIGEMINAL PLATE

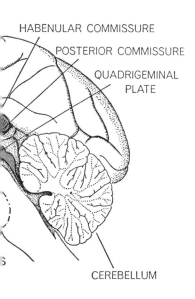

CEREBELLUM

HIPPOCAMPAL COMMISSURE

CORPUS CALLOSUM

HABENULAR COMMISSURE

POSTERIOR COMMISSURE

QUADRIGEMINAL PLATE

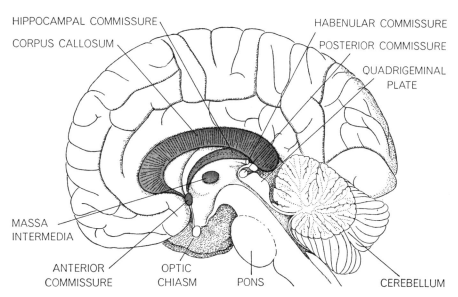

MASSA INTERMEDIA

ANTERIOR COMMISSURE

OPTIC CHIASM

PONS

CEREBELLUM

223

Thanks to a wide variety of experiments with cats and monkeys, involving one-side training and testing of various eye-limb and other combinations, we are now beginning to get a fairly detailed picture of the functions of the corpus callosum. It is needed for correlating images in the left and right halves of the visual field; for integrating sensations from paired limbs, or for learning that requires motor co-ordination of the limbs; for unifying the cerebral processes of attention and awareness, and for a number of other specific activities that involve direct interaction of the hemispheres. Furthermore, the corpus callosum seems to play important roles of a more general nature. Its absence slows down the rate of learning, at least in some situations. And, like other large nerve-fiber tracts, it has a general tonic effect on the brain cells to which it feeds impulses.

Many of these findings in animals have been checked and confirmed recently in studies conducted on a human patient in whom the hemispheres were surgically separated in an effort to control intractable epileptic convulsions. The seizures had been building up for 10 years in this man after a brain injury sustained in World War II. Philip J. Vogel and Joseph E. Bogen, surgeons at the Institute of Nervous Diseases of Loma Linda University in Los Angeles, cut through the corpus callosum and other commissures. The operation was remarkably successful in ending the attacks. Moreover, the patient, a 49-year-old man above average in intelligence, was left without any gross changes in his personality or level of intellect. In the months after the operation he commented repeatedly that he felt much better than he had in many years. In casual conversation over a cup of coffee and a cigarette one would hardly suspect that there was anything at all unusual about him.

With the collaboration of the patient and his physician, Michael S. Gazzaniga of our laboratory has carried out a series of careful tests probing the man's performances with one or both sides of the brain and body. Like most people, the patient is right-handed, and his dominant cerebral hemisphere is the left one. He is able to perform quite normally most activities involving only the left brain and right side of the body. For example, he can easily read material in the right half of his visual field, name and locate objects in that half, execute commands with his right hand or foot and so on. He does, however, have certain difficulties with activities on his left side.

Up to a point the left side of his body can function normally: he appears to see clearly in the left half of his visual field and has good sensitivity to touch and good motor function on his left side. But in any task that requires judgment or interpretation based on language, which is stored only in his left cerebral hemisphere, he clearly shows the effects of the cerebral disconnection. He cannot read any material that falls in the left half of his visual field, so that when he reads with full vision he has difficulty and tires easily. Nor can he write anything at all meaningful with his left hand. As a rule he cannot carry out verbal commands with his left hand or left leg. When an object is presented solely in the left half of his visual field, he may react to it appropriately but he cannot name or describe it. The same is true of an object placed in his left hand when he is blindfolded. While blindfolded he is unable to say where he has been touched on the left side of the body or to describe the position or movements of his own left hand. In fact, if the dominant hemisphere of his brain is occupied with a task, anything happening to the left side of his body may go completely unnoticed. When his dominant left hemisphere is questioned about nonverbal activities that have just been carried out successfully by the left hand via the right hemisphere, it cannot recall them; this is often the case even when both of his eyes have been open and their visual fields unrestricted. Evidently the dominant hemisphere of the brain neither knows nor remembers anything about the experiences and activities of the other hemisphere.

The separation of the two hemispheres is further indicated by certain specific tests. For instance, when the skin on one side of the subject's body is lightly tapped with the point of a pencil, he can locate the point touched with the hand on that side but not with the other hand. When a spot of light is flashed on a screen in one half of the patient's visual field, he can point to it only with the hand on the same side. In generalized motor activities his left hand usually co-operates with the right, but not always. At times the left hand may go off in a distracted way on independent and even antagonistic activities of its own, which can be troublesome.

These findings are generally confirmed in work begun with a second patient who has more recently recovered from the same kind of brain operation. The results in this individual are not complicated by an earlier brain injury, and two months after the operation the overall recovery picture is even better than it was for the first patient. In particular, motor control of the left hand is not so markedly impaired.

It should be noted again that most of the impairments of brain function from such surgery do not show up in the common activities of daily life. They are detected only under special testing conditions, such as blindfolding the subject, restricting his movements to one or the other hand, using quick-flash projection to confine vision to half of the visual field and so on. One can hope that where the impairments do cause difficulty in ordinary activities, they will be correctible by re-education and other measures as further investigation adds to our understanding of the properties and capacities of the bisected brain.

In any case, it is now clear that the loss of the commissural connections between the two halves of the cerebrum does have important and well-marked effects on the functioning of the brain. If the corpus callosum fails to develop at all because of some congenital accident, centers for language and other functions may develop in compensation on both sides of the brain. This seems to have occurred in a nine-year-old boy lacking a corpus callosum, whom we recently tested. As in some earlier cases in the medical literature, he shows almost none of the impairments we observe in the two adult patients.

In other older cases distinct impairments were observed, but they were ascribed to damage in brain areas near the corpus callosum. In the light of present knowledge these cases reinforce the view that damage to the corpus callosum interferes with normal functioning in a number of clearly defined ways. For example, Norman Geschwind of the Veterans Administration Hospital in Boston has recently noted that a patient with a damaged corpus callosum, and similar individuals in the medical literature, have shown effects such as word-blindness, word-deafness and faulty communication between the right and left hands.

Once the enigma of the great cerebral commissure was cleared up and it was firmly established that the commissure really does serve important communication purposes, our interest shifted to more general questions that might be explored by investigation of the bisected brain. Such a brain offered an extraordinary opportunity to examine the many functions and interrelations of parts of the brain, structure by structure and control center by control center.

Bisection of the brain leaves each hemisphere virtually undisturbed. Each half preserves intact its internal organization, the inflow of sensory messages and the outflow of motor commands. Each retains its full set of cerebral control centers and the potentiality for performing nearly all the functions of a whole brain. Even the human brain, in spite of the normal dominance of one side, can adapt itself to carry on fairly well when one hemisphere is eliminated early in life because of a tumor or an injury. A monkey with one cerebral hemisphere removed gets along better than a man in a comparable condition, and a cat does much better than a monkey.

Because of the independence of the two halves of the bisected brain, it is possible to study nearly all brain functions by concentrating on one half while the animal carries

on normally with the other half. The situation affords certain uniquely helpful experimental conditions. Since the experiments are performed with one hemisphere, the identical opposite hemisphere can serve as a built-in control for comparison. Moreover, the fact that one half of the brain suffices to deal with the animal's needs makes it possible to remove or isolate parts of the experimental half, without disabling after-effects to the animal, in order to identify the functions of each part.

A first question to arise in this connection is: How far can the brain be divided without grossly disrupting brain-mediated processes? We have already noted that cutting the cerebral commissures does not seriously interfere with the functioning of the two hemispheres. In monkeys the bisection has been carried down through the roof of the brain stem and completely through the cerebellum, leaving intact for cross-communication only the tegmentum, or floor of the brain stem (figure 21.6). Such monkeys show some motor unsteadiness, weakness and uncertainty, but they eventually recover their strength and stability. Deeper splits through the tegmentum into the upper part of the pons have

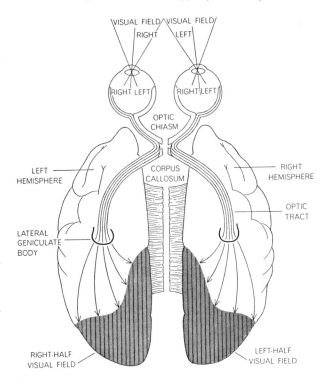

**Figure 21.3 Visual fields** and the visual centers of the brain are related as shown in this diagram of the monkey brain. Cutting optic chiasm and corpus callosum leaves each eye feeding information to one side of the brain only and eliminates the normal overlap of visual fields.

225

been made in the cat by Theodore Voneida of our laboratory. A curious blindness ensued, but it cleared up after several weeks and the animals made a good recovery. The effects on learning and perception of these deepest bisections have not yet been studied in detail. In general, however, it can be said that the two halves of the brain function well even when they are divided down into the upper regions of the brain stem, provided that only cross connections are cut.

The effect on behavior of severing the cross connections between the two halves of the brain is not always simple and unambiguous. An animal with a split brain sometimes behaves as if the two hemispheres were still in direct communication in one way or another. Some of these cases can be explained without difficulty; others are puzzling and call for further investigation.

One case involved the ability to respond to differences in the brightness of light. Thomas H. Meikle and Jeri A. Sechzer of the University of Pennsylvania School of Medicine trained cats to discriminate between brightness differences seen with one eye and then tested them with the other eye. With the corpus callosum severed the cats were able to transfer this learning from one hemisphere to the other when the brightness distinctions were easy to make, but not when they were fairly difficult. The transfer disappeared, however, when cross connections in the midbrain, as well as the corpus callosum, were cut. This case therefore appears to be explainable on the basis that in the cat the process involved is simple enough to occur at a level lower than the corpus callosum. In the monkey and in man, however, the corpus callosum seems to be required for the transfer of even the simplest brightness or color discrimination.

There are types of cross communication that can take place in a split brain because both sides of the brain are directly connected to the motor system or sensory organ involved. For example, each brain hemisphere receives sensory messages from both the right and the left sides of the face and other parts of the head; consequently the separation of the hemispheres does not interrupt the communication of sensations between the two sides of the head. Hearing in each ear

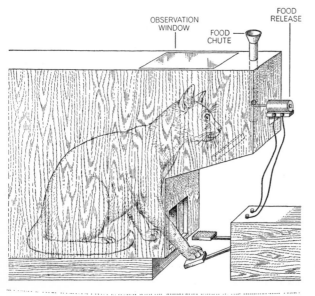

**Figure 21.4 Tactile discrimination** is tested with the apparatus shown in the photograph (*top*) and in the diagram (*bottom*). The animal is trained to distinguish between two pedals with different shapes or surface textures. In a normal cat, whatever is learned with one paw is transferred to the other one. But in a split-brain animal each side must learn a task anew.

is likewise extensively represented in both cerebral hemispheres. The same may apply in lesser degree to certain sensations in the limbs and the rest of the body; this may explain why learning involving hand and arm movements in monkeys with split brains may on occasion transfer from one side to the other.

There is also the possibility of indirect communication between the split halves of the brain through feedback from activity in the body. A motor activity directed from one hemisphere may involve widespread bodily movements that will feed back messages to the opposite hemisphere as well as the active one. For instance, an action performed by one hand is likely to involve adjustments in posture and muscular activity that spread to the other side of the body and thus make themselves known to the other hemisphere. Unifying factors of this sort help to account for the fact that the two sides of the body do not act more independently in a split-brain situation. They do not, however, change the general inference that the two brain hemispheres are for the most part separate realms of knowledge and awareness.

A special case of cross transfer that was at first quite surprising was discovered recently in our laboratory by Joseph Bossom and Charles R. Hamilton. Their experiments dealt with the way in which the brain adjusts itself to overcome the distortions produced by looking through a wedge prism. Such a prism so displaces the visual scene that in reaching for an object the hand misses its mark. With a little practice, however, the eye-brain system soon achieves the necessary corrections to hit the target every time. Bossom and Hamilton trained split-brain monkeys to adapt themselves to the problem using one eye. After the monkeys had learned to correct for the displacement of the prism, they were switched to using the other eye. The learning was fully and immediately transferred – even in monkeys with a deep bisection through the brain-stem roof and cerebellum. This seemed to contradict the earlier experiments showing a lack of transfer of learning from one eye to the other. But when Hamilton followed up with repetitions of the experiments in which the monkey was made to practise the prism adaptation using only one hand, he found that corrective adjustments achieved through the one hand, in combination with either eye, do not transfer to the other hand. This suggested that the central adjustment to deflections of a target by a prism depends primarily on the brain centers concerned with motor activity and bodily sensations rather than on those involved in vision. This interpretation has now been supported in an extension of the study to human subjects. It is still not clear, however, how split-brain monkeys achieve this adjustment so easily when the visual inflow is confined to one hemisphere and the only hand in use is the one governed primarily from the other hemisphere.

Certain other performances under study in our laboratory that appear to involve cross integration in the divided brain are even harder to explain. For example, Colwyn B. Trevarthen and I have found that a split-brain monkey can learn to select the larger (or smaller, as the case may be) of two circles of different sizes presented separately to the two brain hemispheres, the larger to one and the smaller to the other. To make the *relative* size count, the circles are selected from a series of five graded sizes. It would seem that to make the comparison successfully the two hemispheres, although cut apart, must collaborate in some way. Similarly, I have found that split-brain monkeys grasping two handles separately, one in each hand, can pick the larger or the rougher of the pair. Here again five different sizes and five degrees of roughness are paired in random right-left position.

Difficult as it is to avoid the conclusion that the two brain hemispheres are working together in these cases, the strong evidence of many experiments on the independence of the divided hemispheres suggests that one should seek other

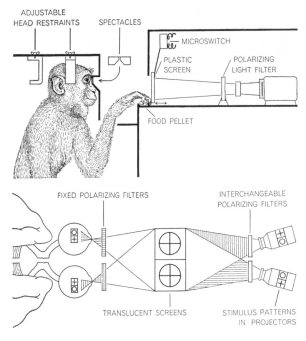

**Figure 21.5 Perceptual conflict** in split-brain monkeys is tested with the apparatus shown in the top drawing. It presents a different image to each eye, as seen in the bottom diagram. While one of the animal's isolated eye-brain systems learns that pushing the panel with the cross is rewarded by food, the other eye-brain system learns to push the circle instead.

explanations. It is conceivable, for example, that a combination of independent strategies used by the two hemispheres might have produced a high score without any real exchange of information. The discrimination of handles by touch might have been aided by cross communication through related sensations of movement or from motor feedback. It is also possible that the apparent communication between the hemispheres may have been achieved by way of interactions taking place in the lower brain stem or even in the spinal cord. These and other possibilities are being investigated.

Another group of observations revealed an interesting and significant difference between animal and human brains. The tests had to do with the ability of one side of the body to respond to visual cues received only by the cerebral hemisphere that directs the opposite side of the body. For example, with the corpus callosum divided and with vision restricted to one hemisphere, the animal is trained to reach out and pick by vision the correct one of two objects; can the subject do this when allowed to use only the hand or paw that normally is associated with the unseeing hemisphere? The cat proved to be able to use either forepaw under these conditions with about equal ease. The monkey does not do so well; sometimes it can co-ordinate its motor response with the visual message and sometimes not. In human patients, on the other hand, this ability is severely

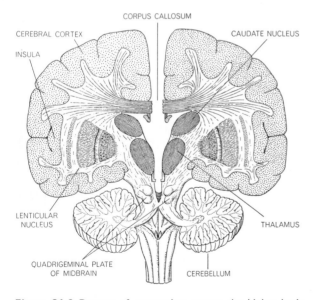

CORPUS CALLOSUM

CEREBRAL CORTEX

CAUDATE NUCLEUS

INSULA

LENTICULAR
NUCLEUS

THALAMUS

QUADRIGEMINAL PLATE
OF MIDBRAIN

CEREBELLUM

**Figure 21.6 Degree of separation** among the higher brain centers that is produced by the surgical procedures discussed by the author is shown in this semisectional diagram of the brain.

disrupted by the severing of the corpus callosum. As we have already noted, in the split-brain patient who was extensively tested the left hand generally is unable to respond correctly to commands or visual stimuli presented only to the left cerebral hemisphere. The patient without prior brain injury does somewhat better, but even so the performance is markedly poorer than that of the monkey.

The same applies to stimuli of other kinds. For instance, when the human patients are blindfolded and hold a pencil in one hand, the other hand is unable to find the end of the pencil if the hand holding the pencil shifts its angle or changes its position in some other way. When monkeys whose corpus callosum had been cut were put to similar tests by Richard F. Mark and me, however, they performed almost normally (figure 21.7). And when all the cross connections down through the roof plate of the midbrain, with the exception of the corpus callosum, were cut, the performance also went well. Subsequent cutting of the corpus callosum in this last situation finally abolishes the performance, showing the participation of the corpus callosum. Even so, the difference between man and monkey in the expendability of the corpus callosum for such hand-to-hand activities remains striking.

Here we are probably seeing a reflection of the evolution of the brain. The appearance and development of the corpus callosum in evolution parallels the appearance and development of the cerebral cortex. As in the course of evolution central controls are shifted from more primitive brain-stem areas to higher stations in the ballooning cerebral cortex, the role of the corpus callosum becomes more and more critical. So also do the phenomena of dominance and specialization in the hemispheres of the cerebrum. In cats and lower animals the two hemispheres seem to be essentially symmetrical, each learning equally and each capable of serving by itself almost as a whole brain. In the monkey the two hemispheres are apparently somewhat more specialized. As the accumulation of memories, or the storage of information, becomes more important in the higher animals, the duplication of memory files in the two brain hemispheres is given up for a more efficient system: the division of labor by the assignment of specialized files and functions to each hemisphere. This evolution has culminated in the human brain. Here a distinct separation of functions prevails: language is the task of the dominant hemisphere and lesser tasks are largely taken over by the other hemisphere.

The question of dominance is crucial for the effective functioning of the brain as the master control system. Bear in mind that the brain is composed of twin hemispheres, with a full set of control centers in each hemisphere that enables it to take command and govern the general behavior of the animal. What happens, then, if the two halves of an animal's split brain are taught to give completely conflicting responses to a given situation?

The devices developed in our laboratory allow a great variety of experiments, using all sorts of combinations of brain control centers with the sensory and motor organs of the body. They can restrict the animal to the use of one eye or the other with one hand or the other, to the tactile sense without vision, to vision in one brain hemisphere and the tactile sense in the other, and so on. A representative apparatus for the monkey, designed for experiments involving visual stimuli and responses with the hand, is shown in figure 21.1. The monkey stations itself behind a barrier that can be adjusted to let it see with both eyes or the right eye or the left eye or neither, and to let it use both hands or only the right or the left. By the use of light-polarizing filters, the visual stimulus (for example a circle) can be split and the two images projected separately to the two halves of its visual field in order to determine if the subject can integrate them. The monkey's responses consist in pressing buttons, pulling levers and so forth; these responses are rewarded when they are correct. We can hook up to this apparatus automatic equipment that is programed to present any of a number of different problems to the animal. In that case the apparatus is attached to its home cage as a kind of porch where the monkey can station itself as the spirit moves it and work at its leisure (figure 21.8).

With this apparatus a split-brain monkey can be trained, let us say, to choose between a triangle and a square as the rewarding stimulus. Looking through its left eye, it learns to select the triangle as the reward; through the right eye, the square. It is trained for a few trials with the left eye, then for a few trials with the right, and this alternation is continued until each eye comes to give a nearly perfect performance, even though the responses with the separate eyes are contradicting each other. As we have already noted, the animal usually evinces no conflict in this paradoxical situation: the left eye unhesitatingly chooses the triangle and the right eye the square. Here the split-brain monkey learns, remembers and performs as if it were two different individuals, its identity depending on which hemisphere it happens to be using at the moment (figure 21.5).

What if the two hemispheres are asked to learn these mutually contradictory answers simultaneously instead of one at a time alternately? Can each hemisphere attend to its own lesson and file one answer in its memory while the other is filing a conflicting answer in *its* memory?

Trevarthen found a way to investigate this question by introducing polarizing filters to present reversed pictures simultaneously to a monkey with both eyes open. A pair of patterns (say a cross and a circle, but any pair of patterns or colors will do) is projected separately to the two eyes. To one eye it appears that the food reward is won by pushing the cross; to the other eye it seems that the circle is being pushed. In other words, for one hemisphere the correct answer is "cross" and for the other it is "circle", but the panel that is pushed is the same in both cases. After the monkey, using both eyes, has learned to push the correct

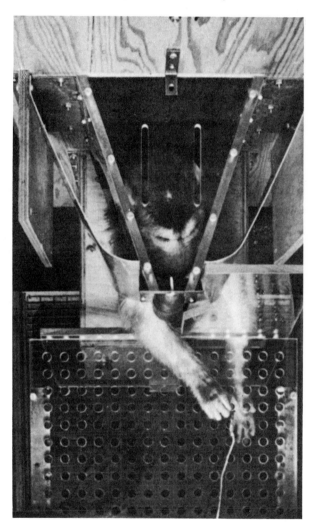

**Figure 21.7 Hand-to-hand coordination** is tested in this experiment. The split-brain monkey cannot see the plastic divider that prevents contact between its hands. By groping, it finds a peanut with its upper hand. It can retrieve the peanut only by poking it down through a hole and catching it with its lower hand. The only cues it has for placing the lower hand are based on a joint-and-muscle sense of the position and movement of the upper hand.

panel 90 per cent of the time, it is tested with each eye separately.

It turns out that there is a strong tendency for one hemisphere (usually the one governing the arm that is first used to push the panels) to learn the answer sooner and more fully than the other. This suggests that active attention by one hemisphere tends to weaken the attention of the second, although the activities of the two have no direct connection. Trevarthen has found, however, that sometimes both hemispheres learn their respective answers fully and simultaneously. That is, the split-brain monkey in these cases divides its attention between the two hemispheres, so that it masters the two contradictory problems in about the same time that a normal, single-minded monkey would be learning one problem.

This doubling of attention is also manifest in Gazzaniga's tests on the split-brain human patient discussed earlier. The test consisted in asking the man to pick a certain figure out of a pair of figures flashed very briefly (for less than a tenth of a second) and simultaneously in each of his visual fields — one pair in the left field and one pair in the right. The subject abruptly points to the correct figure in the left field with his left hand (governed by the non-dominant hemisphere) and at the same time indicates the correct figure in the right field verbally or by pointing (this act being governed by the dominant hemisphere, which controls language and speech). Discussing such responses afterward, the patient typically has no recollection of having pointed with his left hand; the dominant hemisphere seems completely ignorant of what went on in the other one.

These remarkable indications of a doubling of the psychic

**Figure 21.8 Automated equipment** is adapted to tabulating and recording the data from a number of trials conducted with several monkeys over a period of time. The animals work at their tasks at their leisure, moving to apparatus affixed to the rear of their cages.

machinery in the brain raise a number of new questions about the roles played in the learning process by attention, perception and motivation. There are also many intriguing philosophical implications. When the brain is bisected, we see two separate "selves" – essentially a divided organism with two mental units, each with its own memories and its own will – competing for control over the organism. One is tempted to speculate on whether or not the normally intact brain is sometimes subject to conflicts that are attributable to the brain's double structure.

How does an animal with a split brain resolve the dilemma of being conditioned to two directly opposite answers to a given problem? Suppose it is confronted with a situation in which it must make a choice between two "correct" answers? Can it master the conflict or is it paralyzed like the proverbial donkey between a bag of oats and a bale of hay?

The kind of answer that is usually obtained is illustrated in an extension of the experiment with polarizing filters. After the split-brain monkey has been trained so that one hemisphere considers as correct the panel marked by a cross and the other hemisphere considers as correct the panel marked by a circle, one of the eye filters is turned 90 degrees. Now instead of the images being reversed in the two eyes, both eyes see the pair of symbols in the same way – say the cross on the left and the circle on the right. Will the animal, with both eyes open, choose the cross or the circle or waver in confusion between the two? In such tests the monkeys, after only a little indecision and hesitation, make a choice and adhere to it: they consistently select the cross or the circle for a series of trials. That is, one hemisphere or the other takes command and governs the monkey's behavior. This dominance may shift from time to time, each hemisphere taking its turn at control, but it would appear that no serious conflict disrupts any given movement.

Something more akin to conflict between the separated hemispheres is occasionally seen in tests given the human patients. Incorrect responses by the left hand may so exasperate the more sophisticated dominant hemisphere that it reaches across with the right hand to grab the left and force it to make the correct choice. Or conversely, when the literate hemisphere and right hand fail in a block-arrangement test – one of the few things that the left hand and nondominant hemisphere generally do better – impatient twitches and starts occur in the left arm, which may have to be restrained to keep it from intercepting the right. As in split-brain cats and monkeys, however, one hemisphere or the other generally prevails at any given time. Any incompatible messages coming down from the other hemisphere must be inhibited or disregarded.

The experiments discussed in this article are a sample of the large variety of studies with the split brain that are being carried on by our group at Cal Tech and by others in laboratories elsewhere. Work with the split brain has enabled us to pinpoint various centers of specific brain activity, has suggested new concepts and new lines of thought and has opened up a wealth of new possibilities for investigating the mysteries of the mind.

## Bibliography

Cerebral Organization and Behavior, R. W. Sperry in *Science*, Vol. 133, No. 3466, pages 1749–1757, June 1961

Conference on Interhemispheric Relations and Cerebral Dominance, edited by Vernon B. Mountcastle, The Johns Hopkins Press, Baltimore, 1962

Corpus Callosum and Visual Gnosis, R. E. Myers in *Brain Mechanisms and Learning*, a symposium edited by J. F. Delafresnaye, Blackwell Scientific Publications, 1961

Some Functional Effects of Sectioning the Cerebral Commissures in Man, M. S. Gazzaniga, J. E. Bogen and R. W. Sperry in *Proceedings of the National Academy of Sciences*, Vol. 48, No. 10, pages 1765–1769, October 1962

# 22 The biochemical approach to memory

## by *Steven P R Rose*

Other articles in this volume have assembled a picture of the organization of the brain as an interlocking meshwork of cells and processes linked in a manner of almost unimaginable complexity. They describe how the brain is brought into communication with the outside world and how the message, once arrived, may be rapidly dispatched and disseminated through a large proportion of the $10^{10}$ neurons of the cortex by means of their interconnexions, so that the content of any message can swiftly become known to the entire brain. It is against this background that we can now approach the central question: What is the brain for?

This problem has long been the province of theologians and philosophers – more recently psychologists, physiologists and mathematicians. Only within the past few years has it become apparent that it may equally be a question to which biochemistry can contribute a valid answer. What I propose to do here is first demonstrate the relevance of biochemistry to brain function and then describe some of the biochemical answers that are now emerging.

Essentially, the functions of the brain are to process and coordinate information currently available to it from the external environment; to analyse the best course of action to take on the basis of this information; and to instruct the remainder of the organism to act on the basis of this analysis. Of course, the brain has other functions as well. For example, it is involved in the processing, analysing and commanding of events which occur within the organism's domestic economy – such as regional blood supply, rate of heartbeat and discharge of hormones. But these controls generally occur at a lower level of the brain than those concerned with the external environment.

For an organism to respond successfully to changes in external environment, it is desirable for it to have some way of comparing the content of the information reaching it now about the external world with the content of messages which, in the past, have described similar or slightly different situations. It must have a record of the responses it made to past situations and their relative success or failure so that it can draw from its behavioural repertoire an appropriate response to this new, current situation. Evolutionary success among animal species has to a considerable extent gone to those organisms which have been able to expand their ability to store records of past experience so as to make increasingly sophisticated comparisons of *now* and *then* and act accordingly. So much is this the case that for humans a very large proportion of the brain has become involved in this mechanism of recording, storing, sifting and comparing information; relatively smaller portions of the brain are involved solely in the immediate processing of new information or the issuing of commands for present action. It is this sifting process, continually occurring within the brain, which we refer to as consciousness and memory.

If this is what the brain is for, it is the task of the experimentalist to try to describe how these processes occur. There are three interconnected problems. How is the record fed into the brain store? In what form is it stored? And how is it read out from the store when needed? These are, in fact, the problems of learning, of the memory trace and of recall.

At present there is no adequate theory to account for all of these problems – and precious little good experimental data either. The conceptual framework within which the current debate is raging is essentially still that of the 1920–30s, although the language systems and the experimental bases upon which the theories are discussed have altered substantially.

It became apparent early, first from psychological experiments and subsequently, as we shall see, from more biochemical studies, that the process of fixation of the memory trace took place in at least two stages: new information arriving at the brain was placed first in a short-term memory store, then later transferred to a long-term store. Simple psychological tests of an individual's ability to remember a string of numbers read out to him, or the telephone number or name of a person to whom he had just been introduced, indicated that this short-term store was essentially labile and the newly acquired information was

*revised from an article first published in* Science Journal, *May 1967.*

232

easily forgotten. At some time after the memory has been transiently placed in the short-term store, it is transferred to a permanent, long-term store. Here the memory is stable (once we have fixed a name or telephone number, it is relatively hard to forget it again). Estimates of the time taken to transfer the memory from the short- to the long-term store vary from a few minutes up to more than three hours; half an hour is the commonly quoted figure. There is evidence from neurophysiology and neuroanatomy that the anatomical localization within the brain of the short- and long-term stores is different: the short-term store is probably located in the hippocampus, part of the limbic system, located deeper in the brain than is most of the cerebral cortex, while the long-term store is in the cortex itself.

The short term memory store, as I have said, is essentially labile: not only does forgetting often occur naturally during this period, but it can be speeded up by shock treatments which affect the brain – such as insulin therapy, electroconvulsive shock and epileptic fits, or a blow resulting in concussion. All these assaults result in a loss of memory for the events immediately preceding them.

On the other hand, memories transferred to the permanent store are not lost under these conditions. It was this fact that led to the collapse of the early theories of memory, formulated in the 1920s, which followed the discovery that the brain was in continuous electrical activity, as recorded, for instance, by the electroencephalogram (EEG). These theories proposed that, in the storage of permanent memory, a change occurred in some way in the connexions between certain individual neurons, so as to open a new and unique circuit. Round this circuit impulses would continuously travel in a closed loop, forming a permanent electrical or

**Figure 22.1 Early reverberating circuit theory of long-term memory** formulated in the 1920s proposed that a memory was stored by changes in the connexions between certain individual neurons, setting up a new and unique circuit. The simplest circuit possible is between three neurons joined in a triangle. Electrical brain patterns, mirrored in EEG traces, were thought to be the result of these reverberating circuits. The theory was later discarded in favour of a biochemical model.

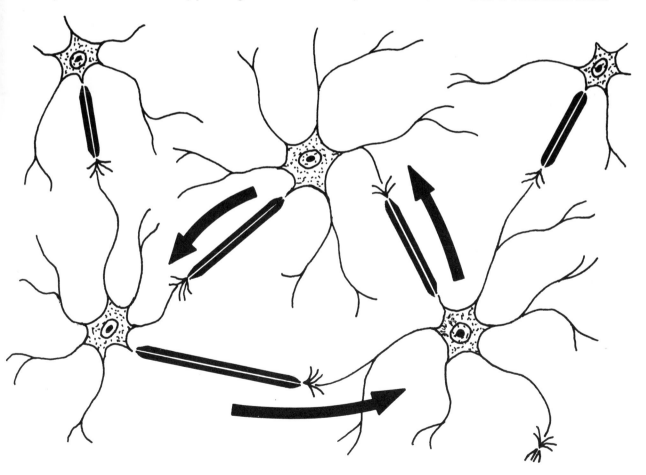

"reverberating" circuit. One of the simplest circuits that can be formed in this way is between three neurons joined in a triangle. As each neuron could participate in many circuits, the amount of information that could be stored in the brain, each "bit" represented by its own unique circuit, is obviously immense – well above the total number of bits (perhaps $10^{11-14}$) that any individual can be calculated to store in a lifetime. It was, argued the exponents of this theory, the sum total of these memories, each with its unique continually reverberating circuit, that was represented by the EEG.

That this theory was inadequate, however, was demonstrated by the fact that long-term memories were unimpaired by assaults which effectively abolish or disrupt for a time the electrical activity of the brain. On the other hand, the lability of short-term memory to these assaults is evidence precisely in favour of some sort of reverberating electrical model. Even more drastic procedures in experimental animals only confirmed what we know from our own personal experience: that memory represents one of the most durable characteristics of an individual, more hard to destroy than almost any other aspect of his existence.

Such durability must imply some permanent, stable change in brain structure in order to accommodate it. One of the easiest changes to envisage would be an alteration in some aspect of the structure of the synapse – the junction between two nerve cells – which made it easier for messages to pass between them. (Unfortunately, we have no way of telling from electron micrographs which of the 10 000 or so synapses each cell makes with its neighbour are really "live" switches, and which are merely "potential" switches needing some alteration in structure, resulting from the cell's acquisition of new information, to make them live.) Alternatively, this stable change in brain structure might involve an alteration of the internal organization of the cell, making it in some way more receptive to messages impinging upon it from the outside world, or more ready to fire on receipt of them.

Either of these changes demands some alteration in the structure of the nerve cell or of its synapses with other cells. In turn, these alterations must require the production of changed amounts of some biochemical substance or substances. Because of the necessity to postulate some permanent change occurring, it is reasonable to argue that the biochemical substances which change must be those which are components of some of the more stable structures within the cell. The implication is that we should search for biochemical changes attendant upon learning and memory fixation among the macromolecular components of the cell – substances such as proteins, nucleic acids and lipids.

This analytical conclusion, which began to be drawn by increasing numbers of workers from the mid-1950s onwards, coincided with several important developments in biochemistry itself, especially the unravelling of the mechanisms of protein synthesis and of the genetic code. And much of the thinking and experimentation that has occurred in the past ten years has been heavily influenced by the belief that protein and nucleic acid synthesis must be bound up in memory storage in a way related to the role of these substances in genetics. Mainly because the nucleic acids are in the geneticist's sense *informational* macromolecules – carrying genetic instructions across generations and bearing the code on which the controlled synthesis of protein depends – the analysis of the role of nucleic acids and proteins in memory storage has become confused with their intrinsic genetic and informational role. I want to try to avoid this confusion. Proteins are essential building blocks of the cell and any change in the shape of the cell or its functional state is almost bound to be associated with changes in the type or amount of protein being produced.

Essentially three types of experiments have been done on the biochemical basis of memory. First, experiments in which substances that either speed up or slow down the synthesis of nucleic acids or proteins have been injected into animals and their ability to learn new tasks or remember old ones examined. Secondly, experiments have been made in which the protein or nucleic acid composition of particular regions of an animal's brain have been examined after the learning of a new task and attempts made to find changes in the quantities or types of protein and nucleic acid present compared with controls. Thirdly, the at first sight unlikely experiment has been made of training animals to perform a particular task, killing them, extracting the proteins and nucleic acids from their brains and injecting them into untrained animals in the hope of "transferring" the memory along with the proteins.

Among the earliest of the first class of experiments are those of Wesley Dingman and Michael Sporn of the National Institutes of Health, Maryland, reported in 1961. Dingman and Sporn used as their inhibitor the substance 8-azaguanine, which is chemically similar to guanine, one of the four bases of which the RNA molecule is composed (the others are adenine, cytosine and uracil). Injections of 8-azaguanine interfere with RNA synthesis: it substitutes for the real base, guanine. Dingman and Sporn trained their rats to swim a simple water maze and showed that once rats had found their way through the maze, injections of 8-azaguanine had no effect on them subsequently remembering the way through. If, however, the 8-azaguanine was injected *before* the rats were taught to swim the maze, it was found that the injected rats made more errors and were slower to learn than controls. Thus, 8-azaguanine, in doses sufficient to inhibit the synthesis of RNA, also diminished the efficiency with which a rat could learn a new maze.

These experiments were quickly followed up by other groups. Louis Flexner and his co-workers at the University of Pennsylvania, using the inhibitor of protein synthesis, puromycin, in mice, found that they too could get a similar effect. Bernard Agranoff and his group at Ann Arbor, Michigan, also used puromycin with goldfish as the experimental animals and found again that, provided the puromycin was injected at an appropriate time prior to the training schedule, inhibition of learning could occur. Similar effects were also found by Samuel Barondes, first at Boston, later at the Albert Einstein in New York. The implication of all these experiments is clear: interference with protein and RNA synthesis, while without effect on the recall of established memories, significantly impairs the brain's ability to lay down new memories. Typically, it seemed to be the case that short-term memory was relatively unaffected, and the lesion occurred in the transfer of the memory from the short-term to the long-term store – that is, in the fixation process.

But there are difficulties in the way of such an interpretation. Thus, Barondes and others have shown that certain drugs which extensively inhibit protein synthesis, such as acetoxycycloheximide, are apparently without effect on memory fixation, at least in some of the experiments. Secondly, the specificity of these inhibitors is not known. While they certainly inhibit protein synthesis, it is far from clear that this is the only biochemical effect they have; the observed memory deficit may be due to some hitherto quite unsuspected side effect, either biochemical or physiological. Barondes, for instance, has noted that puromycin, but not acetoxycycloheximide, tends to produce abnormal electrical patterns in the hippocampus – precisely that brain region which is generally supposed to be the seat of short-term memory. Thirdly, the memory deficit may be the effect of quite other physiological phenomena than those the drugs are affecting direct. In many of the early experiments with puromycin, for instance, the drug was given in sufficiently large doses to result in the animal's death shortly after the experiment. Although smaller doses are currently used, it remains doubtful whether the *only* observable result of the injection of sufficient quantities of a drug to inhibit 95–100 per cent of all protein synthesis in the brain could be that the unfortunate animal was rather bad at learning its way through the maze. Protein synthesis goes on all the time in the brain and is more rapid than in nearly all other tissues of the body. Stopping this important process must surely have other effects as well, yet none have been reported; after the injection of puromycin at low doses the animals are apparently healthy and show no obvious behavioural deficits, other than that of incapacity to fix short-term memories.

A word should be said here too about drugs which *speed up* memory fixation. It has been known for some years that several drugs apparently speed up the rate at which rats learn new tasks, presumably by accelerating the fixation processes. One of the most studied is strychnine, which at low doses enhances electrical activity in the brain. Similar claims have been made for amphetamine (the basis of purple hearts) and nicotine. None of these has yet been shown to affect the rate of protein synthesis in the brain direct. But in late 1965 a group of workers at the laboratories of Abbotts, the Chicago pharmaceutical firm, claimed that a new drug, magnesium pemoline, increased the rate of learning in rats made to jump off an electrical grid and also increased the activity of a key brain enzyme, RNA-polymerase, which is responsible for the synthesis of new RNA. While the firm concerned promptly patented the drug, the initial claims for it, both in terms of its effect on learning and RNA-polymerase, remain to be substantiated. Ronald Smith of Edgewood, Maryland, has reported a failure to find any type of facilitation of human learning by pemoline – in fact, subjects tested with it did significantly worse than those given a placebo. Since then, despite continuing conflicting claims in the literature, interest in this area has diminished.

Thus the data from the drug experiments, while indicative, cannot prove a role for protein synthesis in memory mechanisms. More direct proof should depend on the demonstration of actual changes in the rate of protein and RNA synthesis associated with learning and memory fixation.

There is now a good deal of evidence to suggest that stimulation of a nerve cell – either artificially by placing electrodes upon it or the nerves connected with it, or "naturally" by stimulating the sense or effector organs with which it is connected – can alter the rates of synthesis of both protein and RNA. The physiological stimulus that has been used by G. P. Talwar and his group in Delhi has been the first exposure of the animal to light. We have performed similar experiments in our own laboratory, and both our experiments and the Delhi group's indicate that exposure to light of an animal (rat or rabbit) which has been reared in darkness results in a transient increase (of up to 20 per cent) in the rate of incorporation of isotopically labelled precursors into protein in the visual cortex. Experiments by William Watson in Edinburgh showed that increases in incorporation of nucleic acid precursors into RNA

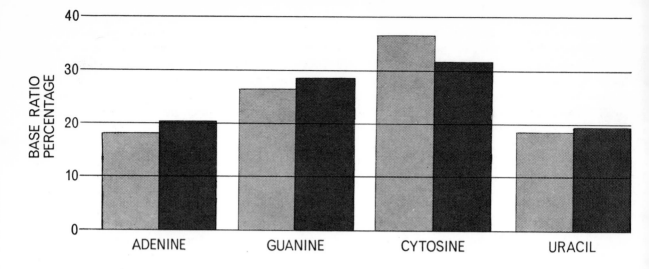

**Figure 22.2 Learning experiment** carried out by Holger Hydén was designed to show what biochemical changes took place when "right-handed" animals were trained to reach for food with their left paws. After the trials were completed the appropriate nerve cells were dissected and analysed for changes in their RNA base ratios — percentages of adenine, guanine, cytosine and uracil. Results showed +9.2 per cent change in adenine and −14.4 per cent in cytosine. Experimental results are shown in dark tone, controls in lighter tone.

occurred during the stimulation of the supra-optic nerve cells of mice (those concerned with the control of body water content) by substituting salt solutions for the normal drinking water for periods of 1–60 days. It must be noted that none of these experiments are strictly speaking concerned with "learning" in the sense of acquisition of, say, a conditioned response; rather, they are concerned with more generalized stimulation.

In more recent experiments, though, we have utilized a more specifically "learning" situation, that of imprinting in the young chick. In conjunction with Drs Bateson and Horn at Cambridge, I have shown that, in the chick exposed to a prominent object for which it learns to show social preference (in common parlance, it tends to regard it as "mother" and moves towards it) there is an increase in the rate of incorporation of radioactive lysine, an amino acid, into protein, and of radioactive uracil, a nucleotide, into RNA. Before either of these events occurs, and after as little as 30 minutes of exposure to the prominent object, an increase in the activity of the enzyme responsible for the synthesis of RNA, RNA polymerase, is detectable in the nuclei of the brain cells. All these changes occur in a specific brain region, the forebrain roof, a region which may be regarded

as including the avian equivalent of the cerebral cortex. It is suggested that in this specific brain region a sequence of events occurs in which a behavioural trigger results in the synthesis of RNA, in the nucleus, followed by the production of new protein in the cytoplasm.

But what is the role of this protein? The type of experiment which helps answer may be one of those in which directed skill acquisition occurs, as in the work of Holger Hydén and his group in Goteborg in Sweden. Nearly 20 years ago Hydén developed a technique for the isolation of large individual nerve cells from specific regions of the brain, by hand dissection under a binocular microscope. In this way he can obtain up to a few dozen of the larger nerve cells from the brain cortex or other regions. The size and weight of these cells are very small (perhaps 0.005 cm in diameter and weighing 0.002 microgrammes). Over a period of several years Hydén has reported a number of experiments in which he has analysed the RNA composition of certain nerve cells in control animals compared to those subject to a variety of stress or learning situations. Some of the larger neurons used are those from the region of the brain concerned with balance, the so-called Deiters' nucleus. Hydén has shown that passive rotation of a rabbit, placed in a box on a rotating wheel (which presumably stimulates these cells) results in a significant increase in their RNA and protein content. But the *composition* of the new RNA produced by this passive stimulation remains the same as that present originally in the cells — there is merely more of it.

On the other hand, in experiments in which the animal's sense of balance is required in the learning of a new task — such as balancing up a 45° wire in order to reach food at the top — nerve cells from this region not only produce more RNA but appear to produce RNA of a significantly differ-

236

ent composition; in particular, the proportion of adenine increases by about 10 per cent compared with the controls and the percentage of cytosine decreases by about an equivalent amount.

More recently Hydén has used a different learning situation in which a "naturally" right-pawed rat is forced to reach for food with its left paw. Similar changes in RNA occur, and, in addition Hydén has been able to analyse the proteins of the hippocampus, supposedly the seat of short-term memory, and the cortex, to show the presence of at least two apparently unique types of protein in the trained animal.

This brings us to the third type of experiment apparently implicating RNA and protein in memory: the "transfer" experiments. These began about ten years ago during investigations by James McConnell and his co-workers at Ann Arbor, Michigan, of the ability of tiny pond flatworms (planaria) to learn. Flatworms normally respond to a light stimulus by stretching towards the light source and to electric shock by curling into a ball. Classical conditioning experiments enabled the flatworms to be taught to respond to the light by curling into a ball instead.

Flatworms, like ordinary earthworms, will regenerate if cut in half; the head end will grow a new tail and the tail end a new head. In the first experiments it was shown that when a trained flatworm was bisected like this, not only did the old head end with its new tail recall its original training (which might be anticipated) but the old tail end, which had grown an entirely new head, also appeared to remember the initial training. Even more sensational results followed when it was shown by McConnell, Allan Jacobson (then at Ann Arbor and now at University of California, Los Angeles) and others that if untrained planaria were fed with the chopped up remains of trained planaria, the "naïve" animals apparently absorbed the learned behaviour along with their cannibalistic diet. These results have produced heated debate ever since, with some groups (such as Melvin Calvin's at University of California, Berkeley) disputing that planaria can be trained effectively at all, and with McConnell, Jacobson and their followers being continually spurred to produce further evidence (much of it reported in the pages of their own journal, once bizarrely named *The Worm-Runners' Digest* but latterly more respectable). Even if they eventually turn out to be correct, the planarian nervous system and the animal's habit of ingesting food in lumps without first breaking down protein and RNA molecules into simpler ones are both so different from the situation in higher animals that extrapolation up the evolutionary scale would seem dubious.

Nevertheless, within the past five years several groups of workers, mainly in the United States, have tried the seemingly impossible experiment of training groups of higher animals to a particular response, extracting RNA or protein from their brains and injecting it into the brain or peritoneal cavity of naïve animals to see if any transfer of the learned response occurs. Several groups have claimed a positive response under these conditions, notably Jacobson and his co-workers at Los Angeles, Frank Rosenblatt at Cornell and D. J. Albert at McGill. Jacobson even claimed to have been able to transfer the response between species, by injecting material from a trained hamster into a naïve rat. Other groups, including Calvin's, have failed to replicate these experiments. While experiments and their rebuttals have been flying back and forth across the pages of *Science* in an emotionally charged atmosphere reminiscent of the debates over extra-sensory perception, it seems wise to reserve judgment on the validity of the effect. Even the "transferers" are divided among themselves as to whether the transfer effect is carried by RNA or by protein or by some contaminant of either. The most recent and persistent claims are those of Georges Ungar of Houston, Texas, who believes he has isolated a short-chain peptide, no more than eight amino acids in length, which codes for "fear of the dark" in mice.

It seems possible that something is passing between the animals, perhaps merely some generalized "alertness factor" which may arouse or stimulate the recipient in some way to increased activity. Experiments by Ewen Cameron and his group at McGill, claiming that improved memory may occur in elderly patients fed with massive doses of yeast RNA, may fall into the same category. It must be emphasized, however, that the biochemical data at our disposal make it most unlikely that any RNA or protein injected into the peritoneal cavity can ever penetrate into the cells of the brain themselves without first being extensively degraded and broken down to much simpler molecules. Indeed, experiments in which isotopically labelled RNA has been injected in this manner have shown that little or none of the label ever gets into the brain at all. Peptides, for this reason, might be much more suitable candidates as "transfer molecules".

We see, then, that over the whole topic of the biochemical basis of memory there stands at present a large question mark. That biochemical changes do occur on the stimulation of brain cells or storage of information seems very probable. That these changes include alterations in the rates of synthesis of macromolecules such as RNA and protein also seems tolerably well established. But whether these changes are confined to these substances alone is not known

– for no one has yet done the experiments to show that similar changes do not occur in, say, the lipids of the brain. It can only be a hypothesis – and some would say an unlikely one at that – that these changes indicate that specific molecules are being made which represent the memory trace.

More likely, in my view, is that what occurs when a memory is fixed is something much more like what the neurophysiologists have long postulated – a change in the probability of a particular nerve cell firing, caused by alteration in the biochemical state of the cell. Most probably, we should look for changes in the capacity of the synapse to transmit a message to the post-synaptic nerve cell. Such a change might be reflected in an increased size of a particular synapse, or altered quantities of transmitted substance within it, or even a more permeable synaptic membrane.

There is indeed some evidence that behavioural stimulation *can* result in changed synapse size and increased numbers of dendritic spines. Perhaps the new protein generated in experiments of the type made by Hydén is transported from the cell body down the axon to the synapse in order to trigger these changes.

While there have been quite a spate of theoretical papers suggesting models of this type, the utility of such models is limited unless they offer testable, alternative hypotheses. Mostly they have not. I would argue that at present it might be better if the theoreticians could cease looking over the biochemist's shoulder for a couple of years so that some outstanding technical issues in this very active controversy could be got out of the way. Then we could present the model builders with a reasonably solid set of data on which to build their constructions.

## Further reading

Macromolecules and Behaviour, edited by J. Gaito, Appleton-Century-Crofts, *New York*, 1966

Aspects of Learning and Memory, edited by D. Richter, Heinemann, *London*, 1966

The Anatomy of Memory, edited by D. P. Kimble, *Science and Behavior Books*, Palo Alto, 1965

Changes in Neuronal RNA During Transfer of Handedness, by H. Hydén and E. Egyhazi, *Proceedings of the US National Academy of Sciences*, Vol. 32, page 1030, 1964

Transfer of Learned Behaviour by Brain Extracts, by F. Rosenblatt and R. G. Miller, *Proceedings of the US National Academy of Sciences*, Vol. 56, pages 1423 and 1683, 1966

Changes in Incorporation of $H^3$-Lysine into Protein in Rat Visual Cortex Following First Exposure to Light, by S. P. R. Rose, *Nature*, Vol. 215, page 253, 1967

Neurochemical Correlates of Learning and Environmental Change by S. P. R. Rose in *Short Term Changes in Neural Activity and Behaviour*, edited by G. Horn and R. A. Hinde, Cambridge University Press, 1970

# 23  Race, intelligence and IQ: a debate

## by A R Jensen, J Hirsch, L Hudson, S P R Rose and M P M Richards

The most recent round in the age-old controversy about whether intelligence is primarily inherited or acquired has been sparked off by an article in the *Harvard Educational Review* (Vol. 39, Winter 1969) by Professor Arthur Jensen. This article has received widespread publicity because it is thought to substantiate two views: that intelligence is predominantly inherited and is therefore unchangeable by education; and that genetic factors account for the lower IQ scores often found for black children who are therefore held to be innately inferior. The segregationists of the southern United States, the Powellite elements of the Tory Party and the "more-means-worse" authors of the Black Paper on Education have all used the "scientific evidence" of Professor Jensen's article to bolster their political aims. In contrast to their uncritical acceptance, and that of the popular press, Professor Jensen's views have not received much support among his fellow scientists. Many eminent psychologists, geneticists and educationalists have been provoked to produce rebuttals and protests but, as is usual, these have been accorded far less publicity than the original article.

The purpose of this present debate is to provide an opportunity for a range of scientists who have special knowledge of the problems to make public their views and to discuss the arguments of Professor Jensen's article with its author.

In this bulletin we print a summary by Professor Jensen of his original article. This is followed by a series of statements by all the speakers in the debate. In the remainder of this introduction we will outline some of the points at which Professor Jensen's arguments have been most attacked.

The development of an individual's characteristics, whether they be his behaviour or his physical traits, are the product

*first published in a Cambridge Society for Social Responsibility in Science special bulletin on a debate on* Education, Race, IQ and Intelligence *held in July 1970.*

*Reprinted with permission. Copyright © 1970 Cambridge Society for Social Responsibility in Science.*

of an interaction between the genetic information received from his parents and the environment in which he develops. This interaction is complex and complete so that it is illogical and impossible to say that any characteristic is the result of either genetic or environmental factors. This would be like trying to assert that the area of a rectangle is the "result" of either its length or its breadth.

However, one can make statements about the origins of *differences* between individuals. Again, this can be illustrated by the analogy of the rectangles. The difference in area of two rectangles could result from a difference in their length or their breadth or both. This can be done statistically (as is explained below by Professor Hirsch) by use of the concept of heritability. The value of a heritability estimate is the proportion of variation between individuals in some trait (*e.g.* their height, or IQ), that can be accounted for by genetic factors. It is very important to note that this is merely a statistical device, it says nothing about individual development and only refers to a group of people. As it is dependent on the interaction of the genetic endowment and the environment, an estimate is only valid for the population and environment for which it is calculated. Changes in the environment for example in educational practice or nutrition (see Professor Rose's statement), will alter the value of the estimate.

So far there is no general disagreement, indeed the principles laid out above are very clearly explained in the first part of Professor Jensen's *Harvard Review* article. The disagreement begins with some of the conclusions and implications that are drawn from the specific discussion of IQ and racial differences in the latter part of his article.

Professor Jensen proposed the figure of 80 per cent heritability for IQ in white American and British people. This means that 80 per cent of the variation between individuals in IQ is related to genetic factors. Many scientists would regard this estimate as high and most would reject Professor Jensen's implication that this high heritability means that attempts to change IQ through educational programmes are doomed to failure. High heritability does not mean that a characteristic is unchangeable or is in some way innate. As pointed out earlier (and by Professor Hirsch and Professor Jensen in his original article) development involves an inter-action of genetic and environmental factors so that the genetic endowment can in no way determine the nature of any individual characteristic.

IQ testing of children in the United States and Britain generally produces lower average scores for the black population. But instead of considering the cultural (see Dr Richards' statement) and environmental (poorer health, housing, school facilities, etc.) differences between these social groups, Professor Jensen implies that the lower IQ scores of black children reflect an innate racial difference. This implication can in no way be derived from the evidence. Certainly the two populations differ. They differ in their genetic make-up *and* the environments in which they live. So a difference in average scores on an IQ test (or any other characteristic) cannot be related to either genetic or environmental factors, it is always a product of both.

IQ tests are used by psychologists to measure intelligence. Various kinds of behaviour are assessed in such tests but they do not cover all, or even many, of the attributes that are referred to by the common language definition of intelligence. Therefore it is important to distinguish two uses of the word intelligence; the common language meaning and the description of the result of an IQ test. Furthermore, an IQ test, like a school examination, reflects a child's performance at one point in time and is in no way a measure of "potential" or future performance as assumed by Professor Jensen. Future behaviour may be inferred from present behaviour but such inferences are always inexact and liable to alteration by environmental changes.

There is wide agreement that the early optimism of the American Headstart programmes of compensatory education has not been reflected in their initial results. However, these programmes were not designed, as Professor Jensen implies, to boost IQ. They were intended to boost the social, educational, medical and political standing of the "deprived" sections of the community. The programmes' success or otherwise cannot be measured in terms of children's IQ scores. The goals of the "war on poverty" are very long term and will involve considerable political and social change throughout all sections of the American community. Whether compensatory education is effective in producing such radical social change is an open question but what is certain is that the heritability of IQ (whether 80, 90 or 20 per cent) is irrelevant to its answer.

Professor Jensen has pointed to the high birth rate of poor black families and has suggested that this will eventu-ally lead to dysgenic changes (that there is or will be positive selection for people with low IQs). Analogous arguments were used in the pre-war years in Britain and the prophets of doom were convinced that the "national intelligence" would show a progressive decline. Over the 50 years that IQ testing has been in existence, the average scores of children in Britain and America have shown a steady increase, thus proving the prophets wrong.

At least for white populations, it is not true that the higher birth rate of the lower socio-economic groups leads to a higher proportion of children in these groups: fewer lower class adults actually marry and have families. So the number of children per adult is less than that for the middle classes.

As Professor Jensen has said, the concern of education is the individual child. Few would disagree with this. But this does not mean that we have to take account of a child's racial or social group membership. Instead we must regard the child as a person with individual feelings, interests, abilities and needs. This is the emphasis behind "progressive" education in primary schools and programmes for comprehensive education. The constant harping on pseudo-scientific "biological" differences between children is only the expression of a political wish to retain the worst social inequalities of the British and American political systems.

# How much can we boost IQ and scholastic achievement? A summary
## by Arthur Jensen

*Compensatory education*

In my article in the *Harvard Educational Review*, I first reviewed the conclusion of a nationwide survey and evaluation of the large, Federally-funded compensatory education programs done by the US Commission on Civil Rights, which concluded that these special programs had produced no significant improvement in the measured intelligence of scholastic performance of the disadvantaged children whose educational achievements they were specifically intended to raise. The evidence presented by the Civil Rights Commission suggests to me that merely applying more of the same approach to compensatory education on a larger scale is not likely to lead to the desired results, namely increasing the benefits of public education to the disadvantaged. The well-documented fruitlessness of these well-intentioned compensatory programs indicates the importance of now questioning the assumptions, theories and practices on which they were based. I point out, also, that some small-scale experimental intervention programs have shown more promise of beneficial results.

I do *not* advocate abandoning efforts to improve the education of the disadvantaged. I urge increased emphasis on these efforts, in the spirit of experimentation, expanding the diversity of approaches and improving the rigor of evaluation in order to boost our chances of discovering the methods that will work best.

### The nature of intelligence

In my article, I pointed out that IQ tests evolved to predict scholastic preference in largely European and North American middle-class populations around the turn of the century. They evolved to measure those abilities most relevant to the curriculum and type of instruction, which in turn were shaped by the pattern of abilities of the children the schools were then intended to serve.

IQ or abstract reasoning ability is a selection of just one portion of the total spectrum of human mental abilities. This aspect of mental abilities measured by IQ tests is important to our society, but is obviously not the only set of educationally or occupationally relevant abilities. Other mental abilities have not yet been adequately measured; their distributions in various segments of the population have not been adequately determined; and their educational relevance has not been fully explored.

I believe a much broader assessment of the spectrum of abilities and potentials, and the investigation of their utilization for educational achievement, will be an essential aspect of improving the education of children regarded as disadvantaged.

### The inheritance of intelligence

Much of my paper was a review of the methods and evidence that lead me to the conclusion that individual differences in intelligence, that is, IQ, are predominantly attributable to genetic differences, with environmental factors contributing a minor portion of the variance among individuals. The heritability of the IQ – that is, the percentage of individual differences variance attributable to genetic factors – comes out to about 80 per cent, the average value obtained from all relevant studies now reported.

These estimates of heritability are based on tests administered to European and North American populations and cannot properly be generalized to other populations. I believe we need similar heritability studies in minority populations if we are to increase our understanding of what our tests measure in these populations and how these abilities can be most effectively used in the educational process.

### Social class differences

Although the full range of IQ and other abilities is found among children in every socio-economic stratum in our population, it is well established that IQ differs on the average among children from different social class backgrounds. The evidence, some of which I referred to in my article, indicates to me that some of this IQ difference is attributable to environmental differences and some of it is attributable to genetic differences between social classes – largely as a result of differential selection of the parent generations for different patterns of ability.

### Race differences

I have not yet met or read a modern geneticist who disputes this interpretation of the evidence. In the view of geneticist C. O. Carter: "Sociologists who doubt this show more ingenuity than judgment." At least three prominent sociologists who are students of this problem – Sorokin, Bruce Eckland and Otis Dudley Duncan – all agree that selective factors in social mobility and assortative mating have resulted in a genetic component in social class intelligence differences. As Eckland points out, this conclusion holds *within* socially defined racial groups but cannot properly be generalized *between* racial groups, since barriers to upward mobility have undoubtedly been quite different for various racial groups.

I have always advocated dealing with persons as individuals, each in terms of his own merits and characteristics and am opposed to according treatment to persons solely on the basis of their race, color, national origin or social class background. But I am also opposed to ignoring or refusing to investigate the causes of the well-established differences among racial groups in the distribution of educationally relevant traits, particularly IQ.

I believe that the causes of observed differences in IQ and scholastic performance among different ethnic groups is, scientifically, still an open question, an important question and a researchable one. I believe that official statements, such as "It is a demonstrable fact that the talent pool in any one ethnic group is substantially the same as in any other ethnic group" (US Office of Education, 1966), and "Intelligence potential is distributed among Negro infants in the same proportion and pattern as among Icelanders or Chinese, or any other group" (US Dept of Labor, 1965), are without scientific merit. They lack any factual basis and must be regarded only as hypotheses.

It would require more space than I am allotted to describe the personal and professional consequences of challenging this prevailing hypothesis of genetic equality by suggesting alternative hypotheses that invoke genetic as well as environmental factors as being among the causes of the observed differences in patterns of mental ability among racial groups.

The fact that different racial groups in this country have widely separated geographic origins and have had quite different histories which have subjected them to different selective social and economic pressures make it highly likely that their gene pools differ for some genetically conditioned behavioral characteristics, including intelligence, or abstract reasoning ability. Nearly every anatomical, physiological and biochemical system investigated shows racial differences. Why should the brain be any exception? The reasonableness of the hypothesis that there are racial differences in genetically conditioned behavioral characteristics, including mental abilities, is not confined to the poorly informed, but has been expressed in writings and public statements by such eminent geneticists as K. Mather, C. D. Darlington, R. A. Fisher and Francis Crick, to name a few.

In my article, I indicated several lines of evidence which support my assertion that a genetic hypothesis is not unwarranted. The fact that we still have only inconclusive conclusions with respect to this hypothesis does not mean that the opposite of the hypothesis is true. Yet some social scientists speak as if this were the case and have even publicly censured me for suggesting an alternative to purely environmental hypotheses of intelligence differences. Scientific investigation proceeds most effectively by means of what Platt has called "strong inference", pitting alternative hypotheses that lead to different predictions against one another and then putting the predictions to an empirical test.

## Dysgenic trends

More important than the issue of racial differences *per se* is the probability, explicated in my article, of dysgenic trends in our urban slums, as suggested by census data showing markedly higher birth rates among the poorest segments of the Negro population than among successful, middle-class Negroes. This social class differential in birthrate appears to be much greater in the Negro than in the white population. That is, the educationally and occupationally least able among Negroes have a higher reproductive rate than their white counterparts, and the most able segment of the Negro population has a lower reproductive rate than its white counterpart.

## Learning ability and IQ

If social class intelligence differences within the Negro population have a genetic component, as in the white population, the condition I have described could create and widen the genetic intelligence differences between Negroes and whites. The social and educational implications of this trend, if it exists and persists, are enormous. The problem obviously deserves thorough investigation by social scientists and geneticists and should not be ignored or superficially dismissed as a result of well-meaning wishful thinking. The possible consequences of our failure seriously to study these questions may well be viewed by future generations as our society's greatest injustice to Negro Americans.

The article also dealt with my theory of two broad categories of mental abilities, which I call intelligence (or abstract reasoning ability) and associative learning ability. These types of ability appear to be distributed differently in various social classes and racial groups. While large racial and social class differences are found for intelligence, there are practically negligible differences among these groups in associative learning abilities, such as memory span and serial and paired-associate rote learning.

Research should be directed at delineating still other types of abilities and at discovering how the particular strengths in each individual's pattern of abilities can be most effectively brought to bear on school learning and on the attainment of occupational skills. By pursuing this path, I believe we can discover the means by which the reality of individual differences need not mean educational rewards for some children and utter frustration and defeat for others.

## Conclusion

Without a doubt, my article has provoked serious thought and discussion among leaders in genetics, psychology, sociology and education concerned with these important fundamental issues and their implications for public education. I expect that my work will stimulate further relevant research as well as efforts to apply the knowledge gained thereby to educationally and socially beneficial purposes.

In my view, society will benefit most if scientists and educators treat these problems in the spirit of scientific inquiry rather than as a battlefield upon which one or another preordained ideology may seemingly triumph.

Present educational practices are failing to provide all segments of our population with the knowledge and skills needed for economic self-sufficiency in our increasingly technological society. Literal equality of educational opportunity falls short of solving this problem. Failure to give due weight to the biological basis of individual and group differences in educationally relevant traits and abilities, as well as to social-environmental factors, may hinder efforts to discover optimal instructional procedures suited to a wide range and diversity of abilities. Inappropriate instructional procedures, often based on the notion that all children can learn best in essentially the same way except for easily changed environmental influences, can alienate many children from ever entering upon *any* path of educational fulfilment.

In our efforts to improve education we should not lose sight of the focal point of our concern – the individual child. This means the biological as well as the social individual, for man's intelligence and educability are the products of biological evolution as well as of individual experience. Not to recognize the biological basis of individual differences in educability is to restrict harmfully our eventual understanding and possible control of the major sources of diversity in human capacities and potentialities. A vigorous renewal of scientific inquiry into the nature–nurture problem will do more to implement the humanitarian goals of a free society than will dogmatic insistence that environment alone is responsible for all educationally and socially important human differences. In the long run, the greatest respect that educators can pay the children in our schools is to take full account of *all* the facts of their nature.

# Heritability and racial intelligence, simplism and fallacy
## *by Jerry Hirsch*

Recently there has appeared a series of papers disputing whether or not black Americans are, in fact, genetically inferior to white Americans in intellectual capacity. The claims and counterclaims have been given enormous publicity in the popular press in America. Some of those papers contain most of the fallacies that can conceivably be associated with this widely misunderstood problem.

The steps toward the intellectual cul-de-sac into which this dispute leads and the fallacious assumptions on which such "progress" is based are the following: (1) a trait (feature) called intelligence, or anything else, is defined and a testing instrument for the measurement of trait expression is used; (2) the heritability of that trait is estimated; (3) races (populations) are compared with respect to their performance on the test of trait expression; (4) when the races (populations) differ on the test whose heritability has now been measured, the one with the lower score is genetically inferior, QED.

In order even to consider comparisons between races, the following concepts must be recognized: (1) the hereditary endowment (genotype) as a mosaic, (2) development as the expression of one out of many alternatives in the genotype's norm of reaction, (3) a population as a gene pool, (4) heritability is not instinct, (5) traits as distributions of scores and (6) distributions as moments.

Since inheritance is particulate and not integral, the genome, genotype or hereditary endowment of each individual is a unique mosaic – an assemblage of factors many of which are independent. Because of the lottery-like nature of both gamete formation and fertilization, no two individuals, other than monozygotes, share the same genotypic mosaic.

The ontogeny of an individual's phenotype (observable outcome of development) has a norm or range of reaction not predictable in advance. In most cases the norm of reaction remains largely unknown; but the concept is nevertheless of fundamental importance, because it saves us from being taken in by glib and misleading textbook clichés such as "heredity sets the limits but environment determines the extent of development within those limits". Even in the most favorable materials only an approximate estimate can be obtained for the norm of reaction. The more varied the conditions, the more diverse might be the phenotypes developed from any one genotype. Of course, different genotypes should not be expected to have the same norm of reaction; unfortunately psychology's attention was diverted from appreciating this basic fact of biology by a half-century of misguided environmentalism. Just as we see that, except for monozygotes, no two human faces are alike, so we must expect norms of reaction to show genotypic uniqueness. Therefore, those limits set by heredity in the textbook cliché can never be specified. They are plastic within each individual but differ between individuals. Extreme environmentalists were wrong to hope that one law or set of laws described universal features of modifiability. Extreme hereditarians were wrong to ignore the norm of reaction.

Individuals occur in populations and then only as temporary attachments, so to speak, each to particular combinations of genes. The population, on the other hand, can endure indefinitely as a pool of genes, may be forever recombining to generate new individuals.

Genetics is a science of *differences*, and the breeding experiment is its fundamental operation. A gene is an inference from a breeding experiment. The operational definition of the gene, therefore, involves observation in a breeding experiment of the segregation among several individuals of distinguishable differences in the expression of some trait from which the gene can be inferred. Genetics does not work with a single subject, whose development is studied, but with populations of individuals.

How does heritability enter the picture? At the present stage of knowledge, many features of animals and plants have not yet been related to genes that can be recognized individually. But the role of large numbers of genes, often called polygenes and in most organisms still indistinguishable one from the other, has been demonstrated easily (and often) by selective breeding or by appropriate comparisons between different strains of animals or plants. Heritability often summarizes the extent to which a particular population has responded to a regimen of being bred selectively on the basis of the expression of some trait. Heritability values vary between zero and plus one. If the distribution of trait expression among progeny remains the same no matter how their parents might be selected, then heritability has zero value. If parental selection does make a difference, heritability exceeds zero, its exact value reflecting the parent-offspring correlation. Or more generally, as Jensen says: "The basic data from which heritability coefficients are estimated are correlations among individuals of different degrees of kinship." However, many of the heritabilities Jensen discusses have been obtained by comparing only mono and dizygotic twins.

A heritability estimate, however, is a far more limited piece of information than most people realize. It is a property of populations and not of traits. A heritability measure provides for a given population an estimate of the proportion of the variance the population shows in trait (phenotype) expression which is correlated with the segregation of the alleles of independently acting genes. There are other, more broadly conceived heritability measures, which estimate this correlation and also include the combined effects of genes that are independent and of those that interact. Therefore, heritability estimates the proportion of the total phenotypic variance (individual differences) shown by a trait that can be attributed to genetic variation (narrowly or broadly interpreted) in some particular population at a single generation under one set of conditions.

The foregoing description contains three fundamentally important limitations which have rarely been accorded sufficient attention: (1) The limitation of any heritability statement to a specific population (2) The limitation of any heritability statement to a specific environment. Everything inside the cell and outside the organism is lumped together and can be called environmental variation – cytoplasmic constituents, the maternal effects now known to be so important, the early experience effects studied in so many psychological laboratories, and so on. None of these can be considered unimportant or trivial. They are ever present. Let us now perform what physicists call a Gedanken, or thought experiment. Imagine Aldous Huxley's *Brave New World* or Skinner's *Walden II* organized in such a way that every individual is exposed to precisely the same environmental conditions. In other words, consider the extreme, but *un*realistic, case of complete environmental homogeneity. Under these circumstances the heritability value would approach unity, because only genetic variation would be present. Don't forget that even under the most simplifying assumptions, there are over 70 trillion potential human genotypes – no two of us share the same genotype no matter how many ancestors we happen to have in common. Let the same experiment be imagined for any number of environments. In each environment, heritability will approximate unity but each genotype *may* develop a different phenotype in every one of the different environments and the distribution of genotypes in terms of their phenotypes must not be expected to remain invariant over such environments. (3) The limitation of any heritability statement to one generation. As gene frequencies can and do change from one generation to the next, so do heritability values. Further, in a recent study of the open-field behaviour of mice, Hegmann and De Fries found that heritabilities measured repeatedly in the same individuals were unstable over two successive days. In surveying earlier work they commented: "Heritability estimates for repeated measurements of behavioral characters have been found to increase (Broadhurst & Jinks, 1961), decrease (Broadhurst & Jinks, 1966), and fluctuate randomly (Fuller & Thompson, 1960) as a function of repeated testing." Therefore, to the limitations on heritability due to population, environment and breeding generation, we must now add developmental stage, or, many people might say, just plain unreliability!

The late brilliant Sir Ronald Fisher, whose authority Jensen cites, indicated how fully he had appreciated such limitations when he commented: "the so-called co-efficient of heritability, which I regard as one of those unfortunate short-cuts which have emerged in biometry for lack of a more thorough analysis of the data". The plain facts are that in the study of man a heritability estimate turns out to be a piece of "knowledge" that is both deceptive and trivial.

*The roots of one misuse of statistics*

The other two concepts to be taken into account when racial comparisons are considered involve the representation of traits in populations by distributions of scores and the characterization of distributions by moment-derived statistics. Populations should be compared only with respect to one trait at a time and comparisons should be made in terms of the moment statistics of their trait distributions. Therefore, for any two populations, on each trait of interest, a separate comparison should be made for every moment of their score distributions. If we consider only the first four moments, from which are derived the familiar statistics for mean, variance, skewness and kurtosis, then there are four ways in which populations or races may differ with respect to any single trait. Since we possess 23 independently assorting pairs of chromosomes, certainly there are at least 23 uncorrelated traits with respect to which populations can be compared. Since comparisons will be made in terms of four (usually independent) statistics, there are $4 \times 23 = 92$ ways in which races can differ. Since the integrity of chromosomes is *not* preserved over the generations, because they often break apart at meiosis and exchange constituent genes, there are far more than 23 independent hereditary units. If instead of 23 chromosomes we take the 100 000 genes man is now estimated to possess and we think in terms of their phenotypic trait correlates, then there may be as many as 400 000 comparisons to be made between any two populations or races.

*A priori*, at this time we know enough to expect no two populations to be the same with respect to most or all of the constituents of their gene pools. Mutations and recombinations will occur at different places, at different times and with differing frequencies. Furthermore, selection pressures will also vary. So the number and kinds of differences between populations now waiting to be revealed in "the more thorough analysis" recommended by Fisher literally staggers the imagination. It does not suggest a linear hierarchy of inferior and superior races.

Now we can consider the recent debate about the meaning of comparisons between the "intelligence" of different human races. We are told that intelligence has a high heritability and that one race performs better than another on intelligence tests.

The people who are so committed to answering the nature–nurture pseudo-question – is heredity or environment more important in determining intelligence – make two conceptual blunders. (1) Their question about intelligence is, in effect, being asked about the development of a single individual. However, they do not study development in single individuals. Usually they test groups of individuals at a single time of life. The proportions assigned to heredity and to environment refer to the relative amounts of the variance between individuals comprising a population, *not* how much of whatever enters into the development of the observed expression of a trait in a particular individual has been contributed by heredity and by environment respectively.

They want to know how innate is intelligence in the development of a certain individual, but instead they measure differences between large numbers of fully, or partially, developed individuals. Let us now take into consideration the norm-of-reaction concept and combine it with the facts of genotypic individuality. There is then no general statement that can be made about the assignment of fixed proportions to the contributions of heredity and environment either to the development of a single individual, because we have not even begun to assess his norm of reaction, or to the differences that might be measured among members of a population, because we have hardly begun to assess the range of environmental conditions under which its constituent members might develop! (2) Their second mistake – an egregious error – is related to the first one. They assume an inverse relationship between heritability magnitude and improvability by training and teaching. If heritability is high, little room is left for improvement by environmental modification. If heritability is low, much more improvement is possible. Note how this basic fallacy is incorporated directly into the title of Jensen's article "How much can we boost IQ and scholastic achievement?" That question received a straightforward, but fallacious answer: "The fact that scholastic achievement is considerably less heritable than intelligence . . . means there is potentially much more we can do to improve school performance through environmental means than we can do to change intelligence. . . ." Commenting on the heritability of intelligence and "the old nature–nurture controversy" one of Jensen's respondents makes the same mistake in his rebuttal: "This is an old estimate which many of us have used, but we have used it to determine what could be done with the variance left for the environment." He then goes on "to further emphasize some of the implications of environmental variance for education and child rearing".

High or low heritability tells us absolutely nothing about how a given individual might have developed under conditions different from those in which he actually did develop. Heritability provides no information about norm of reaction. Since the characterization of genotype–environment interaction can only be *ad hoc* and the number of possible interactions is effectively unlimited, no wonder the search for general laws of behaviour has been so unfruitful – and *the* heritability of intelligence or of any other trait must be recognized as still another of those will-o'-the-wisp general laws. And no magic words about an interaction component in a linear analysis-of-variance model will make disappear the reality of each genotype's unique norm of reaction. Such claims by Jensen or anyone else are false. Interaction is an abstraction of mathematics. Norm of reaction is a developmental reality of biology in plants, animals and people.

# Race, intelligence and learning

## by Liam Hudson

My theme is simple: that when ideology comes in at the door, truth and dispassion fly out of the window. Beyond this, I shall have three points to make: (1) that the research on identical twins reared apart, though interesting, is at present misconceived; and that the evidence produced can only be inconclusive. (2) That the role of the psychologist in such ideologically charged debate must be re-examined. (3) That even if the hereditary view is eventually proved substantially correct, it remains irrelevant to educational practice.

We have picked up the inheritance *v.* environment issue where our elders were forced to drop it by the Second World War. For a quarter of a century after Belsen and Auschwitz, the hereditary view was treated as taboo. As a consequence, the environmentalists have had the field largely to themselves; and extreme environmentalist assumptions are now associated with political radicalism: the young men and women who uproot universities do so in the name of the Infinite Plasticity of Man. Professor Jensen's research represents a reaction — understandable but regrettable — to such excess; and now we have two ideological dinosaurs pawing the ground at one another venting steam.

Hudson's Law of Selective Attention to Data states:

1. That the greater the ideological significance of a particular piece of research, the more selective the experimenter's attention to his own data will be.

2. That the greater his own ideological involvement, the more the experimenter will appeal to external authority: on the one hand to the authority of science; on the other to humane virtues like democracy.

3. That the ideological involvement of research will increase at times of impending political crisis in the society at large.

4. That research cannot be both ideologically relevant and dispassionate, if the experimenter's personal commitment is left inexplicit.

Professor Jensen's recent publications seem to exemplify the action of this law to perfection. He makes assumptions about the validity of the IQ that are unjustified by evidence — and if interpreted literally lead to conclusions that are demonstrably false; he ignores crucial arguments from the other side — among others, that IQs are tested in ways which favour the obedient, conforming and middle-class child. (On this argument, correlations of IQ with either examination results or socio-economic status are circular.) He also ignores the regrettable fact that no-one has yet the least idea of what constitutes an intellectually benign environment — and yet includes "environmental factors" in his equations.

In other respects he systematically misrepresents published evidence — for instance that on the genetic abnormality known as Turner's Syndrome.

His argument hinges on three crucial concepts: genetic endowment, IQ and environment. Two of these concepts are ill-founded. And as my law predicts, he makes strenuous appeals to "objectivity" and to the authority of science. Also, his research shows every sign of springing from, and contributing towards, a rising tide of racial and social tension in the society in which he works.

In truth, the IQ remains what it has always been: a useful technical device. The belief that it can serve, by some magic, to define the limits of our intellectual capability is a myth; one that it has taken psychologists fifty years to sell to the general public, and to themselves — and will take them a further fifty years to buy back again. Logically speaking, and despite the passion it arouses, the practical implication of genetic evidence about IQ remains minimal. If, as is perfectly possible, certain social groups or races eventually prove on average better endowed than others; even if, which seems unlikely, such differences prove categorical — as for instance between monkeys and chimpanzees, cats and dogs — our educational responsibilities remain the same. Namely, to do everything in our power to maximize each child's use of his gifts — whatever those gifts happen to be.

The importance — and the social danger — of research like Jensen's draws nothing from the logical implications of its evidence. Rather it arises — as does the importance of "Powellism" in British politics — from its appeal to more primitive aspects of human involvement: Us and Them, Black and White, Labour and Conservative, Celtic and Rangers. It plays on the human impulses of loyalty and snobbery; our need to think well of ourselves and poorly of our neighbours. Pursued naïvely, scientistically, it leads to the misuse of evidence, to heightened social tension and polarization, and — rapidly — to the abdication of precisely that quality, intelligence, that it originally sought to illuminate.

# The environmental determinants of brain function

## by Steven P R Rose

It is the purpose of this paper to demonstrate the considerable effects that environmental factors have on brain development, structure, function and performance. While certain basic brain mechanisms are clearly genetically specified, "wired in" from birth so to say, including for example, the pathways of the visual system, genetic differences between strains are much harder to demonstrate. Generations of interbreeding are required to produce rat or mouse strains which respond differently in behavioural tests. Such strain differences cannot be demonstrated adequately in wild type populations, nor *a fortiori* in human populations which are not the product of generations of brother–sister crosses being selected for particular characteristics.

On the other hand environmental effects on the brain structure of individuals are profound and well documented. There seems to be a "critical period" of brain development in the interval following birth in many species. This is the period of maximum brain growth. Malnutrition during this period can result in permanent deficits in brain structure and the inter-relations of cells. In humans malnourishment can result in decreases in cranial diameter and hence, probably, of brain size. The relationship between brain weight and body weight seems to be an important one, rather than simply that of brain weight.

These are gross differences. However, less extreme environmental deprivation can also result in deficits. In cats reared in the dark, the visual pathways and cell interrelations do not develop adequately. If groups of littermate rats are reared in one of two conditions – environmental impoverishment of subdued lighting, "white noise" and social isolation, or environmental enrichment, with animals reared together, much visual stimulation, handling and exploratory possibilities – the brain cortex of the enriched group is thicker after a few weeks than that of the impoverished group. Significant differences in brain enzyme content occur. As little as one hour a day of enriched experience is sufficient to produce such differences. Other experiments show that the brain structure is affected by even quite brief exposure to novel or "learning" situations. Under these circumstances changes in the rates of production of certain key biochemical substances within the brain (*e.g.* RNA and protein) can be shown to occur. Concurrently changes in the degree of connectivity of the brain cells takes place.

Conditions which produce many of these "structural" differences can produce behavioural effects in addition. The lability of behavioural performance to quite subtle environmental pressures is shown by experiments in which students are told that one group of littermate rats is "maze bright", and another "maze dull". Within weeks the animals actually respond in the way that the students have been told that they "should do". Similar experiments with human children and their teachers are claimed to have shown that simply re-labelling apparently backward children as "late developers" results in a change of teacher expectation of performance and also of the childrens' actual scores in tests. These environmental influences are, therefore, profound.

Nor are these environmental effects limited to a single generation. Studies of experimental animals have shown that malnourishment in maternal infancy (and even in grand-maternal infancy) can result in behaviourally observable effects in the second generation. These are not genetic effects, though. What they imply is that stress in infancy affects the behaviour of adults in such a way that in due course other stresses appear in the rearing pattern of the adult's own infant. It is not clear how far these studies on rats can be extrapolated to humans. On the other hand it is clear in humans that the childhood pattern of one generation influences the way in which that generation rears its children. Thus we can see that environmental effects can have transgenerational results which may be substantial without any genetic factors necessarily being involved.

In all these studies problems of extrapolation and validity of measure are of major importance. None the less, environmental effects can be shown quite categorically to result in a series of well defined changes in brain structure and performance. No such certainty attends "genetic" conclusions outside the arbitrary laboratory situation of strain isolation and such clear genetic defects as, say, mongolism. It is often suggested that "80 per cent of the variance of intelligence is genetically determined", whatever that might mean. Such a contention is difficult to sustain in view of the environmental data, which would indicate the significance of even pre-natal environmental effects on subsequent performance. What is clear is that behaviour and performance can be markedly altered by the child's environment and that subtle changes can produce quite measurable effects.

In childhood, this critical period extends for at least the first few years of life, a neurobiological observation confirmed by direct IQ measurements. The claim by Jensen in the US and parallel statements made for instance, by Burt or Eysenck in the UK, that there are genetic factors in both race and social class which distribute intelligence unevenly between races and classes is not supported even by the statistics adduced by Jensen himself, as, for instance, Light and Smith have shown. When one inserts into this argument the known environmental effects and their transgenerational implications support for the Jensen conclusions diminishes still further.

Where a change as simple as building into a teacher's expectation that a child is genetically intellectually inferior or superior, is likely to affect performance, it will have a very good chance of being a self-fulfilling prophecy. If we were to extrapolate – perhaps unjustifiably – from the laboratory data we would conclude that the best chance of rearing an intelligent child is to bring it up under conditions in which it has adequate food, continuous love, affection and intellectual stimulation in its environment during the critical periods of development.

## Facts and values: the mystification and misunderstanding of intelligence
*by Martin Richards*

Throughout the whole debate about genetic and environmental factors in intelligence, there has been little or no consideration of the central concept involved, namely "intelligence". The debate takes the results of "objective" tests of intelligence as a starting point and there is no serious questioning of the validity of these tests.

The psychologist draws a distinction between fact and value. Testing is held to be scientific and objective and therefore value-free, and values are only applied when the test scores are used by non-psychologists to influence the future life of the testee. A closer look at psychometric methods shows there are no "facts" which are not value-laden and that, far from being "objectively scientific", psychological testing involves making social and political judgments in the very process of test construction and validation.

What do intelligence tests measure? Though there is some discussion in the psychological literature about the nature of intelligence, the question is usually sidestepped by defining intelligence as what the tests test. This is a good example of the superficiality of academic psychology, for the ability to score highly on an IQ test is certainly not all, or even necessarily part of, what we mean when we say that someone is intelligent. Unfortunately because the psychological and common language uses of the word "intelligence" are often confused or thought to be synonymous, IQ tests have gained a widespread acceptance which is quite undeserved.

Crucial to the whole meaning of IQ are the nature of the questions used in the test. These are very varied. Pragmatic reasons connected with the technicalities of test construction rather than any theoretical framework about intellectual development govern their choice. Test constructors are middle-class white academics and, not surprisingly, the test items represent their values. So three year olds are asked, "Why do we have books?", in one widely used test. This value loading is reinforced by the methods of test validation which include the prediction of academic achievement and social status. It is further increased by the testing situation itself. Middle-class homes tend to foster the relevant motivation – to be correct for the sake of correctness. Why should a black slum child be interested in the white lady's questions about poets and presidents?

Thus it is easy to see how IQ testing can be used in the name of science to maintain a socially and economically privileged élite. This is being done every day throughout the selective educational systems of Britain and America. Streaming in primary schools, the 11+, "streaming guidance" in Comprehensives are all based, at least in part, on IQ tests or, as they are now euphemistically known, tests of scholastic aptitude.

The most pernicious effects of testing are seen when they are applied to social groups that share few of the values of the test constructors. Inevitably, such people, whether they are black Americans, West Indian immigrants in Britain, Kentucky hill children or Kalahari bushmen, are found to be less "intelligent". Because psychologists wish to maintain the pseudo-objectivity of their science, they provide the "scientific" evidence for the claim that any or all of these social groups are inferior. In truth, the only valid scientific claim is that, on average, black children (working class children, Eskimos, West Indians, etc., etc.) are less good at answering questions designed for white middle class children than are the white children.

# 24  Learning to think
## by Harry F Harlow and
## Margaret Kuenne Harlow

How does an infant, born with only a few simple reactions, develop into an adult capable of rapid learning and the almost incredibly complex mental processes known as thinking? This is one of psychology's unsolved problems. Most modern explanations are not much more enlightening than those offered by 18th-century French and British philosophers, who suggested that the mind developed merely by the process of associating ideas or experiences with one another. Even the early philosophers realized that this was not a completely adequate explanation.

The speed and complexity of a human being's mental processes, and the intricacy of the nerve mechanisms that presumably underlie them, suggest that the brain is not simply a passive network of communications but develops some kind of organization that facilitates learning and thinking. Whether such organizing principles exist has been a matter of considerable dispute. At one extreme, some modern psychologists deny that they do and describe learning as a mere trial-and-error process – a blind fumbling about until a solution accidentally appears. At the other extreme, there are psychologists who hold that people learn through an innate insight that reveals relationships to them.

To investigate, and to reconcile if possible, these seemingly antagonistic positions, a series of studies of the learning process has been carried out at the University of Wisconsin. Some of these have been made with young children, but most of the research has been on monkeys.

For two basic reasons animals are particularly good subjects for the investigation of learning at a fundamental level. One is that it is possible to control their entire learning history: the psychologist knows the problems to which they have been exposed, the amount of training they have had on each, and the record of their performance. The other reason is that the animals' adaptive processes are more simple than those of human beings, especially during the first stages of

*first published in* Scientific American, *August 1949.*
*Reprinted with permission. Copyright © 1949 by Scientific American, Inc. All rights reserved.*

the attack on a problem. Often the animal's reactions throw into clear relief certain mechanisms that operate more obscurely in man. Of course this is only a relative simplicity. All the higher mammals possess intricate nervous systems and can solve complex problems. Indeed, it is doubtful that man possesses any fundamental intellectual process, except true language, that is not also present in his more lowly biological brethren.

Tests of animal learning of the trial-and-error type have been made in innumerable laboratories. In the special tests devised for our experiments, we set out to determine whether monkeys could progress from trial-and-error learning to the ability to solve a problem immediately by insight.

One of the first experiments was a simple discrimination test. The monkeys were confronted with a small board on which lay two objects different in color, size and shape. If a monkey picked up the correct object, it was rewarded by finding raisins or peanuts underneath. The position of the objects was shifted on the board in an irregular manner from trial to trial, and the trials were continued until the monkey learned to choose the correct object. The unusual feature of the experiment was that the test was repeated many times, with several hundred different pairs of objects. In other words, instead of training a monkey to solve a single problem, as had been done in most previous psychological work of this kind, we trained the animal on many problems, all of the same general type, but with varying kinds of objects.

When the monkeys first faced this test, they learned by the slow, laborious, fumble-and-find process. But as a monkey solved problem after problem of the same basic kind, its behavior changed in a most dramatic way. It learned each new problem with progressively greater efficiency, until eventually the monkey showed perfect insight when faced with this particular kind of situation – it solved the problem in one trial. If it chose the correct object on the first trial, it rarely made an error on subsequent trials. If it chose the incorrect object on the first trial, it immediately shifted to the correct object, and subsequently responded almost perfectly (figure 24.1).

Thus the test appeared to demonstrate that trial-and-error and insight are but two different phases of one long continuous process. They are not different capacities, but merely represent the orderly development of a learning and thinking process.

A long series of these discrimination problems was also run on a group of nursery-school children two to five years of age. Young children were chosen because they have a minimum of previous experience. The conditions in the children's tests were only slightly different from those for the monkeys: they were rewarded by finding brightly colored macaroni beads instead of raisins and peanuts. Most of the children, like the monkeys, made many errors in the early stages of the tests and only gradually learned to solve a problem in one trial. As a group the children learned more rapidly than the monkeys, but they made the same types of errors. And the "smartest" monkeys learned faster than the "dullest" children.

We have called this process of progressive learning the formation of a "learning set". The subject learns an organized set of habits that enables him to meet effectively each new problem of this particular kind. A single set would provide only limited aid in enabling an animal to adapt to an ever-changing environment. But a host of different learning sets may supply the raw material for human thinking.

We have trained monkeys and children to solve problems much more complex than the ones thus far described. For instance, a deliberate attempt is made to confuse the subjects by reversing the conditions of the discrimination test. The previously correct object is no longer rewarded, and the previously incorrect object is always rewarded. When monkeys and children face this switch-over for the first time, they make many errors, persistently choosing the objects they had previously been trained to choose. Gradually, from problem to problem, the number of such errors decreases until finally the first reversal trial is followed by perfect performance. A single failure becomes the cue to the subject to shift his choice from the object which has been rewarded many times to the object which has never been rewarded before. In this type of test children learn much more rapidly than monkeys.

A group of monkeys that had formed the discrimination-reversal learning set was later trained on a further refinement of the problem. This time the reward value of the objects was reversed for only one trial, and was then shifted back to the original relationship. After many problems, the monkeys learned to ignore the single reversal and treated it as if the experimenter had made an error!

The problem was made more complicated, in another test, by offering the subjects a choice among three objects instead of two. There is a tray containing three food wells. Two are covered by one kind of object, and the third is covered by another kind. The animal must choose the odd object. Suppose the objects are building blocks and funnels. In half the trials, there are two blocks and a funnel, and the correct object is the funnel. Then a switch is made to two funnels and one block. Now the correct object is the block. The animal must learn a subtle distinction here: it is not the shape of the object that is important, but its relation to the other two. The meaning of a specific object may change from trial to trial. This problem is something like the one a child faces in trying to learn to use the words "I", "you" and "he" properly. The meaning of the words changes according to the speaker. When the child is speaking, "I" refers to himself, "you" to the person addressed and "he" to some third person. When the child is addressed, the child is no longer "I" but "you". And when others speak of him, the terms shift again.

Monkeys and children were trained on a series of these oddity problems, 24 trials being allowed for the solution of each problem. At first they floundered, but they improved from problem to problem until they learned to respond to each new problem with perfect or nearly perfect scores. And on this complex type of problem the monkeys did better than most of the children!

One of the most striking findings from these tests was that once the monkeys have formed these learning sets, they retain them for long periods and can use them appropriately as the occasion demands. After a lapse of a year or more a monkey regains top efficiency, in a few minutes or hours of

Figure 24.1 Monkey experiments at the University of ▶ Wisconsin illustrate the process of learning. In the drawing at the upper right a monkey is confronted with two different objects. Under one of them is always a raisin or a peanut. In the drawing at the middle right the monkey has learned consistently to pick the same object. In the drawing at the upper left the monkey has learned consistently to choose one object which differs from two others. In the two drawings below the monkey has learned a much more complicated process. In the drawing at the lower left it has learned that when the board is of a certain color it must choose the object that is odd in shape. In the drawing at the lower right it has learned that when the board is of another color it must choose the object that is odd in color. In all these problems the monkey first learned to solve the problem by trial and error. Later it solved them immediately by understanding.

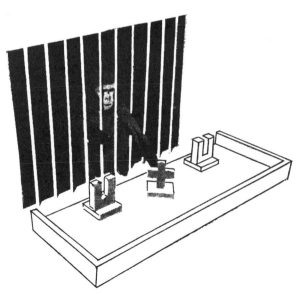

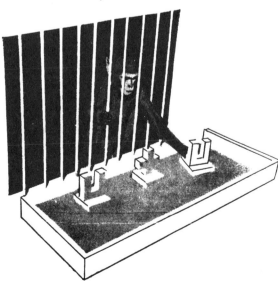

practice, on a problem that it may have taken many weeks to master originally.

All our studies indicate that the ability to solve problems without fumbling is not inborn but is acquired gradually. So we must re-examine the evidence offered in support of the theory that animals possess some innate insight that has nothing to do with learning.

The cornerstone of this theory is the work of the famous Gestalt psychologist Wolfgang Köhler on the behavior of chimpanzees. In a series of brilliant studies he clearly showed that these apes can use sticks to help them obtain bananas beyond their reach. They employed the sticks to knock the bananas down, to rake them in, to climb and to vault. The animals sometimes assembled short sticks to make a pole long enough to reach the food, and even used sticks in combination with stacked boxes to knock down high-dangling bait. That the chimpanzees frequently solved these problems suddenly, as if by a flash of insight, impressed Köhler as evidence of an ability to reason independently of learning. He even suggested that this ability might differentiate apes and men from other animals.

Unfortunately, since Köhler's animals had been captured in the jungle, he had no record of their previous learning. Recent studies on chimpanzees born in captivity at the Yerkes Laboratory of Primate Biology at Orange Park, Fla, throw doubt on the validity of Köhler's interpretations. Herbert Birch of the Yerkes Laboratory reported that when he gave sticks to four-year-old chimps in their cages, they showed little sign at first of ability to use them as tools. Gradually, in the course of three days, they learned to use the sticks to touch objects beyond their reach. Later the animals solved very simple stick problems fairly well, but they had difficulty with more complex problems.

Extending Birch's investigations, the late Paul Schiller presented a series of stick tasks to a group of chimpanzees from two to over eight years of age. The younger the animal, the more slowly it mastered the problems. Some young subjects took hundreds of trials to perform efficiently on even the simplest problems, while old, experienced animals solved them with little practice. None of the apes solved the tasks initially with sudden insight.

Even at the human level there is no evidence that children possess any innate endowment that enables them to solve tool problems with insight. Augusta Alpert of Columbia University tried some of Köhler's simple chimpanzee tests on bright nursery-school children. The younger children typically went through a trial-and-error process before solving the problems. Some of them failed to solve the easiest problem in the series in five experimental sessions.

Eunice Mathieson presented more difficult Köhler-type tasks to a group of University of Minnesota nursery-school children. The results were even more overwhelmingly against the notion that tool problems are solved by flashes of natural insight. The children rarely solved a problem without making many mistakes.

This research, then, supports our findings. In all clear-cut tests — that is, whenever the animals' entire learning history is known — monkeys, apes and children at first solve problems by trial and error. Only gradually does such behavior give way to immediate solutions.

We began by pointing out that psychologists have sought to find in the higher mental processes some organizing mechanism or principle that would explain learning and thinking. We can now suggest such a mechanism: the learning set. Suppose we picture mental activity as a continuous structure built up, step by step, by the solution of increasingly difficult problems, from the simplest problem in learning to the most complex one in thinking. At each level the individual tries out various responses to solve each given task. At the lowest level he selects from unlearned responses or previously learned habits. As his experience increases, habits that do not help in the solution drop out and useful habits become established. After solving many problems of a certain kind, he develops organized patterns of responses that meet the demands of this type of situation. These patterns, or learning sets, can also be applied to the solution of still more complex problems. Eventually the individual may organize simple learning sets into more complex patterns of learning sets, which in turn are available for transfer as units to new situations.

Thus the individual learns to cope with more and more difficult problems. At the highest stage in this progression, the intelligent human adult selects from innumerable, previously acquired learning sets the raw material for thinking. His many years of education in school and outside have been devoted to building up these complex learning sets, and he comes to manipulate them with such ease that he and his observers may easily lose sight of their origin and development.

The fundamental role that language plays in the thinking process may be deduced easily from our experiments. They suggest that words are stimuli or signs that call forth the particular learning sets most appropriate for solving a given problem. If you listen to yourself "talk" while you are thinking, you will find that this is exactly what is happening. You review the different ways of solving a problem, and decide which is the best. When you ask a friend for advice, you are asking him to give you a word stimulus which will tell you the appropriate learning set or sets for the solution of your problem.

This principle is particularly well illustrated by some of our monkey experiments. Though monkeys do not talk, they can learn to identify symbols with appropriate learning sets. We have trained our monkeys to respond to signs in the form of differently colored trays on which the test objects appear. In one test the monkeys were presented with three different objects – a red U-shaped block, a green U-shaped block and a red cross-shaped block. Thus two of the objects were alike in form and two alike in color. When the objects were shown on an orange tray, the monkeys had to choose the green block, that is, the object that was odd in color. When they were shown on a cream-colored tray, the animals had to choose the cross-shaped block, that is, the object odd in form. After the monkeys had formed these two learning sets, the color cue of the tray enabled them to make the proper choice, trial after trial, without error. In a sense, the animals responded to a simple sign language. The difficulty of this test may be judged by the fact that the German neurologist Kurt Goldstein, using similar tests for human beings, found that people with organic brain disorders could not solve such tasks efficiently.

At the Wisconsin laboratories, Benjamin Winsten devised an even more difficult test for the monkeys. This problem tested the animals' ability to recognize similarities and differences, a kind of task frequently used on children's intelligence tests. Nine objects were placed on a tray and the monkey was handed one of them as a sample.

The animal's problem was to pick out all identical objects, leaving all the rest on the tray. In the most complicated form of this test the monkey was given a sample which was not identical with the objects to be selected but was only a symbol for them. The animal was handed an unpainted triangle as a sign to pick out all red objects, and an unpainted circle as a sign to select all blue objects. One monkey learned to respond almost perfectly. Given a

**Figure 24.2 More complicated test** involves teaching a monkey to choose certain objects not by matching but by response to a symbol. In the pair of drawings on the left of this page the monkey is shown a triangular object and pushes forward all the objects of one color. In drawings on the right the monkey, shown a round object, pushes forward objects of another color.

253

triangle, he would pick every object with any red on it; given a circle, he selected only the objects with blue on them (figure 24.2).

All these data indicate that animals, human and sub-human, must learn to think. Thinking does not develop spontaneously as an expression of innate abilities; it is the end result of a long learning process. Years ago the British biologist, Thomas Henry Huxley, suggested that "the brain secretes thought as the liver secretes bile." Nothing could be further from the truth. The brain is essential to thought, but the untutored brain is not enough, no matter how good a brain it may be. An untrained brain is sufficient for trial-and-error, fumble-through behaviour, but only training enables an individual to think in terms of ideas and concepts.

## Bibliography

The Nature of Learning Sets, H. F. Harlow in *Psychological Review*, Vol. 56, No. 1, pages 51–65, 1949

The Mentality of Apes, W. Köhler, Harcourt, Brace & Co., 1925

# Section V
# Social behaviour

In this section we move from the laboratory into the field. One flourishing area of behavioural research over recent years has been that of ethology. Ethologists recognize that there is a danger, implicit in the sophisticated laboratory procedures of neurophysiology and comparative psychology, that the behaviour of an animal under such artificial conditions, while highly significant and interesting to the scientist, may not be so to the animal. What is needed to complement the results produced in the laboratory is information about the behaviour of animals under natural conditions, and particularly about their social behaviour – how they behave towards fellow members of their species. This sort of information is not purely descriptive, although of course, accurate descriptions of behaviour in the wild are necessary. Description is the first step, but having done this, one major question which ethology asks is: "What causes the behaviour which we have just described?" The causation of the elaborate displays performed during courtship and during fights by many species, is one problem which has particularly taxed ethologists, and solving this problem is by no means an easy one. The methods of analysis available to an ethologist are described in Robert Hinde's article, "Courtship and threat display."

Ethologists cannot be content merely to analyse the behaviour of one animal towards another. Many animals live in societies, and these societies, again, need to be described, the factors which hold the society together and determine its characteristics need to be explained, and the adaptive significance of different forms of society need to be explored. One group of social animals in which there has been a great upsurge of interest, particularly over the last ten years, has been the primates: the group containing, among others, the monkeys, apes and man. An extract from an article by John Crook summarizes some of the more recent information about primate societies.

The measured caution and closely argued logic of these two articles might not suggest that the subjects which they discuss could form the substance of several Sunday newspaper articles, and best sellers, and yet this is the case. Two extracts from such popular publications are given. That from *The Human Zoo* by Desmond Morris attempts to find a biological basis for the behaviour of people in positions of power by making comparisons with the behaviour of dominant baboons. The chapter by Konrad Lorenz from his book, *On Aggression*, argues by drawing analogies from the behaviour of other animals that man is innately and spontaneously aggressive. Arguments such as those put forward by Morris and Lorenz have raised heated controversies. To close this section, there is a second article by Robert Hinde which criticizes extravagant extrapolation from the behaviour of non-human primates and other animals to that of man, and in particular, criticizes Lorenz's thesis.

# 25 Courtship and threat display
## by Robert A Hinde

Much of the evidence used in analysing courtship and threat display is based on field observation, and it sometimes involves a modicum of circular argument. It is therefore worthwhile to examine its nature in a little more detail. It can be classified as follows:

## 1 The situation

Often, some evidence can be drawn from the situation in which the behaviour occurs. One example of this may be observed in the case of territorial fighting – threat postures are used primarily on the boundaries, where there is reason to think that tendencies* both to attack and to flee from the rival are in balance. Similarly, if a given display occurs only between potential mates and never between rivals, there is good reason for thinking that a sexual tendency is involved.

## 2 The behaviour which accompanies the display

While displaying, an animal may edge towards or away from the object of its display. Oscillations or hesitation betray the presence of conflict, and the direction of movement indicates which tendency predominates at the moment.

*first published in* Animal Behaviour a Synthesis of Ethology and Comparative Psychology, *2nd Edition, 1970, pages 370–82 (McGraw-Hill, Inc., New York). Copyright © 1970 by McGraw-Hill, Inc. Used with permission.*

---

\* The word "tendency" is used in a rather special sense in this extract. It implies, not only that an animal is likely to behave in a particular way (e.g. a "tendency to attack"), but that certain causal factors are present which are responsible for that behaviour. It does not make any assumptions about the nature of these causal factors and so is particularly useful in studies where their nature is not a matter of primary concern.

Another term which may be unfamiliar is "agonistic behaviour". This refers to a group of behaviour patterns which frequently occur together, and which involves attack, threat, submission and fleeing behaviour. [Editors' note]

In some species the external colouration can be used in a similar way, for changes in the motivational state are mirrored by changes in external colouration produced either by vasoconstriction/dilation or by chromatophores. Examples have been described from many phyla. If a change in colouration is associated with (for example) a change in the probabilities of attacking and fleeing, and also with a change in the frequencies with which various display movements are used, an additional source of evidence as to the nature of the latter is available. A complex case has been analysed in detail by Baerends et al.[1]

## 3 Sequential and temporal correlations

If a particular display is sometimes followed by an attack, and sometimes by fleeing, it is presumably associated with conflicting tendencies to attack and to flee. The underlying assumption here is that the tendency changes more slowly than the overt behaviour, so that the two patterns are likely to share common causal factors (internal or external to the animal) if they are closely associated in time. On this view, the relative strengths of the conflicting tendencies (that is, here, the relative probabilities that each will find overt expression) can be assessed by counting the relative frequencies of, e.g., attacks and fleeing movements which follow the display.

This method was first used by Moynihan[2] to substantiate his view that the various threat postures of the black-headed gull were associated with different absolute and relative strengths of the tendencies to attack and flee from the rival, and has proved a powerful tool. However, some general difficulties in interpreting "sequential associations" must be pointed out. First, many of the changes in behaviour shown by a displaying animal are consequences of changes in the stimulus situation presented by its rival or mate. Apparently important differences between postures seen in the natural situation may in fact be due to differences in the position or orientation of the animal to which the display is directed. This difficulty can be circumvented by recording sequences of behaviour given to motionless dummies, or by selecting for analysis only those sequences in which the behaviour of the second animal did not change.

Another difficulty with this method is that many displays are seldom followed by pure expressions of one or other of the tendencies with which, according to other sources of evidence, they are associated. In one series of observations it was found that the pivoting display (figure 25.1) of the goldfinch was associated with agonistic behaviour in 68 per cent of 152 cases observed and with sexual behaviour (courtship feeding or copulation) in only 8 per cent. Nevertheless, other evidence indicates that a sexual element is important in the display. Pivoting is associated with a call seldom heard in agonistic contexts, is much more common between mates than between flock birds, increases in frequency as the breeding season progresses and is associated with a drooping of the wings which also occurs in other types of behaviour in which the sexual tendency is more conspicuous. Such cases show that understanding of any display demands the use of at least several of the lines of evidence discussed here (*e.g.* Blurton-Jones[3]).

Yet another difficulty is that movements may be associated together in time not because they share causal factors in any ordinary sense, but because they share a low priority among the organism's activities and can occur only in the absence of response tendencies of greater priority. This may be one reason why different "toilet" or "comfort" movements tend to be associated together. Such movements rarely interrupt other types of active behaviour but are themselves often interrupted (Andrew[4]).

## 4 The nature of the display itself

In many analyses of display, the postures are regarded as the basic units. Each posture, however, can be analysed into components — raising of the wings, opening of the beak, spreading the tail and so on. Further understanding of displays has been obtained by using these as the units, each posture being regarded as a combination of components.

In some displays there may be changes in the intensity of particular components and in the number of components present, but the components occur only in certain combinations: $A$, $AB$, $ABC$, $ABCD$ and so on. An example is the "soliciting" posture used by the female chaffinch before copulation.

Another such case, which has been analysed in more detail, is the aggressive display of the Siamese fighting fish, *Betta splendens* (figure 25.2). Here Simpson[6] has shown that a number of measures of the display to a puppet, including the proportion of a test spent with the gill covers erected, are intercorrelated. This type of relationship among different components or measures of a display suggests that

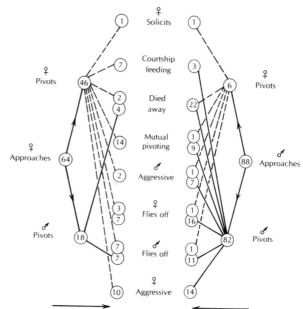

**Figure 25.1 Sequences of behaviour** associated with the "pivoting" display of goldfinches. The figures indicate the number of times each sequence was observed. Read from sides to centre. (After Hinde.[5])

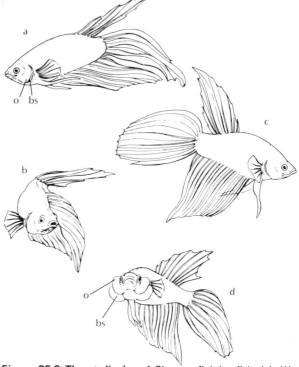

**Figure 25.2 Threat display** of Siamese fighting fish. (*a*), (*b*) non-displaying fish; (*c*), (*d*) displaying fish; *o*, operculum; *bs*, branchiostegal membrane. In (*c*) the fish is broadside, with pelvic fin nearest rival raised. In (*d*) it is facing the rival, with gill-covers raised. (After Simpson.[6])

all vary with the same tendency, but appear at different threshold levels.

At the other extreme the components could, in theory, occur in all possible combinations. For that to be the case, there would have to be as many independently variable groups of causal factors as there are components, and there would be no recognizable "postures", *i.e.* commonly occurring groupings of components.

In practice, most displays lie somewhere between the two. In a study of the agonistic behaviour of the blue tit (*Parus caeruleus*) Stokes[7] assessed the correlations among nine different components. Of the thirty-six possible two-component combinations, a strong correlation ( $p < 0.01$ ) between the components was found in thirty-one. The correlation was in some cases positive; for instance a bird with fanned tail usually raised its wings as well. In others the

**Figure 25.3** (*a*) **Aggressive** and (*b*) anxiety forms of the upright threat posture of the herring gull. (After Tinbergen.[8])

correlation was negative – an erect crest never occurred with wings raised, tail fanned, beak open, or beak down. Stokes made a more detailed analysis of five of the components – position of crest, body, nape, wings and orientation to the second bird. Out of the forty-seven possible combinations of the measures of these five elements, only twenty were actually observed, and eight of them accounted for 576 of the 629 observations in which all these components were recorded. Such results justify the use of crude postures in the preliminary analysis of displays, but indicate that further refinement can be achieved by studying the components independently.

The relation between particular components and subsequent behaviour is not usually a precise one. Stokes[7] studied the relations between the presence of individual components in the agonistic displays of blue tits at a winter feeding station and whether they subsequently attacked, fled or remained where they were. When a bird raised its crest or fluffed its body feathers it subsequently fled on 90 per cent of occasions and never attacked. But for all other components the probability of subsequent attack, escape or staying was 52 per cent or less.

This relatively small correlation between particular components and subsequent behaviour was due in part to interaction between the components. For instance, in an otherwise non-aggressive situation raising of the nape feathers was correlated with an increased likelihood of attack, but when a bird was already in an aggressive posture, the raising of the nape was associated with a reduced incidence of attack. However, as we have seen, these components tend to occur in particular combinations, and these combinations show more reliable relationships with subsequent behaviour. One combination led to escape on 94 per cent of the occasions, another to staying on 79 per cent, and another to attack on 48 per cent.

There are also other types of evidence which suggest that particular components are associated with one or other tendency:

*a* Some components are in fact elements of one of the main types of behaviour occurring in the conflict situation. In the "upright" threat posture of the herring gull the carpal joints are raised, the neck is stretched up and forwards, and the bill pointed downwards: these are components of attacking by wing-beating and pecking from above (figure 25.3). On the other hand, a lateral rather than head-on orientation to the rival, sleeking of the feathers, an upward pointing of the head and an upward instead of obliquely forward position of the neck are components of escape. The posture is, in fact, a combination of these components of attack and flee-ing, and the preponderance of one or the other can be understood in terms of the relative strengths of the associated tendencies.[8] However, a reservation must be made here. The assumption is that the components have the same causal basis in the display as in the other contexts in which they appear. This is often a useful starting point but is obviously not necessarily true in the case of locomotor components. Similarly the head-down display of great tits (*Parus major*) resembles both hammering-in-attack and the hammering move-ment used in opening nuts; further evidence is needed to decide to which it is more closely related.[3]

b *The postures in which the components occur.* If a compon-ent occurs in postures which, on other sources of evi-dence, are known to be threat postures depending on conflicting tendencies to attack and flee, but never occurs in courtship postures, it presumably does not depend on the sexual tendency.

c *The circumstances in which it occurs most often or most markedly.* If a posture varies from one extreme that is very often followed by fleeing, to another that is very often followed by copulation, and if certain compon-ents are absent in the pre-fleeing form but present in the pre-copulation form, they can be said to be asso-ciated with the sexual tendency. Similarly, a compon-ent of a threat posture which is more marked when the bird is inside its own territory than when it is outside it, is likely to be associated with attack.

d *The components with which it is associated.* Vertical stretching of the neck in gulls provides an example here. This may be an intention movement of striking a rival or an intention movement of mounting a mate. The other components with which the neck-stretching is combined provide evidence as to its significance in any particular case.[7,8]

e *Comparative evidence.* Sometimes a comparison of closely related species provides an additional source of evidence. For instance, the facts that the skuas do not raise the carpals in the aggressive upright threat posture and do not use wing-beating in fights give additional weight to the view that wing-raising is an aggressive movement in gulls, which do both.[8]

Using one or more of these methods, the relations be-tween display components and behaviour tendencies have now been assessed in a number of birds and fishes. Although the quantitative relationships may vary with the season,[7] the evidence that many components are associated with a par-ticular behavioural tendency is strong.

However, it cannot be argued that the absence of any components associated with a particular tendency is evi-dence for the absence of that tendency. For instance, Kruijt has argued from other types of evidence that certain dis-plays of the Burmese red junglefowl, though consisting entirely of agonistic components, depend in part on sexual factors. He believes that the latter exert a stabilizing influence on the attack/flee conflict and thus permit expres-sion of the associated ambivalent postures.

## 5 Factor analysis

The methods discussed so far provide a basis for the under-standing of many types of behaviour whose motivation is at first sight obscure. More recently further refinement of method (3) has been achieved by applying the techniques of factor analysis. The method consists of: (*a*) obtaining detailed recordings of sequences of identifiable elements of behaviour; (*b*) assessing the frequency with which each of these elements follows (or precedes) each other element, and hence determining the correlation coefficients between them; (*c*) determining whether these correlations could be deduced from correlations between the elements and a smaller number of hypothetical variables. If they can, then these new variables can be regarded as factors associated with two or more of the behavioural elements and can be said to explain the original correlations.

Wiepkema[9] has analysed the behaviour of the bitterling in this way. The male fish defends a territory round a fresh-water mussel, to which he will admit only ripe females. Such females are led to the mussel and lay their eggs within its gills. The male then ejects sperm while skimming over the siphon of the mussel.

Wiepkema recorded the occurrence of twelve identifiable movements when a territorial male was presented with another male, an unripe female or a ripe female. The correla-tion coefficients between these movements were calculated as indicated above and then subjected to factor analysis. It was found that three factors accounted for about 90 per cent of the total common variance, further factors having no practical significance. The results could therefore be expressed in terms of a three-dimensional model (figure 25.4) in which the dependent variables were represented as vectors. In this model the correlation coefficient between any two activities is represented by the cosine of the angle between them: obtuse angles thus indicate negative correla-tions. The three common factors are shown at right angles to each other, their position being chosen so that each corre-sponds as closely as possible to a group of vectors. The length of each vector indicates the extent to which it can be explained in terms of the common factors introduced, and its projection on to each factor indicates the extent to which that factor is represented in it (*i.e.* its factor loading).

It will be seen that the vectors of four activities (head-butting, chasing, turning beats and jerking) were closely grouped around the positive side of factor 1. These movements have an obvious aggressive function, and thus factor 1 can be called the aggressive factor. Vectors for four non-reproductive activities, which include fleeing, are closely grouped around factor 2; while those for skimming and three other movements used in courtship lie close to factor 3. Factors 2 and 3 can thus be described as non-reproductive and sexual factors, respectively.

Some activities (*e.g.* head-butting, chasing, fleeing, skimming) are almost pure measures of one or other of the

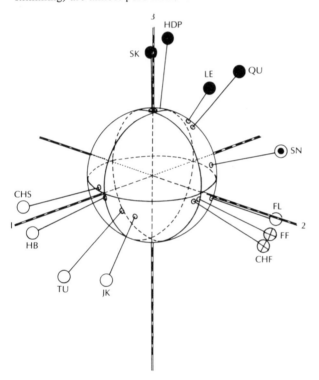

**Figure 25.4 The vector model** of the behaviour of the male bitterling as obtained from a factor analysis of the correlation coefficients between successive activities. The patterns of behaviour are abbreviated as follows: *CHS*, chasing; *CHF*, chafing; *FF*, finflickering; *FL*, fleeing; *HB*, head butting; *HDP*, head-down posture; *JK*, jerking; *LE*, leading; *QU*, quivering; *SK*, skimming; *SN*, snapping; *TU*, turning beat. The positive side of the aggressive factor is indicated by 1, the positive side of the sexual factor by 3, the positive side of the non-reproductive factor by 2. The vectors of the 12 variables are determined by the projections (*i.e.*, factor loadings) of these variables on the three main axes. (After Wiepkema.[9])

factors, since their loadings on the others are almost zero. Others, while having high positive loadings on one factor, also have positive loadings on another: they thus depend on two or more factors. For instance, turning beats and jerking have positive loadings for both factors 1 and 2 and can thus be regarded as expressing both aggressive and non-reproductive tendencies. The latter is in fact probably multiple, the various non-reproductive activities being grouped together on the diagram because they occurred largely in the absence of aggressive or sexual behaviour. This, incidentally, exemplifies the way in which the results of a factor analysis require information from other sources for their full interpretation. Furthermore it is important to emphasize that the results of the factor analysis will be influenced by the decisions taken about the situations to be studied and the types of behaviour sampled.

Such an analysis enables the activities whose vectors have positive loadings for two factors to be arranged in a series of increasing loading by one factor and decreasing loading by the other. For instance, the agonistic movements can be arranged in a sequence of fleeing–jerking–turning beat–head-butting–chasing which corresponds to an increase in the ratio of the aggressive factor to the non-reproductive (fleeing) factor.

Used in this way, the factorial method is a valuable adjunct to the methods used previously for assessing multiple motivation. It remains true, of course, that the method is liable to the various difficulties discussed under (3) above. Furthermore, by itself it gives no information about the nature of the factors.

# 6 Independent manipulation of factors controlling the displays

The most direct approach to the analysis of displays involves experimental manipulation of the supposed underlying tendencies. For example, Blurton-Jones[10] identified the stimulus characters that would cause a pair of tame Canada geese (*Branta canadensis*) to attack him and flee from him; when he combined these characters, the geese threatened him. Later he applied this method systematically in a study of the threat displays of the great tit (*Parus major*). Using hand-reared birds, he found stimulus objects which would elicit attack (a pencil held through the wire of the cage), fleeing (a small lamp bulb) and feeding (food held in forceps). These increased three groups of co-varying responses which other lines of evidence, similar to those discussed in the preceding paragraphs, had shown to be controlled by three separate sets of causal factors. He then used them to create artificial conflict situations. For example, addition of the fleeing–evoking stimulus to the attack stimulus reduced the amount of attacking and increased the amount of display. If the level of attacking was not too high, the fleeing stimulus also increased the proportion of one of the threat displays (the head-up); observational evidence had indicated that this display was related to a stronger tendency to flee than the other displays.

We see, then, that many of the complicated activities shown by fishes and birds during threat and courtship can in large part be understood on the view that tendencies for two or more incompatible types of behaviour are present. Although none of the methods used is in itself conclusive, most studies have used more than one, and the results have been mutually confirmatory. Blurton-Jones's study of great tit threat displays[3] probably represents the most critical and nearly comprehensive application of these methods: he found considerable agreement not only between the different observational approaches but also between observational and experimental ones. Although the cases discussed so far have involved principally conflicting tendencies to attack, flee and behave sexually, these are by no means the only possibilities. For example great tit threat displays may be influenced by a tendency to "stay put", whatever the nature of the latter. A similar point was made earlier by Tinbergen,[8] who showed that one display, "facing away", is performed by a kittiwake (*Rissa tridactyla*) when fleeing is opposed by a tendency either to attack, or to stay on an (owned) nest, or to form a pair-bond with another bird. Even in courtship, tendencies to nest-build, sing, behave sexually, beg, look around and probably others are often involved. Other displays, such as the distraction and mobbing displays given to predators and nest-relief ceremonies, have also been shown to depend on ambivalence. Such conclusions, however, are not to be overinterpreted as implying that all displays, let alone all signals used in intra-specific communications, depend on conflict. When a bird sings, or feeds its mate, conflict is of minor significance.

Furthermore, even when conflict is involved, the interpretation of the signal by the recipient may be influenced not only by the signal itself but also by its context. For instance, many gulls use the "head toss" display in three different situations: in food-soliciting by adult females, as a precopulatory display by both sexes and in hostile encounters (Tinbergen[8]). The common factor is the occurrence of a tendency to escape in conflict with some other tendency which involves approach. The appropriateness of the response by the recipient presumably depends on the context.

# References

1 Baerends, G. P., Brouwer, R. and Waterbolk, H. Tj. (1955), "Ethological studies on *Lebistes reticulatus* (Peters): 1: An analysis of the male courtship pattern", *Behaviour*, Vol. 8, pages 249–334

2 Moynihan, M. (1955), "Some aspects of reproductive behavior in the black-headed gull (*Larus ridibundus ridibundus L*) and related species", *Behaviour Suppl.*, Vol. 4, pages 1–201

3 Blurton-Jones, N. G. (1968), "Observations and experiments on causation of threat displays of the great tit (*Parus major*)", *Anim. Behav. Monogr.* (2), page 1

4 Andrew, R. J. (1956), "Some remarks on behaviour in conflict situations, with special reference to *Emberiza* spp", *Brit. J. Anim. Behav.*, Vol. 4, pages 41–5

5 Hinde, R. A. (1955/56), "A comparative study of the courtship of certain finches (*Fringillidae*)", *Ibis*, Vol. 97, pages 706–745; Vol. 98, pages 1–23

6 Simpson, M. J. A. (1968), "The display of the Siamese fighting-fish, *Betta splendens*", *Anim. Behav. Monogr.* (1), page 1

7 Stokes, A. W. (1962), "Agonistic behaviour among blue tits at a winter feeding station", *Behaviour*, Vol. 19, pages 118–138

8 Tinbergen, N. (1959), "Comparative studies of the behaviour of gulls (*Laridae*): a progress report", *Behaviour*, Vol. 15, pages 1–70

9 Wiepkema, P. R. (1961), "An ethological analysis of the reproductive behaviour of the bitterling", *Archs. néerl. Zool.*, Vol. 14, pages 103–199

10 Blurton-Jones N. G. (1958/1959), "Experiments on the causation of the threat postures of Canada geese", *Rep. Wildfowl Trust*, 1960, pages 46–52

# 26 Evolutionary change in primate societies
## by John Hurrell Crook

Primate species have different ways of moving about. Some swing by their arms in the trees, some jump about in the tree tops, some move on all fours on the ground and some can walk on their hind legs. All these methods of locomotion are reflected in the way their bodies are built. In this sense the relationship between ecology, anatomy and behaviour is well established. However, the nature of primates' societies and the relationships between their social systems and their ecology are only now being elucidated. In this article I shall discuss, in particular, the ways in which the social behaviour of two species of baboon is related to the ecology of their natural habitat in Ethiopia.

Early studies of primate societies were mainly concerned with the reasons for their cohesion and structure in terms of the motivation of individual members. Relatively few field studies were made, only those of C. R. Carpenter being of importance during the 1930s, and the range of contrasts between societies of differing species remained hidden. Only since 1950 have extensive field investigations of a wide variety of species at last begun to provide a reliable basis for a comparative sociology of these animals. The publication of a recent symposium of current knowledge, under the editorship of Irven DeVore, is an important step forward.

The society of a primate species can be adequately described only through a consideration of the three main behavioural features that maintain it. First, there is the system of signals and responses that provides an elaborate communication network allowing rapid transmission of information concerning the motivation of individuals in their encounters with one another. While many of these signals are 'innate' and species specific, it is probable that the meaning given to some of them may vary in different localities and that learning is involved both in their use and in responding to them. Secondly, a social group provides a complex tissue of personal relationships within which a baby monkey has to grow. The 'socialization' process, whereby an infant adopts the roles his sexual and social status impose

on him, is a vital factor ensuring the continuity of the system from one generation to another. Thirdly, a given society appears to be adapted to its environment. Comparisons between the societies of species living in different conditions reveal the functional significance of contrasts between them. Furthermore, within a species, local populations often show contrasts attributable to local conditions and apparently of survival value. Contrasts between terrestrial primate societies, such as those of baboons and macaques, have been especially studied in recent years and appear to be based on the establishment of social traditions under long term environmental selection.

These three aspects of social analysis are commonly treated separately and each field has its own champions and experts. It is becoming increasingly apparent, however, that a society can be adequately characterized only through a comprehensive treatment of all three. In particular, the problem of the relations between the evolutionary adaptations and the local adaptability of primate societies can be approached only in this way.

When I left England in 1964 to spend seven months studying gelada baboons in the Ethiopian highlands only two sorts of society were known among terrestrial primates: the multimale promiscuous type of association (many males and females together) well known in common baboon populations (*Papio cynocephalus* and *P. ursinus*) of the East and South African savannahs; and the one male group "harem" system (troops containing several male "overlords" each with their respective female consorts). The latter had been described by Sir Solly Zuckerman for the hamadryas baboon (*Papio hamadryas*) in the London Zoo and confirmed from the field by Hans Kummer and Fred Kurt. Even so some biologists considered the one male system to be no more than a local variation of the multimale group. Its significance in populations with certain types of ecology was, however, soon to be made apparent.

The late Professor K. R. L. Hall, in a classic field study published in 1965, established that the patas monkey (*Erythrocebus patas*) lived in groups—one male

*first published in* Science Journal, *June 1967.*

surrounded by females and attendant young – but that, unlike Kummer's hamadryas, these were not associated into troops or herds but foraged widely in huge "home ranges" avoiding contact with others of their kind. In the hamadryas, the male "overlord" is a powerful beast strictly disciplining his females to remain within a few metres of him – upon pain of a fierce "neck bite". Patas males, by contrast, are mild creatures adopting the role of watchdog or sentinel for the group while a female may determine the direction of a group's movement. When danger threatens he gives warning and may provide an elaborate distraction display by high speed running and leaping into bushes near the "predator" – or the observer. Male behaviour also tends to maintain the separation of groups through their avoidance of one another.

In Ethiopia I travelled on long foot safaris and by mule caravan in the mountainous area of High Semyen near the ancient city of Gondar in the province of Begemdir. The gelada baboon (*Theropithecus gelada*) is a montane grassland animal found only near crags or precipices to which it orients its whole life. It is found at altitudes between 2 100 metres and 4 500 metres; even so much of its distribution area has been severely modified by human agriculture. To observe it in its more or less natural environment I travelled at high altitudes (about 3 900 metres) on the mountains of Geech and Ambaras – great rolling hogs' backs which are the remains of an old volcano that, swelling like a great boil below the Earth's crust, failed to burst and became stabilized. The eroded edges of these mountains and the great gorges that dissect them produce escarpment and canyon scenery of a quite stupendous grandeur through which the geladas – the biggest mammals in the area – wander like yelping lords. Lion-like in appearance though the great males may be, they are faint at heart, running on the least alarm to the protective crags.

I found that the gelada, like the hamadryas and the patas, had a society based on the one male group. This was, however, by no means easy to determine. Faced with herds of up to 400 members, each one apparently moving at random, I needed two months almost continuous work before the picture clarified. It then transpired that the smallest indivisible population units were "one male groups" and "all male groups" and that herds were composed of congregations of these in favoured feeding areas. The one male group consisted of an adult male with several female consorts whose reproductive cycles, unlike those of hamadryas studied by Kummer, showed no sign of synchronization. Some were pregnant, some were mothers, some in oestrus and some not. The male at any one time associated

closely only with a single (very rarely two) female in oestrus. His relationships with non-oestrus consorts were relaxed. His females, unlike hamadryas wives, could wander up to 200 metres from him and feed happily in quite other parts of the herd.

The appearance of a large party of fused groups thus suggested a random distribution of individuals. However, observations showed that females kept an eye on their male and would periodically move close to him – all coming together within about 200 square metres. Furthermore, if the male got up and proceeded to walk away, his females, wherever they were in the herd, would rise also, gradually approach him and follow him through the herd and even out of it. One male groups were, in fact, not bound to a herd – they were constantly entering it or leaving it. The herd was thus an "artificial" construct arising only in favoured conditions – the real social and reproductive unit was the one male group. Nevertheless, herds could show considerable structuring. In the High Semyen, particularly, where herds patrolled the rich natural grasslands on Geech mountain, a division into a peripheral section of large sub-adult males and a main body, nearer to the cliff line, of one male groups was found. The peripheral males, by reason of more rapid foraging over the ground and a more marked tendency to wander from the safety of the crags, thus appeared to form a protective zone between the harems and any potential predator – in this area mainly ferocious village dogs. When a herd splits up these peripheral males coalesce into "all male groups" the members of which may show considerable loyalty to one another in that membership remains constant over several weeks.

Observations over a period of ten months carried out at several contrasting localities in Ethiopia revealed that the separate wanderings of one male and all male groups greatly increased when food was in short supply or sparsely distributed. Nevertheless, as soon as conditions improved locally in any one area, herds would tend to form. In other nearby places separate groups or small fused parties would still be observed. Although we have yet to carry out critical studies of seasonal changes in food availability, diet and nutritional values the evidence points strongly to the food supply factor being uppermost in determining gelada population dispersion at different places and times.

Kummer and Kurt's work on the hamadryas had given rise to similar thoughts but the separate wandering of the one male parties of their study population had been much less apparent. This was probably owing to the limited numbers of sleeping sites, such as rock cliffs, in their area, which kept the population within bounds. The superabundance of crags and chasms in the gelada habitat means that the

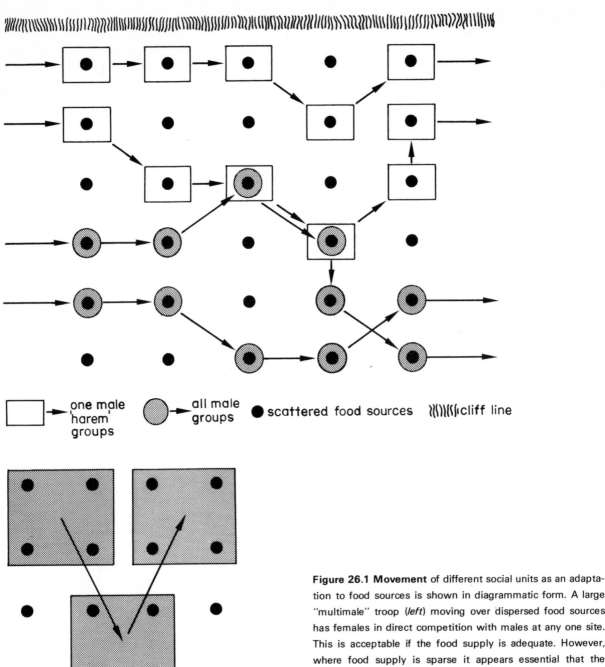

one male 'harem' groups     all male groups     ● scattered food sources     cliff line

troop     ● food source

**Figure 26.1 Movement** of different social units as an adaptation to food sources is shown in diagrammatic form. A large "multimale" troop (*left*) moving over dispersed food sources has females in direct competition with males at any one site. This is acceptable if the food supply is adequate. However, where food supply is sparse it appears essential that the females, as the effective breeding units, should have a high proportion of the available food. Under these circumstances the social units are formed of "one male" and "all male" groups (*above*). Within a one-male group at any one food source the proportion of food available to the females is high because only one large mature male is present. The all male groups, which tend to range along the canyon away from the cliff line, may occasionally exploit the same food sites, but if so it is usually at a different time to the one-male groups.

animals can descend to sleep on them in any numbers at any place. Their geographical distribution is, however, limited to gorge type countryside.

The multimale troop systems of common baboons, rhesus and japanese macaques are already well known. Many males move together with females, juveniles and young in troops that, in savannah at least, are of more or less constant composition. As the females come into oestrus they mate with sub-adult or adult males of low social status, mating only with the despot of the male social hierarchy when in the most receptive condition. Since he thus tends to sire more young than other males, social selection for attributes determining high dominance tends to maintain a markedly hierarchical social structure over generations.

The hamadryas and gelada societies are quite different in this respect. The females normally mate only with their own males and although it is clear that competition for leadership of groups, mainly apparently in sub-adulthood, plays a role selecting for attributes of strength and forcefulness, the absence of a recognizable "peck order" between adult males evidently means that selection for dominance traits is less severe or at least of a different kind.

What advantages accrue to societies based on the one male group and to those consisting of multimale troops? The clue is given by the fact that one male groups occur either in the most arid areas of Africa or in places where the dry seasons are most severe. By contrast, multimale troops occur generally in richer savannah, open woodland or forest fringe conditions where seasonal variations in climate are less extreme. In such areas food is sufficiently abundant for large bodied, dominant males to feed together with smaller females and young. In more severe areas with food sparsely distributed such a big troop would rapidly overexploit every patch of ground through which it moved, and a high proportion of the food would go to the males. The separate foraging of smaller multimale units would be a partial solution but a high proportion of food would still be denied to the females whose role in reproduction is critical and dependent on continuous food availability during pregnancy and lactation. In the one male group fertilization and procreation remain assured and the exploitation of food by the reproductively less important sex is reduced to a minimum. Such units can wander separately over sparsely distributed food supplies with the greater part of the available food going to females. It is important to notice that this is an adjustment primarily to the dispersion of food sources rather than to the total availability of food although it is made necessary by a general reduction in the latter (figure 26.1).

In the gelada the sex ratio over all age groups works out at about 1 : 1. Among adult animals, however, it has dropped to about 1 : 3 (varying locally) in favour of females. The difference arises primarily from the slower maturation rates of males although, in agricultural areas, there is also a higher mortality rate for adult males than for females. Even so a number of adult males are commonly excluded from owning harems and collect with sub-adult males in all male groups that tend to feed and move separately. Thus, although these may often exploit the same general feeding area as the one male units, they do not forage together with them nor do they compete directly with browsing females during their daily range.

The idea that food availability is a prime determinant of these primates' social systems is supported by the following evidence. First, one male groups are found only in the less stable habitats with smaller food supplies and sparse resources which vary seasonally. Secondly, gelada herds are known to occur only in optimum feeding conditions; the population of one male groups is otherwise scattered over the terrain. All male groups show a tendency to feed in different zones from one male groups. Thirdly, the typical multimale group in food rich areas includes large bodied adult males foraging continuously together with females in the same social unit. At the edges of such habitats some reduction in size of the groups has been reported. Fourthly, there is evidence from several species that populations in the less stable environments show more disparate sex-ratios than those in more stable ones. Lastly, in an area in Ethiopia where a one male group society and a multimale group society were found living in the same district the one male group type was found mainly in the food "impoverished" area and spent more time foraging than did the multimale group which was found in the food "rich" area.

This last study was carried out during my final month in Ethiopia together with Pelham Aldrich-Blake. At the monastic settlement of Debra Libanos in Shoa, geladas live in close proximity to doguera baboons (*Papio anubis*). The main contrasts we noted were thoroughly tested for significance using quantitative data (Table 26.1). The importance of the food supply is brought out in several ways. The geladas, eating small objects of low apparent nutritional value, may spend up to 70 per cent of their time at certain times of day in getting their food. Doguera baboons by contrast, which eat larger, more nutritious morsels mainly in woodland, spend comparatively little time feeding and much more time wandering about, manipulating objects and playing. This appears to account in part for their ability to learn complex habits – such as the removal of spines from leaves and fruit of Prickly Pear. They have time in which to educate themselves and the young have time to learn by observation. The more stereotyped gelada behaviour is imposed by its feeding economy.

*Table 26.1.* **Comparison of gelada and doguera populations at Debra Libanos, Ethiopia**

| COMPARISONS | GELADA | DOGUERA |
|---|---|---|
| social units | one male groups } herds<br>all male groups | multimale groups of varying size and constancy |
| dispersion | local herd formation in food rich areas | no variation |
| habitat | scrub, sward, cultivated land | forest – forest fringe |
| diet | seeds, bulbs, grass, insects | fleshy plants, fruit, twigs, bulbs, lichen, olives, insects |
| activity | most of time feeding | more time sitting or moving than feeding |
| habits | terrestrial | arboreal – terrestrial |
| adult sex ratio | approximately 5 times more females than males | approximately 2 : 1 in favour of females |

There seems to be a further fascinating corollary of these contrasts. Females of both the doguera baboon and the gelada have bare patches of skin – secondary sexual characters – that function as signals informing males of the sexual condition of the possessors. These patches change in colour and form with the oestrus cycle. Now while the doguera wears her patch on her bottom the gelada has hers over her chest and surrounding the nipples. Until now it has not been clear why such signals should develop in different areas of the body. A cautious answer can now be suggested. The gelada data show that not only do the animals spend long periods of time feeding but that most of the feeding activity is performed sitting down. Dogueras, by contrast, tend to stroll about collecting food, only sitting down to examine particular morsels. Thus, while signals on the posterior would be easily seen on a doguera, this would be untrue for the gelada. A chest signal is, however, readily observed and occurs in a region already of interest by reason of the babies suckling the nipples when young and the fact that infants commonly "tease" their mothers by playing with them. It may well have been that the nature of the feeding resources, which determine the time spent feeding and the feeding posture, has played a key role in modifying the positioning of structural social signals in these species.

The primate ethologist is now faced with a difficult problem. While the apparent adaptedness of primate societies suggests long term environmental selection, many of the features discussed could be direct functions of contemporary habitat conditions. The ethologist, traditionally a student of "innate" behaviour patterns and their survival value, could easily be misled into making incorrect assumptions concerning the origins of the systems observed. There is, in fact, an increasing wealth of evidence to show that in contrasting areas local populations of the same species may have different sorts of social system. Sometimes indeed variation within a species seems almost as large as that between species. For example, J. S. Gartlan studying vervet monkeys on the rich and largely forested Lolui island in Lake Victoria found territorial behaviour that was totally absent in the impoverished study area at Chobi elsewhere in Uganda. Similarly neither T. Rowell at Ishasha in Uganda nor I at Debra Libanos found troop systems of *Papio anubis* baboons in woodland of the form described for close relatives in the savannahs of south and eastern Africa. The social organization within such species is clearly flexible and responds to environmental changes.

It seems likely that changes in environmental conditions modify primate systems during the passage of time in a highly complex way. Alterations in ecological variables may cause shifts in the relative frequencies of different types of social interaction. For example, relations between adult males play a major role in structuring a social population. This structuring is probably much dependent on the frequency of aggressive encounters which produce avoidance and secondary conditioning both through direct experience and through observational learning. The pattern of such experiences, or natural learning "trials", defines the roles that an animal adopts in relation to its companions. In an ecologically modified population infant and juvenile animals will grow up in a social environment subtly different from that of the previous norm. Their socialization will ensure that they adopt roles acceptable to the new norms of the group. Changes in social tradition may thus arise as direct effects of ecological developments.

One may envisage the probable evolutionary development of one male groups. Following our earlier hypothesis, environmental change will tend to lower the reproductive success of individuals living in groups too large in relation to the local food supply. Among smaller groups those with fewest males will tend to be most successful in terms of procreation. Females living in one male groups, and males temperamentally suited to lead them, will thus gradually gain reproductive advantages over others. Successful one male group societies will tend to be maintained from one generation to another as their young become conditioned to the social structure into which they are born. Environmentally induced modifications in society are furthermore stabilized by socialization to produce the adaptedness and relative fixity of the system as a whole. Individual genotypes are selected as a result of reproductive advantages that accrue through living in certain types of groups maintained primarily by the inheritance of tradition.

Changes in social structure thus allow individuals of particular "temperaments" to gain selective advantages. We have already seen how hamadryas and common baboon societies tend to give reproductive advantages to psychologically contrasting sorts of male. Social selection becomes an important variable determining the genetic basis of individual behaviour. Not only do environmental changes cause shifts in social systems directly but changes in traditional society impose differing selection pressures on the determining factors of innate behaviour. Here we are beginning to trace the complex origins and effects of primate traditions which, with the development of tool use and decreasing dependence upon subsistence diets, gave rise to the cultures of primitive man. At this point perhaps biology assumes a less determining role and history begins.

# 27 Status and superstatus
## by Desmond Morris

In any organized group of mammals, no matter how co-operative, there is always a struggle for social dominance. As he pursues this struggle, each adult individual acquires a particular social rank, giving him his position, or status, in the group hierarchy. The situation never remains stable for very long, largely because all the status strugglers are growing older. When the overlords, or "top dogs", become senile, their seniority is challenged and they are overthrown by their immediate subordinates. There is then renewed dominance squabbling as everyone moves a little farther up the social ladder. At the other end of the scale, the younger members of the group are maturing rapidly, keeping up the pressure from below. In addition, certain members of the group may suddenly be struck down by disease or accidental death, leaving gaps in the hierarchy that have to be quickly filled.

The general result is a constant condition of *status tension*. Under natural conditions this tension remains tolerable because of the limited size of the social groupings. If, however, in the artificial environment of captivity, the group size becomes too big, or the space available too small, then the status "rat race" soon gets out of hand, dominance battles rage uncontrollably, and the leaders of the packs, prides, colonies or tribes come under severe strain. When this happens, the weakest members of the group are frequently hounded to their deaths, as the restrained rituals of display and counter-display degenerate into bloody violence.

*from* The Human Zoo *by Desmond Morris. Copyright © 1969 by Desmond Morris. Used with permission of McGraw-Hill Book Company and Jonathan Cape, London.*

---

* Desmond Morris has argued, earlier in the book from which this extract was taken, that modern, urbanized man lives in conditions comparable to a zoo, conditions which are confined and overcrowded. The city, he says, is a human zoo. Man lives not in the small tribal groupings of his ancestors, but in vast conglomerations, or super-tribes. [*Editors' note*]

There are further repercussions. So much time has to be spent sorting out the unnaturally complex status relationships that other aspects of social life, such as parental care, become seriously and damagingly neglected.

If the settling of dominance disputes creates difficulties for the moderately crowded inmates of the animal zoo, then it is obviously going to provide an even greater dilemma for the vastly overgrown super-tribes of the human zoo.* The essential feature of the status struggle in nature is that it is based on the *personal* relationships of the individuals inside the social group. For the primitive human tribesman the problem was therefore a comparatively simple one, but when the tribes grew into super-tribes and relationships became increasingly impersonal, the problem of status rapidly expanded into the nightmare of super-status.

Before we probe this tender area of urban life, it will be helpful to take a brief look at the basic laws which govern the dominance struggle. The best way to do this is to survey the battlefield from the viewpoint of the dominant animal.

If you are to rule your group and to be successful in holding your position of power, there are ten golden rules you must obey. They apply to all leaders, from baboons to modern presidents and prime ministers. The ten commandments of dominance are these:

*1 You must clearly display the trappings, postures and gestures of dominance.*
For the baboon this means a sleek, beautifully groomed, luxuriant coat of hair; a calm, relaxed posture when not engaged in disputes; a deliberate and purposeful gait when active. There must be no outward signs of anxiety, indecision or hesitancy.

With a few superficial modifications, the same holds true for the human leader. The luxuriant coat of fur becomes the rich and elaborate costume of the ruler, dramatically excelling those of his subordinates. He assumes postures unique to his dominant role. When he is relaxing, he may recline or sit, while others must stand until given permission to follow suit. This is also typical of the dominant baboon, who may sprawl out lazily while his anxious subordinates hold themselves in more alert postures near by. The situation changes once the leader stirs into aggressive action and begins to assert himself. Then, be he baboon or prince, he must rise into a more impressive position than that of his followers. He must literally rise above them, matching his psychological status with his physical posture. For the baboon boss this is easy: a dominant monkey is nearly always much larger than his underlings. He has only to hold himself erect and his greater body size does the rest. The situation is enhanced by cringing and crouching on the part of his more fearful subordinates. For the human leader, artificial aids may be necessary. He can magnify his size by wearing large cloaks or tall headgear. His height can be increased by mounting a throne, a platform, an animal or a vehicle of some kind, or by being carried aloft by his followers. The crouching of the weaker baboons becomes stylized in various ways: subordinate humans lower their height by bowing, curtsying, kneeling, kowtowing, salaaming, or prostrating.

The ingenuity of our species permits the human leader to have it both ways. By sitting on a throne on a raised platform, he can enjoy both the relaxed position of the passive dominant *and* the heightened position of the active dominant at one and the same time, thus providing himself with a doubly powerful display posture.

The dignified displays of leadership that the human animal shares with the baboon are still with us in many forms today. They can be seen in their most primitive and obvious conditions in generals, judges, high priests and surviving royalty. They tend to be more limited to special occasions than they once were, but when they do occur they are as ostentatious as ever. Not even the most learned academics are immune to the demands of pomp and finery on their more ceremonial occasions.

Where emperors have given way to elected presidents and prime ministers, personal dominance displays have, however, become less overt. There has been a shift of emphasis in the role of leadership. The new-style leader is a servant of the people who happens to be dominant, rather than a dominator of the people who also serves them. He underlines his acceptance of this situation by wearing a comparatively drab costume, but this is only a trick. It is a minor dishonesty that he can afford, to make him seem more "one of the crowd", but he dare not carry it too far or, before he knows it, he really will have become one of the crowd again. So, in other, less blatantly personal ways, he must continue to perform the outward display of his dominance. With all the complexities of the modern urban

environment at his disposal, this is not difficult. The loss of grandeur in his dress can be compensated for by the elaborate and exclusive nature of the rooms in which he rules and the buildings in which he lives and works. He can retain ostentation in the way he travels, with motorcades, outriders and personal planes. He can continue to surround himself with a large group of "professional subordinates" – aides, secretaries, servants, personal assistants, bodyguards, attendants and the rest – part of whose job is merely to be seen to be servile towards him, thereby adding to his image of social superiority. His postures, movements and gestures of dominance can be retained unmodified. Because the power signals they transmit are so basic to the human species, they are accepted unconsciously and can therefore escape restriction. His movements and gestures are calm and relaxed, or firm and deliberate. (When did you last see a president or a prime minister running, except when taking voluntary exercise?) In conversation he uses his eyes like weapons, delivering a fixed stare at moments when subordinates would be politely averting their gaze, and turning his head away at moments when subordinates would be watching intently. He does not scrabble, twitch, fidget or falter. These are essentially the reactions of subordinates. If the leader performs them there is something seriously wrong with him in his role as the dominant member of the group.

## 2 In moments of active rivalry you must threaten your subordinates aggressively.

At the slightest sign of any challenge from a subordinate baboon, the group leader immediately responds with an impressive display of threatening behaviour. There is a whole range of threat displays available, varying from those motivated by a lot of aggression tinged with a little fear to those motivated by a lot of fear and only a little aggression. The latter – the "scared threats" of weak-but-hostile individuals – are never shown by a dominant animal unless his leadership is tottering. When his position is secure he shows only the most aggressive threat displays. He can be so secure that all he needs to do is to indicate that he is about to threaten, without actually bothering to carry it through. A mere jerk of his massive head in the direction of the unruly subordinate may be sufficient to subdue the inferior individual. These actions are called "intention movements", and they operate in precisely the same way in the human species. A powerful human leader, irritated by the actions of a subordinate, need only jerk his head in the latter's direction and fix him with a hard stare, to assert his dominance successfully. If he has to raise his voice or repeat an order, his dominance is slightly less secure, and he will, on eventually regaining control, have to re-establish his status by administering a rebuke or a symbolic punishment of some kind.

The act of raising his voice, or raging, is only a weak sign in a leader when it occurs as a reaction to an immediate threat. It may also be used spontaneously or deliberately by a strong ruler as a general device for reaffirming his position. A dominant baboon may behave in the same way, suddenly charging at his subordinates and terrorizing them, reminding them of his powers. It enables him to chalk up a few points, and after that he can more easily get his own way with the merest nod of his head. Human leaders perform in this manner from time to time, issuing stern edicts, making lightning inspections, or haranguing the group with vigorous speeches. If you are a leader, it is dangerous to remain silent, unseen or unfelt for too long. If natural circumstances do not prompt a show of power, the circumstances must be invented that do. It is not enough to have power, one must be observed to have power. Therein lies the value of spontaneous threat displays.

### 3 In moments of physical challenge you (or your delegates) must be able forcibly to overpower your subordinates.

If a threat display fails, then a physical attack must follow. If you are a baboon boss this is a dangerous step to take, for two reasons. Firstly, in a physical fight even the winner may be damaged, and injury is more serious for a dominant animal than for a subordinate. It makes him less daunting for a subsequent attacker. Secondly, he is always outnumbered by his subordinates, and if they are driven too far they may gang up on him and overpower him in a combined effort. It is these two facts that make threat rather than actual attack the preferred method for dominant individuals.

The human leader overcomes this to some extent by employing a special class of "suppressors". They, the military or police, are so specialized and professional at their task that only a general uprising of the whole populace would be strong enough to beat them. In extreme cases, a despot will employ a further, even more specialized class of suppressors (such as secret police), whose job it is to suppress the ordinary suppressors if they happen to get out of line. By clever manipulation and administration it is possible to run an aggressive system of this kind in such a way that only the leader knows enough of what is happening to be able to control it. Everyone else is in a state of confusion unless they have orders from above and, in this way, the modern despot can hold the reins and dominate effectively.

### 4 If a challenge involves brain rather than brawn you must be able to outwit your subordinates.

The baboon boss must be cunning, quick and intelligent as well as strong and aggressive. This is obviously even more important for a human leader. In cases where there is a system of inherited leadership, the stupid individual is quickly deposed or becomes the mere figurehead and pawn of the true leaders.

Today the problems are so complex that the modern leader is forced to surround himself with intellectual specialists, but despite this he cannot escape the need for quick-wittedness. It is he who must make the final decisions, and make them sharply and clearly, without faltering. This is such a vital quality in leadership that it is more important to make a firm, unhesitating decision than it is to make the "right" one. Many a powerful leader has survived occasional wrong decisions, made with style and forcefulness, but few have survived hesitant indecisiveness. The golden rule of leadership here, which in a rational age is an unpleasant one to accept, is that it is the manner in which you do something that really counts, rather than what you do. It is a sad truth that a leader who does the wrong things in the right way will, up to a certain point, gain greater allegiance and enjoy more success than one who does the right things in the wrong way. The progress of civilization has repeatedly suffered as a result of this. Lucky indeed is the society whose leader does the right things and at the same time obeys the ten golden rules of dominance; lucky – and rare, too. There appears to be a sinister, more-than-chance relationship between great leadership and aberrant policies.

It seems as if one of the curses of the immense complexity of the super-tribal condition is that it is almost impossible to make sharp, clear-cut decisions, concerning major issues, on a rational basis. The evidence available is so complicated, so diverse and frequently so contradictory, that any reasonable, rational decision is bound to involve undue hesitancy. The great super-tribal leader cannot enjoy the luxury of ponderous restraint and "further examination of the facts" so typical of the great academic. The biological nature of his role as a dominant animal forces him to make a snap decision or lose face.

The danger is obvious: the situation inevitably favours, as great leaders, rather abnormal individuals, fired by some kind of obsessive fanaticism, who will be prepared to cut through the mass of conflicting evidence that the super-tribal condition throws up. This is one of the prices that the biological tribesman must pay for becoming an artificial super-tribesman. The only solution is to find a brilliant, rational, balanced, deep-thinking brain housed in a glamorous, flamboyant, self-assertive, colourful personality. Contradictory? Yes. Impossible? Perhaps; but there is a glimmer of hope in the fact that the very size of the super-tribe, which causes the problem in the first place, also offers literally millions of potential candidates.

## 5 You must suppress squabbles that break out between your subordinates.

If a baboon leader sees an unruly squabble taking place he is likely to interfere and suppress it, even though it does not in any way constitute a direct threat to himself. It gives him another opportunity of displaying his dominance and at the same time helps to maintain order inside the group. Interference of this kind from the dominant animal is directed particularly at squabbling juveniles, and helps to instil in them, at an early age, the idea of a powerful leader in their midst.

The equivalent of this behaviour for the human leader is the control and administration of the laws of his group. The rulers of the earlier and smaller super-tribes were powerfully active in this respect, but there has been increasing delegation of these duties in modern times, due to the increasing weight of other burdens that relate more directly to the status of the leader. Nevertheless, a squabbling community is an inefficient one and some degree of control and influence has to be retained.

## 6 You must reward your immediate subordinates by permitting them to enjoy the benefits of their high ranks.

The sub-dominant baboons, although they are the leader's worst rivals, are also of great help to him in times of threat from outside the group. Further, if they are too strongly suppressed they may gang up on him and depose him. They therefore enjoy privileges which the weaker members of the group cannot share. They have more freedom of action and are permitted to stay closer to the dominant animal than are the junior males.

Any human leader who has failed to obey this rule has soon found himself in difficulties. He needs more help from his sub-dominants, and is in greater danger of a "palace revolt", than his baboon equivalent. So much more can go on behind his back. The system of rewarding the sub-dominants requires brilliant expertise. The wrong sort of reward gives too much power to a serious rival. The trouble is that a true leader cannot enjoy true friendship. True friendship can only be fully expressed between members of roughly the same status level. A partial friendship can, of course, occur between a dominant and a subordinate, at any level, but it is always marred by the difference in rank. No matter how well meaning the partners in such a friendship may be, condescension and flattery inevitably creep in to cloud the relationship. The leader, at the very peak of the social pyramid, is, in the full sense of the word, permanently friendless; and his partial friends are perhaps more partial than he likes to think. As I said, the giving of favours requires an expert hand.

## 7 You must protect the weaker members of the group from undue persecution.

Females with young tend to cluster around the dominant male baboon. He meets any attack on these females or on unprotected infants with a savage onslaught. As a defender of the weak he is ensuring the survival of the future adults of the group. Human leaders have increasingly extended their protection of the weak to include also the old, the sick and the disabled. This is because efficient rulers not only need to defend the growing children, who will one day swell the ranks of their followers, but also need to reduce the anxieties of the active adults, all of whom are threatened with eventual senility, sudden sickness or possible disability. With most people the urge to give aid in such cases is a natural development of their biologically cooperative nature. But for the leaders it is also a question of making people work more efficiently by taking a serious weight off their minds.

## 8 You must make decisions concerning the social activities of your group.

When the baboon leader decides to move, the whole group moves. When he rests, the group rests. When he feeds, the group feeds. Direct control of this kind is, of course, lost to the leader of a human super-tribe, but he can nevertheless play a vital role in encouraging the more abstract directions his group takes. He may foster the sciences or push towards a greater military emphasis. As with the other golden rules of leadership, it is important for him to exercise this one even when it does not appear to be strictly necessary. Even if a society is cruising happily along on a set and satisfactory course, it is vital for him to change that course in certain ways in order to make his impact felt. It is not enough simply to alter it as a reaction to something that is going wrong. He must spontaneously, of his own volition, insist on new lines of development, or he will be considered weak and colourless. If he has no ready-made preferences

271

and enthusiasms, he must invent them. If he is seen to have what appear to be strong convictions on certain matters, he will be taken more seriously on *all* matters. Many modern leaders seem to overlook this and their political "platforms" are desperately lacking in originality. If they win the battle for leadership it is not because they are more inspiring than their rivals but simply because they are less uninspiring.

## 9 You must reassure your extreme subordinates from time to time.

If a dominant baboon wishes to approach a subordinate peacefully, it may have difficulty doing so, because its close proximity is inevitably threatening. It can overcome this by performing a reassurance display. This consists of a very gentle approach, with no sudden or harsh movements, accompanied by facial expressions (called lip-smacking) which are typical of friendly subordinates. This helps to calm the fears of the weaker animal and the dominant one can then come near.

Human leaders, who may be characteristically tough and unsmiling with their immediate subordinates, frequently adopt an attitude of friendly submissiveness when coming into personal contact with their extreme subordinates. Towards them they offer a front of exaggerated courtesy, smiling, waving, shaking hands interminably and even fondling babies. But the smiles soon fade as they turn away and disappear back inside their ruthless world of power.

## 10 You must take the initiative in repelling threats or attacks arising from outside your group.

It is always the dominant baboon that is in the forefront of the defence against an attack from an external enemy. He plays the major role as the protector of the group. For the baboon, the enemy is usually a dangerous member of another species, but for the human leader it takes the form of a rival group of the same species. At such moments, his leadership is put to a severe test, but, in a sense, it is less severe than during times of peace. The external threat has such a powerful cohesive effect on the members of the threatened group that the leader's task is in many ways made easier. The more daring and reckless he is, the more fervently he seems to be protecting the group who, caught up in the emotional fray, never dare question his actions (as they would in peace-time), no matter how irrational these actions may be. Carried along on the grotesque tidal-wave of enthusiasm that war churns up, the strong leader comes

into his own. With the greatest of ease he can persuade the members of his group, deeply conditioned as they are to consider the killing of another human being as the most hideous crime known, to commit this same action as an act of honour and heroism. He can hardly put a foot wrong, but if he does, the news of his blunder can always be suppressed as bad for national morale. Should it become public, it can still be put down to bad luck rather than bad judgment. Bearing all this in mind, it is little wonder that, in times of peace, leaders are prone to invent, or at least to magnify, threats from foreign powers that they can then cast in the role of potential enemies. A little added cohesion goes a long way.

# 28  The spontaneity
# of aggression
## *by Konrad Lorenz*

I think I have adequately shown elsewhere that the aggression of so many animals towards members of their own species is in no way detrimental to the species but, on the contrary, is essential for its preservation. However, this must not raise false hopes about the present situation of mankind. Innate behaviour mechanisms can be thrown completely out of balance by small, apparently insignificant changes of environmental conditions. Inability to adapt quickly to such changes may bring about the destruction of a species, and the changes which man has wrought in his environment are by no means insignificant. An unprejudiced observer from another planet, looking upon man as he is today, in his hand the atom bomb, the product of his intelligence, in his heart the aggression drive inherited from his anthropoid ancestors, which this same intelligence cannot control, would not prophesy long life for the species. Looking at the situation as a human being whom it personally concerns, it seems like a bad dream, and it is hard to believe that aggression is anything but the pathological product of our disjointed cultural and social life.

And one could only wish it were no more than that! Knowledge of the fact that the aggression drive is a true, primarily species-preserving instinct enables us to recognize its full danger: it is the spontaneity of the instinct that makes it so dangerous. If it were merely a reaction to certain external factors, as many sociologists and psychologists maintain, the state of mankind would not be as perilous as it really is, for, in that case, the reaction-eliciting factors could be eliminated with some hope of success. It was Freud who first pointed out the essential spontaneity of instincts, though he recognized that of aggression only rather later. He also showed that lack of social contact, and above all deprivation of it (*Liebesverlust*), were among the factors strongly predisposing to facilitate aggression. However, the conclusions which many American psychologists drew

*first published in* On Aggression. *Copyright © 1963 by Dr G. Borotha–Schoeler Verlag, Vienna. English translation copyright © 1966 by Konrad Lorenz. Reprinted by permission of Harcourt Brace Jovanovich, Inc. and Methuen & Co. Ltd, London.*

from this correct surmise were erroneous. It was supposed that children would grow up less neurotic, better adapted to their social environment and less aggressive if they were spared all disappointments and indulged in every way. An American method of education, based on these surmises, only showed that the aggressive drive, like many other instincts, springs "spontaneously" from the inner human being, and the results of this method of upbringing were countless unbearably rude children who were anything but non-aggressive. The tragic side of this tragi-comedy followed when these children grew up and left home, and in place of indulgent parents were confronted with unsympathetic public opinion, for example when they entered college. American psycho-analysts have told me that, under the strain of the difficult social adaptation necessary, many such young people really became neurotic. This questionable method of education has apparently not yet died out, for a few years ago an American colleague who was working as a guest at our institute asked if he might stay on three weeks longer, not for scientific reasons, but because his wife's sister was staying with her and her three boys were "non-frustration" children.

The completely erroneous view that animal and human behaviour is predominantly reactive and that, even if it contains any innate elements at all, it can be altered to an unlimited extent by learning, comes from a radical misunderstanding of certain democratic principles: it is utterly at variance with these principles to admit that human beings are not born equal and that not all have equal chances of becoming ideal citizens. Moreover, for many decades the reaction, the "reflex", represented the only element of behaviour which was studied by serious psychologists, while all "spontaneity" of animal behaviour was left to the "vitalists", the mystically inclined observers of nature.

The fact that the central nervous system does not need to wait for stimuli, like an electric bell with a push-button, before it can respond, but that it can itself produce stimuli which give a natural, physiological explanation for the "spontaneous" behaviour of animals and humans, has found recognition only in the last decades, through the work of

Adrian, Paul Weiss, Kenneth Roeder and above all Erich von Holst. The strength of the ideological prejudices involved was plainly shown by the heated and emotional debates that took place before the endogenous production of stimuli within the central nervous system became a fact generally recognized by the science of physiology.

In behaviour research in its narrower sense, it was Wallace Craig who first made spontaneity the subject of scientific examination. Before him, William McDougall had opposed the words of Descartes, "*Animal non agit, agitur*", engraved on the shield of the behaviourists, by the more correct statement, "The healthy animal is up and doing". But as a true vitalist he took this spontaneity for the result of the mystic vital force whose meaning nobody really knows. So he did not think of observing exactly the rhythmic repetition of spontaneous behaviour patterns, let alone of continuously measuring the threshold values of eliciting stimuli, as his pupil Craig did later.

In a series of experiments with blond ring doves Craig removed the female from the male in a succession of gradually increasing periods. After one such period of deprivation he experimented to see which objects were now sufficient to elicit the courtship dance of the male. A few days after the disappearance of the female of his own species, the male was ready to court a white dove which he had previously ignored. A few days later he was bowing and cooing to a stuffed pigeon, later still to a rolled-up cloth, and finally after weeks of solitary confinement, he directed the courtship towards the empty corner of his box-cage where the convergence of the straight sides offered at least an optical fixation point. Physiologically speaking, these observations mean that after a longer passivity of an instinctive behaviour pattern, in this case courtship, the threshold value of its eliciting stimuli sinks. This is a widely spread and regular occurrence; Goethe expresses analogous laws in the words of Mephisto, "*Du siehst mit diesem Trank im Leibe bald Helena in jedem Weibe*,"* and – if you are a ring dove – you do so even in an old duster or in the empty corner of your cage.

In exceptional cases, the threshold-lowering of eliciting stimuli can be said to sink to zero, since under certain conditions the particular instinct movement can "explode" without demonstrable external stimuli. A hand-reared starling that I owned many years ago had never in its life caught flies nor seen any other bird do so. All his life he had taken his food from a dish, filled daily. One day I saw him sitting on the head of a bronze statue in my parents' Viennese flat,

* "With this potion inside you, you will soon see a Helen of Troy in every woman."

and behaving most remarkably. With his head on one side, he seemed to be examining the white ceiling, then his head and eye movements gave unmistakable signs that he was following moving objects. Finally he flew off the statue and up to the ceiling, snapped at something invisible to me, returned to his post and performed the prey-killing movements peculiar to all insect-eating birds. Then he swallowed, shook himself, as many birds do at the moment of inner relaxation and settled down quietly. Dozens of times I climbed on a chair, and even carried a step-ladder into the room – Viennese houses of that period have very high ceilings – to look for the prey that my starling had snatched: but not even the tiniest insect was there.

However, this increase of the readiness to react is far from being the only effect of the "damming" of an instinctive activity. If the stimuli normally releasing it fail to appear for an appreciable period, the organism as a whole is thrown into a state of general unrest and begins to search actively for the missing stimulus. In the simplest cases, this "search" consists only in an increase of random locomotion, in swimming or running round; in the most complicated, it may include the highest achievements of learning and insight. Wallace Craig called this type of purposive searching "appetitive behaviour". He also pointed out that literally every instinctive motor pattern, even the simplest locomotor coordination, gives rise to its own, autonomous appetite whenever adequate stimulation is withheld.

There are few instinctive behaviour patterns in which threshold-lowering and appetitive behaviour are so strongly marked as they are, unfortunately, in intra-specific aggression. Threshold-lowering occurs in the butterfly-fish which, in the absence of a fellow-member of its own species, chooses, as substitute, a member of the nearest related one. It also occurs in the blue trigger fish, which not only attacks the nearest related trigger-fish but also unrelated fish with only one eliciting factor in common with those of its own species, namely its blue colouring. In aquarium cichlids, to whose extraordinarily interesting family life we must give our further attention, a damming of the aggression which under natural conditions would be vented on hostile territorial neighbours, can very easily lead to killing of the mate. Nearly every aquarium keeper who has owned these fish has made the following almost inevitable mistake: a number of young fish of the same species are reared in a large aquarium to give them the chance of pairing in the most natural way. When this takes place, the aquarium suddenly becomes too small for the many adult fish. It contains one gloriously coloured couple, happily united, and set upon driving out all the others. Since these unfortunates cannot escape, they swim round nervously in the corners near the surface, their fins tattered, or, having been frightened out of their hiding-places, they race wildly round the aquarium. The humane aquarium keeper, pitying not only the hunted fish but also the couple which, having perhaps spawned in the meanwhile, is anxious about its brood, removes the fugitives and leaves the couple in sole possession of the tank. Thinking he has done his duty, he ceases to worry about the aquarium and its contents for the time being, but after a few days he sees, to his horror, that the female is floating dead on the surface, torn to ribbons, while there is nothing more to be seen of the eggs and the young.

This sad event, which takes place with predictable regularity, particularly in East Indian yellow cichlids, and in Brazilian mother-of-pearl fish, can be obviated either by leaving in the aquarium a "scapegoat", that is a fish of the same species, or by the more humane method of using a container big enough for two pairs and dividing it in half with a glass partition, putting a pair on each side. Then each fish can discharge its healthy anger on the neighbour of the same sex – it is nearly always male against male and female against female – and neither of them thinks of attacking its own mate. It may sound funny, but we were often made aware of a blurring of the partition, because of a growth of weed, by the fact that a cichlid male starting to be rude to his wife. As soon as the partition separating the "apartments" was cleaned, there was at once a furious but inevitably harmless clash with the neighbours and the atmosphere was cleared inside each of the two compartments.

Analogous behaviour can be observed in human beings. In the good old days when there was still a Habsburg monarchy and there were still domestic servants, I used to observe the following, regularly predictable behaviour in my widowed aunt. She never kept a maid longer than eight to ten months. She was always delighted with a new servant, praised her to the skies, and swore that she had at last found the right one. In the course of the next few months her judgment cooled, she found small faults, then bigger ones, and towards the end of the stated period she discovered hateful qualities in the poor girl who was finally discharged without a reference, after a violent quarrel. After this explosion the old lady was once more prepared to find a perfect angel in her next employee.

It is not my intention to poke fun at my long-deceased and devoted aunt. I was once able, or rather obliged, to observe exactly the same phenomenon in serious, self-controlled men, myself included, when I was a prisoner of war. So-called Polar disease, also known as Expedition Choler, attacks small groups of men who are completely dependent on one another and are thus prevented from quarrelling with strangers or people outside their own circle of friends. From this it will be clear that the damming up of aggression will be more dangerous, the better the members of the group know, understand and like each other. In such a situation, as I know from personal experience, all aggression and intra-specific fight behaviour undergo an extreme lowering of their threshold values. Subjectively this is expressed by the fact that one reacts to the small mannerisms of one's best friends – such as the way in which they clear their throats or sneeze – in a way that would normally be adequate only if one had been hit by a drunkard.

Insight into the laws of this torturing phenomenon prevents homicide but does not allay the torment. The man of perception finds an outlet by creeping out of the barracks (tent, igloo) and smashing a not too expensive object with as resounding a crash as the occasion merits. This helps a little, and is called, in the language of behaviour physiology, a redirected activity (Tinbergen). This expedient is often resorted to in nature to prevent the injurious effects of aggression. But the human being without insight has been known to kill his friend.

# 29  The nature of aggression
## by Robert A Hinde

Understanding a society requires knowledge both of how individuals interact with each other to produce it, and also of how the society influences the nature of the individuals developing within it. These are matters on which biologists and comparative psychologists both have something to say. Unfortunately the very diversity of animals and their societies creates a difficulty. It is too easy to select examples from subhuman species to support any particular view of human society: if you put your blind eye to the microscope you can use ant societies to support democracy, totalitarianism, capitalism, communism or any other system you like. Furthermore, it is easy for the sociologist, the respectability of whose discipline has perhaps not yet gained general acceptance, to forget that biology, and indeed all worthwhile sciences, also still have their problems: not all data are secure, not all interpretations universally accepted.

These dangers are nowhere more marked than in the study of man's aggressiveness; much light can be thrown on it from studies of lower species if – but only if – they are used with humility and discipline. In his recent book, *On Aggression*, Konrad Lorenz – whose familiarity with the behaviour of animals under natural conditions is surpassed by few – used his knowledge of animals to draw conclusions about aggression in man, and to suggest how it can be controlled.

Since his thesis implies acceptance that man's aggressive tendency is virtually unmodifiable, neglects the possibility of improvement in our methods of child rearing, and advocates the already popular occupations of sport, art and science as a solution, it has found a wide audience. Is it well substantiated?

Lorenz's main line of argument is as follows. First, he rejects any equation between aggression and the "non-biological" Freudian death wish. Aggression, he says, is a product of natural selection, bringing increased chances of survival or successful reproduction under natural conditions. The advantage of aggression may lie in the dispersal

*This article first appeared in* New Society, *the weekly review of the social sciences, 128 Long Acre, London W.C.2.*

of individuals so that the available resources are used in the best way possible, or in ensuring that it is the fittest individuals which breed. Fighting may also be useful if it promotes a stable "pecking order" (or social ranking system), and this in its turn may lead to the older and wiser individuals in a group becoming its leaders. The aggression that Lorenz chiefly writes about is "intra-specific" – *i.e.*, it occurs *within* a particular animal species, not between this species and another.

Lorenz argues that aggression, like other "instinctive" patterns of behaviour, is spontaneous. In other words his theory of motivation, like the Freudian one, ascribes the occurrence of behaviour to the building up of an internal drive or drives which must somehow find expression.

If aggressiveness is of adaptive advantage in some contexts, it is disadvantageous in others. The establishment of a territory and aggressiveness directed towards rivals may increase a male's chances of successful breeding, but aggressiveness towards his own mate would decrease them. Devices have therefore been evolved to reduce inappropriate intra-specific aggression. The aggression aroused by a sex partner may be redirected on to a rival male, or inhibited by a submissive posture adopted by the mate. Postures which serve to reduce or deflect aggression in such contexts may, in Lorenz's view, come to be ends in their own right, rituals to be performed for their own sake. In some species they have given rise to complex ritual ceremonies which not only reduce aggression but also enhance personal ties between individuals.

Indeed Lorenz points out that personal ties occur *only* in species which show intra-specific aggression. In many gregarious species, such as shoaling fish and swarming insects, individuals lack aggressiveness towards each other, and also show no particular attachments. Since, in some species, individual bonds seem to arise from the performance of a movement or ceremony whose primitive function was to reduce aggression, Lorenz implies that aggressiveness lies at the basis of personal love.

Man, like most other animals, has evolved a drive

towards intra-specific aggression. But since he lacks formidable natural weapons, Lorenz thinks, he has never evolved effective mechanisms for reducing or diverting inappropriate aggressiveness. Almost overnight he has invented the axe, the arrow and the atom bomb, with no time for natural selection to produce mechanisms similar to those which prevent harmful intra-specific aggression in those lower species which are equipped with claws, canines or other powerful weapons. And he lives in a society which provides little opportunity for the useful or harmless display of his natural aggressiveness.

Here then, in Lorenz's view, lies the problem. Man's spontaneous aggressive drive, evolved through natural selection and originally valuable for survival or reproduction has suddenly become dangerous. What can be done? Before one can consider the solutions which Lorenz offers, one must ask what support his formulation would gain among biologists.

I don't want to become enmeshed in parochial arguments. Many biologists would require Lorenz to state more precisely what he means by aggression. Often he seems to slide from the narrow biological meaning of aggressiveness, indicating patterns of behaviour associated with attack or a readiness to attack another individual, to a broader, perhaps more psychiatric, meaning which includes competitiveness and self-assertiveness. Biologists would also query his happy leaps from fish to man, and many would certainly wonder at the discrepancies between the authorities cited and the bibliography. But these are perhaps minor matters in the present context, more than outweighed by the vividness of his descriptions and the wealth of his observations. There are, however, other crucial points in Lorenz's exposition on which biological opinion would be at least divided. Since Lorenz claims that his facts are verified, and makes many generalisations with a voice of authority, while ignoring the bulk of the experimental literature on his subject, it is as well to reflect on them.

Man's aggression must indeed have a biological basis, and have evolved earlier in his history through natural selection. Furthermore, in intra-specific fighting man, like other species, uses a repertoire of fairly stereotyped expressive movements. Some of these convey threat, others appease: their significance is understood by other individuals. Comparative evidence suggests that the smile evolved as an appeasement movement, but it can perhaps now usefully be described as an end in its own right. Thus at least one of the expressions used in interpersonal relations probably originated in an aggressive context. On such issues the evidence supports Lorenz's account.

But the pivot of Lorenz's argument is his insistence on the *spontaneity* of aggression. Man's problem, he says, arises in part because his aggressiveness wells up in a world where it has no proper outlet. Now spontaneity is a difficult enough concept in any context, but it usually refers to a change in the output of a system without a corresponding change in input. Lorenz uses it in approximately this kind of way, referring to the occurrence of behaviour in the absence of the stimulus situations normally eliciting it. He implicitly associates with this another property – namely that if a certain type of behaviour is not expressed, the underlying drive can or must find expression by activating another type of behaviour.

This implication is a consequence of Lorenz's energy model of motivation. Now, while models of this kind have been of some value in certain contexts (notably, perhaps, to psychoanalysts), they are not accepted by the majority of students of behaviour. This is in part because behavioural energy is so often covertly confused with physical energy: this leads to false explanations. Perhaps more important is that energy models imply that behaviour comes to an end because energy is discharged in action, instead of through the change which it produces in the stimulus situation. Although the use of an energy model is crucial to his thesis. Lorenz does not even attempt to answer the numerous criticisms of such models which have been made during the last two decades, and seems unaware of the dangers which they have for the theoretician.

His own arguments for the spontaneity of aggression do not bear examination. In the first place, many of his examples refer to other types of behaviour. Generalisations about mechanisms which cut across different types of behaviour, let alone across different species, can be at best superficial. Prey-catching, courtship and intra-specific aggression are organised in different ways. This is particularly so in the extent to which they exhibit spontaneity. Lorenz himself argues in another context that each type of behaviour shows spontaneity to a degree which is adaptive in the circumstances in which that type of behaviour is used. So spontaneity of aggression cannot be established by observing other types of behaviour.

A second type of evidence Lorenz gives for spontaneity concerns animals which, in the absence of members of their own species, attack members of another. Yet, as Lorenz himself points out, the animals attacked are those which most resemble the attacker's own species. This aggression could be a response to characteristics shared by the attacked animal and the attacker's own species. Again, Lorenz cites the males of certain Cichlid fish which, in the absence of rival males, attack and kill their own mates. But this is no evidence for the spontaneity of aggression. Lorenz shows elsewhere that the female fish arouses aggressive behaviour which is normally redirected on to another male. In the absence of another male it is hardly surprising that the female is attacked.

Apart from a trivial anecdote about one of his relatives, and some observations on the Ute Indians, which are open to a variety of interpretations, this is almost the whole of Lorenz's evidence for "the spontaneity of aggression".

Lorenz acknowledges that "many sociologists and psychologists maintain" that aggression is primarily a *response* to external factors, but he cites none of the evidence they have produced. He almost totally neglects the long history of support which this view has had among psychologists. He cites Wallace Craig on the courtship of doves as evidence for the spontaneity of instinctive behaviour in general, but he doesn't mention that Craig thought aggression was an "aversion" rather than an "appetite", and that he said animals fight only to get rid of a rival's presence or interference.

Lorenz similarly neglects the view that aggression comes from a frustration of ongoing activity. Yet this can certainly account for a large proportion of human aggressiveness — precisely how much depends on how frustration is defined. There are certainly also cases in which aggression relates primarily to something other than destruction of the object at which it is directed. It aims at winning a parent's attention or a leader's approval. Another case which cannot easily be ascribed to frustration (defined narrowly) is aggression elicited by the approach of another individual, as when a stranger intrudes into a group. This category is the chief cause of aggression in sub-primates.

Whether fighting is due to frustration or to the proximity of another individual it derives principally from the situation, and there is no need to postulate causes that are purely internal to the aggressor. Cases in which animals seem to seek fights are much rarer than Lorenz suggests, and they are mostly related to previous fighting experience in the same situation. If a thesis is to be hung on the spontaneity of aggression, this contrary view, expressed in nearly every textbook of comparative psychology, and held by the great majority of students of animal behaviour, should at least be considered.

The emphasis on the spontaneity of aggression, basic to Lorenz's thesis, thus has little support. Even if spontaneous aggressiveness does occur, there is no evidence that it is *important* in any subhuman species. Nor is there any evidence that, if an animal lacks situations that elicit its "spontaneous" aggression, its aggressiveness must find outlet.

Yet aggression certainly occurs, and we must all share Lorenz's concern. How can we avoid the harmful consequences of man's aggressiveness? The exercise of "moral responsibility" seems by itself to be inadequate. "Cultural traditions" seem to be failing or in a process of metamorphosis.

The first step is to know ourselves, to recognize in advance the situations in which destructively aggressive behaviour is likely to occur, and to avoid them. Lorenz emphasizes the probability of "militant enthusiasm" when a social group, inspired by a leader, feels itself to be threatened by a danger from outside — a situation which certainly can, but need not, be dangerous.

Lorenz stresses especially the avoidance of situations which he sees as facilitating the outlet of aggressive energies through undesirable channels. Those who ascribe aggression to frustration would feel that it is the frustration which must be reduced. Frustration is part of living and starts with the mother's breast, but excessive frustration can be avoided.

Another possible solution is genetic. Perhaps, in the course of generations, selective breeding could reduce man's aggressiveness. Lorenz rejects this because he believes that loss of aggressiveness would bring with it also the loss of its socially desirable consequences. Some of his arguments here are invalid. For instance, the argument that aggressiveness is valuable because it leads to the formation of a dominance hierarchy, which in turn provides a stable social system, loses its force if the value of the stable society is to mitigate the consequences of aggression.

Lorenz thinks that aggression is an essential component of personal friendship. He bases this largely on the observation that species which form bonds between individuals all show intra-specific aggressiveness, and that in many species rituals which play a role in personal bonds have evolved from aggressive movements. This is a non-sequitur. Lorenz also asserts that, without aggressiveness, nearly everything that man does would lose its impetus: "Everything associated with ambition, ranking order and countless other equally indispensable behaviour patterns would probably also disappear from human life." No evidence is cited for this view, and one is left wondering if it depends on the extension of "aggressiveness" to include "self-assertiveness" and similar qualities. These are distinct characteristics, and psychologists are only just developing tools for studying the causal relationships between them. Furthermore, Lorenz himself argues that traits originally dependent on aggressiveness may become causally independent in the course of evolution. This suggests that if genetic selection could produce a race of man less prone to behave aggressively, he would not necessarily also be less prone to smile.

Yet one must agree with Lorenz that different traits do interact, that as yet we know very little of how they do so, and that the consequences of breeding out aggression are unpredictable. It would be a long business and is hardly an answer to current problems.

Lorenz places much hope on the redirection of the aggressive drive on to suitable objects, or its sublimation into socially useful channels. Now if redirection is potentially useful in this way, then Lorenz should surely pay some attention to the theoretical and experimental work which has been done on the factors determining the object on to which thwarted aggression is directed. However, if aggression does not force an outlet for itself when denied its usual expression – then redirection is merely the elicitation, by one object, of aggression initially aroused by another, and loses much of its promise as a solution. Like Lorenz, I too have been impelled to kick tins when angry, but I am not convinced that this effectively lowered my aggressiveness.

Indeed, it could be argued that kicking tins is pleasurable and reinforcing, and that it thus renders aggressiveness more probable on the next occasion that similar circumstances arise. Certainly responses which lead to an animal being confronted by stimuli for aggression are likely to be repeated.

Lorenz regards sport and other competitive activities as valuable in providing a "cathartic discharge of the aggressive urge", and sporting contests as providing an "outlet for the collective militant enthusiasm of nations". He gives no evidence in support of this. The only two studies cited in a recent review by L. Berkowitz produced ambiguous results, and certainly did not support Lorenz. Games may also arouse aggressiveness, and we still know little about the factors that determine which process predominates. Perhaps the arousing effect is more likely to predominate in spectators than players. Certainly the riots associated with football matches would suggest this is so.

Lorenz follows Freud in emphasizing the role of sublimation in a loose sense but offers no proof of its efficacy. What precisely *is* the evidence? His suggestion that common goals in art or science may reduce the probability of aggression towards a rival may be true, but this does not mean that these activities can be used to discharge aggression once it is aroused. Operationally, sublimation implies that activity A renders activity B (in this case, aggression) less likely both during the performance of A and in the succeeding period. But this does not prove that A is driven by, and uses up, "motivation" which might otherwise have led to B. Other explanations are possible. One is that the subject learns to show A in the circumstances which would initially have led to B. Lorenz does not even consider such a possibility, yet it deflects attention from the situations in which aggression is aroused, and on to earlier experience.

It is indeed in the scant attention which he gives to the role of experience that the weakness of Lorenz's prescription lies. For example, he neglects, with little more than a sneer at permissive methods of education, how far the characteristics of individuals can be modified by experience. But many studies of subhuman species indicate that individual experience *can* influence aggressiveness. The social conditions of rearing are known to influence the probability of aggression in intra-species encounters in mice, cats, dogs, monkeys and other animals. The previous experience of success or failure in combative encounters can influence aggressiveness in subsequent ones. Experience of starvation can apparently influence subsequent aggressiveness over food in chaffinches and probably other species.

In man, also, evidence that aggressiveness is influenced by experience is based on numerous detailed studies. Many of these studies are difficult to interpret. We know little enough about how experience produces its effects. We are not yet in a position to specify conditions of rearing which minimize anti-social aggression. But at least we can help to reduce rewards for aggressiveness, such as social approbation, and be aware of the influence which certain types of leader or of mass entertainment may exert. It is surely through the control of individual experience that man's aggressiveness can be tamed.

Therefore, while acknowledging that man, like most higher animals, has a potentiality for aggression, let us not accept the inevitability of its full expression, pinning all our hopes on redirection in situations which may in fact be arousing aggressiveness, or on sublimation. The solution lies rather in an endeavour to understand the roots of behaviour to tease out the aspects of experience which influence aggressiveness and to assess the nature of their effects. We must not be dismayed if some of the attempts which have so far been made to reduce human aggressiveness through early experience now seem bungling and naïve. Let us not merely plan a society to cope with man at his worst, but remember that society can influence the nature of its ingredients.

# Section VI
# Models, machines and minds

In this final section we can begin to look up from the hard-won facts of the laboratory bench or the observation room and consider something of the wider significance of the results of contemporary research. After all, one does not study the brain mainly because it is an interesting piece of tissue in its own right, but because it is the seat of consciousness, the organ of the mind. Before we can ask the relationships between brains and minds, though, we should ask perhaps an easier question: what is the relationship between brains and machines, or models? Could one build, for example, a brain-like computer? It is this relationship which is reviewed by L. D. Harmon and E. R. Lewis, and it has, of course, implications which take us beyond the realm of this book.

The remaining articles in this section are chosen to show the brain scientist at speculation rather than research, examining the relationships between brains and minds. This is an area where the scientist may come into conflict with the professional philosopher, whose chosen domain it is. Is there really a "mind and brain" problem, or is it nothing but a semantic confusion? Philosophers may find the writing of scientists in this area naïve: often they wander blithely across a minefield of ill-perceived logical doubts and paradoxes. Often, too, their "objective" science goes out of the window, while the open assertion of ideological positions, buttressed with selected facts and analyses, enters at the front door; but then, most of "objective" science has its roots in particular ideological viewpoints, and in this vexed region of profound general interest, we may expect to see them coming to the fore.

In choosing the articles for this section, we could indeed have gone back to Descartes who first (in modern times) formulated the mind–body dualism which we would say has obscured analysis for the past 300 years. Nineteenth-century speculations on the role of magnetism and electricity in consciousness, the vigorous agnosticism of biologists such as T. H. Huxley and the resonating phrase "the ghost in the machine", could all have followed. But that would have made another book. We have begun our selection with the heady prose of that most elegant of neuro-physiologists, Charles Sherrington, speculating as Man, on his nature. Sherrington's physiology led in the direct lineage of the Cambridge School, to that of E. D. Adrian, whose writings here are taken from a symposium on brain and conscious experience organized, perhaps surprisingly, by the Vatican. And it is undoubtedly his declared religious position which is reflected too, in Donald MacKay's restatement of human free will, "the bankruptcy of determinism", although the special sense in which he defines his terms makes it possible for those of very different philosophical and ideological outlook to accept his thesis. The final selection, from "a philosopher's symposium", provides the perspective of three philosophers: H. Samuel, A. J. Ayer and Gilbert Ryle, originally from a series of broadcast talks.

No one, however, would suggest that this debate was yet concluded.

# 30 A brief history of neural modelling

## by L D Harmon and E R Lewis

The earliest models of nervous systems arose from considerations of neuromuscular action. The fact that nerves activate muscles was known as long ago as the Ptolemaic period, but only in the past hundred years has man begun to resolve two mysteries inherent in this knowledge: how does nerve conduct, and how does muscle contract? For many centuries these two questions were dealt with as one, so that an early nerve model was usually one-half of a nerve-muscle model.

At least from the time of the pre-Galenic physician, Erasistratus, until well after the time of Glisson in the seventeenth century, the contraction of muscle was thought to be a result of swelling or increase in muscle volume. The commonly viewed picture was that of a long, inflatable tube whose ends came closer together as the tube was pumped up. The postulated role of nerve was to induce this swelling. The theory of nervous conduction, therefore, held that a liquid or gas flowed through pipe-like nerves to inflate the muscles, a concept that probably culminated with Descartes's theories in the seventeenth century.

Descartes[1] compared the nerves of animals with the water pipes in the hydraulic machines and automata of his time. This comparison was not simply metaphorical; Descartes considered these machines to be good models of conduction in nerve. In fact, he used these machines to demonstrate the plausibility of his theories of nervous conduction and muscular contraction. Among these theories, by the way, are some of the earliest discussions of involuntary reflexes and reciprocal innervation of muscle.

Cartesian philosophy viewed life as mechanistic. To Descartes all lower animals were automatons, and their every action could be explained in terms of the laws of nature.[2] Of all the animals only man had a rational element, the soul, and it was located in the pineal gland. The human body, like the animal body, was a machine; however, since it was partially controlled by the rational soul, "*l'âme raisonnable*", it was not an automaton.

According to Descartes, "The animal spirits resemble a very subtle fluid, or rather a very pure and lively flame".[3] These spirits were continuously generated in the heart and ascended to cavities of the brain, which served as a reservoir. (This naïve notion was an inheritance from Galen 1 400 years earlier, but still was a notable advance over Aristotle's view that the function of the brain is to cool the blood.) From the brain the spirits passed through the hollow nerves to the muscles, causing contraction or relaxation depending on their quantity. The flow of animal spirits in a nerve was controlled by valves located at each junction. The valves were either under the direct control of the pineal gland or indirectly controlled by it through flow and pressure differences in different nerves. When the muscles were filled with animal spirits they swelled in the middle and the ends contracted; when emptied they relaxed.

As an example of Descartes's schemes, consider figure 30.1, which is his representation of two reciprocally innervated, antagonistic muscles of the eye.[4] Animal spirits flow through hollow nerves into the muscles $D$ and $E$. There is a one-way valve at the base of each muscle. Valve $g$ (at the bottom of muscle $E$) regulates flow from $D$ to $E$, and valve $f$

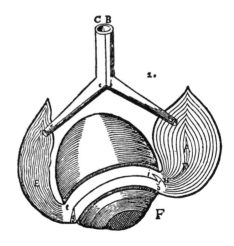

**Figure 30.1 A model** of reciprocal innervation of two muscles of the human eye. For details *see text*. (From Descartes.[4])

*first published in* Physiological Reviews, *1966, Vol. 46 (3), pages 519–530.*

(at the bottom of muscle $D$) regulates flow from $E$ to $D$. If the flow in both nerves were equal, both muscles would be equally tense. In the figure, however, the flow in the right branch is assumed to be greater than that in the left; this has two effects. It causes muscle $D$ to become inflated, and it causes valve $f$ to open and valve $g$ to close. With this valve arrangement: the spirits flowing through $g$ are not held in muscle $E$ but flow on into muscle $D$. Muscle $E$ thus relaxes as $D$ contracts. Valves $f$ and $g$ are controlled by pressure differential. After the eye motion has been completed, other valves (not shown) are adjusted to equalize the forces in the two branches. Valves $f$ and $g$ will then both be half open, and the pressures in muscles $D$ and $E$ will equalize. The animal spirits do not flow centripetally through the nerves, but are eventually lost through pores in the muscles.

Descartes questioned whether or not a subtle fluid flowing through small tubes could be responsible for the rapid, powerful, coordinated actions typical of animals. He relied on previously existing hydraulic automata as models of his system to settle this issue. These machines had been contrived by engineers to do such things as playing musical instruments, pronouncing words or moving in a human- or animal-like way; they were actuated by water flowing through small tubes controlled by systems of valves. Descartes compared the tubes of these machines with nerves, the hydraulic engines and springs with muscles, the water sources or fountains with the heart and the central reservoirs with the cavities of the brain.

The mechanistic views of Descartes influenced many seventeenth-century scientists. Among these was Borelli, who was not only a staunch mechanist but was also a champion of the theory that muscles contract by swelling. Borelli[5] proposed a number of mechanical models of muscle, most of which were based on the rhombohedron. If the edges of a rhombohedron are fixed in length, the distance between opposite vertices will decrease over a considerable range of increasing volume. He used this analogy to show the consistency between swelling and contraction and to calculate the forces necessary for muscle contraction under load.

In the last half of the seventeenth century at least three physiologists, Glisson, Lower and Swammerdam, independently demonstrated that muscle volume did not increase during contractions. In spite of these results the so-called "Balloon Theory" persisted into the eighteenth century. Analogies were still drawn between the heart as a pump for blood and the brain as a pump for nervous spirits.[6] Glisson, on the other hand, had postulated that muscle contracted as a result of intrinsic irritability, a concept that was finally made popular by Haller in the eighteenth century. A muscle was no longer considered simply a passive device waiting to be inflated or swollen by some action of nervous fluid; it was now thought to contain all the components necessary for contraction, needing only a stimulus to set it off.

A new question arose: how could nerves transmit the stimulus to the muscle with the apparently great velocities such as those observed in reflex action? Haller himself proposed several interesting possibilities. One of these was in the form of an analogy; one might call it the croquet model of nerve. Suppose nerve were constructed of a long row of spheres – each in contact with both of its neighbors. If one were to rap the first sphere sharply, the last one would fly off almost instantaneously and would stimulate the muscle, inducing contraction.[7]

Another view was quite prevalent in the eighteenth century. In two very short paragraphs (Queries 23 and 24, included in the second edition of *Opticks*) Newton[8] postulated that nerves were solid but transparent and that excitation was propagated as optical vibrations through them, exactly as he supposed light was propagated in the "æther". In this, as in most matters, Newton's influence was very strong, and these postulates dominated early eighteenth-century concepts of nervous transmission.

Towards the end of the eighteenth century, however, the concept of "Animal Electricity" began to emerge. Even before Galvani published the results of his frog experiments, electricity was accepted as the cause of discomfort when one touched fish such as *Torpedo* or *Electrophorus*. In 1776 Cavendish[9] published *An account of some attempts to imitate the effects of the* Torpedo *by electricity*. This contains a description of what must certainly rank as one of the earliest devices actually constructed and tested as a physiological model. Cavendish built an electric model of the ray, *Torpedo*, and with that model he was able to convince a previously skeptical scientific community that the shock of the ray could indeed be caused by electricity.

The ability of *Torpedo* to produce a shock had been known from very early times.[10] Aristotle, for example, wrote about this phenomenon. Redi and Lorenzini investigated the ray and published accounts of the investigation in 1675 and 1678. Lorenzini postulated that the shock was due to corpuscles or "effluvia" that entered the hand when it touched the ray. Réaumer proposed in 1714 that the shock was due to the sharp contraction of the ray's muscles, which he supposed produced a sharp mechanical blow on the person touching the fish; a similar theory had been proposed earlier by Borelli.

By 1772 several scientists had independently proposed that the shocks of the ray were due to electricity, and Walsh tested the new hypothesis.[10] He determined that the shock was conducted only through electrical conductors. He also found that the shock was diminished as the number of circuits through which it passed was increased. Unfortunately, he could observe no spark across gaps introduced in the circuit and no electrostatic attraction or repulsion, even with the most sensitive electrometers of the day. Many scientists were ready to accept the theory that the shock was the result of electricity, but these two negative results left them in doubt. Another disturbing point was the fact that *Torpedo* could deliver shocks in salt water, a known conductor, and that these shocks were not significantly increased when the fish was in air.

While Walsh continued his attempts to obtain a spark from the discharge of the real *Torpedo*, Cavendish[9] began a series of experiments with artificial torpedoes. First by reasoning and then by means of these experiments, Cavendish satisfied himself and the scientific community that there was "nothing in the phenomena of the *Torpedo* at all incompatible with electricity". His first model ray, shown in figure 30.2, consisted of laminated wood in the shape of a *Torpedo* with a long handle. Pewter plates were attached to the top and bottom of the model, and insulated wires led from these plates to the end of the handle. The entire model was covered with sheepskin and was soaked for several days in salt water to increase the conductance of the wood.

Cavendish submerged the artificial torpedo in a trough of salt water and then placed one hand over each pewter plate while an assistant touched the wires to a battery of charged Leyden jars. He repeated this experiment, varying the charges on the individual jars as well as the total number of series- and parallel-connected jars in the battery. He found that he received a greater shock from a large number of weakly charged jars (low voltage, high capacitance) than from a small number of strongly charged jars (high voltage, low capacitance). If he used enough jars, the shock was equivalent to that of *Torpedo* even when the "force of the current" (*i.e.*, voltage) was not enough to jump even the

smallest gap in the circuit. In addition, the discharge was completed so rapidly that even the most sensitive electrometers of the day were not deflected. Thus the first two objections to Walsh's results were answered.

The third objection proved more difficult. With the jars charged so that the shock of the artificial ray in salt water was equivalent to that of the real ray, the shock in air was much too great. Reasoning that the conductance of water-soaked leather would be greater than that of water-soaked wood and, in fact, closer to the conductance of *Torpedo*, Cavendish constructed another model made of laminated leather. The Leyden jars now required more charge to produce a shock equivalent to that of the wooden model, but the shock in air was no longer greatly dissimilar to that in water. Thus, with the aid of his model, Cavendish answered all of the major objections to the hypothesis of electricity in *Torpedo* and *Electrophorus*.[11]

Fifteen years later, in 1791, Galvani[12] published the results of two experiments: the first showed that electricity could induce contraction in muscle, and the second purportedly demonstrated the presence of electricity in muscle. A third experiment (published anonymously in 1794) is now thought to have definitely proved the existence of electricity in muscle.[13]

All three experiments were discredited, however, by Volta, who attributed the results of the second and third experiments to electricity generated by contacts between dissimilar metals and dissimilar tissues, respectively. Both Volta and Galvani discussed analogies between living tissues and electric devices. Galvani compared muscle to a Leyden jar, or capacitor, which was discharged by nerve, causing contraction. Volta, who denied the presence of electricity in muscle, compared his Voltaic cell with the electric organs of fish. The controversy between Volta and Galvani left the scientific world in a state of confusion; it remained for Du Bois-Reymond to settle the issue once and for all.

Between 1840 and 1850, Du Bois-Reymond[14,15] constructed a pair of very sensitive galvanometers. With them he was able to measure electric currents associated with both nerve and muscle activity. He performed experiments not only with living nerve and muscle, but also with electrochemical analogs of both.

Du Bois-Reymond used these models to extend his thinking and to test his own hypotheses on animal electricity. He used electrochemical analogs, in fact, to develop his "peripolar molecular" theory, which is said to be the forerunner of ionic hypotheses.[6] The analogs themselves were the predecessors of a long series of electrochemical neural models, many of which are still in use today.

Du Bois-Reymond observed what he called the

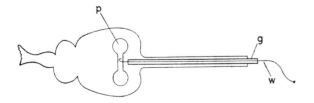

**Figure 30.2 A model** of the electric ray (*Torpedo*). The body was made of wood or leather, with electrodes (*p*) mounted on both sides, each connected to a wire (*w*) that passed through a glass tube (*g*) on the handle. (After Cavendish[9].)

"electrical antagonism between the longitudinal and the transverse sections of muscle", the former being positive with respect to the latter. In reality what he saw was an injury current, but he interpreted his results to mean that an intact muscle has a gross resting potential between its belly (longitudinal section) and its tendons (transverse section). With more refined measurements he found that there were potential differences even within a given section. He attempted to model this potential distribution with a solid copper cylinder, with the cylindrical surface coated with zinc and the ends left bare. The ends represented the transverse section of a muscle and the cylindrical surface represented the longitudinal section. If he applied one end of a wet electrolytic conductor to the zinc and the other end to the copper, a current flowed between the zinc and the copper.

In this configuration, however, the model provided no potential gradations over either the zinc surface or the copper. The cylinder was subsequently submerged in spring water, causing steady currents to flow from zinc to copper. The maximum negativity occurred on the cylinder axis, and the potential was graded from that point to the point of maximum positivity on the cylindrical surface. Du Bois-Reymond measured the currents flowing about this cylinder and found them spatially arranged in a manner similar to the currents in whole muscles.

A flaw still existed in this model. In real muscle the "electric antagonism" existed even in the smallest dissected parts. Thus, if the muscle were cut apart, the smallest obtainable pieces still exhibited a transverse section that was negative to the longitudinal section. This would obviously not be true in the cylinder model. If it were cut in half, parallel to the cylindrical axis, a portion of the zinc surface would be cut away, and part of the longitudinal section would be negative.

Next, Du Bois-Reymond [14,16] proposed a "peripolar molecular" model. In order that every transverse section should always be negative with respect to every longitudinal section (no matter how finely divided the muscle), he assumed that the interior of the muscle was composed of polarized molecules. These "peripolar" molecules, he assumed, were negative at both ends and positive in the center, the negative ends pointing toward the ends of the muscle.

This hypothesis was tested with other zinc-and-copper models. The new models consisted of up to 72 small, hollow, copper cylinders with zinc strips soldered to their sides (figure 30.3 shows a 48-cylinder version). The inside of each cylinder was insulated with varnish. All the cylinders were evenly spaced in a box with the zinc strips oriented in the same direction. The box was filled with an electrolytic

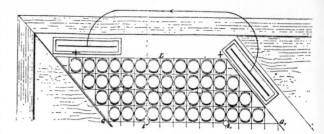

**Figure 30.3 An electrochemical model** designed to test the peripolar molecular theory, consisting of 48 short cylinders (seen on end) with zinc strips mounted on two sides. The entire array was submerged in spring water. (From Du Bois-Reymond.[16])

solution, and the resulting currents were measured with platinum electrodes.

Du Bois-Reymond was satisfied that these measurements justified his "peripolar molecular" hypothesis. A further justification was found in what he called the "negative variation". During a tetanizing stimulus, the muscle current diminished; the "electric antagonism" had vanished. Du Bois-Reymond felt that this could be adequately explained only in terms of very small polar centers that could rapidly be reoriented.

Electrotonic spread was a mystery at first to the mid-nineteenth-century physiologists who observed it. They were unable to explain how a current applied between two points on a nerve could induce potential changes beyond the region bounded by the points. Du Bois-Reymond attempted to explain this phenomenon also in terms of his peripolar molecule. He supposed that each peripolar molecule might be made up of two dipoles with their poles together. Each molecule would thus be electrostatically neutral and there would be no net polarization of the nerve. He then assumed that an applied current would cause all the individual dipoles to align in its direction of flow, resulting in polarization of the nerve. He further assumed that the polarization between electrodes would induce alignment of dipoles in the regions beyond and thus result in electrotonic spread. This explanation was fairly well accepted until Matteucci discredited it by means of another electrochemical model, one of the first *Kernleiter*, or "core conductors".

Matteucci,[17] in 1863, decided to see if electrotonus was strictly a biological phenomenon. To determine whether or not it could be duplicated in nonliving electrochemical systems, he stretched a platinum wire with a cloth sheath in an electrolytic solution and applied a current between two points on the sheath. He then examined the regions beyond the points of current application and indeed found potentials in these regions. The molecular theory of Du Bois-Reymond had hinged on the presence of a pre-existing voltage in nerve – a concept that was then in doubt and later was completely discredited because of the confusion between injury potential and resting potential.[18] Matteucci had now shown that electrotonus was possible in a system having no pre-existing electromotive force (e.m.f.); Du Bois-Reymond's theory of electrotonus was superfluous. Matteucci[17,19] proposed a simpler explanation: electrotonus was due to the spread of electrolysis by diffusion. This explanation, however, was soon replaced by that of Hermann, who also relied on electrochemical models as analogs of nerve.

Hermann[20,21] greatly extended the experiments of Matteucci, working not only with cloth-sheathed wires but also with bare wires immersed in electrolytic solutions. He showed that the electrotonic spread in such models was a result of polarization of the wire surface.

In 1883, Hermann worked with a core model (platinum in zinc sulphate) 2 m long, stimulated at one end with repetitive current pulses. He found electrotonic currents that sometimes attained their maximum value only after the polarizing current was off. As in nerve there were two successive, unequal phases of current, the first being in the same direction as the polarizing current, the second opposite. He attributed the second phase to recovery from polarization.

Whereas Hermann was careful not to draw too strong an analogy between these phenomena and propagation in nerve, Boruttau[22] was not. He experimented with applied alternating current in very long core models of platinum or palladium wire in sodium chloride and found rapid transmission of the negative phase but not of the positive phase. Boruttau equated this with the propagating "negative variation" (spike) in nerve. Most physiologists did not accept this theory, however. Biedermann,[18] for example, put forth a very strong argument against it by pointing out that the propagated negative variation in real nerve followed mechanical and chemical stimuli as well as electrical stimuli, which was not the case with the wire.

In addition to Matteucci, Hermann and Boruttau, a number of physiologists were employing core models to aid in their understanding of the properties of nerve (cf. Taylor[23]). Some of the simplest of these models were devised by Hering.[24] He simply filled hollow grass stems or the exoskeletons of crayfish antennae with saline solution. These models exhibited electrotonic spread even without the central metallic conductor and its progressive polarization. This electrotonus was not analogous to that of nerve, however, in that the polarity gradients within the cylinder were not radially symmetrical, but rather changed sign across the axis of the cylinder.

Between 1900 and 1910, however, the membrane theory began to command the attention of physiologists (see Nernst[25]), and the popularity of core conductors began to wane. *Kernleiter* models were applicable to electrotonic spread, but the newly postulated mechanisms of action-potential propagation were much more exciting. One of the explanations was Bernstein's ionic hypothesis.[26] Along with it came a new electrochemical model, the iron-wire model.

Not long after Bernstein proposed the ionic hypothesis, Lillie[27] became a proponent and introduced into his arguments the first of a long series of discussions of electrochemical models. In 1915 he developed an analog of the injury potential, using a galvanized iron wire immersed in dilute sulfuric acid. When the zinc surface was intact, no chemical or electrical effect was seen. When the outer layer of zinc was removed at some point, a continuous current would flow from the iron to the zinc, and one could observe an "injury potential" that diminished with distance from the point of damage. Lillie drew an analogy between the zinc coat of the wire and the plasma membrane of the nerve fiber.

Lillie's first mention of the analogy between neural propagation and the spread of excitation over "passivated" (oxidized) iron appeared in 1916, although Ostwald had pointed it out in 1900, and Heathcote[28] had subsequently explored it in detail. If an iron wire is immersed in concentrated nitric acid, its surface is oxidized and becomes insensitive to further attack, even when the wire is transferred to dilute nitric acid. If part of the wire is artificially activated (e.g. if the oxide surface is broken by scratching) the activation spreads, and the wire eventually dissolves in the dilute acid. In nitric acid of the proper concentration, however, a local reaction accompanied by bubbles and a darkening of the metal surface propagates over the wire and is followed by complete recovery (return to passivation) of the wire surface. Immediately after repassivation the wire is resistant to activation, recovering its excitability gradually over a period of about 1 min. The passive wire can be activated (stimulated) mechanically, electrically or chemically. Subthreshold stimuli may be temporally summed to produce activation, but a slowly rising electrical stimulus is not nearly so effective as one suddenly applied. Lillie showed that in these and many other ways the iron wire behaves like the nerve fiber, and he concluded from this that the basic mechanisms of response were the same.

One of the strongest objections to Lillie's model came from Hill,[29] who felt that complete reduction of a passive oxide film was too drastic to be a direct analog of nerve transmission. Hill pointed out that the energy released per square centimeter of iron wire during propagation had to be orders of magnitude greater than the energy released during propagation in nerve. Hill did believe, though, that the iron wire was a good nerve model in many other respects and that much could be learned from it — providing its limitations were realized.

Despite the objections raised by Hill, by Rosenblueth, Wiener and others, there was very considerable continued development of Lillie's electrochemical analogs.

Electrochemical models represent only one of many classes of neural models to appear since the time of Du Bois-Reymond. Some of these models were pedagogical, used by their designers to clarify concepts for students or readers of papers. Pflüger[30] (cf. Ref. 18), Hill[31] and Franck[32] used complicated hydraulic models to illustrate their ideas about excitation. Later authors such as Rushton,[33,34] Katz,[35] Hodgkin and Huxley[36] and Grundfest[37] used electrical circuit analogs for this purpose. Rushton[33] also developed an interesting device that was essentially a mechanical neural analog.

Fabre[38] and Schmitt[39] constructed electronic models in the late 1930s to explore theories of excitation. (As part of his model, in fact, Schmitt invented the electronic circuit now commonly used for many applications and universally known as the "Schmitt Trigger".) These neuron models probably were the first to be made with electronic circuits, and they demonstrated a new kind of flexibility and simplicity in model making.

During the 1930s another type of neural model appeared, the mathematical model (Katz[35]). The earliest of these, proposed by Rashevsky,[40] was based on the proposition that processes of excitation in nerve could be described completely by two time factors.

In addition to mathematical models of excitation there appeared several mathematical models of conduction. In this case they were based on linear partial differential equations. Rashevsky[40] and Ruston[34] both proposed such models. Weinberg[41] later demonstrated their equivalence.

Encouraged by the success of differential equations as representations of nervous activity, Rashevsky,[42] Householder[43] and Landahl[44] attempted to extend this form of mathematics to large systems of nerves, treating (without much success) problems of perception and discrimination.

Then in 1943 McCulloch and Pitts[45] published a revolutionary concept in mathematical neural modeling. Viewing the all-or-none behavior of neurons as of first-order importance, they proposed to treat neural systems with discrete rather than continuous mathematics. McCulloch and Pitts applied Boolean algebra and set theory rather than differential equations. They were able to prove that the behavior of all networks of nerve-like threshold elements (now known as "formal neurons") can be treated by the propositional calculus, and that given any logical expression a net of such elements having corresponding function can be found.

The impact of the McCulloch–Pitts theory was stated well by Von Neumann:[46] "It has been attempted to show that such specific functions, logically, completely described, are *per se* unable of mechanical, neural realization. The McCulloch–Pitts result puts an end to this. It proves that anything that can be exhaustively and unambiguously described, anything that can be completely and unambiguously put into words, is *ipso facto* realizable by a suitable finite neural network."

A new kind of mathematical model appeared in 1952; it provided analysis rather than mere description of excitation in nerve. Hodgkin and Huxley[47] had placed microelectrodes inside the giant axon of the squid and measured changes in axon membrane current in response to stepwise changes in membrane voltage. They were able to distinguish two important components of change in the current: (1) a rapidly rising component that immediately passes through maximum and declines to a low level (and which they associated with sodium ions flowing into the axon), and (2) a component that exhibits slower, delayed rise and a very slow subsequent decline (and which they associated with potassium flowing out of the axon).

From their data Hodgkin and Huxley derived four simultaneous differential equations. They showed that the solutions to these equations accounted accurately for the spike potential as well as for its aftereffects.

These four equations constitute the most well known of all neural models, and the Hodgkin–Huxley model of nerve impulse propagation underlies many of the subsequently developed models.

This work of Hodgkin and Huxley caused a resurgence of interest in the use of continuous mathematics to describe and analyze excitation in nerve. This trend, intensified by continuing discovery of many continuously variable (graded) subthreshold properties, led, in subsequent models of many kinds, to the inclusion of continuous properties as well as the discrete ones that the formal neurons had employed.

The advent of digital- and analog-computer concepts and technology, well established by the mid-1950s, added new dimensions to the foundations on which neurophysiological research is based. Nervous systems began to be considered more and more explicitly as processors of information, literally as biological computers. Also, increasingly more conceptual and technical tools became available to meet the accelerating demands of neurophysiological study. So, too, models of many kinds began to come of age.

# References

1 Descartes, R., *De homine figuris et latinitate donatus a Florentio Schuyl* (Leyden: Leffen and Franciscum Moyardum, 1662)

2 Cohen, L. D., Descartes and Henry More on the beast-machine: a translation of their correspondence pertaining to animal automatism. *Ann. Sci.* Vol. 1, pages 48–61 (1936)

3 Fulton, J. F., *Selected Readings in the History of Physiology* (Springfield, Ill.: Charles C. Thomas, 1930)

4 Descartes, R., *Oeuvres de Descartes* (Paris: Léopold Cerf, 1909, Vol. 11)

5 Borelli, A., *De Motu Animalium* (Rome: Bernado, 1680), Vols. 1 and 2

6 Brazier, M. A. B., The historical development of neurophysiology in *Handbook of Physiology, Neurophysiology* (Washington, D. C.: Am. Physiol. Soc., 1959), Sect. 1, Vol. 1, page 1

7 Hoff, H. E., Galvani and the pre-Galvanian electrophysiologists. *Ann. Sci.* Vol. 1, pages 157–172 (1936)

8 Newton, I., *Opticks* (New York: Dover, 1952)

9 Cavendish, H., An account of some attempts to imitate the effects of the *Torpedo* by electricity. *Trans. Roy. Soc (London)* Vol. 66, pages 196–225 (1776)

10 Walter, W. C., Animal electricity before Galvani. *Ann. Sci.* Vol. 2, pages 84–113 (1937)

11 Lewis, E. R., Some biological modelers of the past in *Biological Models*, edited by E. A. Edelsack, H. H. Patee, and L. Fein. (Washington, D.C.: Spartan, 1966, in press)

12 Galvani, L., *De Viribus Electricitatus in Motu Musculari, Commentarius* (Bologna: Ex Typographia Instituti Scientarium, 1791)

13 Galvani, L., *Dell'uso e dell'attivita dell'arco Conduttore Nelle Contrazione dei Muscoli* (Bologna: Thommaso D'Aquino, 1794)

14 Du Bois-Reymond, E., *Untersuchungen über thierische Elektricität* (Berlin: G. Reimer, 1848) Vol. 1

15 Du Bois-Reymond, E., *On Animal Electricity*, translated by H. Bence-Jones (London: Churchill, 1852)

16 Du Bois-Reymond, E., *Ueber das Gesetz des Muskelstromes* (Berlin: Unger, 1863)

17 Matteucci, C., Sur le pouvoir électromoteur secondaire des nerfs, et son application à l'electrophysiologie. *Compt. Rend.* Vol. 56, pages 760–764 (1863)

18 Biedermann. W., *Electro-Physiology* (London: Macmillan, 1898), Vol. 2, pages 227–356

19 Matteucci, C., Recherches physico-chimiques appliquées à l'électro-physiologie. *Compt. Rend.* Vol. 66, pages 580–585 (1868)

20 Hermann, L., Ueber eine Wirkung galvanischer Ströme auf Muskeln und Nerven. (*Pflüger's Arch. Ges. Physiol.* Vol. 6, pages 312–360 (1872)

21 Hermann, L., Zur Theorie der Erregungsleitung und der elektrischen Erregung. *Pflüger's Arch. Ges. Physiol.* Vol. 75, pages 574–590 (1899)

22 Boruttau, H., Ueber temporäre Modification der elektrotonischen Ströme des Nerven. *Pflüger's Arch. Ges. Physiol.* Vol. 68, pages 351–388 (1897)

23 Taylor, R. E. Cable theory in *Physical Techniques in Biological Research*, edited by W. L. Nastuk (New York: Academic Press, 1963), Vol. 6, page 219

24 Hering, E., Theory of the function of living matter. *Brain.* Vol. 20, pages 232–258 (1897)

25 Nernst, W., Zur theorie des elektrischen Reizes. *Pflüger's Arch. Ges. Physiol.* Vol. 122, pages 275–314 (1908)

26 Offner, F., Weinberg, A. M. and Young, G. Nerve conduction theory: some mathematical consequences of Bernstein's model. *Bull. Math. Biophys.* Vol. 2, pages 89–103 (1940)

27 Lillie, R. S. The passive iron wire model of protoplasmic and nervous transmission and its physiological analogues. *Biol. Rev. Cambridge Phil. Soc.* Vol. 11, pages 181–209 (1936)

28 Heathcote, H. L., The passivifying, passivity, and activifying of iron. *J. Soc. Chem. Ind.* Vol. 26, pages 899–917 (1907)

29 Hill, A. V., *Chemical Wave Transmission in Nerve.* (New York: Macmillan, 1932)

30 Pflüger, E., *Untersuchungen über die Physiologie des Elekrotonus* (Berlin: August Hirschwald, 1859)

31 Hill, A. V., Excitation and accommodation in nerve. *Proc. Roy. Soc. (London), Ser. B*, Vol. 119, pages 305–355 (1936)

32 Franck, U. F., Models for biological excitation processes. *Prog. Biophys.* Vol. 6, pages 171–206 (1956)

33 Rushton, W. A. H., A graphical solution of a differential equation with application to Hill's treatment of nerve excitation. *Proc. Roy. Soc. (London), Ser. B.* Vol. 123, pages 382–395 (1937)

34 Rushton, W. A. H., Initiation of the propagated disturbance. *Proc. Roy. Soc. (London), Ser. B*, Vol. 124, pages 210–243 (1937)

35 Katz, B., *Electric Excitation of Nerve*: A Review. (London: Oxford Univ. Press, 1939)

36 Hodgkin, A. L., and Huxley, A. F., A quantitative de-

scription of membrane current and its application to conduction and excitation in nerves. *J. Physiol. (London).* Vol. 117, pages 500–544 (1952)

37 Grundfest, H. Excitation triggers in post-junctional cells in *Physiological Triggers*, edited by T. H. Bullock (Washington, D.C.: Am. Physiol. Soc., 1957), page 119

38 Fabre, P., Retour sur un modèle du nerf (1). *Arch. Intern. Physiol.* Vol. 1, pages 12–32 (1940)

Fabre, P., Retour sur un modèle du nerf (2). *Arch. Intern. Physiol.* Vol. 1, pages 185–196 (1940)

39 Schmitt, O. H., An electrical theory of nerve impulse propagation. *Am. J. Physiol.* Vol. 119, page 399 (1937)

Schmitt, O. H., Mechanical solution of the equations of nerve impulse propagation. *Am. J. Physiol.* Vol. 119, pages 399–400 (1937)

40 Rashevsky, N., Outline of a physico-mathematical theory of excitation and inhibition. *Protoplasma.* Vol. 20, pages 42–56 (1933)

41 Weinberg, A. M., The equivalence of the nerve conduction theories of Rashevsky and Rushton. *Bull. Math. Biophys.* Vol. 2, pages 61–64 (1940)

42 Rashevsky, N., Contribution to the mathematical biophysics of visual perception with special reference to the theory of aesthetic value of geometric patterns. *Psychometrika.* Vol. 3, pages 253–271 (1938)

43 Householder, A., A neural mechanism for discrimination. *Psychometrika.* Vol. 4, pages 45–58 (1939)

44 Landahl, H. D., Contributions to the mathematical biophysics of the central nervous system. *Bull. Math. Biophys.* Vol. 1, pages 95–118 (1939)

45 McCulloch, W. S., and Pitts, W., A logical calculus of ideas immanent in nervous activity. *Bull. Math. Biophys.* Vol. 5, pages 115–133 (1943)

46 Von Neumann, J., The general and logical theory of automata in *Cerebral Mechanisms in Behavior: The Hixon Symposium*, edited by L. A. Jeffress. (New York: Wiley) 1951, page 1

47 Hodgkin, A. L., and Huxley, A. F., Currents carried by sodium and potassium ions through the membrane of the giant axon of *Loligo. J. Physiol. (London).* Vol. 116, pages 449–472 (1952)

Hodgkin, A. L., and Huxley, A. F., The components of membrane conductance in the giant axon of *Loligo. J. Physiol. (London).* Vol. 116, pages 473–496 (1952)

Hodgkin, A. L., and Huxley, A. F., The dual effect of membrane potential on sodium conductance in giant axon of *Loligo. J. Physiol. (London).* Vol. 116, pages 497–506 (1952).

# 31 Man on his nature
## by C S Sherrington

Much as one special organ, the heart, maintains the flow of nutriment throughout the body; so one organ, the brain, is provider of mind for the whole individual. If we smile at so bald a statement we must yet agree that it states the practical situation with which the physician and the surgeon deal.

It shows us too the body in the grip of integration. Much of the body has no demonstrable mind. Of the rest most has mind only lent it, in the form of sensation by proxy. Such of it merely communicates with a certain restricted piece of the body, a particular part of a single organ, and there, so much of the body as feels, has its sensation done for it. There too the body's thinking seems to be done for it, namely, in the brain.

Of man we know even more confidently than of any other concrete life that his mind is correlated with his brain. But let us avoid the sophistication that for the mind to be in the brain is any self-evident proposition. "Many men," wrote Kant, "fancy they feel their thought in their head, but that is a mistake. No experience tells me that I am shut up in some place in my brain." We owe I suppose to medicine in the main the knowledge of where in the body the "seat of the mind", as it is termed, is. But so far from its being a self-evident fact, one of the greatest of biologists, Aristotle, did not subscribe to it although it was accepted by physicians in his time. . . .

Between the study of the mind and that of the brain the gap is wider than between the studies of activity and of visible structure in most organs. Description of the action of a muscle could not dispense with reference to the muscle's visible structure. Reference to the brain at present affords little help to the study of the mind. Ignorance of the "how" of the tie between the brain and the mind there makes itself felt. That is no fault of those who study the mind or of those who study the brain. It constitutes a disability common to both of them. A liaison between them is what each has been asking for. That there is a liaison neither of them doubts. The "how" of it we must think remains for science as for philosophy a riddle pressing to be read.*

Knowledge, medical and other, allocates the "seat" of the mind, as the phrase is, to the brain. That localization has importance for medicine. It may be asked, however, whether for the scope of what we have before us here, it has importance. It would seem to have importance and in this way.

The two concepts, mind and energy, which our experience finds, using the one where the other fails, cover all our experience, are both of course in themselves creations of thought. But what they respectively stand for still remains divided as having nothing in common except time and this curious one and only point of spatial relation, namely "collocation in the brain".

Medicine's localization of the mind in the brain is therefore not only in medicine itself the greatest of all the brain localizations. It is from the more general point of view a lonely datum correlating mind with place. In that respect the evidence it brings is of fundamental interest. It assures us that, as known to us at least, mind is always and without exception individual mind. That is to say, mind in the general and aggregate as known to us is always many contemporary minds. It tells us that the mental as we know it is always in actuality a limited and impermanent individual system.

In many of its bearings the relation between mind and energy seems, although touching life at countless points, too subtly elusive to be captured for examination. In this one instance, however, the elusiveness seems set aside; for the brain and the psyche lie together, so to say, on a knife's edge. Whatever the solution of the problem we can here feel this. That in the energy-pattern which is the brain, two sets

*extracts from* Man on his Nature, *Gifford Lectures 1937–1938 as edited by G. N. A. Vesey in* Body and Mind, *Readings in Philosophy (George Allen and Unwin Ltd, 1964).*

* *Cf.* Viscount Samuel, *Nature,* February 1939; C. S. Myers, *Realm of Mind,* p. 112, W. McDougall, *Outline of Psychol.,* at end.

of events happen such as, to human knowledge, happen nowhere else the perceptible universe over. In that universe, sampling it, standing where we do on our planet's side, ourselves compact of energy, nowhere does our glimpse detect in all the immensity of energy any relation of energy except to energy save in this one instance, the brain. There energy and mind seem in liaison as to place.

Mind, always, we know it, finite and individual, is individually insulated and devoid of direct liaison with other minds. These latter too are individual and each one finite and insulated. By means of the brain, liaison as it is between mind and energy, the finite mind obtains indirect liaison with other finite minds around it. Energy is the medium of this the indirect, but sole, liaison between mind and mind. The isolation of finite mind from finite mind is thus overcome, indirectly and by energy. Speech, to instance a detail, illustrates this indirect liaison by means of energy between finite mind and finite mind. I have seen the question asked "why should mind have a body?" The answer may well run, "to mediate between it and other mind". Philosophical speculation might be tempted to suppose the main *raison d'être* for energy in the scheme of things to be this. Energy provided as a medium of communication between finite mind and finite mind. It might be objected that such a view is undiluted "anthropism". To that we might reply, anthropism seems the present aim of the planet, though presumably not its enduring aim. Man will, we may think, go; and anthropism cannot be when man is gone.

If we suppose the planet's programme be expression of an aim, then trying to read that programme to learn whither the aim would, surely we do well to draw what inference we can. It may be that the aim towards which what we observe as progress moves includes the human as step to a further stage, of which we may forecast it will be supra-human. If mind, as we experience it and argue it in others, seem to itself that which the programme of the planet has aimed at, and if "more mind" seem what the planet would and the communication between mind and mind foster more mind, then to hesitate to read this message because it seem "anthropic" is to be blind to our cause and to that of our planet, of which latter cause, it would seem for the moment, ours is a part.

For energy to be the only means of communication between finite mind and mind seems at least a significant fact in the economy of life. It is a special service rendered to life by energy. It is also yet one instance more of the unity of the complex of which energy and mind seem the two ultimate constituents, for unless mind have working contact – "*contact utile*" – with energy, how can energy serve it? . . .

The body is of cells and like the rest of the body the brain is of cells. Have then the cells of the brain mind and the body's other cells not? Supposing a cell to be sentient, surely we have little chance of knowing whether it be so. A well-versed observer of the one-celled animal world has said that were an amoeba as big as a dog we should all acknowledge its mind. We could then put many more questions to it, but, with all deference, I am not clear that mind would be recognizable in the answers given. Aristotle knew the exposed human brain insentient when touched or manipulated. For him to remark the fact it must have seemed to him noteworthy. Today the surgeon reports that he removes large areas of the cortex of the brain – the cortex is the region where brain and mind meet – from conscious patients without their noticing difference or change. This insentience of the brain may have conduced to Aristotle's view of the heart rather than the brain lodging the mind. But we can understand that the brain in order to feel may have to be approached in a right way. If the brain be mechanism and the mind be related mechanism then it will surely be so. The wireless set answers to turning the switch but not to shaking the box. The connection of the brain with mind seems to rest on the organization of the brain, and that organization is cell-organization. Does knowledge of that organization help us to understand the organization of the mind?

The organization might bring out by additive processes a cell-attribute too slight for detection in the single cell yet obvious when summed. What evidence is there in general of mind attaching to any single cell? . . .

A brain-cell is not unalterably from birth a brain-cell. In the embryo-frog the cells destined to be brain can be replaced by cells from the skin of the back, the back even of another embryo; these after transplantation become in their new host brain-cells and seem to serve the brain's purpose duly. But cells of the skin it is difficult to suppose as having a special germ of mind.

Moreover, cells, like those of the brain in microscopic appearance, in chemical character and in provenance, are elsewhere concerned with acts wholly devoid of mind, *e.g.* the knee-jerk, the light-reflex of the pupil. A knee-jerk "kick" and a mathematical problem employ similar-looking cells. With the spine broken and the spinal cord so torn across as to disconnect the body below from the brain above, although the former retains the unharmed remainder of the spinal cord consisting of masses of nervous cells, and retains a number of its nervous reactions, it reveals no trace of recognizable mind.

That the brain derives its mind additively from a cumulative mental property of the individual cells composing it, has therefore no support from any facts of its cell-structure. For a class-room to exhibit an isolated brain-cell and label it large "The organ of thought", may be dramatic pedagogy; it is certainly pedagogical over-statement. The cell-organization of the brain may be the key to the secret of its correlation with mind; but not, it would seem, by individual mental endowment of its constituent cells.

On the brain, it is true, devolves the managing of those of our acts of which we are directly aware. Looked at along the evolutionary series the brain it is with whose development has progressed the control of those acts which we most directly control. In it are carried to their highest pitch the nerve-actions which manage the individual as a whole. It integrates the individual as a system of motor acts, and the integrated act is the response to an integrated situation, integrated likewise by the brain, but especially by mind.

We are back at the close tie between motor act and mind. We saw it was primitive. We see it here still operative although no longer primitive. Control of act and awareness of act meet. I cannot by any effort of my will evoke my knee-jerk. Likewise I do not directly experience it. When it is elicited I seem to look on at it, as I might at a motor-car moving. It is not so with my hand sketching; I do control its act and do directly experience it acting. My experience then is that it is "I" doing the drawing. If I am told, as indeed science tells me, that I, as mind, have had nothing to do with this act of drawing except as an onlooker, I find that puzzling.

The dilemma goes further. The motor behaviour of the individual is our only contact with his individuality. Indirect indication of him though it be, we in that way interpret him and allow him "values", moral, aesthetic, etc. We infer he will do a generous act because we have inferred of him a generous mind. We attribute his acts to his mental character which we have inferred from his acts. We even fancy that our mental opinion of him can influence our own motor behaviour towards him. I have come to regard my words as an outcome of such thought as I have. When I ask science to tell me how all this is so, science vouchsafes me no reply. If I ask again she tells me it is none of her business; that though spoken words are energy, thoughts are not. . . .

Activity of the brain involves great numbers, not to say, vast numbers, of nerve-cells cooperating. Yet the means of securing that cooperation is by impulses via the nerve-fibres connecting cells. A large and an essential part of even the highest brain activity must therefore consist of nerve impulses.

We turn to the actual cells of the brain. They, if we pursue the simile of the telephone system, are not the mere wires but are the actual exchange; they do the re-transmitting. They too have now come under examination by electrical methods. Their changes of potential are of two kinds; the more usual fall and an opposed rise of potential. Since in these situations the neural process is known to be of two kinds, one activation, the other arrest of activation, these changes of opposed electrical sign suggest a significant fit into the physiological picture. And there are too, as we saw, the rhythmic electrical waves which can be picked up by pad-electrodes placed on the head. They come probably from the surface-sheet of the brain cells. The rhythm of the beat is not too quick to be easily distinguishable by us were it perceptible to our consciousness at all. But our consciousness knows nothing about it. Through all the ages no suspicion of it has dawned upon us. Not even when now told of it do we feel it. The seat of the rhythm is in the visual region of the brain; vision sees nothing of it. Yet with the shift of mind the beat is altered; to open the closed eyes immediately disturbs it. It is possible to upset the rhythm by trying, without opening the eyes, to see something. A flash of light on the eye and a whole series of waves can be picked up from the visual part of the brain.

Physiology has got so far therefore as examining the activity in the "mental" part of the brain when activity there is in normal progress. The desideratum to carry observation into the telephone-exchange itself with that exchange normally at work seems thus at last fulfilled. But has it brought us to the "mind"? It has brought us to the brain as a telephone-exchange. All the exchange consists of is switches. What we wanted really of the brain was it would seem, the subscribers using the exchange. The subscribers with their thoughts, their desires, their anticipations, their motives, their anxieties, their rejoicings. If it is a mind we are searching the brain for, then we are supposing the brain to be much more than a telephone-exchange. We are supposing it a telephone-exchange along with the subscribers as well. Does your admirably delicate electrical exploration vouchsafe us any word about them? Its finger is ultra-sensitive, but energy is all that it can feel. And is the mind energy?

The "subject" whose eye opens and whose brain-waves then alter, experiences as the most significant fact of the moment the mental change that he now sees something whereas before he did not. Do the concurrent electrical potentials contribute anything at all to the conception of, or to the understanding of, this visual experience?

It is now some seventy years since the words of a great biological leader of his time to his hearers were "the thoughts to which I am now giving utterance and your thoughts regarding them are the expression of molecular changes in that matter of life which is the source of our other vital phenomena" (Huxley). The terminology is a little "dated", but is the main position thus set forth altered today? The concomitance in time and place between the "molecular changes" and "the thoughts" is still all we have correlating the two. Regarded as a paradox it has become more intriguing: regarded as a gap in knowledge more urgent. . . .

The sixteenth-century physician Jean Fernel would have smiled at this difficulty which presents itself to us. For him there is no difference between thought and the rest of living. The cause of the brain's thinking was for him the life-spirit in it. That spirit has the brain for habitation, its temporary dwelling. He would tell us that what his boat is for the time being to the mariner, such the brain is for the time being to this spirit. That the brain should obey and do what the spirit would he finds no more remarkable than that the boat obeys the handling of him who sails it. But we recall a railway-coach attached to its locomotive solely by goodwill between guard and driver and it did not arrive.

For Fernel there was duality but that duality created a situation of no difficulty. Its members, matter and spirit, combined in perfectly satisfying cooperation. Matter was the servant. Spirit, mind, was the master. Perhaps that was from the Phaedo, where we remember the soul rules, the body obeys. Today the duality is there; and combination is there, but the footing on which the combination rests, so obvious to Fernel, is for our inquiry still to seek. Perhaps the "servant and master" phrase had in view an assertion of free-will. But where in nature shall we find "servant and master"? Where our knowledge halts our description will resort to metaphor. Long will man's fancy deal with the tie between body and mind by metaphor and often half forget the while that metaphor it is. Regarding this problem will a day come when metaphors can be dispensed with? . . .

The energy-concept, we saw, embraces and unifies much. The scheme seems coterminous with the perceptible. Therein lies its immensity and also its limitation. Immense as it is, and self-satisfying as it is, and self-contained as it is, it yet seems but an introduction to something else.

For instance a star which we perceive. The energy-scheme deals with it, describes the passing of radiation thence into the eye, the little light-image of it formed at the bottom of the eye, the ensuing photo-chemical action in the retina, the trains of action-potentials travelling along the nerve to the brain, the further electrical disturbance in the brain, the action-potentials streaming thence to the muscles of eye-balls and of the pupil, the contraction of them shar-

pening the light-image and placing the best seeing part of the retina under it. The best "seeing"? That is where the energy-scheme forsakes it. It tells us nothing of any "seeing". Everything but that. Of the physical happenings, yes. A tiny patch of a particular radiant energy disturbing the surface of the body in a region specially reactive to it; it connects that patch with an energy-path entering the eye, then with one carrying brainward from it, a shower of repetitive electric potentials. It locates these in a certain region of the brain, which it therefore indicates as concerned with what occurs in us through the eye. It also accounts to us for all the manoeuvring of the eye-balls as they catch the photo-image and sharpen it and place the eye centrally under it, so too for our turning of the head to help the eyes.

But, as to our *seeing* the star it says nothing. That to our perception it is bright, has direction, has distance, that the image at the bottom of the eye-ball turns into a star over-head, a star moreover that does not move though we and our eyes as we move carry the image with us, and finally that it is the thing a star, endorsed by our cognition, about all this the energy-scheme has nothing to report. The energy-scheme deals with the star as one of the objects observable by us; as to the perceiving of it by the mind the scheme puts its finger to its lip and is silent. It may be said to bring us to the threshold of the act of perceiving, and there to bid us "goodbye". Its scheme seems to carry up to and through the very place and time which correlate with the mental experience, but to do so without one hint further. If the energy-scheme exhaust motion and embrace all "doing" then the act of perceiving would seem not to be motion and it would seem, is not "doing". Otherwise it would be included. So with the whole of mental experience, the energy-scheme leaves it aside and does not touch it. Our mental experience is not open to observation through any sense-organ. All that the energy-scheme submits *is* thus open. The perceptible and the energy-scheme are co-extensive, for both are for us rooted in sense. Our mental experience has no such channel of entrance to the mind. It is already of the mind, mental. We can turn no sense-organ upon it. Such expressions as "internal sense" mislead if they are taken literally. The mental act of "knowing" we are aware of, but we cannot sensually observe it. It is experienced, not observed. . . .

The sense-organs are specifically fitted to pick up, *i.e.*, to "receive", stimuli which by their means the body can react to. But they do not all of them or at all times by so doing affect "sense". The energy-mind problem asks "how can they affect sense?" Sense is an aspect of the mental; how then can the physical receptor affect sense? That the physical receptor, *e.g.* the eye, connects with the roof-brain does not remove the difficulty. How can a reaction in the brain condition a reaction in the mind? Yet what have we sense-organs for, if not for that? This difficulty with sense is the same difficulty, from the converse side, as besets the problem of the mind as influencing our motor acts.

I would submit that we have to accept the correlation, and to view it as interaction; body $\rightleftharpoons$ mind. Macrocosm is a term with perhaps too mediæval connotations for use here; replacing it by "surround", then we get surround $\rightleftharpoons$ body $\rightleftharpoons$ mind. The sun's energy is part of the closed energy-cycle. What leverage can it have on mind? Yet through my retina and brain it seems able to act on my mind. The theoretically impossible happens. In fine, I assert that it does act on my mind. Conversely my thinking "self" thinks that it can bend my arm. Physics tells me that my arm cannot be bent without disturbing the sun. Physics tells me that unless my mind is energy it cannot disturb the sun. My mind then does not bend my arm. Or, the theoretically impossible happens. Let me prefer to think the theoretically impossible does happen. Despite the theoretical I take it my mind *does* bend my arm, and that it disturbs the sun.

Organic evolution, with its ways and means, appears to the biologist to treat and handle body and mind together as one concrete individual. To a human spectator it may well appear that the long series of animal creation has its *raison d'être* as a mechanism *for* evolving mind. He inclines to regard his own mind as the precious product which was the desideratum. But in that he may be suffering from "anthropism". The human mind is not a goal. Nature has started the bird's brain after already putting potentially the human on its way, that is, has started another and inferior mind after reaching the ground-plan of the human mind. Be that as it may, he regards his mind as associated with his brain which is also a part of him. He sees his brain so placed that certain nerve-paths reaching inward from specialized bits of the body, the eye, the ear and so on, bring physical events, as it were by some natural magic, into such relation with the mind that they affect it. In other words, as we said, the theoretically impossible happens.

At the core of this difficulty is the attribute "unextended" as applied to the finite mind. It is difficult to reconcile this attribution with certain facts. The mind of the individual, finite mind, as judged by an impressive concensus of opinion, has "place". It has "whereness"; nor does it matter for our purpose of the moment what "where" it has. It has a "where". Speaking for myself, although I can allow dialectically a Euclidean point and admit its artificiality to be a helpful convention, it is beyond me to conceive or figure or imagine even approximately a concrete anything as having whereness without magnitude. A thing without extension as

descriptive of the mind, even though negatively descriptive, fails for me to be more than a conventional symbol. Kant seems, I would think, to have had something of a not dissimilar difficulty, when he wrote of the human soul that it "resides in a place of a smallness impossible to describe".

Accepting finite mind as having a "where" and that "where" within the brain, we find that the energy-system with which we correlate the mind has of course extension and parts and exhibits, moreover, marked spatial organization of those of its parts correlating in space and time with the finite mind. The roof-brain is a veritable labyrinth of spatial construction. With different parts of that labyrinth observational inference connects different mental actions. Thus, different ranges of memory are injured by brain-affections of different seat. There is a "visual" part, an "auditory" part and so on. Again, in this "mental" part of the brain "touches" from different points of the skin are registered at separate brain-points, and each psychical "touch" has according to its place its particular psychical "local-sign". Space relations of the brain seem then to count mentally. Different "wheres" in the brain, in short, correlate with different mental actions. Nor is it that an "unextended" mind simply jumps from one spot to another. Two or more different activities of mind correlating with different "wheres" in the brain are commonly in action contemporaneously. It may be asked whether these separate regions are not mere separate channels of physiological approach to a mind-focus of Euclidean-point character. But their relation to mind is closer and more "mental" than that. We have, I think, to accept that finite mind is in extended space.

Again, the change in living organisms which evolution produces is, as examination of them proves, a recollocation of the elemental parts. It is a rearrangement, a reshuffling, and often an addition of more such parts. The mind of the organism is embraced as well as the body by the evolutionary process. This would seem presumptive evidence that the mind has parts which can be reshuffled and amplified under evolution. But reshuffling, recollocation, implies extension in space. The mind to undergo it would seem to occupy extended space.

Again if "things" through nerve can act on finite mind — and most of us would admit that to be the basis of perceiving — it then becomes difficult to suppose action between energy and mind is unilateral only, solely energy $\rightarrow$ mind. The action should be reaction. In that case mind influences energy. My mind seems to act on my "material me" when at breakfast I lift my coffee cup with intent to drink. I infer a like situation in the chimpanzee when he peels his banana before eating it. Reversible interaction between the "I" and the body seems to me an inference validly drawn from evidence.

The "how" of it has the difficulty that finite mind is not an object of sense. There are at least two ways of being insensible, in other words, imperceptible. One way is to be quantitatively too little, *i.e.* below threshold. Another is to be inadequate to any sense-organ. Our sense-organs miss a number of the world's qualities and quantities of energy. Scientific devices help us partly out of this disability. Thus, nervous impulses in a fish's organ of smell may be insensible by our unaided sense-organs, but when Adrian to study them converts them into a noise like rattling rifle-fire, the roomful of us can hear them. By scientific means our powers of sense can in such ways be much extended. Yet the mental itself remains obstinately inaccessible to sense, and to all these extensions of it.

It may be so because it is not of the category of energy at all. Here we have of course to remember that in looking for mind as energy we are not looking for a form of energy then to translate it into mind. Of that we have abundant instances already. Thus, radiant energy via nerve into seeing, or into heat-sensation, or pain. That would be to look merely for forms of energy which nerve can transmute through sense into the mental. What we look for is an energy which *is* mind. In short we seek whether mind is energy; whether for instance seeing, feeling, pain, thinking, etc., are manifestations of energy – *are* energy. No evidence as yet assures us of this. No organism seems furnished with any sense-organ which takes into its purview even the place pertaining to its finite mind. We may perhaps take that as equivalent to saying that no advantage would accrue to the organism if its mind were an object of sense to itself and therefore it is not so. . . .

We have, it seems to me, to admit that energy and mind are phenomena of two categories. In that case the phasic appearance of a mental system alongside the energy-system of the developing body has the difficulty that the mental seems to spring suddenly out of nothing. But we have already dealt with instances in ourselves where mind is clearly inferable although not directly recognizable by us. If that be so in ourselves, still greater is the difficulty of observing mind objectively, that is as object, when, by its very nature, it is insensible, *i.e.* not accessible to "sense". Mind as attaching to any unicellular life would seem to me to be unrecognizable to observation; but I would not feel that permits me to affirm it is not there. Indeed, I would think, that since mind appears in the developing soma that amounts to showing that it is potential in the ovum (and sperm) from which the soma spring.

The appearance of recognizable mind in the soma would then be not a creation *de novo* but a development of mind from unrecognizable into recognizable. It is at this point therefore that on these admissions we become committed to dualism. But while accepting this duality we remember that Nature in instance after instance dealing with this duality treats it as a unity. Evolution evolves it as one. In this body-mind individual, with its two cohering systems, bodily and mental, even as the former component exhibits both inherited and acquired features, so too does the latter. . . .

Latterly our theme touched more than once the question of the relation between the two concepts "energy" and "mind". I would venture here to turn specifically to that relation. To leave its argument, as that appears to me, merely tacit, might seem to invite mystery in a matter on which I would wish to arrive at clear expression. But over and above that there is an importance proper to the question. It has theoretical importance; that is perhaps generally admitted. But its claim to practical importance is apt to raise a smile. Yet the question surely touches the reading of man's situation in his world.

We need not think of it as an issue between idealism and materialism. Nor does it touch so-called "reality"; our world is in any case an act of mind. It asks rather whether the world, as our mind apprehends it, is for one part of it known to us in one way, for its other part known to us in another, the two ways not of essential parity. One form in which the question states itself is how far the world as known to us is fundamentally of one kind throughout. We may then regard the question as that of dualism or monism in a limited scope, that is, with no reference to reality. To me what ultimate reality may be is one of those questions which rise to the mind, and that the mind of itself has not the means to answer.

We saw ground for thinking that in the evolution of mind a starting point for "recognizable" mind, lay in its connexion with motor acts. Motor behaviour would seem the cradle of recognizable mind. I incline to endorse the challenging remark, that, "the most fundamental function of mind is to guide bodily movement so as to change our relation to objects about us". Moreover the motor act is that which seems to clinch the distinction between self and non-self. The doer's doings affirm the self. Lotze's trodden worm contrasting itself with the world found of the two its trodden self the greater. We may wonder at such anthropoid reflection on the part of the worm, but we grant the statement expresses fairly the view native to the "self". The worm shares the impulse as motion though not as thought. And surely even as early as the "suffering self" arose the "doing self". As far back in the evolutionary tree as intuitions go among them must be that of a subjective "doing".

The concept "self" taken with all its connotations has become vastly far-reaching and intricate. Yet it would seem to have at its core an element relatively simple, germane to our question here. The awareness or consciousness of each of us, prominent in certain of our motor acts, relates the self to the act. The awareness is of course an example of what in the abstract is spoken of as mind. It seems a law of mind to connect its phenomena by relations. The awareness attaching to these motor acts relates the conscious "self" to the acts as doing them.

In our awareness when doing these acts there would seem awareness both of the self and of its act, and a connexion between them. This awareness-complex comes traceably from two sources. One source is sensual. The motor act in its bodily execution consists of changes in several bodily parts, for instance, changes of length and tension in muscles, etc. The muscles besides being motor instruments are sense-organs. The muscular act therefore affects sense. There is perception of the act. Sensual perception has, as always, spatial reference. Its awareness carries reference to the bodily parts operating the act, for instance to a limb, a finger or what not. It is an awareness which, as the phrase goes, "projects" spatial reference, in this case into the moving limb, finger or what not concerned in the act.

But there is in the conscious motor act an awareness also of the "I-doing". This latter awareness is not derived from sense. It is the "I's" direct awareness of itself acting. A difference between it and the awareness derived from sense is that while that which derives from sense has, as we said, spatial projection, this which is not derived from sense has no spatial projection. It is awareness of the self "doing" but it is not projected....

In the complex of awareness belonging to a conscious motor act there is, along with the awareness of the "I-doing" which is unprojected, the sense-derived awareness of the bodily act which is projected, for instance, referred to the moving limb. This latter is by spatial projection separated from the unprojected "I". The bodily movement is therefore distinguished from the "I". The mind, finding relations between phenomena, seeks also to couple some phenomena as cause and effect. This bent or tendency has served it well. Whatever it may mean, it has helped to sift events conjoined by sequence in time. The mind relates the "I-doing" in the conscious motor act causally with the act. The unprojected "I" is the "cause" and the projected motor act is the "effect".

In this attribution we need not suppose that any conscious logical argument is at work. Rather it would be a naïve unargued assumption. One of those unanalysable workings of the mind which are practically tantamount to inference but are drawn unconsciously and often so quickly that the conclusion is reached before there would seem time for full comprehension of the data....

This "I" which when I move my hand I experience as "I-doing", how do I perceive it? I do not perceive it. If perception means awareness through sense I do not perceive the "I". My awareness and myself are one. I experience it. The "I-doing" is my awareness of myself in the motor act. It is my mental experience in that phase of my activity. It is, if we prefer, my experience of "self" explicit in action. In it my "self" is not an object which I can examine through sense. As compared with the latter I am at the disadvantage that I cannot submit this to others besides myself to examine and report on. It is private to myself, but each of us can examine his own case. For examining it, all we can do is to attend to what we are aware of in it.

This may be felt too trustful of introspection. If introspection be our impressions of our own consciousness those impressions, although perforce individual, may yet be representative. However, we have to be on our guard. The term introspection can, as is often insisted, be misleading. It might suppose that we can turn some perceptual process upon the "I" and watch it and treat it as an object of perception, so to examine and analyse it. Kant was one of those who continued late to use the term "inner sense", although he does not always make it clear with what meaning. The physiology of sense has advanced greatly since his time. The "I" can never come into the plane of objects of sensual perception. It *is* "awareness". Even if the mind had a sense-organ which were turned inward, so to say upon the mind itself, what would it fulfil? Broadly taken, and briefly, and crudely put, if the purpose of sense be to translate events physical and chemical into mental, what use would it serve in application to the mind which is already mental? Besides the "I", since it is awareness, would still remain not "sensed". The mind is no part of the perceptible.

But the mind does experience itself. Memory attaches to that experience. The self can remember and re-live at second-hand and reflect upon its experience of itself. It can think over what its experience in "doing" was. That perhaps is more effective than the divided effort of trying to examine the awareness actually while the awareness is in process.

Of two components which can be traced in the awareness of a conscious motor act, one, we saw, is the immediate awareness belonging to the "I-doing", the other the sensual awareness accompanying the bodily act. The second is in some instances, by disease or injury, stripped away. The dual complex of the conscious act is to that extent analysed.

This happens when a limb though its motor power is retained is robbed of all sensation. The patient then does not sense his limb. He does not know where his limb is, unless he sees it. In bed he may "lose" his arm. But the motor act is still evoked and consciously although there is no sensual perception of the limb. The "I" still experiences itself in acting. The residual awareness in this insentient condition of the limb is therefore in so far not sensually given. It is the "I's" direct awareness of itself in action.

It is true the motor act executed by the insentient limb is clumsy. That it is executed at all and consciously "at will" is here the point. The launching of it as a conscious act although the sensory basis for it, and the sensual perception of it, are wanting, indicates that this "I-acting" is not derived from sense perception but is directly given. . . .

These two concepts (energy and mind), and they are two concepts of one mind, divide, and between them comprise, our world. One of them, the spatial, which we may call the energy-concept, derives by way of the senses. The other, as we saw, is not derived by way of any sense. We saw why. The mind has no sense which it can turn inwards so to say upon itself. The idea which mind forms of itself lacks extension in space, because sense is required for such extension as a datum, and mind does not derive its idea of itself through sense. . . .

How can the phenomena of the two (space-time energy and non-space mind) interact? The more the biologist studies life the less I fancy does it seem to him like life to have a loose wheel spinning. Yet how shall a spatial wheel cog into unextended mechanism or the non-spatial drive a spatial wheel? Spinoza, thinking of Descartes' interaction between the rational soul and the pineal gland, wrote, "I would fain be told how many degrees of movement the mind can give to this little pineal gland, and with what force it can lift it. I feel surprise that so great a man and philosopher, one who has laid it down as his rule to draw conclusions only such as are self evident, and to assert nothing of which he has not a clear and distinct perception, he who so often has reproached scholasticism with explaining the obscure by qualities which are occult, allows himself an hypothesis more occult than all the occult qualities put together." Actually the dilemma is now become for many acuter still, if that be possible. The pseudo-"go-betweens" have vanished. Not that they in truth, I think, ever existed for either Spinoza or Descartes; the latter likened the animal spirits to fine fire, *i.e.* they were physical.

"Energy" proves itself a closed system, shutting out "mind". They may be juxtaposed, but they do not blend. An instance where perhaps particularly they approximate is at the mental process and the cerebral process. There on one side electrical potentials with thermal and chemical action, compose a physiological entity held together by energy-relations; on the other a suite of mental experience, an activity no doubt; but in what, if any, relation to energy! A suggestion has been made that we must redefine "energy" so as to bring "mind" into it. We have not in our power to re-fashion a concept shaped by our sense-perception. Again, it has been ingeniously said that had in the development of Science biology preceded physical science, a concept reached by Science would have embraced "mind" and "energy" together, merging them without disparity. But who shall jockey "space" out of its natural rights?

The puzzle might seem not altogether unlike that in regard to the physical interpretation of light, and indeed of "matter" generally. The electron, following its discovery, acquired charge, mass, spin and a special dynamics of its own. But that was not enough to carry the observational data which accrued. Matter, like light, was found to possess both the properties of particles and the properties of waves. Louis de Broglie put forward an equation expressing the correlation of the particle-behaviour and the wave-behaviour of matter. This budded into a synthesis. It achieved success in accounting for, and even to the extent of predicting, many observed facts. But its basal assumption that a particle is associated with a system of waves is, I imagine, accepted as an assumption and left unaccounted for.

So our two concepts, space-time energy sensible, and insensible unextended mind, stand as in some way coupled together, but theory has nothing to submit as to how they can be so. Practical life assumes that they are so and on that assumption meets situation after situation; yet has no answer for the basal dilemma of how the two cohere. There is no more of course than mere analogy between this mind-energy complex which teases biology and that other the wave-particle dilemma which has been teasing physics. In the latter case both of its terms are at least assimilable in the measure that each is describable by space into time. Both are in short physical. The biological dilemma is of another order. In it the two terms are divergent to the degree that while the one is sensible the other is insensible. How then account for conjunction between two incommensurables? The physical dilemma however treated as parable does offer a certain pragmatic counsel. To carry on in biology as if the two terms, mind and energy, whose connexion we cannot describe, are conjoined and to do so for the reason that to observation they act connectedly. With all humility, I imagine that physics argues "wave and particle seem, although we do not know how they can do so, to go together as one. We accept that without understanding it". Newton's essential modernity showed itself in no way more than in his acceptance of what he declared he could not account for. Our parable would preach acceptance of energy and mind as a working biological unity although we cannot describe the how of that unity.

Practical life regards, for instance, our thoughts as answerable for what we say. It proceeds as though qualities of mind, *e.g.* memory, courage, rightness of inference and so on, affect the acts we do. Law proceeds on the same assumption, in its corrective system as elsewhere. Parent and schoolmaster regard well-bestowed praise as promotive of well-doing. Society in general regards mind as productive of acts. While our conception of the mind as unextended seems to preclude mind from interacting with any energy-system, the body inclusive, every-day life assumes there is interaction and that our mind shapes our conduct. Here ethics surely takes the same view as does daily life.

Of this dilemma Nature herself, if we may so apostrophize her, takes no notice. She proceeds as if no such dilemma existed. Nothing is clearer than that in her process of Evolution she evolves in living creatures characters which, largely as they spell advantage or disadvantage to the individual life, tend to survive or disappear. We have seen life *per se* to be a system of energy. Since life is a system of energy a character to be of advantage or disadvantage to that system must influence that system. Nothing is clearer than that mind has evolved. Mind therefore has had survival value. Mind it would seem then has an influence which Nature finds can count for advantage to the energy-system colligate with it, the body. Mind, as we know it, is never any other than embodied mind. Hence such properties as size, shape, movement, etc., are assessed by mind as being of account. Nature in her process Evolution, although we do not know her as ethical, proceeds as if believing in a working relation between mind and body as does our human ethics.

If the "I-doing", which stands at some disadvantage, as we saw, for observing itself, had, instead of assuming that it was the "cause" of its motor act, regarded itself simply as colligate with the act, a part with it of one event, the seeming inconsistency between the two concepts in this situation would disappear. There would then be no need to ask for interaction. Then, that Nature deals with both as one explains itself. The evolution of the one is of necessity the evolution of the other. There is no causal relation between them; they are both inseparably one. Their correlation is unity. The "I" can accept itself as one aspect of the act. The "I-perceiving" is not then a "cause" within the spatial world.

The "I-experiencing" is just a part of the act it experiences. The relation is not as cause and effect but as parts of one event. So the relation between the "I-doing" and what is done is not cause and effect, but two colligate and concurrent components of one event. The "I-doing" becomes thus in effect another aspect of its motor act. Its motor act and it are one. Its motor act can be called rightly a "conscious motor act". That is exactly what it is. Its awareness is part of it. It can also rightly be called a willed act, unless by that it is intended to say "will" causes the motor act. This cannot be phrased more adequately I think than by some words in the *De Anima*, although their context is somewhat different from the present. "We must add that to speak of the soul as feeling angry is no more appropriate than to speak of the soul as weaving or building. Perhaps, in fact, it is better to say not that the soul pities or learns or infers, but rather that the man does so through his soul." The motor act and the "I-doing" appear as two parts of one event, one fitting the spatial concept (energy), the other the non-sensual concept (mind). This is akin to regarding the finite mind as a sort of esoteric activity bound up with the cerebral activity, an inner phase of which the nervous activity is the outward phase.

# 32 Consciousness
## by E D Adrian

One can scarcely come to a meeting of this kind* without being reminded of the basic problems that have shaped Western philosophy, the problems of substance and shadow, reality and appearance, mind and matter. They are problems that have been debated since Plato and they have led to all the main developments of philosophic doctrine. As natural scientists I expect most of us prefer to remain uncommitted: our own picture of the universe is clearly not the whole truth but it has been too useful to be far from it and it can always be adapted to include fresh evidence. Yet if we are physiologists it may be difficult to maintain this Olympian detachment. If we are concerned with the sense organs and the central nervous system we are bound to be aware of the difficulties which arise, or have arisen in the past, in relating activities which seem to be shared by the body and the mind.

In his book on *The Analysis of Mind*, Bertrand Russell said this: "Few things are more firmly established in popular philosophy than the distinction between mind and matter. Those who are not professional metaphysicians are willing to confess that they do not know what mind actually is or how matter is constituted, but they remain convinced that there is an impassable gulf between the two and that both belong to what actually exists in the world." It would seem then that the physiologist has that impassable gulf to face as soon as he allows himself to look up from his apparatus.

But Russell wrote that more than forty years ago. I am not at all sure that it is still the popular belief that mind and matter cannot be mixed. There may be a few elderly simple people who are still convinced of the gulf, but the philosophers of our time have all argued so persuasively against it that most of us are prepared to admit that our conviction of it might have been due to some misunderstanding. However

*first published in* Brain and Conscious Experience, *edited by J. C. Eccles, 1966, Ch. 10, pp. 238–246. Copyright © 1966 by Pontificia Academia Scientiarum, Citta del Vaticano. Reprinted by permission of Lord Adrian.*

---

* On brain mechanisms and consciousness [*Editors' note.*]

much we distrust the metaphysicians, we cannot overlook the fact that the gulf between mental and material can scarcely be called self-evident. It is, or used to be, anathema in the USSR and there must be a large number of the human race who have never suspected its existence.

The change in popular opinion in the twentieth century seems to have been due, in part, to the influence of Mach and William James and the spread of the experimental method into psychology. At all events, by the beginning of the century it was becoming more respectable for psychologists to use some kind of monism as a working hypothesis and even to be whole-hearted behaviorists. McDougall in England kept the flag of dualism flying for a time, but the controversy was becoming a back number by 1914 when the interest had shifted to the more romantic areas revealed by Freud.

Since that time, metaphysicians of all shades have shown a notable unanimity in rejecting the dualist position. They are agreed that the layman's separation of mind and matter will never do and they have given no support to the physiologists who assert that a thought is not the kind of thing which can be expected to depolarize a membrane. They tell us that those who hold such views have no clear conception either of mind or of matter and have been led into error by theological dogma and the ambiguities of language.

Unfortunately their agreement in rejecting dualism has not been coupled with agreement in accepting anything else. Various compromises have been put forward, things or processes which can be viewed as physical or mental according to their context, like Whitehead's *Structures of Activity*, or Russell's *Sensibilia* or Broad's *Sensa*. It is discouraging to find that each of these explanations, which seems so logical when we read it, should fail to satisfy more than the few professional critics whose explanation has been on the same lines; yet it is some encouragement to learn of so many different ways of escape from the mind-body dilemma, and scientists can say, rather patronizingly, that in metaphysics the advance is bound to come by disputation rather than by experimental evidence.

Now physiology and psychology are experimental

sciences and they have advanced considerably in their proper spheres during the present century, but have they done any better than metaphysics in bringing mental activity into the same picture as matter, or, alternatively, in showing that it is bound to be excluded? Certainly not much better, but at least it can be said that the gulf has been narrowed, that they have brought mind and matter closer together.

It has never seemed to be necessary to go outside the elastic frame of natural science in describing the action of the sense organs and the signals they send to the brain, but now we can add that there is no need to invoke extra-physical factors to account for any of the public activities of the brain itself. Nowadays a mechanical man could certainly be built to do all, or almost all, that we do ourselves. Someone would have to design and make it, but it could be made to behave as intelligently as we do. The "Universal Turing Machine" can turn its band to any problem. Machinery, in fact, could be constructed to produce most of the facets of human behavior – far more than would have been dreamt of in the period when Condillac imagined the statue coming to life. The comic papers do not exaggerate. Our present-day statue could be designed to speak its thoughts, to answer our questions, to express anger or joy, to recognize friends, form habits and solve problems. It could be made to report introspections and to tell us its hopes and fears.

According to Ross Ashby, and I think we must accept what he says, a machine made on his plan could equal the human brain in the search for knowledge. Naturally there would be differences; unless great pains were taken in its design, we should not expect the robot brain to be so flexibly organized, its different departments might not be so well integrated, and quite apart from such failings we should recognize it as part of a machine and not of a man because it would be made of metals and plastics instead of living cells. We have to admit, however, that to this extent the behaviorist hypothesis seems adequate. As far as our public behavior is concerned, there is nothing that could not be copied by machinery, nothing therefore that could not be brought within the framework of physical science.

Yet for many of us there is still the one thing which does seem to lie outside that tidy and familiar framework. That thing is ourself, our ego, the I who does the perceiving and the thinking and acting, the person who is conscious and aware of his identity and his surroundings. As soon as we let ourselves contemplate our own place in the picture we seem to be stepping outside the boundaries of natural science.

It was William James's rejection of consciousness that made everyone more critical of this particular ghost. He saw no need for separating the thinker and the thoughts and reported that his own search for the "I" revealed only feelings of tension, chiefly in the mouth and throat. At that time, Bergson's philosophy was in the ascendant, and as late as 1911 Bergson maintained that we have a direct and communicable knowledge of our own consciousness. For James, however, consciousness was not an entity but a function, simply the function of knowing.

There are, of course, logical or linguistic difficulties about assigning any meaning to the statement, "I am immediately aware that I am conscious", or even, "I know my own mind." In fact, one has only to read any of the numerous books and papers and reports of symposia in the past ten years to realize the various muddles we are in when we try to give precision to arguments about consciousness or mind. Ryle has made much of these in arguing against the dualist position, the ghost in the machine. But, in general, the psychologists seem to be much more troubled by the grammatical and logical difficulties than are the philosophers. These are on the whole more tolerant and anxious to rescue whatever meaning our statements contain.

How then are we to account for our conviction that we have an immediate awareness of ourselves and that this is the one thing which a machine could not copy?

I used to regard the gulf between mind and matter as an innate belief. I am quite ready now to admit that I may have acquired it at school or later. But I find it more difficult to regard my ego as having such a secondhand basis. I am much more certain that I exist than that mind and matter are different.

Apart from those who are insane, "out of their mind", one does not come across people who do not believe in their individuality, though there are many who do not believe in the separation of mind and matter. Belief in one's existence seems to depend very little on deliberate instruction.

But here we have to rely on evidence which must be derived by introspection. We could construct a machine which would tell us that it was conscious, but we should not believe it. When our fellow men say they are conscious, we believe them because they are much more like ourselves; but we know that many of their ideas and ours have been planted in them and in us by parents or schoolfellows; and, for all we know, some of our beliefs about our minds and our awareness may have been acquired in that way. The "I" that I know has been exposed to all the influences of the outside world since my birth. If we wish to reach through to the mind, the individual that has been influenced, we might try to discount all these extraneous factors by comparing the introspections of a great variety of people.

This is easier said than done, for it is usually necessary to elicit introspective reports by direct questioning and it is then more than likely that the report will be unintentionally influenced by the questioner. The horses of Elbefeld were accustomed to giving their master the answer he wanted and the human subject can be equally obliging when the answer will do no one much harm. Questions about the ego need careful framing and impersonal asking if they are to avoid the danger of suggesting the answer which would fit our particular beliefs. It was partly this unreliability of introspective reports which made the behaviorists disregard consciousness in their study of human activity.

Now, in the study of the human ego, introspections are almost all that we have to guide us, but some of the difficulties may not be as serious as we may think. The particular difficulty that the questioner may influence the answer recalls the uncertainty principle in physics, which limits the knowledge we can gain about any individual particle. Observation of that particle is bound to affect its position and velocity, but this does not make it impossible to define the behavior of a system made up of a large number of particles. In a similar way, some kind of statistical treatment might help to compensate for the disturbing effect of the questioner who asks us to report our private data.

Few of us would wish to embark on large-scale statistical comparisons of introspective data, but there are various problems in the psychosomatic field which seem to be badly in need of such treatment. It may be too much to expect that we shall ever find a way of submitting the theories of Freudian psychoanalysis to tests as exacting as those we should use in physics. In our present state of knowledge, it may be more illuminating to express the conflicts of the spirit by parables and myths than by weights and measures – and in any case it would now be very difficult to find people in the Western hemisphere who have not been already biased by popular opinion.

But there is a field of some promise, where the data are less emotionally charged, and it is one more closely related to particular physiological events. This is the field of perception, and I shall mention developments in that field which may be relevant to the problem of our conscious activities, though they might also be used to illustrate the weakness of introspective evidence. There was one, concerned with what is called eidetic imagery, which is in danger of being forgotten nowadays; it dates from the period when German psychology was still under the inspiration of Kraepelin's psychiatric classification and the psychologists then were particularly anxious to divide humanity into different bodily, mental and temperamental types, the asthenic, the pyknic, the schizoid and so on. Kretschmer's book on *Physique and Character* was published in 1921. Not long after, Jaensch, at Marburg, began to study the perceptual images following optic stimuli and found that they could be used as a guide to the mental and constitutional type. His work on eidetic images roused great interest, for he described them as something between sensations and images. Like physiological after-images, they are always seen in the literal sense, but we do not all see them. They are more often reported by literary or artistic Frenchmen or Spaniards than by scientific Britons or Americans. Sometimes they are little more than sensations and are then seen like after-images, in the complementary colors; sometimes they are more like memory images, with more detail and variety and appearing in the original colors. Jaensch said that eidetic imagery of this latter kind was rare among average adults, but much commoner in children, and that the eidetic disposition is correlated with nationality, with the particular kind of school teaching and with certain constitutional factors depending on the thyroid gland.

He found that in schools in certain districts, 85–90 per cent of the children were eidetics. He considered that some of his colleagues had failed to recognize the eidetic type and pointed out that the difference between actually seeing and merely imagining is particularly clear when the eidetic image develops gradually. "Now I see this . . .", "Now that is beginning to appear", children will say, pointing to a particular spot on the screen. "I know that . . . was also there, but I do not *see* it." In spite of the critics (Allport, *Brit. J. Psychol.*, *XV*, 1924), Jaensch maintained that eidetic phenomena were easily recognizable and reproducible. He was able to develop theories of perception and of education based on their occurrence.

For a time it looked as though Jaensch had discovered something which might be an important bridge between the physiological processes of sensation and the resulting mental experience, but the emphasis was on its value in typology. The general impression seems to have been that, although eidetic imagery exists, Jaensch went too far in thinking that a particular type of response was at all characteristic of the mental and bodily type. The nature of the image seems to depend much more on the situation than on the individual, though it may well be a valuable clue to the way in which visual material is incorporated in the mental organization.

At present, at all events, the study of the body image seems a much more profitable line to follow. It brings together the psychologist, the psychoanalyst and the clinical neurologist, and it is usually associated with the name of Paul Schilder who was all three. He made observations on eidetic imagery and hypnagogic visions, but was particularly concerned with images dealing with the subject's body and limbs in relation to the outside world, with the boundary between the body and its surroundings, with its relations with space and time and movement. It is to some extent his preoccupation with our ideas of ourselves in relation to the world that distinguishes Schilder's description of the body image from that of earlier workers, Head for instance. The conclusion he reaches is that the body image is constructed gradually, by trial and error. Consciousness is not an independent phenomenon, but consists of the process of trial and error in perception and thought "until the object and the outside world is reached. Consciousness is the attempt to bring experience within a context, we may call this context the ego, from an analytic point of view." The ego, in fact, is a synthesis of our experiences from birth (or before it).

His book *The Image and Appearance of the Human Body* has the subtitle *Studies in the constructive energies of the psyche*, and some of it is hard going for those who are not at home in a Freudian landscape. Some of it also reviews our mistrust of introspective reports, particularly when they have been elicited by someone who was clearly a quick-witted and sympathetic examiner with views of his own.

For instance, when Schilder deals with the physiological basis of the body image, he says that "our tactual perception of the skin is felt distinctly below (about 2 cm below) the surface of the optic perception of the body. When we touch an object and gradually diminish the pressure exerted on it, the object and the space between the object and the skin disappear but the sensation in the skin remains. There is at the same time a distinct sensation that the skin is bulging as if reaching for an object."

I have to admit that I do not recognize this description in my own sensations, and there are other passages where, although I can recognize what he describes, I suspect that I should not have done so without his prompting. He quotes, for instance, the reports of six subjects who were asked to imagine a white line, of others asked to describe their sensations in an elevator descending rapidly and then coming to rest. I will not tell you the reports, for you would then be biased for or against them.

Nor shall I try to summarize the more theoretical treatment he undertook, his views on the libidinous structure of the body image and on the difference between his attitude and that of Gestalt psychology. But his views on the physiological basis of the body image include a great many observations made from a more direct physiological and clinical standpoint. He believed that there is no action in which the postural model of the body does not play an important part, and "No sensory experiences that lack spatial qualities". (The term *perception* means that something is going on in space.) Effort or experiment leads to more unified space experience. The body image too is constructed

gradually; it can be changed by clothing, by spectacles or a walking stick. "When people wear enormous masks at the Carnival in Nice they are not merely changing the physiological basis of their body image, but are actually becoming giants themselves."

Schilder does not regard the body image as more than one essential ingredient of the ego, though, like the ego, it is organized by memory and experiment and cannot be maintained without constant effort. I am not convinced that I have understood his description of consciousness as a social act dependent on the resistances of the world, but it consists in "trying to see the context of our experiences by comparing those we find in our outer and inner world". I can only recommend his two books, *Mind, Perception and Thought* and *The Image and Appearance of the Human Body*. Although I cannot follow all the arguments and think some of the evidence is not convincing, at least he makes it clear that our ego and our awareness have many features which are related to bodily events. He makes it very difficult to maintain the belief in an impassable gulf between mind and body.

I am not sure whether more observations on these lines can lead us much further, for what is most needed is corroborative evidence based on data which are not merely reports of introspection but are open to public observation. Fortunately we have evidence of a different kind in the studies of Baldwin, Piaget and others on the development of intelligent behavior in the child. The picture which Piaget draws is again of a gradual process of establishing the boundary between the self and the external world. He distinguishes first a phase of "absolute realism", where there is no boundary at all, when the child is exclusively concerned with things and confuses himself and the world; then the phase of "immediate realism", where the instruments of thought, names and words are distinguished from the things but are situated in them. This may last up to eight or nine years, to be followed by the stage of "mediate realism", where they are not in the things but in the body, and finally by the adult phase of "subjectivism", where the thoughts are within ourselves.

Piaget finds that the child's awareness of his own thoughts takes place invariably after the age of seven or eight. It is dependent on social factors through contacts with others. He quotes an interesting passage from Edmund Gosse's account of his own childhood. He had lied to his father and not been found out: he suddenly realized not only that his father was not infallible but that there was a secret belonging to Edmund Gosse and to someone who lived in the same body with him. "There were two of us and we could talk together. It is difficult to define impressions so rudimentary, but it is certain that it was in this dual form that the sense of my individuality now suddenly descended upon me."

Piaget points out that as long as the child believed in his father's omniscience, his own self was nonexistent, in the sense that his thoughts and actions seemed to him common to all. The moment he realized that his parents did not know all, he straightway discovered the existence of his subjective self. It shows how the consciousness of self is not a primitive intuition but results from a dissociation of reality and shows also to what extent this dissociation is due to social factors, to the distinction the child makes between his own point of view and that of others.

There is, of course, a large element of introspection in such evidence, but not in the evidence which shows that it may be seven years or more before the child's ideas of space, size and direction are organized. Without that organization the distinction between the self and the world can scarcely be as definite as it will be in the adult. That particular ingredient of the ego must be built up by experience. I have to admit that this seems to have little relevance to the question whether a machine could ever become conscious, but it does seem to me to make the question less important.

I will try to sum up the position as I see it now. William James said that his search for the ego revealed only feelings of tension, chiefly in the mouth and throat. No doubt his thoughts took shape to the accompaniment of slight movements of verbalization. Nowadays we should expect to find the whole sensory input from exteroceptors and proprioceptors contributing to the tension, and it is probably better to think of the ego as a summary of the whole structure which has built up the individual since the child began to answer to its name.

But words like "structure", "organization" or "pattern" can often give a false sense of scientific respectability, and they have been used too often as a way of escape from our difficulties. It will be better to avoid them and to end up by giving you the general conclusions reached by the distinguished neurologist Francis Schiller, at a symposium on Brain and Mind in 1951. His paper is called "Consciousness Reconsidered". He is led to conclude that exclusively physiological and exclusively introspective accounts of the subject are incompatible and give rise to artifacts. Although they are complementary, integration of knowledge is hard to achieve because their points of reference and scales of observation are wide apart. "Consciousness" is a logical construction. The ego is a convenient abbreviation, an abstract of a multiplicity of objects from which it is developed. It arises when unconscious processes are integrated; its base line in the individual and in the animal kingdom is arbitrary.

That seems to me to be a reasonable position to have reached. It differs little from Schilder's and Piaget's in essentials. The physiologist is not forced to reject the old fashioned picture of himself as a conscious individual with a will of his own, for the position allows some kind of validity to the introspective as well as to the physiological account.

It admits that the two are incompatible but does not maintain that they must always be so. It would certainly be absurd to suppose that the scientific account will not be altered. Physics has synthesized ideas which once seemed quite incompatible and will probably do so again with great profit; possibly our picture of brain events or of human actions may be changed so radically that in the end they will account for the thinker as well as his thoughts.

# 33 The bankruptcy of determinism

## by Donald M MacKay

Ever since Heisenberg's Uncertainty Principle shattered the deterministic image of physics nearly half a century ago, there has been something of a tug of war between those who hailed it as restoring the scientific respectability of "free-will", and others who argued that it made no practical difference to the physical determinateness of brain function. Both sides took it for granted that *unless* the chain-mesh of cause-and-effect in the brain could be shown to be significantly incomplete, our sense of freedom in making a choice must be dismissed as an illusion, a sign of mere ignorance of the true state of affairs. In this article I want to undercut the traditional debate by questioning the assumption on which both sides were agreed. I hope to show that even if the workings of our brains were as mechanical as planetary motion, our freedom in choosing would be no illusion, but a matter of fact. If I am right, all attempts to debunk human responsibility on grounds of scientific determinism are demonstrably bankrupt.

To clear our minds, let us imagine ourselves back in the days of pre-Heisenberg physics, when it was supposed that a "snapshot" of the positions and velocities of all particles in a closed physical system could in principle determine the whole of its past and future. We call such a system "physically determinate", meaning that for anyone *outside* it there exists already a definite answer to any question about its future (or its past) which he would be correct to accept and mistaken to reject. For example, we call planetary motion "determinate" if future planetary events, such as eclipses, have specifications that can be proved to *exist now* to be discovered, with a demonstrable claim to our assent. No one may in fact know these specifications, but if we believe anything contrary to them, we are under an illusion.

On the other hand, as Sir Karl Popper showed some years ago (*British Journal for Philosophy of Science*, vol. 1, pages 117 and 173), even a computing machine of unlimited capacity would be unable completely to predict the future of a physical system *of which it was itself a part*; so the restric-

*This article first appeared in* New Scientist, *the international weekly review of science and technology, 128 Long Acre, London W.C.2.*

tion to individuals outside the system is important. If an individual is himself part of the system in question, the logical path becomes treacherous indeed; and the denial of freedom of choice by determinists is I think a direct consequence of a logical sideslip at this point.

Very little is yet known of the detailed relation between what a man perceives, thinks or believes and what goes on in his brain. There is plenty of evidence that the two are not independent (see, for example, the symposium *Brain and Conscious Experience*, edited by J. C. Eccles, Springer-Verlag, 1965); but it falls far short of proof that they are completely correlated. For our present purpose, however, it will be enough to ask what *would* follow *if* all of our mental activity were rigorously represented by some activity of our brain mechanism, so that no change could take place in what we perceived, thought, believed, etc., without some corresponding change taking place in the state of that mechanism. To work out the implications of this, the toughest form of the mechanistic assumption, may make it easier to come back to the ambiguities of present evidence with an open mind.

Here then is Joe Snooks, whose brain (we suppose) rigorously represents what he believes to be the case at any moment. We equip ourselves with some remote monitoring devices whereby we can get all the data we need from his brain in order to make our predictions without disturbing Joe. (Here already we are transgressing the bounds of physical possibility, but the determinist will want us to imagine this as possible "in principle", so let us do so and see how much – and how little – good it does his case.)

For any future state of affairs let us now ask our key question: does a specification of this state exist which has an unconditional claim on Joe's assent, even though he may not know it? Would he be correct to believe it, and incorrect to disbelieve it, whether he likes it or not? Consider, for example, the time of the next solar eclipse. We can see that Joe's brain would have to change from its present state if he were to believe a specification of this; but we can verify that any physical repercussions of the change would have a negligible effect on the solar system. Thus the claim of such a specification is demonstrably unconditional, granted the assumptions on which it is based. Anyone who believes it is correct; anyone who disbelieves it is in error. The event in question is in this sense *inevitable*.

But now what about the future state of Joe's brain itself? In particular, suppose we focus on the part or aspect of its mechanism that represents what Joe believes: Joe's *cognitive system*. We (presumably) can in principle frame a complete specification of this for ourselves; but if we ask whether *Joe* would be correct to believe our current specification, the answer must clearly be "No". Assuming that our specification is correct before Joe believes it, it cannot be so afterwards; for as soon as Joe believes it his brain must be in a new state different from the one it specifies. Nor would it help if we could invent a complete specification that would become correct *provided* that Joe believed it; for then *unless* Joe believes it it will be incorrect; so in spite of all our efforts, Joe would not be in error if he disbelieved it. In short, *no complete specification of Joe's cognitive system exists* that has an unconditional, take-it-or-leave-it, claim on Joe's assent. For Joe, the present and immediately future states of his cognitive system are in this sense *indeterminate* until after the time in question.

Note that this indeterminacy of Joe's cognitive mechanism (for Joe) has nothing to do with any *physical* indeterminacy in his brain workings. Our conclusion has not depended on either denying or asserting strict causality in the sense of classical physics. Regardless of physical theory, it stands simply as a logical consequence of assuming that the state of a man's brain represents (among other things) what he believes – the very assumption that is often thought by determinists to *deny* the reality of our human freedom!

To avoid confusion with Heisenberg's Principle, I have suggested the name "logical indeterminacy" to denote this curious attribute of our brain-workings. It applies, of course, not only to our cognitive system, but also to any future brain activity whose course depends on details of that system that are indeterminate for us.

But we have not yet exhausted the oddity of this situation. Joe Snooks' brain admits of no complete present or future specification that has an unconditional claim to Joe's assent. So far, so good. Yet we admitted that there was nothing in principle to stop *us* (isolated from Joe by a one-way connexion so that we cannot significantly disturb his brain) from having a correct and complete specification, extending into the future as far as the laws of physics will allow. Surely (it might be argued) if we are correct in what we believe, Joe must be mistaken in not believing the same? Oddly enough, the contrary is the case. So far from being mistaken in *not* believing what we do about his brain, Joe

would be mistaken if he did believe it! For if he believed it his brain must be in a different state from that described by our specification. No complete specification of Joe's brain exists that both Joe and we could be correct unconditionally to accept, until after the event.

In other words, the situation we are dealing with here is *relativistic*. In order that we, the detached onlookers, should be correct in what we believe about Joe's brain, it is necessary (logically necessary) that Joe himself should not believe the same. The evidence that determines for us the present and future details of Joe's brain workings has no power to refute Joe's view of his future as indeterminate; for it is something that Joe would be systematically in error to accept. For him, as a participant in the situation, our prediction has no definitive, take-it-or-leave-it status, since its correctness depends precisely upon whether he takes it or leaves it!

The situation here has a parallel in one we have learned to live with in the physical theory of relativity. We are familiar in that context with the idea that two people may have to differ in their accounts of a situation if they are related to it in different ways (for example, moving with different relative velocities); and that neither can then claim to have the "one true view". This does not mean that each can believe what he likes. On the contrary, one and only one account is correct from each standpoint, and the two are quite precisely related. But it does mean that their two beliefs *cannot be identical if both are to be correct*. And this, no more and no less, is what our argument compels us to say about the detached observer's view and the participant's view of future human actions.

To test the strength of the argument, let us take the most favourable case imaginable by the determinist. Suppose that from our observations of Joe's brain and its environment we can write down, well in advance, a whole series of predictions that we keep secret until after the events, and then triumphantly produce to Joe as a proof of our success. By showing him a cine film of the calculating process, we convince him beyond doubt that our mechanistic theory of his brain is correct. Would not this show at least retrospectively that he was mistaken in believing that he was facing genuinely *open* possibilities?

It would not. It would show, of course, that the outcome was *predictable by us*. What it would not show is that it was *inevitable for him*. It cannot do so, for it cannot produce a specification of the outcome that Joe would have been unconditionally correct to accept before he made up his mind. In this sense, no matter how many detached observers could predict the outcome, Joe – and you and I – are *free* in choosing. We cannot logically escape (or be denied) responsibility for our choices on the grounds of their predictability by non-participant observers.

All this has an obvious bearing on the use of evidence from brain science to determine whether a criminal should be denied responsibility for his actions. If our argument is correct it is clearly not enough to prove that an action "had a physical cause", or could have been predicted by non-participants. What matters is whether its causes were such that, before it took place, they determined the outcome *inevitably for the man himself*.

As we have seen, there could be many cases in which the chain-mesh of cause-and-effect in the brain was as tight as we please, but no such inevitable outcome could have been specified in advance. If, however, as in certain kinds of brain damage, epileptic seizures, *force majeure* or the like, the cognitive system is bypassed or overridden, the situation is quite different. There may well exist now a specification of a future action with an unconditional, take-it-or-leave-it claim on the man's assent; in other words, the outcome is not now open for him to determine, but inevitable.

This suggests a possible mechanistic criterion of *diminished responsibility*. Clearly there could be a whole range of intermediate cases in which what we believe about the outcome of our choice would have progressively less effect on its predictability for us. (Think, for example, of the slow stages by which a drug may take over control of a man's priorities.) In such cases we can usefully think of responsibility as diminished in proportion as the outcome becomes unconditionally specifiable for the man concerned. Ideally, it is about this that we want the brain scientist or the psychiatrist to tell us. Evidence that the outcome was predictable by *others* is not enough in itself to justify depriving anyone of the right to be treated as a responsible agent.

Perhaps because it questions deep-rooted habits of thought, the present argument is easily misunderstood as proving only that we are "free subjectively but determinate objectively". It is particularly important to see the mistake in this, since the essence of the argument is that in treating people as free we are recognizing an objective fact about them: namely, the non-existence of an unconditional specification of their future actions, *for them and for us*.

The point is that when we are in dialogue with another individual, our brains form a mutually coupled system. Thus not only is your immediately future brain-state necessarily indeterminate in detail for you; it is also indeterminate for *me* when I am in dialogue with you. So in social interaction the individuals concerned are objectively correct in recognizing that each is indeterminate (in detail) for *all* members of the dialogue. Not even the most fully equipped of non-participant observers could produce a completely detailed specification of the future of the community that could survive the scrutiny, let alone claim the unconditional assent, of any member of it.

It may seem almost suspiciously strange that this logical oddity should turn up in connexion with the brain, when we have not run into it elsewhere; but it is easy to see that in fact it belongs to a family of related oddities which beset us in science whenever a factor classically treated as negligible has turned out not to be so.

Broadly speaking, the process of gaining scientific knowledge has three stages, in which information is respectively (1) generated, (2) transmitted and finally (3) absorbed. At each we have to pay for our information by accepting limitations which were classically thought to be trivial.

1. Generation of information requires *interaction*. This interaction cannot be reduced below the limit set by Planck's constant.

2. Transmission of information requires *time*. This time cannot be reduced below the limit set by the velocity of light. In each of these cases, when the scientific spotlight has been turned upon the process itself, we have had to recognize that the corresponding costs could no longer be neglected. The result has been the familiar paradoxes of quantum theory and relativity theory.

The basis of the present argument is that on the assumption made by mechanistic brain theory itself, (3) absorption of information requires a *change in brain-state*. Thus when the scientific spotlight is turned upon the process of cerebration itself, we need hardly be surprised that this cost in turn proves no longer to be negligible. It is by reckoning with it consistently, I suggest, that we can see the bankruptcy of all attempts to use brain science to deny human responsibility.

# 34 The physical basis of mind
## by Viscount Samuel, A J Ayer
## and Gilbert Ryle

### by The Rt Hon. Viscount Samuel

In so short an article, I can only offer baldly my own conclusions on the question debated in this most interesting, and indeed exciting, discussion, without attempting any survey of the previous contributions.

The discussion has been an approach, from the side of physiology, to one of the oldest and most fundamental of the problems of philosophy – the relation between mind and matter. For centuries, philosophers of different schools have made strenuous efforts to resolve one into the other. Some have sought to show that mind is nothing more than an emanation, in the course of evolution, from matter; others that matter is nothing more than a concept of mind, which alone is real. Those efforts have been unsuccessful: neither view has won general assent.

The materialists appear to ignore the obvious lessons of daily experience. We see, every moment, events which cannot be accounted for by derivations, however subtle, from physical or chemical processes. Watch a chess-player deliberating for a quarter of an hour whether to move his queen here or a pawn there. At last he stretches out his hand and does the one or the other: or he may do neither; using his vocal organs, he may say, "I resign this game". The physiologist may reveal the nervous and muscular mechanism which operates the hand or the tongue, but not the process which has decided the player's action. Or consider a novelist making up a story, a musician writing a symphony, a scientist engaged in a mathematical calculation; or, indeed, something much simpler, a bird building its nest, and choosing the right materials for each stage; or a cat waiting for a pause in the traffic before crossing the street. All these, and all such, are engaged in some process that is different in kind from electrical attractions and repulsions, or from the

*from radio broadcasts first published in* The Physical Basis of Mind – A Philosophers' Symposium, *1950 (Basil Blackwell, Publisher, Oxford).*

---

The scientific contributions referred to were similar to the contributions of Sherrington and Adrian reproduced as earlier chapters. [*Editors' note.*]

processes that unite particles into atoms, atoms into molecules, molecules into objects, and move them about relatively to one another.

The idealists do not account for the fact, which we are bound to accept from astronomy, geology, and anthropology – if we think at all, and if we accept anything at all – that the stars and the planets and this earth existed aeons before man existed; that the universe carried on its activities then – and may properly be assumed to carry them on now – independently of man's perceiving and observing, timing and measuring. The material universe cannot, therefore, be a product of human thought. If it is said that matter may still be an emanation of mind – the mind of God – that is merely an evasion, removing the problem outside the scope of the argument.

The whole effort – to resolve mind into matter or else matter into mind – is the outcome of what T. H. Green called "the philosophic craving for unity". But a craving is something irrational, and we had better beware of becoming addicts. What ground is there for requiring any such unification, either of the one kind or of the other? An essential duality in nature is the alternative that is left.

For those who have proceeded on that assumption, it has been natural and usual to regard the living conscious body as the province of mind and the outside material universe as the province of matter. But this view puts the boundary between the two in the wrong place. Scientists have clearly established that the acceptance of sense stimuli, the transmission of their effects along the nerve fibres, and their activation of different parts of the brain, are mechanical. Whether the approach is from biophysics or biochemistry, anatomy or pathology, the conclusion is the same – these are material activities, obeying mechanical laws. We must conclude that these processes, although inside the body, are not essentially different from the physical processes that are going on outside; rather they are a continuation. When we feel an electric shock, the nerve fibres that carry the current are performing a function similar in kind to that of the copper wire between the battery and the hand. When we hear a sound, the mechanism of the auditory organs, including the relevant part of the brain, is specialized, no doubt, but is not fundamentally of a different order from the air-waves which had carried the sound. It follows that the meeting-place between mind and matter in our own experience is not where we had supposed it to be; it is not at the boundary between body and not-body, but is internal.

That, however, does not solve the problem; it merely shifts it. Some meeting-place there must be to account for the brain-mind relation. And we are bound to assume that, although the two are of different orders, they must have something in common, because there is a meeting-place; because the two interconnect and interact; because body (including brain) does in fact condition and influence mind, and mind does in fact condition and influence body.

The painter or sculptor is conditioned and influenced by his materials; the composer by the musical instruments that exist in his time; the architect by the available building materials; the craftsman by his tools; the captain and crew by their ship. But also the artist, composer, architect, craftsman or navigator chooses the things that he will use and decides the purposes that they shall serve. So with mind and body.

This discussion has helped to clarify the whole problem by establishing the fact that the meeting-place is not at the points where external stimuli impinge upon the nervous system; it is at the points where mind accepts and utilizes the sense-data offered by the brains. But the discussion has not been able to answer the question what it is that takes over at those points; and therefore it could not even begin to consider how the connexion may be made.

Here again our scientists are substantially agreed. Professor Le Gros Clark has said: "No more than the physiologist is the anatomist able even to suggest how the physicochemical phenomena associated with the passage of nervous impulses from one part of the brain to another can be translated into a mental experience." Dr Penfield has compared the mechanism of nerve-cell connexions to a telephone switchboard. He asks: "What is the real relationship of this mechanism to the mind?" He says that "there is a difference between automatic action and voluntary action: ... that something else finds its dwelling-place between the sensory complex and the motor mechanism, that there is a switchboard operator as well as a switchboard." Sir Charles Sherrington has written elsewhere, "That our being should consist of *two* fundamental elements offers, I suppose, no greater inherent improbability than that it should rest on one only." Again, "We have to regard the relation of mind to brain as still not merely unsolved, but still devoid of a basis for its very beginning." And he has ended his stimulating contribution to the present discussion by saying, "Aristotle, 2 000 years ago, was asking how is the mind attached to the body? We are asking that question still."

That, it seems, is where we are now at a standstill. Until science and philosophy can help us to move on from that position we cannot hope that the universe will, for us, be rationalized.

## by A J Ayer

I wonder if Lord Samuel has made it completely clear exactly what the problem is that the philosophers are here called upon to solve? The scientists who spoke in this series have shown very fully and convincingly how various mental processes — thinking, feeling, perceiving, remembering — are causally dependent upon processes in the brain, but to some of them at least the character of this connexion still appears mysterious. Thus, Sir Charles Sherrington remarked that "it is a far cry from an electrical reaction in the brain to suddenly seeing the world around one, with all its distances, colours, and chiaroscuro"; and Professor Adrian confessed to the same "misgivings" when he says that "the part of the picture of the brain which may always be missing is of course the part which deals with the mind, the part which ought to explain how a particular pattern of nerve impulses can produce an idea; or the other way round, how a thought can decide which nerve cells are to come into action."

If this is a genuine problem, it is hard to see why further information about the brain should be expected to solve it. For however much we amplify our picture of the brain, it remains still a picture of something physical, and it is just the question how anything physical can interact with something that is not that is supposed to constitute our difficulty. If what we are seeking is a bridge across a seemingly impassable river it will not help us merely to elevate one of the banks. It looks, indeed, as if some of the previous speakers were hoping to discover in the brain something describable as the locus of the mind; as if mind and brain could be conceived as meeting at a point in space or as somehow shading into one another: but to me this is not even an intelligible hypothesis. What would it be like to come upon this junction? By what signs would you recognize it if you found it? Descartes had the same problem, and he met it by suggesting that mind and body came together in the pineal gland; but how this conjecture could conceivably be tested he did not explain. The reason he had the problem — the reason why we have it still — is that matter and mind were conceived by him from the outset as distinct orders of being; it is as if there were two separate worlds, such that every event had to belong to one or other of them, but no event could belong to both. But from these premises it follows necessarily that there can be no bridge or junction; for what would the bridge consist of? Any event that you discovered would have to fall on one or other side of it. So, if there is a difficulty here, it is not because our factual information is scanty, but because our logic is defective. Perhaps this whole manner of conceiving the distinction between mind and matter is at fault. In short, our problem is not scientific but philosophical.

Let us consider, then, what can be meant by saying that a particular pattern of nerve impulses "produces" an idea, or that "a thought decides" which nerve cells are to come into action. What are the facts on which such assertions are based? The facts are that the physiologist makes certain observations, and that these observations fall into different categories. On the one hand there are the observations which lead him to tell his story about nerve cells and electrical impulses. That is to say, the story is an interpretation of the observations in question. On the other hand there are the observations which he interprets by saying that the subject of his experiment is in such and such a "mental" state, that he is thinking, or resolving to perform some action, or feeling some sensation, or whatever it may be. It is then found to be the case that these two sorts of observations can be correlated with one another; that whenever an observation of the first type can be made, there is good reason to suppose that an observation of the second type can be made also. For example, when the scientists make observations which they interpret by saying that such and such nerve cells are undergoing such and such electrical disturbances, they can also make observations which are interpreted by saying that the subject is having sensations of a certain type. Again, when they are able to make such observations as are interpreted by saying that the subject is resolving to perform some action, they can also make further observations which are interpreted by saying that certain impulses are passing through certain of his nerve fibres. It seems to me that when it is asserted that the two events in question – the mental and the physical – are causally connected, that the pattern of nerve impulses "produces" the sensation, or that the thought "decides" which nerve cells are to operate, all that is meant, or at least all that can properly be meant, is that these two sets of observations are correlated in the way that I have described. But if this is so, where is the difficulty? There is nothing especially mysterious about the fact that two different sets of observations are correlated; that, given the appropriate conditions, they habitually accompany one another. You may say that this fact requires an explanation; but such an explanation could only be some theory from which the fact of this correlation could be deduced. And in so far as the theory was not a mere redescription of the facts which it was intended to explain, it would serve only to fit them into a wider context. We should learn from it that not only were these observations correlated, but certain further types of observation were correlated with them. To ask *why* something occurs, if it is not simply equivalent to asking *how* it occurs, is to ask what other things are associated with it. Once the facts are fully described, there is no mystery left.

If there seems to be a mystery in this case, it is because we are misled by our conceptual systems; not by the facts themselves but by the pictures which we use to interpret the facts. The physiologist's story is complete in itself. The characters that figure in it are nerve cells, electrical impulses, and so forth. It has no place for an entirely different cast, of sensations, thoughts, feelings and the other *personnae* of the mental play. And just because it has no place for them they do not intervene in it. The muddle arises from trying to make them intervene, as I am afraid Lord Samuel does. We then get a confused, indeed an unintelligible, story of electrical impulses being transmuted into sensations, or of mental processes interleaved with disturbances of the nervous cells. The picture we are given is that of messengers travelling through the brain, reaching a mysterious entity called the mind, receiving orders from it, and then travelling on. But since the mind has no position in space – it is by definition not the sort of thing that can have a position in space – it does not literally make sense to talk of physical signals reaching it; nor are there such temporal gaps in the procession of nervous impulses as would leave room for the mental characters to intervene. In short, the two stories will not mix. It is like trying to play *Hamlet*, not without the Prince of Denmark, but with Pericles, the Prince of Tyre. But to say that the two stories will not mix is not to say that either of them is superfluous. Each is an interpretation of certain phenomena and they are connected by the fact that, in certain conditions, when one of them is true, the other is true also.

My conclusion is, then, that mind and body are not to be conceived as two disparate entities between which we have to make, or find, some sort of amphibious bridge, but that talking about minds and talking about bodies are different ways of classifying and interpreting our experiences. I do not say that this procedure does not give rise to serious philosophical problems; how, for example, to analyse statements about the thoughts and feelings of others; or how far statements about people's so-called mental processes are equivalent to statements about their observable behaviour. But once we are freed from the Cartesian fallacy of regarding minds as immaterial substances, I do not think that the discovery of causal connexions between what we choose to describe respectively as mental and physical occurrences implies anything by which we need to be perplexed.

## by Gilbert Ryle

The story is told of some peasants who were terrified at the sight of their first railway-train. Their pastor therefore gave them a lecture explaining how a steam-engine works. One of the peasants then said, "Yes, pastor, we quite understand what you say about the steam-engine. But there is really a horse inside, isn't there?" So used were they to horse-drawn carts that they could not take in the idea that some vehicles propel themselves.

We might invent a sequel. The peasants examined the engine and peeped into every crevice of it. They then said, "Certainly we cannot see, feel, or hear a horse there. We are foiled. But we know there is a horse there, so it must be a ghost-horse which, like the fairies, hides from mortal eyes."

The pastor objected, "But, after all, horses themselves are made of moving parts, just as the steam-engine is made of moving parts. You know what their muscles, joints and blood-vessels do. So why is there a mystery in the self-propulsion of a steam-engine, if there is none in that of a horse? What do you think makes the horse's hooves go to and fro?" After a pause a peasant replied, "What makes the horse's hooves go is four extra little ghost-horses inside."

Poor simple-minded peasants! Yet just such a story has been the official theory of the mind for the last three very scientific centuries. Several, though not all, of the scientists in this series have automatically posed their problem in this very way. I think that Lord Samuel still accepts the whole story, and that Professor Ayer would like to reject it, but does not see how to do so. For the general terms in which the scientists have set their problem of mind and body, we philosophers have been chiefly to blame, though we have been obsessed, not by the rustic idea of horses, but by the newer idea of mechanical contrivances. The legend that we have told and sold runs like this. A person consists of two theatres, one bodily and one non-bodily. In his Theatre A go on the incidents which we can explore by eye and instrument. But a person also incorporates a second theatre, Theatre B. Here there go on incidents which are totally unlike, though synchronized with those that go on in Theatre A. These Theatre B episodes are changes in the states, not of bits of flesh, but of something called "consciousness", which occupies no space. Only the proprietor of Theatre B has first-hand knowledge of what goes on in it. It is a secret theatre. The experimentalist tries to open its doors, but it has no doors. He tries to peep through its windows, but it has no windows. He is foiled.

We tend nowadays to treat it as obvious that a person, unlike a newt, lives the two lives, life "A" and life "B", each completely unlike, though mysteriously geared to the other. Ingrained hypotheses do feel obvious, however redundant they may be. The peasants in my story correctly thought that a steam-engine was hugely different from a cart and automatically but incorrectly explained the difference by postulating a ghost-horse inside. So most of us, correctly thinking that there are huge differences between a clock and a person, automatically but incorrectly explain these differences by postulating an extra set of ghost-works inside. We correctly say that people are not like clocks, since people meditate, calculate and invent things; they make plans, dream dreams and shirk their obligations; they get angry, feel depressed, scan the heavens, and have likes and dislikes; they work, play and idle; they are sane, crazy or imbecile; they are skilful at some things and bunglers at others. Where we go wrong is in explaining these familiar actions and conditions as the operations of a secondary set of secret works.

Everybody knows quite well when to describe someone as acting absent-mindedly or with heed, as babbling deliriously or reasoning coherently, as feeling angry but not showing it, as wanting one thing but pretending to want another, as being ambitious, patriotic or miserly. We often get our accounts and estimates of other people and of ourselves wrong; but we more often get them right. We did not need to learn the legend of the two theatres before we were able to talk sense about people and to deal effectively with them. Nor has this fairly new-fangled legend helped us to do it better.

When we read novels, biographies and reminiscences, we do not find the chapters partitioned into Section "A", covering the hero's "bodily" doings, and Section "B", covering his "mental" doings. We find unpartitioned accounts of what he did and thought and felt, of what he said to others and to himself, of the mountains he tried to climb and the problems he tried to solve. Should an examiner mark the paper written by the candidate's hand but refuse to assess the candidate's wits? Theorists themselves, when actually describing people, sensibly forget Theatre A and Theatre B. Sir Charles Sherrington paid a well-deserved compliment to Professor Adrian, but he did not pay one cool compliment to Professor Adrian "A" and another warmer compliment to Professor Adrian "B".

In saying that a person is not to be described as a mind coupled with a body I am not saying, with some truculent thinkers, that people are just machines. Nor are engines just wagons or live bodies just corpses. What is wrong with the story of the two theatres is not that it reports differences which are not there but that it misrepresents differences which are there. It is a story with the right characters but the wrong plot. It is an attempt to explain a genuine difference – or rather a galaxy of differences – but its effect, like that of the peasants' theory, is merely to reduplicate the thing to be explained. It says, "The difference between a machine like a human body on the one hand and a human being on the other is that in a human being, besides the organs which we do see, there is a counterpart set of organs which we do not see; besides the causes and effects which we can witness, there is a counterpart series of causes and effects which we cannot witness." So now we ask, "But what explains the differences between what goes on in the Theatre B of a sane man and what goes on in that of a lunatic? A third theatre, Theatre C?"

No, what prevents us from examining Theatre B is not that it has no doors or windows, but that there is no such theatre. What prevented the peasants from finding the horse was not that it was a ghost-horse, but that there was no horse. None the less, the engine *was* different from a wagon and ordinary people *are* different not only from machines, but also from animals, imbeciles, infants and corpses. They also differ in countless important ways from one another. I have not begun to show how we should grade these differences. I have only shown how we should not grade them.

One last word. In ordinary life (save when we want to sound knowing) we seldom use the noun "Mind" or the adjective "mental" at all. What we do is to talk of people, of people calculating, conjuring, hoping, resolving, tasting, bluffing, fretting and so on. Nor, in ordinary life, do we talk of "Matter" or of things being "material". What we do is to talk of steel, granite and water; of wood, moss and grain; of flesh, bone and sinew. The umbrella-titles "Mind" and "Matter" obliterate the very differences that ought to interest us. Theorists should drop both these words. "Mind" and "Matter" are echoes from the hustings of philosophy and prejudice the solutions of all problems posed in terms of them.

# A glossary of zoological terms as used in the articles by A S Romer and E J W Barrington

*actinopterygians* A group of bony fish consisting of teleosts (*q.v.*) and a few other forms.

*amniotes* Reptiles, birds and mammals.

*Amphioxus* A small, fish-like animal which, although related to vertebrates, lacks a brain, skull and bony or cartilaginous skeleton.

*Annelids* A group of animals including earthworms, leeches and ragworms.

*anurans* Frogs and toads.

*Apoda* A group of legless amphibia.

*arthropods* An enormous invertebrate group including insects, spiders, scorpions, crabs, lobsters and many others.

*Aurelia* A type of jellyfish.

*bifurcate* Divides into two.

*bipolar neuron* A neuron with two main processes.

*branchial* Relating to the gills.

*bulla* The bony region of the skull which encloses the middle ear.

*cephalic* Pertaining to the head.

*cephalopods* A group of molluscs including the squids, octopus, cuttlefish and others.

*Chondrichthyes* Fish with cartilaginous skeletons, such as sharks and rays.

*cranial* Relating to the head

*crossopterygians* A group of fish, now virtually extinct, which included the ancestors of land-living vertebrates. One living form, the coelacanth.

*crustaceans* A group of arthropods which includes crabs, lobsters, barnacles and wood lice.

*cyclostomes* A group of fish which lack jaws, including lampreys.

*Dibranchiata* The group of animals to which all living cephalopods except *Nautilus* (*q.v.*) belong.

*Diptera* The group of insects to which belong the flies, gnats and mosquitoes.

*distal* The end of a structure, furthest from the main axis of the body.

*diurnal* Active during the day.

*dorsal* Structures which lie close to the upper surface of the body, or closer to it than other structures with which they are being compared. The term applies regardless of changes in orientation of an animal. Thus a dog's dorsal surface is its back, regardless of whether it is lying on its stomach or on its back.

*ectoderm* The outer layer of cells in the embryo.

*elasmobranchs* Sharks and rays. For present purposes can be regarded as equivalent to *Chondrichthyes*.

*epidermis* The outermost layer of cells of plants and animals.

*epithelium* A sheet of cells which form a lining or covering.

*flexure* A bend, kink or fold.

*foramen* A hole, especially in a part of the skeleton.

*gnathostomes* Vertebrates with jaws. *i.e.* all vertebrates except cyclostomes.

*hagfish* A cyclostome.

*Hemichordata* A group of worm-like animals, possibly distantly related to vertebrates.

*histology* The study of tissues (*e.g.* muscle, bone, *etc.*)

*Hymenoptera* The group of insects to which belong the bees, wasps and ants.

*hyoid arch* A skeletal structure lying just behind the jaws.

*hyomandibular* Dorsal element of the hyoid arch, adjacent to the spiracle. Often used as an adjective, meaning pertaining to the region of the hyomandibular.

*hypoglossal nerve* A nerve which originates directly from the brain in vertebrates.

*interstitial fluid* The fluid which bathes the cells of the body.

*intra vitam* A method of staining cells by injecting dyes direct into a living animal.

*labyrinthodonts* A major group of fossil amphibia.

*lamprey* A cyclostome.

*Limulus* A marine arachnid (the group to which spiders belong) called the king crab.

*littoral* Relating to the shore line.

*Locusta* The locust.

*mastoid* Part of the mammalian skull just behind the ear.

*medial* also *median* On or near the midline of a bilaterally symmetrical animal.

*mesenchyme* Rather irregular branching cells found in embryo. Give rise to bone, blood and connective tissue.

*mesoderm* A term given to a layer of cells in embryos which lies between the outer and innermost layers of cells. Structures which develop from this layer are termed mesodermal.

*molluscs* The group of animals which includes snails, slugs, oysters, octopus and many others.

*monotreme* An egg-laying group of mammals which includes the duck-billed platypus.

*morphology* The study of the form and structure of organisms.

*multipolar neurons* Neurons with more than three main processes.

*nerve root* Part of the nerve that originates from the spinal cord or brain.

*nerves V, VII, IX, X* Nerves originating directly from the brain in vertebrates which are identified by Roman numerals.

*nauplius larva* A distinctive larval form found in many crustacea (*q.v.*).

*Nautilus* A cephalopod distinguished from other living forms, but similar to many fossil forms, in possessing a well developed external shell.

*occiput* The posterior part of the skull where it joins the vertebral column.

*Onychophora* A group of animals intermediate in some structures between the annelids and some of the arthropods.

*ophidians* Snakes.

*ossicle* A small bone.

*otic* Relating to the ear.

*pallial* Relating to a gill.

*Patella* The limpet.

*phylogeny* Evolutionary-history.

*placentals* All mammals with a placenta *i.e.* virtually all mammals except for duck-billed platypus, kangaroos and their relatives.

*Platyhelminthes* A group of flat worms.

*polychaetes* A sub-division of the annelids (*q.v.*) which includes the ragworm and lugworm.

*protoplasm* The living material of the cell.

*proximal* The near end of a structure – *see* distal.

*sabellids* A group of polychaetes which live in tubes.

*somatic motor neurons* Neurons carrying impulses to the somatic muscles.

*somatic muscles* The muscles of the trunk, tail (where applicable) and eyeball of vertebrates. They are innervated by somatic motorfibres.

*Somatic sensory fibres* Carry impulses in from the skin, muscles and tendons.

*spiracular gill cleft* (*or spiracle*) The most anterior gill of many fish, much reduced in size.

*statocyst* An organ of balance.

*sulcus* A groove on the surface of the brain.

*swim bladder* A bladder which many fish possess and use in adjusting their density.

*Tarsius* A primate related to lemurs and bush babies. It is small and has enormous eyes.

*teleosts* A sub-group of the actinopterygians (*q.v.*) containing the great majority of existing fish (*e.g.* perch, salmon, carp, mackerel).

*temporal region of skull* The region behind and above the eye.

*terminal* At the end.

*tetrapods* Amphibia, reptiles, birds and mammals.

*trigeminal nerve* A nerve which arises directly from the vertebrate brain.

*Turbellaria* A sub-division of the platyhelminths.

*urodeles* Newts and salamanders.

*vagus nerve* A nerve which arises directly from the vertebrate brain.

*ventral* The lower surface of an animal – *see* dorsal.

*vertebral canal* The hole in the vertebrae through which the nerve cord passes.

*vesicle* A sack-like or bag-like structure.

*visceral muscles* The muscles of the gut and gills. They are innervated by visceral motor fibres.

*visceral sensory fibres* Nerve fibres which conduct impulses from the gut and other internal organs to the brain or spinal cord.

# Index